MANAGEMENT, WORK AND ORGANISATIONS

Series editors: **Gibson Burrell**, The Management Centre, University of Leicester
Mick Marchington, Manchester School of Management, UMIST
Paul Thompson, Department of Human Resource Management,
University of Strathclyde

This series of new textbooks covers the areas of human resource management, employee relations, organisational behaviour and related business and management fields. Each text has been specially commissioned to be written by leading experts in a clear and accessible way. The books contain serious and challenging material, take an analytical rather than prescriptive approach and are particularly suitable for use by students with no prior specialist knowledge.

The series is relevant for many business and management courses, including MBA and post-experience courses, specialist masters and postgraduate diplomas, professional courses, and final-year undergraduate courses. The books will become essential reading at business and management schools worldwide.

Published

Paul Blyton and Peter Turnbull
THE DYNAMICS OF EMPLOYEE RELATIONS (3rd edn)

Sharon C. Bolton
EMOTIONAL MANAGEMENT IN THE WORKPLACE

Peter Boxall and John Purcell
STRATEGY AND HUMAN RESOURCE MANAGEMENT

J. Martin Corbet
CRITICAL CASES IN ORGANISATIONAL BEHAVIOUR

Keith Grint
LEADERSHIP

Marek Korczynski
HUMAN RESOURCE MANAGEMENT IN SERVICE WORK

Karen Legge
HUMAN RESOURCE MANAGEMENT: anniversary edition

Stephen Proctor and Frank Mueller (eds)
TEAMWORKING

Helen Rainbird (ed.)
TRAINING IN THE WORKPLACE

Jill Rubery and Damian Grimshaw
THE ORGANISATION OF EMPLOYMENT

Harry Scarbrough (ed.)
THE MANAGEMENT OF EXPERTISE

Hugh Scullion and Margaret Linehan
INTERNATIONAL HUMAN RESOURCE MANAGEMENT

Adrian Wilkinson, Mick Marchington, Tom Redman and Ed Snape
MANAGING WITH TOTAL QUALITY MANAGEMENT

Diana Winstanley and Jean Woodall (eds)
ETHICAL ISSUES IN CONTEMPORARY HUMAN RESOURCE MANAGEMENT

For more information on title in the Series please go to www.palgrave.com/business/mwo

Invitation to authors

The Series Editors welcome proposals for new books within the Management, Work and Organisations series. These should be sent to Paul Thompson (p.thompson@strath.ac.uk) at the Dept of HRM, Strathclyde Business School, University of Strathclyde, 50 Richmond St Glasgow G1 1XT

Other books by Karen Legge include:

POWER INNOVATION AND PROBLEM-SOLVING IN PERSONNEL MANAGEMENT
EVALUATING PLANNED ORGANIZATIONAL CHANGE
CASES IN INFORMATION TECHNOLOGY, PEOPLE AND ORGANIZATIONS (edited with
  C. Clegg and N. Kemp)
CASE STUDIES IN ORGANIZATIONAL BEHAVIOUR AND HUMAN RESOURCE
  MANAGEMENT (edited with D. Gowler and C. Clegg)

Human Resource Management

Rhetorics and Realities

Anniversary edition

Karen Legge

First published 2005 by
PALGRAVE MACMILLAN
Houndmills, Basingstoke, Hampshire RG21 6XS and
175 Fifth Avenue, New York, N.Y. 10010
Companies and representatives throughout the world

PALGRAVE MACMILLAN is the global academic imprint of the Palgrave
Macmillan division of St. Martin's Press, LLC and of Palgrave Macmillan Ltd.
Macmillan is a registered trademark in the United States, United Kingdom
and other countries. Palgrave is a registered trademark in the European
Union and other countries.

ISBN 1–4039–3600–5

This book is printed on paper suitable for recycling and
made from fully managed and sustained forest sources.

A catalogue record for this book is available from the British Library.

A catalog record for this book is available from the Library of Congress.

10   9   8   7   6   5   4   3   2   1
14   13   12   11   10   09   08   07   06   05

Printed and bound in Great Britain by
Creative Print & Design (Wales), Ebbw Vale

In memory of Dan Gowler

'The best and brightest'

Contents

List of Figures

List of Tables

Acknowledgements

The first edition of this book was written largely at a time of great personal sadness, following the death of my husband and partner, Dan Gowler. The support I received – both personal and professional – from colleagues and friends at that time and subsequently has been more generous and meant more to me than I can say. It would be invidious to single out names, so my heartfelt thanks go to all my friends at the Department of Behaviour in Organisations (now Department of Organisation, Work and Technology), Lancaster University; Templeton College, Oxford; The Management School, Imperial College (now Tannka Business School); the MRC/ESRC Social and Applied Psychology Unit (now the Institute of Work Psychology), University of Sheffield; the School of Industrial and Business Studies, University of Warwick (now Warwick Business School); Manchester Business School; Bath, Birkbeck, Cardiff, Glasgow, Hull, LBS, Leeds, LSE, Loughborough and Southampton Universities. Special thanks go to those whose patience I have tried sorely – Gibson, Mick, Paul and Stephen, my editors at the publishers and Sue, who never complains at hieroglyphics still written in 2H pencil by the last computer illiterate (in 1994 that was!).

Above all, though, this book would never have been completed without the love and support of my families at Uxbridge Road and Elstead, to whom this book belongs as much as to Dan. To you, kids, especially – here's looking at you!

Ten years on, still looking at you, kids!

The author and publishers wish to thank the following for permission to reproduce copyright material:

Blackwell, *Journal of Management Studies* and John Purcell, for Figures 2.1 and 2.2, from J. Purcell and A. Gray, 'Corporate personnel departments and the management of industrial relations: two case studies in ambiguity' (1986) and from J. Purcell, 'Mapping management style in employee relations' (1987); Routledge, *International Journal of Human Resource Management* and John Storey, for Figures 2.3 and 2.4, from J. Storey and N. Bacon, 'Individualism and collectivism: into the 1990s' (1993); Blackwell and John Storey, for Figures 2.5, 3.1 and 3.3 from *Developments in the Management of Human Resources* (1992);

Harvester Wheatsheaf and Mick Marchington, for Figure 2.6, from M. Marchington and P. Parker, *Changing Patterns of Employee Relations* (1990); Blackwell, *Journal of Management Studies* and David Guest, for Figures 3.2 and 3.5, from D. E. Guest, 'Human resource management and industrial relations' (1987); Routledge and Richard Whittington, for Figure 4.1, from R. Whittington, *What is Strategy and Does it Matter?* (1993); Open University Press, Keith Sisson and John Storey, for Figures 4.2, 4.3 and 4.4, from John Storey and Keith Sisson, *Managing Human Resources and Industrial Relations* (1993); *Organisational Dynamics*, for Figure 4.5, from R. E. Miles and C. C. Snow, 'Designing strategic human resources systems' 1984); Blackwell, for Figure 4.6, from M. Goold and A. Campbell, *Strategies and Styles* (1987); Routledge and *International Journal of Human Resource Management*, for Figure 4.7, from C. Hendry and A. Pettigrew, 'Human resource management: an agenda for the 1990s' (1990); also John Wiley and *British Journal of Management*, for Figure 4.7, from C. Hendry and A. Pettigrew, 'Patterns of strategic change in the development of human resource management' (1992); *Journal of General Management*, for Figures 4.8 and 4.9, from P. Miller and D. Norburn, 'Strategy and executive reward: the mismatch in the strategic process' (1981); MCB University Press and *International Journal of Management*, for Figure 5.1, from G. L. Mangum and S. L. Mangum, 'Temporary work: the flipside of job security' (1986); Jossey Bass, for Figure 6.1, from E. H. Schein, *Organizational Culture and Leadership* (1985); Free Press, for Figure 9.1, from M. Beer, B. Spector, P. Lawrence, D. Quinn Mills and R. Walton, *Human Resource Management: A General Manager's Perspective* (1985); John Wiley, for Figure 9.2, from M. A. Devanna, C. J. Fombrun and N. M. Tichy, 'A framework for strategic human resource management', in C. J. Fombrun *et al.*, *Strategic Human Resource Management* (1984); *Employment Gazette* (various issues), for data in Tables 8.1–8.3; Blackwell and *British Journal of Industrial Relations*, for data in Table 8.2, from J. Waddington, 'Trade union membership in Britain 1980–87: unemployment and restructuring' (1992).

Introduction

This book is intended to provide MBA students with a critical overview and evaluation of the nature of Human Resource Management (HRM) in the UK. Its aim is to situate changing rhetorics and approaches to managing employee relations – or people at work, or the human resource in the circuit of capital accumulation – in their socio–politico–economic context. The concern is not to explicate in a prescriptive manner the minutiae of 'best practice' management techniques that form the hand tools in the work of managing employees. Good introductory 'how it should be done' texts already exist that fulfil this function admirably (see, for example, Torrington and Hall, 1987). For practitioners requiring greater detail and even more evangelism about specific techniques – anything from graphology in selection testing to outplacement counselling for the 'delayered', management publishers and consultancy organisations are ready with expensive step-by-step maps to the holy grail of the 'optimum utilisation of human resources in pursuit of organisational goals'. The purpose of this book is rather to situate such activities (critically evaluated and deconstructed) in the context of managerial rationales, constraints and opportunities. (We'll leave aside for the moment whether such constraints and opportunities are 'real' or 'enacted'.)

Nor is there any intention to draw comparisons with human resource management as practised in other countries. Given my own reservations about the meaningfulness of broad-brush international surveys, such as the Price Waterhouse Cranfield survey (Brewster and Hegewisch, 1994), in order to achieve any depth of situated analysis it would require extensive use of detailed nationally-based research studies from all over the world. As time and space constraints have prohibited this option, I have preferred not to draw comparisons which, at best, might be superficial and stereotyped and, at worst, misleading. However, for readers interested in comparative work on HRM some useful papers and texts exist (for example, Brewster and Tyson, 1991; Kakabadse and Tyson, 1993; Kirkbride, 1994; Torrington, 1994; Brewster, 1995; Kochan and Dyer, 1995; Scullion, 1995; Sparrow and Hiltrop, 1994) although international comparative studies are more developed in the areas of employee/industrial relations than in HRM specifically (see, for example, Bean, 1994; Bamber and Lansbury, 1993; Hyman and Ferner, 1994; Ferner and Hyman, 1992; Niland et al., 1994).

If this is the general approach, why not a critical text on our old, tried and trusted(?) friend, personnel management, instead of new-fangled faddish HRM? It is precisely these less than flattering attributions about HRM that make it so interesting. Is it really any different from personnel management, or is it the old product, in a new glitzy customer-aware package – as Armstrong (1987) put it, 'old wine in new bottles'? If it is little different from personnel management, why the hype? It will be argued in this book that the importance of HRM, and its apparent overshadowing of personnel management, lies just as much and (possibly more so) in its function as a rhetoric about how employees should be managed to achieve competitive advantage than as a coherent new practice. It is a rhetoric chiefly espoused by British and American senior managers shaping up to heightened global competition from nations their countries once defeated in war. And why the appeal of HRM's particular rhetoric? Because its language (of integration, flexibility, commitment and quality, to take Guest's (1987) model) celebrates a range of very WASP (White, Anglo–Saxon, Protestant) values (individualism, work ethic, those of the American Dream) while at the same time mediating the contradictions of capitalism (Legge, 1989a; Guest, 1990b; Keenoy, 1990b). That the latter is a topical activity there can be little doubt. For not only did the enterprise cultures of the 1980s highlight and exacerbate these contradictions, but the changing mood of the 'Caring 1990s' may arguably demand their amelioration, or at least the rhetorical appearance of amelioration.

The importance of HRM as a rhetoric that speaks to the concerns of a wide range of stakeholder groups – personnel and line managers, government and academics – should not be underestimated. For while normative models exist of the essential characteristics of HRM and analysis of how it differs from comparable models of personnel management, there is evidence that such models of HRM are rarely realised extensively or completely in practice. While exemplars of its strategic implementation do exist, from case study and survey evidence the general picture is one of techniques associated with HRM receiving widespread support but implementation being largely *ad hoc*, opportunistic and fragmented.

But this is to anticipate discussion that will be developed later in the book. The book's structure and contents are as follows. First, analysing a little of its history and a lot of its recent typologies, Chapter 1 identifies the nature of personnel management as a starting point and benchmark for subsequent discussion. Four models of personnel management are identified: the normative, the descriptive–functional, the critical–evaluative and the descriptive–behavioural model. In exploring these models, the argument is presented that personnel management may be typified as a bundle of ambiguities and contradictions leaving personnel managers historically with a 'kind of generalized inferiority complex' (Herman, 1968). Not surprisingly this provokes recurring attacks of navel-gazing. The early 1980s, under the first shock waves of the enterprise culture, saw a bout of just such attacks (for example, Thurley, 1981), leaving personnel management ripe for its periodic reassessment, remoulding and re-marketing – this time as HRM. Chapter 2 continues this analysis by considering the models of the range of styles in which personnel management, and employee relations generally, has been conducted in different organisational settings in the recent past. Consideration is given to the contextual and ideological factors associated with the adoption of different styles. The importance of ideas about individualism and collectivism in relation to espoused styles is explored, along with the product and labour market and other contextual factors that result in the practice of a pragmatic opportunism. With the scene set, Chapter 3 takes an overview of the emergence and nature of HRM and considers its similarities to, and differences from, personnel management. Two normative models of HRM are identified, the 'soft', or 'developmental humanism' model of the Harvard School (Beer, Katz, Kochan, Lawrence, McKersie and Walton), and the 'hard', or 'utilitarian–instrumentalism' model of the Michigan School (Devanna, Fombrun and Tichy) (see Hendry and Pettigrew, 1990; Keenoy, 1990b).

Guest's (1987) version of a 'soft' normative model of HRM is now chosen as a framework for a critical dialogue about the tensions between 'hard' and 'soft' HRM models, both in theory and in implementation, that will be conducted throughout the book. Each of the constituents of Guest's model: integration, flexibility, commitment and quality are considered in the light of these tensions, in Chapters 4–7.

Chapter 4 considers three aspects of integration in relation to HRM: the integration or 'fit' of human resource policies with business strategy; the integration or complementarity and consistency of mutuality policies aimed at generating employee commitment, flexibility and quality; the internalisation of the importance of human resources on the part of line managers. While these issues are explored theoretically and empirically, it is suggested that much hinges on how we conceptualise the nature of strategy. Arguably, the act of *consciously* matching HRM policy to business strategy is only relevant if one adopts what, empirically speaking, is the *least* realistic model of the strategy-making process. Further, is matching HRM policies with strategy necessarily advisable? What evidence is there that senior managers in the UK have explicit, well formulated and consistent HRM policies, let alone that these are consciously integrated with business strategy?

Chapter 5 turns to issues of flexibility. The nature and extent of corporate restructuring in the UK is considered in the context of two major debates: that of post-Fordism and flexible specialisation and of Atkinson's model of the flexible firm. The chapter explores the broader background of academic debates in which HRM concerns with flexibility need to be situated; evaluates the empirical evidence derived from surveys and case studies, of enhanced flexibility, whether at the level of task or organisational design in UK firms and accounts for the continuities and changes identified in the empirical evidence, and their significance for HRM. The central importance of 'flexibility' as a discourse and ideological agenda emerges.

Chapter 6 turns to the *leitmotiv* of 'soft' models of HRM: the hoped-for movement from behavioural compliance to employee commitment and enhanced performance via programmes of culture change that highlight values of quality to be achieved through greater employee involvement. This chapter critically dissects the notion of commitment and considers the feasibility and utility of cultural change programmes in the light of both the problematic nature of the key concepts involved and the empirical evidence of exemplar culture change programmes. The conclusions drawn are largely sceptical.

Chapter 7 deals with the fourth element in Guest's model, looking at the relationship between HRM and quality. Focusing on the nature of Total Quality Management (TQM) and Just-in-Time (JIT) in manufacturing industry and on the rhetoric of quality in the public and private service sectors, the chapter considers how shifting definitions of quality may be used to address different models of HRM and enlist different groups of stakeholders. In many circumstances it is clear that 'quality' exists mainly as a beguiling discourse to mask the hard practices of labour intensification and unit resource cut-back, just as discourses about 'customer sovereignty' cloak the market manipulations of quasi-monopolistic and oligopolistic organisations.

Because it has been widely debated, by Guest amongst others (for example, Guest, 1989b, 1995), that HRM makes important assumptions about, and has critical implications for, trade unionism, Chapter 8 considers the relationship between HRM, industrial relations and trade unionism, with special reference to the so-called 'new realism' forms of industrial relations. Against a background of the erosion of 'traditional' British industrial relations, following a decade and a half of the enterprise culture, with associated restrictive trade union legislation and major economic recessions, the following questions are addressed. What is 'traditional' industrial relations, and does it still exist? What changes have occurred, why, and are they likely to be reversed with a change of government? If the industrial relations system now exhibits a 'new realism', is this compatible with the 'hard' and 'soft' models of HRM, and in what sense?

Up to this point in this book, a conventional 'textbook' approach has been adopted – an implicitly positivistic stance in which various propositions about HRM have been explored (perhaps 'tested' is too strong a word!) in the light of available empirical evidence. The analysis, hopefully, has been logical, ordered and rational. Yet the 1980s saw the rise, in academic and literary circles, of an anti-positivistic, 'postmodern' mode of analysis, aimed at 'deconstructing' texts in a spirit of relativistic, 'serious playfulness'. And what, you might ask *is* postmodernism? I am tempted to reply in the words of a bemused commentator in the *Independent* (24 December 1987) who concluded 'The word has no meaning – use it as much as possible!' (This response, as you will later discover, is postmodernist – if unwittingly – in both form and content.) More prosaically, 'postmodernism' may be seen to embody two distinct and epistemologically different perspectives. The first is a notion of 'periodisation' – that we now live in new post-Fordist times, that equally may be labelled as times of 'radical' or 'late' 'modernity' or of 'disorganised capitalism', as well as the 'post-modern' age (see Parker, 1992; Giddens, 1990; Lash and Urry, 1987; Clegg, 1990). These new 'post-modern' times, however, may still be researched from an out-and-out modernistic, positivistic standpoint of deductive reasoning, hypothesis testing and so forth. The second 'postmodern' perspective is that of the epistemological shift, already identified above, away from the absolutist facticity of positivism to a relativistic 'deconstruction' of discourse.

So, in Chapter 9, in concluding this critical analysis of HRM, it seems appropriate to locate it in a much broader socio–cultural context than that considered in Chapter 3. In a 'post-modern' world and from a 'postmodern' epistemological perspective, what, as a socio-cultural artifact, does HRM represent? Can it be seen just as a phenomenon of 'post-modern' times or is more to be gained by viewing it from a postmodern epistemological perspective? How do these different perspectives speak to the 'hard' and 'soft' models of HRM? As will be seen in Chapter 9, attempts to grapple with these issues is a complex matter. Suffice to say here that the focus of Chapter 9 is to bring together strands of argument in the other chapters that identify HRM in terms of rhetoric and discourse. Here HRM is 'deconstructed' as a phenomenon whose importance lies largely in its existence as a rhetoric and discourse that serves the interests of a range of influential stakeholders who have an interest in hype-ing the extent and depth of its facticity. 'Deconstructing' HRM here has a serious intent, for in pulling apart its assumptions, exploring its paradoxes and contradictions, postmodern analysis is used 'as a positive technique for making trouble; and an affront to every normal and comfortable habit of thought' (Norris, 1982, p. xi).

Finally in Chapter 10, I return to a conventional analysis to consider the foreseeable future of HRM in the light of future socio–economic trends consequent on investment patterns, globalisation, EU membership and possible governmental change. The quotation mark in the title of that chapter is intentional, but my conclusion probably renders it superfluous.

Preview/postscript for anniversary edition

'Times they are a-changing': *Human Resource Management, Rhetorics and Realities* ten years on*

Introduction

It is ten years since I wrote the first edition of *Human Resource Management, Rhetorics and Realities* (HRMRR-1) and the durability of the story it tells is evident from its continuing flourishing sales. Nevertheless, both empirically and conceptually, time and circumstances have moved on and our perceptions of and the key research questions concerning HRM have changed with them. A decade on, with this Anniversary Edition of the book, it is now appropriate to reflect on these changes and tell the next episode of the story. This chapter constitutes both a 'Preview' and a 'Postscript': a 'Preview' for those who are already familiar with the arguments in HRMRR-1, many of which are still relevant today, and a 'Postscript' for those approaching the text for the first time.[1]

Changing context

In this extended chapter, I intend to do three things. First, I wish to consider how the setting of the story has changed. No longer is Japan lauded as the miracle, iconic economy and the 'German economic miracle' has lost much of its lustre. The rise of China and India are now the focus of interest. Furthermore, in the first edition, although I made some reference to globalisation (pp. 115, 328–9), it was a passing mention in the context of considering whether HRM was a post-modern phenomenon and was discussed in relation to 'disorganised capitalism' (Lash and Urry, 1987). This concept needs to be revisited and more firmly located in debates about the implications of globalisation for sustained competitive advantage and for organisational design. Further, the first edition deliberately focused on the UK experience. Although the emphasis in this chapter has not materially changed, acknowledgement must be made to the growing body of empirical research on 'international' HRM. This includes both studies on European HRM (see, for example, Brewster and Larsen, 1999; Brewster *et al.*, 2000) and on HRM world-wide (see especially the *International Journal of Human Resource Management*; also Sparrow, 2004). The focus in this Preview/Postscript chapter though is on seeing the UK through the institutionalist perspective of 'national business systems' (e.g., Whitley, 1992, 1999) and 'varieties of capitalism' (Hall and Soskice, 2001). This perspective focuses on how the politico-legal, cultural, financial and educational and training systems, within a particular society, define what counts as legitimate ways of doing business, the 'rules of the game' that determine how the stakeholders of the business system in a particular setting relate to each other (see, for example, DiMaggio and Powell, 1991; Greenwood and Hinings, 1996).

Then, although mention was made of the service sector, particularly in relation to public sector services (pp. 266–71), the private sector services, the fastest growing sector of developed economies, received little attention. The vast numbers of studies about McDonaldization and call centres require some critical analysis. Nor can the fashionable 'knowledge worker' be ignored. Indeed, one such manifestation, the consultant, has been active in propagating fads and fashions in HRM practice over the last ten years. Throughout HRMRR-1, much was made of the relationship between 'hard' HRM and labour intensification in manufacturing, but hardly a word was said about 'emotional labour' (the management of emotions and provision of behavioural displays associated with feelings in interactions with customers/clients) and associated 'burn out' in the service sector. This calls for some critical analysis and reflection. Korczynski's (2002) text in this series is an excellent resource on the service sector.

Finally, at the time of writing in 1995 in the UK, the Conservative government was still, if somewhat shakily, in power. At the end of HRMRR-1, I speculated on whether a Labour government would provide an economic, industrial and social climate more conducive to the flourishing of 'soft' (what we would now call 'high commitment management' (HCM)) HRM. My conclusion was pessimistic: that 'the widespread implementation of the "soft" normative model of HRM appears as a mirage, retreating into a receding horizon' (p. 367). Was this pessimism justified? Has the much touted 'Third Way' (Giddens, 1998, 2000b; see also Hutton, 1995), beloved of New Labour, reversed the Conservative governments' employment relations 'reforms' and/or stimulated the adoption of 'high commitment' HRM?

Changing debates

Secondly, I wish to chart the conceptual developments in research on HRM. Clearly debates that were central to UK HRM research even ten years ago – for example, 'Is HRM different from personnel management?', 'Why has HRM emerged?' (HRMRR-1, Chapters 1 and 3) – are now moribund. This is partly due to US dominance in setting research agendas, given the priority which the Higher Education Funding Council of England (HEFCE) Research Assessment Exercises (RAE) place on publications or citations in top-ranking US journals, and partly due to an established consensus on the issues involved. There is little point in discussing the niceties of the differences between personnel management and HRM when, in the US, HRM is just another term for personnel management. In any case it was a bit of a straw man debate. Whether HRM was considered to be different from personnel management – in the UK at least – largely depended on the point of comparison. Sharp distinctions and contrasts emerged if the normative aspirations of HRM were compared with the descriptive practices of personnel management, but otherwise faded into several different emphases, all of which, though, pointed to HRM, in theory at least, being an essentially more central, strategic task than personnel management (Boxall, 1992). There is no longer much point in discussing reasons for the rise of HRM. There is a consensus that globalisation and the 'Japanese Janus', deregulation, electronic technologies, privatisation/enterprise culture/cultures of excellence, decline in trade union power awakened *some* senior managers to the importance of human resources in the achievement of sustained competitive advantage in a world of perceived intensified competition. How dated all this now sounds – along with the presentation of Marks & Spencer and BA as exemplar organisations in the development of cultures of excellence! In both cases, complacency born of the 'Icarus paradox' (Miller, 1990) and misreading of the marketplace have allowed competitors with more 'agile' business models – notably Tesco, Next, easyJet and Ryanair – to outstrip them in profitability and growth in market share.

The world moves on. Even what was recognised as a novel development in HRMRR-1 – the discussion of HRM as a post-modern/postmodern phenomenon (pp. 326–37, 341–53) – has now a slightly *passé* feel. Postmodernism, in a similar manner to managerial consultancy fashions (cf. Abrahamson, 1996; Kieser, 1997), has fallen somewhat out of fashion in the analysis of HRM.[2] It could be argued that although this has been a marked trend from the mid 1990s, it was reinforced, post 9/11, by postmodernism's collision with the pre-modern and the consequent re-embrace of the security blanket of modern epistemologies (Legge, 2002a). (See also Burrell, 1997, for an early recognition of the relevance of the pre-modern to organisation studies.) With some honourable exceptions (for example, Keenoy, 1999; Special Issue, *Organization*, 1999), there has been a retreat from postmodernist approaches to HRM, although some discourse analysis, largely from a critical theory perspective, lingers on (for example, Knights and McCabe, 2000). In part under the influence of US academic imperialism, modernist, positivistic perspectives are now dominant. Indeed, in the very year that HRMRR-1 was published, seminal papers by two leading US researchers, Huselid (1995) and MacDuffie (1995) were rooted in that perspective. The favoured theoretical foundations of today's debates and research are institutionalist and resource-based value theories, reflected in evidence-based approaches that privilege the search for causal relationships in the service of performativity (for two excellent indicative overview publications, see Boxall and Purcell, 2003, and Guest, 1997).

So what are the debates on HRM in the first decade of the 21st century? *The* major concern has been to conceptualise and test the links between HRM and business strategy and performance, a concern which reflects the fashion in auditing societies of evidence-based theorising (Power, 1997). Such research involves three basic questions: how are we to conceptualise HRM, and performance, and how are we to establish the relationship between the two?

Leaving aside the first two questions until later in the chapter, it is the third question that is central to recent debates. Underpinned by resource-based value theory (Barney, 1991) there has been recognition that strategic HRM *potentially* should be a source of sustained competitive advantage. But *is* strategic HRM (however defined) linked to performance (however defined)? If it is, is this on a universalistic (additive), configurational (patterned) or contingency (idiosyncratic) basis (Delery and Doty, 1996; Purcell, 1999)? Should organisations seek 'best fit' or 'best practice'? What are the methodological problems in establishing the validity and generalisability of such relationships? Conceptually speaking, is the 'psychological contract' the key to opening the 'black box' of employee behaviour as the lynch-pin between HRM policy and practice and performance outcomes (Flood *et al.*, 2001; Guest, 1998; Guest and Conway, 1997, 1998, 2000, 2001)?

Finally, in discussing the goals of HRM, alongside the more business-oriented, orthodox goals of labour productivity and organisational flexibility, Boxall and Purcell (2003, pp. 11–13) identify that of 'social legitimacy'. This is not only a major aspect of the institutionalist perspective in its broader sense, but contains ethical overtones. It points to a growing interest in debates about the ethics of HRM, in the context of globalisation, organisational flexibility and the pursuit of cost effectiveness/ profit (Legge, 1998, 2000a; Winstanley and Woodhall, 2000). It also reflects the socio-political climate of New Labour and its fondness for rhetoric about a stakeholder, 'fairer' society. Of course, ethical concerns have never been far from HRM. The notion of 'a fair day's work for a fair day's pay' is central to the work of personnel management/HRM, signalling the need to achieve both the control and consent of employees via 'efficiency and justice' as the old Institute of Personnel Management (1963) used to put it (see HRMRR-1, pp. 56–60). Now that stock markets and NGOs alike speak in the language of the 'triple bottom line', ethical considerations in the treatment of a broad range of stakeholders has become centre-stage.

In the rest of this 'Preview/Postscript' chapter, I wish to explore these issues and debates from a critical perspective and to speculate on future directions of HRM research and practice.

Changing context

Globalisation, organisational design and employment

Definitional issues

In HRMRR-1 globalisation was simply defined in Giddens' (1990, p. 64) terms as 'the intensification of world wide social relations which link distant localities in such a way that local happenings are shaped by events occurring many miles away and vice versa' (HRMRR-1, p. 328). This definition embodies some interrelated ideas, of 'accelerating interdependence' (Ohmae, 1989), of 'action at a distance' (Giddens, 1990) and of 'time–space compression' (Harvey, 1989). 'Accelerating interdependence' is understood to be the growing intensity of international enmeshment among national economics and societies, such that developments in one country impact directly on other countries. 'Action at a distance' refers to the way in which actions of social agents in one locale can come to have significant and unintended consequences for the behaviour of 'distant others'. 'Time–space compression' refers to the manner in which globalisation appears to shrink geographical distance and time. In a world of near instantaneous communication, distance and time no longer seem to be major constraints on patterns of human organisation and interaction (Held *et al.*, 1999, p. 5 fn 2).

Scholte (2000, pp. 15–16) adds to this. In his view, globalisation contains ideas of internationalisation (cross-border flows of resources); liberalisation (removing government imposed restrictions on such flows); universalisation (a sense of the world-wide); westernisation/modernisation (the spread world-wide of the institutions of modernity) and the deterritorialisation/spread of superterritoriality. As a result 'social space is no longer wholly mapped in terms of territorial places, territorial distances and territorial borders'. Held *et al.* (1999, p. 16) bring all these ideas together in their comprehensive definition, that globalisation can be thought of as:

> A process (or set of processes) which embodies a transformation in the spatial organisation of social relations and transactions – assessed in terms of their extensity, intensity, velocity and impact – generating transcontinental or interregional flows and networks of activity, interaction, and the exercise of power.

In these terms, events as diverse as 9/11 and its aftermath, the use and abuse of immigrant labour, the rapid growth of China's and India's economies, the collapse of the market for 'legal' CD singles and the recognition of 'ethnic' cuisine as the favoured takeaway food in the UK all reflect common processes and outcomes of globalisation.

The debates

At the societal level, wide-ranging debates have raged about the cultural and institutional effects of globalisation. Cohen and Kennedy (2000: chapter 20) identify four:

- economic globalisation is nothing new;
- a materialist culture will give rise to uniformity and disempowerment;
- a clash of civilisations will lead to cultural conflict and violence; and
- globalisation will lead to a dystopian future.

Against this an optimistic scenario may be painted of a technology-enabled near utopia.

At the level of organisations and markets the debates which predominate are those between the 'hyperglobalists' and the 'globalisation sceptics'. The 'hyper-globalists', whether optimists such as Ohmae (1989), or pessimists, such as Streeck (1997), argue that world economic integration is occurring on an unprecedented scale, with transnational companies integrating national and local economies into global and regional networks. Depending on your viewpoint, the result is either an exciting 'borderless economy', enhancing the world's long-term prosperity (Ohmae, 1989) or a 'runaway world' (Giddens, 2000a) of a global economy that has escaped both the regulation of the nation state and weak compensatory global institutions. From this perspective the process of globalisation is leading to homogenisation and convergence in organisations' strategies, structures and processes and in consumer choice, along with a new global division of labour that widens the income gap between the 'haves' and the 'have-nots' both within and between societies.

In contrast, there are the 'globalisation sceptics' – often institutionalists – who argue that the novelty, extent and intensity of globalisation is exaggerated and that organisations continue predominantly to reflect their embeddedness in national and local institutions and cultural values (Granovetter, 1985; Hirst and Thompson, 1999; Rugman, 2000; Whitley, 1999). First, much is made of the different patterns of organisational strategising and behaviour as compared to the west that emerge not only from the erstwhile Asian Tigers – so fashionable in the 1980s and early 1990s, the Japanese *keiretsu* and the Korean *chaebols* – but *within* western developed countries too. The contrast is frequently made between the 'liberal market economies' (LMEs) of Anglo-America and the coordinated economies (CMEs) of Germany, North Europe and, to a lesser extent, of France. The LMEs are characterised by market coordination of economic actors, lightly regulated labour markets, capital allocated via stock markets and short-termism, which tends to result in high levels of labour and capital mobility, rapid industry adaptation and a relatively low wage, low skill economy. In contrast, in the CMEs, markets are subject to state regulation, collective bargaining and legislation control the labour market, and banks provide long-term capital to firms. While this inhibits labour flexibility and capital mobility, it encourages the development of a high skill, high value added economy and a high trust system of industrial relations (Hall and Soskice, 2001). From this position any notion of convergence seems exaggerated.

Secondly, the argument goes that the process of internationalisation is nothing new, that few multinationals are truly 'global' companies, being heavily dependent on their home markets, that most foreign direct investment, financial flows and trade are still between and within the 'Triad' of the USA, EU and Japan, that multinationals are not beyond regulation and control and that the 'death of the nation state' has been much exaggerated. The upshot is that there is no trend towards convergence and homogenisation. Rather, firms fit different niches within the world economy, those that match their capacities and capabilities (Morgan, 2001, p. 113).

The compromise view is one that has been termed 'transformationalism' (Held *et al.*, 1999, p. 7). This suggests that the complexities of the interactions between global economic, technological, political, military, migratory and cultural interactions are such that we cannot predict the outcomes other than that 'systems of transnational production, exchange and finance weave together ever more tightly the fortunes of communities and households on different continents' (Held *et al.*, 1999, p. 8 cited in Morgan, 2001). This has echoes of chaos and complexity theory (Stacey *et al.*, 2000)! The best guess at the level of the organisation is that as firms internationalise they evolve and adapt their strategies, structures and processes to new contexts to produce 'hybridised' forms and practices 'out of selective adaptation, innovation and change' (Morgan, 2001, p. 114). At the risk of sounding flippant, this is precisely the process termed 'creolisation' that appears to be on-going with consumer products, such as the adaptation of 'ethnic' foods to western tastes.

Organisational and HRM implications

Where does this leave us in relation to organisational design and HRM, particularly with reference to the UK? The directly connecting links lie in a globalised division of labour, not just at the level of job tasks, but in regional specialisations in terms of industries, skills and the production of raw materials, that are a response to the mantra that globalisation leads to and reflects enhanced competition. Consequently there is a need for ever more 'responsive' and 'flexible' organisations and employees. I will explore this in a bit more detail.

First, the global division of labour has resulted in the developing Third World and EU accession states specialising as providers of cheap labour and commodities, while the developed First World countries of the so-called Triad (Rugman, 2000) concentrate on skills that enable the production of high value added goods and services of all kinds. In the west, this has been reflected in a shift of employment away from labour intensive commodity goods manufacturing as such production is outsourced to cheap labour economies, to the service sector, such as financial and business services, retailing and 'in-person' services (Reich, 1991). The service sector comprises three different sorts of work: highly skilled, 'professional'/'knowledge work' (for example, R&D experts, investment analysts, advertising and IT consultancy, traditional professions); semi-skilled, routine back-office work, heavily reliant on operating IT packages (for example, call centre work, data inputting in financial services) and front-line customer/client facing work (for example, holiday reps, care workers, hairdressers) which, not withstanding the often high levels of personal skills and emotional labour involved, is *generally* labelled as semi- or low skilled.[3] Such work and its HRM implications are discussed in detail in the next section.

Secondly, while *theoretical* rationales about how to achieve sustained competitive advantage might differ, the end result reinforces the message about the desirability of a flexible, 'lean' organisation. Thus institutional theorists argue for the tendency towards institutional isomorphism, whether by 'coercive' means (state or other powerful actors propel firms to take on a particular institutional form), 'normative' direction (transfer of techniques, such as JIT, BPR, Sigma 6, by so-called 'experts' from one setting to another) or sheer imitation ('mimetic' isomorphism) when organisations imitate what seem to be recipes for success and, hence, come to resemble each other (DiMaggio and Powell, 1983). The present 'best practice' seems to be the development of the hollowed-out, 'lean' organisation, as 'rationalisation' has the potential to boost share prices in an Anglo-American culture of 'impatient capital'. Resource-based value theorists argue that keeping up with the leaders does not deliver sustained competitive advantage; rather this depends upon the organisation developing its own unique, scarce and inimitable competencies (Barney, 1991; Wernerfelt, 1984). However, in practice, this may lead in not dissimilar directions. One distinctive capability identified by Kay (1993) is the 'architecture' of supplier and employee relations, that is developing appropriate relational forms, be it trust in interpersonal relations (Hosmer, 1995) or involving subcontracting or networking organisational forms (which may depend on trust or contract). Similarly, if an organisation's core competencies relate to employee know-how that cannot just be brought in, but represents job and organisational knowledge that is unique to the organisation, can only be learned inside and is only valuable to the firm itself (e.g., Ohmae's (1989) 'transnational organizational man' or woman), or if it depends on know-how that might be transferable, but is difficult to secure and retain (e.g., Reich's (1991) 'symbolic analyst'), then an appropriate competitive *and* cost effective organisational form might be a minimalist 'core' supported by a 'periphery' of workers on non-standard contracts and a network of subcontractors ('outsourcing') and contract labour agencies ('insourcing'), scattered throughout the world. Where this occurs, we see the enactment of Atkinson's (1984) model of the flexible firm writ large.

Thirdly, the achievement of competitive advantage in the global economy is often *pragmatically* associated with responsiveness to the sovereign customer, equated to the speedy delivery of the right product/service, of the right quality, at the right time and at the right price. 'Rightness' of product/service suggests an understanding of the consumer's needs: hence the need to get closer to the customer via blitzing the slow, unresponsive, long lines of communication of bureaucracy, through business process engineering. In theory, this means a move from function-centred to process-oriented organisational forms and practices; from linear-sequential work organisation towards parallel processing and multidisciplinary teamworking; towards integrating previously fragmented tasks so that fewer people take less time to perform the process in question. In practice this is often associated with delayering and downsizing. The achievement of 'right' quality is often associated with the introduction of Total Quality Management and (again) functionally flexible teamworking. 'Right' time suggests the introduction of 'just-in-time' production of goods and services and the elimination of waste, which may include 'unnecessary' workers. 'Right' price, particularly in relation to relatively standardised, labour intensive products or services, means the reduction of labour costs, by optimising numerical as well as functional flexibility. Again, the model of 'lean', or some would say 'anorexic', organisation is reinforced.

The empirical data on the long-term success of such initiatives is very mixed (see Legge, 2000b). Certainly, the evidence with respect to business process engineering, in particular, is that very few initiatives achieve the desired breakthrough in performance, partly because of their internal contradictions and, partly, because of their generally narrow technicist view of organisational change and neglect of the human dimension in implementation (Grey and Mitev, 1995; Grint and Willcocks, 1995; Mumford and Hendricks, 1996; Oram and Wellins, 1995; Willmott, 1994).

It is against this background that the conceptual debates about the nature of HRM and its relationship to performance must be set. Of central importance is the issue raised here: is the link with performance on a universalistic, configurational or a contingency basis? This will be considered when I turn to the debates. Meanwhile, this discussion of globalisation draws attention to the rise of the service sector in the west and it is to this that I now turn.

The service sector

Since writing HRMRR-1, the private service sector in developing economies has experienced accelerating growth, particularly with the outsourcing of much commodity manufacture to developing countries. By 2003 the service sector accounted for 80 per cent of employment in the UK (*Labour Market Trends*, 2004). The stereotypical worker in UK industry is no longer the blue-collar, male, manual factory worker, still the focus of much empirical research on HRM pre-1995, in the guise of empowered/oppressed workers in 'lean' 'Japanese' car manufacturing plants. Symptomatic of this change is the sorry tale of the Rover UK car company. In HRMRR-1, Rover was celebrated as moving towards lean manufacturing and HRM under the benign influence of collaboration with Honda. Following the breakdown of that relationship and a short-lived marriage with and divorce from BMW (who were glad to divest the business, minus its crown jewels of Land Rover and the new Mini for £1), Rover, in 2004, with its miniscule market share, aging models and no money to invest in a new range, teeters on the edge of bankruptcy. Instead it is the female or unisex worker in retail or financial services, working in a shop, back office or call centre. Korczynski (2002) provides an excellent summary of many of the HRM issues involved in managing service sector employees and below I highlight some of his major arguments.

The nature of service work

In this chapter I will focus on the private service sector. Suffice to say, since HRMRR-1, in the public services in the UK, the trends identified there of ever-intensified target-setting, surveillance and auditing and governmentally-inspired 'new initiatives' have continued apace. 'Value for money' and 'customer charters' have now been augmented by public–private partnerships in the pursuit of cost-effective 'service delivery'. The issues identified in HRMRR-1 concerning public sector managerialism remain relevant.

Turning to private sector services, as noted in HRMRR-1 (pp. 245–6), services differ from products in that they are intangible, perishable, variable (in customer expectations of and behaviour in the service interaction), simultaneously produced and consumed, and inseparable (customers are involved in the production of many services) (Reeves and Bednar, 1994). Further, different types of service work may be differentiated according to such factors as the degree of customer contact time, extent of customisation, degree of discretion in meeting customer needs, degree of focus on people or equipment, source of value added – front or back office and the extent to which the focus is on a separate product or on the service process (Fitzgerald et al., 1991, cited in Korczynski, 2002, pp. 9–10).

On this basis and building on the ideas of Leidner (1993), Mills (1986) and Lashley (1997), Korczynski (2002, p. 11) identifies three broad categories of service work. At the bottom of the hierarchy is the 'service factory', typified by fast food workers, where the product acts as a buffer between the producer and consumer and where the organisational focus is on the efficiency of product delivery rather than on the customer interface service process. In the middle of the hierarchy, in the 'service shop', the service process is an important part of the product being delivered, the focus is on both front and back offices, and there is an important degree of intangibility. The top of the hierarchy, professional services, comprises the so-called 'knowledge work' where service interaction *is* the product and the focus is on interaction rather than on a back office producing a separate product. While there has been a burgeoning literature on knowledge workers – largely associated with related debates on knowledge management and the development of 'learning organisations' (see 'Changing debates' below), Korczynski argues that the growth of service work lies in the middle category, in interactive service work, 'where it is not thinking or even technical skills which are of increasing importance to most employers ... but "person to person" skills' and even the 'aesthetic' skills deemed essential by the 'style' labour market (Thompson et al., 2001, pp. 926, 930–4).[4] This is borne out by the UK and US statistics. In the UK, only 10 per cent of new jobs can be classified as knowledge work and in the USA current trends predictions suggest that knowledge working will account for only 13 per cent of employment growth (DfEE, 2000; Hatch and Clinton, 2000; Henwood, 1996; *Labour Market Trends*, 2000 – all cited in Thompson et al., 2001, p. 925). Most service sector employment growth is occurring in retail serving, security guarding, personal care in private health and residential care services and in the hospitality services (Crouch et al., 1999).

Contradictions in the 'customer-oriented bureaucracy' and HRM

Building on these classifications, Korczynski (2002: Chapter 4) introduces the important notion of the 'customer-oriented bureaucracy', of particular relevance to the 'service shop'. Here the tensions are recognised between the demands for cost minimisation *and* delivering customer-oriented service-process quality. These tensions are reflected in such dual imperatives as achieving a 'quantity *and* quality focus', 'efficient task completion *and* customer relationship', 'maintaining internal stability *and* adapting to customer variability'. Authority derives from formal rationality *and* from the customer as king, while control reflects both 'imperfect bureaucratic measurement *and* customer-related norms' (see Korcynski, 2002: Table 4.2).

Clearly the nature of HRM practice is likely to vary depending on the type of service work in question. HRM in a 'service factory', where the focus is on cost minimisation and efficient product delivery, as in fast food and in *some* retail chains and call centres, is likely to replicate the 'hard' HRM observed in manufacturing plants with similar imperatives – what commentators now refer to as the 'low' road to work design and employment conditions (see, for example, Ackroyd and Proctor, 1998; Bacon and Blyton, 2000; Batt, 2000; Delbridge, 2003; Holman, 2003; Taylor and Bain, 1999). HRM for professional knowledge workers, assuming they are recognised as possessing the job or organisational knowledge deemed essential to the organisation's effectiveness, is likely to have the characteristics of 'soft', 'high commitment management' (HCM), as part of the 'golden handcuffs' operative in the 'war for talent' (Flood *et al.*, 2001; Melian-Gonzalez and Verano-Tacorante, 2004). But for HRM in the 'customer-oriented bureaucracy' of the 'service shop', such as call centres that aim to optimise sales through 'relationship management', such clear-cut dichotomies are insufficiently nuanced to cope with the requirements and tensions arising out of the dual imperatives of providing a service that achieves instrumental rationality or efficiency and 'the (formally irrational) enchanting myth of [customer] sovereignty' (Korczynski, 2002, pp. 79–80). HRM then becomes an exercise in combining both 'hard' and 'soft' approaches to walk the tight-rope between the Scylla of bureaucratic controls and the Charybdis of necessarily allowing employees some discretion in managing the customer interface. Korczynski (2002, pp. 65–9, 195) outlines the strategies that may be employed to mediate such contradictory imperatives in order to maintain this 'fragile social order' – an order made fragile through 'labour-stretching' and the 'customer moving from enchantment to disillusion'. These include the use of rhetorics of teamworking and shared values and the provision of coping mechanisms, such as 'stress management and emotional self-defence strategies' (Zemke and Schaaf, 1989, p. 65) counselling and creating a 'fun' environment in order to mediate the contradictory imperatives (Kinnie *et al.*, 2000a, b).

The complexities of HRM in the service sector arise from contradictions embedded in, but over and above, those associated with customer-oriented bureaucracy. There is a classic literature on the emotional labour associated with service work and employees' strategies of resistance to both customers' and employers' demands for such labour (for example, Hochschild, 1983, Van Maanen, 1991; see also Fineman, 1993; Fineman and Sturdy, 2001; Korczynski, 2002: Chapter 8). Hochschild (1983), for example, develops the well known argument that emotional labour leads to alienation on the part of the service worker as a result of the commodification of emotion, structured inequality in relation to customers and managerial imposition of feeling rules. However, Korczynski (2002) argues that Hochschild's identification of conditions of *objective* alienation ignores the possibility that emotional labour and the customer's response to it may be major sources of job satisfaction for those successfully enacting such labour. When employees have some autonomy in their expression of emotional labour, and have socially embedded relationships with customers/clients, as in many of the traditional 'caring' jobs in public sector service, real satisfactions for both parties may result and 'spaces' and 'fine lines' may be drawn that facilitate the management of the inherent tensions. Indeed, the tensions that HRM may be called upon to manage in the 'customer-oriented bureaucracy' may arise when employees perceive themselves to be constrained by its instrumental rationality from delivering the degree of individual care and attention that they consider appropriate.

Korczynski's subtle and insightful analysis of work in the customer-facing 'service shop' areas of the service sector calls into question the simple-minded analysis of the so-called 'new service management school' writers (see, for example, DuPuy, 1999; Heskett *et al.*, 1997; Schneider *et al.*, 1993; Zeithaml and Bitner, 1996). The latter take a simplistic approach to HRM in the service sector, arguing for a virtuous circle of 'soft' HCM policies aimed at creating a service culture, whereby employees' and customers' satisfaction 'mirrors and reinforces each others'. Korczynski (2002, Chapter 2) demonstrates that not only is there no empirical support for such a model and that so-called exemplar case studies reveal a 'darker side' (2002, p. 194), but that the model itself rests on dubious unitaristic assumptions. Equally, he accepts that the 'customer-oriented bureaucracy' model of HRM is not appropriate to all customer-facing service sector jobs, even allowing for the exclusion of professional knowledge workers. Sales workers, often in financial services, who are actively involved in stimulating customer demand, may be said to have a sales rather than a customer orientation. When this involves the employees' and the firms' interests being prioritised and the customer being manipulated (as in the recent financial products mis-selling scandals), an instrumental relationship between the employee and customer is likely to exist. In these circumstances, Korczynski (2002, Chapter 6) points out, there is a largely contracted out relationship between the sales force and employer and HRM systems are noticeable by their absence other than in the systems of financial incentive. If service becomes an important element in the sales package, then HRM has a major role in encouraging a more service-oriented culture, although Korczynski suggests that such a development may be contested by carpet-bagging, front-line employees.

The fashionable-but-elusive knowledge worker

Finally, we have the 'knowledge worker', a highly fashionable subject for academic research and debate,[5] although constituting a small minority of service sector workers (Special Issues, *Journal of Management Studies*, 2001; *Organization*, 2000a; *British Journal of Management*, 2004a; Newell *et al.*, 2002). This fashion owes much to the conceptualisation of the knowledge worker as *the* wealth generator of the networked 'information society' and as the lynch-pin of the 'learning organisation' (Castells, 1996; Easterby-Smith *et al.*, 1999; Nonaka and Takeuchi, 1995; Senge, 1990). Knowledge workers are distinctive because, unlike other service sector workers such as those serving call centres or data processors in the back offices of financial services organisations who are receivers and users of knowledge and, hence, *knowledgeable* workers (Thompson *et al.*, 2001), they *generate* knowledge. Hence the definition of knowledge workers as those for whom 'knowledge is simultaneously an input, medium and output of their work' (Newell *et al.*, 2002, p. xii). That said, commentators have got into a tangle in trying to sharpen the concept further, mainly through problems of deciding what sort of knowledge they are talking about (e.g., Blackler, 1995; Gibbons *et al.*, 1994; Polanyi, 1966); what different categories of knowledge worker might be identified (e.g., Reed, 1996); and in what sorts of organisations – often loosely referred to as 'knowledge intensive firms' (KIF) or 'professional service firms' – they might be found (e.g., Alvesson, 1993, 1995; Lowendahl, 1997; Maister, 1994; Scott, 2001; Starbuck, 1992). A problem with these attempts at categorisation is that, given the pervasiveness of 'knowledge', the categories are rarely discrete and the boundaries are fluid (Legge, 2002b). The distinction between a 'knowledgeable' and 'knowledge' worker is often debatable. For example, how do you categorise the young graduate accountant, working in a consultancy organisation, but effectively applying standardised, ready 'solutions'? In a very general sense, who *isn't* a knowledge worker?

What is agreed, however, is that 'true' knowledge workers – in Reed's (1996, p. 586) terms, those whose knowledge base is 'esoteric, non-substitutable, global and analytical' are a productive asset rather than a cost to a firm; that they generally expect and require high levels of task autonomy; and that often being co-located or enjoying very close relationships with their clients, they are vulnerable to poaching activities of client and competitor firms. This has direct implications for the design of appropriate HRM systems for their management (Newell *et al.*, 2002). A 'best practice' approach would argue for a 'high commitment management' strategy addressed to what Newell *et al.* identify as the four key motivators for knowledge workers: personal growth, operational autonomy, task achievement and high financial rewards (Flood *et al.*, 2001; Melian-Gonzalez and Verano-Tacorante, 2004). An HCM strategy might be reinforced by efforts to develop a strong culture as a means of normative control over employees' necessarily high levels of operational autonomy. Prior to its demise, Arthur Andersen was a good example of such an approach (Grey, 2003). Such a strategy recognises a KIF's dependency on the retention of both human and social capital. Social capital is about the networks of either strong or weak ties (Granovetter, 1973) between employees that promote shared understandings or 'communities of practice' which facilitate effective knowledge sharing, development and exploitation (Brown and Duguid, 1991; Edelman *et al*, 2004; Lave and Wenger, 1991; Nahapiet and Ghoshal, 1998). Given the path-dependent nature of such social capital, it may be seen as a resource from the perspective of resource-based value (RBV) theory and, hence, a source of sustained competitive advantage.

A 'best fit' approach might differentiate HRM strategy according to the business strategy pursued by the KIF. For example, Hanson *et al.* (1999) (cited in Newell *et al.*, 2002, pp. 73–5), distinguish between KIFs that follow a 'codification' strategy ('knowledge is carefully codified and stored in data bases where it can be accessed and used readily by any one in the company' (p. 107)) and those that follow a 'personalisation' strategy ('knowledge is closely tied to the person who has developed it and is shared mainly through direct person-to-person contacts' (p. 107)). They suggest that these contrasting strategies, which may also differentiate hierarchical levels within the same firm, call for different approaches to recruitment and selection, training and development and for reward systems.

The 'Third Way'?

The death of private sector collectivism

A few years after the publication of HRMRR-1, the Workplace Employee Relations Survey (WERS 1998) provided a snapshot of the state of employee relations systems in the UK at the end of the decade (Cully *et al.*, 1999). What stands out is the extent of the retreat from traditional forms of collectivism over the last two decades of the twentieth century. Guest (2001a) provides a good summary of the findings (see also Special Issue, *British Journal of Industrial Relations*, 2000b; Millward *et al.*, 2000). In a nutshell, collective representation in Britain is now largely a public sector phenomenon, with 56 per cent of employees in the public sector belonging to a union, compared with only 26 per cent in the private sector. Further, where union members exist in a workplace, but where there is no recognition, the non-recognition rate is much higher in the private sector at 30 per cent than in the public sector at 3 per cent. Again, 60 per cent of workplaces have no worker representatives, including 25 per cent where unions are actually recognised. Where consultative committees exist, in only 34 per cent of public sector and 20 per cent of private sector workplaces, they are more likely to be recognised as influential if they are composed of non-union representatives and particularly where they are appointed by management rather than elected by workers. Finally, the agenda for collective bargaining appears impoverished. Of the WERS list of nine conventional items for bargaining, there was no negotiation with union representatives over *any* of these issues in half the workplaces where unions were recognised. Where negotiation did take place, on average union representatives negotiated on only 1.1 of the 9 issues, while non-union representatives negotiated on even less, 0.9 issues. Nor were issues covered much more comprehensively by consultation: the average number covered by consultative committees was 2.9 where union representatives were involved and 3.7 where non-union representatives were involved.

These statistics reflect two depressing factors from the unions' point of view: their failure to organise new private manufacturing and service sector workplaces, set up since 1980, and their failure to recruit 18–29-year-old workers over the same period (Machin, 2000).

What we have here is a picture of collective representation surviving in organisations that epitomised the Fordist/Keynesian/corporatist settlement – the public sector and large manufacturing plants. For the rest of the private sector and particularly the flourishing service sector the norm is now non-unionisation and without worker representation. The reasons for this decline are not hard to find. There are the structural reasons – a shift to sectors (private service) and workforces (women) that traditionally have not been unionised – and the cultural changes that underpin the structural changes. These cultural changes are epitomised by Conservative governments' advocacy in the 1980s and 1990s of neo-liberal economics, individualism and an enterprise culture in Britain (Keat and Abercrombie, 1991).

If collectivism is on the decline, nevertheless with the advent of New Labour, is the socio-economic climate more conducive to 'soft' HCM than the neo-liberalism of the Conservative governments of the 1980s and 1990s? If it is, this is not (could not be) reflected in WERS 1998 statistics, given Labour had been in power for only one year at the time of collection (Cully *et al.*, 1999). In 1998, the statistics revealed the stony ground that confronted New Labour in the workplace. Only 14 per cent of responding workplaces had high commitment HRM in place (defined as eight plus out of fifteen 'high commitment' practices), as opposed to 29 per cent which had three or less; 22 per cent of which, with three or less HCM practices and no unions, may be defined in Guest's (1995, 1999) memorable phrase, as 'black holes'. More HCM practices existed where there was a recognised trade union reflecting the fact that more practices existed in larger workplaces and in the public sector. Only 1 per cent of private sector workplaces both recognised a trade union and had HCM in place – even in terms of WERS' restricted definition.

Stakeholding and partnership?

When New Labour came to power in 1997, the union movement and many left-of-centre voters hoped for at least a partial reversal of the Conservative governments' 'reforms'. In this they were disappointed. New Labour came to power on a platform which, it claimed, represented a form of social democracy more in tune with contemporary globalised capitalism than the corporatist Keynesian policies of 'Old Labour', but avoiding the uncaring excesses of neo-liberalism (Giddens, 1998; Hutton, 1995). While there is some debate as to whether or not New Labour policies are sufficiently thought-through, innovative and coherent to be presented as a truly 'Third Way' in socio-economic management (Crouch, 2001), this is a convenient label under which to explore New Labour's approach to employee relations, since it came to power.

As Hay and Watson (1998, p. 15, cited in Howell, 2004, p. 6) point out, the approach of New Labour has been to act 'as if the globalization hypothesis were an accurate description of reality'. As a result, the focus has been to adopt policy that encroaches as little as possible on labour flexibility, while at the same time seeking to promote a workplace context in which 'the productivity and creativity of workers is properly harnessed for the good of the firm' (Howell, 2004, p. 14). This has resulted in a three-legged policy: the maintenance of much Conservative industrial relations legislation; a stress on individual rights enforced through legislation; an emphasis on 'stakeholding' and 'partnership'.

As already stated, much of the Conservative governments' legislation, involving the regulation of and limits to industrial action and associated picketing, was left intact. It is significant that New Labour's mantra with regard to trade unions is the call for 'modernisation', which seems to embrace the idea that the way forward is 'to extend individual rights, rather than rights acquired through union membership' (Waddington, 2003, p. 338). Through policies such as the reversal of the opt-out from the Social Protocol of the EU and the introduction of a National Minimum wage, the role of the state was identified as supporting the provision of fairly minimalist individual rights rather than strengthening the institutions of collective bargaining. This flies in the face of the conventional 'Old Labour' pluralist view that 'collective procedures are the custodians of individual rights' (Brown et al., 2000, p. 627) and that the proper concern of industrial relations institutions is 'to correct the imbalance of power in the workplace' (Howell, 2004, p. 14). Instead, New Labour has adopted an essentially unitarist view, that the interests of business and workers are not opposed and that 'win-win' agreements can be reached through 'partnership'. While the idea of partnership focuses on employer–employee/union relationships, this concept was broadened through the notion of stakeholding (in the early days of New Labour government), to include consumers, lenders, debtors and the community. As Howell (2004, p. 13) puts it:

> All but the most minimal definition of stakeholding was disavowed by New Labour in advance of the election, but it remains an alternative discourse, suggesting inclusiveness, social solidarity and fairness, in contrast to the atomism, individualism and exclusive concern with profitability allegedly characterizing Thatcherism.

Yet this is also a discourse which presents the pluralism of 'Old Labour' as encouraging a conflictual, 'them and us', approach to industrial relations, too focused on distributional issues, with worrying echoes of 'beer and sandwiches at No. 10' and of the 'Winter of Discontent', rather than on productivity. The tensions between 'New' and 'Old' Labour are exemplified by New Labour's Prime Minister, Tony Blair, in 2002, labelling public sector unionists as 'wreckers' and firefighters as 'Scargillite', for voting to take industrial action (Waddington, 2003, p. 335). In 1995, in HRMRR-1, such language would have been associated with the Thatcherite Right rather than with a Labour government.

As I write, relationships between trade unions and the Labour government are fraught, not least because the proposed reforms of the public sector services, irrespective of the associated welcome investment, are seen by the unions as likely to undermine the last bastion of collective organisation. A way forward, advocated by both government and the TUC, is to promote 'partnership' between employers and trade unions. This is reflected in the Labour government's *Fairness at Work* document (DTI, 1998), translated a year later into the Employment Relations Act (1999) and the provision of a Partnership Fund to finance new partnership arrangements, and in the TUC's *Partners for Progress: New Unionism in the Workplace* (TUC, 1999). As with the concept of stakeholding (Stoney and Winstanley, 2001), there is confusion as to its precise meaning (see Martinez Lucio and Stuart, 2004, for a general discussion). Guest and Peccei (2001), for example, identify three different models – pluralist, involving use of representative systems; unitarist, emphasising direct participation, financial and psychic states; and hybrid, combining elements of both in a mutual gains model. Further, partnership, as with stakeholding, can be viewed from normative (principles), descriptive (practices) and instrumental (outcomes) perspectives (Donaldson and Preston, 1995).

Guest and Peccei's (1998, 2001) studies of partnership in the UK, focusing on those predisposed in its favour (that is, the membership of the Involvement and Participation Association (IPA)) contain both good news and bad news with respect to the Labour government's and the TUC's aspirations. The good news is that where mutuality principles are matched by consistent and complementary practices, then the outcomes, in terms of employee attitudes and behaviours and associated organisational outcomes, such as positive employee relations and productivity, are likely to be positive. This is particularly marked when partnership constitutes a bundle of direct and representative participation, job design and quality initiatives and employee share ownership and where a high trust dynamic exist (Guest and Peccei, 2001, p. 232). The bad news is that even among this IPA sample, the level of direct participation in work decisions and of representative participation in wider policy decisions is low, implying relatively low levels of management trust in employees and their representatives. Further, it appears that not only is the scope of partnership activities largely determined by management, but that greater emphasis is placed on ensuring the employees' contribution than promoting employee welfare (Guest and Peccei, 2001, p. 231). Further, where partnership deals exist in the UK, they are often born out of crisis and depend on the enthusiasm of a small group of people, thus raising questions about their sustainability. More generally, on the basis of WERS 1998 data, 'new' industrial relations, defined as an amalgam of industrial relations and HRM practices, is almost non-existent in the private sector and is not associated with positive attitudes in the public sector (Guest, 2001a, pp. 102–3; Guest and Conway, 2004). Employee involvement, too, while increasingly extensive, is often introduced in a faddish, piecemeal fashion, lacking line management support, with what little time spent on it involving employees only passively (e.g., downward communication) (Marchington, 2001).

It is not surprising then that some leftward leaning commentators, notably Kelly (1999), are very sceptical of this 'way forward', regarding it rather as a path to trade union incorporation, where employee flexibility is demanded by the employer, but where unions can never endorse collective action. However, a pluralist union strategy of direct confrontation, in the present economic and political climate arguably seems to hold little hope of greater success (Charlwood, 2004; cf. Heery *et al.*, 2003).[6] For senior TUC officials, as Guest (2001a, p. 104) argues, partnership is 'much the most attractive game to play'. Indeed, Ackers and Payne (1998, p. 529) have argued that unions, responding to the 'ethical turn' of business 'should play back the rhetoric of employee involvement and become active agents in the workplace and wider society'. One argument is that this should go hand-in-hand with campaigning for legislation and 'advocating closer ties with Europe and the European [pluralist] ethos of social partnership' (Guest, 2001, p. 104). In this union leaders may be unduly optimistic. Not only does Undy (1999) argue that the 1999 Employment Relations Act is likely to be the conclusive piece of New Labour legislation in settlement with the unions, but that the UK business system is not conducive to high trust pluralist forms of partnership. As Britain lacks most of the coordinating institutions associated with coordinated market economies and tends increasingly towards the institutions of a liberal market economy, the institutional supports for any partnership that does not imply 'enterprise-confined, co-operative unions as subordinate "partners"' do not exist (Smith and Morton, 2001, p. 121). As Howell (2004, p. 19) succinctly puts it:

> The Third Way in industrial relations is institutionally incoherent, in that it is seeking changes in one sphere without challenging the fundamentally liberal market orientation of the rest of the political economy. In this sense, the Third Way can be thought of as a policy of adaptation specific to centre-left governments in weakly coordinated liberal market economies.

Having sketched out some themes relating to the changing context of HRM, in order to situate the changing nature of the debates about HRM, I now turn to the debates themselves.

Changing debates

Strategy, resource-based value theory and the 'learning organisation'

In HRMRR-1, two chapters were devoted to defining HRM and reflecting on its relationship with strategy. Much of the material in those chapters, in defining strategy and looking at the 'fit' between different forms of HRM and strategy, is echoed in today's debates. Nevertheless, the language, orientation and focus of today's debates have seen some shift in emphases.

Gone is the language of 'hard' and 'soft' HRM (Storey, 1987) and of 'utilitarian instrumentalism' and 'developmental humanism' (Hendry and Pettigrew, 1990), to be replaced by the US alternatives of 'high commitment management' (HCM) and 'high performance work systems' (HPWS) (Becker and Gerhart, 1996; Huselid, 1995). Although these terms are sometimes used synonymously, there is an important distinction that to some extent mirrors the earlier UK ones. HCM focuses on job security, job design and employee development as the route to high productivity/profits *and* to high employee satisfaction/commitment. HPWS focuses on practices correlating with high financial performance, such as incentivised pay, de-emphasising job security and the use of internal labour markets and is concerned *only* with high productivity/profits. Further, in HRMRR-1, there was a tendency to imply that matching HRM with strategy would entail choosing either a 'hard' or 'soft' HRM strategy, depending on whether the organisation was pursuing a cost leadership or high value added strategy. Now it is generally recognised that it is not a question of 'either'/'or', but of 'both'/'and' (Keenoy, 1999; Watson, 2004).

Boxall and Purcell's (2003) definition of strategic HRM fits well this 'both'/'and' position. Having identified first, viability and, secondly, sustained competitive advantage as *the* central, 'first-order', strategic goals for all organisations, they suggest that HRM's contribution to such goal achievement is through meeting three, second-order, goals, namely desired types and levels of labour productivity (cost effectiveness), organisational flexibility (short-term responsiveness and long-term agility) and social legitimacy (employment citizenship).

This definition of strategic HRM is consistent with a shift in orientation, away from outward-looking, market-focused, external 'fit' models to inward-looking, firm-focused, resource-based value (RBV) models of strategy (for a good summary paper, see Wright *et al.*, 2001a). As already touched upon, resources are considered to be any feature of the firm that is value creating (and preferably rare, inimitable, non-substitutable and appropriable) (Barney, 1991), including the talents and interactions of employees, even if, unlike proprietary technologies and systems, the firm does not own them. While resources are not immune to 'Schumpeterian shocks', or radical innovations that redefine technologies and the nature of businesses, barriers to imitation have been identified. These comprise such factors as unique timing, teamwork and learning (first mover advantage, path dependency), social complexity (complex patterns of coordination inside and outside the firm, strong clusters of 'human and social capital') (Lovas and Ghoshal, 2000, p. 883 cited in Boxall and Purcell, 2003, p. 77) and causal ambiguity (ambiguity about the cause/effect relations that explain a firm's performance). (The latter characteristic is somewhat controversial and debated – see Boxall and Purcell, 2003; McWilliams and Smart, 1995; Priem and Butler, 2001.)

The RBV perspective argues that a firm's ability to achieve success in the long run rests on its ability to understand its core competencies or those that its needs to develop for future viability as well as competitive advantage. Hamel and Prahalad (1994, pp. 217–28, cited in Boxall and Purcell, 2003, p. 79) identify a 'core competency' as:

'● A bundle of skills and technologies that enables a company to provide particular benefits to customers
● Not product specific
● Represents ... the sum of learning across individual skill sets and individual organisational units
● Must ... be competitively unique
● Is not an "asset" in the accounting sense of the word
● Represents a "broad opportunity arena" or "gateway to the future".'

Leonard's (1998) approach is similar, presenting what she terms 'core capabilities' as 'knowledge sets' composed of four dimensions: 'content' dimensions which include relevant employee skills, knowledge and technical systems and the process dimensions which include managerial systems, values and norms. Because these dimensions are interlocking and systemic, they can become 'core rigidities' over time, *unless* firms can renew themselves by 'double-loop' organisational learning (Argyris and Schön, 1978). Capabilities are dynamic: over time one firm's core capability (such as outstanding quality or customer service) is likely to be copied by competitors and firms that seek sustained competitive advantage must discover new ways in which to differentiate themselves. What starts as a firm's distinctive capability within a particular business sector over the years tends to become a 'table stake' or 'ticket to play', the norm within that sector (Hamel and Prahalad, 1994, p. 226). (Think of quality and reliability in cars, once the distinctive capability of Japanese manufacturers and now the global norm.) The crucial factor then in the RBV approach to organisational analysis is the recognition that 'it is the firm's ability to learn faster than its rivals, and adapt its behaviour more productively, that gives it competitive advantage' (Boxall and Purcell, 2003, p. 83; see also Kamoche and Mueller, 1998). From this perspective firms should place a high priority on becoming 'learning organisations', developing 'organisational agility' and skills of 'knowledge management' (see, for example, Brown and Duguid, 1991; Dyer and Shafer, 1999; Easterby-Smith and Lyles, 2003; Easterby-Smith *et al.*, 1999 ; Nahapiet and Ghoshal, 1998; Newell *et al.*, 2002; Nonaka and Takeuchi, 1995; Senge, 1990).

This is all very fine in theory. A problem is that, like many fashionable concepts, the more one probes the concept of a learning organisation, the more problematic it becomes. For example, conceptually it appears to confuse levels of analysis. After all, it is people that learn and to suggest that 'organisations' learn is to reify an abstract concept. In theory, 'organisational learning' may be said to have taken place when individual or small group knowledge is codified into routines that then become the 'new technologies' embedded within the organisation such that the knowledge persists even in the event of its original creators leaving. (An example of this might be the embedding and development of a new IT system within an organisation, after the consultants that have sold the system have left.) But this is to take a structural rather than a processual perspective on knowledge creation, to privilege codified above tacit knowledge and 'knowledge' before 'knowing'. The orthodoxy today is to see knowledge creation as rooted in social action and practice, as emergent in 'communities of practice' (Brown and Duguid, 1991; Blackler, 1995; Newell et al., 2002).

There are many definitions of what constitutes a learning organisation, but Marquardt and Reynolds' (1994) list of characteristics captures most of the salient points. A learning organisation:

- embraces uncertainty and change;
- has a holistic, systemic view of the organisation;
- has a shared organisation-wide vision;
- creates new knowledge as part of its competitive strategy;
- has a culture of high trust, feedback and disclosure; encourages empowerment at all levels;
- links employees' self-development to the development of the organisation as a whole;
- encourages managers to act as mentors, coaches and facilitators;
- has leaders who encourage risk-taking and experimentation and so on.

Salaman (2001, pp. 346–7) puts it rather differently. He sees the 'learning organisation' as a sanitised version of the discourse of enterprise ('organization and employee as actively and autonomously committed to the achievement of flexible, responsive relationships with clients and employers') that subsequently 'replace[s] an overtly commercial, market focus with the gentler psychological developmental language of learning'.

Although organisations may publicly aspire to become learning organisations (e.g., Ford), the path is fraught with practical difficulties (let alone the conceptual ones) that render its wholesale achievement highly questionable. To begin with, as Weick and Westley (1996, p. 440) perceptively remark, 'Organizing and learning are essentially antithetical processes which means the phrase "organizational learning" qualifies as an oxymoron. To learn is to disorganize and increase variety. To organize is to forget and reduce variety'. Thus, while organisations can live with single-loop learning, the double-loop learning of the learning organisation is inimical to it. Further, the collectivist, democratic, unitarist assumptions of the learning organisation run counter to the individualist, hierarchical and pluralist nature of conventional organisations in capitalist economies. Issues of power and culture are involved here.

The very fact of organisations' persistence and stability over time gives rise to horizontal boundaries that establish areas of expertise and vertical levels that differentiate power and rewards. Such structures generate sectional interests, which, in the context of scarce resources, give rise to power struggles and, as Salaman (2001, p. 348) puts it, 'the possibility of deference and careerism [are] strong motivation[s] to distort, divert, censor data'. When knowledge is power and the source of rewards, those looking for promotion have no incentive to share their 'scarce' knowledge with potential competitors, unless directly rewarded for doing so (see Husted and Michailova, 2002; Swart and Kinnie, 2003). Nor are workers likely to share their tacit knowledge with management (what Marxists refer to as 'mining the gold in the workers heads') without tangible rewards. Managers may be unwilling to become coaches and facilitators if this undermines their ability to justify their differential status and reward.

Further, shared values about conformity, deference, not treading on people's toes, group loyalty, risk avoidance are inimical to the learning organisation's advocacy of freedom of speech, challenging taken-for-granted assumptions, welcoming criticism. Moreover, shared cognitive structures or 'recipes', while advantageously reducing data processing time when conditions are stable, may become counterproductive under changed circumstances, as those erstwhile 'strong culture' heroes of HRMRR-1, Marks & Spencer and BA, found out to their cost. 'Recipes', a form of codified organisational learning, restrict an organisation's ability to learn by restricting environmental analysis or by influencing how data are analysed (Daft and Weick, 1984; Weick, 1995). Rather than flexibly responding to new signals from the environment, managers create their own environments through shared sense-making and then respond to these enactments in ways that make them real. This is inconsistent with the learning organisation's advocacy of managers reflexively questioning their own basic assumptions.

Finally, there is the issue of whether a national business system is likely to facilitate or inhibit the development of a learning organisation. While Japan is often seen as facilitative, the UK's tendency towards a liberal market economy is inhibitive. Keep and Rainbird (2000), for example, characterise the UK economy as chronically short-termist, with a preference for a growth strategy of merger and acquisition (facilitated by deregulated financial markets) rather than organic growth via R & D investment, for a long working hours culture (leaving people with little time or energy for training), and with an obsession with shareholder value and the bottom line. These factors are not facilitative to the development of a learning organisation. Indeed, despite all the talk of developing learning organisations as the route to sustained competitive advantage, Keep and Rainbird point to the prevalence of lean and mean organisational forms in the UK (see also Ackroyd and Proctor, 1998):

> The notion that a set of universalistic trends and competitive pressures is compelling organizations towards competition based on organizational learning is seriously flawed. Alternative avenues to competitive advantage remain viable, at least in the UK, and price-based competition continues to thrive above all in the service sector ... many organizations, far from opting for the high skills route to competitive success remain wedded to standardized, low specification goods and services where the main factor of competitive advantage is consistent delivery of relatively simple goods and services at a low price. This Fordist or Neo-Fordist strategy is in turn reflected in Tayloristic forms of work organization that minimize the opportunities for creativity and discretion. (Keep and Rainbird, 2000, p. 185)

Such organisations, in a deregulated labour market, are likely to be at the forefront of cost-reducing delayering, downsizing and outsourcing exercises, with their attendant effects on employee trust and skill development (Grugulis et al., 2003). Low trust is hardly conducive to collaborative learning.

Nevertheless, the learning organisation matches well the RBV view of organisations that promote employees as *the* source of competitive advantage, even if for most UK organisations advocating the learning organisation, this remains a utopian aspiration rather than a realistic achievement (see, also, Knights and McCabe, 2000). There is a political dimension too in its very advocacy, despite the fact that it is political factors that are likely to undermine its achievement.

It is hardly surprising then that the RBV view of organisations, by treating employees and HR systems as *potentially* a source of sustained competitive advantage, is popular with reflective HR practitioners and academics alike and, even among the less reflective, may become the next consultant/practitioner fad. Fitting HR policy to business strategy always leaves HR policy and practice as reactive, if no longer as powerless as traditional personnel management. The RBV perspective accords a more proactive role to HRM as it can be valued not just for reinforcing predetermined business strategies, but for developing strategic capability, improving the long-term resilience of the firm.

Universalistic 'best practice' or contingent 'best fit'?

If strategic HRM centrally involves the integration of HRM with business strategy, we need to reflect on just what is meant by 'integration'. This issue was dealt with extensively in Chapter 4 of HRMRR-1, which critically evaluated various models of internal and external 'fit' and the arguments remain relevant. Apart from those mentioned in the chapter, there is now the model of Baron and Kreps (1999). They identify desirable internal 'fit' as involving three types: 'single employee consistency' or mutually consistent and supportive policies in relation to employees – no 'deadly combinations' to use Delery's (1998) colourful phrase; 'among employee consistency' or consistency of employment conditions for employees doing similar work; and 'temporal consistency' or consistency in how employees are treated over a reasonable period of time. As discussed in HRMRR-1 (Chapter 4), these forms of integration and their interrelationships are problematic at a conceptual, empirical and prescriptive level.

It is not surprising then that there is only *limited* empirical support for any widespread and close matching of business strategy and HR policy and practice (see HRMRR-1, pre-1995; Boxall and Purcell, 2003, post-1995). Furthermore, from a prescriptive position, there is an argument that this is not necessarily desirable as it may inhibit the flexibility required to cope with new opportunities and market changes (Boxall, 1992; Wright and Snell, 1998). Similarly, it has been suggested that advocacy of close 'internal' integration 'over-simplifies the paradoxical elements involved in managing people' (Boxall and Purcell, 2003, p. 57). For example, an organisation may require a highly committed, 'empowered' workforce, while at the same time pursuing a strategy of downsizing, as is the case for companies in the airline and car manufacturing industries (Pil and MacDuffie, 1996, cited in Boxall and Purcell, 2003, p. 57). External fit may undermine the possibility of achieving internal fit.

A further problem is that while external fit with business strategy would argue a *contingent* design of HRM policy, internal fit or consistency – at least with the human resource values associated with HCM/HPWS – would argue a *universalistic* approach to employment policy. Can this contradiction be reconciled without stretching to the limit the meaning of HRM as a distinct approach to managing people at work?

This distinction is critical as the contingent and universalistic approaches rest on very different and contradictory theoretical perspectives about organisational competitiveness. The universalistic approach is consistent with one reading of institutional theory and arguments about institutional isomorphism (DiMaggio and Powell, 1983; Paauwe and Boselie, 2003). In other words, the assumption here is that organisations that survive and prosper do so because they identify and implement the most effective, 'best' policies and practices. As a result successful organisations get to look more and more like each other through practices such as benchmarking. In HR terms this equates with the belief that treating employees as assets via the HCM/HPWS models will always pay off, irrespective of circumstance, and that the effects are additive (the greater the number of 'best' HR practices that are implemented, the greater the positive effect on performance) (see, for example, Pfeffer, 1994; see Marchington and Grugulis, 2000, for a critique of Pfeffer's work). Further, in what is sometimes described as a configurational approach, it is also claimed that an integrated 'bundle' of HCM/HPWS practices will have positive, non-linear, synergistic effects on performance (MacDuffie, 1995). Contingency approaches, on the other hand, are consistent with the RBV theories that argue that sustained competitive advantage rests not on imitating so-called best practice, but on developing unique, non-imitable competencies (Barney, 1991). This approach rests on the recognition of the importance of *idiosyncratic* contingencies that result from path dependency, social complexity and causal ambiguity (Collis and Montgomery, 1995). From this perspective organisational performance is not enhanced by merely following 'best' HR practice (the HCM/HPWS models) but from knowledge about how to combine, implement and refine the whole potential range of HR policies and practices to suit the organisation's idiosyncratic contingencies (Boxall, 1996; Wright *et al.*, 1994).

There has been some attempt to reconcile these two approaches. For example, Boxall and Purcell (2003, p. 69) suggest that it is helpful to distinguish between the 'surface level' of HR policy and practices in an organisation and an 'underpinning level' of processes and principles. They write:

> We are most unlikely to find that any theorist's selection of best practices (the surface layer) will have universal relevance because context always matters, as descriptive research demonstrates. It is, however, possible to argue that there are some more effective ways of carrying out the generic HR processes (such as selection) which all firms would be wise to follow. More powerfully, it is possible to argue that there are certain *desirable* principles which, if applied, will bring about the more effective management of people (authors' italics).

Further, building on the work of Wright and Snell (1998), Guest (2001b, p. 1093) proposes what he terms a 'contingent strategic contingency model'. In other words, it might be argued that in capital intensive manufacturing, HCM/HPWS models may always be preferable as labour costs are a small proportion of total costs and high quality, committed labour can facilitate the optimum exploitation of high cost plant and materials. In the service sector, however, there is a choice, depending on business strategy, between the 'high road' of HCM/HPWS and the 'low road' of a low waged, Tayloristic, highly controlled employment strategy. Empirical research has yet to provide clear support for this proposition.

This brings us to what has become *the* key debate about strategic HRM, in both the USA and UK: what is its relationship to organisational performance?

The performance link

Is strategic HRM linked to organisational performance on a universalistic (additive), configurational (patterned) or contingency (idiosyncratic) basis (Delery and Doty, 1996)? The greatest support appears to be for the universalistic model: that the greater the extent to which the characteristics of the HCM/HPWS model are adopted, the greater the association with organisational performance (see, for example, empirical studies in both the UK and USA by Batt, 2002; Delaney and Huselid, 1996; Delery and Doty, 1996; Guest, 1997, 1999; Guest *et al.*, 2003; Huselid, 1995; Ichniowski *et al.*, 1997; MacDuffie, 1995; Patterson *et al.*, 1997; Pfeffer, 1994; Youndt *et al.*, 1996). (For support of the contingency position, see Arthur, 1992, 1994; Sanz-Valle *et al.*, 1999.)

However, on examination, the empirical evidence for such universalism is more equivocal than it might appear at first sight.

The problems stem from methodological concerns with research design (see Becker and Gerhart, 1996; Edwards and Wright, 2001; Guest, 2001b; Legge, 2001; Marchington and Grugulis, 2000; Ramsay et al., 2000; Rogers and Wright, 1998; Wright and Gardner, 2003; Wright et al., 2001b) and from empirical observation (see Cully et al., 1999; Gittleman et al., 1998; Osterman, 1994). As already said in the introduction, considering the relationship between HRM and performance, the three most basic questions are: how are we to conceptualise HRM, how are we to conceptualise performance and how are we to conceptualise the relationship between the two?

For testing the relationship between HRM and performance, from a positivistic perspective, the first requirement is a theory-derived conceptualisation of HRM and its precise specification as an independent variable. Clearly positivists cannot work with the subtleties and sophistication of Keenoy's (1999, p. 16) approach, which, likening HRM to a hologram, regards it 'not as a concrete, coherent entity but as a series of mutually implicated phenomena which is/are in the process of becoming'. For a positivist, HRM must be a precisely specified variable not a process. Process, in theory, pertains to the relationship between HRM and performance, not to HRM as a concept. That said, in treating HRM as a variable, positivists have not acted consistently, either at the level of theorising or in terms of specifying and measuring the concept of HRM.

At the level of theorising there have been the competing 'strategic', 'descriptive' and 'normative' perspectives (Guest, 1997). Nor has there been agreement about specification or measurement. For example in operationalising the concept of pay, as Wright and Gardner (2003) point out, does one assess the presence or absence of contingent pay, or does one specify a variety of approaches for tying pay to performance (merit pay, bonuses, stock options, profit-related pay, commissions and so on)? One could also specify the range of different performance criteria to which pay could be tied. The fact that most studies opt for the simple measure of presence/absence is worrying as this tells us nothing about how effectively the practice is implemented (see Ramsay et al., 2000). With reference to contingent pay, for example, Purcell (1999, p. 27) reminds us that 'Bowey and Thorpe (1986) found that it was not the type of pay system that affected the outcome but the use of consultation in the design phase – i.e., that process was more important than content'. As for measurement, although the concept of contingent pay is included in MacDuffie's (1995), Huselid's (1995) and Arthur's (1992) list of 'high performance practices', each measures it differently. For example, Huselid uses the proportion of the workforce covered by profit sharing, gainsharing and merit pay, while Arthur used the percentage of employment costs accounted for by bonus or incentive payments (Becker and Gerhart, 1996, p. 793).

Leaving aside the issue of specification, questions have also been raised about the validity and reliability of measures of HR practices. Most of the American studies already cited involve large-scale postal surveys of 'single respondents answering quick questions', to quote John Purcell (1999, p. 28). Purcell questions whether one senior management respondent can possibly have knowledge of the whole firm and also of the desirability of question 'that encourages the respondent to tick a box and not go to the file to find the answer'. Further, the use of single respondents grows more problematic the more complex and diversified the firm. It is especially suspect when the respondent is asked to make judgements on how the firm compares with others, particularly in relation to matters of performance (see below).

If there is a question mark over the validity of the data in these studies, their reliability (and, hence, generalisability) is also suspect. While most studies rely on single respondents (and, hence, issues of internal consistency dominate), a multiple-respondent study by Gerhart et al. (2000), designed to examine sources of variance in the measurement of HR practices, found 'frighteningly low' levels of overall reliability of HR practices measures. They noted that the statistic commonly used in multiple respondent studies [rwg] was inappropriate because it only assesses 'agreement' within one firm rather than 'reliability' across firms. However, although they found almost no interrater reliability for more 'objective' measures of HR practices, they report better interrater reliability on subjective measures (involving Likert-type scales) of the effectiveness of the HR function.

Despite these difficulties, as Guest et al. point out (2003, p. 294), it cannot be denied that the large majority of studies find an association between HR practices and performance *whichever* operational definition of HRM is used. Indeed, Edwards and Wright (2001, p. 570) argue that diversity in measures of HRM may be a positive rather than a negative factor:

> if different empirical measures come up with broadly similar results, then surely the basic hypothesis is strengthened. Yet the studies may be showing only that managing people in a coherent and disciplined way is more effective (in some sense) than not doing so.

Turning to the conceptualisation and measurement of performance, US commentators have tended to take a rather limited conceptualisation, generally in terms of productivity and financial performance. A study by Rogers and Wright (1998) (cited in Wright and Gardner, 2003) reviewed 29 empirical studies containing 80 separate observations of an empirically tested link between HRM and organisational performance. They categorised the performance measures into HR (turnover being the only employee measure they found), organisational (for example, productivity, quality, customer satisfaction), financial accounting (for example, return on assets) and financial markets (for example, Tobin's q the difference between the market- and book-value of a firm's assets). They found that only 3 effect sizes were reported relating HR to human resource outcomes, but 34 relating to organisational, 24 to accounting and 19 to financial market outcomes. No sign here of the 'balanced scorecard' approach to performance advocated by

David Guest (1997, p. 266) and to some extent achieved in Guest's (1999) own study of employee reactions to HRM and in the WERS (1998) survey, which tapped employee attitudes to work and their assessments of the climate of employee relations (Cully et al., 1999, Chs 6, 8 and 12). The lack of American studies on employee outcomes seems misguided as all the theoretical rationales of how HR affects organisational performance rest on the assumption that its is *through* these employee outcomes.

Apart from the very limited and questionable conceptualisation of organisational performance and, with the exception of European commentators (Boselie et al., 2001; Boxall and Purcell, 2003; Guest, 1997; Paauwe and Richardson, 2001), no recognition that these are but social constructions, there are problems with measurement. As Wright and Gardner (2003) point out, with the notable exception of Huselid's (1995) study, there is a tendency not to assess multiple performance measures in any single study. As a result researchers are unable to examine the interrelationships among outcomes, although Huselid's study suggests these may be significant (at least some of the effect of HR practices on firm performance was mediated by the reduction in employee turnover). Problems such as these, though, pale into insignificance when compared to those associated with examining the *relationship* between HR and performance.

A first issue is the practical one of trade-offs in selecting an appropriate level of analysis in testing HRM/performance relationships (Wright and Gardner, 2003). Plant-level studies (for example, MacDuffie, 1995; Youndt et al., 1996) have three strengths: the risk of variance in HR practices is minimised; the respondent(s) is likely to have first-hand knowledge of the HR practices – both espoused and in-use – increasing the validity of the responses; there is the potential of providing the most proximal measures of performance. The drawback is that research at this level may not allow assessing 'fit' with business strategy and there are the perennial issues of generalisability (see Purcell, 1999, p. 31).

Business-level studies are optimal for assessing relationships between HR practices and business strategy, but given that businesses often have multiple locations, categories of employee and jobs, as indicated earlier, precise assessments of HR practices become problematic, especially if the research design relies on just one senior management respondent.

The bulk of research linking HR practices and performance has been conducted at corporate level (see Wright and Gardner, 2003) given the reliance on financial measures of performance, as it is at this level that much of the publicly available financial data exists. However, this exacerbates problems associated with the validity of single respondent assessments given the complexity of assessing HR practices over a range of businesses, the problem that there may be variance between the business strategies across businesses within some corporations (hence identifying *a* business strategy is likely to be problematic) and, because these studies cross industries, the difficulty in partialling out all of the industry effects.

At first sight, this may appear to be here just a methodological issue rather than a theoretical one (that is, the researcher needs to be careful to match appropriately the research question with the level of analysis). However, what is worrying theoretically is that if the majority of the research studies remain located at the corporate level, given the American obsession with measures of financial performance, this is not conducive to assessing the enacted aspects of employee behaviour that constitute the intervening variable in explaining the relationship between HR practices, operating and financial performance. It is difficult to see how such studies can *test* causal relationships, as opposed to making theory-derived inferences about the correlations they find.

This brings us to some major difficulties: causality, implicit performance theories and the 'black box'.

First, with some exceptions (see Becker and Gerhart, 1996, Table1) the majority of the American studies are cross-sectional rather than longitudinal and, hence, as intimated above, while causality may be inferred from correlation, technically it is not tested. This gives rise to three possibilities. A causal relationship may exist in the direction inferred, that is, HRM policies and practices give rise to positive outcomes. However, as Purcell (1999, p. 30) points out, even if this did exist, it might reflect no more than a temporary 'Hawthorne' effect in response to a change programme. (Of course it is possible, with the same direction of causality, that HRM, particularly 'hard' HRM, may give rise to negative outcomes, or as Guest and Hoque (1994b) report, positive outcomes on organisational performance measures but negative outcomes on HR/employee outcomes.) Alternatively, reverse causality may exist. In other words, just to take the financial outcomes, as a firm becomes more profitable or its share price rises, it may invest in 'high commitment/ performance' HRM practices, such as expenditure on training or profit sharing. As Wright and Gardner (2003) point out, this may be due to a belief that such practices will further increase performance, from a belief that they will reduce the risk of performance declines, or they might stem from a belief in the justice and efficacy of wealth distribution. However, it is the profits that generate HR practices rather than vice versa. A further possibility, identified by Wright and Gardner, is that the observed relationship between HR practices and performance may stem not from any true relationship (that is, 'true' from a positivistic perspective), but from the implicit theories of organisational survey respondents. Their argument on this latter point is as follows.

Implicit performance theories (e.g., Brown and Perry, 1994; Golden, 1992; McCabe and Dutton, 1993) suggest that respondents' implicit theories of relationships between variables of interest bias their responses to survey questions. So, for example, if a respondent has little detailed knowledge of the HR practices in her firm (highly likely if the firm is large, diverse and multisited), but knows that the firm is performing well in terms of productivity and profitability, she may infer that 'high performance' HR practices *must* exist, given this level of performance, based on the implicit theory that such practices are related to high performance. In their own study (Gardner, Wright and Gerhart, 1999, cited in Wright and Gardner, 2003) some support was found for implicit theories about the HR/performance relationship, in a simulated study. Gardner, Wright and Gerhart presented line managers, HR managers, MBAs and HR Masters students with scenarios of high- and low-performing firms and then had them estimate the use of HR practices in each firm. They report that all four groups estimated significantly greater usage of 'high performance' HR practices in high- as opposed to low-performing firms. This suggests that the observed relationship between measures of HR practices and firm performance may simply be an artifact of the implicit theories about their relationship held by respondents. Furthermore, Guest *et al.* (2003), in an empirical study of 366 companies, found that while the greater use of HRM was not associated with higher productivity when *objective* performance measures were used, there was a strong association between HRM and both productivity and financial performance when using *subjective* performance measures. When a rigorous test of causality was used, namely employing objective performance measures, controlling for past performance and testing for change in performance, then no significant association between HRM and performance were found.

Finally, there is the vexed issue of the 'black box'. It is widely recognised, even by adherents to this research agenda and its associated positivistic research designs (for example, Becker and Gerhart, 1996; Guest, 1997; Wright and Gardner, 2003) that little has been done to unlock the 'black box' of the processes that link HRM (however conceptualised) with organisational performance (however conceptualised). But unless this is done, for example, by developing models that include theory-derived, key intervening variables, it is not possible to rule out unequivocally alternative causal models that explain empirical associations between HR practices and organisational outcomes (Becker and Gerhart, 1996, p. 793; Purcell, 1999, p. 29).

The question then becomes how many and what intervening variables should there be in the 'black box' (employee behaviour?, employee skills?, strategy implementation?, operating performance?) (Becker *et al.*, 1997; Becker and Huselid, 1998) and how should these variables be specified? For example, 'operating performance' might be defined and measured in terms of customer satisfaction, customer retention, sales revenues, quality defects, scrap, down-time, productivity, labour costs; employee behaviours in terms of productivity, creativity and discretionary effort (Becker *et al.*, 1997; Wright and Gardner, 2003). Then there is the issue of distinguishing between espoused and actual HR practices and employee skills and behaviours (Wright and Snell, 1998). And, as Wright and Gardner (2003) point out, the greater the number of intervening variables identified and the greater the level of specificity, the greater the multiplicative effect in determining the processes of a model, as the model building requires specification of the relationships between each of the specifications of the major intervening variables.

If this complexity is problematic when a universalistic approach to HR practices/ performance relationships is adopted, it becomes additionally so when a contingency or configurational approach is preferred. With contingency models of the HRM/performance relationship there are issues of causal ambiguity and path-dependent contingencies that add up to idiosyncratic choices (Boxall, 1992; Collis and Montgomery, 1995; Purcell, 1999). Causal ambiguity refers to the numerous and subtle interconnections between contingent factors that makes each organisation's experience, in a sense, unique. Path dependency recognises the emergent nature of strategy and the dependence of policy choices on the organisation's history and culture. Put the two together and the resultant idiosyncratic contingency suggests that each organisation has to make choices of HR policy and practice based on its judgment not just of appropriateness to business and operational strategies but what 'suits' the history and culture of the organisation, what 'feels' right (Purcell, 1999, p. 35). Such potential complexity sits uneasily with the large-scale surveys and quantitative approaches of positivism.

Turning to empirical observation, we are confronted by puzzling findings. If we are to accept at face value the research studies that suggest there is a universalistic relationship between HCM/HPWS and organisational performance, why do we find such relatively little implementation of this model of HRM? I have already mentioned the absence of any widespread, extensive adoption of HCM practices in UK organisations (Cully et al., 1999). Similarly, in the US, Gittleman et al.'s (1998) comprehensive survey found that of six work organisation practices (teamwork, TQM, quality circles, peer review of employees' performance, worker involvement in purchase decisions and job rotation) 58 per cent of firms had none of these practices. Putting the findings of the empirical studies together (including those of Osterman, 1994) there seems to be a consensus that HCM/HPWS are more prevalent in the public sector (UK) and in private sectors competing on quality, whether in products or services, exposed to international competition and employing more advanced technology. As far as workplaces are concerned, HCM/HPWS are more likely to be found on the greenfield sites of large (and in the UK) foreign-owned and unionised organisations. But all this would point to the logic of the contingency 'best fit' approach rather than that of 'best practice'. It may also point to the possibility that LMEs, typified by short-termism, are inimical to the development of HCM.

Indeed, as several commentators have observed, the implementation of any management 'best practice' is likely to fall foul of vested interests, politicking, organisational history and culture (Dunlop and Weil, 1996). What is defined as 'best practice' is going to be influenced by national culture and institutions, as is clear from the differing HR implications of the 'patient capital', coordinated market economy institutions of Germany as compared to the short-termism of the liberal market economy of Anglo-America. Indeed, it has been suggested that, in the Anglo-American world, in the last fifteen years or so, the dominant emphasis in practice has been on short-term survival rather than the development of long-term resource-based advantage, with the widespread, *ad hoc* adoption of 'hard' policies of delayering, downsizing and increasingly contingent forms of employment, even if, simultaneously, senior management aspire to a committed, involved workforce (Boxall, 1996; Pil and MacDuffie, 1996).

Future directions of research on the strategic HRM and performance relationship

Despite the difficulties outlined above, interest in the HRM/performance relationship seems here to stay. Most commentators, already cited, have suggestions for the improvement of research designs (for example, more within industry, business and plant-level designs, more consistent and valid measures of HR practices, more longitudinal studies, a 'balanced scorecard' approach to organisational outcomes, opening up the 'black box' and so on). Guest (1997) and Purcell (1999) present two contrasting ways forward, one from a universalistic and one from a contingent perspective.

Guest (1997, 1999) suggests that expectancy theory might provide a theory of process to link HRM practices and performance, as it links motivation and performance. Specifically, expectancy theory proposes that, at the individual level, high performance depends on high motivation, coupled with the necessary skills, abilities, appropriate role design and perception. This equates skills and abilities with quality, motivation with commitment and role structure and perception with flexibility. HR practices designed to foster these HR outcomes (for example, selection and training for abilities and skills/quality; contingent pay and internal promotion for motivation/commitment and teamworking design for appropriate role design and perception/flexibility) should facilitate high individual performance. This in turn should contribute to high performance outcomes (for example, high productivity, low absenteeism and labour turnover) giving rise (other things being equal) to desired financial outcomes. In empirical studies of employees' reactions to HCM/HPWS policies (Guest, 1999; Guest and Conway, 1997, 1998, 2000, 2001) Guest suggests that the psychological contract may be a key intervening variable in explaining the link between such HR practices and employee outcomes such as job satisfaction, perceived job security and motivation. Furthermore, although Guest's research is cross-sectional and, hence, raises the usual caveats about causality, the inferred direction of his empirical findings is supported by a similar longitudinal study (Patterson *et al.*, 1997).

Nevertheless, Guest acknowledges the limitations of these models in terms of explaining organisational outcomes. While we may be able to measure the impact of HR practices on *HRM* outcomes (quality, commitment and flexibility), the measurable impact on *organisational* and *financial* outcomes is likely to become progressively weaker because of the range of potentially intervening variables. Guest also suggests that we need a theory about the circumstances when human resources matter more and a theory about how much of the variance between HR practices and performance can be explained by the human as opposed to other factors.

Purcell (1999, pp. 36–8), building on the resource-based value view of strategy, has some interesting observations here. He recognises that, on the one hand, claims that bundles of 'best practice' HCM/HPWS are universally applicable leads into 'a utopian cul-de-sac', ignoring dual labour markets, contingent workers and business strategies that do not require such expensive practices to achieve financial success. On the other hand, the search for a contingency model of HRM is a 'chimera', 'limited by the impossibility of modelling all the contingent variables, the difficulty of showing their interconnection, and the way in which changes in one variable have impact on others, let alone the need to model idiosyncratic and path dependent contingencies'. The way forward, Purcell argues, is the analysis of how and when HR factors come into play in the management of strategic change. Purcell suggests that we should explore how organisations develop successful transition management, build unique sets of competencies and distinctive organisational routines and, in situations of 'leanness', with greater dependency on all core workers, develop inclusivity and trust. The focus of research on strategic HRM (indeed, the focus of strategic HRM itself) should be on 'appropriate HR architecture and the processes that contribute to organisational performance in the short and medium term, and which positively contribute to the achievement of organisational flexibility and longevity'. Suggestions as to how this might be done are outlined in Boxall and Purcell (2003).

Whether the future research on strategic HRM focuses on the psychological contract or on the processes of transition management, it can only benefit from the insights derived from qualitative, preferably longitudinal, critical case studies. In particular, such studies, by their ability to explore in depth contextual contingencies and employee sense-making, can contribute to opening the 'black box' of the processes that link HRM to organisational performance.

The ethics of HRM

Since writing HRMRR-1, there has been a growing interest in business ethics generally, reflected in concerns about the environment and animal rights, the effects of globalisation and, in the wake of corporate scandals such as Enron and WorldCom, issues of corporate governance. This has rubbed off onto HRM (see, for example, Special Issues of *Organization*, 1995, 2003b; Legge, 1998, 2000a; Parker, 1998; Winstanley and Woodall, 2000; Woodall and Winstanley, 2001). The reasons for this interest are implicit in much of the preceding discussion. There was a reaction against the perceived excesses of the enterprise culture, which, for some, embodied the 'unacceptable face of capitalism'. Milton Friedman's (1970) assertion that 'the social responsibility of business is to increase profit', while in tune with the enterprise culture, rang a discordant note with the stakeholding leanings of New Labour. There are concerns about the implications of globalisation and the associated mantra about the search for competitive advantage which, often in practice if not in theory, are equated with cost cutting and labour intensification. The short-termism of Anglo-American business systems and their apparent single-minded obsession with organisations' financial performance often appears to disregard human dignity at work (Hodson, 2001). In the 1980s, HRM commentators might have considered debates about the ethicality of multinationals to be of specialist interest. Now, the outsourcing of much commodity production (and services, such as call centres) from the west to developing countries, as part of a strategy of flexible organisation, has brought close to home the issues of the ethicality of child labour and the 'hollowing out' of UK and US household name companies. The changing nature of the UK workforce places questions about equality and diversity firmly on the agenda. Above all, as is evident in much of the preceding discussion, the concept of trust, identified years ago in Alan Fox's (1974) seminal work, now permeates many problematic issues about employee relations and organisational design. These include generating employee commitment and honouring their psychological contracts, developing social partnerships between employer, employees and unions and managing joint alliances and extended supply chains (see Special Issue, *Academy of Management Review*, 1998; Special Issue, *International Journal of Human Resource Management*, 2003a).

Good technical discussions applying western deontological and teleological ethics (Kant, Nozick, Rawls, Mill, Aristotle) to HRM and employment relations abound (see, for example, Woodall and Winstanley, 2001; Legge, 2005). However, the two most influential books in fuelling ethical debates about HRM and globalisation are the polemics by Richard Sennett, *The Corrosion of Character*, and by Naomi Klein, *No Logo*. In the next section I wish to explore the interrelationships between their arguments and the implications for HRM.

The Corrosion of Character?

Richard Sennett, an Aristotelian, argues that organisational 'flexibility' has deeply damaging effects on workforces in Anglo-American post-industrial societies as it prevents people from developing a long-term, coherent narrative that can render their lives meaningful to them. While recognising the well-known dysfunctions of bureaucracy and Fordism, in particular, the deadening of the spirit, initiative and spontaneity, Sennett (1998, p. 43) argues that routine can protect as well as demean, 'decompose labor, but [it can] compose a life'. In other words, the work might be routine, but contains 'traction' as well as tedium (well recognised in Baldamus' classic study (1961) and in that of Jahoda (1972 [1933]) on unemployment), giving structure to the days, weeks and years. The 'metric of time' might be oppressive, but through its formal negotiation (whether of overtime, holidays, or seniority rules) and its informal 'fiddling' (work-study, time-based incentive schemes) could provide an arena of empowerment. Long service in one organisation might conceivably generate a sense of community and mutual commitment, even loyalty and *esprit de corps* among colleagues and workmates that had grown old together, united by shared, if not always pleasant, experiences. Bureaucracy and Fordism, both icons of modernism, are rooted in modernism's meta-narrative of progress. Hence, if all else failed, employees could give meaning to their lives through a belief, underwritten by the Keynesian settlement, that their steady, stoical endurance and deferred gratification would provide the foundation for the upward mobility of their children. As Sennett (1998, p. 44) concludes: 'to imagine a life of momentary impulses, short-term action, devoid of sustainable routines, a life without habits, is to imagine indeed a mindless existence'.

But, Sennett suggests, flexibility in all its manifestations, is pushing us in the direction of a meaningless work life. Work is becoming 'illegible' at many levels. For example, for routine production and service workers, equipment that is designed to be user friendly to facilitate speed of response has the complexity built into the machines rather than the operations. Its lack of comprehensibility renders our engagement with work superficial, since we lack deep understanding of what we are doing. The lack of challenge on the one hand and the inability to cope with potential challenges in the event of machine breakdown undermines any identification with the task, in the context where the side-bets inherent in long-term stable work, which might have provided substitute identification, no longer exist. Among managerial and professional workers in delayered organisations, job moves, whether inside or outside the organisation, often constitute 'ambiguous lateral moves', as the vertical moves, characteristic of the old bureaucracies, disappear, and it is only after the event that 'retrospective losses' may be clear. No longer is it clear, either, whether voluntary 'career' moves between organisations are the best strategy to optimise financial gain, particularly in a world of continual downsizing, when 'last in' is likely to be 'first out'. Yet failure to move in a society that idolises change, not to take the gamble that it might be career-enhancing, is to accept oneself in advance as a failure. Then, in fast-moving organisations, particularly the media, financial services and ICT industries, the emphasis may be on youth, with a devaluing of experience, particularly as recognition of seniority and experience may appear to be a reversion to the habits of bureaucracy. Finally, the feeling that experience and track record no longer count, may result from the favoured control mechanisms of decentralised and supposedly responsive organisations: surveillance and auditing (see also Lyon, 1994; Power, 1997; Sewell, 1998; Townley, 1994). The first contains the message of low trust and the second that one is only as good as one's last game, that there is no longer any notion that past record counts, that the accumulation of credit, of a character that is valued for its own sake, is irrelevant.

To Sennett, 'teamworking, ' part of the vocabulary of flexibility, epitomises many of the corrosive trends he identifies. 'Teamworking', he argues, emphasises the group, but for groups to hold together, they tend to keep to the surface of things by avoiding difficult, divisive personal questions. One difficult issue that cannot be confronted is that team members may be competitors and that the 'leader', now represented as a 'facilitator', is really the boss, but one who holds power while denying responsibility because that has been delegated to the team. Management is now a matter of peer pressure or a mixture of 'concertive' and 'chimerical' controls (Barker, 1993; Sewell, 1998). Equally, the team can deny responsibility, because 'change' is the responsible agent and everyone is a victim. The existence of power without authority in teams encourages the deep acting of a mask of cooperation and respect for team members, while looking for opportunities for freeloading, escaping responsibility for failed projects and claiming ownership of successes. The short-term projects and fluid team membership do not allow for the development of loyalties and trust.

The ethical question that Sennett leaves us with is: 'how can a human being develop a narrative of identity and life history in a society composed of episodes and fragments', in a world where flexibility no longer refers to tensile strength but to global trends that threaten to bend, if not break us? Sennett's voice is not alone. Almost twenty years previously, MacIntyre (1981), also an Aristotelian, was making similar observations. He argued that role fragmentation, inauthenticity ('the most effective manager is the best actor') [p. 107] and an unbalanced development of potentiality (hence the present maxim: 'no one on his deathbed has said "I wish I'd spent more time at the office"; many have said "I wish I'd spent more time with my family"') deprive us of the opportunity to develop a substantial integrated narrative of our lives. As a result, we fail to render our lives meaningful to ourselves and to the community as a whole (see, also, Special Issue, *Organization*, 1995).

Now it is easy to criticise Sennett's argument as one-sided, overblown and as the nostalgic musings of an ageing unreformed Keynesian socialist,[7] but it serves as a corrective to the utilitarian-inspired eulogies about the challenge of portfolio careers in flexible organisations in an exciting boundaryless world. Certainly, where flexible labour is about treating employees as a variable cost to be minimised rather than an asset to be nurtured and valued, the very words that are associated with such employment – the 'contingent', 'peripheral' workforce – along with the individualised contracts offered, point to the organisation loosing its bonds of obligation to its employees.[8] This may result in treating them as a commodity, contrary to Kantian and Aristotelian ethical premises. 'Outsourcing' and 'insourcing' exacerbates this commodification of employees because when workers are not technically employed by an organisation yet whose quality of employment is an indirect outcome of its policies, it is likely to be a case of 'out of sight, out of mind'. This has worrying echoes. The longer the supply chain, often stretching to the other side of the world, the more that workers are placed contractually outside the boundaries of the organisation, the greater the extent to which proximity is replaced by physical, social and psychological distance, the more likely it is that fellow human beings are then transformed into objects different from ourselves, for whom we feel no responsibility (cf. Bauman, 1991). A recent UK example is the exploitation (and invisibility) of migrant and asylum-seeking immigrants working for gangmasters in agricultural, fishing and food processing industries (*Guardian*, 27 March 2004). Purcell (1997) cites some overhead transparencies used in a presentation by the employment agency Addecco, suggesting the key advantages of using agency labour, that encapsulates the commodification of labour contractually outside the boundaries of the organisation:

- 'Enhances flexibility (turn on and off like a tap)
- No legal or psychological contract with the individual
- You outsource the management problems associated with non-core staff
- Greater cost efficiency (on average 15 to 20 per cent)'.

Mickey Mouse and the meaning of life

Turning to Naomi Klein's (2000) *No Logo*, her analysis suggests that one answer we may seek to Sennett's (and MacIntyre's) question about rendering our lives meaningful, only serves to reinforce the trends of global flexibility that 'corrode character'. Her argument is as follows.

It is a cliché that in a postmodern world many of us seek identity through our consumption rather than production and that such consumption is less about use-value than of meaningful images, values and experiences. These are often contained in the global brands that are the marketing triumphs of the global corporations, the engines of global flexibility. Brands, Klein argues, are not so much products as symbols of lifestyles and their character is to colonise the potentially competing sources of meaning, such as sporting events, institutions of learning and the media. While nation states symbolised their conquest of peoples and colonisation of territory by implanting a national flag, so the global companies implant their logos over areas of captive consumption.

It starts when logos grow 'so dominant that they have essentially transformed the clothing on which they appear into empty carriers for the brands they represent' (Klein, 2000, p. 28). Then the logos look to extend their colonising reach. The first tactic is sponsorship. As the 'feel-good' experience is all-important to consumer brands, there is a 'natural' association with leisure and pleasure. Hence sporting events and rock concerts are the first to be sponsored. This extends further in the development of fluid, synergistic partnerships between celebrity people and celebrity brands, such as between Michael Jordan and Nike. A variant of this is when the creator of a superbrand is accorded star status in the eyes of the consuming public, as in the case of Virgin and Richard Branson. Then, in a world of deregulation and privatisation, as government spending on public services dwindles, educational institutions and the arts generally, anxious to make up the shortfall, are ripe for partnerships with large corporations. This includes universities seeking sponsored Chairs, research and buildings, schools granting exclusive vending rights to Coca-Cola or Pepsi in exchange for equipment or art galleries extensions being named after their sponsor, such as the Sainsbury Gallery at the National Gallery in London. The search for profitable synergies through cross-promotional tie-ins, often facilitated by merger, is the next step and one exemplified by Disneyworld. From the initial children's films have sprung a raft of enterprises: videos, theme parks and hotels, Disney superstores, the *Disney Magic* cruise ship, which may visit Disney's privately-owned island in the Bahamas, Castaway Cay. There is even a gated and protected Disney township development in Florida, 'Celebration'. Disney bought ABC, which then broadcast its cartoons and films, and stimulated demand for a trip to Disneyland or Disney stores. As Klein (2000, p. 146) puts it, such activities 'combine buying with elements of the media, entertainment and professional sports to create an integrated branded loop'. A further step in brand dominance is signalled by the elimination of independent competition. This is done through the establishment of mega chains, such as Walmart, which undersells competitors; the blitzing out of competition by setting up chain store clusters – Starbuck's tactic; and the introduction of palatial flagship superstores, which act as a 3-dimensional advertisement for the brand (Klein, 2000, p. 132). The global corporations' final victory in this process of colonisation is signalled by their powers of censorship. This is direct, as when ABC suppressed a negative Disney-related story. It is also indirect as when Walmart's and Blockbuster Videos' refusal to stock material that they consider might undermine their image as a shop for the whole family, results in musicians, journalists and other media workers self-censoring their records, videos and magazine products in order not to risk the loss of shelf space (Klein, 2000, pp. 165–71). Here we have the irony that icons of capitalism are suppressing freedom of choice and individual rights to freedom, the major ethical justification of capitalism.

Sennett's and Klein's work are complementary. If we seek to achieve a meaningful identity, denied to many of us at work, through the consumption of *meaning full* brands, whether knowingly or not, we collude with those very global corporations that have been instrumental in creating working conditions that 'corrode character' in the first place. There are many ironies in this process. When we speak of shopping as 'retail therapy', the implication is that it unwinds the stresses induced by the flexibalisation deemed necessary for the production of the products and services that we now seek to consume. As producers we are stressed by the labour intensification of functional flexibility and the 'contingent worker' status afforded us by numerical flexibility, as shoppers we welcome low prices and extended opening hours. In purchasing brands we may feel we acquire a distinctive image, yet in following 'fashion' we lose uniqueness. We may deplore the instabilities in our working life, yet embrace it in some of our consumption as we seek to identify and follow the latest trends. We may want fashion, but in purchasing 'brands', by definition, we are also seeking security and predictability, 'something you can rely on' – the antithesis of many people's working lives. We may mourn the lack of value accorded to seniority and experience today, yet we purchase brands that look to 'cool' youth cultures for inspiration (Klein, 2000: Chapter 3). We may find no meaning in poorly paid, casualised 'McJobs', but as consumers, whether of fast food, financial services or supermarkets, we collude with our conversion into unpaid, part-time workers. We act as waiters in fast food restaurants, as bank clerks when we engage with call centres and cash machines, as garage attendants at petrol stations and as shop assistants – not to mention the pushing and tidying away of shopping trolleys – in supermarkets. In our roles as consumers we underwrite the flexibalisation that gives rise to the 'corrosion of character'. The irony is that those most in need of alternative experiences to compensate for a 'McJob' working life are the least able to afford them.

Ethics and HRM

It is against this background that we can consider the role of human resource management in relation to the ethics of employment. As was discussed in HRMRR-1 (pp. 56–60), the personnel function is centrally concerned with achieving both the control *and* consent of employees or, to put it in Marxist terms, to assist in the extraction of surplus value through obscuring the commodity status of labour. The 'high commitment management' (HCM) model of human resource management seeks to secure the consent and commitment of employees to organisational values and demands by treating them as valuable assets and with respect. Ethically speaking, this strategy may be motivated by a belief in stakeholder ethics, New Labour's favoured stance. Such a position is consistent with the unitarism of human resource management. Insofar as it is linked to a belief in fostering a unitary, inclusive and supportive culture, there may be elements of communitarianism, a close cousin of Aristotelianism. However, although HCM may appear Kantian in its respect for the person, the likely instrumentality of that respect rules out a truly Kantian ethical position. The ethical standpoint that appears to be most clearly embodied in HCM, not surprisingly, is a major ethical justification of capitalism: utilitarianism. The 'black holes' and 'bleak houses' identified by Guest and Sisson respectively (see HRMRR-1, p. 359) might appear to be basing their employment practices on the ethical position outlined by Friedman (1970).

Nevertheless, what prevails as the *enacted* ethics of human resource management in workplaces is likely to be the outcome of an on-going process of informal negotiation between different organisational stakeholders, reflecting emergent power/knowledge relations in which *most* employees are not as powerful as their employers. However, mindful of the circuit of capital, the voices of employees as consumers are likely to be influential in a capitalist society, but at the risk of cooptation into the ethics of utilitarianism.

Indeed, as Klein (2000) herself suggests, there already exists an activist backlash against brands. There is 'culture jamming', the touching up of billboards and other advertising media in a way that subverts the original message. There is anti-corporate and anti-globalisation activism, including boycotts over the use of child labour in the developing world and over a range of environmental issues (environmental pollution, rain forest destruction, GM crops). There have been attacks on the symbols of globalisation, such as McDonald's. Such debate and protest has been facilitated by the use of the Internet.

In the long term, though, the Kantian, trust-building ethic of 'Do as you would be done by', that may harness employees' productive creativity by providing dignity and trust at work (Hodson, 2001), might be most beneficial to all organisational stakeholders.

The future of HRM and HRM research

What of the future for HRM? This question can be considered from two perspectives: the nature of HRM practice and approaches to HRM research.

The future of HRM in the UK, at the level of practice, is likely to involve those perennial issues that require a balancing act. One might predict a continuing, pragmatic recognition that core knowledge working employees with scarce and valuable skills are likely to require some form of HCM, that may be considered 'too expensive' to extend to low skill, easily replaceable employees. Even so, judging by present empirical data (see, for example, Melian-Gonzalez and Verano-Tacorante, 2004), such knowledge workers are likely to be the lucky minority and there are no guarantees that HCM will accompany them all their working lives without continuous refurbishing of their skills in the light of changing organisational demands. One might predict the continuing need to respond to the often conflicting demands of the regulatory environment and of the marketplace and the imperative of cost control in a context of short-termism. One expression of this may be the challenge of coping with an increasingly diverse workforce given skills shortages and the influx of workers from the enlarged EU, let alone the rest of the world. The need to gain both the control and consent of employees, as ever, will be the *leitmotiv* of human resource management (Hyman, 1987). In coping with these challenges one might guess that, as in the past, practitioners will be susceptible to the fads and fashions of the consultancy industry (Clark and Fincham, 2002). Presently Kaplan and Norton's (1996, 2001) ideas about a 'balanced scorecard', not to mention the mirage-like learning organisation, are the latest fashions in HRM's perennial quest for centrality and credibility.

Just at the time when the key ideas of resource-based value theory penetrate the thinking (if not necessarily, the practice) of practitioners, I would predict that the academic debates, while not abandoning the RBV perspective, will tend to refocus outward to explore more fully the institutionalist approaches.[9] This is likely to have two foci.

First, there is interest, *within* particular sectors of industry and national economies generally, of how human resource management practices become *homogenised* through isomorphism. Thus Paauwe (1996, 2004), Paauwe and Boselie

(2003) and Boselie *et al.* (2001, 2003), in the Netherlands, have been exploring the effects of coercive, normative and mimetic isomorphism (DiMaggio and Powell, 1983) in producing particular patterns of HRM and HRM and performance relationships in what they term highly institutionalised (hospitals and local government) and less institutionalised (hotels) sectors. Here 'institutionalised' is defined in terms of such factors as labour legislation, collective bargaining regulation, works councils with their legal prerogatives, unionisation – all employee-friendly characteristics of coordinated market economy institutional settings. Their research reveals two particularly interesting findings. First, that due to institutional pressures, twelve out of sixteen of Pfeffer's (1994) so-called 'best practices' are so prevalent in the Netherlands that they cannot be the source of competitive advantage against other Dutch companies (Paauwe, 1996). Secondly (and relatedly), the effect of HRM on performance is lower in highly institutionalised sectors than in less institutionalised sectors, where there is more leeway with respect to HRM choices.

The second focus of the institutionalist perspective is likely to be continuing work on *heterogeneity* in HRM *between* institutional settings. I would predict fruitful work in exploring the different nature of HRM and HRM/performance relationships between liberal market economies and coordinated market economies. The development of HRM practices in economies moving from state regulation to private enterprise is another developing area. Particular attention may be paid to the former East European economies, now members of the EU, and to what is likely to be the economic superpower of the 21st century, China (see, for example, Special Issue, *International Journal of Human Resource Management*, 2004b).

Finally, while not dismissing the highly quantitative studies on HRM and performance, I would support Korczynski's (2002) and Edwards' and Wright's (2001) plea that we cannot understand the nature of HRM unless we understand the nature of the work, the social relations and the dynamic of the economy in which it is embedded. This calls for rich, longitudinal case studies (see, for example, Hope Hailey, 1997) and an historically and culturally informed understanding of organisations' institutional settings. Further, the submerged voice of those who experience HRM initiatives (see Guest, 1999; Knights and McCabe, 2000) needs to be given more prominence, not only for ethical reasons, but to counteract the managerialist agendas that are implicit in much HRM and performance research.

Notes

* It should be noted that this chapter draws on and adapts some material already published in Legge (2000a), Legge (2001) and in Legge, K. (2003) 'Strategy as organizing', in Cummings, S. and Wilson, D. (eds), *Images of Strategy*. Oxford: Blackwell, 74–104.

1. I have decided not to update HRMRR-1, chapter by chapter, for three reasons. First, much of what is contained in that text is still valid today. Second, it nevertheless stands as a statement of the emergence of HRM in an historical context of rising neo-liberalism,

which the Preview/Postscript chapter updates. Third, if I were to substantially rewrite the book from a 21st century standpoint, I would use the Postscript/Preview chapter as a framework and write a *different* book. This would be something of an amalgam between the approach adopted in this Preview/Postscript chapter and those of the excellent Boxall and Purcell (2003) and Paauwe (2004). The emphasis would be predominantly institutionalist, but with some critical deconstructive discourse analysis and greater use of actor network theory.

2. Nevertheless, in organisation studies generally, postmodernism still finds a welcome refuge in *Organization*, a journal founded in the year HRMRR-1 was published and in the Standing Conference in Organisational Symbolism (SCOS). The focus of such work tends to be on discourse analysis and on organisational aesthetics. With the exception of 'Human and Inhuman Resource Management: Saving the Subject of HRM', Special Issue, *Organization*, 1999, the work undertaken from a postmodern perspective today rarely focuses on HRM, but on organisation/organising generally.

3. 'In-person' services also contain highly skilled and paid work, particularly when the target client group is affluent and the service being purchased is a lifestyle choice, less about use-value and more about image (du Gay, 1996). Yet while a Michelin-starred media chef is light years away from a McDonald's fast food worker and might more accurately be perceived as a knowledge worker, sadly, in employment terms, far more people work in the fast food industry!

4. According to Thompson *et al.* (2001, p. 931), 'Aesthetic labour is defined as a supply of embodied capacities and attributes possessed by workers at the point of entry into employment. Employers mobilize, develop and commodify these capacities and attributes through processes of recruitment, selection and training, transforming them into competencies and skills which are then aesthetically geared towards producing a "style" of service encounter deliberately intended to appeal to the senses of customers, most obviously in a visual or aural way'.

5. Much of the research about knowledge workers is framed in debates about the nature of organisational knowledge, its creation and management in knowledge-intensive firms. As this is seen to be a hot topic in post-industrial societies, much research money has been available in both Europe and North America, spawning many Special Issues of journal papers in this area. See, for example, Special Issues, *Journal of Management Studies*, 1993, 2001; *Organization Studies*, 2003c; *British Journal of Management*, 2004a. The same applies to the proliferation of Special Issues on the 'learning organisation'.

6. For more up-beat and optimistic interpretations of the present position and future of UK trade unionism, see Gospel and Wood (2003) and Kelly and Willman (2004).

7. Sennett is also well known for his early classic *The Hidden Injuries of Class* (with Jonathan Cobb, 1977, Cambridge University Press).

8. It should be noted, however, that Guest *et al.* (2000) found that working on a fixed term contract correlated with perceptions of fairness on the part of their *knowledge worker* IPD survey respondents. This was explained by respondents' perception that a transactional contract protected them from the open-ended commitments 'expected' by an overly demanding organisational culture. Further, given their high employability, a fixed term contract allowed them to negotiate conditions that offered a good balance between work and the rest of their lives' activities.

9. This is not to suggest that these two approaches are incompatible, just that institutional setting will influence the application of RBV theory. See, for example, Oliver (1997).

1

What is personnel management?

Introduction: four models

As outlined in the Introduction, this book is concerned with contradictions and paradoxes in personnel management and HRM. Hence it is fitting to start with a paradox. The question 'What is personnel management?' may appear straightforward enough. But in many ways it is reminiscent of the old philosophy exam question and answer:

'Is this a real question?
Yes, if this is a real answer!'

The paradox here is that what at first sight appears a neat conclusive answer in fact raises a whole series of questions – about what constitutes the form and substance of a 'real' answer. And it is the search for a satisfactory answer that reveals that the initial question is not as straightforward as it looks. To achieve an answer that is not only neat in form but satisfactory in content requires the unpacking of the substance of the question.

'What is personnel management?' then, requires consideration of (a) personnel management and (b) how we are using the notion of what it 'is'. Let's start by attempting to define 'personnel management'. Immediately before we address its substance, we might remember that 'personnel management' and the 'personnel function' are terms that are often used synonymously both in the academic literature and, more particularly, by practitioners. But the term 'function' itself can have several meanings. Quite apart from its mathematical and sociological usage, managers use the term in two distinct yet overlapping senses. The 'personnel function' can refer either to an *activity* (by implication arising from the system's/ organisation's 'need') or to the activity's *institutionalised* or *departmental* presence within the organisation. In this latter case it is synonymous with the 'personnel department' (Legge, 1978, pp. 18–19).

But the activity and the departmental presence are not identical, even if they do overlap. As an activity, personnel management must necessarily spread beyond the

43

confines of the personnel department and involve line managers, marketing, finance and so on. Indeed, evidence from the most comprehensive recent surveys (at the time of writing the Workplace Industrial Relations Survey (WIRS) 2 and 3) would suggest that personnel *specialists* are the exception rather than the rule in most workplaces. While this reflects the fact that 'most' workplaces employ under 50 people, even in the large companies in which most people in the UK are employed, personnel specialists are not invariably present in their divisional and head offices (Millward and Stevens, 1986, pp. 20–3; Millward *et al.*, 1992, pp. 27–35; see also Legge, 1988, pp. 19–21). As will be discussed later, the fact that personnel management as an activity and as a specialist department are not coterminous gives rise to numerous problems of ambiguity and perceived credibility for personnel specialists.

Leaving this aside for the moment, can we at least differentiate the personnel management activities in which all managers participate and those reserved for specialists? Again, no simple answer presents itself. Specialists in smaller companies tend to be less 'specialist' than those in larger companies, and to perform a different, often less ambitious role (Tyson, 1985). The nature of the involvement of non-specialist managers (as well as the roles adopted by specialists) is likely to vary from company to company, reflecting not just size, but the business strategy and the philosophy and style of personnel management that the company chooses to adopt (see, for example, Tyson and Fell, 1986; Purcell, 1987; Marchington and Parker, 1990). (I return to this issue in Chapter 2.)

So, if personnel management can refer to an activity or a specialist department, the boundaries between which are unclear, can we at least identify in the broadest terms what that activity is, irrespective of who carries it out? Here we meet with our second issue: how are we using the notion of what personnel management 'is'? There seems to be four options. We can refer to what personnel management aspires to do, what ideally in essence it 'is'. This we might label the *normative* model, as 'is' and 'should be' are equated. Or, we can recognise the functions we think it actually serves, irrespective of our evaluative assessment of such functions. We could call this the *descriptive–functional* model. A third model is a descriptive statement but with clearly critical overtones. This we call the *critical–evaluative* model. Finally, we can identify the behaviours, warts and all, of those who see themselves as occupying a personnel specialist role. Let us call this the *descriptive–behavioural* model. To clarify these distinctions, we will consider each of these models in turn.

Normative model[1]

Most personnel management textbooks offer variants on the standard normative definition of personnel management as 'the optimum utilisation of human resources in pursuit of organisational goals'. Here is a selection, first, of some US definitions:

Pigors and Myers (1969)
Since management aims at getting effective results *with people*, personnel administration is a basic management function or activity permeating all levels of management in any organization ... Personnel administration is ... organizing and treating individuals at work so that they will get the greatest possible realization of their intrinsic abilities, thus attaining maximum efficiency for themselves and their group, and thereby giving the enterprise of which they are a part its determining competitive advantage and its optimum results.

Megginson (1972)
It is believed that the most significant aspect of personnel management is to be found through the direction and control of the human resources of an organization in its daily operations ... the successful performance of the personnel function necessitates that each manager orient himself within his total business environment in order to help achieve the various organizational programs and objectives [Note the sexist language!].

Glueck (1974)
Basically personnel is concerned with the matching of people to the jobs that must be done to achieve the organisation's goals.

Jucius (1975)
Personnel management is defined here as follows: The field of management which has to do with planning, organizing, directing and controlling the functions of procuring, developing, maintaining and utilizing a labor force, such that the

(a) Objectives for which the company is established are attained economically and effectively.
(b) Objectives of all levels of personnel are served to the highest possible degree.
(c) Objectives of society are duly considered and served.

Compare these with the classic definition of the (then) Institute of Personnel Management (IPM) (now Institute of Personnel and Development (IPD)):

IPM (1963)
Personnel management is a responsibility of all those who manage people, as well as being a description of the work of those who are employed as specialists. It is that part of management which is concerned with people at work and with their relationships within an enterprise. Personnel management aims to achieve both efficiency and justice, neither of which can be pursued successfully without the other. It seeks to bring together and develop into an effective organisation the men and women who make up an enterprise, enabling each to make his own best contribution to its success both as an individual and as a member of a working group. It seeks to provide fair terms and conditions of employment, and satisfying work for those employed.

Analysing these statements, it would appear that normative models of personnel management highlight some common themes. It seems that personnel management is about selecting, developing, rewarding, and directing employees in such a way that not only will they achieve satisfaction and 'give of their best' at work, but by so doing enable the employing organisation to achieve its goals. Furthermore, personnel management is the task of all managers, not just of personnel specialists alone. If these are common themes some differences are implicit when comparing the US with the UK IPM definition. The US definitions clearly assume a unitary frame of reference: achieving the 'greatest possible realisation of [employees'] intrinsic abilities' is assumed to be not only perfectly compatible with 'attaining the maximum efficiency for themselves and their group', but a precondition of the organisation's achieving its 'optimum results'. In contrast the IPM definition, contrasting efficiency and justice, takes a markedly more pluralist stance. Such a stance becomes even more pointed when we look at the position of the descriptive–functional models.

Descriptive–functional model

These definitions of what personnel management is, tend to appear in UK rather that US texts and reflect a pluralist perspective. By way of example consider these of Sisson (1989) and Torrington and Hall (1987).

Sisson (1989)
The term personnel management is used here to describe the policies, processes and procedures involved in the management of people in work organisations ... [this collection of papers] is primarily concerned with personnel management as a system of employment regulation: the ways in which people in work organisations are selected, appraised, trained, paid, disciplined, and so on ... [it] is concerned with the regulation for which managers are primarily, if not exclusively, responsible.

Torrington and Hall (1987)
Personnel management is a series of activities which: first enable working people and their employing organisations to agree about the objectives and nature of their working relationship and, secondly, ensures that the agreement is fulfilled.

Both definitions state clearly that the function of personnel management is – not should be – the regulation of employment relationships. Neither assumes that the regulation is directed towards some fixed God-given set of organisational goals, but rather implies (or, in the case of Torrington and Hall, explicitly states) that the goals as well as the means to achieve them are open to negotiation. Sisson's mention of discipline suggests that employers and employees will not necessarily agree or pursue the same goals or means of achievement. The existence of different stakeholders within an organisation identifies the necessary function of regulation. If an organisation is to survive, regulation is necessary – and hence is the prime function of personnel management.

Critical–evaluative model

Almost unique among the definitions provided of personnel management is that of Watson (1986).

Watson (1986)

Personnel management is concerned with assisting those who run work organisations to meet their purposes through the obtaining of the work efforts of human beings, the exploitation of those efforts and the dispensing with of those efforts when they are no longer required. Concern may be shown with human welfare, justice or satisfactions but only insofar as this is necessary for controlling interests to be met and, then, always at least cost.

As Watson (1986, p. 176) himself admits, he created this definition, which is unlikely to appear in standard textbooks or management policy statements, in order 'to point up the justificatory overtones and comforting mystifications' of the normative models. As with the Sisson and Torrington and Hall definitions, Watson recognises the existence of different stakeholders in the organisation and that their interests are likely to differ. But, in contrast, he does not see the management of the employment relationship as one of regulation of equal interests. By his own admission, from a deliberately 'loaded' perspective, by way of correction to the normative models, Watson invites us to consider personnel management as an activity in which one stakeholder, the employer, has substantially more power than the employed, and the 'management' of the employment relationship is essentially exploitative rather than regulatory. It should be noted that the three models of personnel management that we have identified so far, generally speaking, rest on three different world views. The normative models (particularly the American ones) rest on a unitary perspective; the descriptive–functional models, on a pluralist perspective, and the critical–evaluative model on a radical perspective (see Burrell and Morgan, 1979; Morgan, 1986).

Descriptive–behavioural model

If we have identified what personnel management ideally aims to do, and what function it actually serves, what, in practice, are the behaviours of personnel specialists in their efforts to enact either of these models? Here, (perhaps signalled by Watson's definition) we come down to earth with a bump. For many of the descriptions of what personnel specialists actually do at best convey an air of disappointment and at worst are positively disparaging, even insulting. A few examples will suffice to paint a rather depressing picture.

Torrington and Hall (1987, p. 3) open their book by reminding us of a scene from *Dirty Harry*. Harry Callaghan, having overstepped the mark in the use of forceful persuasion in his policing activities, is summoned by his superiors and informed that he is to be transferred to personnel. With a curling lip and contemptuous look he snarls 'Personnel is for assholes'. The message is clear: Personnel is crap. While Harry's language might be a little extreme, it is not far removed from typical line managers' assessment. Guest (1991a), for example, refers to American managers' view of personnel managers as having 'Big hat, no cattle', while Keenoy (1990a, p. 6), quoting a manager from Marks & Spencer, refers to the 'personnel ghetto'. These quotations from the early 1990s hark back to Drucker's famous assessment of personnel management in the early 1960s

> Personnel administration ... is largely a collection of incidental techniques without much internal cohesion. As personnel administration conceives the job of managing worker and work, it is partly a file clerk's job, partly a housekeeping job, partly a social worker's job and partly fire-fighting to head off union trouble or to settle it ... the things the personnel administrator is typically responsible for – safety and pension plans, the suggestion system, the employment office and union's grievances – are necessary chores. I doubt though that they should be put together in one department for they are a hodge-podge ... They are neither one function by kinship of skills required to carry out the activities, nor are they one function by being linked together in the work process, by forming a distinct stage in the work of the managers or in the process of the business. (Drucker, 1961, pp. 269–70)

The reference to the incoherence of personnel managers' activities, reminds me of a joke about personnel management often recounted and received with relish by managers at the bars of Business Schools. It goes like this:

> Three professionals, an architect, an accountant and a personnel manager were discussing which (apart from the obvious one) was the oldest profession. The architect said: 'Well, of course, it's architects because, if you remember your Bible, God created Heaven and Earth, and of course that's essentially an architectural job.' 'Ah', said the accountant, 'but before he created the world, God created order out of chaos, and surely that's the essence of accountancy, so accountants must be the oldest profession.' 'Wrong', says the personnel manager. 'Where do you think the chaos came from?'

A second joke (equally well received) reflects managers' and employees' often disappointed expectations of what personnel managers actually do as compared to their stated functions and aspirations:

> There are three great lies:
> (1) 'I will love you forever'
> (2) 'The cheque is in the post'
> (3) 'I am from the personnel department and I am here to help you'.

In the eyes of other management groups, whether in the US or UK, perennial criticisms of personnel managers centre around their perceived lack of influence with senior management, their being 'out of touch' with business and the rest of management's problems and their promising more than they deliver. Ritzer and Trice's study in 1969, in the US, found that their sample of American managers saw their personnel departments as

(1) 'Reacting to, rather than anticipating, problems.
(2) Passive – not an initiator nor a stimulator.
(3) Defending the status quo rather than being creative and attempting to exercise leadership.
(4) Carrying out management decisions, but not helping to shape management thinking.
(5) Not standing up to be counted.
(6) Not a risk-taker.
(7) Not business oriented.
(8) Not involved in the personnel aspects of business decisions.
(9) Having very little influence with management.
(10) Operating in a vacuum. (Ritzer and Trice, 1969, p. 5)

Foulkes (1975, and Foulkes and Morgan 1977), also in the US, in the mid-1970s, records virtually identical perceptions of their personnel departments on the part of the American line managers from a range of organisations, whom he interviewed and taught. Nor did the British studies at that time paint a different picture.

For example, the personnel managers in Watson's (1977, pp. 92–5) sample, when asked what they disliked about personnel work, presented what might be seen as a mirror image of the perceptions of the US line managers cited above. Not only did they dislike routine administration ('I like the Personnel but hate the f ..... g. Admin') but those aspects of the work that embodied the sorts of unflattering stereotypes already identified by line managers:

'It's the attachment of women to it – the welfare image'
'We've got to stop them treating us as inefficient bumbling do-gooders'
'We're not seen a part of management by management'
'We are only used to fire-fight'
'Having to draw back from using power you haven't got'
'Our lack of status and people and knowing what to do'
'Being a service department, not being seen as contributing to the organisation'
'The lack of a clear personnel philosophy in the company.'

Issues of low status and lack of a coherent set of activities also emerge from Legge's (1978) study of the same period. In the same vein she identified that in the late 1970s the line managers interviewed, generally speaking, appeared to have a confused and stereotyped perception of the activities of personnel specialists. All agreed that an organisation's personnel department existed to provide a service to the line, and that the line had the right to decide what this service should be. But when encouraged to state what kind of service ideally they would wish to have provided, many of the managers were at a loss to suggest anything other than the provision of routine service, the 'necessary chores', as Drucker put it. Superficially, criticisms related much more to the inadequacies of *how* this service was carried out than its scope. But the accompanying complaint that personnel specialists were 'out of touch' with the operating areas of the company suggested an awareness of the *results* of inadequate diagnostic, planning and developmental activities (beloved of the normative models of personnel management) even if this was not matched by an articulated recognition of where the *cause* lay. Overt expressions of satisfaction with the existing narrow scope of personnel management, as they experienced it, Legge commented at the time, sat uneasily with criticisms of content that implicitly questioned the scope of personnel activities in practice.

But these are observations of studies of the late 1970s. Surely, it might be argued, after the invigorating changes of the 1980s, the behaviours of personnel specialists must have changed and, with them, the perceptions of line managers? Flicking through an issue of *Personnel Management* in the early 1990s, I noticed an article by Keith Allen entitled 'Personnel management on the line: how middle managers view the function'. The subtext is revealing:

> Using the results of a small survey on the attitudes of middle management to the personnel function, Keith Reynolds Allen describes how personnel is currently falling short of managers' expectations.

The voiced complaints are all too familiar

> Other questions showed that 54 per cent thought personnel provided irrelevant information or even information and ideas that clashed with business reality (49 per cent). A high proportion (62 per cent) saw the function as providers of low level administrative information, and 68 per cent saw it as being mainly concerned with legal compliance and hiring and firing lower-level staff.

> Several groups of comments were made to justify this negative view of the human resource function. One group included phrases such as: 'turn line managers against them by late, irrelevant, time consuming policies'; 'issue meaningless statistics'; 'unaware of business reality'; 'being rigid' and 'being only reactive'.
> The kindest conclusion that can be drawn from this study is that the human resources function has some way to go before it is really part of management.

Leaving aside the representativeness of the survey, it is interesting that the same negative stereotypes emerge and that the official practitioner journal of the (then) Institute of Personnel Management (now Institute of Personnel and Development) is prepared to publish them. This points to an issue that has dogged personnel specialists throughout their history. We might call it an obsession with their credibility.

The credibility gap

In the light of the behavioural model it is hardly surprising, to quote Herman (1968), that personnel managers have 'a kind of generalized inferiority complex'. Both Watson's (1977) and Legge's (1978) studies of the mid- to late 1970s revealed personnel managers to be obsessed by the issue of their credibility with other management groups. In the 1980s, Thurley (1981) asked if the personnel function in the UK was 'a case for urgent treatment?', while Tyson (1985, p. 22) commented tellingly:

> If all the managers were to write in their diaries each day "What have I done today to make the business successful?" would the personnel manager have an embarrassingly short entry to make? Were we to believe all the critical articles and books published during periodic crises of confidence suffered by personnel specialists, the answer would be yes.

The initiation of Thatcherite economic policies in the early 1980s did little to assist the growing confidence that personnel managers had begun to develop in the late 1960s and 1970s as interpreters and implementers of successive Labour governments' protective employment legislation, mediators of trade union pressure, and managers of employees' rising expectations and consequent organisational change (Legge, 1978, 1988; Tyson and Fell, 1986). An environment of recession, rising unemployment and restrictive trade union and employment legislation gave rise to images of 'macho managers' trampling roughshod over carefully constructed accommodations with trade unions and progressive employee relations systems, to the hand-wringing of their personnel specialists. Articles such as Manning's (1983) 'The rise and fall of personnel', arguing that the occupation was an aberration caused by post-war full employment, were reflective of a difficult climate for personnel specialists, even if the message of their 'fall' was much exaggerated (see Legge, 1988). That confidence is still lacking is reflected in yet another headline in the June 1991 issue of *Personnel Management*, proclaiming ' "Investors in people" scheme could provide route for personnel to achieve credibility'. The implication of such a statement is, of course, that personnel still lacks credibility. Why is this?

At one level, we can answer this quite simply. Lack of credibility might be seen as a direct result of the contrast between the high aspirations of the normative models and of failure to deliver as reflected in the behavioural model. Thurley (1981, p. 26) put the problem well when he stated that personnel specialists

> are caught in a mismatch between a pretentious abstract model of human resource management and the reality of a fragmented set of activities carried out with little recognition of their value by other managers.

A management group that preaches one message but practices another runs the risk of not being taken seriously. But this is only the surface expression of a deeper issue signalled in Watson's critical–evaluative model. Personnel management's function of employment regulation points us to an underlying cause of tensions between normative aspirations and enacted behaviour. Both the activity and personnel specialists are driven by contradictions that promote ambiguity of action. The chief contradictions are those embedded in capitalism. However before showing how and why this is so, a little history is necessary to set the scene.

A short history of personnel management in the UK

Readers seeking more detail than I intend here are referred to Niven's (1967) classic history *Personnel Management 1913–63*, and for subsequent years and alternative analyses, Tyson and Fell (1986), Legge (1978, 1988) and Torrington (1989).

The history of personnel management reflects a tension between two potentially incompatible orientations, which might be called the 'personnel' and the 'management' approaches to the function (Thomason, 1975) or the 'caring' versus 'control' approaches (Watson, 1977). The early history reflected a 'personnel', 'caring', or welfare approach. Following Torrington's (1989) terminology and analysis, the roots of personnel management (well before the emergence of a specialist role) lay in the activities of the mid-19th century 'social reformers', such as Shaftesbury and Owen, who sought, in legislation on hours and conditions, to ameliorate the lot of factory workers (particularly women and children). Their example influenced a select band of predominantly Quaker and other non-conformist employers (for example, Cadbury, Rowntree and the Lever Brothers), in the early 20th century, to introduce female welfare officers, 'acolytes of benevolence', into their factories to dispense benefits such as canteens, medical provision and sick pay to deserving and, again, often female employees. Although, undeniably, the motivation was very largely the Christian charity of paternalist employers, straws in the wind pointed in another direction.

In 1912 Edward Cadbury, in his book *Experiments in Industrial Organisation*, writing of Bournville, made the vital connection between welfare and efficiency: 'the supreme principle has been the belief that business efficiency and the welfare of employees, are but different sides of the same problem' (cited in Niven, 1967, p. 24). This connection became fully explicit during the First World War, particularly in relation to the munitions factories. It paved the way for what might be seen as a transitional role for personnel management, that of the 'humane bureaucrat'. In the inter-war years the connection between welfare and efficiency was being broadened to include not only the physical environment of work, but activities aimed at getting a good fit between the individual worker and a particular job. Thus personnel specialists (now increasingly men) became engaged in role specification, recruitment, and selection, training, keeping records for the monitoring and investigation of absence and labour turnover and of dismissals. As Torrington (1989, p. 58) puts it: 'The personnel manager was learning to operate within bureaucracy, serving organisational rather than paternalist employer objectives'. Torrington also points out that the more innovative of the specialists were beginning to look to the social sciences for ideas about managing people at work, 'with scientific management (Taylor, 1911), administrative management (Fayol, 1949) and the Human Relations movement (Mayo, 1933) all finding enthusiastic devotees among personnel managers'. The choice of social science exemplars is revealing and open to two interpretations. On the one hand, it might be argued that the choice of scientific and administrative management shows a growing concern with notions of rationality and efficiency, while adherence to human relations shows an awareness of the limitations of rational models of management control and a continuing tradition of concern for the welfare and development of individuals at work. A more cynical view might suggest that human relations conveniently linked paternalist welfarism with the search for efficiency, as it proposed that concern for workers as people, requiring a measure of respect and self-fulfilment, would mean greater efficiency and lower costs. Ideas of efficiency through management control and concern for the lot of the workers could come together as the human relations movement asserted the feasibility of a form of control through motivation. As we will see later, such ideas have resurfaced through certain models of HRM and the concept of 'responsible autonomy' (Friedman, 1977).

The Second World War and its aftermath of relatively full employment saw the emergence of the role Torrington (1989, pp. 58–9) terms 'consensus negotiator'. The war brought with it both the direction of labour and the prohibition of strike activity, and hence a myriad of Essential Works Orders, Control of Engagement Orders, and National Arbitration Orders. This brought together a legal, administrative and negotiating aspect to what were increasingly being called 'Labour Officer' roles. (It was in 1931 that the Institute of Industrial *Welfare* significantly changed its name to the Institute of Labour *Management*.) The fact that the occupation was reserved (i.e., male 'labour officers' were exempt from military service) signified that men were beginning to take over the function, a process that was accelerated with the increasing strength of male-led and dominated trade unions. Bargaining with trade unions was seen to be a man's role. The commitment to full employment and union recognition by the post-war Labour government, combined with the establishment of the welfare state, gave further opportunities for extending the link between personnel management and efficiency, whilst undermining the importance of the 'feminine' task of welfare. Full employment prioritised the tasks of recruitment and selection and, with the enhancement of union density and power, that of wage negotiation. The welfare state provided as of right many of the benefits previously in the gift of the employer. The rise of the nationalised industries at this time and some continuance of a war-time spirit of collective endeavour, encouraged the development in some industries of various forms of joint consultation, a further responsibility for the 'consensus negotiator'.

From the 1960s onwards three other developments in the personnel role have emerged, particularly in large companies, reflecting a preoccupation with the effectiveness of the organisation as a whole. The first, what Torrington refers to as 'organisation man', was in part a reaction to the predominance of the 'consensus negotiator' role, particularly following the plant bargaining and relatively high levels of industrial unrest in the late 1960s and 1970s. The personnel specialist as 'organisation man', attempted to develop a more open, effective organisation culture, both between managers, and management and workforce. Achieving an open flexible organisation able to adapt effectively in a changing world was the aim, and resulted in much attention to organisational and management development and experiments in more 'open' organic forms of organisational design (see Chapter 6). The organisational development (OD) experiments of the 1960s and 1970s at Shell, Pilkington and ICI, although of no enduring impact, are illustrative of this development (Hill, 1971; Blackler and Brown, 1980; Warmington et al., 1977; Pettigrew, 1985). In its emphasis on effectiveness rather than efficiency and use of cultural change techniques based on group dynamics, such personnel activity was termed 'deviant innovation' by one commentator (Legge, 1978). 'Deviant' innovation was defined as an attempt by personnel specialists to gain acceptance for a different set of organisational success criteria, reflective of social as much as business values, by which their contribution could be judged. It must be remembered that this was the period of social liberalisation and protest, of Flower Power, the Great Society – and of Vietnam. The emphasis was on developing 'new philosophies of management', more open and trusting organisational cultures capable of responding flexibly to the challenges of new technologies and employee and consumer expectations. Today we might call it legitimacy through developing 'learning organisations' (Easterby-Smith, 1990). In the 1960s and early 1970s, the language was much more in terms of 'the death of bureaucracy' (Bennis, 1966). Not surprisingly many hard-nosed line managers were highly sceptical of this development in personnel management. They found in OD's explicit use of social science theory, whether in process consultancy or socio–technical systems analysis, a perverse mixture. On the one hand OD was seen to be a form of devious manipulation, managers describing its activities as 'propaganda', 'brain-washing' and, in one extreme case (referring to 'T' groups) 'wholly wrong and almost evil' (Blackler and Brown, 1980, p. 54; Pettigrew, 1985, p. 295). On the other it was seen to be 'wishy-washy', 'being nice', 'not to be taken too seriously' and without a proper concern for profit (Blackler and Brown, 1980; Pettigrew, 1985).

A more durable form of 'deviant innovation' at this time was the development of what Farnham (1990) has termed the 'third party role' of personnel management or, to continue with Torrington's (1989) terminology, 'legal wrangling'. The social values in this case derived not from those embedded in OD but from employment law that incorporated certain societal values (health and safety at work, equal opportunities) which override the self-interest of individual employers. From the

1970s onwards personnel specialists have developed an important role in interpreting the mass of employment laws enacted by Parliament and, increasingly, by the EU. Particularly in the 1970s when the legislation was protective rather than restrictive of the rights of employees and trades unions, personnel managers could seek credibility as the experts guiding the line managers away from misguided (il)legal *faux pas*.

The last role Torrington (1989, p. 59) identifies, that of the 'manpower analyst', emerged partly in reaction to that of the 'organisation man'. The tight labour markets of the 1960s, followed by the economic turbulence of the oil shocks of the early and late 1970s, rising inflation and 'stop–go' government policy coalesced to raise issues about the costs and benefits of substituting capital, or new technology, for labour and renewed concern for short-term efficiency. Either way, a major personnel management responsibility came to be seen as achieving the closest possible fit between numbers and skills required and those achieved. Manpower planning was seen as a potentially prestigious role aimed at achieving optimum head count. In developing this activity personnel specialists might be seen as opting for a 'conformist innovator' role – equating efficiency with organisational success and, in emphasising cost benefit, bureaucratic/utilitarian values, conforming to their colleagues' concern with the 'bottom line'.

A further typology of personnel management roles is that of Tyson and Fell (1986). Rather than situating roles directly in an historical context, they identify three styles of enacting the personnel function, current in present-day organisations, that derive from the welfare, industrial relations, manpower control and professional traditions of personnel management. These are the 'clerk of works', the 'contracts manager' and the 'architect' (shades of my earlier joke about architects, accountants and personnel managers!). As these are largely operating styles of personnel management that need to be interpreted contextually, I will reserve detailed discussion of them until Chapter 2. But, in anticipation, it may be useful at this stage to draw some comparisons between the traditions Tyson and Fell identify, their models and Torrington's historically situated roles. The following loose parallels are suggested. The 'clerk of works' role, deriving from the welfare tradition, has overtones of the 'acolytes of benevolence' and the 'humane bureaucrat'. The 'contracts manager', deriving from the industrial relations and manpower control traditions, mirrors the 'consensus negotiator', with touches of the 'legal wrangler' and 'manpower analyst'. The 'architect', deriving from the professional tradition, depending on organisational strategy and climate, is likely to resemble the 'organisation man' or the 'manpower analyst'.

The place of HRM in this historical development of the personnel management activity will be considered in Chapter 3. But, in order to do so, we first need to be clear about how these roles reflect the nature of management control in organisation. Put in a more partisan fashion let us consider personnel management as reflecting the contradictions of capitalism and patriarchy.

Personnel management: instrument and victim of the dilemmas of capital?

The fact that personnel specialists oscillate between the 'personnel' and 'management', between 'caring' and 'control' aspects of the function, can be attributed to their role in mediating a major contradiction embedded in capitalist systems: the need to achieve both the control *and* consent of employees. In Marxist terms, personnel management exists to assist in the realisation of surplus value through obscuring the commodity status of labour (see for example, Braverman, 1974; Burawoy, 1979, 1985; Hyman, 1987). In Weberian terms, it exists to mediate the tensions between formal, or instrumental, and material, or substantive, rationality (Watson, 1977). On what arguments do such assertions rest?

First, let us consider the Marxist view, which will be elaborated in Chapter 9. This rests on several assumptions: that in a world of competition for scarce resources, a ruling class, that owns and controls the means of production, seeks to accumulate maximum surplus or profit, via the circuit of capital. The circuit of capital involves the purchase of labour and the production *and* realisation of its surplus value. Thus in the market place the employer – read capitalist – buys the labour capacity of the nominally 'free' worker at its exchange value. The worker is 'free' in the sense that she or he can sell their labour capacity to another employer but, unless entering their ranks, given capital's ownership and control of the means of production, cannot realise the potential value of their labour, without enacting this exchange relationship. But labour capacity only creates value for the employer in use. Hence the employer's aim is to maximise the difference between the exchange and use value of labour capacity and then realise this difference or surplus value, through the sale of resultant commodities/services in the market place.

Extraction of surplus value raises the question of control. 'Employers need to exercise control over labour, both at the level of general directive powers and over working conditions and tasks' (Thompson and McHugh, 1990, p. 39). In doing so – and here Weber's ideas about rationalisation dovetail quite neatly – employers exercise a formal rationality by organising the means of production, via the division and coordination of labour, according to rationally calculable principles, in order to extract surplus value with maximum efficiency. This *may* (but *not inevitably*) involve cheapening the cost of labour at the point of production by (a) treating workers as a variable cost and (b) work intensification. How is this done?

Edwards (1979) argues that control systems have three elements: direction and specification of work tasks; evaluation, monitoring and assessment of performance; the systems of discipline and reward to elicit cooperation and compliance. The control modes through which these activities are enacted may be personal (direct supervision), technical (control built into the technology, as through the control of the assembly line) and bureaucratic (rules used to define and evaluate work tasks and to govern the application of sanctions). Edwards also argues that employers consciously segment their labour markets, particularly on the basis of gender and race, in order to undermine potential labour solidarity, through the creation of vested interests (e.g., of white, male, craft workers) and competition between workers.

Such control strategies may treat labour as a variable cost through casualisation, redundancy or short time, or through the relocation of plants to areas where, through unemployment, culture or government (in)action, labour is disempowered and low cost (i.e., Edwards' segmented labour market strategy). Work intensification has traditionally resulted from Tayloristic forms of work organisation with associated tight external controls, whether close supervision (personal control); incentive payment systems (bureaucratic control); assembly line pacing (technical control) and so on. Reducing labour costs has also involved strategies of deskilling and, depending on relative costs, the substitution of capital for labour (bureaucratic and technical control).

Now it might well be argued that the picture painted here is simplistic. For a start, it would be inappropriate to see 'management' as one interest group, united in the conscious exploitation of labour (or in any monolithic strategy). As Hyman (1987, p. 30) says 'since management is itself a collective labour process, internal coherence cannot be assumed *a priori*'. Different functional specialisms have different sectional interests and priorities. Even colleagues within the same department may be in competition, just as much as in cooperation, with each other. The interests of different levels in the management hierarchy are not always compatible. Organisations differ too. As Thompson and McHugh (1990, p. 42) point out, not all work organisations are based on commodity production or are capitalist in character. In particular, those in the public service sector (education, hospitals, social services, etc.) are (or used to be) concerned with services in use not for profit. Without the imperative to accumulate surpluses, surely they have no motive to extract maximum surplus value?

Up to a point all this may be true. But, managers are generally in a loose coalition about the importance of the 'bottom line'. Organisations may differ, but given it is impracticable for public sector services to pursue investment, pricing and pay policies which would put them 'outside the general market conditions set by the predominance of private enterprise' (and particularly when the government of the day advocates the virtues of private enterprise and a market economy) the differences may be more apparent than real (Westergaard and Resler, 1975, cited in Watson, 1977). The public sector is equally under pressure (often through public accountability and government control of the purse-strings) to pursue formal rationality and, as such, is likely to prioritise cost reduction, and the avoidance of deficits, if not the generation of surplus. The introduction of managerialist principles into public sector services in the 1980s (see Chapter 7) has accentuated such pressures.

A more telling critique is contained within the Marxist argument. The full circuit of capital involves not just the purchase of labour and the achievement of surplus value at the point of production, but its realisation through the sale of commodities/services in the market place. The 'purchase' of labour, as already suggested, implies that it is 'free' – free to develop a 'calculative' attitude to the effort–reward bargain on offer, and 'free' to go to another employer (Watson, 1983, p. 25). 'Free' labour may well object to the implications of formal rationality for its terms and conditions of employment and resist, not just by absenteeism and labour turnover, but by go-slows, strikes, sabotage and manipulation of the effort–reward bargain. Not only is such resistance likely to impede the efficient extraction of surplus value but, in so doing, subvert its realisation.

And here again Weber's ideas about rationality and Marx's about the realisation of surplus value are not incompatible. For, following Weber, Watson (1977, pp. 33–6) points out that *formal* rationality has to go hand in hand with *material* rationality or the achievement of the employer's ultimate goal through the use of rational calculation. The ultimate goal in a capitalist society is often (but not invariably) profit *realised* in the market place. The problem is that 'formally rational techniques [may] subvert materially rational ends' (Watson, 1977, p. 192).

Both at the extraction and realisation of surplus value 'efficient' control contains the seeds of its own decay, or what Watson (1986, p. 53, pp. 182–3) terms the 'paradox of consequences'. Employers cannot always prescribe tasks in detail, particularly when the work is highly complex and the achievement of quality standards (so necessary to realise surplus value in the market place) requires the exercise of employee discretion. In the interests of a flexible response to variances in day-to-day operational processes the employer would not wish to remove all worker discretion – as we all know from the problems associated with employees 'working to rule'. Furthermore, although employers may wish to extract surplus by minimising labour costs, too aggressive a pursuit of this strategy may be self-defeating, not only through the potential loss of labour to higher-paying employers, but through the disabling of employees as potential direct and indirect purchasers of the goods and services produced. Unless employees also act as purchasers, surplus value cannot be realised in the economy at large, as evidenced in major economic recessions. Employers, then, may buy the right to control their employees' work, but in the interests of the achievement and realisation of surplus value (or, one might say, in the interests of achieving material rationality) they must give some leeway to their employees, on a daily basis, to exercise some control over the means of production, albeit ultimately in the employers' interests as much as the employees'. In both cases, employers must enlist their employees'/customers' cooperation to ensure that their discretion as both workers and consumers is exercised for, rather than against, capitalism's interests. In a sense, then, personnel management and advertising are two sides of the same coin (to quote Burawoy, 1985) of 'hegemonic' control.

For Burawoy (1979) argues that, if the employer wishes to fully extract and realise surplus value, she or he must 'obscure the commodity status of labour' to achieve control by surrendering it, by 'manufacturing consent'. Consent is generated by engaging workers in collusive games with management (for example, in manipulating the effort–reward relationship, through competing in conditions of optimal uncertainty to 'make-out'). Their freely-entered participation serves to make workers acquiesce in their role in the process of production, because just as the social relations of production define the rules of the game, so the game playing itself generates consent to these rules (Burawoy, 1979, pp. 81–6). Despotic, or coercive control is supplemented, if not completely replaced, by 'hegemonic'–ideological control (Burawoy, 1985). But 'manufacturing consent' carries its own contradictions for employers wishing to achieve a material rationality defined in terms of optimising the full circuit of capital. The creation of commitment to the job (whether via collusive game playing or a paternalist employee relations strategy) may result in employee inflexibility and conservatism. Efficient labour and administrative processes often call for cohesive relations within a workforce and standardisation of their terms and conditions of employment, negotiated through representatives accountable to and for groups of employees. Yet such cohesion and standardisation is likely to generate a collective solidarity which employees may use against the employer's interests. Hence all 'personnel' policies, containing the seeds of their own decay, need continual monitoring, modification and, at times, radical revision (Watson, 1986, pp. 182–4).

It is against this backcloth of the contradictions of capitalism and the tensions between formal and material rationality that the functions and behaviours of personnel specialists can be re-interpreted. It was not for nothing that Braverman (1974, p. 87) refers to personnel departments, 'practitioners of "human relations" and "industrial psychology"' as the 'maintenance crew for the human machinery'. The early development of their 'welfare' role (the 'social reformers' and 'acolytes of benevolence') coincided with what today might be called 'the unacceptable face of capitalism' and, subsequently, with the period when line management's application of formal rationality to extract surplus value at the point of production was being recognised as dysfunctional. 'Welfare' sought to ameliorate the effects and mask the functions of such rationality. Personnel specialists' involvement in recruitment, selection and training ('the humane bureaucrat') emerged at a time when most direct labour was treated as a variable rather than a fixed cost. The consequent frequent hiring and firing, induction and training not only made it sensible to have a specialist function perform this and related 'terms and conditions of employment' activities but, by doing so, enabled a dissociation between the sale of labour power and the performance of the labour process, thus (to echo Hyman, 1987, p. 42) 'obscuring the exploitative basis of the capital–labour relation'. Other roles that personnel specialists have adopted, notably that of the 'organisation man' and, in the 1970s, the 'legal wrangler' may be seen, rather, as strategies aimed at 'manufacturing consent'.

However the role that expresses personnel specialists' function as mediator of the contradictions of capitalism most clearly is perhaps that of the 'consensus negotiator'. If the 'manpower analyst' role is expressive of personnel's function in pursuing formal rationality, the 'consensus negotiator' is there to 'represent to management the effect of decisions on people and defend those people' (personnel manager cited in Watson, 1977, p. 177). Watson (1977, p. 63) clearly expresses the basic dilemma which underlies this role:

> The members of personnel departments are forced to pay attention to both the formally rational criteria of productivity, profit, effectiveness and the rest as well as the human needs, interests and aspirations of employees which, if not attended to, may lead to the formally rational means subverting the substantively rationally concerned ends of the ultimate controllers of the organisations.

Not surprisingly, then, the personnel specialist is commonly identified (and they often identify themselves) as the 'man in the middle', 'placator', 'oiler of the works', 'buffer' or 'safety valve' (Watson, 1977, p. 62). But, although the 'in-between', 'mediating', 'on the fence' role is recognised and, at least among Watson's sample of personnel managers, generally accepted, it is as 'manufacturers of consent', not as champions of labour for its own sake, that this role is adopted. Watson's respondents were clear that 'in the final resort' personnel managers 'always side with management' and that it is the *appearance* as a neutral mediator that is sought, not its 'reality' (Watson, 1977, pp. 175–7).

Any mediatory role, as with the proverbial Janus, runs the risk of giving an impression of two-facedness, with attendant loss of credibility. When problems of credibility are further compounded by a history and appearance of oscillating between two different interests, 'personnel' and 'management', mediation goes hand in hand with ambiguity. At this point personnel specialists become just as much victims of the contradictions of capitalism as their instruments. But, before we consider the outcome – personnel specialists as victims of ambiguity – we need to look briefly at a related contradiction and source of further ambiguity: the problem of patriarchy.

The problem of patriarchy

Western industrialised societies are invariably patriarchies (cf. Hofstede, 1980; Walby, 1986; 1990). That is, they are societies in which, through a system of social structures and practices, men dominate and exploit women in cultural/linguistic and economic terms. (*Note*: even the word 'woman' is merely 'man' with a qualifying suffix, while the gender connotations of the word 'man-agement' are self-evident.)[2] The origins of patriarchy are complex. Some would argue it lies in biological differences. Others, that women, by exchanging unpaid domestic labour to secure their children's upkeep, in an explicit marriage contract (or cohabitation) enter an implicit contract through which men control their labour and activities generally. Marxists maintain that patriarchal relations are produced by and serve the interests of capital by providing a cheap way of securing day to day care of workers and producing the next generation of workers. However it is not the place here to delve into such debates that are, in any case, well covered by writers such as Barrett (1980) and Walby (1990). Suffice to say here that, alone among the management functions, personnel specialists through the welfare origins of the occupation have been saddled with a 'feminine' and, hence, a downgraded image in patriarchal society. But not only is the early history of personnel management illustrative of its feminine origins, it is also susceptible to a feminist analysis (Legge, 1987).

Statistics suggest that, in a very literal sense, personnel management, as a specialist occupation, started life as women's work. Not only were the pioneers of personnel management women – for example, Adelaide Anderson, Mary Wood and Eleanor Kelly – but all but a handful of the estimated sixty to seventy welfare workers in factories at the outbreak of the First World War were women. When, at the 1913 conference, the precursor of the Institute of Personnel Management (IPM) was formed, all but five of its thirty-four founder members were women, including the first president, Mary Wood. By 1927 membership was 420 but fewer than twenty members were men. Between 1918 and 1931, of the eleven institute presidents, six were women. Although in the latter statistic a familiar trend might be observed to be emerging (men represented in higher officers disproportionately to membership), it would be fair to say that women dominated the early profession (Niven, 1967). Admittedly it was men, such as Seebohm Rowntree, Edward Cadbury, George Hargreaves, Charles Jacob and David Crichton that played major sponsorship roles in allowing opportunities for the role of welfare officer to develop in their organisations. But perhaps it is ironic that these champions of early legislation and welfarism generally were very often non-Conformists and (especially) Quakers who, excluded in earlier times from the universities, professions and public office and diverted into lower status occupations in trade and industry, might almost be regarded as 'honorary women'. (It is interesting in this context that Hofstede (1980) considers that Quakers represent a feminine subculture in the United States, promoting values of 'service', pacifism and so forth.)

The early days of personnel management may be also analysed from a feminist perspective. For its origins may be seen to embody several of what Lipman-Blumen (1984, p. 74) terms 'control myths'; that is 'social stereotypes about the "true nature" of women and men [which] once internalized, serve as self-control mechanisms, used by both genders to regulate their own behavior'. Now, as already discussed, personnel management arose out of 19th century factory legislation, which was directed at the plight of women and children, not at that of men, although the latter worked in similar conditions. Note here two implicit control myths, that 'women [like children] are weak, passive, dependent and fearful' and that 'men have women's best interests at heart; women can trust men to protect their welfare' (Lipman-Blumen, 1984 pp. 76, 92). Hence women must rely on men in Parliament to pass protective legislation (which, at the same time, as Lipman-Blumen (1984, p. 94) points out, 'guarded women from a wide range of higher paid, resource generating jobs') while men could organise and fight for better conditions and wages (Niven, 1967, p. 17). It was in the wake of such legislation that the first factory inspectors were appointed (in 1893) and, hard on their heels and sponsored mainly by Quaker employers, there came the first 'lady social workers' or 'social secretaries' such as Mary Wood, appointed to Rowntree's in 1896 and first president of the IPM, as already mentioned, in 1913.

The activities of these pioneers may be interpreted as embodying further control myths. As early as 1864, an official document (cited by Niven, 1967, p. 16) stated that 'a female overlooker, married and of mature age is as essential to prosperity, the good government and the *moral* character of a factory as the material with which the workers are employed' (emphasis added). Furthermore, when Mary Wood was appointed to the Rowntree's factory one of her first duties, which she herself identified, was to curb rowdy behaviour in the dining room and, through raising the moral tone of the factory, partly by placing flowers in the workrooms and organising lunch-time concerts and lectures, to attract 'more respectable girls'. Quite apart from an implicit repetition of the control myth that equates women with children, here we see lurking just below the surface of explicit pronouncement the myth that 'women's sexuality is inexhaustible, uncontrollable, and even dangerous to men' (Lipman-Blumen, 1984, p. 86). Furthermore this control myth may be seen as implicitly reinforcing other power relationships. 'Rowdiness' and 'poor discipline' (read 'self-assertion' and 'independence'?) are not notably characteristics desired in a direct labour force by an economy dominated by market or hierarchy.

But the nature of the work of the pre-First World War 'social workers' – who saw their tasks mainly in terms of the 'selection and education of employees, and the provision of health and safety, recreative and social institutions' (Niven, 1967, p. 23, citing Cadbury, 1912) – can also be seen, perhaps most clearly, as reflecting stereotypically 'feminine' activities. As such these underwrite the control myth that 'women are more altruistic, more nurturing and thus more moral than men' (Lipman-Blumen, 1984, p. 83). A corollary of this myth, that women meet their own achievement needs through the success of others (usually men, or those enacting male roles) has to the present day dogged that status of the personnel function as mere 'advisers' to line management. But, equally important, this early identification of personnel management with *female* welfare activities in a patriarchal society, inevitably meant that the function would carry a legacy as being of low status and unimportance, at least in comparison to central male activities, such as production, finance and so on. That this legacy still haunts the personnel function is borne out by Jenkins' (1986) and Collinson's (1987, 1988) work on discriminatory practices in recruitment and selection. Commenting on personnel managers' subordinate service role at operational level and consequent failure to ensure the implementation of formalised selection practices, Collinson (1991, p. 62) notes

> Within the conventional organizational pecking order, line managers [are] usually elevated in importance as 'providers' and producers of wealth and profit. By contrast, the personnel function in many companies [is] downgraded, even dismissed, as a 'welfaristic soft option', whose role [is] best confined to administration. This asymmetrical relationship between personnel and line management could be said to mirror the conventional domestic division of labour, since the status of the (male) organizational breadwinner is elevated above the 'unproductive' (female) welfare and administrative function.

The problem for personnel specialists is how to overcome this legacy. The emergence of the different specialist roles identified earlier, may be seen not just as functional imperatives – the emergence of activities to cope with the problems and opportunities of the time, with the 'paradox of consequences' – but as a conscious strategy to background the feminine myths (realities?) of origin and create a male image. For male personnel managers are faced with a double problem in developing a career in an occupation with a feminine image. At a very personal level, as men, they may find it an ambiguous situation to be performing a 'feminine' job. As one of Watson's (1977, p. 60) respondents commented, expressing, perhaps unconsciously, his ambivalence, 'its [the problem of] getting rid of the image of the guy who keeps the sanitary towel machine stocked up'.

At another level, if personnel specialists wish to have influence in their organisations, they have to confront a general paradox about power in and out of occupations. That is, when women have power within an occupation it is generally the case that that occupation has yet to attain power (Dasey, 1981) or is losing power within organisations or society (Smith, 1982). When the situation is reversed – for example, when the roles of consensus negotiator, or *man*power analyst or legal wrangler are seen to contribute to business success – the converse holds: women's position in that occupation is threatened and their contribution is downgraded. This is what appears to have taken place – at least from the end of the Second World War to the end of the 1970s – in personnel management in Britain (for a detailed analysis of the steady decline, from the heady early days, of woman's position in personnel management, see Long, 1984; Legge, 1987).

Watson (1977, pp. 189–90) makes an interesting observation about male personnel managers' role in this decline. He argues, from his own experience as well as his research in the 1970s, that in order to undermine the feminine image of the occupation male personnel managers often deliberately discriminated against women applicants for junior personnel jobs and blocked the potential promotion of those women already in post. Judging by IPM membership patterns in the post-war years there is some evidence that this may have occurred, at least as far as recruitment is concerned (Legge, 1987). But, in doing so, personnel managers could be caught on the horns of a dilemma. Their actions involved contravening the spirit, and possibly the letter, of the equal opportunities and equal pay legislation that it was their responsibility to implement. This could cause a certain ambivalence if at the same time the personnel manager was seeking to augment his status and credibility in the organisation by developing the 'male' role of 'legal wrangler'. If, on the other hand (highly unlikely), the personnel manager highlighted his 'legal wrangler' role by engaging in a high profile attempt to implement the provisions of such legislation, by recruiting and promoting women in personnel, he ran the risk that, in a patriarchy, this would serve to undermine the credibility and influence of the specialist function.

Finally, it could be argued that male personnel managers' dilemmas about the feminine image of the occupation contain a further problem. The backgrounding of this image is problematic in itself. For to deny 'welfare' is to deny the very origins and foundation of personnel as a *specialist occupation*. This is a dangerous argument to pursue as it may raise questions about the validity and necessity for such a specialist occupation at all. Furthermore, denying welfare denies a lubricant in oiling the works of capitalism, which again challenges the necessity for a specialist 'oiler of the works'. Denying welfare denies too a role in which personnel specialists may be both visible and seen in a positive light by the employees, whose required cooperation justifies their existence.

As the instruments and victims of both capitalism and patriarchy, it is not surprising that personnel specialists often see themselves, as compared to other management groups, as peculiarly beset by ambiguity. It is to some of these daily experienced ambiguities that, in conclusion, we now turn.

Conclusion: personnel managers as victims of ambiguity

On a daily basis personnel managers are confronted by ambiguities that arise directly out of problems in defining personnel management which themselves reflect and are exacerbated by the contradictions of capitalism and patriarchy. These ambiguities lie at the heart of personnel specialists' perennial concern with the issue of credibility.

First, there is the problem of demonstrating unequivocally, the contribution of personnel, as an *activity* to organisational success. This is because its raw material, people, are proactive as well as reactive, and cannot be shielded from extra-organisational influences to the same extent as other resources once within the organisation's boundaries, and are less easily manipulable than inanimate objects. Hence, if 'desirable' behaviours are in existence (high labour productivity, low labour turnover and absenteeism, no strikes) it cannot be demonstrated unequivocally that this is the result of good personnel management. It may reflect the motivations of individual employees but as a result of their assessments of their domestic circumstances, the economic environment and so on. Difficulty in demonstrating a direct relationship between personnel management *activities* and valued organisational outcomes presents particular difficulties for the *specialist department*.

Notably there are problems in the adoption of surrogate measures of success. Suppose, in spite of the difficulties in demonstrating direct causation, 'success' becomes defined as the absence of any 'personnel problems' that might disrupt the smooth running of the organisation. As Watson (1986, p. 182) points out, this might lead to the specialist department becoming almost invisible, with the risk that it will be starved of resources and left out of decision-making. As Batstone (1980) has argued, personnel departments and strong 'troublesome' unions could be regarded as having a symbiotic relationship. Furthermore, lack of 'personnel problems' is too inclusive a measure given the 'omnipresent' nature of personnel management as an activity. Because every management function involves the execution of 'personnel' activities, the personnel department cannot lay an exclusive claim to such 'successes' as a compliant, productive workforce (see Guest and Hoque, 1994a). Indeed, the necessary diffusion of aspects of the personnel function into other management functions, taken to its extreme, can lead to line management debating whether the function needs a departmental presence at all. Alternatively, though, specialist designed personnel programmes or systems, by definition, have to be implemented within other management departments and often involve non-personnel managers. As a result, the success or failure of a personnel programme, even within its own terms, is often removed from the direct control of the personnel specialists themselves. If it is successful, line managers can claim the success, if a failure even as a result of poor non-specialist implementation, then the personnel department can be scapegoated.

If, on the other hand, the department chooses to enhance its visibility by measuring 'success' by the number of activities and new initiatives it takes on, it may run the risk of collecting the 'hodge-podge' of miscellaneous activities that Drucker so decried, and which may further confuse the question of its 'real' contribution to organisational success.

Second, apart from this problem in demonstrating success, the 'omnipresent' nature of personnel management gives rise to other ambiguities. Because all managers, in a sense, engage in personnel management, the work does not appear to be a truly specialist activity involving unique knowledge and skills. It is too 'substitutable'. Furthermore, potential expert knowledge bases that might be 'uniquely' held by personnel specialists as compared to other managers (e.g., the social sciences) are often viewed suspiciously by management groups as a whole (social sciences having the additional misfortune, in the light of earlier discussion, of having a 'feminine' 'soft' image). As Watson (1986, p. 182) points out, the issue of expertise places personnel specialists into a double bind. If they *are* able to convince their managerial colleagues of some expertise (say, in industrial relations law, grievance handling, counselling) they are liable to be dumped with messy personnel problems and problematic personnel decisions. Personnel specialists then run the risk at best of being overloaded (a situation with which they may collude if trying to 'collect' activities and appear indispensable) or, at worst, of being scapegoated. Furthermore, line managers are then likely to lose touch with their own staff and are rendered less effective in their own personnel management role – as are the overloaded specialists. If, on the other hand, personnel specialists lay no claim to specialist knowledge or expertise, they may end up ignored by other managers except as the collector of garbage-can activities.

The double-binds associated with the issue of unique expertise do not end here. They have also to be seen in the light of the tensions and problematic nature of line–staff relationships. As has already been discussed in this chapter, one source of expertise, and a route by which personnel specialists have sought to enhance their image and power throughout the post-war period, has been through emphasising their role as industrial relations experts (or 'consensus negotiator' or 'contracts manager' to use Torrington's and Tyson and Fell's terms respectively). In some measure this was a strategy that succeeded, particularly in the 1970s and early 1980s (Legge, 1988). But the growth in the 1970s of large corporate personnel departments was not an unmixed blessing for enhancing personnel specialists' influence. Interpreting the results of the first Warwick Company Level survey, conducted in 1985, Purcell argues that it is possible that heavy involvement in the management of trade union relations, and the associated institutions and procedures of industrial relations, led to the personnel function becoming segmented into an isolated department:

> Personnel is thus seen as an essentially operational responsibility unconnected with strategic management. It has primarily a gatekeeper function: the act of divorcing trade unions from strategic management considerations is undertaken at the cost of personnel itself being excluded from, or seen as having little contribution to make to, strategic management. (Marginson *et al.*, 1988, p. 76)

Over a decade earlier, Winkler (1974, pp. 211–12, cited in Watson, 1977, p. 174) made a very similar point in discussing how company directors appeared very isolated from personnel and industrial relations problems:

> Psychologically, isolation functions as a defence mechanism. If labour problems arise, the director has a double repository for blame: not just recalcitrant workers, but the subordinates to whom he delegated the task of keeping them quiet.

Again personnel specialists' potential for being scapegoated is raised. Not surprisingly then Watson (1977, p. 185) identifies his respondents' frequent stress on the importance of avoiding mistakes.

The confusions associated with being nominally an advisory function, but being pushed towards executive action, do not end here. Although, in theory, specialist personnel departments are there to offer advice, this conflicts with their ultimate rationale of 'keeping the organisation as a whole going on a long-term basis through maintaining the staffing resource and coping with the conflicts and contradictions which arise whenever and wherever people are employed' (Watson, 1986, p. 205). This demands, in the interests of the organisation as a whole, that personnel managers sometimes have to act to constrain line managers' pursuit of sectional interest that can cause unfortunate precedents elsewhere in the organisation. The rationale of consistency in the interests of the whole, given legislative, union and head office constraints, can lead to 'advice' becoming 'mandatory', and regarded by some managers as 'dictatorial intrusion' on how they manage their own staff (Watson, 1986, p. 205). The resulting resentment at perceived 'unnecessary' constraints, can intensify line management's tendency to scapegoat their personnel departments when opportunity arises.

The problem of demonstrating a unique contribution to organisational success in the employment of a unique expertise, at worst, has resulted in a series of vicious circles, from which it is difficult for personnel departments to extricate themselves (see Figure 1.1). The following is a typical pattern that emerges, but perhaps most notably in those labour intensive companies, where the demands of competitive product and labour markets, combined with highly interdependent workflow processes, stimulate *ad hoc* decision-making and management. Line management, although nominally satisfied with the service it receives from the personnel department, having defined its scope narrowly, excludes the department from 'mainstream' marketing, production and investment decisions. Neglect of the personnel dimension at this level can give rise to unequivocally personnel problems (such as in the areas of recruitment and training) that, falling within the scope of even the most narrowly traditional department, have to be coped with, often without full knowledge of their causes, but with extreme urgency. Crisis management results. This may involve stop-gap measures, creating unfortunate precedents for future bargaining, while offering only a partial or inadequate solution to the problems involved. Line management then gains an unfavourable impression of the department's ability to handle even those problems that come within its scope, and has reservations about any extension of its area of responsibility. This in turn inhibits the recruitment of talent to such a 'clerk of works' (Tyson and Fell, 1986) personnel department, encourages turnover amongst those with either the talent or professional training to aspire towards a more demanding role for the department, and effectively deskills those that remain (Jenkins, 1973; Poole, 1973).

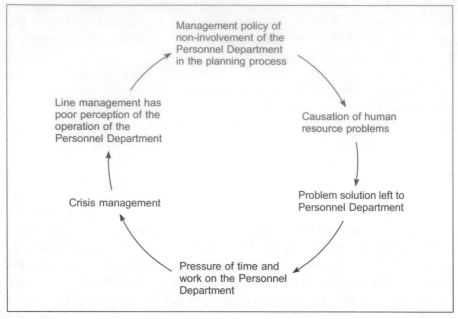

Management policy of
non-involvement of the
Personnel Department
in the planning process

Line management has
poor perception of the
operation of the
Personnel Department

Causation of human
resource problems

Crisis management

Problem solution left to
Personnel Department

Pressure of time and
work on the Personnel
Department

Source: Legge 1978, p. 56.

Figure 1.1   A vicious circle in personnel management

Further, while it is difficult to encourage the most professional personnel
managers to take over such a department, even the provision of training and
development for existing staff would not necessarily break the vicious circle. For, if
this occurred, and the department tried to break out of its traditional 'canteens, hire
and fire' image and involve itself in sophisticated personnel management and
policy-making decisions (Tyson and Fell's 'architect' function) the personnel
specialists' involved would probably lack the credibility and bargaining power to
gain the information and support from other departments (still seeing them in their
old image) necessary for them to assume new areas and modes of operation.
Without the use of relevant information and without political support within the
organisation for the personnel department to assume a more adventurous role, such
new activities as it undertakes, starved of resources, are likely to be unsuccessful.
This, in turn, confirms the old stereotype and the view that it is not worth
cooperating with the personnel department, as it has demonstrated that it is not
competent to operate in these areas anyway. Thus a vicious circle of information
denial, lack of support and credibility is set up and maintained.

If we compare, on the one hand, the position of a strong personnel department
able to constrain parochial line managers with mandatory advice in the interests of
consistency, with that of the weak marginalised department stereotyped above, if
would seem that personnel specialists cannot win. I quote Watson (1986, p. 204),
discussing managerial perceptions of their personnel departments:

If personnel specialists are not passive administrative nobodies who pursue their social work, go-between and firefighting vocations with little care for business decisions and leadership then they are clever, ambitious power-seekers who want to run work organisations as a kind of self-indulgent personnel playground.

To return to the main theme explored in this chapter, it is suggested that these ambiguities and paradoxes arise out of the contradictions of capitalism and patriarchy already explored. To a large extent they emerge from the tensions of seeking to achieve both control and consent, formal and material rationality, of holding a balance between the 'personnel' and 'management' aspects of the function. They also reflect the fact that, in attempting to mediate these contradictions, personnel specialists are confronted by the 'paradox of con-sequences' – that the very systems which are established to generate control and consent can also develop into sources of further disorder and uncertainty (Watson, 1986, p. 53, pp. 182–3).

It is not surprising, then, that personnel management has an enduring problem of establishing credibility. In its task of managing the contradictions of capitalism, personnel specialists become prey to a series of ambiguities and double-bind situations, from which extraction is difficult, if not to say impossible. In the decade of the enterprise culture and into the 1990s human resource management is being presented as a model of managing people at work that is more credible than personnel management.

Is it? Is human resource management really different from the models of personnel management we have explored in this chapter?

Before we can approach these questions, we need to look further at the different styles in which 'traditional' personnel management is enacted in different types of organisations. Personnel management style in context, then, is the focus of Chapter 2.

Notes

1. I have used the term 'normative' to label models that present aspirations of what personnel management and, subsequently, in Chapter 3, what human resource management ideally should be. In order to make such prescriptions, such normative models, with varying degrees of explicitness, rest on conceptual frameworks, or theoretical reasonings, that identify key concepts, their interrelationships and predicted effects or outcomes (This assumes, of course, that the conceptual underpinnings of the normative models are invariably positivistic – see Chapter 9.) Hence when I talk of 'normative' frameworks I am including the conceptual frameworks on which they rest. (Equally, of course, all descriptive or evaluative models of personnel or human resource management rest on implicit or explicit theoretical assumptions.) For further discussion of the distinctions between prescriptive, descriptive and conceptual models of HRM, see Storey (1992b, pp. 30–41.)

2. I use the word 'connotations' advisedly. The actual derivation of the word 'management', properly speaking, has nothing to do with the word 'man'. Rather it is derived from the Italian verb 'maneggiare', which means 'to handle a horse'.

2

Styles of managing the employment relationship

Whether personnel management is perceived to be about 'the optimum utilisation of human resources', or about the 'regulation of the employment relationship', or about 'managing the contradictions of capitalism and patriarchy', how have these different orientations been expressed in the ways in which personnel specialists and line managers enact what they see to be personnel management or 'managing employee relations'?

In this chapter, the focus shifts from the question of '*what* is personnel management?' to that of '*how* is it enacted?', given different perceptions of what in essence it is or should be. In other words, can the *modus operandi* or styles of managing the employment relationship, associated with the history and specialist roles outlined in Chapter 1, and with particular organisational contexts, yet to be discussed, be identified?

This chapter falls into three main sections. First, there is an attempt to define what is meant by personnel management or employee relations 'style'. Is it, for example, the same as an employment 'strategy'? In what sense? Next, some well known models of personnel management and employee relations styles are critically examined. These include those of Fox (1966, 1974), Purcell and Sisson (1983), Purcell (Purcell and Gray, 1986; Purcell, 1987), Friedman (1977), Tyson and Fell (1986) and Marchington and Parker (1990) and, latterly, that of Storey and Bacon (1993). Finally, the relationship between choice in personnel management style and such contextual factors as organisational ownership, structure and size, and the nature of product and labour markets is considered. The question is then posed as to whether certain personnel management styles equate with what is now termed 'human resource management'. The answer to that question is tackled in Chapter 3 and further explored in subsequent chapters.

Personnel management and
employee relations styles

At its simplest 'style' refers to a way of doing something. In characterising a 'style', activities are classified by criteria relevant to whatever typology of 'style' is being developed. But here's the problem. What criteria, and on what basis are they selected?

Commentators on personnel management 'style' are divided as to what extent 'style' and 'strategy' may be equated. The position taken depends partly on how strategy itself is conceptualised, whether from the traditional, rationalistic standpoint (for example, Chandler, 1962), or from a 'processual' stance (for example, Mintzberg, 1978) (for further discussion, see Chapter 4). A rationalistic position sees strategy as a process of planning and implementation that is conscious, proactive, long-term, integrative and enterprise-wide. As such it is seen as emanating from the top/centre of the organisation (responsible for choices and planning) and moving smoothly to operating levels (responsible for implementation), in an iterative cycle of planning – implementation – feedback – planning and so on. Such models tend to concentrate on the planning/choice activities at the centre, with far less attention paid to implementation at operating levels. In its most extreme form, such a perspective on strategy gives the appearance of assuming implementation is automatic and unproblematic and that 'espoused theory' is the same as 'theory-in-use' (Argyris and Schön, 1978). It also assumes more consensus between functions and levels in the hierarchy than is evident. The 'processual' view, on the other hand, identifies strategy less in the rhetorics of intentionality at the centre and more in the often non-articulated, but emergent and recurring patterns of decisions and action throughout the organisation that retrospectively show some coherence (Mintzberg, 1978). Some commentators reckon that there is a danger here of 'imputing rationality from the consequences of actions which, with the benefit of hindsight, appear as conscious and intentional' (Marchington and Parker, 1990, p. 58). Perhaps such a view of strategy is best seen as similar to Brunsson's idea of 'action rationality' (Brunsson, 1982).

One commentator, Purcell (1987), has explicitly attempted to conceptualise personnel management 'style' and, in doing so, comes close to equating it with a modified version of the rationalistic model of strategy. 'Style', Purcell argues, cannot be inferred from the outcomes of management/employee interaction, but arises out of the attitudes, beliefs and frames of references of those involved, and resides in their conscious, if constrained, choices. It may be identified not so much from the study of outcomes 'but of originating philosophies and policies which influence action' (1987, p. 534). Nevertheless it is different from management attitudes, as the latter do not always translate into action. To count as 'style', according to Purcell, conscious management choices must be translated into policy (even if there may be a 'frequent shortfall between aspiration and outcome') and additionally be capable of being 'periodically redefined' (Purcell, 1987, p. 535). In sum, Purcell (1987, pp. 535, 546) identifies style as 'akin to business policy and its strategic derivatives', as necessitating 'a guiding set of principles which delineate the boundaries and direction of acceptable management action in dealing with employees', and which is 'firm-specific', 'ubiquitous and continuous'.

I think this definition contains some unresolved tensions, particularly if it is to guide the construction of a typology of style. This is largely due to Purcell's insistence on the distinction between attitudes, 'guiding principles' and behaviour in inferring style. It raises the old distinction between 'espoused theory' and 'theory-in-use'. For example if style must be 'ubiquitous and continuous', but also capable of being 'periodically redefined', where are we left if discontinuities between (new) rhetoric and (old) action occur? Is it that style is being redefined and new actions will inevitably emerge (and what's the guarantee of that?) or that a style no longer exists, as rhetoric and action are inconsistent? How close does action have to be to espoused philosophy for a 'style' to exist? Of course these problems disappear if we recognise that technically we can only infer attitudes from behaviour (whether interactive or self-reflexive behaviour). Furthermore, the creation of typologies derives from the process of the observer imputing meaning to the behaviours she observes. Forms of intentionality, for example, can be imputed from an articulated choice or from apparent non-choice/reactivity. This, in fact, is precisely what Purcell and Sisson (1983) did, most usefully, in identifying a style they labelled as 'standard modern' from the opportunistic, reactive, pragmatic actions of certain managements. Furthermore, imputing style from observed behaviours (which include the rhetorics about employment relationships offered to the observer) allows the possibility of 'style' being identified from the behaviours of actors at the operating level (where employment policies may be developed and certainly are implemented). It also accepts the possibility that, particularly in highly diversified, multiplant organisations, where different plants, let alone subsidiary companies, may have very different historical traditions, internal labour markets and product market conditions, several different 'styles' may coexist in one organisation.

Hence I consider that typologies of personnel management style are best developed by imputing meaning to patterns of observed behaviours, treating 'philosophies' and 'articulated guiding principles' as one behaviour (a rhetorical performance) amongst others. I would suggest that 'styles' of managing employee relations can be identified and typologies constructed (as they have been done) without adhering to Purcell's overly restrictive definition. Indeed Mintzberg's (1978) more encompassing approach to the identification of strategies seems to be that implicitly adopted in the derivation of most typologies of personnel management style.

Typologies of personnel management and employee relations styles

Frames of reference: the contribution of Fox (1966, 1974)

Fox's (1966) early Research Paper for the Donovan Commission contained ideas that have been highly influential in the typologies of personnel management style that subsequently emerged. Fox argued that managements' employee relations style might be typified as expressing, what he termed, either a 'unitary' or 'pluralist' frame of reference (akin to Purcell's 'guiding principles').

Following Morgan's (1986, pp. 188–9) analysis, these two frames of reference may be contrasted in terms of their stance towards organisational stakeholders' interests, their conceptions of conflict and power, and the imagery that is typically employed. Thus managers holding a 'unitary' frame of reference emphasise that management and employees hold common interests (for example, the survival and growth of the organisation) and that, given this unity, conflict is aberrant (dysfunctional, transitory and caused by 'troublemakers'). Given the emphasis on unity and the backgrounding of conflict, power is not an issue. Instead, ideas about authority and leadership underwrite the unilateral exercise of a managerial prerogative directed at guiding the organisation towards the achievement of common goals. The imagery is of 'leading' the 'team' in the 'right' direction (political pun not intended, but apt!). In contrast, a 'pluralist' frame of reference recognises that organisational stakeholders legitimately may have different interests (for example, over how the profit 'cake' is to be divided), and that it is to be expected that different interest groups will bargain and compete to gain a share in the balance of power and to achieve a negotiated order out of diversity. Hence conflict is normal and often, although not always, functional as a means of energising the organisation, stimulating learning and change and facilitating mutual accommodation, through exploring and resolving rather than suppressing differences. Power is the medium for conflict resolution, and its balance may legitimately shift over time. The imagery is that of a 'coalition', that of 'allies' and 'opponents', of power used in an arena of bargaining.

Although not developed by Fox, a third frame of reference has been identified by critical theorists of a Marxist persuasion (for example, Clegg and Dunkerley, 1980; Burrell and Morgan, 1979). This 'radical' frame of reference is more one attributed by observers of management about certain management styles than publicly claimed by managers themselves, unless in an overtly politicised, 'macho' environment (as was the case in some of the nationalised industries in the early 1980s). The radical frame of reference, to quote Morgan (1986, p. 186) views society as comprising antagonistic class interests, characterised by deep rooted social and political cleavages, and held together as much by coercion as by consent. Conflict in organisations is inevitable due to incompatible objectives that reflect opposed class interests. Power is unequally distributed in organisations, power relations in organisations are reflections of those in capitalist society at large, and are closely linked to wider processes of social control (for example, the legal and education system). The imagery is of 'fighting', 'warfare' and 'battlegrounds', and outcomes are expressed not in terms of consensus (as in the unitary model) nor accommodation (as in the pluralist model) but in victory or defeat, winning or losing the battle. This is well caught in Wedderburn's (1986, pp. 85–6) comments about the way a Conservative government and its supporters, in the early 1980s, presented some 'militant' unions, notably the National Union of Mineworkers (NUM) as led by demagogues threatening democracy.

> Those who opposed the new policies increasingly ran the risk of being seen not as critics with whom to debate and compromise (the supreme pluralist virtue) but as a domestic enemy within, which must be defeated ... In such circumstances the old tradition of compromise was squeezed out: (quoting government spokesman) 'The mining dispute cannot be *settled*. It can only be *won*'.

It was from this frame of reference in the early 1980s that the rise of 'macho management' was identified (Purcell, 1982; Mackay, 1986), even if this was subsequently found to be somewhat exaggerated (Marchington, 1985; Legge, 1988).

The unitary and pluralist frames of reference were used by Fox (1974, pp. 297–313) to develop a typology of patterns of management – employee relations, resulting from a combination of the frames of reference held by the two parties. For example, the 'traditional' pattern occurred when managers and employees both held unitary frames of reference; 'sophisticated paternalism', where employers were pluralist and employees unitary; 'classical conflict' (similar to the radical frame of reference), where employers were unitary and employees pluralist. This categorisation formed the basis of a much cited typification of (originally) five employee relations styles (Purcell and Sisson, 1983), the rationale for which has been further refined in two subsequent publications (Purcell and Gray, 1986; Purcell, 1987).

Purcell *et al.*'s typology: enter individualism and collectivism

The five styles were labelled 'traditionalist', 'sophisticated paternalist' (later updated to 'sophisticated human-relations'), 'consultors' (later 'consultative'), 'constitutionalists' (later 'constitutional') (both the latter two 'sophisticated moderns' in Fox's (1974) terms) and 'standard modern'. Although Purcell (1987) was later to reject the 'standard modern' as a 'true' style (failing as it did to fulfil the essential requirements of his reconceptualisation of 'style'), in the original publication (Purcell and Sisson, 1983, p. 116) it was considered the most prevalent, comprising 'by far the largest' group of companies.

Before describing these ideal typical styles, it may be useful to first consider Purcell's subsequent conceptualisation about their underpinnings. Moving on from

Fox's ideas about unitary and pluralist frames of reference, Purcell suggests that the typology may be seen to rest on the concepts of individualism and collectivism. Whereas Fox saw unitary and pluralist frames of references as mutually exclusive, Purcell, somewhat questionably, sees individualism and collectivism 'not as opposites but as two facets of the managerial belief system toward employees' (Purcell and Gray, 1986, p. 213). Initially Purcell and Gray (1986, p. 213) defined individualism as relating to 'policies based on belief in the value of the individual and his or her right to advancement and fulfilment at work' and collectivism as 'a recognition by management of the collective interests of groups of employees in the decision-making process'. Although subsequently this definition of individualism was not substantially altered, that of collectivism was elaborated. The recognition of the right of employees to have a say in aspects of management decision-making was seen to have two aspects (Purcell, 1987, p. 538). Collectivism may be expressed through the existence and recognition of union or non-union-based democratic structures of collective bargaining and/or participation. Equally it concerns the degree of legitimacy afforded to such collective structures by management and, hence, the extent to which management either welcomes and cooperates with or barely tolerates such structures (p. 539).

In their first use of the dimensions of individualism and collectivism, Purcell and Gray (1986) saw each as representing a continuum from 'high' to 'low' and cross-cutting to present four quadrants (see Figure 2.1). Into these quadrants they assigned the styles for managing employee relations already identified in Purcell's earlier publication (Purcell and Sisson, 1983). So what are these styles?

The first two, the 'traditional' and 'sophisticated paternalism/human relations' may appear very different at first sight, representing the 'controlling' and 'caring' sides of personnel management respectively. But both share a unitary orientation and have little sympathy with collectivism. The 'traditional' style is one where both collectivism and individualism scores are low. As what might be considered the unacceptable face of a unitarist frame of reference, the 'traditional' style is characterised by labour being viewed as a factor of production, as hands to be exploited or a cost to be minimised. Unions are opposed and vilified and attempts at unionisation met with victimisation. This management style may be typified by left-wing observers in terms of the radical frame of reference, although such managements' predilection for the use of casual marginalised labour (for example, disempowered groups such as racial minorities, women and the young) to facilitate strategies of labour intensification and cost minimisation, often results in little overt resistance. The Grunwick photo processing company, employing largely Asian labour and at the centre of a major dispute over union recognition in 1976–7 is often cited as an example of this style under challenge (Rogaly, 1977).

Where individualism is high and collectivism is low, Purcell and Sisson identified 'sophisticated paternalism'. Employees are viewed as the company's most valued resource, and the emphasis is to inculcate employee loyalty, commitment and

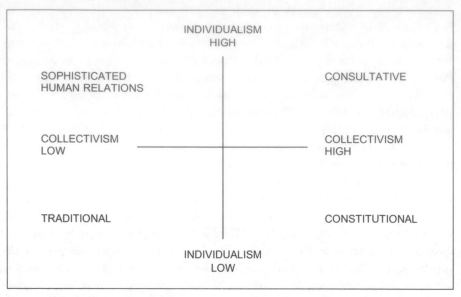

INDIVIDUALISM
HIGH

SOPHISTICATED
HUMAN RELATIONS

CONSULTATIVE

COLLECTIVISM
LOW

COLLECTIVISM
HIGH

TRADITIONAL

CONSTITUTIONAL

INDIVIDUALISM
LOW

Source: Purcell and Gray (1986).

Figure 2.1   Purcell and Gray's model of employee relations styles

dependency, via above average pay, internal labour market structures with promotion ladders, employee appraisal linked to merit awards and intensive attitudinal as well as skills training. Collectivist structures may exist in the form of consultative committees, but although much emphasis is placed on intensive communications with employees to identify grievances and to preach the company message, the preferred means are through procedures to harness individual or work group attitudes (surveys, briefing groups, quality circles). Unions are not welcomed and the aim of the 'caring' personnel policy is to make unionisation appear unnecessary or unattractive to employees. As Marchington and Parker (1990, p. 78) suggest this style has elements of both unitary and pluralist frames of reference, although in my view the unitary predominates. Companies identified as typifying this style are Marks & Spencer and, prior to its massive financial problems and restructuring in the 1990s, IBM. In both companies employees are often seen by outsiders as being 'lettered IBM (or M & S) all the way through'.

The second two styles are those where collectivism, in terms of the existence and recognition of union institutions, is high. Purcell and Sisson's (1983) two 'sophisticated modern' styles, the 'consultative' and the 'constitutional' are contrasted in terms of their sympathy with individualism. The 'consultative' style, scoring high on both collectivism and individualism, in practice resembles 'sophisticated paternalism'/human relations, except that unions are recognised. Management attempts to coopt the unions almost as partners, and engages in broad ranging discussions over a whole range of issues, including plans for change. Emphasis is placed on achieving individual commitment (via internal labour markets, training, profit sharing) but in a context where consultation and bargaining with the unions is taken for granted. Other vehicles of employee participation are encouraged (joint working parties, briefing groups, consultative committees containing employee representatives apart from union officials), but these are regarded as supplementing the communication process rather than as substitutes for, or undermining, management–union relationships. Again this style has both unitary and pluralistic elements, but in contrast to 'sophisticated paternalism', pluralism predominates. ICI and Cadbury–Schweppes in the private sector, and local authorities and public services in the public sector are generally recognised to typify this style. More recently Sisson (1989, p. 9) has suggested that the Nissan subsidiary near Sunderland exemplifies this style, but even allowing for the existence of union agreements in that plant, I would dispute whether 'sweetheart' deals and single-unionism reflects completely Purcell's understanding of collectivism, if the aspect of intentionality and legitimacy is considered. Certainly the pronouncements of Peter Wickens, Personnel Director of Nissan (UK) in its early developmental period, have more of a ring of a unitaristic 'sophisticated paternalism'/human relations.

In the quadrant where collectivism is high (at least in terms of the existence of union structures) and individualism is low, Purcell and Gray (1986) assign Purcell and Sisson's (1983) 'constitutional' style. Unions are recognised, but grudgingly as unavoidable, rather than welcomed into a constructive dialogue. Management prerogatives are jealously guarded through highly specific collective agreements which are carefully administered and monitored on the shopfloor. Management's emphasis is on the need for stability, control and containment of conflict, in order to minimise or neutralise union constraints on operating and strategic management. But although 'collectivist' in institutional terms, the degree of legitimacy accorded to the unions is low. It is 'containment-aggression by grudging acknowledgement' (Purcell, 1987, p. 539, citing Walton and McKersie, 1965, p. 189). In terms of values, as opposed to structures, the 'constitutional' style comes closer to the 'traditional' than the 'consultative' style. From an observer's radical frame of reference, the constitutional style expresses a Cold War between labour and capital. As Marchington and Parker (1990, p. 79) put it 'peace is maintained by a respect for the other side's disruptive potential'. It is generally considered that this style is most prevalent in Fordist production systems, and where there is a tradition of legalistic employee relations. This is a style considered to be more in evidence in the US than in Britain (given, until recently, a tradition of voluntarism in British industrial relations). Not surprisingly Ford itself was often quoted as the exemplar of such an employee relations style, although, as Marchington and Parker (1990, p. 79) point out, its recent attempts to introduce employee involvement may now make this typification less appropriate (see also Storey, 1992b).

The fifth style identified by Purcell and Sisson (1983) falls outside the collectivism/individualism quadrants and, indeed, with Purcell's (1987) more restrictive conceptualisation of 'style', is denied the status of being a 'true' style at all. Termed the 'standard modern', this approach to employee relations is characterised as pragmatic and opportunistic. There is no consistent policy about the recognition of trade unions, recognition often depending on past history, or inherited with company acquisition. Employee relations is viewed as the responsibility of operational management at unit or divisional level and not as a strategic issue. There can be marked differences in approach between different establishments or divisions in a multiplant company and between different levels in the hierarchy. The importance attached to employee relations management reflects product and labour market conditions. When union power is high and product and labour markets buoyant or if legislative needs dictate, negotiation and consultation are the order of the day. If the reverse conditions prevail, or major technical changes threaten existing practices, unions may be 'rolled back' as management seeks to regain its prerogatives. In essence, employee relations tends to be viewed as 'firefighting': 'it is something which is assumed to be non-problematic until events prove otherwise' (Purcell and Sisson, 1983, p. 116). GEC is generally quoted as an exemplar of such an approach.

Purcell's (1987) elaboration of the individualism/collectivism dimensions throws further light on the similarities and contrasts of these management styles. Presenting the two dimensions in graph rather than cross-cutting form, he characterises their extremes and mid-points. Thus 'high' individualism involves treating employees as a resource and hence points to an employee relations strategy of employee development. 'Low' individualism is typified by treating employees as an exploitable commodity, and a strategy of tight labour control. Mid-way between the two is paternalism 'limiting the freedom of the subject by well meant regulations' (Purcell, 1987, p. 537). While 'high' collectivism is typified by 'cooperative' relationships with employees' collective organisations and 'low' collectivism by a unitary frame of reference, the mid-point is seen as management engaging in 'adversarial' relations with collective institutions. If, in the light of their characterisation, the five management styles are located on this graph (an exercise Purcell did not attempt), the similarities, on the one hand, between the traditional and constitutional style and, on the other, between sophisticated paternalism/human relations and the consultative style, and the contrasts between the two styles is highlighted. The similarities between sophisticated paternalism/human relations and the consultative style is particularly marked in those situations where, in spite of no union recognition, the sophisticated paternalist/human relations managers have built extensive communication channels with groups of employees. More difficult to locate on this graph is the standard modern style as, by definition, its appearance changes with circumstances. Perhaps it is best expressed as a dotted diagonal line, with the potential to span the range of possibilities (see Figure 2.2).

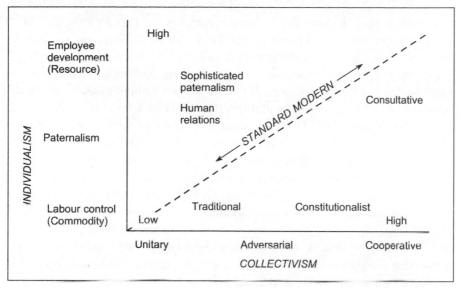

Source: Purcell (1987).

Figure 2.2 Purcell's model of mapping managerial employee relations styles

Marchington and Parker's (1990) critique and revision of Purcell's typology

On the basis of extended case study research in four unionised multiplant companies, in chemicals, food processing, retail, and engineering, in the mid-1980s, Marchington and Parker (1990) proposed some amendments to Purcell's individualism/collectivism dimensions. Having tried to fit their companies along the individualism/collectivism axes, they identified a number of problems with them. First, they query whether a mid-point along the individualism dimension can always be equated with paternalism, particularly when the mid-point is achieved by companies in the process of change and which exhibit elements of both a development/resource and labour control/commodity approach. Second, they argue – rightly, I think – that it is debatable whether the extremes of the individualism dimension are mutually exclusive, as 'all employers are concerned about controlling labour costs', in spite of the fact that some may aim to treat employees as a resource to be developed. Compare, for example, a BT mission statement ('Westminster District Vision') that 'the manner in which employees are treated means that they see Westminster District as a caring responsible employer' with subsequent proposals for radical reductions of the head count. Furthermore, Marchington and Parker (1990, p. 235) did not find that managers regarded either developing employees or treating them as a commodity as having anything to do with individualism or collectivism *per se* – which is not surprising if the strategies are not seen as mutually exclusive.

Turning to the collectivist dimension, Marchington and Parker (1990, pp. 235–7) query whether the existence and recognition of union institutions can really be regarded as managements' commitment to collectivism, 'because all the employers are doing is to find a mechanism for maintaining and securing order in the workplace' (pp. 235–6). Managers may prefer to work without unions, but if order is maintained with unions, so be it; if not, they may be fearful of the consequences of initiating derecognition. Unions' institutions may survive intact but managers (as Marchington and Parker found) may choose to side step and marginalise them by creating new mechanisms of employee involvement (see Storey, 1992b).

Hence Marchington and Parker propose that in place of the individualism and collectivism dimensions, it might be more appropriate to build on Purcell's ideas about employee development and the legitimacy accorded to unions. On the basis of their research they suggest dimensions based on management's approach to employees and to unions: the investment orientation (to employees) and the partnership orientation (to the unions). As with the Purcell dimensions, companies can score high or low on either dimension.

Responsible autonomy and direct control: enter Friedman (1977)

Although predating Purcell's and Marchington's typifications of managerial styles of employee relations/personnel management, Friedman's (1977) categorisation of the two basic approaches to exercising control over labour fits well with their analyses (and indeed is acknowledged to have directly influenced Marchington's research) (Marchington and Parker, 1990, pp. 80–3). Based on human relations industry-area case studies, the most comprehensive being on the car industry in the Coventry area, Friedman suggests managers have the choice between allowing employees 'responsible autonomy' (RA) and exercising 'direct control' (DC) over them. Responsible autonomy 'attempts to harness the adaptability of labour power by giving workers leeway and encouraging them to adapt to changing situations in a manner beneficial to the firm. To do this top managers give workers status, authority and responsibility'. In contrast, direct control 'tries to limit the scope for labour power to vary, by coercive human relations, close supervision and minimising individual workers' responsibility. [This] tries to limit its particularly harmful effects and treats workers as though they were machines'. Here, clearly expressed in Friedman's identification of the two approaches, is the tension between achieving control and consent that arises out of the contradictions of capitalism, discussed in Chapter 1. The one strategy (RA) is reflected in the 'caring' face, and the other (DC) in the 'controlling' face of personnel management.

Now, admittedly there are criticisms of Friedman's dichotomy of styles: that it oversimplifies by collapsing a range of approaches (such as Purcell and Marchington identify) into only two, and that it fails to consider whether both approaches may be pursued with the same group of employees simultaneously

(Wood and Kelly, 1982, pp. 84–5). There is the problem too of management intentionality – what might appear to be consistent with either an RA or DC strategy might express other intentions – as with pseudo-participation or close (but supportive) supervision. As Marchington and Parker (1980, p. 83) point out 'the conceptualisation of RA and DC as opposite ends of a continuum implies a clarity in management initiatives, a coherence in management organisation, and an omnipotence in management activity which cannot be taken for granted'.

That said, if we accept Friedman's dichotomy of styles for what it is – a potentially useful heuristic – we can find echoes and consistencies with Purcell's and Marchington and Parker's approaches. For example, if management believe in investing in employees and in seeking partnership rather than conflict or containment with the unions, we might expect them to adopt personnel policies consistent with a 'responsible autonomy' approach. Indeed, our very categorisation of such a management style might rest on our identification of such policies in practice. We might also expect to observe the policies of 'responsible autonomy' to be more in evidence in firms choosing a 'sophisticated paternalist' or 'consultative' style of management, at least in relation to their core employees, than a 'traditionalist' or 'constitutionalist' management style. Observation of policies of 'direct control' might lead us to identify 'traditionalist' and possibly 'constitutionalist' management styles. Indeed, there is something of the 'chicken and egg' about the relationships between these typologies. Do we predict that management, expressing the 'guiding principles' explicit in Purcell's and Marchington's typologies, will tend toward one or other of Friedman's strategies, or is it by our identification of policies largely consistent with either of these strategies, that we label a workplace's personnel management style according to Purcell's and Marchington's typologies?

Storey and Bacon's 'criteria-based' approach

More recently, Storey and Bacon (1993), concerned by the industrial relations focus and static nature of Purcell's and Marchington and Parker's typologies, have sought to develop a new 'criteria-based' approach that, in common with Friedman, addresses work organisation as an intrinsic aspect of employee relations style, and aims to throw light on current developments and to locate change.

Storey and Bacon (1993) argue that the concepts of individualism and collectivism require further unpacking. In relation to Purcell's model (see Figure 2.2) they suggest that 'employee development' cannot necessarily be equated with greater 'individualism' as Japanese style development is marked by groupism. Similarly, traditional British craft apprenticeships were fully compatible with union collectivism. In a sense, too, Taylorism, based on work fragmentation, could be seen as an example of 'individualisation'. Individualism and collectivism might be better explored, they argue, by establishing criteria representing industrial relations, work

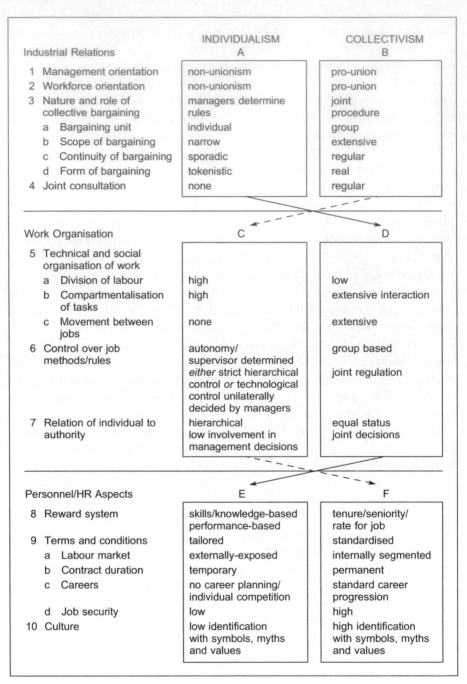

Industrial Relations	INDIVIDUALISM A	COLLECTIVISM B
1 Management orientation	non-unionism	pro-union
2 Workforce orientation	non-unionism	pro-union
3 Nature and role of collective bargaining	managers determine rules	joint procedure
a Bargaining unit	individual	group
b Scope of bargaining	narrow	extensive
c Continuity of bargaining	sporadic	regular
d Form of bargaining	tokenistic	real
4 Joint consultation	none	regular

Work Organisation	C	D
5 Technical and social organisation of work		
a Division of labour	high	low
b Compartmentalisation of tasks	high	extensive interaction
c Movement between jobs	none	extensive
6 Control over job methods/rules	autonomy/ supervisor determined *either* strict hierarchical control *or* technological control unilaterally decided by managers	group based joint regulation
7 Relation of individual to authority	hierarchical low involvement in management decisions	equal status joint decisions

Personnel/HR Aspects	E	F
8 Reward system	skills/knowledge-based performance-based	tenure/seniority/ rate for job
9 Terms and conditions	tailored	standardised
a Labour market	externally-exposed	internally segmented
b Contract duration	temporary	permanent
c Careers	no career planning/ individual competition	standard career progression
d Job security	low	high
10 Culture	low identification with symbols, myths and values	high identification with symbols, myths and values

Source: Storey and Bacon (1993).

Figure 2.3 Storey and Bacon's model of criteria for exploring individualism and collectivism in organisations

organisation and personnel management practices and then assessing each criterion in relation to individualism or collectivism. For example, the criteria to assess work organisation are identified as the technical and social organisation (division of labour, compartmentalisation of tasks, movement between jobs), control over job methods/rules and relation of individuals to authority. To take just one criterion, if the division of labour is high, the criterion is scored as individualistic and, if low, is collectivist. If a criterion of personnel management – namely, reward system – is scored as resting on skills/knowledge, or is performance-based, the criterion is scored as individualistic, if it is scored as resting on tenure/seniority/rate for the job it is scored as collectivist (see Figure 2.3). And so on.

Clearly, in the classification of the criteria, there is much room for discussion, but Storey and Bacon's (1993) intention is to construct a classificatory device that allows for the identification of different patterns of individualistic/collectivist relationships along *different* dimensions of the employment relationship and to explore movement between eight logical types (see Figures 2.3 and 2.4). Two types, Types 2 and 5, they consider unlikely to exist in reality. In Type 2, the extent of management control, through individualised industrial relations and work organisation, makes it unlikely that there would be any pressure for a collective approach to personnel management. Type 5 is also unlikely because the individualistic organisation of work and personnel management systems makes a

---

Type '1' situations: where management exercises strong control through individualised treatment of all aspects of employee relations (route A–C–E on Figure 2.3).

Type '2' situations: where both industrial relations and work organisation are individualised but HR policies are collectivised (route A–C–F).

Type '3' situations: where unions are opposed, work organisation is collective and sophisticated HR policies are pursued (route from B towards A, and then to D and E).

Type '4' situations: where a non-union stance is harnessed to an enhanced form of work organisation while HR policies remain collectively organised (route A–D–F).

Type '5' situations: where IR is collectivised yet work organisation and HR are dealt with on an individualised basis (route B–C–E).

Type '6' situations: where the maintenance of a traditional industrial relations pattern is associated with a high division of labour and standardised terms and conditions (route B–C–F).

Type '7' situations: where a collective approach to industrial relations and work organisation is combined with an individualised approach to HR (route B–D–E).

Type '8' situations: where a collective approach to all aspects of employee relations is pursued (route B–D–F).

Source: Storey and Bacon (1993).

Figure 2.4 Storey and Bacon's model of combinations of individualism and collectivism in employee relations

collectivist approach to industrial relations inappropriate. Types 1 and 8 (completely individualistic or collectivist) are 'all of a piece' and unlikely to change, being styles to which their adherents have high commitment. The four remaining types all represent mixes of individual and collectivist elements in their employee relations strategies. Type 3 represents policies of non-unionisation with enhanced work organisation and sophisticated human relations policies (for example, IBM, Digital, Marks & Spencer). Type 4 represents companies which have recently moved towards individualising industrial relations and aspire to the more sophisticated human relations policies found in Type 3 companies, while developing collective forms of work organisation, through multiskilling and teamworking (for example, in some oil and chemical companies). The Type 6 category contains companies which have sought to move away from individualised forms of work organisation within a highly proceduralised context (for example, Ford). Type 7 represents a pattern where individualised human relations personnel policies coexist alongside collectivist industrial relations and work organisation (for example, Japanese transplant factories in the UK).

Tyson and Fell's 'building site' analogy

If personnel management is about 'regulating the employment relationship' (descriptive–functional definition) it is not surprising that imagery to do with constructive relationships and by extension 'construction', have formed the basis of a rather different typology of personnel management style. Tyson and Fell (1986, p. 23), thinking in terms of personnel management's contribution to 'the building of the business', have identified human relations modes of operation, already referred to in Chapter 1, the 'clerk of works', the 'contracts manager' and the 'architect'. This typology differs from that of Purcell et al., and of Marchington and Parker in that it does not derive from Fox's frames of reference nor his early typology, nor does it rest on the individualism/collectivism or investment/partnership dimensions developed by Purcell and Marchington and Parker and Storey and Bacon. It further contrasts with the latter authors and with Friedman in that the styles are not focused on managerial value orientations towards employees and unions *per se*. Rather the typology expresses ideal-type roles that personnel specialists might be expected to enact in different organisational contexts. 'Roles', in this typology, are defined as 'a number of consistent expectations about how [personnel managers] will act in situations to which they are usually exposed' (Tyson and Fell, 1986, p. 24).

Tyson and Fell (1986, pp. 22–3) argue that these 'consistent expectations' concern four parameters of the personnel function. These are: the decision-making approach of senior management, the planning horizon adopted for personnel activities, the degree of discretion afforded to the personnel specialist, and the extent to which such specialists are involved in creating the organisation's culture, 'with the concomitant styles of management expected by top managers and employees'. These parameters relate to four major tasks that personnel specialists are involved with, namely representing the organisation's central value system; maintaining the boundaries of the organisation; providing stability and continuity; and adapting to organisational change (Tyson and Fell, 1986, pp. 39–40).

Bringing these parameters and tasks together, Tyson and Fell identify the characteristics of their human relations 'operating styles' (p. 24). The 'clerk of works' is allowed little discretion, short to immediate planning horizons, and is wholly subservient to line managers. The role is reactive and *ad hoc*, and centres on providing routine, administrative services to the line, and welfare provision to employees. Such systems as exist are created in an *ad hoc* way, and involve the *post facto* recording of standard employee centred/legal requirements information. The main systems are likely to be financially oriented – to provide head count, payroll and performance against budget data. The personnel specialist who enacts this role will report to line management and, rather than being a trained specialist, is likely to have moved into this role, on promotion, from a clerical position. This operating style may achieve satisfactorily the maintenance of boundaries (routine recruitment) and stability and continuity (administering basic routines) but will play no part in consciously representing a central value system or adapting the organisation to change. This, in Drucker's words, is the 'file-clerk' style of operating the personnel function.

The 'contracts manager' monitors an infrastructure of well established, rule-based, unionised industrial relations policies, 'the expert on the existing contract, ensuring that every sub-clause is fulfilled' (Tyson and Fell, 1986, p. 23). Although line managers perform the main industrial relations activity, the 'contracts manager' has some discretion in interpreting existing procedures, agreements and contracts in the light of new circumstances. Working to a medium-term planning horizon, he (invariably 'he' rather than 'she') gives service and advice to middle and senior line management, provides knowledge of systems, IR practice and precedents, and generally acts as the agent of senior management. The infrastructure of procedures, bargaining and consultation systems proclaim an 'espoused' industrial relations policy, but it is recognised that the contracts manager is adept at working a more pragmatic 'operational' policy. To sum up, 'the accent is on making the existing system work better' (p. 26). As such, and with an espoused industrial relations policy, the contracts manager may be recognised as representing the central value system of the firm, maintaining its boundaries and providing stability and continuity, but not to the forefront in helping the organisation adapt to change (p. 46). The 'contracts manager' style of operation is caught in Tyson and Fell's (1986, p. 23) description:

> His knowledge of the system and his pragmatism, his reputation for getting things done quickly, effectively, and for maintaining the existing relationships, grants him a senior job where top management want the here and now well controlled, irrespective of the future.

The 'architect', in contrast, combines both high discretion and a long-term planning horizon. These are earned, or justified, by his or her role in integrating personnel policies with business strategy, indeed, developing explicit policies to give effect to the corporate plan. Such a manager 'regards himself [*sic*] as a business manager first and a "professional" personnel manager second' (p. 26). The 'architect' is expected to be proactive in the development of policy to initiate and manage organisational and environmental change. In doing so, the personnel manager acts as consultant to and partner with senior management. This mode of enacting the personnel function – participating in human resource planning with the top management team – is of sufficiently high status to attract not just career professional personnel specialists, but line managers either permanently or for career development. This is the role of personnel manager as 'organisational diagnostician' (Lupton, 1964; Legge, 1978), as the 'long-term designer and planner, creative, flexible and mindful of the need for change' (Tyson and Fell, 1986, p. 23). It is in this operating mode that Tyson and Fell see personnel management as fulfilling all four of its potential tasks (p. 46). Whether the 'architect' personnel manager and human resource management, in reality, are one and the same will be considered in Chapter 3.

It is tempting to locate these styles of management hierarchically (i.e., 'architect' = personnel director; 'contracts manager' = divisional/plant personnel manager; 'clerk of works' = plant personnel officer or personnel assistant). However, as Tyson and Fell (1986, pp. 35–6) point out, this would be simplistic. 'A personnel assistant, for example, may have been recruited with an "architect" view of personnel management, whereas the personnel director could have been promoted from long experience of running industrial relations to be personnel director, with a "contracts manager" perception of the function'. In a multiplant company history and circumstances may encourage the adoption of different operating modes in different companies or toward different groups of employees. Different models may be found in the same company during processes of transition. Tyson and Fell argue, however, that if different operating modes exist at different levels of the hierarchy or towards different groups of employees, or in different plants in a multiplant company, ensuing inconsistencies and conflict are likely to result in a predominant style emerging (shades of Purcell *et al.*, and Marchington's typologies) (p. 36). Whether this is so, in my view, however, is likely to depend, in a multiplant company, on the degree of diversification, decentralisation and autonomy accorded to its constituent parts. This issue will be developed later in this chapter.

Storey's (1992b) typology

In his much cited *Developments in the Management of Human Resources*, Storey (1992b) presents a typology of personnel management styles derived from empirical research that is reminiscent of that of Tyson and Fell (see Figure 2.5). The typology

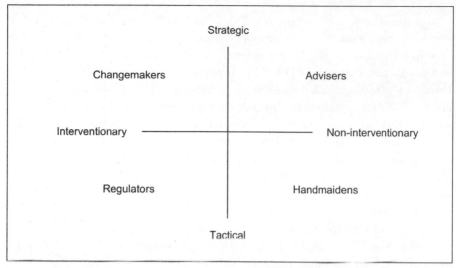

Source: Storey (1992b).

Figure 2.5   Storey's model of types of personnel management

is based on two cross-cutting dimensions: the strategic/tactical and the interventionary/non-interventionary. Four main styles of personnel management enactment are suggested: the 'handmaidens' (tactical/non-interventionary); advisors (strategic/non-interventionary); regulators (tactical/interventionary) and the 'changemakers' (strategic/interventionary).

'Handmaidens' are those whose reactive contributions are very much customer-led – personnel's activities being closely scrutinised by line management, with an explicit understanding that any parts of the service (for example, training) that was judged not be of value to the business or could be obtained cheaper elsewhere, would be dropped. In such circumstances, personnel's defence is mainly to point out the consequences if various services were cut. This is an 'up-market' variant on the 'clerk of works' role and, as Storey (1992b, p. 174) points out, at a lower level, like the 'clerks of works' 'handmaidens' are involved in the routine 'trash-can' services, such as welfare, combined with some reactive industrial relations firefighting, that is anathema to personnel 'professionals'.

'Advisors' are those personnel managers who have concentrated on refusing to be dumped with routine firefighting problems by the line and instead have developed a role as internal consultants advising on new initiatives and encouraging line management to run their own units with specialist advice. Such managers refuse the role of custodian of agreements or troubleshooters and accept that major employee relations initiatives are increasingly devised by the line, if with their own 'expert' input. Such a role contains the strategic vision of Tyson and Fell's 'architect', but lacks its proactivity.

'Regulators' are very similar to Tyson and Fell's 'contracts managers', if somewhat more proactive. They formulate, promulgate and monitor observances of employment rules, ranging from personnel procedure manuals to joint agreements with trade unions. As Storey (1992b, p. 169) puts it: 'these [are] the "managers of discontent", seeking order through temporary, tactical truces with organised labour'. Their interventions rarely involve engagement with wider business strategy – rather, they act as the traditional industrial relations buffer that insulates main board members from potential intrusions of 'problematic' labour issues into strategic decision-making (cf. Marginson *et al.*, 1988, p. 76). Nevertheless, in recent years, 'regulators', mindful of the criticisms about the slowness of procedure and the need for tough decisions that do not lend themselves to negotiated compromise, have developed a more proactive 'bargaining-for-change' approach (see, for example, Ford, UK) (Storey, 1992b, pp. 179–80).

Finally, Storey's 'changemakers' appear very similar to Tyson and Fell's 'architects'. These personnel managers seek to integrate systematically personnel policy with the 'needs of the business'. Their contribution, which is similar to that proposed by both the normative models of personnel management *and* human resource management (see Chapters 1 and 3) is highly interventionary and strategically oriented, the 'antithesis ... [of] ... bargaining, ... *ad hocery* ... and ... "humble advice"' (Storey, 1992b, p. 180).

Summary

Finally, what connections might be made between the various typologies? It is tempting to paint some pretty pictures in bold colours. Thus we could see the 'architect' or 'changemaker' as a 'sophisticated paternalist' or 'consultor', pursuing policies of investment in employees and partnership with unions, fully committed to 'responsible autonomy' for people-as-resources – at the leading edge of human resource management (see Chapter 3). Equally we might wish to identify a 'contracts manager' or 'regulator' as a constitutionalist, treating employees as commodities/costs, in connivance rather than in partnership with the unions, and maintaining a strategy of direct control over a blue collar workforce. The 'traditional' company might be seen as operating with a 'clerk of works' or 'handmaiden' personnel officer – that is, if it had any personnel specialist at all on its cut-to-the-bone payroll – highly unlikely as WIRS 3 would indicate (Millward *et al.*, 1992). Appealing though they might be such pictures at best are stereotypes and at worst a gross simplification, as Storey and Bacon's (1993) work suggests. Logically, an 'architect's' or 'changemaker's' vision could encompass all but the 'traditional' styles of operating, and her strategy might be to differentiate between 'core' and 'peripheral' employees in choice of 'responsible autonomy' or 'direct control' policies. A 'contracts manager' or 'regulator' might well be operating in a consultative company – even if the rules and systems he monitored and interpreted differed in content and coverage from those of a constitutionalist organisation. 'Clerks of works' or 'handmaidens' are probably found at the plant level irrespective of the dominant or emerging new styles of personnel management. Organisations may be developing a mixture of individualist and collectivist policies in relation to industrial relations, work organisation and personnel management practices and in respect of different groups of employees (Storey and Bacon, 1993). But this raises the second concern of this chapter. Leaving aside speculation, can we identify *empirically* any relationship between choice of a particular personnel management/ employee relations style and organisational context?

Personnel management styles in context

Case study and survey data would suggest that different personnel management styles are associated with different configurations of organisational ownership, size, strategy and structure — not to mention past history and product market conditions (see, for example, Sisson and Scullion, 1985; Purcell and Gray, 1986; Ahlstrand and Purcell, 1988; Legge, 1988; Marginson *et al.*, 1988; Sisson, 1989; Marchington and Parker, 1990; Marginson *et al.*, 1993). The evidence is fragmentary rather than complete, suggestive rather than conclusive, so an element of speculation remains.

A single style?

That said, before associating particular styles with particular configurations, there is a prior issue. Can we identify factors that either encourage or discourage the adoption of one consistent organisation-wide style, within a multiplant (even multisubsidiary) company, irrespective of what that style might be?

Sisson and Scullion's (1985) early work is useful here. Divisionalised organisations, in which strategic and operational management are separated, take two forms depending on the nature and extent of diversification: the multi-divisional structure and the critical function structure. Sisson and Scullion (1985) suggest that where growth has taken place via diversification, often by merger and acquisition, as in the case of BTR or Hanson, the corporation takes on a classic multidivisional form. That is a structure of subsidiary companies, linked together in divisions or groups, or operating independently, and which, in turn, comprise further subordinate companies and divisions, which may be yet further decentralised by product or geography into separate business units. Here the divorce between strategic and operating management is more or less complete, and managers in individual businesses, although controlled through centralised budgetary and information systems, are nonetheless highly autonomous as far as operating decisions go. In contrast, in a small minority of businesses, such as Sainsbury, Ford or IBM, where growth has been via the development of a single business or range of products and where consequently the potential for integration is high, head office managers retain control of one or more 'critical functions' of operating management (for example, merchandising in Sainsbury or Marks & Spencer, production in Ford), although the company might be decentralised geographically or by product. In such companies, operating managers in business units are likely to experience far less autonomy than those in multidivisional corporations, their units being regarded as cost rather than – as in the latter – profit centres.

One upshot of this is that the role played by the corporate personnel department is likely to vary according to the type of organisation structure and ethos prevailing. Where a 'critical function' or 'single business' structure exists and personnel is defined as a 'critical function' (as in Marks & Spencer and IBM), a large and (relatively) powerful corporate personnel department is likely to flourish as it assists the overall control of operations from the centre. Moreover, lack of diversification is conducive to running the organisation as a large internal labour market (Hendry and Pettigrew, 1986). In contrast, where the diversified corporation takes a multidivisionalised form, it is arguably less likely that a large department will exist as standard policies and approaches will be impractical and inappropriate. Instead, strategic personnel policy is likely to be formulated by the personnel department located at subsidiary company or divisional level, and at unit level as far as operational matters are concerned (Sisson and Scullion, 1985). Hence an organisation-wide personnel management style is more likely to emerge in a critical function or a single business structure rather than in a diversified, multidivisional structure, because of the greater power and influence of the corporate personnel department. So goes the argument.

The evidence to support this argument is largely positive (Legge, 1988, pp. 57–9). Admittedly the first Warwick IRRU Company Level Survey, conducted in 1985, contrary to predictions, found no significant relationship between diversification or level of profit centre and the existence and scale of a specialist personnel staff at head office. However, perhaps not too much weight should be put on this finding, when assessing the support for Sisson and Scullion's general argument, as they admit that, due to time lags and institutional inertia, the 'fit' between strategy and structure may not be perfect. By the time of the second Warwick Company Level survey, conducted in 1992, the picture is much clearer, possibly due to the amount of company re-organisation reported (Marginson et al., 1993, Table 2.5). The size of the corporate personnel department was found to be linked not only to the overall size of the enterprise (as in the 1985 survey) but to the degree of diversification, conglomerates having a smaller central service as compared with single business companies (Marginson et al., 1993, Table 4.3). Firms organised along territorial or spatial lines, like those without any intermediary or divisional structures, were relatively intensively staffed unlike the classic multidivisional firms, structured along business or product market lines, found amongst conglomerates. Further, the wider the scope of the division the smaller the relative size of the corporate personnel office.

In the 1985 Warwick Company Level survey all evidence pointed to corporate personnel departments in highly diversified companies allowing their establishments greater autonomy than those enterprises whose activities were concentrated in a single business. Thus, for example, Marginson *et al.* (1988) reported that enterprises which were more diversified across industrial sectors in employment terms were more likely to give their establishments a degree of autonomy over personnel and industrial relations decisions, whereas enterprises whose activities were concentrated in a single business were more likely to instruct their establishments. Furthermore, enterprises that were more financially devolved, either in that operating establishments were profit centres or that such profit centres could retain funds for strategic investment purposes, gave their establishments more autonomy, whereas financially centralised enterprises were very likely to instruct establishments over personnel and industrial relations decisions. Enterprises whose activities were concentrated in a single business were significantly more likely to have a binding policy on communication, involvement and participation than were more diversified enterprises, and enterprises where profit responsibility was devolved, were more likely to have policies which were more advisory in nature. Establishments' perceptions of their relative autonomy were consistent with these findings, in that establishments in enterprises which produced heterogeneous rather than homogeneous products and services, and those able to retain a proportion of funds generated for investment purposes, felt that they had significantly greater discretion over industrial relations decisions.

The findings of the 1992 Warwick Company Level survey are consistent, in this respect, with those of the 1985 survey. The large corporate personnel departments associated with single business companies are more likely to issue instructions, monitor compliance and collect data, hold regular meetings with personnel managers at unit and business level and be associated with the presence of enterprise-level industrial relations structures than the smaller corporate personnel departments associated with conglomerates or more diversified business enterprises (Marginson *et al.*, 1993, pp. 32–4).

One, further, relevant finding emerges from the 1992 Warwick Company Level survey, that is, the importance of having a personnel director at main board level. First, the presence of such a director is associated with relatively large corporate personnel departments (3 personnel managers per 1000 UK employees compared to 1.4 where there was no director) which are more likely to be involved in making and applying personnel policy than smaller ones (see Marginson *et al.*, 1993, Table 4.9). Second, the presence of a personnel director seems associated with a more sophisticated 'changemaker' or 'architect'-style personnel function. Thus such firms were more likely to have certain key personnel policies – such as in equal opportunities – and to organise regular meetings of personnel managers; personnel directors were involved in pushing for productivity improvements; they took part in the review of business units and the career decisions on senior managers and their pay; they were more likely to have a dedicated training and development budget; to have worked alongside colleagues in finance in designing and running performance, profit and share ownership reward systems; and were more likely to be party to strategies for corporate change. They were also more often involved in making decisions about pay assumptions in business-unit budgets (Marginson *et al.*, 1993, pp. 33–7; Purcell, 1994). Further, in the light of subsequent discussion, it should be noted that it is overseas-owned companies that are more likely to have a large corporate personnel department, much more likely to have a personnel director on the main board *and* a specialist personnel manager on site than their UK counterparts (Millward *et al.*, 1992).

So which style, where?

The evidence we have about *which* personnel management styles are associated with which organisational and market configurations points to the overriding importance of degree of diversification and product market strategy, along with size and ownership.

On the basis of their research, Purcell and Gray attempted to typify the circumstances in which the five styles identified in Purcell and Sisson's (1983) typology are likely to occur, and the expected role of corporate personnel management. Given the relatively restricted research base, there is inevitably some speculation here – but it is informed speculation. Purcell and Gray suggest that the 'traditional' style is most likely to be found in small owner-management companies or possibly franchises. Product markets would be likely to be highly competitive with competing firms having low market share, leading to an emphasis on cost control, with low profit margins. There would be few, if any, personnel specialists. In contrast, 'sophisticated paternalism/human relations' is characteristic of US-owned, single industry, large, financially successful organisations, with a high market share in growth industries, such as the electronics and financial services sectors. As we have already seen such organisational contexts are likely to have strong corporate personnel departments, that develop and implement organisation-wide policies. The 'consultative' style is similarly characteristic of large single industry companies, often with high market share. In contrast with the 'sophisticated paternalist' context, though, the organisations tend to be British- (and, Purcell would argue, Japanese-) owned, in industries (such as process) with relatively low labour costs. Again the central personnel departments would be likely to be strong, but as likely to produce policy guidelines and advice, as well as directives when required. Purcell and Gray suggest that the context characteristic of the 'constitutional' style is the large single industry unionised company, organised in large plants for large batch and mass production of relatively standardised products. Labour costs form a significant proportion of total costs, and product market conditions are often highly competitive. There is a strong emphasis on the auditing and control function of the central personnel department. If we consider 'opportunism' to be a style, it would appear to be most common in conglomerate, diversified companies that have grown by acquisition and merger. It is particularly characteristic of diversified companies in engineering and heavy manufacturing with long traditions of unionisation. In such contexts the personnel function is often weak at corporate level with specialists at operating level having a reactive firefighting role, in response to union pressures and legislative requirements. The influence of personnel specialists in such organisations is likely to vary over time, depending upon how problematic the labour supply is perceived to be in the achievement of business targets.

So, as a broad generalisation, 'opportunism' would seem characteristic of large, diversified companies, 'sophisticated paternalism' or the 'consultative' style characteristic of large, single business, successful firms with high market share, and the 'tougher' 'traditional' and 'constitutional' styles characteristic of competitive market conditions in which control of labour costs is a high priority. If the centrality of business strategy and product market conditions is recognised by Purcell and his colleagues, their influence on personnel management style has been further explored by Marchington and Parker (1990).

Strategy, product markets and personnel/employee relations style

In a very useful discussion of research published in the 1980s, Marchington and Parker (1990, pp. 84–100) identify three types of study that have dealt with the relationships between product markets and employee relations strategies and style. Some studies have provided in-depth analyses of specific plants, companies or industries at a particular point in time, which describe key features of the product market and link these to employee relations strategies and practices (for example, Goodman *et al.*, 1977; Purcell, 1981; Marchington and Loveridge, 1983; Purcell and Gray, 1986). Then there are those studies which examine changes in the management of the labour process in the context of longer run historical adjustments in product market conditions (for example, Fox, 1974; Friedman, 1984). Finally, there are the studies of a particular industry or company, over a period of time in the 1970s and 1980s, illustrating changes in employee relations following a major readjustment in the product market (for example, Batstone *et al.*, 1984; Capelli, 1985; Kochan *et al.*, 1984). These studies point up two lessons: one, that competitive, particularly adverse product market conditions constrain managerial choices in their adoption of a particular management style and, two, nevertheless, even in response to major changes (such as deregulation), some choice remains as to which style may be adopted (see, especially, Capelli, 1985). If the choice adopted in constraining conditions usually involves pragmatism and cost cutting, this is not always so – as evidenced in the 1980s by Ford's attempts at employee involvement (Werther, 1985), and Goodrich's diversification response to intense competitive pressure with the introduction of radials in the US tyre market (Capelli, 1985).

Insightful though these case studies are, they fail to provide a systematic explanatory model of links between markets and employee relations systems and style. Building on earlier speculative models by Thurley and Wood (1983) and Thomason (1984), Marchington and Parker (1990) have done much to rectify this omission. With insights derived from the case study work referred to above, and from the inductive analysis of their own research data, they have developed a useful framework to explain the relationships between product character, market power, trade union activity, employee behaviour and management style (see Figure 2.6).

Taking 'market power' first, Marchington and Parker argued that management discretion in choice of preferred style is greater when market constraints are low, that is, when the organisation has monopoly and monopsony power. Using what is basically a Porterian analysis (Porter, 1980, 1985), monopoly (supplier) power is considered likely to be greater when demand for the company's specific product(s) or service(s) is growing and there are barriers to entry for potential competitors. Such conditions are conducive to an increasing market share and profitability. Conversely, if demand is falling and vulnerable market share is under attack from new competitors with a substitute product, then management is likely to feel highly constrained by competitive pressure in the marketplace. Similarly, the degree of customer pressure (or lack of it) offers constraints (or opportunities). If customer demand for an organisation's products or services is stable and predictable, and if

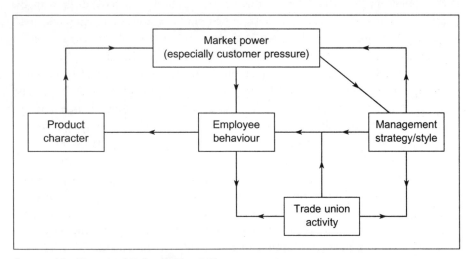

Source: Marchington and Parker (1990, p. 247).

Figure 2.6 Marchington and Parker's model of management, employee relations and market power

customers constitute uncoordinated individual consumers who purchase from a monopoly producer, this clearly presents the supplier organisation with little customer pressure. When the opposite situation prevails – demand fluctuating and unpredictable, a small number of large, possibly coordinated customers, with a range of available suppliers – the supplying organisation is likely to feel the boot on the customer's foot (monopsony power). This is not to imply that market power is deterministic. By their choice of products or services to be supplied, geographical markets in which to compete and, importantly, the basis of their competitive advantage, senior management can influence the character of the markets they confront. But, once these choices have been made, managements have to respond to the markets in which they trade and, in theory at least, choose an employee relations style consistent with their marketing strategies/corporate objectives. But, as Marchington and Parker point out, management can also legitimise choices about management style, made for ideological reasons, by presenting the market to their employees as more deterministic than it is.

Employees are also likely to be influenced by market pressure, either directly (by contact with customers, flow of work through a department, indicative of the state of the order book, social contacts, media reporting) or indirectly, through management's interpretations and messages to the shopfloor (newsletters, briefing groups, etc.). Where there is no union organisation employees may have difficulty in contesting managements' interpretations of market pressure, but, where unions exist, through their use of alternative information networks or the union's research department, the potential exists for some challenge to statements perceived as biased or inaccurate.

Trade union activity and management style are likely to be mutually reinforcing. Where, given low competitive and customer pressure, management may feel free to choose an investment oriented style, there is a good chance that, unless marginalised, trade unions will be prepared to cooperate in a partnership relationship with management, and that employees will also be supportive of this approach. Where market pressure is intense, and managements feel constrained to treat employees as costs to be minimised/commodities to be maximally utilised, it is likely, if the organisation is unionised, for relations to be adversarial. In both cases, management style and union and employee response are likely to be mutually justificatory and reinforcing.

In the final part of their model Marchington and Parker suggest that employee behaviours can influence the product market, through their impact on the character of the product or service the company markets. If management has chosen to compete on delivery dates or quality or customer care, employee commitment (or lack of it) to these objectives can have a major effect on whether management aspirations are achieved. Again, the relationships hypothesised in the model are likely to be mutually reinforcing. If an investment style is adopted employees may be more ready to cooperate, which in turn is likely to reinforce management's commitment to this style. If, on the other hand, market pressure results in the choice of an employee as cost/commodity style, employees may equally choose to withhold cooperation, to work 'without enthusiasm'. This in turn may confirm management's choice of style and commitment to Tayloristic beliefs, in the necessity for minimising employee discretion, with further loss of cooperation. In both cases, management style is likely to reinforce existing patterns of management/union relations, which in turn will reinforce emergent patterns of employee behaviours and their effects on the product character and subsequently the market.

Marchington and Parker's emphasis on the primacy of the product market in influencing (but not determining) management's choices about the basis of their competitive advantage and resulting management style finds echoes in Capelli and McKersie's (1987) research. On the basis of their study of reactions of US employers to changes in and intensification of competition, Capelli and McKersie suggest that management have adopted one of two strategies: 'asset management', or 'value added'. 'Asset management' involves shifting a firm's capital from high cost/low profit businesses to those that are more profitable. To critics it gives rise to charges of 'asset stripping' and may involve large-scale closures, divestment and diversification. The employee relations style associated with this business strategy is essentially opportunistic. In the businesses into which money is pumped, an investment oriented approach may be adopted, if the basis of competitive advantage is seen as quality products or services for a niche markets. But for employees in the asset-stripped companies, and in those remaining businesses which compete on cost, an employee-as-commodity style is far more likely to emerge. Where the released assets are invested in developing country manufacturing, employee relations styles are likely to mirror the prevailing practice of the chosen country and industrial sector.

In contrast, the 'value added' approach, rather than shifting assets between businesses, aims to increase profitability within existing businesses. This is typically the approach adopted by single business companies (for example, motor and computer manufacturing, airlines, food retailing chains). It may involve a production-driven, cost-reduction (for example, Ford) or a marketing (for example, British Airways) approach. In conditions of recession a marketing approach may be overtaken by a cost-reduction one (for example, British Airways) or, in conditions of growth, vice versa (tour operators). Again, the employee relations style is likely to reflect choices about the basis for competitive advantage, but the effects of recession are likely to trigger opportunism in all but those most committed to an investment oriented approach for ideological reasons.

Ownership

The importance of ideology in choice of personnel management style finds its clearest expression in the part played by ownership, either at an early stage in an organisation's development or in the labour management traditions of ownership–nationality. In Chapter 1, the part played by Quaker and non-establishment entrepreneurs in the early history of personnel management in Britain was noted. In Purcell and Sisson's terminology, all could be classified as 'sophisticated paternalists', and such traditions have persisted in the companies they founded – at least until the adverse market pressure of recent years. Other well-known entrepreneurs – Marks and Sieff of Marks & Spencer, Watson of IBM and Hewlett and Packard of the same company (HP) have left legacies in a similar mould which emphasise an investment orientation toward employees, as members of the company-as-extended-family. Harvey-Jones' proclaimed consultative, open style management philosophy (see Harvey-Jones, 1988) sits easily within the traditions established by the Mond Brothers (Purcell and Sisson, 1983). But not all founding fathers took the same view towards their employees. Ford, *par excellence*, saw employees as commodities and, in spite of recent attempted developments, the tradition of Cold War industrial relations dies hard.

Leaving aside the influence of single individuals or families, the ethos associated with an organisation's focal task can permeate the style of personnel management adopted, over long periods of time. Thus local authorities, with traditions of public service and democratic validation have long been associated with a consultative style of personnel management. Changes in management style, in the public sector generally (see Chapter 7), have gone hand in hand with a major ideological shift, on the part of government, away from espousal of the values of public service to those of the marketplace. However, whether we observe the influence of founding fathers or task ethos, in either case its longevity is associated with the organic growth of a single business or service, not diversification by merger or take-over (Purcell and Sisson, 1983, p. 117).

The influence of ownership nationality, whether British, US, German or Japanese will be developed in subsequent chapters, where there is space to subject the stereotypes to critical examination. One pattern may be noted here, however. Judging by survey evidence of the 1980s and 1990s overseas-owned companies are more likely to have a strong corporate personnel function, a personnel director on the main board, a written employee relations policy which is consistently implemented, to use sophisticated personnel policies of employee development, communication and involvement and to be less likely to recognise trade unions than British companies (see Legge, 1988; Marginson *et al.*, 1988, pp. 121, 263; Marginson *et al.*, 1993). Similarly, at establishment level, twice the proportion of overseas-owned as UK-owned employed designated personnel specialists – as many as a third of the former did so as compared with 15 per cent of UK-owned establishments. This difference persisted even when taking into account size of establishment (Millward *et al.*, 1992, p. 33). This evidence suggests a possibility that overseas-owned companies are more likely to adopt a sophisticated human relations style of management than UK companies. Interestingly, while the 1985 Warwick

Company Level survey found that overseas companies differed little from their UK counterparts in terms of diversification across broad industrial sectors, in 1992, overseas-owned companies were substantially more likely to be diversified than UK-owned non-multinationals, but similarly diversified as compared to UK multinationals (Marginson et al., 1988, pp. 45–6; Marginson et al., 1993, pp. 7–8). This suggests that ownership, over and above any possible 'single business' effect, does seem to be a factor too.

Conclusion: changing personnel management styles

Early in this chapter I discussed what is meant by personnel management style and the contexts in which one style is likely to be enacted organisation-wide, irrespective of what that style might be. Subsequently, various typologies of style have been identified and compared, and the contexts in which each is most likely to emerge discussed. Management's choices about the basis of its organisation's competitive advantage, resulting product market strategies, and ideological preferences associated with founding fathers or the ethos of the focal task, appear as important explanations for decisions about the style in which the personnel function is performed. But this analysis should carry two caveats.

First, in the discussion of style, it was suggested that it might be best inferred from patterns of observed behaviours, treating 'philosophies' and articulated 'guiding principles' as one behaviour, a rhetorical performance, among others. This is important as 'espoused' policy is frequently at odds with personnel management/employee relations practice (see Brewster et al., 1983). 'Espoused' policy is usually more coherent and aspirational, less pragmatic and opportunistic than operational practice. Well-articulated, neat, strategies emanating from senior management may be modified or resisted both by those managers who are supposed to implement them and by the subordinates for whom they are ultimately designed. Managers may display opposition on the basis of function or hierarchy, or they may resist implementing rules to allow themselves more leeway in dealing with subordinates, or the policy may be diluted unintentionally through acts of omission rather than commission. Furthermore, subordinates may resist espoused policy either overtly or covertly, resulting in formal renegotiation or more usually, informal compromises and tacit understandings about how far a policy may be 'pushed' (Marchington and Parker, 1990, pp. 63–9). It is important to emphasise the likely gap between espoused and operational policy as much of the discussion about the nature of human resource management with some honourable exceptions (for example, Pettigrew's and Storey's work) still rests presently on statements of 'espoused' policy rather than rigorous examination of enacted practices. Although from an interpretative point of view both behaviours (i.e., rhetoric and enacted practices) are equally 'real', it will be important in subsequent chapters to consider how this potential 'gap' may affect any statement about 'what is HRM?'.

The second caveat is that the analysis presented in this chapter has tended to emphasise continuities at the expense of changes in style (cf. Storey and Bacon, 1993). This is perhaps inevitable, given that the discussion has focused on typologies which by their nature are static classificatory devices, regardless of any supposed infusion of dynamism through the use of continua. But discontinuities there clearly are. For example, it was suggested earlier that ideological shifts on the part of government, toward a market-based philosophy, has resulted in changes in personnel management style in the public sector (or erstwhile public sector). Under successive governments determined to cut back the institutions of the 'nanny state' and to expose those that escape privatisation to the rigours of a quasi-market and to cut-backs in public spending, there is evidence to suggest that the traditionally 'consultative' style of the public sector is being eroded. In its place, it has been suggested, is emerging an adversarial 'macho management' style, defined by Purcell (1982, p. 3) as 'tough ... almost contemptuous of unions and negotiating procedures', eager to assert management prerogative and to roll back long-established trade union rights by imposing, by diktat if necessary, new working practices, tighter discipline and new employment contracts (MacInnes, 1987b; Legge, 1988). 'Set-piece battles' (to quote MacInnes) have taken place in the (then) public sector coal and steel industries, in the railways and in the Civil Service (GCHQ). Guerrilla warfare and Cold War typified the relationship with the teachers in the late 1980s and early 1990s as suspension of bargaining rights was followed by an imposed review body, and perceived inadequate pay increases went hand in hand with the additional workload of the National Curriculum.

Quite apart from the public sector, if we follow Marchington and Parker's and other commentators' views on the influence of product market conditions on management's choice of personnel management style, it must be recognised that over time, particularly for companies whose market position is under more competitive and customer pressure, style is likely to change. While there is no convincing evidence that employers in the *private* sector have used the recession of the early 1980s as a stimulus to adopting a 'macho' management style, the decreased company profitability of the early 1990s' recession certainly undermined the security of an investment orientation (see for example, Legge, 1988, pp. 60–2; Marchington and Parker, 1990, p. 257). The evidence of WIRS 3 (Millward *et al.*, 1992, pp. 363–4) in 1990 is of an increased prevalence of what Sisson (1993, p. 207) terms a 'bleak house' scenario in the growing number of non-unionised workplaces: fewer procedures and fewer health and safety representatives, fewer channels of information and consultation, less information from management and fewer personnel specialists, more dismissals, more compulsory redundancies, more labour turnover, more low pay alongside a greater dispersion of pay, that is more often performance-related and more market-determined. This picture seems reminiscent of a 'traditional' personnel management style rather than the 'modern' styles identified earlier.

It is against this backcloth of discontinuity, as well as continuity, that the emergence of human resource management (HRM) must be seen. What is HRM? Why the interest? Who espouses it? How is it enacted? What are its effects? These questions, and their answers, form the core of the rest of this book.

3

What is human resource management?

HRM ... It's a posh way of describing a personnel manager ... but it goes a bit farther than that.

> (A caller to BBC Radio 4's *Call Nick Ross* phone-in
> (15 October 1991) describing his occupation)

Introduction

In the last ten years, in both the UK and USA, the vocabulary for managing the employment relationship has undergone a change. 'Personnel management' has increasingly given way to 'human resource management' (HRM) or, better still, to 'strategic human resource management'. Nor is this shift exclusively confined to those followers of fashion, the commercial management consultants. It may be charted first in the writings of US academics and managers (for example, Tichy *et al.*, 1982; Fombrun *et al.*, 1984; Beer *et al.*, 1985; Walton and Lawrence, 1985; Foulkes, 1986). Quickly, however, the term was taken up by both UK managers (for example, Armstrong, 1987; Fowler, 1987) and UK academics (for example, Hendry and Pettigrew, 1986; Guest, 1987; Miller, 1987; Storey, 1987; Torrington and Hall, 1987). By the end of the 1980s and the beginning of the 1990s the floodgates were open. Although both the WIRS 3 survey of 1990 and the second Warwick Company Level survey of 1992 reported that only a small minority of personnel specialists have 'human resource' in their titles (Millward *et al.*, 1991, p. 29; Marginson *et al.*, 1993, Table 4.1) this was not evident from the media. Not only were job advertisements in the professional magazines and in the appointments pages of the quality press as likely to ask for a 'Human Resource' as a 'Personnel' manager, but erstwhile 'personnel management' courses were being retitled and the content refocused, 'new' courses in HRM were being set up (see, for example, the Open University's 'Human Resource Strategies' MBA module), guided by the incumbents of newly established professorships in HRM, and a large literature emerged exploring both the theoretical debates and empirical manifestations that are associated with this term (see, for example, Storey, 1989, 1992a, 1992b; Guest, 1987, 1989a, 1989b, 1990b, 1991; Hendry *et al.*, 1988, 1989; Hendry and Pettigrew, 1990; Keenoy, 1990a, 1990b, and Blyton and Turnbull, 1992). Reflecting and reinforcing this interest in HRM is the emergence, in 1990, of two new academic journals, entitled, respectively *Human Resource Management Journal* and *International Journal of Human Resource Management*, eclipsing the long-established specialist journal, *Personnel Review*.

Of course, this is hardly the first time that the language of management has changed: the shift over the years away from traditional unionised manufacturing industries towards process industry, high-tech manufacturing and the service sectors, with accompanying changes in occupational and employment structures and union density had already been mirrored in managers' increasing tendency to refer to 'employee' rather than 'industrial' – let alone 'labour' – relations, well before the perceived slackening in trade union pressure in the politico-economic environment of the 1980s. But whereas that shift reflected some changes in the practice of management (for example, moves towards staff status in process industries) can the same be said of this latest shift in vocabulary? Is HRM different in substance or emphasis from personnel management? If so, in what ways and what might such a shift signify?

In this chapter, answers are sought to three questions implied in its title:

- What is HRM?
- Is it any different from personnel management?
- Why did it emerge in the 1980s?

What is human resource management?

In discussing personnel management in Chapter 1, four different models were identified: the normative, the descriptive–functional, the critical–evaluative, and the descriptive–behavioural. In theory it should be possible to identify the same range of models with reference to HRM. And, in practice, it is. In subsequent chapters I will attempt to develop a descriptive–behavioural model of HRM, in considering the gap between the normative models and company practice, as it is being revealed by recently published and on-going research studies. At this point, though, I will concentrate on the other three – in particular on the normative and critical-evaluative models of HRM.

Normative models[1]

As in Chapter 1, let us start with some quotations about what HRM is supposed to be, drawn from both US and UK sources.

First, some US definitions

Fombrun, Tichy and Devanna (1984)

just as firms will be faced with inefficiencies when they try to implement new strategies with outmoded structures, so they will also face problems of implementation when they attempt to effect new strategies with inappropriate HR systems. The critical management task is to align the formal structure and the HR systems [selection, appraisal, rewards and development] so that they can drive the strategic objectives of the organization.

Beer and Spector (1985)

We have come to believe that the transformation we are observing amounts to more than a subtle shift in the traditional practices of personnel or the substitution of new terms for unchanging practices. Instead the transformation amounts to a new model regarding the management of human resources in organizations. Although the model is still emerging, and inconsistencies in its practice are often seen, we believe that a set of basic assumptions can be identified that underlie the policies that we have observed to be part of the HRM transformation. The new assumptions are:

- proactive, system-wide interventions, with emphasis on fit, linking HRM with strategic planning and cultural change (cf. old assumption: reactive, piecemeal interventions in response to specific problems).
- people are social capital capable of development (cf. people as variable cost).
- coincidence of interest between stakeholders can be developed (cf. self-interest dominates, conflict between stakeholders).
- seeks power equalization for trust and collaboration (cf. seeks power advantages for bargaining and confrontation).
- open channels of communication to build trust, commitment (cf. control of information flow to enhance efficiency, power).
- goal orientation (cf. relationship orientation).
- participation and informed choice (cf. control from top).

Walton (1985)

The new HRM model is composed of policies that promote mutuality – mutual goals, mutual influence, mutual respect, mutual rewards, mutual responsibility. The theory is that policies of mutuality will elicit commitment which in turn will yield both better economic performance and greater human development.

Foulkes (1986)

Effective human resources management does not exist in a vacuum but must be related to the overall strategy of the organisation ... Too many personnel managers have a tendency to create and function in their own little worlds, forgetting that their primary value is helping to realize top and line management goals.

The British definitions again may be contrasted with the American:[2]

Hendry and Pettigrew (1986)

What, from a review of the existing literature does 'strategic HRM' appear to mean?

We start out by noting that there are two themes which overlap one another: the first contained in the term 'strategic', the second in the idea, or philosophy, of 'human resources'. The latter suggest people are a valued resource, a critical investment in an organisation's current performance and future growth. The term 'strategic'... in this context has both established and new connotations [these are]

1.   the use of planning;
2.   a coherent approach to the design and management of personnel systems based on an employment policy and manpower strategy, and often underpinned by a 'philosophy';
3.   matching HRM activities and policies to some explicit business strategy; and
4.   seeing the people of the organisation as a 'strategic resource' for achieving 'competitive advantage'.

Guest (1987)

The main dimensions of HRM [involve] the goal of integration [i.e., if human resources can be integrated into strategic plans, if human resource policies cohere, if line managers have internalised the importance of human resources and this is reflected in their behaviour and if employees identify with the company, then the company's strategic plans are likely to be more successfully implemented], the goal of employee commitment, the goal of flexibility/adaptability [i.e., organic structures, functional flexibility], the goal of quality [i.e., quality of staff, performance, standards and public image].

Compare these normative models of HRM with what comes close to a *descriptive–functional* definition, offered by Torrington and Hall (1987):

Torrington and Hall (1987)

Human resources management is directed mainly at management needs for human resources (not necessarily employees) to be provided and deployed. There is greater emphasis on planning, monitoring, and control, rather than on problem-solving and mediation. It is totally identified with management interests, being a general management activity and is relatively distant from the workforce as a whole.

Underpinning personnel management are the twin ideas that people have a right to proper treatment as dignified human beings while at work, and that they are only effective as employees when their job-related personal needs are met. Underpinning human resources management is the idea that management of human resources is much the same as any other aspect of management, and getting the deployment of right numbers and skills at the right place is more important than interfering with people's personal affairs.

In the majority of these normative definitions several common themes stand out: that human resources policies should be integrated with strategic business planning and used to reinforce an appropriate (or change an inappropriate) organisational culture, that human resources are valuable and a source of competitive advantage, that they may be tapped most effectively by mutually consistent policies that promote commitment and which, as a consequence, foster a willingness in employees to act flexibly in the interests of the 'adaptive organisation's pursuit of excellence'.

The 'hard' and 'soft' versions

However on closer examination of these definitions, two different emphases – not *necessarily* incompatible – can be identified as to what HRM should be. At the risk of some stereotyping and oversimplification, these have been termed the *'hard'* model, reflecting a *'utilitarian instrumentalism'*, and a *'soft'* model, more reminiscent of *'developmental humanism'* (Storey, 1987; Hendry and Pettigrew, 1990). The 'hard' model stresses HRM's focus on the crucial importance of the close integration of human resources policies, systems and activities with business strategy, on such HR systems being used 'to drive the strategic objectives of the organisation' as Fombrun *et al.* (1984, p. 37) put it. This requires – as the Hendry and Pettigrew (1986) definition makes clear – that personnel policies, systems and practices are not only logically consistent with and supportive of business objectives, but achieve this effect by their own coherence. From this perspective the human resource, the object of formal manpower planning, can be just that, largely a factor of production, along with land and capital and an 'expense of doing business', rather than 'the only resource capable of turning inanimate factors of production into wealth' (Tyson and Fell, 1986, p. 135). This perception of 'resource' appears to underline Torrington and Hall's descriptive–functional model of HRM, with its reference to appropriate factors of production ('numbers' and 'skills') at the 'right' (implicitly the 'lowest possible') price. In their model, too, the human resources appear passive ('to be provided and deployed') rather than (to quote Tyson and Fell) 'the source of creative energy in any direction the organisation dictates and fosters'. In essence, then, the 'hard' model emphasises the 'quantitative, calculative, and business strategic aspects of managing the headcount resource in as "rational" a way as for any other economic factor' (Storey, 1987, p. 6). Its focus is ultimately human *resource management*.

In contrast, the 'soft' 'developmental humanism' model, while still emphasising the importance of integrating HR policies with business objectives, sees this as involving treating employees as valued assets, a source of competitive advantage through their commitment, adaptability and high quality (of skills, performance and so on) (see the Guest, 1987, model). Employees are proactive rather than passive inputs into productive processes; they are capable of 'development', worthy of 'trust' and 'collaboration', to be achieved through 'participation and informed choice' (Beer and Spector, 1985). The stress is therefore on generating commitment via 'communication, motivation and leadership' (Storey, 1987, p. 6). If employees' commitment will yield 'better economic performance' it is also sought as a route to 'greater human development' (Walton, 1985). In this model, then, the focus is on HR policies to deliver 'resourceful' humans (Morris and Burgoyne, 1973), on *human resource* management.

Clearly these rather different emphases are not *necessarily* incompatible. Indeed most of the normative statements contain elements of both the 'hard' and 'soft' models. Where an organisation pursues a strategy of producing high value added goods and services, in a knowledge-based industry, where it adopts a policy of value added growth rather than asset management (Capelli and McKersie, 1987, pp. 443–4), treating (at least its core) employees as resourceful humans to be developed by humanistic policies makes good business sense. This is conveyed in the definitions of Hendry and Pettigrew (1986) and of Beer and Spector (1985), Walton (1985) and by Guest (1987). But what of the organisation that as part of its asset management chooses to compete in a labour intensive, high volume, low cost industry, generating profits through increasing market share by cost leadership? For such an organisation the HR policies that may be most appropriate to 'driving strategic objectives' are likely to involve treating employees as a variable input and a cost to be minimised. This is a far cry from the employee relations philosophy embodied in the models of Beer and Spector (1985), Walton (1985) and Guest (1987).

Contradictions

This raises a major theme that will be developed in subsequent chapters. The potential tensions in the normative models of HRM, expressed in this 'hard'/'soft' dichotomy, are indicative of a range of contradictions implicit in these models. A short introduction to these contradictions may be found in Legge (1989a). Suffice to say at this point that these normative models of HRM are problematic at two levels. First, at the surface level, there are the problems stemming from ambiguities in the conceptual language of both the 'hard' and 'soft' models (see Keenoy, 1990b, pp. 9–10). The key concept in the 'hard' model is that of 'integration'. But 'integration' appears to have two meanings: integration or 'fit' with business strategy and the integration or complementarity and consistency of 'mutuality' employment policies aimed at generating employee commitment, flexibility, quality, and the like. This double meaning of integration has been referred to also as the 'external' and 'internal' fit of HRM policies (Baird and Meshoulam, 1988). The problem is that while 'fit' with strategy would argue a *contingent* design of HRM policy, internal consistency – at least with the 'soft' human resource values associated with 'mutuality' – would argue an *absolutist* approach to the design of employment policy. Can this contradiction be reconciled without stretching to the limit the meaning of HRM as a distinct approach to managing HRM? Indeed, should we focus on HRM as a 'special variant' of personnel management, reflecting a particular discipline or ideology about how employees should be treated? Or should we regard it as a variety of very different policies and practices designed to achieve the desired employee contribution, judged solely 'against criteria of coherence and appropriateness (a less rigid term than "fit")?'. In which case would we be treating HRM as a 'perspective on personnel management, not personnel management itself'? (Hendry and Pettigrew, 1990, pp. 8–9; also Guest, 1989a). Such dilemmas and confusions that make it difficult to 'pin down' the meaning of HRM are neatly expressed in Storey's (1992b, p. 27) 'mapping' of the various meanings of HRM (see Figure 3.1) and will be considered further below.

The problems inherent in this double meaning of 'integration' find echoes in similar ambiguities – and resultant contradictions – in the conceptual scaffolding used to develop the 'soft' model of 'developmental humanism'. 'Flexibility', for example, can express values of employee upskilling, development and initiative (as in the functional flexibility of core employees) or the numerical and financial flexibility to be achieved by treating labour as a variable cost to be minimised input

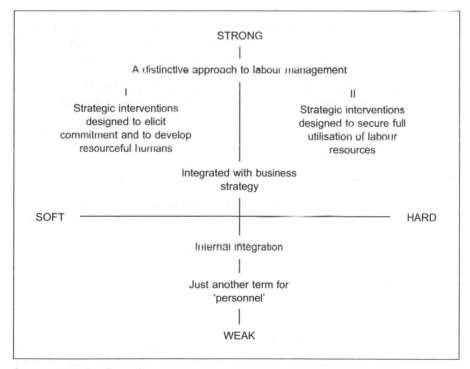

Source: Storey (1992b, p. 27).

Figure 3.1   Storey's model of mapping the various meanings of HRM

(Atkinson, 1984). Is the right 'quality' of an organisation's workforce to be judged against absolutist standards or relative to business strategy? What exactly is the employee to be committed to? What too of the potential tensions *between* policies aimed at enhancing these different values?

But, secondly, at a deeper level, it may be suggested that HRM, no less than personnel management, is confronted by a contradiction of capitalism: that is, responsibility for accommodating the dilemma that, although the 'labour commodity' is a major means to further the interests of dominant groups in capitalist society, it is liable to subvert those interests (Watson, 1977). Does HRM have the potential to cope more effectively with this tension than traditional approaches to personnel management? Implicit in this is an assumption that rather than being a perspective *on* personnel management, HRM is different to, and distinct *from* personnel management.

Before turning to consider the critical–evaluative models of HRM this assumption needs to be tested and explored.

Is HRM different from personnel management?

Both managers and academics, particularly in the UK, have recognised the problem of identifying clear differences between personnel management and HRM. Fowler (1987, p. 3), for example, argues that substantively there is little new in HRM:

> What's new [personnel managers will ask] about the concept that 'the business of personnel is the business' (to quote the theme of a Personnel Management essay competition of yester-year). What is new about the view that employees give of their best when they are treated as responsible adults? Haven't these been at the heart of good personnel practice for decades? To which the answer is, of course, yes.

Such words are echoed by Armstrong's (1987, p. 32) comment that:

> It could indeed be no more and no less than another name for personnel management, but, as usually perceived, at least it has the virtue of emphasising the need to treat people as a key resource, the management of which is the direct concern of top management as part of the strategic planning processes of the enterprise. Although there is nothing new in the idea, insufficient attention has been paid to it in many organisations. The new bottle or label can help to overcome this deficiency.

Nor is Armstrong alone in suggesting a re-labelling process. Guest (1987, p. 506) points out that a number of personnel departments have become 'human resource departments' without any obvious change in roles, just as the new editions of several long-standing textbooks have changed title but little else. Scepticism about there being little substantive difference between 'human resource management' and traditional personnel management is further reinforced by the practice, particularly in the US, of using 'human resource management' as a generic term and one interchangeable with 'personnel management'.

In order to identify possible differences between personnel management and human resource management, we can take two approaches. First, we can ask whether their normative models differ; secondly, whether their descriptive–behavioural models – their respective practices – differ. As Guest (1987, p. 507) suggests, we cannot really ask what human resource management looks like in practice unless we have a model about what it should constitute. Otherwise we run the danger of accepting as HRM any practices so labelled, even if indistinguishable from what a few years ago we would have termed 'personnel management'. In theory, once a normative model of HRM is established and empirical research undertaken, several outcomes are logically possible: the normative models of personnel management and HRM might be similar but their practices (descriptive–behavioural models) differ; their normative models might differ, but their practices be similar; both their respective normative models and respective practices might be similar, or both, respectively, might differ. It is in the final case that we might be most confident that HRM and personnel management really *are* different approaches to managing employees. Examining the normative models is amenable to the conceptual analysis of published statements, but identifying similarities or differences in the practice of personnel management and HRM is a matter of empirical observation. Fortunately, we now have a range of detailed case material that enables us to compare personnel and HRM practice, and this will be considered in subsequent chapters. Let us start, though, by comparing their respective normative models, as outlined in Chapter 1 and in the preceding section above.

Similarities

First, a close comparison suggests that there are clear similarities between the two.

1. Both models emphasise the importance of integrating personnel/HRM practices with organisational goals. Particularly in the case of the American commentators, it cannot even be said that the language has changed – Pigors and Myers (1969) speak of 'determining competitive advantage' and Megginson (1972) of 'orienting to the total business environment'.
2. Both models vest personnel/HRM firmly in line management.
3. Both models, in the majority of instances, emphasise the importance of individuals fully developing their abilities for their own personal satisfaction to make their 'best contribution' to organisational success. The similarity of the two models in this respect is underlined when comparing Torrington and Hall's model of personnel management with the other commentators' models of HRM. For their conception of the ideas underlying *personnel management* 'that people have a right to proper treatment as dignified human beings while

at work, and they are only effective as employees when their job-related personal needs are met' is identical to the values underlying all the 'soft' version HRM models.

Furthermore, their statement elaborating this position, that speaks of the desirability of 'mutuality' and 'reciprocal dependence' between employer and employee in order for the employer to obtain 'commitment to organisational objectives that is needed for organisational success' (Torrington and Hall, 1987, p. 11) uses the same language as Walton's (1985, p. 36) HRM model: 'the new management strategy involves policies that promote mutuality in order to elicit commitment which in turn can generate increased economic effectiveness and human development.'

4. Both models identify placing the 'right' people into the 'right' jobs as an important means of integrating personnel/HRM practice with organisational goals, including individual development. Glueck's (1974) and Cuming's (1975) statements about *personnel management's* function in this respect are virtually identical to that of Tichy *et al.* (1982, p. 51) that an 'essential process' of strategic *human resource management* 'is one of matching available human resources to jobs in the organisation'. The recognition that this matching process is nevertheless a dynamic one, given the rate of environmental and organisational change, and that employees really should be selected and developed in ways that enhance their adaptability and flexibility, is common to both HRM models and to what might be termed the 'deviant innovation' model of personnel management as embracing OD value systems and practice (c.f. Guest, 1987, pp. 514–15; Legge, 1978, pp. 87–9).

So, is there any difference between the normative models of HRM and those of personnel management? One is tempted to say 'not a lot'. And, indeed, the sharp contrasts that Guest (1987) elicits in his comparison of what he terms personnel management and human resource management 'stereotypes', in spite of his disclaimers, appear to owe much to an implicit comparison of the *descriptive* practice of personnel management with the *normative* aspirations of HRM, rather than comparing like with like (see Figure 3.2). The same might be said of Storey's (1992b) more recent comparison (see Figure 3.3). However, both stark comparisons *and* assumptions of similarities should be treated with caution. Even at the level of normative analysis – let alone empirical observation – neither personnel management nor HRM is a singular model, but each is conceptualised in a variety of guises. Perhaps the sharpest contrasts may be found in comparing British personnel management models with US HRM models, or paradoxically, the 'hard' and 'soft' versions of the HRM model.

Furthermore, similarities are evident when we compare both the normative and descriptive–functional models of HRM with those of the employee relations style associated with the enactment of personnel management (see Chapter 2). The 'soft'

	Personnel management	Human resource management
Time and planning perspective	Short-term reactive *ad hoc* marginal	Long-term proactive strategic integrated
Psychological contract	Compliance	Commitment
Control systems	External controls	Self-control
Employee relations perspective	Pluralist collective low trust	Unitarist individual high trust
Preferred structures/ systems	Bureaucratic/mechanistic centralised formal defined roles	Organic devolved flexible roles
Roles	Specialist/professional	Largely integrated into line management
Evaluation criteria	Cost minimisation	Maximum utilisation (human asset accounting)

Source: Guest (1987, p. 507).

Figure 3.2   Guest's stereotypes of personnel management and human resource management

'developmental humanism' model of HRM is reminiscent not only of Fox's unitary frame of reference (with the emphasis on compatibility of stakeholders' interests, shared vision and culture), but of styles based on an individualistic, investment orientation to employees. There seems little difference, for example, between the Beer and Guest 'soft' models and sophisticated human relations. Each appears as a very similar variant of personnel management.

Torrington and Hall's (1987) descriptive–functional model also has overtones of unitarism and individualism, but in a rather different sense. Referring back to Purcell's (1987) continua, here unitarism is not about shared vision but about management's denial of the legitimacy of collectivist aspiration (and hence anticipating a potential challenge). Individualism reflects a view of labour control, as commodity, rather than an investment orientation.

In contrast, the 'hard' 'utilitarian–instrumentalism' model of HRM, emphasising as it does the close integration of human resource policies, systems and activities with business strategy, could resemble *any* of the identified employee relations styles (except the opportunistic 'standard modern') depending on the strategy chosen to achieve competitive advantage. This contingent rather than absolutist modelling of HRM would present it as a perspective *on* rather than a variant *of* personnel management. But in enacting either 'soft' or 'hard' models of HRM, the role of management points to Tyson's 'architect' model.

DIMENSION	PERSONNEL AND IR	HRM
Beliefs and assumptions		
1 Contract	Careful delineation of written contracts	Aim to go 'beyond contract'
2 Rules	Importance of devising clear rules/mutuality	'Can-do outlook; impatience with 'rule'
3 Guide to management action	Procedures	'Business-need'
4 Behaviour referent	Norms/custom and practice	Values/mission
5 Managerial task vis à vis labour	Monitoring	Nurturing
6 Nature of relations	Pluralist	Unitarist
7 Conflict	Institutionalised	De-emphasised
Strategic aspects		
8 Key relations	Labour–management	Customer
9 Initiatives	Piecemeal	Integrated
10 Corporate plan	Marginal to	Central to
11 Speed of decision	Slow	Fast
Line management		
12 Management role	Transactional	Transformational leadership
13 Key managers	Personnel/IR specialists	General/business/line managers
14 Communication	Indirect	Direct
15 Standardisation	High (e.g. 'parity' an issue)	Low (e.g. 'parity' not seen as relevant)
16 Prized management skills	Negotiation	Facilitation
Key levers		
17 Selection	Separate, marginal task	Integrated, key task
18 Pay	Job evaluation (fixed grades)	Performance-related
19 Conditions	Separately negotiated	Harmonisation
20 Labour–management	Collective bargaining contracts	Towards individual contracts
21 Thrust of relations with stewards	Regularised through facilities and training	Marginalised (with exception of some bargaining for change models)
22 Job categories and grades	Many	Few
23 Communication	Restrict flow	Increased flow
24 Job design	Division of labour	Teamwork
25 Conflict handling	Reach temporary truces	Manage climate and culture
26 Training and development	Controlled access to courses	Learning companies
27 Foci of attention for interventions	Personnel procedures	Wide ranging cultural, structural and personnel strategies

Source: Storey (1992b, p. 35).

Figure 3.3 Storey's dimensions of personnel/IR and HRM

Differences

The differences between the normative models of personnel and human resource management are more those of meaning and emphasis than substance – but nonetheless 'real' for that.

1. First, many statements about personnel management when placed in the context of the texts from which they are derived, seem to see it as a management activity which is largely aimed at non-managers. Apart from management development (often treated as a separate activity or function) personnel management appears to be something performed on subordinates by managers rather than something that the latter experience themselves – other than as a set of rules and procedures that may constrain their freedom in managing their subordinates as they think fit. HRM, on the other hand, not only emphasises the importance of employee development, but focuses particularly on development of 'the management team' (see, for example, the interviews with Bob Beck, Alan Lafley and Clifford J. Erlich in Foulkes, 1986). This shift of emphasis appears related to two other differences.

2. The second is that while both personnel management and HRM highlight the role of line management, the focus is different. In the personnel management models, line's role is very much an expression of the view that all managers manage people, so all managers in a sense carry out 'personnel management'. It also carries the recognition that most specialist personnel work still has to be implemented within line management's departments where the workforce is physically located (see, for example, Legge, 1978, pp. 22–3). In the HRM models, HRM is vested in line management as business managers responsible for coordinating and directing all resources in the business unit in pursuit of bottom line results. Not only does the bottom line appear to be specified more precisely than in the personnel management models, with much emphasis on quality of product or service (see for example, Storey, 1987, p. 16; Upton, 1987), but a clear relationship is drawn between the achievement of these results and the line's appropriate and proactive use of the human resources in the business unit. Personnel policies are not passively integrated with business strategy, in the sense of flowing from it, but are an integral part of strategy in the sense that they underlie and facilitate the pursuit of a desired strategy.

    Storey's (1992b, Chapter 7) identification of line management moving away from a reactive tactically oriented role as 'production manager' to the proactive, but still technically oriented role as 'manufacturing manager', and finally to the proactive and commercially oriented 'business manager' role is indicative of this change.

3. The third difference is that most HRM models emphasise the management of the organisation's culture as the central activity for senior management. Although the OD models of the 1970s proclaimed a similar message, these

were not fully integrated with the run-of-the-mill normative personnel management models of the 1970s. OD was always seen as standing slightly apart from 'mainstream' personnel management and, in fact, was generally kept separate in a formal institutional sense, with separate OD consultants, not always with a background in, or located within the personnel department (see Pettigrew, 1985). Above all, it was often presented as a fringe activity, an initiative that was 'nice to have' but essentially the gilt on the gingerbread, to be dispensed with at the first hint of financial cut-backs (along with training!) (Keep, 1989). Peters and Waterman's (1982) linking of 'strong cultures' with financial success (however spurious), along with American management's fascination with the linkages between a stereotyped 'Japanese' employment culture and Japanese economic strength, has raised the development and management of an appropriate culture as the strategic or 'transformational' leadership activity, that gives direction, a sense of purpose and involvement to all organisational members (see the next section and Chapter 6). It is through an integrated and internally consistent set of HR policies in relation to recruitment, selection, training, development, rewarding and communications, that the organisation's core values can best be conveyed, according to the normative HRM models. Integration, therefore, is a doubly important issue – not just integration of HRM policies with strategy, but the internal integration and consistency of HRM policies themselves to enact a coherent 'strong' culture. The normative personnel management models do not present personnel policies as senior management's instrument for reinforcing or changing organisational values in a manner consistent with preferred business strategy.

These three differences in emphasis all point to HRM, in theory, being essentially a more central strategic management task than personnel management in that it is experienced by managers, as the most valued company resource to be managed, it concerns them in the achievement of business goals and it expresses senior management's preferred organisational values. From this perspective it is not surprising that Fowler (1987, p. 3) identifies the real difference between HRM and personnel management as 'not what it is, but who is saying it. In a nutshell HRM represents the discovery of personnel management by chief executives'. If this is so what factors stimulated such a belated discovery?

The emergence of HRM in the 1980s

The emergence of a rhetoric of HRM in the 1980s in the US and UK may be seen as resultant of several changes, experienced in both countries, in both product and labour markets, changes mediated by technological development and a swing to right-wing political ideologies. Several buzz words signify these changes: intensification of international competition, globalisation, the Japanese Janus (threat/icon), cultures of excellence, information technology, knowledge working, high value added, the enterprise culture. The phrase that encapsulates them all is 'the search for competitive advantage'. The effect of these factors lies in their reinforcing interrelationships as much as in their separate existence.

Market changes

The 1980s were marked by the increased globalisation of markets, and intensification of competition (Sisson, 1989, 1990; Blyton and Turnbull, 1994, Chapter 3). The rise of the Pacific economies – first Japan, then South Korea, Taiwan, Singapore and so on, combining modern technology with (initially) relatively cheap labour – has posed a massive challenge to European and US economies. From a US point of view, the EU poses another; from a UK point of view, our competitive position is challenged within the EU by the greater effectiveness of German, French and, arguably, Italian economies. The shift from 'command' to 'market' economies in Eastern Europe not only further enlarges the international economy but, given relative labour costs, represents another competitive threat (or marketing opportunity, given pent up consumer demand).

This globalisation of markets, facilitated by an IT-induced speeding up of world-wide communication, has gone hand in hand with the emergence of multinational companies, operating on a world-wide basis. This has resulted in an international division of labour, where regions specialise according to their source of competitive advantage (cheap, low skilled labour providing low cost assembly; well educated, high skilled knowledge workers providing high value added goods and services; commodity producers) (Nolan and O'Donnell, 1991). Not only is production located where it is most cost effective, but multiple-sourcing of products and services is used to encourage internal competition to enhance effectiveness (Sisson, 1989, p. 28). Furthermore, production is organised for effective access to chosen markets – hence, from a UK point of view, the patterns of inward investment to gain access to EU markets (for example, Japanese investment in 'screwdriver' factories) and the outward investment into continental Europe and the US, the latter assisted by Conservative government policies of financial deregulation. (For a more extended discussion of globalisation, see Chapter 9.)

Deregulation combined with instabilities in the global political order (reduction of trade barriers; breakdown of international trade treaties such as Bretton Woods, providing stable exchange rates; major politico–economic shocks to commodity prices such as oil; recessions of 1973–4, 1979–81, 1989–93 ending the long post-war Keynesian period of stability and growth; the US/Japanese trade imbalance culminating in the Stock Market crash of 1987) have all increased the volatility of trading.

Focusing on the UK, this intensification of international competition has forced many companies to become more strategically aware. As discussed in Chapter 2, should they pursue a policy of 'asset management' or 'value added'? (Capelli and McKersie, 1987). This has encouraged analysis of their sources of competitive advantage. If we take manufacturing industry in the UK, such an analysis confronts management with a series of dilemmas surrounding investment policy and working practices. Manufacturing in the UK was rooted in mature industries such as general engineering, steel and glass production, shipbuilding, textiles, where competition is price sensitive. If a firm chooses a 'value added' strategy, two main courses of action are open: to increase efficiency and/or to go up-market with higher quality, high design input products that are less price sensitive. Both strategies, logically, require investment in human and technical capacity, often involving new working practices, if long-term repositioning is to be achieved. Here both the 'hard' and 'soft' HRM models have a palatable message. The 'hard' model looks to the integration of human resource policies with business strategy. Will cost effectiveness best be achieved by relocating production to low cost areas and/or with market access advantages (see, for example, the strategies of GKN, IMI and Pilkington)? Or, if higher quality, greater customer responsiveness is required, what about those 'soft' HRM policies that speak of generating greater employee flexibility and commitment, necessary if integrated manufacturing systems require multiskilling, TQM, JIT and so forth?

The HRM models speak equally to those organisations, often originally based in manufacturing, that have preferred to adopt an 'asset management' policy of closures, divestment and diversification in pursuit of profitable investment. All evidence points to the UK increasingly becoming a *relatively* low skill, low hourly labour costs, low productivity (and consequently, high unit labour costs) economy, beset by a structural deficit arising from a manufacturing base too small to support the consuming population (see House of Lords, 1985; Legge, 1988; Coutts and Godley, 1989; Evans *et al.*, 1992). Thus, for many, given this weakness of the UK economy, a long-term investment policy in British manufacturing industry has been judged an ineffective use of assets due to the extent of the investment gap in new plant, infrastructure, education and training as compared to continental European and Pacific competitors which does not bode well for economic health (see Streeck, 1985; Keep, 1989). Such views received reinforcement in both the early 1980s and in the early 1990s when government monetarist policies, involving the lethal combination of high interest and exchange rates, have made investment very expensive and profitability very uncertain. Diversification away from manufacturing (e.g., BAT), closure of unprofitable plant (e.g., BTR) and overseas investment (e.g., Hanson) have seemed a better route to profitability. In such circumstances the 'hard' model of HRM preaches an important message: tailor the management of its labour resource to the business strategy of each constituent business unit – take a contingent rather than absolutist approach to what HRM should involve for each business.

These product market changes are mirrored in labour market changes in the UK and US (Sisson, 1990, pp. 2–3). The long-term shift in employment from manufacturing to the service sector,[3] exacerbated by the 1979–81 recession (for a discussion, see Legge, 1988; MacInnes, 1987), and the greater technical sophistication of much surviving manufacturing, has resulted in a decline in manual jobs relative to non-manual jobs. This has had several knock-on effects. First, the workforce has become increasingly polarised between those undertaking jobs requiring the skills of 'knowledge workers', and consequently high levels of education and training and those performing routinised, low skill service jobs (check-out, shelf-filling, fast-food catering). Secondly, the workforce is becoming feminised, as it has become the norm for women to work with only a minimal break for child rearing and as service sector jobs are available.[4] Thirdly, due to demographic trends, the workforce will become increasingly 'middle-aged' in the 1990s. Again the unitaristic message of the HRM models finds a less hostile environment than in the days when the 'worker' was seen as predominantly young, male, manual working in unionised manufacturing industry. Today, arguably, managers can see the advantages of coopting rather than confronting 'core' knowledge workers, aiming for commitment via cultural management and marginalisation of unions, rather than compliance through collective bargaining. Further, growth in employment has occurred in a sector (private service) and among a category of employees (women – and working part-time[5]) that traditionally are not highly unionised (see Chapters 5 and 8).

Finally, a major labour market change since the late 1970s has been the sharp rise in redundancies declared in Britain, peaking in the recessions in the early 1980s and 1990s, and the high endemic levels of unemployment.[6] The effect of unemployment and redundancy was put succinctly by Ron Todd (then Chief Negotiator at Ford and later General Secretary of the TGWU) in 1983, when he declared 'we've got three million on the dole, and another 23 million scared to death' (cited in Blyton and Turnbull, 1994, p. 52). While fears of unemployment may have encouraged 'resigned behavioural compliance' rather than the 'commitment' on the part of employees, advocated by 'soft' model HRM (see Chapter 6) it certainly strengthened management's hand and weakened union resistance to changes in work practices and personnel policies aimed at enhancing flexibility, quality – and labour intensification (see Chapters 5 and 7; also Metcalf, 1989; Guest, 1991a).

The Japanese 'Janus' and models of excellence

Janus, the Roman god of doorways, gates and openings, looks in opposite directions, with a friendly and a hostile face. At the risk of stereotyping, this image is not inappropriate to the UK's and US's reaction to Japan. On the one hand, Japan's hostile face is recognised as an erstwhile war-time enemy, that has now turned the tables on an overgenerous victor, using 'unfair' tactics in economic combat. On the other hand, though, is a sneaking admiration and envy: after the destruction of allied bombing and nuclear attack, how ever could the Japanese have become the second most powerful world economy, in the space of forty years? What lessons can we learn from the benign face of economic success?

The 'lessons' learnt in the early 1980s, stemmed from influential publications – Ouchi's (1981) *Theory Z*, and Peters and Waterman's (1982) *In Search of Excellence* – that claimed a similarity between company 'excellence' (defined largely in terms of financial criteria) and the adoption of management practices reminiscent of those of Japan. In the eyes of these influential texts this boiled down to combining the 'hard' – tight controls on results – with the 'soft' – facilitating autonomy in definitions of priorities, decisions and actions (Wood, 1989a, p. 383). The argument was that American management practice had traditionally placed too much emphasis on a centrally imposed rationality, expressed through excessive emphasis on the measurable, involving the manipulation of complex structures to achieve compliance and results. The Japanese, on the other hand, prioritised creating a shared vision, a culture of collective commitment to achieving organisational goals, often expressed in philosophical rather than in quantitative terms (for example, 'quality', being the 'best', Komatsu's vision of 'encircling Caterpillar'). The Americans had neglected this 'transformational ' leadership, in favour of a shorter-term 'harder' transactional style. But the comforting message was that all was not lost. Where US companies had adopted management practices that resembled those of the Japanese ('Theory Z', Peters and Waterman's 'eight attributes') they had achieved financial success. The lesson was clear: cultural management that secured the commitment of employees as valued assets – hallmarks of the 'soft' HRM model – should be the order of the day. Supported by the six 'pillars' of Japanese employment practice (lifetime employment, company welfare, quality consciousness, enterprise unions, consensus management and seniority-based reward systems) – all suitably adapted to the local context, of course – this would facilitate the adoption of other Japanese practices (Kanban [JIT]; Kaizen [continuous improvement]), that call for flexible utilisation of resourceful humans.

It should be noted that the underpinning of this equation of Japanese management, including human resource management practices, with success in US companies is shaky to say the least. First, the research design and empirical basis of Peters and Waterman's research is highly suspect, raising doubts as to the genuine excellence (even financial!) of the companies identified, and the reliability of the eight attributes (for an excellent critique see Guest, 1991b). Second, the typification of Japanese management practice rests on crude stereotypes that neglect such important qualifications as Japan's dualistic industrial structure and the extent to which traditional HRM policies have ever been universally applied and, indeed, are in the process of erosion in the light of demographic change, internationalisation, and technological development (for a short summary see Thompson and McHugh, 1990, pp. 202–6; for longer accounts see Clark, 1979; Godet, 1987; Mroczkowski and Hanaoka, 1989; Bartlett and Yoshihara, 1988; Whittaker, 1990; Okubayashi, 1986). Nevertheless, the imagery of the Japanese Janus and the rhetoric associated with models of excellence resonates with the messages contained in the 'soft' HRM model.

The enterprise culture

If market changes, the Japanese Janus and models of excellence pointed both to an intensification of competition and strategies for meeting it, at a macro level, government ideology and resultant policies, in the UK and US, provided just the right growing medium (or should I say, compost) for the ideas contained in HRM models to flourish.

In both the UK and US in the 1980s, under Mrs Thatcher and President Reagan, national government swung to the political right. Although their respective economic policies differed (compare, for example, the monetarism – later relaxed – of the early days of the first Thatcher government with the runaway budget deficits of the Reagan years), at the level of ideology both administrations preached the virtues of a 'rugged entrepreneurial individualism' (Guest, 1990b, p. 31), of the central value of 'enterprise' to national economic well-being.

Enterprise, though, as Keat (1991) and Fairclough (1991) point out, has a dual meaning. It can convey the meaning of a noun – 'the commercial enterprise' – as well as that of a verb – to be 'enterprising', by taking risks, showing initiative, self-reliance and so on. In the UK, in the 1980s, government attempted to equate these meanings in the politico–economic environment it had sought to create.

The desirability of the model of the 'commercial enterprise' – that is, the privately-owned firm operating in a free market economy – found expression in policies aimed at extending the domain of the 'free market' and intensifying competition therein. Such policies included a rejection of Keynesian demand management economic policies, aimed at the maintenance of full employment – 'the business of government is not the government of business' as one finance minister declared – in favour of monetarist supply management, aimed at squeezing inflation out of the economy, through the control of the money supply (M3, PSBR). Levels of employment then find their own 'natural' level through the operation of the forces of supply and demand in the marketplace. Firms' survival and growth depends on their 'leanness' and 'fitness' in dealing with the rigours of the marketplace, no longer featherbedded by artificially protective fiscal measures. There has been an end of exchange controls, a deregulation of financial services and the removal of non-market restrictions governing the conduct of some professions. For organisations formerly protected by public funding and ideologies at odds with the marketplace (public good/need) there has been institutional reform designed to introduce market principles and commercially modelled forms of organisation. Hence, in the UK, the 1980s and 1990s saw the privatisation of state-owned industries and public utilities and the introduction of quasi-markets in the organisation of public services (for example, the 'opting-out' of schools, 'trust' status and 'fund management', purchaser–provider relations in the NHS, market-testing in the Civil Service, competitive tendering in local authorities). Expressive of these changes has been the introduction of the concept of 'consumer' into situations where the terminology of professional dominance (c.f., 'student', 'patient', 'client') previously prevailed. Whether in the service or manufacturing, public or private sectors 'meeting the demands of the "sovereign consumer" [has become] the new and institutional imperative' (Keat, 1991, p. 3).

Used as a verb, 'enterprising' has connotations of initiative, energy, indepen-dence, boldness, self-reliance, and a willingness to take risks and to accept responsibility for one's actions. In this sense an enterprise culture is one in which the acquisition and exercise of these qualities is valued and encouraged. In the UK such encouragement has taken the form of attempts to neutralise and reverse the influence of institutions that are supposedly inimical to the spirit of enterprise: the trade unions and the welfare state.

The trade unions have been considered doubly inhibiting. On the one hand they are seen by protagonists of the enterprise culture as fettering the free will of 'captive' individuals through imposing the shackles of collective bargaining and by impeding the free working of market forces by such institutions as the closed shop, restrictive practices and legal immunities. On the other hand, they are regarded as protective of employees' collective interests in a way that encourages the diminution of individual responsibility and aspiration, creating a culture of dependency.

Such a view, in the early to mid-1980s, not only resulted in a rejection of conventional incomes policies, and a general shift from direct to indirect taxation, but an approach to employment legislation designed to weaken trade union power and strengthen the employer's hand *vis-à-vis* employees in the fight against inflation. Thus, the two Orders of July 1979 served to restrict employment protection, particularly in relation to unfair dismissal. The Employment Acts 1980 and 1982 largely dismantled the 'minimum conditions' props to collective bargaining – the latter being completely side-stepped by legislation imposing a pay settlement in the case of the teachers' pay dispute in 1987. The Employment Acts 1980 and 1982, and the Trade Union Act 1984 collectively chopped back union immunities in relation to industrial action, with restrictive clauses, in particular, on picketing, secondary action, action to extend recognition and negotiation, the definition of trade disputes, dismissal of strikers and strike ballots. Similarly, the 1982 and 1984 Acts, by imposing liability on unions in tort, undermined union strength and security. The same effect was aimed for in the 1980 and 1982 Acts, by the attack on the closed shop (or as the government saw it, freeing a 'conscript army' of unionists). In the same spirit, the 1984 Act sought to 'democratise' internal trade union affairs by compelling ballots in trade union elections and over the continuance of the political levy. The Employment Act 1988 placed further restrictions on trade unions with respect to balloting before industrial action and the election of officials and declared the post-entry closed shop unenforceable. The Employment Act 1990 made the pre-entry closed shop illegal and placed further constraints on industrial action. Finally, the Trade Union Reform and Employment Rights Act 1993 strengthening balloting and notification provisions with respect to industrial action, weakened the 'check-off' system and abolished the majority of the wage councils. Little by little unions' freedoms and immunities with respect to industrial action and civil redress and the supports for recruitment and healthy finances have been whittled away (see Chapter 8).

Gone was the image of trade union leaders walking the corridors of power in Whitehall and enjoying 'beer and sandwiches at No. 10'. Consistently, in the early-mid 1980s, the government refused to discuss economic issues with the Trades Union Congress (TUC). Instead, in the public sector, it lent ideological and financial support to managements' attempts to reassert control, at the risk of prolonged strike action (1984 dispute at the Department of Health and Social Security (DHSS) in Newcastle, the coal miners' strike 1984–5, the Railtrack dispute in 1994). Individuals' membership of unions, in special cases, was considered as incompatible with their status as employees (Government Communications Headquarters (GCHQ) dispute); some 'militant' unions, notably the National Union of Mineworkers (NUM), were presented as led by demagogues threatening democracy and their 'defeat' celebrated as a victory against 'the enemy within'. In a nutshell, successive Conservative governments have sought to marginalise trade unions through restrictive legislation, strike defeat, unemployment and the ending of their role in policy-making bodies.

Turning to the welfare state, UK governments of the 1980s and early 1990s considered that receiving as of right a wide range of welfare and unemployment benefits, pensions, housing, even aspects of education and health, have also contributed to attitudes of dependency and passivity. Hence, to quote Keat (1991, p. 5)

> Along with increasingly stringent criteria for the receipt of benefits by right, in which the principle of need is modified by a strongly voluntaristic conception of desert, a key strategy is to encourage the commodification of previously state-supplied goods, replacing them by consumer purchasable products – e.g., private pensions, health insurance, home ownership, and so on. Individuals become non-dependent and 'responsible' by taking financial responsibility for these matters, as consumers; and the sphere of consumption thus becomes an important training ground for the enterprising self.

The two meanings of the enterprise culture come together in the view that the management of commercial enterprises is the field of activity in which enterprising qualities are best put to use and developed. As enterprising qualities are seen as virtues, this justifies and validates the workings of a free market economy. At the same time, in order to maximise the benefits of a 'free enterprise' economic system, firms and their participants must be seen to act in ways that express enterprising qualities (Keat, 1991, pp. 3–4).

Now, clearly, major criticisms can be raised about many of the assumptions that lie behind this vision of enterprise culture and the politico–economic policies that have been adopted in its pursuit.[7] But as a political rhetoric presenting a particular gloss to the intensification of competition discussed earlier, its message is consonant with assumptions embodied in both the 'hard' and 'soft' models of HRM. The individualistic values (and anti-union bias) that pervade the rhetoric of the enterprise culture are consistent with the individualistic and unitarist values of stereotypical normative HRM models. Its emphasis on the primacy of the market and the need to create enterprising individuals and firms to compete successfully in the marketplace finds echoes in the 'hard' model's emphasis on external integration – of the match between strategy and environment, and of HRM policy, procedures and practices with business strategy. The image of enterprising individuals as keen to take responsibility, goal oriented and concerned to monitor their progress toward goal achievement, motivated to acquire the skills and resources necessary to pursue these goals effectively, seeing the world as one of opportunity rather than constraint (Keat, 1991, pp. 5–6) is consistent with the values of commitment and flexibility embodied in the 'soft' model. One could argue too that the rhetoric about the sovereignty of the consumer is consistent with the ideas about quality, also central to the 'soft' model. Finally the ideas about competitive advantage that pervade HRM and the models of excellence are part of the rhetoric of a free market economy, the bed-rock of the enterprise culture.

HRM revisited: the critical–evaluative models

It is against this backdrop, contextualising the emergence of HRM, that a very different set of models may be introduced. Several commentators (for example, Legge, 1989a; Guest, 1990b, 1991a; Keenoy, 1990a, 1990b; Keenoy and Anthony, 1992) have recognised a puzzle. On the one hand there is much hype about the change from personnel management to HRM, on the other, little evidence that either of the HRM models already outlined are being implemented consistently or on a scale commensurate to the hype (cf. Storey, 1992b). (The extent to which the normative models of HRM *are* being implemented will be analysed in detail in the following chapters.) Indeed, as has already been discussed, it can be argued that there is little difference between *normative* models of HRM and personnel management, although there are clear contrasts between the normative models of HRM and the *descriptive–behavioural* model of personnel management.

Furthermore, if we accept the contingent perspective of the 'hard' HRM model, it allows for the equation of HRM with most of the existent employee relations styles; if we accept the absolutist perspective of the 'soft' HRM model, it looks very similar to the long-established sophisticated human relations model (see, also, Marchington, 1992). So why all the excitement?

Sceptical commentators would take the following critical view. The importance of HRM lies not in the objective reality of its normative models and their implementation, but in the phenomenological reality of its rhetoric (see Chapter 9). It should be understood as a cultural construction comprising a series of metaphors redefining the meaning of work and the way individual employees relate to their employers. Just as a metaphor gives new meaning to the familiar by relating it to the unfamiliar (and vice versa), so those that comprise HRM can give a new, managerially prescribed meaning to employment experiences that, within a pluralist perspective, might be considered unpalatable.

Keenoy and Anthony (1992) present this argument in its strongest form. They suggest that HRM is a rhetoric aimed at achieving employees' normative commitment to a politico–economic order, in which the values of the marketplace dominate all other moral values. As they suggest: 'once it was deemed sufficient to redesign the organisation so as to make it fit for human capacity and understanding: now it is better to redesign human understanding to fit the organisation's purpose' (p. 239). The language of the HRM models is the instrument of such cultural change. For, from a postmodernist perspective, it is inappropriate to regard rhetoric as somehow separate from or lesser than the 'real' world: rhetoric *is* the real world. For example, in late capitalist societies of today, products are differentiated by image as much as by substance; as consumption dominates production we buy the image associated with the product rather than the product itself (cigarettes, coffee, jeans). In an extreme form, it is argued, capitalism is now concerned with the production and exchange of cultural forms: the material product is merely the vehicle for the 'real' product: the image. (A good example of this would be the Moscow branch of McDonald's.) The latter may incorporate the consumer 'itself': we are differentiated by our patterns of consumption – by purchasing the product, the consumer acquires access to the product; by consuming it, the consumer becomes part of the advertisement and, hence, 'the consumer *becomes* the image' (Keenoy and Anthony, 1992, p. 237). Keenoy and Anthony conclude:

> In principle, cultural constructions, such as HRM policies and practices, can be seen to embody this most advanced form of commodification process. The culture (a product) is employed to create the images (products), which in turn are used to reconstruct the culture (a product). The inherent potential of such circularity, du Gay and Salaman (1990, p. 12) suggest, is such that employee identities can 'be built around cultural change programmes, can be chosen, in an analogous way to the consumer's choice of life style'. There is, it would seem, nothing more to be said. (p. 287)

How then has HRM rhetoric been used to construct appropriate employee identities and belief systems? And, to what purpose?

HRM and the American Dream

It could be argued that the early hyping, particularly of the 'soft' model of HRM, in the US, owes more to the values it embodies, than any widespread, consistent application of its practices or unequivocal evidence of its success. According to David Guest's (1990b) persuasive analysis, HRM has been talked up in the US because its values echo persistent themes in the American Dream.

Guest's argument is as follows. The American Dream, 'a goal to pursue, in part a counter to cynicism and despair', views America as a land of opportunity in which individuals by hard work and self-improvement can achieve the highest measure of success – from the 'log cabin to the White House'. However, opportunities are not handed to the individual on a government-provided plate. It is up to the individual to create his/her own opportunities by pushing back the frontiers – whether the West, the 'final frontier' of Space – or even the new frontier of the challenge of foreign, particularly Japanese, competition. The frontier mentality, Guest (1990b, p. 390) suggests, includes elements of the 'self-reliant small businessman who sets up on his own and takes on all comers, ... the desire for a challenge against a powerful unknown adversary'.

The American Dream had taken a battering under the failure of the Great Society and Vietnam under the Johnson years, Watergate under Nixon, and the Iran Hostages under Carter. Enter Reagan, a genuine Hollywood frontiersman, with a simple message that recaptured the American Dream:

> America is back in business, but back on its own terms. The solutions to Japanese competition can be found in America's own backyard, in getting back to basics. It was 'morning in America' again, and America was feeling good about itself. (Guest, 1990b, pp. 390–1)

Guest suggests that three central themes underlying HRM resonate with the American Dream. First, a belief in the potential for human growth is central to the 'soft' model of HRM, and reflects all-American themes of motivation, ranging from McGregor's (1960) Theory Y, Maslow's (1943) hierarchy of needs, and Herzberg's (1966) motivator–hygiene theory. Irrespective of the naivety and lack of empirical support for these theories, not only do they capture the values of middle America but, in emphasising opportunities for progress and growth, based on individual achievement, they epitomise the values of the American Dream. 'And like the American Dream, the ultimate goal is nebulous, it is some idealized and seldom attained state captured in Maslow's elusive concept of self-actualization' (Guest, 1990b, p. 391). Such theories, too, emphasise the importance of 'becoming', of developing rather than arrival. This, Guest argues, is also consonant with the American Dream, quoting Moore (1969) to the effect that

In the American ideological baggage, the man who professes to be satisfied has 'given up'. He has left the rat race and entered the treadmill, where progress is foredoomed. Contentment is not a permissible goal; in fact it is downright immoral.

Such motivation theories, emphasising as they do, progress and growth, while central to the OD and Quality of Working Life (QWL) movements of the 1960s, fell out of favour in the more sceptical 1970s. The advent of the Great Rhetorician, Reagan, and renewal of a confident America, brought back such theories into fashion, riding in an HRM vehicle.

Second, Guest argues, HRM expresses an optimistic desire to improve the opportunities for people at work. Managers would like to create opportunities for human growth in the workplace – if time, resources and a lifting of constraints enabled them to do so. 'HRM provides an opportunity to espouse the Dream and to display at least the good intention to turn it into reality … [although] in most cases this is no more than a fantasy, a dream' (Guest, 1990b, p. 392).

Finally, HRM reflects those aspects of the American Dream that highlight the value of strong leadership, backed up by a strong organisational culture, both reflecting the spirit of 'rugged, entrepreneurial individualism'. Guest points out how the war stories of the excellent companies foster such an image around their founding fathers (for example, Tom Watson of IBM). The qualities emphasised are those of transformational leadership, 'the ability to generate commitment and enthuse others to innovate, to change and indeed conquer new frontiers in the marketplace or on the shopfloor' (Guest, 1990b, p. 393). Even within bureaucracy, individual initiative can be expressed and old frontiers challenged by entrepreneurship. Even if all Americans can no longer fulfil the aim of owning their own business, they can take 'ownership' of their own business or work performance within the transforming bureaucracy.

Guest concludes by suggesting that the marrying together of the 'soft' HRM model with the American Dream has converted 'legends' of HRM practice, that serve to reinforce an ideal, into myths that serve 'to obscure the less than pleasant reality'. Thus stories about General Motors and Lockheed are of their achievements in promoting HRM initiatives such as quality circles, not about their simultaneous closure activities elsewhere in the organisation. The importance of HRM then becomes the ability of its rhetoric to provide myths that sustain managerial legitimacy through its close association with the founding myth of the American Dream. If so

> then the main impact of HRM in the United States may have been to provide a smokescreen behind which management can introduce non-unionism or obtain significant concessions from trade unions … Like the myths of the cowboy and the wild west which served to obscure the reality of the massacre of the Indians, so HRM can serve to obscure the assault on the union movement in the USA. HRM then, presents the benevolent face of American management; and its practitioner is the James Stewart of the new industrial frontier. (Guest, 1990b, p. 393)

An alternative view of HRM as rhetoric – and one that has focused on the UK context – is to identify it as a mask for the less acceptable face of the enterprise culture (Legge, 1989a; Keenoy, 1990b; Keenoy and Anthony, 1992). The argument goes as follows.

The enterprise culture, as has already been discussed, presents an ideology that prosperity and social justice are best achieved through enterprising individuals exercising their talents and initiative in private business enterprises, in a free market economy. But, as Keenoy and Anthony point out, how is this optimistic philosophy to be squared with observation of the consequences of deregulation: a sharpened exposure of both organisations and individuals to the 'competitive edge'? How is the vision of a UK economic miracle – less tarnished in the late 1980s, prior to the lengthy recession of the early 1990s – to be reconciled with massive unemployment through cost-cutting exercises and high levels of failure among newly established businesses set up by those very same enterprising individuals? One argument is that HRM, with its 'brilliant ambiguities' (Keenoy, 1990b), provides a language that effects 'an occlusion between the imagery of the "enterprise culture" and the experienced reality of increased competition' (Keenoy and Anthony, 1992, p. 235).

Legge, Keenoy and Anthony all develop similar arguments. Legge (1989a), for example, suggests that the 'new label' of HRM provides a different language from that of personnel management. In the UK 'personnel management' evokes images of do-gooding specialists trying to constrain line managers, of weakly kowtowing to militant unions, of both lacking power and possessing too much power. The new HRM language of the enterprise culture, in contrast, asserts a new dynamic image: of line management's right to manipulate *and* ability to generate and develop resources. The dual usage of the concept 'resource', with its simultaneous passive and proactive connotations, and its 'hard' and 'soft' version HRM models, is very useful here. While the language and policies of the 'hard' version model can be used on employees peripheral to the organisation, those of the 'soft' version can be used to reassure and secure 'core' employees whose resourcefulness is deemed essential for the achievement of competitive advantage.

Good examples of this are the rhetorics used to disguise potential mismatches between a 'hard' external integration and the values of the 'soft' mutuality model, and in presenting redundancy. First, rhetoric is used to suggest mismatches between the demands of 'hard' and 'soft' models is illusory. Actions that may appear to epitomise the treatment of individuals as a variable cost, rather than resource, in the interests of business strategy, e.g., chopping out dead wood whose performance is not up to standard, tying rewards closely to individual performance, transferring employees to other jobs and parts of the organisation in the light of business requirements, is in fact providing an opportunity for employees to develop their resourcefulness and competencies. If some employees prove unequal to the challenge and have to be 'let go' or if business circumstances dictate that some have to be sacrificed in the interests of the organisation as a whole, this is really an example of 'tough love', or 'care which does not shy away from tough decisions' (Barham *et al.*, 1988, p. 28; Peters and Waterman, 1982, pp. 96, 240).

The use of 'tough love' as a rhetorical device to mediate this contradiction may be illustrated by quotations from two managers, cited in Barham *et al.*, (1988) and Foulkes (1986) respectively. First, in a booklet setting out its management principles, an insurance company's chief executive asserts:

> The needs of our business will be most effectively attained if the needs of people for fulfilment, success, and meaning, are met. If people are in poor shape, the company's objectives are unlikely to be achieved. Yet the needs of the business still come first. People need to be developed, but this will not be achieved by treating them with soft care, by allowing issues to be smoothed over without being properly addressed. To treat people without care will cause them and, therefore the business, to diminish. Experience suggests that the needs of people and the business will be best met if we treat ourselves with 'tough love'. This is very different from 'macho' management, which basically does not involve care. Tough love requires courage. Respect for the individual does not mean pandering to the individual's weaknesses or even wishes. Involving people through tough love to secure both their development and good performance requires managers to take initiatives ...

> People, of course, are far and away the most important resource in any company. But they are not more than that. It is very easy to forget when endeavouring to develop people and to care for them, and even to love them, that the needs of the business must come first. Without that, there can be no lasting security. A fool's paradise in which effort is concentrated only on the present well being of the staff, without regard for the future, will eventually disintegrate and it may well be the staff that suffer most. (Barham *et al.*, 1988, p. 28)

Note here that 'putting the needs of the business first', is presented as an intrinsic part of 'tough love', and that 'love', as opposed to 'soft care' – or even 'pandering to the individual's ... wishes', is a question of sometimes being 'cruel to be kind'. Without toughness the staff may be the ones to 'suffer most'. 'Care' for the individual appears essentially as respect for employees' ability to be 'developed' in ways that the organisation deems appropriate and, implicitly, to be 'man (or woman) enough to take it' if personal sacrifice for the good of the organisation is required. Indeed the very denial that 'tough love' is at all like 'macho' management only serves to reinforce the suspicion that in its manifestation to unfortunate employees exhibiting 'individual weaknesses' it may appear indistinguishable.

The assumptions of paternalism and a unitary frame of reference which pervade the quotation above are echoed in the words of a vice-president of ITT, cited in Foulkes (1986, p. 382):

> The positive fact is that the removal of a marginal, unproductive or unnecessary surplus employee, provided it's legally and ethically handled, almost always improves the morale

of the average and above-average employees, who are, after all, the people the company most wants to retain. It is demoralising to a good, productive employee to observe a fellow worker who is consistently dogging it – and getting away with it.

It is the personnel manager's responsibility to see that the level of employee performance and productivity is always as high as possible, even when the achievement of that objective requires the unilateral removal of unsatisfactory employees.

The rhetoric of 'tough love' then glosses the potential tensions between 'external fit' and commitment to 'soft' HRM values. Development, flexibility and adaptability are defined by the organisation and in its own interests. The company's interests and those of its employees are equated. If an individual's abilities and performance are defined as inappropriate by the company, given the identification of employee and organisational interests, that person must inevitably be redefined as no longer an employee, and a tough decision may have to be made in loving concern for the employees the company wishes to retain, who depend on its survival and growth.

Leaving aside the sacking of 'inadequate' individuals, HRM provides a new rhetoric to obfuscate mass redundancies (Keenoy and Anthony, 1992, pp. 241–4). Not only is a euphemistic language provided – 'outplacing', 'downsizing' – better, still, 'rightsizing', 'manpower transfer', 'headcount reduction', even 'workforce re-profiling', but as Keenoy and Anthony point out, the reality of redundancy is not only marginalised, but represented as a positive act.

> At times the reality of job loss seems to be banished altogether from our linguistic experience of the enterprise culture; a mere footnote in the voluminous strategy documents. British Telecom, in their 1990 report to shareholders, noted: 'Our profit figure includes an exceptional charge of £390 million relating to our restructuring – particularly manpower release costs – and associated provisions for refocusing our operations' (BT *Annual Review*, 1990, p. 2). The planned sacking of some 19,000 employees (7.7 per cent of the total workforce) becomes a minor distraction between the 'profit figure' and the projected developments which were doubtless designed to have beneficial consequences for next year's 'profit figure' ... The following year, at one point, the workforce reduction is attributed to 'good cost control and the effects of our capital investment programme' while elsewhere it is *reported that BT's workforce was reduced by 18,000 during the year, by simplifying the management structure and improving productivity.* Operating profit ... increased by 10%. (BT *Annual Review*, 1991, pp. 2, 14 – emphases added by Keenoy and Anthony, 1992, p. 242)

Keenoy and Anthony (rightly in my view) consider this rhetoric as seeming both to preserve the image of the company and to sanitise the reality of the workings of 'free' market forces. Free markets are supposed to bring economic opportunity and wealth, not to destroy people's livelihoods. Management too is absolved of responsibility for harsh decisions – all it is doing is virtuously acceding to the imperatives of a free-market that knows best how to allocate resources so that the fittest survives.

On the basis of such analyses, Keenoy (1990b) proposes that the reality of HRM is as both a legitimatory and reality creating rhetoric. First, it acts to mediate the crises of the early 1980s and early 1990s recessions, of intensified competition combined with high unemployment and a consequent loss of employee confidence in the work ethic (i.e., employees not 'naturally' acculturated into the enterprising individual ideology). It does this by providing 'a legitimatory managerial ideology to facilitate an intensification of work and an increase in the commodification of labour' (Keenoy, 1990b). Second, the rhetoric of HRM becomes an agent of change, 'concerned with the management of beliefs, with the manufacture of acquiescence in corporate values, with the production of images'. Via the 'soft' model it persuades employees to interpret in an appropriate light (as 'empowerment' or 'responsible autonomy') the organisational changes induced by adherence to the 'hard' model (team surveillance, temporal flexibility, performance-related pay). Hence it is possible to consider the symbolic rather than the social construction of reality as the central concern of strategic HRM (Keenoy and Anthony, 1992). Or as Legge (1989, p. 40) put it:

> The language of 'tough love' seeks to coopt the assent of both those who may suffer as well as those who may benefit from its effects. Ironically, it is the contradictions embedded in HRM that have facilitated the development of this rhetoric even if they simultaneously render strategic action problematic.

Conclusion: HRM in action

Having considered normative, descriptive–functional and critical–evaluative models of HRM, we now need to go on to identify what is enacted in practice – quite apart from the rhetoric considered briefly in the preceding discussion.

In looking at what HRM 'should be' two different perspectives have been identified. The one sees HRM in a contingent light – as a strategically oriented perspective on personnel management cohering with business strategy. This contingent perspective seems to owe most to the 'hard' version of the HRM model – and is the one favoured by Pettigrew and his colleagues at Warwick in the UK, and by the Michigan School (Fombrun, Tichy, Devanna) in the US. The other sees HRM in absolutist terms – as a special variant of personnel management, typified by the 'mutuality' model of the Harvard School in the US, and Guest's representation of such principles in the UK. Just what the model might look like in substantive rather than categorising terms has been succinctly summarised by Sisson (1994b, pp. 7–9) (see Figure 3.4).

Subsequent chapters will consider how, and the extent to which, the proclaimed implementation of HRM in organisations appears to follow either of these perspectives. The issue of integration, dealt with in Chapter 4, will be considered largely from a contingent perspective; those of flexibility, commitment and quality from an absolutist one. In particular, in those latter chapters, I will evaluate organisational practices using Guest's (1987) framework as a map – or perhaps an image intensifier (see Figure 3.5) (see also Noon, 1992). As a map it focuses attention on the relationships between valued outcomes of HRM – the core components of Guest's normative model (strategic integration, commitment, flexibility and quality), the policy choices in areas of organisational and job design, recruitment, selection, appraisal, training, development and reward that in theory should deliver these outcomes, and their contribution to the achievement of organisational success criteria.

Beliefs and Assumptions
Business and customer (internal and external) needs are main referent. Search for excellence and quality and continuous improvement are dominant values. Aim to go 'beyond contract'; emphasis on 'can-do' outlook and high energy. Widespread use of team analogy and metaphors. High levels of trust. HRM central to business strategy.

Managerial Role
Top managers are highly visible and provide a vision for the future that employees can share. They also offer transformational 'leadership', setting the mission and values of the organisation. Middle managers inspire, encourage, enable and facilitate change by harnessing commitment and cooperation of employees; they also see the development of employees as a primary role.

Organisation Design
'Federal', highly decentralised, 'flat' organisation structures. Job design congruent with organisation structure, technology and personnel policies. 'Cross-functional' project teams and informal groups responsible for particular products or services or customers; they 'contract' contribution to organisation with jobs defined in terms of team role. Teams enjoy large measure of autonomy and there is great deal of 'task' flexibility, if not interchangeability, between members.

Personnel Policies
Numerical flexibility, i.e. core and periphery workforce. Time flexibility, e.g. annual hours etc. Single status, i.e. reward, etc. of core employees reflects contribution. Selection – emphasis on attitudes as well as skills. Appraisal – open and participative with emphasis on two-way feedback. Training – learning, growth and development of core employees are fundamental values; lateral as well as upward career advancement with emphasis on 'general' as well as 'specific' 'employability'. Equal opportunities. Reward systems – individual and group performance pay; skill-based pay; profit and gain sharing; share ownership; flexible benefits package, e.g. 'cafeteria' principle. Participation and involvement – extensive use of two-way communication and problem-solving groups.

Source: Sisson (1994b, p. 8).

Figure 3.4   Sisson's model of the HRM organisation

A theory of HRM		
HRM policies	Human resource outcomes	Organisational outcomes
Organisation/job design		**High** Job performance
Management of change	Strategic integration	**High** Problem-solving Change
Recruitment selection/socialisation	Commitment	Innovation
Appraisal, training, development	Flexiblity/adaptability	**High** Cost-effectivenes
Reward systems Communication	Quality	**Low** Turnover Absence Grievances
	Leadership/culture/strategy	

Source: Guest (1987, p. 516).

Figure 3.5   Guest's normative HRM model

Notes

1. See Chapter 1, n.1.
2. Again, some differences may be observed between the US and British models. The American models of HRM, in a similar manner to their models of personnel management, assume a unitary frame of reference: that 'there is a long-run coincidence of interests between all the various stakeholders of the organisation', as Beer and Spector (1985, p. 283) would put it. Even where potential union problems are recognised, cooptation is identified as the way forward: 'other managers have decided to actively promote more cooperative relations with their existing unions ... [concluding] that they could not successfully transform their workforce management strategy without the active support of the unions' (Walton, 1985, p. 61). The British models adopt a rather different position. While Armstrong's 'revised' model (1987) merely makes some gestures in the direction of a pluralistic stance, other commentators, in recognising that the HRM model is essentially unitaristic, and marginalises the role that trade unions might play in organisations, find this a source either of logical inconsistency within the model or of practical unfeasibility in its execution. Thus, on the other hand, Fowler (1987, p. 3) asks 'Is it really possible to claim full mutuality when at the end of the day the employer can decide unilaterally to close the company or sell it to someone else?', while, on the other, Guest (1987, p. 520) suggests that 'for many, the unitaristic implications of human resource management could only begin to have an appeal following a much more radical shift of ownership and control in industry'.

3. In 1971, 36·4 per cent of all employees in employment in Britain worked in manufacturing; by 1992 this had fallen to 21·4 per cent. Conversely, in 1971, 52·6 per cent of employees worked in service industries; by 1992 this had risen to 71·6 per cent of employees. The severity of decline in manufacturing was particularly marked in coal, oil and gas extraction; metal manufacturing, ore and other mineral extraction; motor vehicles and parts; and textiles, leather, footwear and clothing. The strongest growth was in private sector services; banking, insurance and finance sector, hotels and catering and other services (personal services, recreational and cultural services) (*Employment Gazette*).

4. Women's share of employment has increased from 37·9 per cent in 1971 to 46·1 per cent in 1991 (*Employment Gazette*).

5. In June 1992 45 per cent of female employees worked part-time. In 1971 15·4 per cent of all employees worked part-time, by June 1992 this figure had risen to 25·2 per cent. The vast majority of all part-time working (93·2 per cent in 1992) in Britain is located in the service sector and undertaken by women (81 per cent in 1991) (*Employment Gazette*).

6. In 1979 unemployment was just under 1¼ million. By 1983, following recession, this rose to over 3 million, peaking eventually at 3·21 million in February 1986. In spite of economic growth, unemployment only fell to 1½ million by June 1990, before rising to over 3 million again by January 1993. Although the UK is now emerging from recession (August, 1994) unemployment remains at around 2 million in spite of the demographic changes that have resulted in a marked reduction of young people entering the labour market. Redundancies peaked in the recession of the early 1980s but rose again in that of the early 1990s. Turnbull (1988b) reckons that the official statistics, based on redundancies involving ten or more workers, substantially underestimates the numbers that have been made redundant in the 1980s and early 1990s. Further, such figures do not include job losses through planned natural wastage, early retirement and so forth. In this context, it should be noted that in the second Warwick Company Level 1992 survey, 37 per cent of respondents reported that delayering had taken place in their companies in the last five years and 65 per cent and 44 per cent of finance respondents assumed increased labour productivity and decreased headcount respectively in their payroll budgets (Marginson *et al.*, 1993, Tables 2.5 and 3.3).

7. For example, following Keat (1991, pp. 7–9) it might be argued that the image of enterprising producers belongs to an earlier period of competitive capitalism, of small-scale owner-managed firms, not the large-scale, globally organised companies, with ownership and managerial control separated, that dominate the 'free' markets of today. Further is consumer sovereignty somewhat illusory given the use of sophisticated marketing and advertising techniques to shape and control consumer choices? Proponents of the enterprise culture would counter these arguments by pointing to the increasing sophistication of consumers who demand high quality, differentiated, sometimes even 'green' products; of producers' recognition that business is 'market-led'. They would highlight the post-Fordist theories pointing to decentralisation and autonomy of small business units and so forth. A further counter argument might suggest that 'market-led' production owes more to the dominance of large retailers than consumers *per se*, that the autonomy of small business units is illusory given centralised financial controls and investment decision-making, etc.

4

HRM and 'strategic' integration with business policy[1]

The goal of integration lies at the heart of Guest's (1987) model of HRM. For Guest, integration has three aspects: the integration or 'fit' of human resources policies with business strategy; the integration or complementarity and consistency of 'mutuality' employment policies aimed at generating employee commitment, flexibility and quality; the internalisation of the importance of human resources on the part of line managers. While this chapter will deal with all three aspects, it will concentrate on the first. What assumptions do we make when considering the feasibility of integrating HRM with business strategy? What evidence is there that senior managers in the UK have explicit, well formulated and consistent HRM policies, let alone that these are consciously integrated with business strategy? Before we can tackle these questions, it is necessary to consider what is meant by 'business strategy'.

What is strategy?

At first sight this appears a straightforward question. We can trace the derivation of the concept back to the Greek word 'strategos', a general, which in turn comes from roots meaning 'army' and 'lead' (Bracker, 1980 cited in Whittington, 1993, p. 14). This immediately points to notions of strategy being a senior management activity, involving directing the organisation towards some goal or goals. This is borne out by other definitions. Miller (1993, pp. 7–8), for example, sees strategic management as being about

the present and future direction of the organisation. It includes:

- assessing the organisation's internal competencies and capabilities,
- assessing environmental threats and opportunities,

133

- deciding the scope of the organisation's activities,
- creating and communicating a strategic vision,
- managing the process of change in an organisation

Although, perhaps, too all-embracing, this definition is not inconsistent with that of Kay (1993, pp. 8–9) who suggests that 'the subject of strategy analyses the firm's relationship with its environment, and a business strategy is a scheme for handling these relationships'. Kay goes on to state that strategy is about the achievement of competitive advantage which, in his view, is based upon an organisation identifying, developing and applying to relevant markets its distinctive capabilities, which are most often derived from the unique character of its relationships with its suppliers, customers or employees. Similarly, Miller (1991, p. 23) sees strategy as a 'market-oriented concept ... fundamentally concerned with products and competitive advantage'.

Such conventional definitions often differentiate between different levels of strategy, from corporate, 'first-order' strategy, dealing with the long-term direction of the firm and the scope of its activities, market positioning, locations and so forth, to 'business', second-order strategy, dealing with internal operating procedures and relationships between different parts of the organisation, through to functional, or third-order, strategy, that involves different functions, including HRM, devising broad strategies to support business strategy and achieve functional performance objectives (Miller, 1991, p. 23; Miller, 1993, p. 9; Purcell, 1989, pp. 70–3). The assumption is that the strategy process is a 'cascade', where the top of the waterfall is the corporate level, and subsequent levels are logically 'downstream' or dependent on directions established at corporate level. Hence Chandler's (1962) classic dictum that structure (how a firm is organised to achieve its goals – a second-order strategy) follows strategy (the type of business undertaken at present and in the future – a first-order strategy). (Whether this assumption of a logical, linear relationship is valid will be considered later in the chapter.)

While all very fine, such definitions sound warning bells, for implicitly they are presenting a normative model of what strategy *should be* rather than a description of the behaviours that *are enacted* under the loose label of strategy. To explore the latter we need other approaches to the concept. Recent work by Whittington (1993), in my view, proves very helpful here.

Four approaches to strategy

Whittington suggests that theories of strategy may be typologised in terms of four generic perspectives, based on their position on two axes, relating to continua of outcomes (profit-maximising ↔ pluralistic) and of processes (deliberate ↔ emergent). The perspectives thus identified, Whittington terms 'classical' (profit-maximising, deliberate), 'evolutionary' (profit-maximising, emergent), 'processual' (pluralistic, emergent) and 'systemic' (pluralistic, deliberate) (see Figure 4.1).

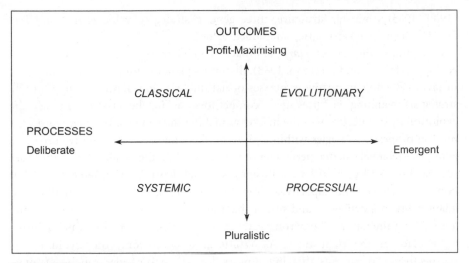

Source: Whittington (1993).

Figure 4.1 Whittington's model of generic perspectives on strategy

The '*classical*' approach, referred to briefly in Chapter 2, embodies the assumptions contained in the orthodox definitions of strategy given above. In other words, profitability/competitive advantage is seen as the supreme goal and rational, top-down planning as the means to achieve it. Strategy formulation is the activity of senior management and strategy implementation, to which relatively little attention is paid, is the responsibility of operational managers. Strategies are presented as emerging from a conscious, rationalistic, decision-making process, fully formulated, explicit and articulated, a set of orders for others, lower down the organisation, to carry out. The separation of strategy formulation from its implementation is facilitated by the creation of multidivisional structures that remove senior management from operational responsibilities, allowing them to focus on first-order strategy formulation. The intellectual forebears of this model derive from military practice – the heroic general presiding over a rigid hierarchy of obedient subordinates – and from economics. The latter tradition has not only provided the idea of the rational economic man [*sic*], exercising both 'reason' (the ability to foresee consequences and discern advantage) and 'self-command' (the ability to defer immediate gratification in favour of long-term interests), but ideas about industry structure (Porter, 1980, 1985) and transaction costs in business organisation (Williamson, 1985). As such, while looking outward, to market constraints and opportunities, the focus is internal, on the value of planning in relation to market positioning. Whittington (1993, p. 30) identifies this perspective as characteristic of Anglo–Saxon cultures and of the period of stable markets, steady growth and the 'Pax Americana' of the 1950s and early 1960s. Classic writers in this tradition are Ansoff (1965), Chandler (1962, 1977) and, more recently, Porter

(1980, 1985) (industry structure, three generic strategies, value chain) and Kay (1993) (distinctive capabilities and added value).

In contrast, the *'evolutionary'* approach, rooted in the theory of 'population ecology' (Hannan and Freeman, 1988), discounts planning for profit-maximisation, in favour of the competitive processes of natural selection. Rather than corporate strategists planning victories over competitors, as in the classical model, the evolutionary perspective sees the market as picking the winners. In other words, the most appropriate strategies within a given market emerge as competitive processes allow the relatively better performers to survive while the weaker performers are squeezed out and go to the wall. Business survival depends on differentiation, but doubt is cast on the capacity of organisations to achieve differentiation and adaptability in a deliberate and sustainable way, given the rate of, and problems in, anticipating the nature of environmental change. Rather it is a case of being in the right place at the right time. As Whittington points out, the 'evolutionary' perspective even suggests that investing in long-term strategies can be counter-productive as flexibility, evolutionarily speaking, is inefficient and investors in long-term strategies of innovation, diversification and change can always be undercut by the short-term, inflexible, low-cost producer that concentrates on achieving a perfect fit with the present environment. Furthermore, from this perspective, the search for any long-term sustainable competitive advantage is undermined by the efficiencies of the market for information, whereby competitors can imitate and take advantage of innovators' learning, and thus erode their competitive advantage. The only real competitive advantage, then, is relative efficiency and close control of the transaction costs of organising and coordinating (Williamson, 1985). If deliberate strategising is ineffective, economic health may be achieved by a stream of new entrants into any market niche, from which the environment can select the best. If this is so, management's best strategy might be to abandon any formal long-term planning, experiment with as many small initiatives as possible, back the winners and abandon the failures (Peters, 1992). This perspective, rooted in economics and a Darwinian biology, focuses externally on markets, and on implicit strategies of efficiency to achieve survival, hopefully combined with profit-maximisation. Not suprisingly, Whittington considers this very much the perspective of the UK and US right-wing enterprise cultures of the 1980s. Hannan and Freeman (1988) and Williamson (1985) are identified as classic proponents of this point of view.

The *'processual'* perspective (briefly touched upon in Chapter 2) has little faith in either the omniscience or feasibility of rational strategic planning nor in the natural efficacy of the market. Instead, 'both organisations and markets are often sticky, messy phenomena, from which strategies emerge with much confusion and in small steps' (Whittington, 1993, p. 22). If rationality rests on agreement on goals and knowledge of alternatives and consequences, it is unlikely to survive the complexities and uncertainties of organisations and markets. Agreement is unlikely given the complexity and range of different stakeholders' interests in a world of scarce resources. Knowledge of alternatives and consequences is prey to individuals' cognitive limitations, such as the inability to consider a great range of factors at the same time, lack of resources and motivation to conduct comprehensive information searches, the biases in our interpretation of data, our propensity to accept courses of action that are 'good enough' rather than seeking to optimise (Cyert and March, 1963). Not only is pure rationality unfeasible, but its desirability may be questionable. As Brunsson (1982) has argued, decision rationality may constitute action irrationality, through undermining decision-makers' motivation and commitment to act. Rather, a 'bounded rationality' resulting in 'satisficing' behaviours, acceptable to the 'dominant coalitions', is the reality of strategy-making.

Strategic management, then, is not encapsulated in some 'grand plan' aimed at profit-maximisation, but is entrenched in management's 'causal maps', 'routines', and 'standard operating procedures' that emerge as a result of political compromise shaped by prevailing organisational culture and sub-cultures. Strategic change, as a result, is slow. Rather than risking the 'internal civil war' that may result from pursuit of radical change, 'organisations opt simply for "adaptive rationality", the gradual adjusting of routines as awkward messages from a dynamic environment eventually force themselves on managers' attention' (Whittington, 1993, p. 24). This is feasible because, in the view of processualists, unlike that of evolutionists, markets are often tolerant of underperformance, given the market power firms often possess and the imperfections of information flows in the market place.

As Whittington (1993) points out, a processualist perspective inverts many of the assumptions of the classical perspective. Rather than strategy cascading down and driving the organisation, it is recognised as a way managers try to simplify and order a world too complex and chaotic for them to understand, let alone control. Strategic planning constitutes a set of heuristics that act as 'comforting rituals, managerial security blankets in a hostile world' (Whittington, 1993, p. 25). Rather than strategy formulation preceding implementation, strategy is often discovered or recognised in action. A strategic intent may be identified in retrospect, as actions, taken separately, show a loose coherence over time. Strategy formulation and implementation are thus inextricably entangled in a continuous, formative, adaptive process. As such, strategy-making has been conceptualised as a 'craft' rather than as the analytical science of the classicist (Mintzberg, 1987). As Whittington (1993, p. 25) puts it

> The craftswoman is intimately involved with her materials: she shapes her clay by personal touch, imperfections inspire her to artistic improvisation, hands and mind work together in a process of constant adaptation. So should it be with strategy. In a world too complex and full of surprises to predict, the strategist needs to retain the closeness, the awareness and the adaptability of the craftsperson, rather than indulge in the hubris of grand long-range planning.

Strategy emerges, then, in the small successive steps of 'logical incrementalism' rather than in big pre-planned strides (Mintzberg and Walters, 1985; Lindblom, 1959). Rather than looking outwards towards chaotic markets, this perspective looks inwards towards building distinctive competencies acceptable to the cultures of those coalitions eager to develop them.

Whittington (1993) regards this perspective as characteristic of the 1970s, when successive oil shocks, stagflation and a breakdown of confidence in Keynesian economics, awoke recognition of market uncertainty and consequent pressures for change in a world of perceived scarcer resources. This, in turn, sharpened structural conflicts and political awareness in organisations. Rooted in cognitive psychology and micro-sociology, key writers from this perspective are Cyert and March (1963), Wildavsky (1975), Mintzberg and Walters (1985), Mintzberg (1987) and Pettigrew (1973, 1985).

Finally, there is what Whittington terms the '*systemic*' perspective. This perspective emphasises how strategic goals and processes are shaped by the social systems in which they are embedded; by factors such as class, profession, national culture, ethnicity, religion and gender. From this perspective the norms that guide strategy derive not so much from individuals' cognitive limitations as from the cultural rules of the local society; the processes of strategy formation reflect not just organisational micro-politics but the institutional interests of broader society. Hence, for example, the very different strategic goals of US and Japanese companies, the former prioritising return on investment and share price increase, the latter preferring market share to rate of return on investment and proportion of new products over share price increase (Abegglen and Stalk, 1985). This, Whittington argues, reflects the different capital market structures of Japan and the US. In Japan, where corporate shareholders are interlinked through the mutually supportive *keiretsu* groupings of banks and companies, investors are typically loyal and patient, unlike those of the more fluid capital markets of the US and UK. Indeed the institutional investors in the UK, such as pension funds, are often legally obliged to seek the best short-term returns on investment. Similarly, the acceptability of state intervention in industrial affairs differs not only between 'interventionist' Japan and 'non-interventionist' US, but within Europe (cf. 'interventionist' France and Germany, 'non-interventionist' UK). The similarity between the UK and US, Whittington attributes to a shared Anglo–Saxon culture that values individualism and free enterprise.

From this perspective, the classical model of strategy can be seen as a social construction reflecting the values, beliefs and institutions of the society from which it emerged. Thus, its belief in the efficacy of rational planning to achieve profit-maximisation reflected the stability and optimism of the 1950s and 1960s period of economic growth and American domination of the world economy. Its emphasis on top-down management and profit-maximisation mirrored and supported the bureaucratically organised capitalist society of that period – just as the processual and evolutionary models reflect the uncertainties of the 1970s, the enterprise culture of the 1980s and the general drift towards 'disorganised' capitalism (Lash and Urry, 1987). Hence, Shrivastava's (1986) conclusion, that 'orthodox strategic management is not a neutral, objective scientific discipline, but an ideology that serves to normalise the existing structures of American society and universalise the goals of its dominant élite' (Whittington, 1993, p. 32). As an ideology it may also be considered to serve the interests of an emergent professional managerial class. Knights and Morgan (1990) (cited in Whittington, 1993, pp. 36–7) suggest that the development of normative models of corporate strategy represents an attempt by professional managers to construct a claim to legitimacy in the absence of that stemming from the established rights of ownership enjoyed by earlier generations of entrepreneurs, who had no need to invent the discipline of corporate strategy. As Whittington (1993, p. 37) puts it 'whether practically effective or not, the point about the formally rational apparatus of classical strategy-making is that it cloaks managerial power in the culturally acceptable clothing of science and objectivity'. Finally, the classical model may be seen as expressive of the voluntaristic western values of free-will and self-control, in contrast to those of more deterministic cultures, that attribute outcomes to fate, luck or God's will (Boyacigiller and Adler, 1991, cited in Whittington, 1993, p. 30). In a society that values rationality, the rational apparatus of strategic planning serves to cloak the very limited rationality and messiness of organisational life.

Whittington (1993, p. 38) suggests that the systemic perspective challenges the universality of any single model of strategy. Rather 'the objectives of strategy and modes of strategy-making depend on the strategists' social characteristics and the social context within which they operate'. But this is not to take a deterministic line. As Whittington (1993, p. 37) suggests and his own study of organisations' strategies in recession and recovery (Whittington, 1989) bears out,

> societies are too complex and people too individualistic to expect bland uniformity. Neither Japanese enterprises nor professional managers will always behave in just the same way. The rich complexity of most societies offers a plurality of resources and norms of conduct, capable of enabling and legitimating a wide range of business behaviours. Individual strategists are able to build from the diverse and plural features of their particular social systems unique and creative strategies of their own.

Compare, for example, the strategies of Weinstein at GEC with those of Branson of Virgin Atlantic, and, within the same sector, Branson's strategies with those of Marshall at BA.

Whittington summarises the systemic model by describing its strategy as 'embedded', its rationale as 'local', its focus as external but looking towards societies rather than towards markets, as in the evolutionary approach. Its intellectual roots in sociology and social anthropology, it sees the processes of strategy-making and choice of objectives as reflecting the rationalities of the locally dominant social groups. Key authors writing from this perspective are identified as Granovetter (1985) and Marris (1964). Finally Whittington (1993, p. 41) sees this perspective as that which will be dominant in the 1990s because

> the end to the Manichean opposition between capitalist America and the Communist Soviet bloc should allow a more nuanced appreciation of the different textures of market economies and the rich variety of their linkages with the rest of society. The success of the Far Eastern economies, the entry of East European countries into the capitalist world and the closer interaction of West European countries are compelling proper appreciation of the diversity of practice within capitalist economies.

Matching strategy and HRM

Clearly the feasibility and even what is meant by integrating HRM policies with business strategy will very much depend on which perspective on strategy and strategy-making one adopts. Arguably the act of *consciously* matching HRM policy to business strategy is only relevant if one adopts the rationalistic 'classical' perspective. From the point of view of the 'processual' perspective there may be no clearly articulated business strategy with which to match HRM policy. The 'evolutionary' view may suggest that the whole business of consciously matching strategy and HRM policy is a delusion and waste of time: the market will decide if they are appropriate. The 'systemic' view would suggest that even the concept of corporate strategy may be unfamiliar in some cultures as would be the conscious articulation of HRM strategies, or, indeed, the very idea of HRM itself! Rather, if there is an integration between the direction that the organisation takes and its choice of employees and how they are treated at work, this may just reflect an underlying coherence in national, industrial or professional cultures in which the organisation is embedded. However, before considering such problems in integrating business strategy and HRM policies, what approaches have been suggested from a classical perspective?

Business life cycles, competitive advantage and strategic management styles

The most popular approaches to the integration of business strategy with HRM policies, from a rationalistic perspective, are normative models suggesting how HRM policies – in particular those related to recruitment and selection, training and development, appraisal and rewards – should 'fit' either the stage of development arrived at or the strategic orientation/management style adopted in pursuing survival or growth. Typically the organisation's stage of growth is characterised in one of two ways. First, it may be in terms of the organisational life cycle: start-up, growth, maturity and decline (somewhat similar to the Boston Consultancy Group's portfolio planning growth-share matrix for evaluating the growth prospects and investment requirements across a number businesses within a diversified corporation, with its product life cycle stages of 'wild cat' (start-up), 'star' (growth), 'cash cow' (maturity) and 'dog' (decline)) (Kochan and Barocci, 1985; Baird and Meshoulam, 1988; Lengnick-Hall and Lengnick-Hall, 1988; Purcell, 1989) (see Figure 4.2). Second, stage of development may be characterised in terms of product or geographical diversity achieved (e.g., single product; single product, vertically integrated; growth by acquisition of unrelated businesses; related diversification of product lines through internal growth and acquisition; multiple products in multiple countries) and by the associated organisation form (e.g., owner-manager agency; functional, separate self-contained businesses; multi-divisional; global organisation) (Fombrun *et al.*, 1984) (see Figure 4.3). With each stage of development particular configurations of HRM policies are deemed appropriate. Thus, in terms of rewards, a start-up organisation should 'meet or exceed labour market rates to attract needed talent' (Figure 4.2); a single product functional structure (the 'start-up' equivalent), is likely to provide rewards that are 'unsystematic and allocated in a paternalistic manner' (note the difference between the former's prescriptive and the latter's descriptive approach, although their observations are not necessarily incompatible).

A second approach is to consider the match between strategic orientation/ management style and HRM policies. Notable here is Schuler and Jackson's (1987) strategic orientation typology, based on Porter's (1980, 1985) generic strategies for achieving competitive advantage under different industry conditions (see Figure 4.4) and Miles and Snow's (1984) (see Figure 4.5) and Goold and Campbell's (1987) management style typologies (see Figure 4.6). Schuler and Jackson suggest that each of the three Porterian business strategies – innovation, quality enhancement and cost reduction – require a different set of 'needed role behaviours' or essential employee behaviour patterns. These, in turn, suggest different HRM policies in relation to job design, employee appraisal and development, reward, participation and so forth (see Figure 4.4). Thus, for example, while innovation requires a high degree of creative behaviour and, hence, jobs that require close interaction and coordination among groups of individuals, cost reduction, in contrast, requires relatively repetitive and predictable behaviour and, hence, relatively fixed and explicit job descriptions that allow little room for ambiguity. (The validity of these simplistic assumptions will be critiqued below.)

Miles and Snow (1984) identify three effective[2] types of strategic behaviour, associated organisational characteristics and supportive HRM strategies, which they term 'defender', 'prospector' and 'analyser' (see Figure 4.5). A 'defender' strategy is characterised by a narrow and relatively stable product-market domain, single, capital intensive technology; a functional structure; and skills in production efficiency, process engineering and cost control. Miles and Snow cite Lincoln

Human resource functions	Life cycle stages			
	Start-up	Growth	Maturity	Decline
Recruitment, selection and staffing	Attract best technical, professional talent	Recruit adequate numbers and mix of qualified workers. Management succession planning. Manage rapid internal labour market movements	Encourage sufficient turnover to minimise lay-offs and provide new openings. Encourage mobility as re-organisations shift jobs around	Plan and implement workforce reductions and reallocation
Compensation and benefits	Meet or exceed labour market rates to attract needed talent	Meet external market but consider internal equity effects. Establish formal compensation structures	Control compensation	Tighter cost control
Employee training and development	Define future skill requirements and begin establishing career ladders		Mould effective management team through management development and organisational development	Maintain flexibility and skills of an ageing workforce
Implement retraining and career consulting services				
Labour employee relations	Set basic employee relations philosophy and organisation	Maintain labour peace and employee motivation and morale	Control labour costs and maintain labour peace. Improve productivity	Maintain peace

Source: Storey and Sisson (1993, p. 61), adapted from Kochan and Barocci (1985, p. 104).

Figure 4.2 Kochan and Barocci's model of critical human resource activities at different organisational or business unit stages

Strategy	Structure	Human resource management			
		Selection	Appraisal	Rewards	Development
1 Single product	Functional	Functionally oriented: subjective criteria used	Subjective measures via personal contact	Unsystematic and allocated in a paternalistic manner	Unsystematic largely job experience: single function focus
2 Single product (vertically integrated)	Functional	Functionally oriented: standardised criteria used	Impersonal: based or cost and productivity data	Related to performance and productivity	Functional specialists with somegeneralists: largely rotation
3 Growth by acquisition (holding company) of unrealted businesses	Separate self-contained businesses	Functionally oriented, but varies from business to business in terms of how systematic	Impersonal: based on return on investment and profitability	Formula-based includes return on investment and profitability	Cross-functional but not cross-business
4 Related diversification of product lines through internal growth and acquisition	Multi-divisional	Functionally and generalist oriented: systematic criteria used	Impersonal: based on return on investment, productivity, and subjective assessment of contribution to company	Large bonuses: based on profitability and subjective assessment of contribution to overall company	Cross-functional, cross-divisional, and cross-corporate: formal
5 Multiple products in multiple countries	Global organisation (geographic centre and world-wide)	Functionally and generalist oriented: systematic criteria used	Impersonal based on multiple goals such as return on investment, profit tailored to product and country	Bonuses: based on multiple planned goals with moderate top management discretion	Cross-divisional and cross-subsidiary to corporate: formal and systematic

Source: Storey and Sisson (1993, p. 65), adapted from Fombrun *et al.* (1984).

Figure 4.3 Fombrun *et al.*'s model of HRM links to strategy and structure

Strategy	Employee role behaviour	HRM policies
1 *Innovation*	A high degree of creative behaviour	Jobs that require close interaction and coordination among groups of individuals
	Longer-term focus	Performance appraisals that are more likely to reflect longer-term and group-based achievements
	A relatively high level of cooperative, interdependent behaviour	Jobs that allow employees to develop skills that can be used in other positions in the firm
		Compensation systems that emphasize internal equity rather than external or market-based equity
	A moderate degree of concern for quality	Pay rates that tend to be low, but that allow employees to be stockholders and have more freedom to choose the mix of components that make up their pay package
	A moderate concern for quantity	
	An equal degree of concern for process and results	Broad career paths to reinforce the development of a broad range of skills
	A greater degree of risk taking	
	A high tolerance of ambiguity and unpredictability	
2 *Quality enhancement*	Relatively repetitive and predictable behaviours	Relatively fixed and explicit job descriptions
	A more long-term or intermediate focus	High levels of employee participation in decisions relevant to immediate work conditions and the job itself
	A moderate amount of cooperative, interdependent behaviour	A mix of individual and group criteria for performance appraisal that is mostly short-term and results orientated

A high concern for quality	A relatively egalitarian treatment of employees and some guarantees of employment security
A modest concern for quantity of output	Extensive and continuous training and development of employees
High concern for process	
Low risk-taking activity	
Commitment to the goals of the organisation	

3 *Cost reduction*

Relatively repetitive and predictable behaviour	Relatively fixed and explicit job descriptions that allow little room for ambiguity
A rather short-term focus	Narrowly designed jobs and narrowly defined career paths that encourage specialisation, expertise and efficiency
Primarily autonomous or individual activity	Short-term results orientated performance appraisals
Moderate concern for quality	Close monitoring of market pay levels for use in making compensation decisions
High concern for quantity of output	Minimal levels of employee training and development
Primary concern for results	
Low risk taking activity	
Relatively high degree of comfort with stability	

Source: Storey and Sisson (1993, p. 69), adapted from Schuler and Jackson (1987, pp. 209–13).

Figure 4.4 Schuler and Jackson's model of employee role behaviour and HRM policies associated with particular business strategies

Organisational/Managerial Characteristics	Type A (Defender)	Type B (Prospector)	Type AB (Analyser)
Product-market strategy	Limited stable product line Predictable markets Growth through market penetration Emphasis: 'deep'	Broad changing product line Changing markets Growth through product development and market development Emphasis: 'broad'	Stable and changing product line Predictable and changing markets Growth mostly through market development Emphasis: 'deep' and 'focused'
Research and development	Limited mostly to product improvement	Extensive emphasis on 'first-to-market'	Focused, emphasis on 'second-to-market'
Production	High volume-low cost Emphasis on efficiency and process engineering	Customised and prototypical Emphasis on effectiveness and product design	High volume, low cost: some prototypical Emphasis on process engineering and product or brand management
Marketing	Limited mostly to sales	Focused heavily on market research	Utilises extensive marketing campaign
Organisation structure	Functional	Divisional	Functional and matrix
Control process	Centralised	Decentralised	Mostly centralised, but decentralised in marketing and brand management
Dominant coalition:	CEO Production Finance/accounting	CEO Product research and development Market research	CEO Marketing Process engineering
Business planning sequence	Plan-Act-Evaluate	Act-Evaluate-Plan	Evaluate-Plan-Act
Basic strategy	Building human resources	Acquiring human resources	Allocating human resources
Recruitment, selection, and placement	Emphasis: 'make' Little recruiting above entry level	Selection based on weeding out undesirable employees	Emphasis: 'buy' Sophisticated recruiting at all levels

Staff planning	Formal, extensive	Informal, limited	Formal, extensive
Training and development	Skill building Extensive training programmes	Skill identification and acquisition Limited training programmes	Skill building and acquisition Extensive training programmes Limited outside recruitment
Performance appraisal	Process oriented procedure (for example, based on critical incidents or production targets) Identification of training needs Individual group performance evaluations Time-series comparisons (for example, previous year's performance)	Results oriented procedure (for example, management by objectives or profit targets) Identification of staffing needs Division/corporate performance evaluations Cross-sectional comparison (for example, other companies during same period)	Mostly process oriented procedure Identification of training and staffing needs Individual/group/division performance evaluations Mostly time-series, some cross-sectional comparisons
Compensation	Oriented toward position in organisation hierarchy Internal consistency Total compensation heavily oriented toward cash and driven by superior/subordinate differentials	Oriented toward performance External competitiveness Total compensation heavily oriented toward incentives and driven by recruitment needs	Mostly oriented toward hierarchy, some performance considerations Internal consistency and external competitiveness Cash and incentive compensation

Source: Miles and Snow (1984, pp. 43–9).

Figure 4.5 Miles and Snow's model of business strategies and HRM systems

Electric as a typical example. A 'prospector' strategy is typified by the continual search for new product and market opportunities and experimentation with potential responses to emerging environmental trends. 'Prospector' characteristics include a diverse product line; multiple technologies; a product or geographically divisionalised structure and skills in product research and development, market research and development engineering. Hewlett Packard is identified as a typical 'prospector'. 'Analysers', according to Miles and Snow, operate in two differing types of product-market domain – one relatively stable, the other changing. Given different market demands 'analysers' enact a diversity of behaviours. Thus they are characterised by a limited product line; search for a small number of related product and/or market opportunities; cost-efficient technology for stable products and project technologies for new products; mixed (frequently matrix) structure; and skills in production efficiency, process engineering and marketing. Miles and Snow identify Texas Instruments as a typical 'analyser'. The logic of these different strategies is that the organisation's HRM policies should differ, depending on strategy. For example, Miles and Snow suggest that the basic HRM strategy of 'defenders' will be to 'build' human resources, that of 'prospectors' to 'acquire' human resources and that of 'analysers' to 'allocate' human resources.

The different approaches to HRM, in theory, have very different implications for policy choices. If we take the examples of selection and development, for instance, Miles and Snow suggest that a 'defender' company should typically engage in little recruiting above entry level, with selection based on 'weeding out undesirable employees', while training and development should involve extensive, formal skills-building programmes (i.e., the 'make' approach). In contrast, 'prospectors' should seek to 'buy-in' talent – a strategy that should involve sophisticated recruitment at all levels, with selection involving pre-employment psychological testing, training being limited, the emphasis being on skills-requirements identification and their acquisition in the labour market. By implication Miles and Snow suggest that the 'analyser' companies should match recruitment, selection and development strategies to the nature of the product market (stable, innovative) and the stage of the product life cycle and thus engage in 'make' (stable product market, 'cash cow') or 'buy' HRM policies (innovative products, 'rising star') as appropriate to the different market domains.

Finally, we consider Goold and Campbell's (1987) typology of strategic management styles (see Figure 4.6). Goold and Campbell, in their study of sixteen UK-owned diversified companies, asked how the corporate office managed its relationship with business units to ensure that value is added to the units' performance, given five major tensions that require resolution. The tensions were identified as between multiple perspectives vs clear responsibility; detailed planning reviews vs entrepreneurial decision-making; strong leadership vs business autonomy; long-term objectives vs short-term objectives; flexible strategies vs tight controls. Two factors appeared important: the extent to which the corporate office

Strategic planning companies push for maximum competitive advantage in the businesses in their portfolio. They seek to build their portfolios around a small number of 'core' businesses, often with coordinated global strategies. The style leads to a wide search for the best strategy options, and tenacious pursuit of ambitious long-term goals. But decisions tend to be slower, reaction to poor performance is less decisive and there is less ownership of strategy at the business unit level. Financial performance is typically strong with fast organic growth, but, from time to time, setbacks are encountered. Companies with this style were BOC, BP, Cadbury Schweppes, Lex, STC and UB.

Financial control companies focus more on financial performance than competitive position. They expand their portfolios more through acquisitions than through growing market share. The style provides clear success criteria, timely reaction to events, and strong motivation at the business level resulting in strong profit performance. But it can cause risk aversion, reduce concern for underlying competitive advantage, and limit investment where the payoff is long term. Although financial performance in these companies has been excellent, with rapid share price growth, there has been less long-term organic business building. Companies with this style were BTR, Ferranti, Hanson Trust and Tarmac.

Strategic control companies balance competitive and financial ambitions. They support growth in strategically sound and profitable businesses, but rationalise their portfolios by closing down or divesting other businesses. The style focuses on the quality of thinking about strategy, permits businesses to adopt long-term strategies, and fuels the motivation of business unit managers. But there is a danger that planning processes can become superficial and bureaucratic, and that ambiguous objectives can cause confusion, risk aversion and 'political' manoeuvring. Strategic control companies have achieved profitability improvement and share price recovery, but have seen less growth and fewer major initiatives. Companies with this style were Courtaulds, ICI, Imperial, Plessey and Vickers.

Source. Goold and Campbell (1987, pp. 10–11).

Figure 4.6 Goold and Campbell's strategic management styles

had planning influence and the extent to which it sought to exercise control influence. Three types of control influence were identified that reflected the amount of attention given to annual budget targets and monthly monitoring and sanctioning of results: flexible strategic control, tight strategic control and tight financial control. Combining the planning and control dimensions, Goold and Campbell (1987, p. 10) identify three strategic management styles: strategic–planning, financial–control and strategic–control (see Figure 4.6 for details and examples).[3] Although they themselves have little to say about the HRM policies that appear associated with these different styles, Purcell's (1989) analysis, based on their research, draws some clear inferences.

Purcell (1989, p. 86) argues that in many ways financial-control companies adopt the logic of portfolio planning, minimising the interdependences and maximising the autonomy of business units within the constraints of tight financial control. However, the management style found in such companies is likely to be analogous to that found in the 'dog' companies, emphasising cost-cutting, margins increased and investment avoided unless there are clear pay-backs over short periods. The resultant HRM policies – if they can be called that in the light of associated pragmatism and opportunism – are likely to resemble those associated with the 'hard' model of HRM. People are a resource to be utilised with maximum short-term efficiency goals in mind. Conversely, strategic–planning companies, with their willingness to take a longer-term view, their commitment to growing 'core' business to achieve value added (in contrast to the financial-control companies' preference for 'asset management') provide an environment more conducive to the values and policies associated with 'star' businesses and embodied in the 'soft' model of HRM.

Scanning these attempts at fitting HRM policies to various typologies of strategic behaviour, some very general themes emerge. First, that HRM is seen largely as a third-order strategy deriving from second-order strategies (internal operating procedures, relationships between parts of the firm), which in turn derive from first-order strategy (long-term direction of the firm, scope of activities, markets, locations, etc.). Is this so empirically? Should it be so? We return to these questions later.

Secondly, in terms of very broad generalities, it is possible to identify some common agreement as regards polar opposites in the various typologies. Thus, at the risk of gross oversimplification, it is possible to see much in common between a strategic–planning firm, that is a 'prospector', contains 'stars' in its portfolio, is in a growth phase, is committed to innovation and adopts 'soft' HRM policies for its 'star' businesses. Conversely, we can look at 'dog' businesses, declining within a financial-control company, that pursue a policy of stringent cost cutting to defend their other businesses, and introduce policies resembling (if they were not so pragmatic) the 'hard' model of HRM. But, generally speaking, the typologies are too general and simplistic to give much guidance. For example, a strategic–planning company could arguably fall into any of Miles and Snow's three effective categories. Are strategic–control companies classic 'analysers' or 'defenders'? Are financial–control companies classic 'defenders' – or prepared to prospect opportunistically? Equally they might be seen as classic 'analysers', adapting to the multiple environments in which their diversified businesses are located. Miles and Snow talk of 'prospectors' 'acquiring' human resources and 'defenders' 'building' them. But it could be equally argued that if prospectors are enacting their markets as part of a strategic–planning strategy, competing on innovation or quality enhancement, the logic is to develop skills and distinctive competencies and to 'build' human resources. This is certainly the logic of Kay's (1993) approach to strategy and appears to be the message from Schuler and Jackson's (1987) typology (see Table 4.3). Conversely, if 'defenders' are cash cows and are seeking to reduce or at least contain costs, to what extent will they be committed to 'building' the skills of their employees, when it might be cheaper in terms of overheads to buy them in? Also, to what extent *are* 'defenders' committed to cost-cutting if their market share is large, if stable, and profit margins are high? Purcell (1989, p. 78) suggests that in some circumstances such businesses may equally be marked by paternalism and indulgency patterns. Further, as regards innovation/prospector typologies, there seems to be a contradiction about the appropriate approach to appraisal – Schuler and Jackson considering that appraisals should reflect 'longer-term and group-based achievements', while Miles and Snow emphasise a 'results-oriented procedure, for example, management-by-objectives or profits targets'. Do the HRM policies proposed in the various typologies apply equally to all employees, or only to 'core' and/or managerial employees? The problem is that the very simplifications involved in developing essentially normative typologies endow them with the characteristics of blunt sledgehammers rather than those of sharp dissecting instruments. In which case, what is their utility? Is there any empirical support for their prescriptions?

Problems with the 'matching' approach

A critique can be levelled at the contingent 'matching' approach on three grounds: a critique of the rationalistic approach to strategy formulation (let alone, strategy *formation*) involved and specific critiques of the models outlined above; a critique of the empirical support for strategy – HRM 'fit'; a questioning of the prescriptive validity of such an approach.

Conceptual critique of strategy models

As will be clear from my earlier discussion of strategy modelling, the matching approach assumes the classical rationalistic approach to strategy formulation and ignores the other three approaches. This allows the presentation of clear, simplistic models that assume a top-down, unitaristic planning process and that first-order strategy formulation will inevitably and logically precede third-order HRM strategy. In particular, it ignores the systemic approach that allows strategy formation to be embedded in organisational and societal cultures, shaped by numerous stakeholders and the processual approach that recognises it to be a multi-level, multi-stage, iterative, incremental, 'messy' and political process (Hendry and Pettigrew, 1990; Boxall, 1992). In the best tradition of the American hegemony of the 1950s and early 1960s, the image of strategy-making presented in these models is one that is 'sanitized for our protection'. The rationalism reflects aspirations for, and belief in, control. The models chiefly reflect a rhetoric of corporation man, uneasily at odds with the entrepreneurial images of the 'excellence' school.

If we turn to the models themselves – stages of development (note: logical, ordered, linear progression), the portfolio planning models and the Porterian derivative of Schuler and Jackson – more specific criticisms can be raised. Take the life cycle concept. As Hendry and Pettigrew (1992, p. 140) point out, the idea of organisations moving sequentially from one predictable stage to another is debatable; their own evidence and that of others (Birley and Westhead, 1990;

Hendry *et al.*, 1991) suggesting recurring patterns of crisis and renewal. The scope for revitalising an industry or firm by means of new technologies (Abernathy *et al.*, 1981) and putting it on a different growth path undermines the life cycle model. Thus, 'there are now no longer mature industries; rather there are mature ways of doing business' (Porter and Miller, 1985 cited in Hendry and Pettigrew, 1990, pp. 16–17). Secondly, the life cycle is often implicitly equated with (and confounded by) organisational size. Thirdly, company life cycle is largely a reflection of product life cycle, which, as a concept, is itself subject to similar criticisms about the inevitability of moving through sequential stages (Hendry and Pettigrew, 1992). Wensley (1982) has suggested that the use of portfolio models, such as the Boston Consulting Group's market growth-share matrix, because of the difficulty in projecting the impact of activities to increase market share, means that such characterisation of businesses may simply become a self-fulfilling prophecy. Further, such portfolio approaches have consequently been criticised for stifling organisational renewal rather than stimulating it (Chakravarthy, 1984; Porter, 1987).

The Porterian model suffers from Porter's assumption that firms must make a clear choice between lowest cost, widespread differentiation or focus strategies (translated into cost-reduction, quality enhancement and innovation in Schuler and Jackson's model). Porter explicitly advises against 'getting stuck in the middle', on the assumption that success comes when managers resolve contradictions or paradoxes.

> Since higher quality costs more money to deliver, it is the opposite of low cost; they are contradictory forces that cannot be present at the same time, paradoxes between which managers must choose if they want to succeed. (Stacey, 1993, pp. 92–3)

However, as Hendry (1990) has pointed out, there is no economic reason why a firm should not be a below-average-cost producer and yet achieve above-average quality that allows the charging of above-average prices. Indeed the Japanese have consistently sought enhanced quality and reduced cost simultaneously via such techniques as flexible manufacturing and JIT delivery and inventory systems (see Chapter 7). But if organisations simultaneously pursue quality and cost reduction how are we to interpret Schuler and Jackson's simplistic classifications as outlined in Figure 4.4?

The conceptual problematics and fuzziness that permeate the major strategy models used to 'match' HRM policies with strategy raises doubts about their operationalisation in empirical research and the consequent validity of such studies' findings.

The empirical critique

Given the reservations expressed about the rationalistic approach and conceptual limitations of the strategy models used in 'matching' HRM policies, it is not surprising that they have been mainly employed at a normative level to derive prescriptions, rather than those prescriptions being empirically tested. Such studies that accept these models at face value and which have attempted some empirical testing, have produced very limited and fragmented evidence in their support (Golden and Ramanujam, 1985).

There is some empirical evidence that organisational or product life cycle is a determinant of HR practices, and that an appropriate fit between life cycle stage and HR practices may be associated with better firm performance, *if* one accepts the presence of the confounding variable of size (Rowland and Summers, 1981; Kuhn, 1982; Smith-Cook and Ferris, 1986; Christianson, 1986). Other studies have documented linkages between particular strategies and selection (Cohen and Pfeffer, 1986), compensation (Balkin and Gomez-Mejia, 1987; Kerr, 1985) and training and development (Kerr and Slocum, 1987). However, none of these studies have related these linkages to firm performance. Buller and Napier's (1993) study of mid-sized firms suggests that firms employing different strategies or operating at different stages in their development tend to emphasise different HR practices. In addition, firms in an initial or high growth stage of development tend to emphasise fewer HR activities and generally have a lower degree of strategy–HR integration than firms in more mature stages of development. Further, their findings provide no clear evidence that strategy–HR integration is related to firm performance, although there are suggestions that integrating HR activities with strategy may be more beneficial in mature rather than in fast growing firms. However, in summarising a range of short case studies, telephone interviews, and survey research (most with very low, c. 20 per cent, response rates) (for example, Rowland and Summers, 1981; Tichy *et al.*, 1982; Lorange and Murphy, 1984; Nkomo, 1984; Mills, 1985; Buller, 1988) Buller and Napier (1993, p. 79) conclude that as far as the general integration of HR policies and practices with strategy goes 'although the HR function is moving towards a greater strategic role in many firms, high levels of S–HR integration did not yet exist in the majority of firms'. Against this, Fox and McLeay (1992), in their study of 49 companies, drawn largely from the UK engineering and electronics sectors, found a positive relationship, over a ten year period, between practices in the areas of recruitment and selection, management education, training and development, performance appraisal, remuneration and rewards and company level career planning, as applied to managers, their integration with corporate strategy and financial performance, adjusted for sector average performance.

Work on the Porterian model is similarly inconclusive. Jackson *et al.* (1989, cited in Boxall, 1992, p. 67), in a survey study of 267 firms, found some support for the proposition that organisations pursuing an innovation strategy seek to develop personnel practices for hourly workers 'broadly consistent with that thrust', but that practices varied with manufacturing technology, industry sector, organisational structure and size, and union presence. Further, personnel practices were substantially different for managerial and hourly employers across the whole sample. However, while the study does not disprove the matching model of HRM, it 'provides few answers', by the authors' own admission (Jackson et al., 1989, p. 782). Leaving aside low response rates, the survey research design does not allow the inference of causality and, in any case, the study contained no measures of organisational effectiveness. A lack of longitudinal in-depth case studies in the American work, combined with a penchant for small-scale, low response rate surveys, gives only fragile empirical support – if that – for a weighty prescriptive infrastructure.

The more detailed survey work emerging from the first and second Warwick Company Level surveys (Marginson et al., 1988; Marginson et al., 1993; Purcell, 1995) and the in-depth longitudinal case studies of Pettigrew and his colleagues in the UK (see, for example, Sparrow and Pettigrew, 1988a, 1988b; Hendry and Pettigrew, 1990; Pettigrew and Whipp, 1991; Whipp, 1992; Hendry and Pettigrew, 1992) paint a more tentative and critical picture, recognising the limitations of the rationalistic models of strategy and the complexities of disentangling the interrelationships between organisational strategy and HRM policies and between HRM polices and practices.

Sisson and his colleagues, having identified in the early 1980s that the prevailing management style in managing employee relations was 'pragmatic' or 'opportunistic' (see Chapter 2), sought evidence for a more strategic approach developing in the mid- to late 1980s. Hence, in the first Warwick Company Level 1985 survey respondents at corporate and divisional levels were asked whether the company or division had 'an overall policy or philosophy for the management of employees', whether it was written down in a formal document, and whether employees were given a copy. Managers were further asked to describe the approach or philosophy in their own words. Subsequently, the answers to these questions were correlated with the answers to the questions about specific policies and practices to see if the overall policy or philosophy which respondents professed to follow was actually reflected in specific policies and practices. At first sight the results looked impressive: 84 per cent of head office managers claimed that their company had an overall philosophy about employee management. Notably, companies which were financially centralised in terms of profit responsibility, those in the service sector and those overseas-owned were significantly more likely to have an overall approach than others in the sample. However, of those replying positively to this question, only 52 per cent (50 per cent of all companies) said the policy was written down in a formal document, and only 22 per cent said that they gave a copy of the document to their employees. (The equivalent responses by divisional managers were similar.) Further, when respondents were asked to describe their employee relations philosophy, many managers had great difficulty in detailing its features. Vague references were made to 'forward looking', 'caring', 'looking after' and 'fairness'. When categories of replies such as stress on 'employee involvement' and 'communication' were compared with the detailed profile of practices drawn from other parts of the interview schedule there was found to be no correlation at all (Sisson and Storey, 1993, pp. 71–2; Marginson *et al.*, 1988, pp. 116–20). Not surprisingly, the researchers' overall assessment was that

> it is difficult to escape the conclusion that, although the great majority of our respondents claim that their organisations have an overall policy or approach towards the management of employees, with the exception of a number of companies which are overseas owned, or financially centralised, or operating in the service sectors, it would be wrong to place very much store by this ... the general weight of evidence could seem to confirm that most UK owned enterprises remain pragmatic or opportunistic in their approach. (Marginson *et al.*, 1988, p. 120)[4]

Further, data from both the first and the second Warwick Company Level surveys, from WIRS 2 and from a range of studies in the 1980s on the involvement of personnel considerations and the personnel function in strategic decision-making is similarly consistent with a pessimistic view on the likelihood of any widespread integration of human resource policies with corporate and business strategies.

For example, in the first Warwick Company Level 1985 survey personnel and industrial relations considerations were not taken into account at corporate level, in just under half the companies, when it came to budget formulation and investment decisions, and in a quarter of companies in relation to acquisitions, with a similar picture evident in divisions (Purcell in Marginson *et al.*, 1988, p. 74). This is consistent with Hickson *et al.*'s (1986, p. 80) view, analysing strategic decisions taken over a period from the mid-1960s to the late 1970s that personnel managers' role in relation to such decision-making could be described as 'fringe lightweights, infrequent involvement and infrequently influential'. In the same vein Hunt and Lees (1987) reported that human assets are rarely considered in decisions on company acquisition policy and that personnel managers are involved in only relatively peripheral aspects, such as the transfer of pension rights (echoes of the 'clerk of works' or 'handmaiden' role!). Data from WIRS 2 and a range of case studies suggest that personnel managers play only a very marginal role in the introduction of technical change, and then at the implementation rather than the decision making stage (Legge, 1989b; Daniel, 1987; Legge, 1993).

By the time of the second Warwick Company Level 1992 survey, the picture has improved somewhat. Respondents from both the personnel and finance functions were asked about the role played by personnel in relation to a range of strategic decisions that had clear human resource implications – merger/acquisition, investment in new locations, expansion of existing sites, divestment of existing businesses, closure of existing sites, rundown of sites, joint ventures (see Marginson *et al.*, 1993, Table 4.14 and pp. 36–7). Respondents were asked, in relation to up to four such events, first, whether personnel *issues* were taken into account and, second, whether the personnel *function* was involved in drawing up proposals, evaluating financial consequences, taking the final decision and implementation.

In the first case, with the exception of mergers and acquisitions where it is 70 per cent, in three-quarters of the major change events, it was claimed that personnel issues *were* taken into account. However, in regard to the involvement of the personnel function, a less rosy picture emerges. First, according to both finance and personnel respondents, it is in the implementation of decisions that the personnel function is most likely to be involved and in the actual taking of the final decision that they are least likely to be involved. In the most important stage as far as the integration of human resources and corporate and business strategies goes – the drawing up of proposals – personnel claimed to be involved in half and in some cases in over three-quarters of the events. However, finance respondents reckoned that this occurred in only a third to a half of the cases. Thus, according to the finance respondents, in merger and acquisition decisions personnel were *not* involved in drawing up proposals in two-thirds of the cases, in 70 per cent there was no personnel involvement in evaluating the financial consequences and in 82 per cent personnel did not have a role in making a final decision. Even in implementation, in five of the seven types of decision listed, the majority of finance respondents had not experienced personnel involvement.[5] Furthermore, the corporate personnel function took part in the critical business unit review meetings in only just over a third of cases (Marginson *et al.*, 1993, Table 4.13). Marginson *et al.* (1993, p. 37) conclude

> If one of the defining characteristics of human resource management is the explicit link with corporate and business strategies then this survey has failed to find it for the majority of large companies in the UK.

Purcell and Ahlstrand's (1994) study of multidivisional organisations reaches similar conclusions about personnel specialists' involvement in strategy formulation.

> What they are allowed to do limits their role in the management of change. In the process, their role in strategy formulation, while often dreamed of, remained marginal. Personnel managers are caught in the middle. They know the theory, perhaps, but have not the power to enact it.

The case study work of Pettigrew and Whipp confirms this sceptical view. Analysing the case studies of strategic change in Jaguar and Associated British Publishers (ABP) Whipp (1992) draws several general conclusions about these companies' ability to integrate business strategy and HRM policy and practice. First, that both companies could not hope to immediately link strategic thinking with HR planning as strategic management was absent before the 1980s, as in many UK firms. Second, both organisations, even by the end of the 1970s, had hardly developed even a reactive personnel management approach. Third, 'where attempts were made to improve business performance in the way people were managed, they proved to be fragile, unstable and highly difficult to sustain' (p. 51). Whipp cites, by way of example, Jaguar's slow and painful attempts to develop an organisational learning capacity. This he shows to be a long spiral process 'moving through cycles of observation, reflection, hypothesising, experimentation, action'. Whipp goes on to comment:

> Learning goes way beyond training, embracing structural adjustment, the use of experimentation, the development of new language and the reshaping of values ... Knowledge then has to be codified and diffused within the organisation and entrenched knowledge and beliefs broken down ... the relation between such learning and strategy formation and implementation is reciprocal. (p. 51)

Whipp argues that this slow iterative process had to be developed reciprocally with any attempt to link business strategy and HRM. Even then the social, political and educational forces of the competitive process are neither static nor often susceptible to control. At Jaguar, even the development of a learning capacity did not enable it to maintain independence as competitive pressures heightened. Hence 'the hope that HRM can be easily linked to the competitive performance of a firm is illusory' (p. 52).

Whipp's implicit use of processual and systemic models of strategic formation in analysing Jaguar and ABP, finds explicit support in Pettigrew's longitudinal in-depth case studies (Hendry and Pettigrew, 1992). Pettigrew argues that the mechanistic matching of strategy with HRM policies and practices[6] ignores the complex processes whereby strategy and HRM, symbiotically interwoven, emerge in the broader process of managing organisational change. Such a process will be moulded by 'outer context' factors such as the socio–economic, technical, political–legal and competitive environment, 'inner context' factors, such as organisational culture, structure, politics/leadership, task-technology, business outputs, and the 'HRM context' factors such as its role, definition, organisation and HR output. These will mould and in turn be influenced by the business strategy content and the HRM content (see Figure 4.7). The upshot is that 'matching' is not the issue. Rather it is a question of being sensitive to the opportunities and constraints afforded for the development of HRM that emerge out of complex patterns of strategic and structural change. From this perspective, which Pettigrew illustrates with extended case histories of Barclaycard, Pilkington, Wang, GKN, IMI, Pilkington and ICL, it appears that structural change is often a necessary *precursor* to strategic change by shifting the power base away from stakeholders supportive of existing strategies. Similarly information systems may need to be developed to put across new messages before new strategic directions can emerge. Further

> Human resource change may be a vital part of this change process through new appointments, the formation of new top teams and other groups, the disbanding of competing power centres, promotion of a new culture and other forms of political and personnel change ... In the longer view ... HRM can contribute to the making of strategy

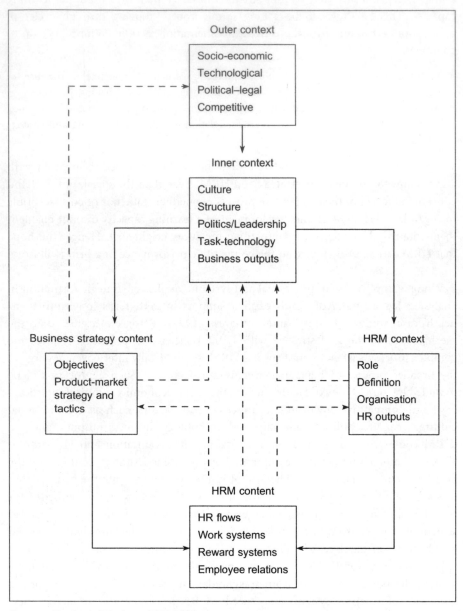

Outer context

Socio-economic
Technological
Political–legal
Competitive

Inner context

Culture
Structure
Politics/Leadership
Task-technology
Business outputs

Business strategy content

Objectives
Product-market
strategy and
tactics

HRM context

Role
Definition
Organisation
HR outputs

HRM content

HR flows
Work systems
Reward systems
Employee relations

Source: Hendry and Pettigrew (1990, 1992).

Figure 4.7 Hendry and Pettigrew's model of strategic change and human resource management

and to initiating change. Certainly, the management of structural (and associated cultural) change, *as a necessary precursor to making strategy*, becomes a key HRM activity. (Hendry and Pettigrew, 1992, p. 154, added emphasis)

Pettigrew argues that rather than testing for some mechanistic 'match' between various HRM policies and practices and strategic patterns (however conceptualised) a more fruitful line of empirical research would be to focus on the *processes* of strategic and HRM change. To this end he proposes a series of hypotheses about conditions favouring the development of HRM. These are

1. Increasing complexity in the product portfolio, but a complexity matched by coherence, in which increasing variety in product-markets stops short of the unrelated product situation.
2. Increasing complexity in internal organisation structures to manage the portfolio situation.
3. The use of decentralization and similar structural devices to devolve responsibility and increase employee involvement.
4. A shift in preoccupations from industrial relations 'fire-fighting' to the development of skills and competencies.
5. The existence or survival of a central personnel function.
6. The role of crisis in focusing the need for new approaches.
7. The importance of top leadership in legitimizing ideas. (Hendry and Pettigrew, 1992, pp. 154–5)

The second Warwick Company Level 1992 survey offers some support to these hypotheses. For example, with reference to hypothesis 1, conversely the greater a firm's diversification and the more unrelated the different parts of multisite companies are, the more likely it is that there will be a small corporate personnel department and that business units will be given greater freedom to determine their own human resource policies, which are likely to be seen as a purely operational matter (see Marginson *et al.*, 1993, Table 2.8c and Table 4.3a). Human resource management in such a case has no part to play in the formulation of corporate strategies that will critically affect what sort of personnel policies can be, and are, applied by operating subsidiaries. In contrast, considering hypotheses 5 and 7, the survey found that the presence of a personnel director on the main board makes a considerable difference to the possibilities of integration between human resource management and corporate strategy (see also comments in Chapter 2). For example, representation of the personnel function in business unit review meetings occurred in 30 per cent of cases where there was no director but rose to 48 per cent where there was a director. Further, the local unit manager was more likely to be involved in the review meetings too in companies with a main board personnel director. The presence of a main board personnel director also increased the influence of personnel *vis à vis* finance in relation to the design and administration of profit and share schemes, in the provision of information on pay determination and in the design of performance-related pay. Similarly personnel's likelihood of a decision-making role in relation to career development for senior managers increased from 58 to 78 per cent if a main board personnel director was in place. Again, the existence of a main board personnel director also increased the likelihood of regular meetings taking place between personnel managers at unit level and those in the field. Such meetings occurred in less than half of the companies without a main board personnel director but in just over three-quarters where there was one. However, it should also be noted that a main board personnel director was in post in only 30 per cent of the companies surveyed and were far more likely to exist in foreign-owned companies (Marginson *et al.*, 1993; Purcell, 1995).

An examination of the processes of strategic and HRM change calls into question 'whether managers have a genuine free choice of strategic stance' (Sisson and Storey, 1993, p. 72) in any case. As Sisson and Storey point out, transformational change, in American industrial relations along the lines of a 'new industrial relations' (see Chapter 8) by Kochan *et al.* (1986) has proved a lot more difficult to implement than the authors initially imagined. Consistent with Pettigrew's position, Sisson and Storey acknowledge that 'companies (and strategic business units or divisions) are not islands unto themselves. They find it very difficult to act independently of prevailing legal, social and political norms and structures' (p. 72). Indeed Kochan and his colleagues now acknowledge their naivety in under-estimating the difficulties in effecting top-down, rationalistic change

> 'strategic' human resource management models of the 1980s were too limited ... because they depended so heavily on the values, strategies and support of top executives ... While we see these as necessary conditions, we do not see them as sufficient to support the transformational process. A model capable of achieving sustained and transformational change will, therefore, need to incorporate more active roles of other stakeholders in the employment relationship, including government, employees and union representatives as well as line managers. (Kochan and Dyer, 1992, p. 1, cited in Sisson and Storey, 1993, p. 73)

The prescriptive critique

Leaving aside the evidence that the integration of strategy and HRM is at best a lengthy, complex and iterative process and, at worse, that there is little evidence to suggest that widespread integration is achieved, is the close matching of strategy and HRM policies desirable anyway?

Clearly integration raises some problematic issues, particularly if one is concerned to achieve both integration with business strategy ('external integration') and the integration or complementarity and consistency of 'mutuality' employment policies aimed at generating employee commitment, flexibility and quality ('internal integration') (Baird and Meshoulam, 1988).[7] First, is it possible to have a corporation-wide, mutually reinforcing set of HRM policies, if the organisation operates in highly diversified product markets and, if not, does it matter in terms of organisational effectiveness? Second, if business strategy should dictate the choice of HRM policies, will some strategies dictate policies that – unlike most normative HRM models – fail to emphasise commitment, flexibility and quality? If these questions are relevant to an organisation with market diversity in Miles and Snow's terms, they are writ large for conglomerates operating not only in different markets in one industry, but in a range of industries and even countries.

Taking the first point, if a highly diversified corporation is to match its HRM policies to a wide range of very different product-market requirements then clearly the logic of such a position is that different policies would emerge in different divisions or subsidiaries. As we have already seen, the findings of the second Warwick Company Level 1992 survey support this idea in that highly diversified companies allowed their business units greater industrial relations autonomy than companies with a single or related business. Conversely, Miller (1987) does well to draw to our attention that many of the companies generally recognised as pursuing company-wide, internally consistent HRM policies – for example, Hewlett Packard or Marks & Spencer – are notable for low levels of business (as opposed to product) diversification, of 'sticking to the knitting'. However, whether the pursuit of different sets of HRM policy in a diversified corporation 'matters' is another question, assuming such an organisation sought integration only at the financial level and allowed its business units a high level of autonomy. All that would then be required for congruence would be that each unit adopt policies that were consistent with its own business strategy and mutually reinforcing – irrespective of the extent to which they contradicted HRM policies pursued in other business units elsewhere in the corporation. While, as a consequence, no organisation-wide 'strong' culture would be likely to develop, arguably this would not be necessary as integration, other than financial, would not be sought either. (I say 'arguably' as some commentators maintain that stock market confusion over a clear corporate image can lower share prices (Ahlstrand and Purcell, 1988).)

Against this, strong unit sub-cultures, a claimed ingredient of competitive advantage, might well develop. A problem would only arise if there developed a perceived requirement to integrate two or more sub-units in a manner that required integration at operating level and, hence, of personnel. Then not only would the difficulty of merging distinct sub-cultures be likely, but perception of potential inequalities and inconsistencies between erstwhile autonomous units' HRM policies might undermine the trust and commitment that is supposed to develop from perceptions of congruence.

In relation to this question Miller (1987) makes a further interesting observation. To suggest that to achieve competitive advantage each business unit in a diversified corporation should tailor its HRM policy to its own product-market conditions, irrespective of potential inconsistencies with HRM policies being pursued elsewhere in the corporation, is to assume that the business units are market-driven. While this may be true of individual units within the corporation, it is not necessarily so for the corporation as a whole. As Miller points out, the success criteria of diversified conglomerates are defined in financial terms and largely sought through the manipulation of corporate assets. 'The success of Hanson Trust will depend not on building competitive advantage in the businesses within the portfolio ... but by acquired growth' (Miller, 1987, pp. 359–60). Such a corporate strategy though may not lead to organisational effectiveness as broadly understood 'and, indeed, there is a creeping criticism that these businesses, as a result of their failure to engage world markets, are bad for the economy' (Miller, 1987, p. 359). Indeed, it is increasingly the view – summed up in Peters and Waterman's (1982) injunction to 'stick to the knitting' that unrelated diversification, while it might produce short-term financial success, has serious potential drawbacks. The unrelatedness of the constituent businesses does not allow the development of synergies between them. Further, its extreme outward-looking market orientation diverts attention away from the analysis of the firm's internal strengths and weaknesses and consequently from the identification and development of its unique capabilities. Such capabilities, often resting on the knowledge, adaptability and commitment of employees, it is argued, are the real basis of long-term competitive advantage (Kay, 1993; Purcell, 1995). They are also clearly the focus of 'soft' model HRM.

However, if a multi-business conglomerate's success is sought through acquisition, asset stripping and attention to its price–earnings ratio on the stock markets, its HRM 'policies' – if not entirely pragmatic – may logically call for actions (e.g., compulsory redundancy, reward based on short-term performance results) which, although consistent with such a business strategy, are unlikely to generate employee commitment. Even where a company does seek competitive advantage in the market for its products or services, patterns of demand and cost structures may argue that, at least at the level of non-managerial employees, flexibility is more effectively achieved through Tayloristic work organisation, treating labour as a variable input, and exploiting the secondary labour market rather than through enhancing the skills and quality of the workforce. This would appear to be the chosen strategy of much of the High Street, whether fast food chains or a large part of the retail sector. In cases such as these, the 'hard' version of human resource *management* appears more relevant than the soft version of *human resource* management. In other words, matching HRM policies to business strategy calls for minimising labour costs, rather than treating employees as a resource whose value may be enhanced, in terms of Guest's model, by increasing their commitment, functional flexibility, and quality. Furthermore, where such cost-minimisation policies are pursued in relation to direct employees, lack of integration may occur at another level. It may be in such companies that 'soft' version HRM policies are followed for *managerial* staff, resulting in a lack of internal consistency which may further undermine the commitment of direct employees.

The attempts to reconcile this contradiction – that matching HRM policies to business strategy ('external fit') may involve the denial of 'internal fit' with core 'soft' HRM value – have taken two forms. As already discussed in Chapter 3, there is the argument that the lack of consistency in the two forms is illusory. The language of 'tough love' is used to mediate this contradiction. Secondly, an alternative approach to reconciling these potential contradictions is to point to changes in business strategy. Thus, the argument has been presented that even in sectors where, traditionally, cost-minimisation has been the order of the day (e.g., in mass production, supermarket retailing), given the levels of cost-effectiveness achieved in

The objective of the business	The main business activities	The chief executive should be
Growth	1 Pursuit of increased market share 2 Earnings generation subordinate to building dominant position 3 Focus on longer-term results 4 Emphasis on technical innovation and market development	A Young, ambitious, aggressive B Strong, development and growth potential C High tolerance for risk taking D Highly competitive by nature
Earnings	1 Pursuit of maximum earnings 2 Balanced focus on short range/long range 3 Emphasis on complex analysis and clearly articulated plans 4 Emphasis on increased productivity, cost improvements, strategic pricing	A Tolerates risk, but does not seek it B Comfortable with variety and flexibility C Careful but not conservative D Trade-off artist; short/long, risk/reward
Cash flow	1 Pursuit of maximum positive cash flow 2 Sell off market share to maximise profitability 3 Intensive pruning of less profitable product/market segments 4 Intensive short-range emphasis/minimise 'futures' activities	A Seasoned and experienced B Places high premium on efficiency C High tolerance for stability no change for sake of it D *Not* a dreamer, turned on by results now

Source: Miller and Norburn (1981).

Figure 4.8 Miller and Norburn's model of matching managers to strategy

the early 1980s, competitive advantage can now best be achieved by enhancing the quality of the product or service – an argument that has taken something of a knock in the recession of the early 1990s. Hence commitment must be generated in employees directly manufacturing the product or at the customer interface – whether through participative structures and policies of employee involvement or through training and development. Rover's 'Working with Pride' programme of quality circles and employee involvement (Storey, 1987; Arthur, 1994) and Bejam's training programmes (Upton, 1987) have been cited as typical senior management initiatives to improve quality. Again it is difficult to know where rhetoric ends and

The objective of the business	The main business activities	The chief executive's remuneration should be
Growth	1 Pursuit of increased market share 2 Earnings generation subordinate to building dominant position 3 Focus on longer-term results 4 Emphasis on technical innovation and market development	High, incremental, incentive element based on market share (with identified ceiling) No incremental element to basic salary No pension scheme if under 35 Few fringe benefits Payments in lump sums
Earnings	1 Pursuit of maximum earnings 2 Balanced focus on short range/long range 3 Emphasis on complex analysis and clearly articulated plans 4 Emphasis on increased productivity, cost improvements, strategic pricing	High, incentive element based on earnings (without identified ceiling) Stable element in salary – incremental, with fair number of steps Fairly large fringe benefits package (based on cafeteria principle)
Cash flow	1 Pursuit of maximum positive cash flow 2 Sell off market share to maximise profitability 3 Intensive pruning of less profitable product/market segments 4 Intensive short-range emphasis/minimise 'futures' activities	No incentive element (except perhaps based on group profits) High basic salary, few incremental steps

Source: Miller and Norburn (1981).

Figure 4.9 Miller and Norburn's model of matching reward systems to strategy

the extent to which compliance with the normative 'soft' version HRM model is really sought or achieved on the shop floor. Certainly the managers Storey (1987, p. 17) cites suggest a gap between 'espoused theory' and 'theory-in-use'. Furthermore, this line of argument comes close to suggesting a higher degree of homogeneity in business strategy among organisations than the commentators cited earlier perhaps would suggest.

Turning to more general issues, the classic top-down rationalistic model, in which HRM follows from and is sequentially matched to business strategy as already discussed, has been queried empirically by Pettigrew and his colleagues. They, along with other commentators (Butler, 1988; Lengnick-Hall and Lengnick-Hall, 1988; Boxall, 1992) have also questioned whether such a reactive implementationist role *is* appropriate for HRM. Rather, as already suggested, HRM may be promoted as a proactive tool to create new structures and cultures in which new strategy-making may occur (Gunz and Whitley, 1985). A reciprocal relationship between HR policy-making and business strategy is considered a preferable option.

Further, a tight matching of HRM policies with business strategy may be both impractical and disadvantageous. For example, matching managerial personalities, skills and styles with the requirements of different business activities (see Figure 4.8), with their behaviour directed by an appropriate reward system (see Figure 4.9), 'assumes a rigidity of personality and a stereotyping of managers that is untenable, as well as an unrealistic precision in the selection process' (Kerr, 1982; Chakravarthy, 1984 cited in Hendry and Pettigrew, 1990, p. 17). Boxall (1992, pp. 68–9) argues that additionally it is unwise to lock management skills and incentives into a particular competitive response. Rather, it would seem preferable to develop managers who can perceive the need for and have the ability to respond appropriately to a range of competitive conditions, given the rate of environmental change. Again, creating a capacity for organisational learning seems a 'better' prescription if one adopts a processual or systemic model of strategy-making.

Internal integration: the issue of the internal consistency of the 'soft' HRM model

Leaving aside potential contradictions between integration of HRM policy with business strategy and the ability to achieve an integrated company-wide HRM policy; between policy matched to business strategy and the 'soft' HRM model, indeed between the 'hard' and 'soft' versions of the model itself, contradictions may be found in the goals of commitment, flexibility and quality, and of 'strong' culture, sought by the 'soft' version of the model.

First, there seems to be some confusion over the concept of commitment. Although the issue is dealt with in detail in Chapter 6, a few words are appropriate here. Guest (1987, p. 513) in querying 'commitment to what?', identifies 'multiple and perhaps competing commitments to organisation, career, job, union, work group, and family'. If we assume that HRM emphasises high standards of performance – 'the excellent companies are measurement-happy and performance-oriented ... borne of mutually high expectations and peer review' (Peters and Waterman, 1982, p. 240) – and quality of product/service, individuals' job commitment would seem important, along with their desire to develop their skills and competencies. But with the higher level of commitment to a particular set of skills, arguably, there may occur a decrease in an employee's preparedness to be as flexible between jobs, or willing to accept a redefinition of a job that might diminish elements to which a commitment has been made.

Hendry and Pettigrew (1988, p. 43) suggest an interesting sidelight on this potential conflict in their discussion of multiskilling at Hardy Spicer:

> Retraining itself has unforeseen consequences. One effect is the belief that it adversely changes attitudes to production. Learning to overcome equipment faults means that the particular interest then lies in the exercise of these skills, and the job is only really interesting when the machine breaks down. As the managing director put it: 'we taught them everything but the importance of the production ethic. You could almost hear them saying to the machine "break down, break down".'

Secondly, HRM appears torn between preaching the virtues of individualism and collectivism. At first sight most commentators, observing its backgrounding of collective, union-based employee relations and its highlighting of individual skills and development, along with individually assessed performance-related pay, assert that it is individualistic rather than collectivist in orientation (see, for example, Guest 1987; Storey, 1987). In this they are supported by much management rhetoric. For example, according to a manager at BMW:

> At BMW there is a new concentration on the individual. We have got to achieve as far as we can a self-organising company and this means that there has to be more individual responsibility. (Barham et al., 1988, p. 54)

But, at the same time, there is a parallel emphasis on team work (see Chapters 5 and 6) whether in the form of quality circles or functional flexibility and, above all, on the individual's commitment to the organisation, represented not just as the sum of the individuals in it, but rather as an organic entity with an interest in survival. Storey and Bacon's (1993) criteria-based approach to individualism and collectivism in HRM (see Chapter 2) is a somewhat belated recognition of this tension. However, the potential conflict between emphasising the importance of the individual on the one hand, and the desirability of cooperative team work and employee commitment to the organisation on the other, is often glossed over through the general assumption of unitaristic values. For example, from Norsk Data comes the observation:

Norsk Data is made up of individuals like yourself. We have the 'Norsk Data Spirit'. If you'll be yourself, and use your whole personality in your job, the rest of the team will stand behind you and your efforts. (Barham *et al.*, 1988, p. 30)

This quotation also points to why HRM stresses the development of a strong corporate culture – not only does it give direction to an organisation, but it mediates the tension between individualism and collectivism, as individuals socialised into a strong culture are subject to unobtrusive collective controls on attitudes and behaviour (see Chapter 6).

However, thirdly, there exists a potential tension between the development of a strong corporate culture and employees' ability to respond flexibly and adaptively. Following Brunsson's (1982) arguments, 'objective' ideologies (defined as ideas shared by all organisational members), when 'conclusive' (that is, clear, narrow and consistent) in one sense – speed of response – can promote adaptability. This is because decisions can be made quickly as the conclusive ideology – read 'strong' culture – acts as an effective filter on the acceptability of an action, eliminating lengthy discussion while generating commitment to implementing it. But this 'adaptability' is only when the action required involves no radical departure from the tenets of the 'strong' culture, as conclusive ideologies rule out changes that challenge their assumptions. IBM's inability to recognise the swing of markets away from mainframe to personal computers is often cited as an example of the blindness induced by a strong culture. Leaving aside the strong bureaucratic cultures that inhibit risk taking and innovation *per se* (Golzen, 1988), the development of a culture congruent with and supportive of a particular business strategy can act as a block to employees adopting different behaviour in response to changing market demands in a similar manner to the inflexibilities generated by too close a 'match' between HRM and business policies referred to earlier. Further discussion and illustration of this point is contained in Chapter 6.

The integration of HRM
with line management

A final aspect of integration that Guest (1987) identifies is that of integrating HRM into line management. This occurs when line managers, as business managers, recognise that they are responsible for coordinating and directing *all* resources in their business unit, including human resources, in pursuit of the bottom line. In such circumstances, it is argued, they will see the importance of using human resource policies – whether of a 'hard' or 'soft' nature – systematically and consistently to support their operating goals and, hence, at the most senior levels, business strategy. What evidence do we have for this form of integration?

First, the general lack of systematic strategic thinking among corporate and divisional managers about managing human resources, discussed earlier

(Marginson *et al.*, 1988; Marginson *et al.*, 1993; Sisson and Storey, 1993) must not be forgotten and the exemplar case study evidence of large organisations presenting a contrary picture must be seen against this background. Nevertheless, case studies originating in the Warwick Centre for Corporate Strategy and Change and in the Industrial Relations Research Unit suggest that HRM *considerations* are increasingly recognised in the initiation and implementation of organisational changes that are rooted in technical change and, hence, seen as the concern of line managers. These changes, all highly dependent on the development of new technologies, have taken two major forms: those in operational management (such as TQM, MRP, JIT and CAM) (see, in particular, Chapter 7) and those in organisational design (not just the development of new team-based work systems, consequent on operations management changes, but strategic initiatives such as decentralisation to single business units and the 'delayering' of swathes of middle management 'support' staff, redefined in 'hard' HRM terms, not as a 'resource', but as an 'overhead'). As is discussed in Chapters 6 and 7, both types of change are designed to serve similar, if potentially incompatible, ends: cost-cutting, quality enhancement and increased flexibility and customer awareness both inside and outside increasingly permeable organisational boundaries (cf. the Schuler and Jackson typology of business strategies).

The evidence presented in the case study material of Hendry, Pettigrew and their colleagues (Hendry and Pettigrew, 1987; Hendry and Pettigrew, 1988; Hendry *et al.*, 1988; Pettigrew *et al.*, 1988; Hendry, 1991; Pettigrew and Whipp, 1991) and that of Storey (1992b) suggests that human resource considerations are raised at the initiation stage of operational management and organisational design changes, but as already discussed in relation to WIRS 2 and the Warwick Company Level surveys, that the extent to which traditional personnel specialists are involved is questionable. Hendry *et al.* (1988) suggest that HRM, particularly at policy-making levels, is becoming the province of managers with a high degree of business credibility – a credibility not always found in specialist personnel departments (see Chapter 1). Significantly they state:

> For personnel functions there is not just an issue of developing skills in new areas but also one of needing to link together business, technical and HRM skills. Our research suggests that there is unfortunately a shortage of people with such skills and competences within firms. The problem, however, is not just the shortage of people with sufficient skills and competences: it is also one of recognising the legitimacy of HRM. Putting capable personnel professionals into punishing environments is not a successful strategy. *For this reason, the trend detectable in some firms towards putting line managers into the most senior positions to oversee the personnel function, may represent a breakthrough in the acceptance of HRM issues at the highest level.* (1988, p. 41, added emphasis)

More recent evidence from Storey's (1992b) research supports this picture of some measure of integration of HRM into line management. First, in his 'core' companies, HRM was becoming increasingly vested in senior and middle line management, not just as a delivery mechanism for new approaches in employee relations, but as 'the designers and drivers of the new ways' (1992b, p. 194). In Smith and Nephew, Ford, Bradford City Council and Peugeot–Talbot, senior management were increasingly giving HRM issues a high profile in their general deliberations on business strategy while, at the same time, maintaining that personnel policy itself had been taken over by the executive (1992b, pp. 172, 204). As a director of manufacturing at Peugeot–Talbot UK stated:

> The central personnel function is now basically a co-ordinating activity. The personnel director leads for us in the formal negotiations with the trade unions. But on the major policy shifts in areas such as communications, management, quality, team building, problem-solving teams and the like, these are matters for the executive. (1992b, p. 204)

Secondly, the major initiatives undertaken to achieve competitive advantage were often rooted in technical change generally and in IT specifically (TQM, MRP, JIT, organisational designs which place operatives in teams or created 'cells', computer-aided manufacture). Thirdly, the prime movers in both initiating and managing such change were manufacturing managers rather than the 'notably reticent', 'foot-dragging' personnel specialists (1992b, p. 194).[8] Indeed, there was a general recognition by both personnel specialists and line managers of this state of affairs. Just as the personnel director of a manufacturing company acknowledged

> I have to admit that TQM and the Top Management Workshops represent two of the main thrusts in our management development strategy and, to be perfectly honest with you, they are now major planks in our human resource strategy as a whole. You are correct in saying that neither of them was launched by us. We sort of inherited them ...

so, in one of the process companies, a manufacturing manager, referring to issues surrounding the introduction of TQM, MRP II and the achievement of enhanced flexibility stated: 'I don't see that personnel helped us in this!' (1992b, p. 183, p. 201). The vesting in line management of HRM initiatives rooted in technical change, Storey argues (1992b, p. 196), reflects the 'crucial fusion' of devolved management and the non-proceduralised approach of HRM, with its emphasis on direct communications with employees, participation and involvement, hands-on management style, on-the-job coaching and development.

One corollary of 'downsizing' (cuts in staff numbers at all levels, to cut costs) and 'delayering' (reducing numbers of levels in the hierarchy to achieve greater customer responsiveness) is often devolved accountability, with the creation of Strategic Business Units (SBUs), target-setting, introduction of multi-faceted performance indicators and devolved budgeting. The creation of SBUs at lower levels within organisations has given line managers both a broader remit and enhanced legitimacy as the key contributors to the 'bottom line'. As mentioned in Chapter 3, in many of Storey's case study organisations, the old style, technically oriented, reactive 'progress chasing' production manager has been transformed into a proactive (albeit technically oriented) 'manufacturing manager' 'actively seek[ing] to find new ways of reducing costs, or improving quality and of employing labour, materials and plant in new configurations which will add value to the processes in hand' (1992b, p. 198). In some cases this transformation has gone one step further, with the manufacturing manager evolving into a proactive, but commercially oriented 'business manager', aware of the total organisation and its interface with the wider environment of customers and suppliers, 'competent in SWOT analysis, planning, target-setting, finance, marketing and the management of change' (1992b, p. 198). (Note here Storey's implicit assumption of the business's manager's use of rationalistic strategic–planning techniques, which is highly questionable.) In both cases, line managers have increasingly become generalists, directing a team of support functions towards the achievement of business goals. As Storey quotes the director of manufacturing at Peugeot–Talbot: 'The manufacturing manager is king' (1992b, p. 202).

This transformation, where it has occurred, has given line management the responsibility for a wider mix of employees and for the management of change. This, in turn, brings human resource issues higher up line management's agenda as the new initiatives in operations management and organisational design have implications for a whole host of HRM issues such as recruitment, selection, training and achieving attitudes and behaviour that deliver the required quality and flexibilities. As Storey points out, line management is both the object of HRM inspired initiatives in such areas as well as the designer and deliverer of its repercussions to the shopfloor.

While this evidence is supportive of Guest's normative injunctions, it must be remembered that it is derived from a relatively small number of case studies, some of which are exemplars of HRM initiatives in UK industry (e.g., Rover, Jaguar, GKN, Hardy Spicer, Whitbread) (see, for example, Arthur, 1994). To what extent this level of integration is typical of UK industry – particularly in the light of the research evidence presented earlier in this chapter and in the light of Guest's (1995) view that many organisations may be retreating into a 'black hole' of no systematic HRM or institutional industrial relations (see Chapter 10) – is highly debatable.

Conclusions

Several points emerge from the preceding analysis and discussion. First, the conventional frameworks for integrating business strategy and HRM assume a classical, rationalistic, top-down model of strategy-making that itself is normative rather than empirically grounded and might best be seen as an expression of the Anglo–American hegemony and values of the 1950s and early 1960s. It is not surprising, then, that conceptually such frameworks are problematic and that there is little convincing empirical evidence in their support. The processual framework, that is better grounded empirically, would suggest – as Pettigrew's, Hendry's and Whipp's case studies bear out – that integrating HRM and business strategy is a highly complex and iterative process, much dependent on the interplay and resources of different stakeholders. As strategies are emergent, 'their coherence accruing through action and perceived in retrospect' (Whittington, 1993, p. 26), their integration with HRM is generally a similarly tentative and exploratory process, often existing largely in retrospective rationalisations, couched in the appropriate rhetoric. The evolutionary approach to strategy would argue that conscious attempts to integrate strategy and HRM policy are at best a hit and miss affair, at worse an irrelevancy. Certainly for those 'selected out' by the market, opportunistic pragmatism and firefighting is likely to have been the last-ditch prevailing approach to employee relations. For the survivors, factors quite apart from HRM policy, such as exchange and interest rates and shareholder sentiment, may determine survival or failure.

However, the systemic model of strategy is useful in suggesting *why* the integration of business strategy and HRM policies is the exception rather than the rule in the UK. The systemic model sees strategy-makers as embedded in social networks and their characteristic values and beliefs. From this perspective Sisson (1990, 1993) has analysed why it is that UK industry appears characterised by a short-termism in developing business strategy that fosters an opportunistic pragmatism and inhibits the long-term envisioning conducive to developing a 'soft' model HRM strategy.

Sisson's argument is as follows. UK short-termism reflects a relatively fluid capital market, in which strategies of aggressive acquisitions and divestments are easy,[9] and in which public companies rely heavily on large investments from pension funds, investment trusts and other institutional shareholders. As already stated, such institutions are often mandated to generate the best dividends they can for their own stakeholders and hence are sensitive to, not to say fickle about, short-term results. In consequence, as this message is conveyed to companies, managers' performance horizons are adjusted to meet annual and half-yearly reporting schedules. This places a premium on behaviours and investments that have a quick pay-back, and acts to inhibit long-term and potentially risky [read 'innovative'] investment projects. Hence, as Sisson and Storey (1993, p. 76) point out, an endemic tendency exists in UK industry for 'managers to have recourse to opportunistic quick-fix agreements, fire fighting solutions; and Tayloristic job design methods which are built on command and control rather than more time-consuming consensus methods'.

Further, this proclivity is both reflected in and reinforced by the numbers of accountants in senior positions in British organisations and the dominance of an accountancy logic and accountancy-driven managerial control systems (Armstrong, 1989). This, in itself, reflects the absence of well-educated and trained managers from different disciplines combined with the well known cultural prejudice against engineering qualifications as a route to senior management in British industry (Glover and Kelly, 1987). Further, as already touched on, short-termism is reinforced by the UK predilection for multidivisional diversified organisations, often leaning towards a financial–control strategic style (Goold and Campbell, 1987). In relation to the electronics industry a McKinsey NEDO report (1988) suggested this resulted in a failure

> to take advantage of the opportunities for synergy which large company status should confer. Fragmentation and devolution to constituent businesses had become so prevalent that, when wedded to the often associated financial control system, the result was a set of small businesses having to respond to short-term financial goals. (Sisson and Storey, 1993, p. 77)

This short-termism is further reflected in the traditional lack of investment in training and development in UK society and industry (Finegold and Soskice, 1988; Keep, 1989; Handy, 1987; Constable and McCormick, 1987), in contrast to the provision in competing countries, notably Germany and Japan (Steedman and Wagner, 1987; Lane, 1990). In both the latter countries training is seen as investing in a core workforce, whose expected long tenure encourages such investment and facilitates a longer-term view. The latter is further reinforced by the close long-term relationship between specific banks and companies in Germany (e.g., the Deutsche Bank and Daimler-Benz continuous relationship since the 1920s) and the *keiretsu* groupings of interlocking shareholder banks and associated corporations in Japan (Whittington, 1993). As Beaumont (1993, pp. 26–8) points out it is the mutually reinforcing nature of HRM policies and the business context that can provide either a virtuous circle (as in the case of Germany and Japan) or a vicious circle (as in the case of the UK) as far as the generation of long-term strategy and competitive advantage is concerned. Lane demonstrates this message:

> A system of VET (vocational education and training) is far more than merely an instrument for the production of technical skills ... the German system creates not only a distinct social structure in business organisations but also a host of behavioural and attitudinal patterns. These shape interactions in labour markets and in the field of employment, in industrial relations and work organisation, and even in the area of technological innovation. These various social consequences of the German skill structure constitute strong 'push' and 'pull' factors which, together with recent changes in the market environment and in technology, have led management to adopt new production concepts. These have enabled enterprises in many industries to maintain or improve their competitive position in world markets. (Lane, 1990, cited in Beaumont, 1993, pp. 27–8)

Hence, if we regard strategy-making in UK organisations from the systemic perspective, the likelihood of the integration of a carefully articulated business strategy with long-term 'soft' HRM policies in much of UK industry would appear something of a forlorn hope. Possibly it may be sighted in strategic–planning, high-technology companies, with sufficient market-dominance to be able to compete on product/service uniqueness, rather than principally on price. But for many companies, given the nature of the UK context, perhaps the most realistic expectation is of a thinking pragmatism reminiscent of the 'standard modern' employee relations style. Insofar as such short-term opportunistic policies are internally consistent, and that some conscious connection is made with business strategy (compete on cost → cut the cost base → get rid of overhead → let's downsize), a rhetoric might be created of integrating business strategy with 'hard' model HRM.

Notes

1. I am very grateful for the valuable comments of John Purcell, Templeton College, Oxford, on an earlier draft of this chapter.
2. Miles and Snow (1978) in fact identify a fourth style of strategic behaviour, 'the reactor' – where managers perceive change and uncertainty but are unable to respond effectively. They lack a consistent strategy and act when the environment 'forces' them to do so. As this 'strategy' is, by definition, a pragmatic, 'non-strategy', for the purposes of this argument, it has been excluded.
3. These styles bear some resemblance to Hill and Hoskisson's (1987) distinction between financial, synergistic and vertical economies in the way multidivisional firms are structured (financial, resembling financial-control, synergistic and vertical control could resemble strategic-planning or strategic-control depending on the precise strategies adopted).
4. This conclusion echoes that of Brewster et al. (1983) who, in the early 1980s, found a gap between the 'espoused' strategies voiced by senior management and the 'operational' policies actually implemented at workplaces.
5. There is a good reason to believe the finance respondents' estimates rather than those of personnel. Not only might one expect the personnel respondents to exaggerate their involvement (cf. Brewster and Burnois, 1991; Gennard and Kelly, 1994), but it seems strange that their claimed involvement in all instances exceeds the extent to which they claim that personnel issues were taken into account (Marginson et al., 1993, p. 37). Of course if these responses are taken as valid and consistent it paints an even more depressing picture of the personnel function's influence on corporate strategy!
6. HRM here being defined as a sense of coherence and appropriateness in employment decisions – where aspects of the employment systems are internally consistent with one another and are aligned with business strategy (Hendry and Pettigrew, 1992, p. 137).
7. The Pettigrew school, of course, would not have a problem here, defining internal integration not in relation to consistency with the 'mutuality' model, but solely in terms of the internal consistency of employment policies and practices (see n. 4 above).
8. In contrast to Storey's (1992b) cases, Marchington et al.'s (1993) IPM (now IPD) sponsored case study research into TQM initiatives found that personnel specialists did 'play a sizeable part in the operation of quality management at these organisations' (p. 31), although the role played varied in breadth and depth. Some personnel managers

were involved at operational level, whether adopting a prominent high-profile 'internal contractor' role or a less visible 'facilitator' role (the most common stance). Others were involved at the strategic level whether in a high profile 'change agent' role (a minority) or less prominently, as a sounding board or 'hidden persuader'. (See also Wilkinson and Marchington, 1994.)

9. There is evidence to suggest in both the UK and US that increases in directors' pay is only very weakly related – if at all – to corporate performance, whether measured using stock market data or accounting data on earnings per share. Rather, corporate growth is an important determinant of upward changes in directors' remuneration (Crystal, 1991; Colvin, 1992; Gregg *et al.*, 1993). Not only is this finding at odds with the rationalistic, classical model of strategy, which would argue that directors should represent shareholders' interests, but it suggests that directors may well pursue mergers and acquisitions out of self-interest, regardless of their economic merit. When short-termism is reinforced by managerial self-interest a lethal combination is in place. I am grateful to John Purcell for drawing this issue to my attention.

5

HRM: towards the flexible firm?

In his model of HRM, Guest (1987) sees flexibility as having three components: relating to organisational design, job design and employee attitudes and motivations. For organisations to have the capacity to manage planned change and to be adaptive to uncertainties and unanticipated pressures at all levels in the organisation the structure must avoid the rigidities associated with hierarchical machine-like bureaucracies, entrenched, powerful interest groups and inhibitive demarcations among work groups. Instead, organisations should seek flexibility via organic structures, extensive decentralisation and delegation of control and, therefore, through the design of jobs. Job design should seek to achieve 'functional flexibility' (i.e., polyvalency and multiskilling) among the workforce (Atkinson and Meager, 1986) and the relaxing of inappropriate professional and craft demarcations. Furthermore, 'the issue of flexibility can be taken further – for example, in relation to core and periphery workers, the nature of the employment contract and the location of work' (Guest, 1987, p. 514). Guest concludes by suggesting that flexibilities in organisational and job design can only be achieved if employees display 'high organisational commitment, high trust and high levels of intrinsic motivation'. Hence, he suggests, many large bureaucratic institutions are presently incapable of meeting these conditions, which limits their ability to pursue 'soft' HRM policies.

Guest's argument echoes those of many of the fashionable American gurus of organisation theory such as Drucker (1988), Peters (1987, 1992), Peters and Waterman (1982), Kanter (1984, 1989) and Kanter *et al.* (1992) who have long advocated the virtues of 'tight–loose' structures, whether profit centres or single business units, partnerships, alliances, joint ventures and various forms of relational contracting. The challenge is clearly stated: to achieve the flexibility for rapid responsiveness to customer needs while retaining effective cost control. The solution to this reworking of the old issue of simultaneously achieving requisite integration and differentiation (Lawrence and Lorsch, 1967) is seen to lie, on the one hand, in differentiating via devolved accountability and focusing on areas of core competencies and, on the other, integrating via central financial controls and shared vision (see Chapter 6). The processes involved are now fashionably termed 'business process re-engineering', and involve (in Grint's somewhat sceptical words), 'closing the distance between supply points, production, assembly and customer, by decentralising, using process teams, building awareness, developing a vision based on strategic objectives, smashing functional barriers, creating involvement, streamlining information systems, and a few other assorted odds and ends' (Grint, 1994, p. 181).

A strategy that facilitates the achievement of both of these objectives is flattening the organisation's hierarchy through delayering with accompanying downsizing. Jaques (1964, 1990), applying his time-span of discretion ideas, has argued that hierarchies have become overelaborated in order to provide for career structures and rewards rather than through functional necessity. Superfluous managerial layers are dysfunctional through failing to add real value to the work of subordinates, through slowing the transmission of information, impeding decision-making and cramping accountability. Further, erstwhile functional managerial layers are now being called into question as the information processing and coordinative activities supplied by layers of middle management are now largely superseded by the application of information technology (Drucker, 1988). Either way, delayering and devolved accountability seem the route to both cost-savings and greater responsiveness to the customer – whether in banks (e.g., National Westminster, TSB), telecommunications (e.g., BT), oil and chemicals (e.g., BP) or the public sector (e.g., the NHS).

Clearly such strategies have very direct HRM implications concerning reward and career development structures and the maintenance of employee commitment among survivors, not only beset by fears about job insecurity (see reports in *Daily Telegraph*, 9 January 1995, for example), but confronted by reduced promotion prospects and possible work overload. How too is the paradox resolved that, while the fashionable solution to the above is for the employer to enhance employee 'employability' (Kanter, 1989), delayering often involves the removal of erstwhile training grades?

Ideas from the industrial economists, about agency theory (Alchian and Demsetz, 1972) and transactions costs analysis (Williamson, 1975) have also stimulated thinking about new organisational forms. Such theories have challenged conventional, taken-for-granted assumptions about the inevitability of large organisation forms, vertically integrated through hierarchy, by posing the question 'why organisation?'. Using concepts such as the 'free-loader' and the 'principal-agent' relationship (agency theory) and ideas about complexity/uncertainty, bounded rationality, small numbers, opportunism and 'information impactedness' (transactions costs analysis) questions may be asked as to the determinants of organisational boundaries – what activities are best coordinated and controlled 'in-house' and which are best transacted in the marketplace (the 'make or buy' decision)? This has stimulated interest in looser organisational forms (for example, franchising, subcontracting, joint ventures, 'customer–contractor quasi-markets', as in the NHS) where erstwhile internalised transactions or activities, coordinated and controlled by means of hierarchy, are now reassessed as being more cost-effectively and/or responsively enacted in the marketplace.

This general concern with flexibility and customer responsiveness, quite apart from the centrality of flexibility to Guest's (1987) HRM model, must first be seen against the background of the socio-economic and cultural changes in the UK and US discussed in Chapter 3. Market competition, the Japanese Janus, models of excellence and the enterprise culture all point to the desirability of enhanced responsiveness to the customer and the sweeping away of institutional rigidities that might impede a flexible response. But this is not all. While not explicit, save in his choice of references, Guest's characterisation of flexibility – and, indeed, its inclusion in his model – owes much to wider, fashionable academic debates about the future of work in western capitalist societies. Such debates are themselves reflective of the 'dynamic environmental "shocks" induced by slower economic growth, globalisation and intensification of competition, a rising rate of product innovation, and the impact of advanced forms of information technology' (Thompson and McHugh, 1990, p. 191) that are part and parcel of the socio-economic changes identified above. The debates I refer to are those surrounding the concepts of the 'second industrial divide' and 'flexible specialisation' (Piore and Sabel, 1984; Kern and Schumann, 1984, 1987; Aglietta, 1979; Wood, 1989b) or, more generally, the 'post-industrial society' (Bell, 1974; Handy, 1984) and the Institute of Manpower Studies' (IMS) model of the 'flexible firm' (Atkinson, 1984; Atkinson and Meager, 1986; Pollert, 1987, 1988a, 1991). (See also Chapter 9.)

Some aspects of flexibility in relation to organisational design – decentralisation and delayering – have already been touched on in Chapter 4 and briefly above and will not be considered further here. The flexibility (or perhaps lack of it?) achieved via employee commitment (to what?) is the focus of the next chapter. The present chapter concentrates on three issues central to questions about flexibility and HRM:

- The broader background of academic debates in which HRM concerns with flexibility need to be situated.
- The empirical evidence, derived from surveys and case studies, of enhanced flexibility, whether at the level of task or organisational design in UK firms.
- Accounting for the continuities, and changes, identified in the empirical evidence, and their significance for HRM.

The debates: 'flexible specialisation' and the 'flexible firm'

Before embarking on the themes of this chapter, it is necessary to offer some definitions of flexibility, as a benchmark to subsequent discussion, particularly as the concept has been used rather differently in different debates.

In the context of 'flexible specialisation' to quote Smith (1989, p. 203):

'Flexibility' refers to labour market and labour process restructuring, to increased versatility in design and the greater adaptability of new technology in production. 'Specialization' relates to niche or custom marketing, the apparent 'end of Fordism', mass production and standardization. Hence the concept unites changes in production and consumption.

In contrast, in the flexible firm model (and implicitly in Guest's HRM model) flexibility is defined less abstractly and in terms of three facets: functional, numerical and financial flexibility (Atkinson, 1984):

- *functional* flexibility refers to a firm's ability to deploy employees between activities and tasks to match changing workloads, production methods or technology. It is often loosely associated with polyvalency and multiskilling. This is the form of flexibility that comes closest to the flexibility referred to in flexible specialisation.
- *numerical* flexibility refers to a firm's capacity to adjust labour inputs to fluctuations in output, via the use of 'non-standard employment contracts', designed to achieve flexibility through outsourcing and undermining of permanency of the employment relationship.
- *financial* flexibility refers to a firm's ability to adjust employment costs to reflect the state of supply and demand in the external labour market, in a way that is supportive of the objectives sought by functional and numerical flexibility. As far as direct wage costs go, this involves a move away from uniform and standardised pay structures, possibly located in a national negotiating framework, towards more individualised systems containing a greater element of variability, dependent upon performance.

Flexible specialisation: the proposals

Since the late 1970s much academic and popular debate has centred on the 'future of work' in the light of technological developments, loss of confidence in the post-war Keynesian economic order and subsequent recognition of discontinuous change (Drucker, 1989; Lash and Urry, 1987). There is much confusing bandying around of a series of closely related concepts: neo-Fordism, post-Fordism and flexible specialisation, that may appear virtually identical to the uninitiated but have subtly differentiated meanings to the cognoscenti. The key commentators in this debate are Piore and Sabel (1984), Kern and Schumann (1984, 1987), Aglietta (1979), Hirst and Zeitlin (1991), and Lash and Urry (1987). Many of the arguments involved are summarised and critiqued, in greater detail than here, in Wood (1989b) and in Pollert (1991).

The essence of the debate is as follows. The first 'industrial divide' (Piore and Sabel, 1984) occurred with the development and diffusion of 'Fordist' mass production in the early 20th century. Fordism may be characterised as a system of mass production of standardised goods designed for mass consumption, manufactured by semi- or unskilled labour operating dedicated mechanised equipment in Tayloristic systems of fragmented, specialist, work-studied job design. Fordism directs an instrumental rationality at achieving economies of scale and defines the HRM 'problem' as one of achieving labour control largely through substituting labour by machinery (Kern and Schumann, 1987). It is the regime of production – and of accumulation (Aglietta, 1979) – that reached its apogee in the long period of sustained post-war economic growth. But the world-wide changes already referred to have called into question the continued viability of Fordism, and this 'crisis of Fordism' (Aglietta, 1979) or 'second industrial divide' (Piore and Sabel, 1984), it is argued, calls for new regimes of production and accumulation. The answers are variously neo-Fordism, post-Fordism and flexible specialisation. Which answer is favoured depends on the precise analysis of the causes of the crisis of Fordism.

For the proponents of neo-Fordism (regulation theorists such as Aglietta, 1979) this crisis of Fordism arose because it had been too successful. Assembly lines had reached a pinnacle of perfectly balanced optimisation of labour and capital inputs and as a result there were limits to further productivity under existing Fordist arrangements. Some questioned whether it was easily applicable to the faster growing service sectors of western economies (Aglietta, 1984). Neo-Fordism is essentially about going beyond Fordism without negating its fundamental principles. As Wood (1989b, pp. 20–2) points out, it involves a restructuring of tasks towards job enrichment; increased automation in order to enhance overall coordination and control, and increased internationalisation of production, along the lines of the world car strategy (Marsden et al., 1985). While commentators, such as Aglietta, saw such strategies as a solution to the crisis of Fordism, others, such as Sabel (1982), saw neo-Fordism as a step away from the rigid control model of Fordism, but only a step towards its ultimate rejection in favour of flexible specialisation.

Flexible specialisation, it is argued, is the alternative to, rather than reform of, Fordism. Identifying a saturation in the demand for standardised products, a fragmentation of markets, and the emergence at the same time of a new more flexible information technology, Piore and Sabel (1984) suggest that this allows manufacturers to reconsider strategies of capital and labour utilisation. The new technologies offer the possibility of reducing break-even points, allowing viability to small and medium batch production, even in what were traditionally mass production industries. Economies of scale can then be replaced by economies of scope,[1] whereby the flexible organisation of production and use of widely applicable, rather than product-specific or functionally dedicated, technology allows a firm to attain higher quality standards and smaller batches, without increasing production costs, and hence to service relatively small, more diverse markets (see Wood, 1989, p. 13). 'Once such choices are made, manufacturing economies are locked into a technological trajectory' (Thompson and McHugh, 1990, p. 192). The Taylorist strategy of designing fragmented, low discretion, specialist jobs needs to be replaced by a high degree of multiskilling and flexibility of deployment, as well as the exercise of 'craft' judgement and skill. Furthermore, flexible specialisation, so it is argued, can reverse the pattern of increased dominance of large firms in the economy, and of an international division of labour, in which labour intensive, low skill assembly is located to low labour cost areas of the developing world, and research and development retained in the parent companies' home country. Instead there could be a re-emergence of what Sabel (1989) calls 'regional economies' built round a network of decentralised, flexible small firms, between which cooperation and competition is balanced, so as to encourage continuous innovation and adaptability. Regions with a surviving 'craft' tradition, such as the oft-cited Veneto and Emilia Romagna in North Italy, are identified as seedbeds for experiments in flexible specialisation. The final claim is that such a strategy, in contrast to Fordism, through policies of decentralisation, participation and involvement, encourage the high-trust ideologies that may result in collaborative industrial relations and the generation of a 'yeoman democracy', thus providing a more democratic solution to present economic crises (Piore and Sabel, 1984; Wood, 1989, p. 14; Reed, 1992, pp. 230–1). As Wood (1989, p. 13) rightly points out, this scenario, which starts descriptively by identifying trends in markets and technology and making analytic projections about logical trajectories, ends as a normative manifesto in favour of a 'diverse, but well-integrated, network of small and medium sized organisations, embedded within local cultures and ideologies based on community structures which foster collective involvement and high trust relations' (Reed, 1992, p. 234).

So, what of post-Fordism? Wood (1989, p. 27) building on Coombs and Jones' (1988) ideas, suggests that it may be differentiated from both neo-Fordism and flexible specialisation on the basis of how the new technology is used and on the basis of territoriality. Neo-Fordism in this framework is typified by technology used to substitute labour and improve quality, without necessarily changing the horizontal or vertical division of labour; and with more fully fledged inter-nationalisation, with a spatial division of labour within firms and a supply of uniform products (world car) to all markets. Flexible specialisation, in contrast, is likely to have a highly fragmented labour process, concentrate on bespoke manufacturing in which conception and execution are collapsed, with the customer coming to the production location. Post-Fordism, unlike neo-Fordism, is likely to involve changes in the vertical division of labour, an emphasis on product innovation, improved design capability, relations with suppliers and responsiveness to local markets. Unlike flexible specialisation, though, product and process conception and development remains ahead of sales and production, and involves prototypes and experimentation.

However, 'post-Fordism' is also used in a more general sense, to refer to broader changes in regimes of regulation and accumulation, that involve socio–politico–cultural changes – as, for example, Lash and Urry's (1987) notion of 'disorganised capitalism'. In this sense, post-Fordism merges with conceptions of post-industrial (Bell, 1974) and post-modern (Clegg, 1990) organisation and society: away from the logic of mass production towards that of individualised consumption; away from technological determinism and dedicated equipment towards technological choice and flexible micro-electronic equipment; away from bureaucratic rationality and its associated emphasis on hierarchy, centralisation and specialisation towards 'the proliferation and free play of discursive rationalities' (Reed, 1992, p. 229) and associated entrepreneurial, decentralised, self-regulating, flexible networks and the dissolution of boundaries; away from planning towards strategy; away from time–space fragmentation towards time–space compression; away from the absolute and standardised towards the relative and eclectic (see Murray, 1989; Lyotard, 1984; Best and Kellner, 1991; Harvey, 1989; Moult, 1990; Fox, 1990). And, as befits such discontinuous change, that is reflected in commentators' propensity to talk of 'the end of' almost everything, a unifying theme is flexibility – whether of rationalities, choices or structures. (For further discussion, see Chapter 9.)

Flexible firm: the proposals

It is against this background of macro-level debates that the widespread dissemination and clichéd status of the Institute of Manpower Studies' model of the 'flexible firm' must be seen. Arguably, much of the interest and controversy (Pollert, 1987, 1988a and 1991) it has excited arises because its proposals resonate with those emerging from the flexible specialisation/post Fordism debates.[7] Essentially the model reflects the tensions between production strategies designed to achieve versatility via outsourcing (of goods, services and labour), and those that seek versatility through tapping the skills, adaptability and creativity of the workforce. The first response undermines the permanency of employment, and/or externalises it via subcontracting and outsourcing. The second seeks to incorporate employees ever tighter into managerial concerns and business objectives, via team building, quality circles, multiskilling and employees' communications programmes. As Marginson (1991, pp. 33–4) points out, both strategies reflect the need for companies to become more responsive in terms of price, quality and variety of goods and services they produce and, hence, more versatile in resource deployment, in the light of internationalisation and enhanced competition. But whereas outsourcing reflects the displacement of administrative coordination by financial controls, flexible production methods can be a strategy to overcome the potential problems of production coordination and quality control that externalising production may result in. The tensions in the model reflect therefore the broader issues of transaction costs in markets vs hierarchies (Williamson, 1975).

In brief, Atkinson (1984) proposes that employers seek an optimal balance between functional, numerical and financial forms of flexibility through segmenting the labour force into core and peripheral groups (see Figure 5.1). The core group, which conducts the organisation's key firm-specific continuous activities, enjoys job security and the possibility of career development in the internal labour market, in return for the obligation (opportunity?) to be polyvalent and multiskilled. It is from this group that the organisation derives *functional* flexibility. The peripheral group, from which *numerical* flexibility is sought, comprises three categories of employees.

First, there are those who perform relatively routinised or deskilled tasks (whether manual or white-collar) which require an element of firm-specific

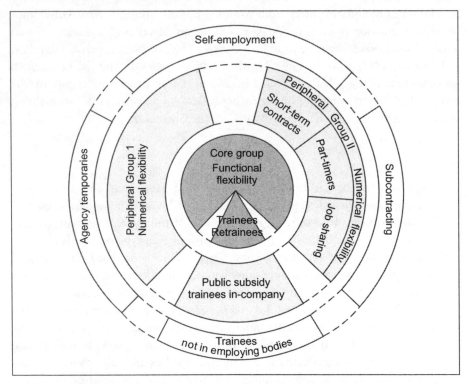

Source: Mangum and Mangum (1986, p. 14).

Figure 5.1   Atkinsin's model of the flexible firm

training, but which offer few career prospects. Their employment, in the organisation's secondary internal labour market, while theoretically continuous (whether full- or part-time), is vulnerable to market or technical change. Secondly, in the primary external labour market, are those with specialist non-firm-specific skills, required by an organisation on an intermittent, discontinuous basis (e.g., systems analysts, TQM consultants) and who can demand a high fee for specific items of service. Finally, there are those tasks (e.g., cleaning, catering, routine security) which can be contracted out to small firms employing some of their own 'core', but largely casual, temporary unskilled labour, drawn mainly from the secondary, external labour market, whose pay and conditions are likely to be poor, given the level of unemployment that existed through much of the 1980s and which, with recession (the demographic 'time bomb' notwithstanding), has returned in the early 1990s.

In theory, if we assume this model might be enacted in the equally hypothetical post-Fordist age, who might comprise these different groups, to some extent, will be influenced by the speed of adoption and choices about the use of the new technologies. For example, Child (1985), Child et al. (1984) suggests that direct manual workers are only likely to be part of the stable core where the type of task still requires the direct operative's discretion and judgement, permits flexibility of physical movement, of time budgeting and possibly sequencing. Such a situation would be more likely to prevail where investment is in micro-electronic cybernetic control systems (process production) and in flexible manufacturing (small batch production involving complex machining and variability in specification). However, it would be accompanied by the elimination of much semi-skilled and traditional supervisory employment and the loss of traditional craft jobs, as minor maintenance would be undertaken by polyvalent operatives and major maintenance contracted out to specialist engineers (in administrative, professional, technical (APT) grades) of the capital equipment engineering firms' service companies. Alternatively, in situations where product market competition is based on cost-effective standardised mass production, archetypal of Fordism, and where the task characteristics involve repeated routine operations, with little uncertainty and few exceptions, new technology may be used to deskill erstwhile craft and semi-skilled jobs, relocating such employees who retain employment firmly in a peripheral group (Wilkinson, 1983). Nor are such trends confined to manual labour in manufacturing industry. Child et al. (1984) argue that new technologies enable clerical and technical work in all sectors (e.g., banking, medical laboratories) to be increasingly divided into its routine and less routine elements, deskilling the majority and skill-enhancing a minority of increasingly polyvalent employees. Furthermore, where demand for labour input is uneven or discontinuous (as in retailing, or in the demand for some specialist professional services) new technologies can be employed (e.g., by giving more precise information on customer flows; by enabling 'networking') to facilitate the substitution of part-time or temporary contract employees for full-time staff.

Hence at both macro- and micro-levels, in models of economy and society and of the firm and its labour markets, a manifesto is proposed that enhanced flexibility will be (and should be) the key to appropriate labour utilisation and HRM. Indeed, both the debates have overlapping themes: responsiveness to markets, the facilitating role of information technology, the cutting of overhead/'small is beautiful', all of which imply restructuring. Or, from a more ideological standpoint, 'a celebration of market and consumer sovereignty; a legitimation of the view that the solutions to organisational and economic problems lies [sic] in altering the behaviour of labour; the resurrection of a dual labour market analysis; and a futurological discourse underwritten by a post industrial analysis in which flexibility marks the vital break from the past' (Thompson and McHugh, 1990, p. 215 – referring to Pollert's ideas). But how sound are the theoretical foundations of these proposals, and what is the empirical evidence for their strategic enactment?

'Flexible specialisation' and the 'flexible firm': the counterblast

Although flexibility is an important agenda item and part of the rhetoric of managers today, a certain amount of scepticism must be raised about both the 'flexible specialisation' and the 'flexible firm' models that form the backdrop to the largely pragmatic initiatives in HRM towards enhanced flexibility. The criticisms raise four general issues:

1. In relation to both models it is often unclear whether the commentators are talking descriptively, about what is, or prescriptively, about what should be.
2. In both models central concepts are either inadequately specified or used tautologically. As a result the theories often appear ambiguous and difficult to test.
3. In so far as one can test the models, in both cases, there seems to be a lack of coherent empirical data to support their often sweeping generalisations.
4. Hence, the question is raised: how much real change is taking place? In relation to flexible specialisation commentators are questioning whether such new structures and working patterns that *can* be identified really represent advanced capitalist societies' break with Fordism – 'a total "institutional paradigm shift" in which one industrial order gives way to another' (Reed, 1992, p. 233). Or is it rather 'one ideal-typical model or strategy of production and regulation co-present with others in a complex historical ensemble' (Rustin, 1989 cited in Reed, 1992, pp. 235–6)?

As for the 'flexible firm' model, the empirical evidence would point less to a strategic HRM initiative in organisation design and labour utilisation and (with a few exceptions) more to a conventional exercise in pragmatism and opportunism.

Let us look at these criticisms in more detail before drawing implications for the enactment of the 'hard' and the 'soft' HRM model.

Flexible specialisation: pie in the sky or a bridge too far?

As I have already discussed the tendency of the 'flexible specialisation' protagonists to alternate between descriptive analysis and prescriptive advocacy, I will concentrate on the other criticisms, in particular 2 and 3 above.

Conceptual specification

The concept is not well specified and therefore difficult to test. For example, what counts as flexibility? As Wood (1989, pp. 15–16) queries 'In the case of car plants ... is flexibility simply the ability to alternate styles, product models in the same size range, models of significantly different size ranges, cars or trucks, or cars one day or week, another product the next?'. Block (1985, cited in Wood, 1989) asks whether the appropriate referent should be the firm, industry or even locality. Hyman (1991, p. 281) goes further, pointing out the hidden ideological content of the very concept of flexibility that makes it 'more a rhetorical slogan than ... an analytical instrument'. His comments are worth quoting at some length:

> The language of flexibility 'is heavily value-laden: outside the realm of moral principles, flexibility is invariably a good thing and rigidity a bad one' (Salvati, 1989;44) ... the idea of *absolute* flexibility is an impossibility, an absurdity [... for purposive action and interaction to occur there must exist some relatively stable structural regularities ...]: explicitly or implicitly the debate is rather about the *level* and *distribution* of regularity and variability. To define certain social realities as rigidities (rather than points of stability) and others as flexibilities (rather than areas of uncertainty) is to impose a particular evaluation, to commend a particular *distribution* of options and constraints, and hence to propose a particular structure of social power. Thus the issue is not rigidity versus flexibility but what *kinds* of rigidity? And in terms of policy, what institutional rules and arrangements should be sustained, which altered or abandoned, and which new rigidities established? Here the ideological dimension is of crucial importance, for a key influence on the discourse of flexibility is *who gains or loses* from a particular set of institutional arrangements, and *whose interests* would benefit or suffer from their alteration.

The lack of specification and covert ideological overtones of the concept reflect the ambiguity underlying its simultaneous descriptive and prescriptive usage. Flexibility is a slippery concept indeed, in spite of the apparently straightforward definitions given earlier in the chapter.

Testing the model: dilemmas and data

Apart from the difficulties in conceptual specification and the hidden value assumptions, the 'flexible specialisation' debate in its presentation of what amounts to an ideal-typical model of production and regulation, draws too sharp contrasts with existing modes. For example, there is an assumption that Fordist production systems are not only the paradigm for mass production but that mass production dominates advanced capitalist economies. But, as Williams *et al.* (1987) and Pollert (1991) point out, even within large technologically advanced organisations associated with manufacturing and mass production, a variety of technologies and production systems coexist. 'The assumed connection between production systems, technologies and production outcomes needs to be broken; semi-skilled flow line work, for example, need not be confined to standardised mass production, but can be adapted to flexible small batches' (Pollert, 1991, p. 18). Furthermore, mass production does not always use dedicated equipment to make standardised products but can handle diversification within flow lines. As Wood (1989, p. 28) states: 'There was considerable flexibility in Fordism – indeed central to Taylorism was the idea of workers being disposable and hence the association of routinisation and low training times with numerical flexibility'. Commentators such as Williams *et al.* (1987) dispute whether Fordism was ever dominant outside the US and note the continued importance, particularly in engineering, of small and medium batch production. Linn (1987, cited in Wood, 1989, p. 29) notes that even in assembly line systems as many work off the line as on it. The dominance of Fordism as a model of the past, it has been argued, is used as something of a paper-tiger in the flexible specialisation debate as it 'elides too many differences and establishes an uninformative stereotype' (Williams *et al.*, 1987, p. 423).

If the Fordist stereotype is exaggerated, so too are the supposed flexibilities associated with the new technologies and production systems. The flexible specialisation thesis, it is argued, not only overestimates the prevalence of programmable technology, but is overoptimistic about the actual flexibilities achieved even when it is in place (Jones, 1988, 1989; Legge *et al.*, 1991). 'Much of the literature on computer-based production contains a large element of hype; the more prosaic reality is of limitations to flexibility, systems deficiencies and defects, problems of compatibility between machinery installed at different times and difficulties of matching changing product strategies to equipment potential' (Hyman, 1991, p. 267). As Wood (1989b, p. 16) points out, the emphasis in much manufacturing is on improving control, coordination and quality within existing capital installations, through improved routeing, disposable tools and product design rather than through programmable process flexibility. Further, even when flexible technologies arc adopted, flexibility in one area may inhibit that in another. Thus flexibility in response to the customer via JIT may equally mean decreased flexibility in the production process due to single sourcing and the dependency between buyer and supplier.

The stereotype of the emergence of reskilling and the new craft worker in the flexible specialisation thesis is also overstated – partly because of its almost exclusive concentration on manufacturing industry, which, in any case, is a declining source of employment in advanced economies (Wood, 1989; Hyman, 1991). There is no technical inevitably in either upskilling or deskilling: the choice made will be related to broader management strategies (Legge et al., 1991, pp. 14–17). There is evidence though, especially in the expanding service sector, that information technology generally has been used to routinise and intensify labour (Meegan, 1988) and increasingly to polarise skills along traditional gender lines (Cockburn, 1985; Rubery et al., 1987). As Hyman (1991, p. 267) states: 'In this sense the "second industrial divide" may mean literally, a growing polarisation in conditions of work.' (This will be considered further, when examining evidence for the flexible firm model.)

The flexible specialisation thesis may also be criticised in terms of its assumptions about markets. The notion that mass markets are in terminal decline to be superseded by niche markets holds very little water. Just as there have always been small specialist niche markets, so too there still exist massive markets for mass produced consumer durables, based on families of interrelated products, and supplying a large stable replacement demand (Williams et al., 1987). Many of the new electronic leisure products that lie at the heart of Japanese manufacturing success are mass produced and standardised. Even where markets are becoming more fragmented and product differentiation increasing, is this demand- or supply-led? Particularly given the market-enactment power of the multinationals, fragmentation reflects more often an attempt to manipulate demand and to create a market than new consumer tastes (Thompson and McHugh, 1990, p. 214). Indeed, Pollert (1991, pp. 18–19) does well to remind us of the rigidities of niche marketing. 'The niche company may be innovative, but only in the short term; the large retailer and large producer can quickly capture that product and exploit its entrenched advantage in the market.' Note the problems experienced by 'Sock Shop' and 'Tie Rack'.

In its concentration on the technology and social organisation of production and on the structure of consumer goods markets, the flexible specialisation model neglects the financial structure of capitalism and government involvement in economic affairs (Hyman, 1991). As a result multinational conglomerates are presented almost as a contingent element of mass production that can be sloughed off with its too readily anticipated demise. But this ignores the increasing centrality of multinationals in the international division of labour and the subordination of small-scale localised production to their market power. Multinationals may be prepared to develop strategic alliances and networking arrangements with such firms – but only as part of their global strategy to maintain old modes of accumulation within the world economy (Hudson, 1989).

This conclusion goes hand-in-hand with scepticism about the resurgence of artisanal industrial districts. First, the same examples – the Veneto and Emilia Romagna in Italy and Baden-Württemberg in Germany – are continually cited, with insufficient attention to their specific histories of well-established vocational training and the technological transfer in the late 19th century which fostered the development of an entrepreneurial class, but which render them atypical (cf. Sheffield and Birmingham). While the networks of small firms are responsive to changes in consumer fashions in industries such as textiles, it is arguable whether, in comparison to the multinationals, they can innovate in sectors requiring heavy expenditure in R & D. Amin (1991) argues that recent research on the small firm in the 'Third Italy' demonstrates that high exploitation, not a revival of artisan prosperity, underlies competitive success, while a long-term perspective on the prospects of industrial districts suggests that large capital is reasserting its dominance. And, as Wood (1989, p. 24) suggests, not only does semi-skilled work continue to provide the bulk of employment in these areas, but 'Benetton', the supposed exemplar of the industrial district, has come to resemble not 'a nexus of firms all flexibly specialised and employing highly committed skilled workforces', but 'a network dominated by the large firm modelled largely along the lines of Atkinson's flexible firm'. Wood rightly raises the question

> Ought we not to be emphasising the similarities between the strategies of Benetton and the leading car companies: the globalisation, increased automation, adoption of just-in-time procedures and the intensified use of the computer for design, production and stock control ... Is the Benetton Economy ... a world of flexible specialisation or of Japanese-led revitalised Fordism? (Wood, 1989b, p. 25)

Furthermore, with reference to the UK, Johnson (1991) sees the vaunted 'renaissance' of the small firm as misleading. Rather, the growing number of small firms reflects the contraction of the large firm sector and its associated job shedding practices, as many of the new 'entrepreneurs' were unemployed before starting up and resumed standard employment with the expansion of the economy (see also Rainbird, 1991). Similarly, Felstead (1991) argues that franchises, rather than representing decentralised small business units, reflect an extension of the standardised Tayloristic labour process and an arrangement whereby larger firms cost-effectively gain access to wider markets.

In the light of the evidence it is tempting to see the manifesto of flexible specialisation as just that: comforting rhetoric about the possibility of a new industrial order at a time when observers are only too conscious of the multiple sources of instability in global economic relations. Moreover it is a rhetoric that backgrounds a less palatable scenario – of an ever strengthening grip of the multinational corporation on national and global economies able, if not necessarily predisposed, to ride roughshod over democratic and community-based institutions.

If the 'flexible specialisation' thesis has received a critical hammering, this pales into insignificance compared to the battering of the flexible firm model. Good summaries of the criticisms may be found in Thompson and McHugh (1991, pp. 215–17) and Wood (1989, pp. 4–9), but the real vitriol resides in the writings of Pollert (1988a, 1988b, 1991). The criticisms focus on three issues: sloppiness in conceptual specification; lack of unequivocal empirical support for the model as description; the covert ideological agenda embodied in the model as prescription.

Conceptual specification

A host of problems surrounds the identification of what exactly is 'core' and what is 'periphery'. First, it is apparent that the concepts of 'core' and 'periphery' can be and, indeed, *are* interpreted by managers in different ways: as the nature of the employment contract, the conditions of service associated with it, the status of the job or the workers performing it, and as whether the tasks comprising a job were a main activity of the workplace or ancillary to it (Hunter *et al.*, 1993, p. 398). This gives rise to a series of difficulties. The identification of what is 'core' can easily become circular: core workers have secure employment, and the existence of such employment is used as evidence for the presence of a core (Pollert, 1987). If, to overcome this problem, the core is defined in terms of both employment status and tasks, further difficulties emerge. Some groups may have relatively secure employment (e.g., university messengers) but not be regarded as a core part of the organisation; others, identified as peripheral (e.g., part-time and casual women employees in retailing, mail-order and hotel and catering trades) may be central to its functioning (Wood, 1989b, p. 5; Walsh, 1991; Wong, 1993).[3] If, instead, functional flexibility is considered to be the defining characteristic of the core, it implies that part-time workers, subcontracted labour, and distance workers are all involved in narrow specialist tasks, which is not necessarily true. Consider, for example, the work of a junior school supply teacher. Indeed, as Hyman (1991, pp. 259–60) points out, it is simplistic to equate core = skilled = flexible, periphery = unskilled = inflexible, particularly in the light of intensified market competition that encourages strategies of financial flexibility using numerical flexibility as a tactic. Hence Whittington (1991), using case studies of R & D professionals, shows how a group which conventionally might be considered 'core' has experienced fragmentation of employment, as large firms are increasingly managing R & D through market mechanisms (involving competitive contracting, decentralised internal profit centres) rather than by bureaucratic control. Finally, there is the problem of dual status (Wood, 1989b, p. 6). A worker might simultaneously be defined as part of the 'core' or 'periphery' depending on the point of reference. She may work as part of the core of a specialist consultancy firm, but count as part of the periphery of a large flexible firm that is utilising her subcontracted services.

This lack of clarity about the empirical referents of the terms 'core' and 'periphery' can cause confusion in both testing the model and evaluating empirical studies of it. But a further confusion exists when attempting to separate out the descriptive and prescriptive dimensions of the model. The 'flexible firm' model at one level represents an ideal type of what the Institute of Manpower Studies (IMS) considers to be an appropriate employment strategy, in pursuit of 'the bottom line', in conditions of environmental uncertainty. It is a *strategy* for managing in a cost-effective manner the organisation's internal and external labour markets. At another level, it claims to describe employment *practices* that are on-going in firms. These rather different perspectives on the model point to two different research questions. If the model is seen as a strategy to aspire to, what evidence do we have to suggest that managers are consciously and systematically *changing* employment practices in order, as a matter of *strategy*, to enhance the three forms of flexibility identified in the model? Of course, this again raises the issue considered in Chapter 4 as to how we conceptualise 'strategy' (Procter *et al.*, 1994). If, on the other hand, the model is seen as a description of on-going employment practices, is it offering anything more than a recognition of labour market segmentation, which is hardly a new idea or practice (see, for example, Doeringer and Piore, 1971)? If there is evidence that the employment practices identified in Atkinson's model exist in UK organisations, does this represent the continuity of traditional labour market segmentation or a strategy in pursuit of the HRM ideal?

The evidence

What is going on out there? The evidence we have derives from two sources: surveys (in particular WIRS 1, 2 and 3, the first and second Warwick Company Level surveys, that of ACAS, the Employers' Labour Use Strategies survey (ELUS), the Labour Force survey (LFS), the Labour Research Department survey (LRD), and the IMS panel study of large firms[4] and case studies). By their nature surveys tend to reveal continuity, while case studies highlight change (Legge, 1988; Morris and Wood, 1991). In summary the evidence would broadly point to the following:

1. That while there is some increase in the use of *numerical* flexibility, this is often building on practices of long-standing and, with the arguable exception of the public sector, is undertaken pragmatically and opportunistically, rather than as part of a coherent strategy of adopting the flexible firm ideal type.
2. Such *functional* flexibility as has occurred is a modest and incremental change towards job enlargement and overlapping job descriptions and functions, but with little multiskilling.

3. Some *financial* flexibility is logically inherent in the adoption of numerical flexibility. However, insofar as financial flexibility is additionally associated with the adoption of performance-related pay [PRP], there is little evidence of its cost effectiveness. Rather, it appears as an instrument and symbolic of attempts to generate an entrepreneurial, market oriented culture and to signal disapprobation of collectivist and bureaucratic values.
4. Nevertheless, flexibility is now part of management's *rhetoric* and has become a catch-all label to describe on-going efforts to optimise labour utilisation, both qualitatively and quantitatively, in pursuit of competitive advantage.

The evidence for these assertions is as follows:

Numerical flexibility

Leaving aside, for simplicity, the problems of conceptual specification, let us accept Atkinson and Meager's (1986) identification of part timers, those employed on fixed-term contracts, temporary labour from private agencies, freelancers and outworkers as 'peripheral'. What evidence is there for their increased and strategic use in the interests of numerical flexibility?

Data from the Labour Force Survey (LFS) 1981–8 would suggest a relatively modest increase in the use of non-full-time employees over this period, rising from 30 per cent of those in employment in 1981 to 36 per cent 1988 (see Hakim, 1990, Table 1; Casey, 1991, Table 10 6). But the largest share of this growth is represented by an upsurge in the numbers of the self-employed, who are likely to be labour only subcontractors (Hakim, 1988) or as Rainbird (1991, p. 214) puts it 'disguised ... and self-exploiting ... wage labour'. Further, while there has been a substantial but steadier growth in part-time work, there has been almost no significant growth in temporary work. This growth in 'non-standard' employment, both relatively and absolutely, is greater for men than for women, with one-fifth explicable in terms of changes in the industrial structure. The smaller amount of change for women appears to be directly attributable to changes in employment practice, most notably in the public sector, with changes in manufacturing being smaller (Marginson, 1991; Casey, 1991). Furthermore, Casey's (1991) analysis of LFS data would suggest that only minorities of part-time and temporary workers were 'involuntary' in the sense that they were unable to find full-time jobs.

Evidence from the Employers' Labour Use Strategies survey, covering the period 1983–7, points in the same direction. The percentage of non-standard labour in the workforces of ELUS firms grew by around 2.5 percentage points over the four years, most of this growth, in contrast to the LFS survey, being accounted for by increasing use of temporary, agency-temporary and self-employed labour. However, upwards of 25 per cent of employers reported that non-standard labour formed a larger part of their labour force compared with 1983. This was consistently well above the percentages reporting a relative decline in use. The increases were similar across regions, industries and establishment sizes and between public and private sectors. As Hunter *et al.* (1993, p. 389) comment, 'these findings indicate that non-standard labour was indeed becoming more important during the 1989s, although in quantitative terms the changes could not be described as dramatic'.

The results from the most comprehensive and systematic of surveys, WIRS 1, 2 and 3 series (comparing 1980, 1984 and 1990) similarly reveal little evidence for any large-scale increase in the flexible forms of working they examined (part-time, fixed-term contract, freelance and homeworkers). Insofar as a trend may be detected it is of stable or declining figures for non-standard employment in private manufacturing and services, but with a rise in the public sector. Thus while WIRS 2 found that the same percentage of workplaces (19 per cent) reported some use of employees on short fixed-term contracts in 1984 as in 1980, this had risen to 22 per cent in 1990. This rise disguises a drop of 2 per cent in private manufacturing and a rise of 10 per cent in the public sector. Again, the proportion of managers who reported using freelance workers, declined from 22 per cent in 1980 to 14 per cent in 1984, but rose to 16 per cent in 1990. This disguises small falls in private manufacturing and services, but a rise of 4 per cent in the public sector. The figures for homeworkers/outworkers declined between 1980 and 1984, but then remained virtually stable in 1990. In contrast, the WIRS surveys have shown a slow but steady rise in part-time working, rising from 14 per cent of workplaces in 1980, 16 per cent in 1984 to 18 per cent in 1990. This is consistent with LFS survey results, if not with those of ELUS. This growth reflects the use of increasing proportions of part-time workers in the public sector and the growth in the number of workplaces in the private services sector. Notably, though, WIRS 3 found a reported increase in subcontracting in the second half of the 1980s (no data from earlier surveys), particularly in the most highly unionised parts of the public sector (Millward *et al.*, 1992, Chapter 9). In summary, then, such increases in non-standard employment that the WIRS surveys record over the decade, while relatively modest, seem to reflect changes in industrial structure and government policy *vis à vis* the public sector.

The first Warwick Company Level survey, conducted in mid-1985, focused on head office policy towards, and establishment use of, temporary contracts, outworking and subcontracting. Just over half the establishments reported employing temporary workers and less than half this number reported an increase in its usage (i.e., around a fifth of the sample). Much use of temporary staff appears to focus on traditional activities e.g., seasonal work, holiday cover, secretarial 'temps' and so on. Only a minority of head office managers (32 per cent) claimed that changes in policy towards the use of temporary contracts over the past five years had led to an increase in their usage (Marginson *et al.*, 1988, p. 12). Similarly, Atkinson and Meager's (1986) NEDO study found that 38 per cent of their companies claimed to have increased their use of temporary work since 1989

(Marginson, 1991, p. 36). The ACAS (1988) survey reported that 59 per cent of their establishments employed temporary workers, of which 24 per cent reported increasing their use of temporary workers over the previous three years. Nevertheless, 35 per cent had either decreased their use of temporary staff or experienced no change as compared to three years previously.

Geary's (1992) case study data of three electronics factories throws some interesting light on these equivocal and sometimes contradictory survey data. In all of his case study companies management's preferred strategy was to minimise its dependence on temporary employees whenever possible, using them in the traditional fashion to meet production peaks and as a buffer against changes in demand. The perceived advantages of employing temporaries was less due to lower wage and non-wage costs then being able to adjust manning levels to workloads without incurring major severance costs. But in one case, Astra, where the proportion of temporaries had reached 70 per cent, due not just to market volatility, but to severe manpower restrictions placed on the plant by the US corporate headquarters, local management saw this as a positive disadvantage, First, it led to animosity between temporaries and permanent employees, which impacted negatively on the sought-for teamwork. Secondly, such conflicts as arose required time-consuming intervention from supervision, taking them away from more productive tasks. Thirdly, there was concern among line managers that unsuitable candidates were recruited, resulting in loss of product quality. Management was concerned too that temporaries were inhibited from 'speaking out' in suggesting improvements to the production process, or in wishing to rotate between tasks, or in expressing dissatisfactions, believing that it ruined their chances of gaining permanency. There was the further problem that many managers felt the use of temporary status as 'a crude control device' (Geary, 1992, p. 260) facilitating labour intensification, was inconsistent with an espoused policy of equal and consistent treatment of all employees. In essence, as Geary (1992, pp. 267–8) points out, a policy of large-scale employment of temporaries by creating a new status divide, resulted in a new rigidity rather than flexibility. As a result 'when management themselves came to see employment flexibility as a rigidity, when it was defined as dysfunctional to their interests, they sought to establish more *rigid* and *stable* forms of employment'

Hunter *et al.*'s (1993, p. 398) analysis of their own case study data chimes with Geary's conclusion. They similarly found that in some cases employers' initial decisions to seek numerical flexibility were being questioned or reversed, due to the costs incurred by absenteeism, lack of commitment and loyalty and a loss of quality. 'In other words, when the full productivity implications were taken into account, the *prima facie* attraction of cheaper labour mixes often disappeared.'

Evidence for increases in subcontracting, at first sight look more impressive. For example, the first Warwick Company Level 1985 survey reports that, of the 83 per cent of establishment-level respondents who engaged in subcontracting, 37 per cent reported an increase in its use over the last five years (i.e., 1980–5). Furthermore, 56 per cent of head office managers reported a change, the majority of whom said it led to increased subcontracting. Atkinson and Meager (1986, p. 28) found that seven out of ten of their respondents had increased their use of distancing since 1980. Of these, 90 per cent had increased their use of subcontracted ancillary services and 51 per cent their use of non-ancillary services. Similarly MacKay's study (1987, Table III, p. 4) found that just over 30 per cent of her interviewees report an increase, present or impending, in the use of subcontracting.

However these figures should be kept in perspective. The other side of the coin is that 60 per cent of the Warwick Company Level survey (1985) establishment-level respondents and, by implication almost half of the head office managers, reported no change over the last five years in their subcontracting practices, while of MacKay's interviewees, if almost 70 per cent reported an increase in their use over the previous three years, 46 per cent reported a decline in the use of subcontractors, or no change. While Atkinson and Meager's figures appear unequivocal, it should be borne in mind that their samples were small (72 and 31 firms), not statistically representative (see n. 4) and, in the case of the smaller sample, the firms were selected 'because they were known to have introduced changes to work organisation specifically to promote greater flexibility, or because they represented clear examples of flexibility already achieved' (Atkinson and Meager, 1986, p. 4).

Taking these data together, it cannot be emphasised too strongly that, due to selective bias in several of the surveys (notably in Atkinson and Meager, LRD, ACAS and ELUS) and differences in timing and sectoral coverage, great care needs to be taken in their interpretation. In particular, Marginson (1991, pp. 40–1) shows how, in the Atkinson and Meager and in the ACAS surveys, data are reported in such a way (e.g., by filtering out the companies which have not sought to increase numerical flexibility; by conflating levels of use with degree of change) as to highlight change at the expense of continuity. Furthermore an erroneous impression of massive increases in non-standard employment may owe something to the fact that such non-standard workers as exist may be non-standard on more than one count (i.e., they may be both temporary and part-time, or part-time and self-employed), while the fastest growth that has occurred has been among very small (no more than eight hours per week) part-time jobs (Casey, 1991). That said, a consensus of opinion (see, for example Marginson, 1991; Casey, 1991; Hyman, 1991), in the light of the survey data, seems to be that while changes in the direction of enhanced numerical flexibility *have* taken place, particularly in the service sector, these have not been dramatic and often represent a development of traditional practice.

Thus, in the ELUS survey employers were asked to select from lengthy lists the reasons for employing each form of non-standard labour. These responses were often classified as traditional (e.g., demands for short-term cover), supply-side (reflecting preferences of employees or potential recruits) or new (e.g., due to uncertainties surrounding compulsory competitive tendering exercises in the public sector) (see McGregor and Sproull, 1992; Hunter *et al.*, 1993). *Traditional reasons dominated for each type of labour considered* (part-timers, temporaries, agency temporaries and the self-employed), although supply-side explanations were quite important for employers of part-time and self-employed labour. New rationales were most frequently cited in relation to temporary workers and the self-employed, but were reported in only 3 per cent of the part-timers (Hunter *et al.*, 1993, Table 1). However, when reasons for the *increased employment* of non-standard labour were explored, the new rationales were more frequently reported (Hunter *et al.*, 1993, Table 3).

The question then arises as to whether the use of non-standard labour is part of a deliberate manpower strategy to implement some approximation of the flexible firm model. And here we have the problem, discussed in Chapter 4, of what approach to the conceptualisation of strategy it might be appropriate to adopt. In the ELUS survey the questions about whether manpower decisions were guided 'by some sort of manpower strategy or plan' and whether 'this manpower strategy view(s) the workforce as divided into a central core and an outer periphery of workers' implicitly assume a classical, rationalistic approach to strategy formation. The case study work conducted by Hunter *et al.* (1993, p. 386) took an equally rationalistic view of what constituted a manpower strategy, requiring evidence of a statement of objectives relating to manpower utilisation in the medium or longer term, based on some kind of analysis or appreciation of differential costs of alternative labour contract mixes; awareness of the relation between these objectives and other practices such as selection, recruitment and training, so that they should be mutually reinforcing; and some association of manpower objectives with overall business and/or corporate strategies.

A criticism of this approach, as we saw in Chapter 4, is that strategy making in real life rarely conforms to this rationalistic model. However, if for the moment we accept this conceptualisation of strategy, a consensus emerges that among employers it is the exception rather than the rule. Hakim (1990) in her analysis of the ELUS data, found that not only could just a minority (35 per cent) be classified as 'strategists' in relation to manpower planning, but of these, only a third could be classified as 'core–periphery' strategists. Indeed, she additionally found examples of 'anti core–periphery strategy', in which priority was given to maintaining the jobs in the core workforce and eliminating or minimising the periphery (cf. Geary, 1992). Hunter *et al.* (1993, p. 396) confirm these results, concluding that approximately a ninth of ELUS respondents 'could be seen to fit loosely the flexible firm model', but that even this estimate was probably too high given sampling biases. In relation to their case study data, they found no evidence of formal statements of organisational policy on manpower utilisation and little evidence of a strong linkage between labour use objectives and related personnel practices in recruitment, training and remuneration. The main explanation for the use of non-standard contracts throughout the case studies was the presence of 'immediate business needs' in the private sector and of spending constraints and compulsory competitive tendering requirements in the public service sector. Hunter *et al.* (1993, pp. 397–8) concluded

> Manpower measures were operated on a much shorter time scale than the business planning process, so that there was a lack of harmony and integration between them … The overriding impression was one of *ad hoc* measures to keep the business viable in the face of greater competitive pressure, to meet temporary needs, or (in the case of multi-establishment organisations) to satisfy divisional head offices; while in the public sector the drive came from cash-limited budgets and imperatives from above requiring either compulsory tendering or strict adherence to a manpower head count.

This view is supported by evidence from the first Warwick Company Level survey and ELUS, that moves towards greater numerical flexibility are *mainly* piecemeal, opportunistic and *ad hoc* rather than as a result of strategic intent. The first Warwick Company Level 1985 survey at first sight would suggest the possibility of a coherent strategy in that the changes appear to be originating at head office. 40 per cent of corporate-level managers claimed that policy had changed towards the employment of temporary staff and 58 per cent that it had changed towards the use of outworking and subcontracting. However responses from establishment level suggest a gap between espoused policy and what is enacted at plant level. Of the establishments reporting increased use of temporary contracts, only 14 per cent claimed that this was as a result of a policy decision taken at a higher level. Most claimed that it was a result of local initiative. Again with subcontracting, of those establishments reporting a change in its usage, 39 per cent said that it was as a result of a policy decision at a higher level, whereas 60 per cent said that it resulted from local initiative.

Turning to the second Warwick Company Level 1992 survey on each of five areas (securing task flexibility, use of temporary workers and fixed-term contracts, subcontracting, working time flexibility and use of part-time workers) around two-thirds of companies had no company-wide policy. Where there was a policy, between a quarter and a third of cases had a policy on one issue but not on another. Marginson *et al.* (1993, p. 49) suggest that this overall lack of tight connections is consistent with the view that firms tend not to have a considered policy on flexibility for, if they did, policy on one area would be tightly tied to that on others. They conclude

> Though these data cannot be compared exactly with the 1985 survey, they point in the same direction. Policies on labour flexibility seem to be rather rare, and to be spread rather randomly across companies. (p. 49)

They add that their findings as a whole are 'consistent with the now familiar argument that firms rarely have developed coherent policies for seeking labour flexibility, tending instead to respond to particular contingencies and/or to rely on specific opportunities as they arise' (p. 49).

However, there is one major exception to this line of argument. All the data cited above point to the fact that the one sector in which the core–periphery model undoubtedly has been strategically enacted is in the public sector services, primarily through the use of subcontracting via competitive tendering and contracting out. Here, the Conservative Government as legislator and paymaster has the power and the will to translate espoused policy into action to an extent unfeasible among private sector organisations. Rather than such policies being opportunistic and pragmatic they comprise part of a coherent strategy promoting the primacy of the free market, buttressed by a rhetoric advocating reductions in public expenditure, the introduction of 'business principles' into the management of public sector services, in the interests of efficiency and effectiveness for the client as customer and tax payer (Kelly, 1991).

Functional flexibility

Much of the survey and case study evidence relating to functional flexibility has been summarised by Elger (1991), while excellent recent case study evidence, placed in the context of broader HRM initiatives, may be found in Storey (1992b), Newell (1991), Hendry (1993), Clark (1993) and Preece (1993).

Elger (1991) focusing on UK manufacturing industry draws some interesting conclusions from a range of survey data – the IMS panel study of large firms, WIRS 1 and 2, ACAS, LRD and Cross' survey of largely process industries (NEDO, 1986; Daniel, 1987; ACAS, 1988; LRD, 1986; Cross, 1988) – and from case studies that largely, but not exclusively, focus on the motor industry (Holloway, 1987; Starkey and McKinlay, 1989; Marsden et al., 1985; Smith, 1988; Garrahan and Stewart, 1992, c.f. Jones and Rose, 1986; Terry, 1989). While recognising the non-representativeness of the ACAS, LRD and Cross surveys, the 'particularities' of the case study material, and 'the heterogeneity of change and restructuring, with significant regional, sectoral, occupational and gendered variations' (Elger, 1991, p. 63), nevertheless some conclusions emerge that are not inconsistent with the later case study data of Storey (1992b), Newell (1991), Hendry (1993), Clark (1993) and Preece (1993).

First, while there is plenty of evidence to suggest a fairly widespread movement towards enhanced task flexibility, the degree of flexibility both sought for, and achieved, in the vast majority of cases appears more modest than celebratory accounts of multiskilled teamworking or craft-based flexible specialisation might imply. Elger's (1991, p. 51) analysis of the IMS data, for example, indicated that 'the extent of the change appeared largely determined by managerial juggling of technical, organisational and training cost considerations', and the emphasis on flexibility was qualified by managerial awareness of the continuing advantages of retaining specialist skills. Storey (1992b, p. 91) on the basis of his case study research, comes to the same conclusion:

> Management may expressly want a limited number of experienced workers to remain dedicated to a particular task – swapping and changing round would be regarded as wasteful and even dangerous. Similarly the costs of achieving flexibility – whether incurred through training or through extra payment for skill attainment – may also deter.

Second, as a result, many managers' objectives were relatively modest. Elger (1991) cites such concerns as the reduction of 'porosity' and the intensification of effort, as much by cutting down pauses and waiting time as by increasing the pace of work directly.

Third, the intent of the changes, as a result, has rarely involved radical skill enhancement. More characteristic is the achievement of limited craft overlap, sometimes requiring retraining, or the small enlargement of a craftsman's job, but without 'violation of any group's "core trade"' (NEDO, 1986, p. 45, cited by Elger, 1991, p. 50). Sometimes attempted moves towards the supercraftsman or the spanning of core-trade boundaries have come unstuck through union resistance (see, for example, Storey's (1992b, p. 87) account of the problems in achieving mechanical-electrical/electronic teams of maintenance engineers at Birds Eye Walls). Sometimes crossover between electrical and mechanical skills is seen as not attainable, for technical reasons, other than at the margins, although flexibility between mechanical craftsmen may be sought, as at Ford at Dagenham and Halewood (Storey, 1992b, pp. 91–5). Where multi-trade working for craftsmen is sought (as at Peugeot–Talbot) it may be for only a small élite, 'the brighter of the toolmakers', management not requiring more extensive upskilling, nor wanting to pay for it (Storey, 1992b, p. 96).

Widespread change, but of a job enlargement rather than a job enrichment nature, has taken place for semi-skilled operatives, particularly in the motor industries. Typically, this has involved some relaxation and reorganisation of job boundaries among operatives, involving inspection and routine maintenance, often capitalising upon the self-diagnostic capabilities of modern equipment.

Fourth, the extent of the flexibilities sought and achieved depends much on prior technological choices and decisions about investment, head count and labour costs. Thus while Plessey Naval Systems 'Flexibility Agreement' with the (then) EEPTU contains the rhetoric of total flexibility, in practice this pointed more to the use of managerial prerogative over labour deployment in a Tayloristic work system, for, as Storey (1992b, p. 90) suggests 'as the bulk of the work was becoming more standardised and deskilled the implied necessity for skill enhancement proved to be somewhat illusory'. Similarly Peugeot–Talbot's requirement for multiskilled 'A+ grade' craftsmen was seen to vary across plants depending on technological investment and sophistication (Storey, 1992b, p. 96). In contrast, much functional flexibility via job enlargement and labour intensification, coupled with management effort to enhance its control over resulting flexibilities, has occurred almost by the back door as reductions in headcount as part of cost cutting exercises have resulted in smaller numbers of employees covering an unchanged – or enhanced – set of production requirements. Flexibilities achieved informally by headcount reductions may subsequently be formalised as concessions are bargained from employees eager to attract investment as a guarantee against potential plant closure.

The qualificatory messages of the research cited above is underlined by recent case studies of greenfield sites. It is a commonplace that if 'soft' HRM initiatives are to be found anywhere in a form resembling the ideal-type models, it is on exemplar greenfield sites (Guest, 1987). Yet the evidence would suggest that even here functional flexibility is limited for very practical if pragmatic reasons. At Pirelli's greenfield site at Aberdare, Clark (1993) found that in spite of a negotiated agreement that all non-management staff could be deployed totally flexibly between tasks and different areas of the factory (within the constraints of their level of training) in practice full flexibility was neither achieved nor sought. Furthermore, by mid-1990 there was some contractual retreat from the notion of full flexibility, by agreement to 'cap' the number of skill modules an employee could undertake and by prescribing 'primary' and 'secondary' areas of responsibility.

Clark points out that there were six reasons for the abandonment of full functional flexibility. First, there was a recognition of the 'horses for courses' principle – that many employees were more suited to, and interested in, some areas of work than others. Second, was the importance of specialist knowledge (identified earlier by both Elger and Storey), and the company's recognition of its importance in enabling staff to produce consistently good quality work or, as in sales, maintaining a personal relationship with industrial customers. Third, there was strong management and employee interest in the latter's 'ownership' of particular work areas, with the greater possibility of commitment to, and achievement of, high quality work. The fourth reason related to both the cost and availability of training. Total flexibility involved very high levels of both direct and indirect training costs. The direct costs lay in the sheer volume of training potentially to be provided if there was no formal limit on the number of skill modules that an employee might achieve in the interests of full flexibility. The indirect costs lay in the linking of non-consolidated payments to the achievement of skill modules. Added to this was the problem of availability of suitably qualified and experienced trainers to up-grade existing employees' skill at a time when a priority was the provision of training for newly recruited staff. The fifth reason was skill retention, as experience showed that skills were often forgotten if there was too great a gap between skill acquisition, putting them into practice, and regularly reinforcing them by practice. Finally, and somewhat paradoxically, flexibility was limited by the comparatively tight staffing levels in the new factory. Clark (1993) points out that tight staffing levels had two contradictory effects on the possibilities for flexibility. On the one hand, particularly in maintenance, tight staffing levels led to an enhancement of required flexibility between fitters and electricians and in their deployment in different areas of manufacturing. In contrast administrators achieved very little flexibility as the tightness of the staffing levels, *combined* with the distinctiveness of most of the jobs (cf. wages clerk, export sales, personnel assistant) inhibited the take-up of the necessary training. Staff could simply not be 'spared' for training in a different unrelated task.

Newell's (1991) findings at 'Brewco' and 'Grimco'[5] point also to the limitations in the amount of flexibility sought and achieved. At 'Brewco' management did not seek flexibility between the eight manufacturing units, only job enlargement within each unit. At 'Grimco' process operators undertook minor engineering work, or assisted a multiskilled tradesman with more major engineering work, while such tradesmen assisted operators to run the line as required. However, the feasibility of process operators undertaking engineering tasks, in an environment where post-commissioning training was perceived as inadequate, was called into question by an error in valve replacement that resulted in an explosion that halted the process for three days. Experience of functional flexibility, even on a greenfield site, can result in ambitious plans being tailored to the practicalities of operational constraints. Garrahan and Stewart's (1992) study of Nissan's greenfield site at Sunderland suggests that the much vaunted common grading and teamworking in practice involved only limited flexibility, focused primarily on switching among related work routines within the team. Instead, they argue, productivity is mobilised through stress via reduction in buffer stocks, the elimination of off-line inspection and rectification, and the maximisation of line speeds, underpinned by 'a compelling ethos of competitive team working' (Elger, 1991, p. 62).

Even if the degree of functional flexibility sought and achieved is more modest than celebratory accounts and messianic 'flexible specialisation' manifestos might imply, its importance should not be underestimated. First, the resulting job enlargement and labour intensification does indicate management's enhanced control over the labour process. Survey evidence of the 1980s (see Legge, 1988) consistently points to increased labour intensification, as does the Percentage Utilisation of Labour Index (Bennett and Smith-Gavine, 1988a, 1988b) (see also, Guest, 1990a). Second, as Clark (1993) points out, where enhanced flexibility has been sought if not fully achieved, or modified in the light of experience, the rhetoric surrounding it, combined with other initiatives (such as single status, single-unionism, more selective recruitment, enhanced commitment to training and communications) can have a climate-changing effect. Particularly on greenfield sites, employees may increasingly 'take-it-for-granted' that, within the limitations of their training and capabilities, they will be as flexible as operations require (see also Newell's discussion of the 'Grimco' case). Many small changes 'at the margin' may nevertheless add up to substantially increased managerial control over the workforce and, in conditions of high levels of unemployment, a workforce prepared to show behavioural compliance – and possibly commitment – to such changes.

Significantly though, while models of numerical flexibility appear to underwrite existing gender divisions of labour (which in one sense inhibit flexibility), those of functional flexibility as applied in practice appear to have done little to break down this form of demarcation.

Financial flexibility

Given that numerical flexibility refers to a firm's capacity to adjust labour inputs to fluctuations in output, it is logically a form of financial flexibility in that organisations are treating labour as a variable rather than a fixed cost. That said, although non-standard labour, generally speaking, is more likely to be employed in low wage sectors of the economy (e.g., private services), according to Hunter et al. research (1993, p. 395) there is little evidence within firms of differential payments for workers on non-standard contracts compared to corresponding standard contract employees. Issues of fairness and the motivational impact of differential remuneration for the same job appeared more important to respondents than achieving such complete financial flexibility. Nevertheless, subcontracting ancillary operations (such as security and catering) or competitive tendering operations in the public sector often allowed employers to take advantage of differentials between minimum rates in the industry that was the main business of the workplace and rates in the [low pay] security, catering or cleaning industries. While it could have been perceived as unfair simply to reduce the pay of direct employees to reflect external market rates, it was possible to achieve a similar result by changing the boundaries of the employment to exclude these workers (p. 395). However, even here, there were limits to this process, due to concerns about loss of control over work done by subcontractors and deterioration in the quality of the labour supplied.

Turning to performance-related pay [PRP] many of the problematic issues that surround its introduction and relevance to achieving financial flexibility have been admirably summarised by Kessler (see, in particular, Kessler and Purcell, 1992; Kessler, 1994).

Kessler (1994) identifies three types of performance-related pay: individual merit and performance-related systems based on some form of appraisal of the individual using various inputs (traits, skills, 'behavioural characteristics', such as coopera- tiveness) or output (objectives achieved) indicators; individual bonuses (e.g., piecework, sales commission) and collective bonuses (e.g., gain-share schemes). The evidence is that, first, over the 1980s and early 1990s, there has been a substantial growth in individual performance and merit-based schemes (Long, 1986; Cannell and Long, 1991; Cannell and Wood, 1992; Casey et al., 1991; Millward et al., 1992; Marginson et al., 1993; Kessler, 1990). Secondly, the concentration of these schemes is among non-manual rather than manual employees. Thirdly, these schemes are now quite widely dispersed throughout managerial and white-collar hierarchies and across a range of sectors. Fourthly, apart from appraisal-based systems linked to skills acquisition there appears to be a *declining* interest in individual bonuses for manual workers (see Kessler, 1994, pp. 469–73). Hence there appears to be something of a contradiction here. While, according to the theory, we might expect *peripheral* workers to be most associated with schemes treating labour as a variable cost, in practice, as far as PRP goes, it appears that it is the *core* workers that are more involved. (This, of course, may reflect the fact that financial flexibility among the 'periphery' is more readily achieved by use of non-standard contracts. That is, flexibility is already achieved through economies in hourly labour cost.)

It is difficult to assess the contribution that PRP makes directly to financial flexibility as there has been very little academic research or company evaluation of its effectiveness in achieving traditional payment system objectives (i.e., recruitment, retention, motivation and equity) let alone those associated with the values of the enterprise culture (National Research Council, 1991; Thompson, 1992 – both cited in Kessler, 1994). In theory, PRP is meant to achieve some direct financial flexibility through 'targeting and directing pay to "those who deserve it" and in this respect ... providing better "value for money" than inflexible across the board increases related to the cost of living or service' (Kessler, 1994, p. 481). As Kessler points out, though, the effects might be the reverse to those intended, if additional merit elements supplement the continued provision of general cost of living increases, not to mention added costs of administration. But there is evidence that it has also been used symbolically to signal a range of desired organisational changes. These include developing a market oriented, entrepreneurial, individualistic culture, whether on greenfield sites or to replace the 'corporate paternalism and bureaucratic centralism' of lately privatised industries or remaining public sector services (see Chapters 6 and 7); to weaken the influence of trade unions and undermine collective bargaining as the primary means of pay determination; to revitalise and strengthen the role of the line manager and to enhance employee commitment to the organisation (Kessler, 1994, pp. 478–81; see also Batstone *et al.*, 1984; Wickens, 1987; Petch, 1990; Storey, 1992b).

The extent to which these change oriented objectives are achieved is open to question – particularly if employee cynicism results due to problems of implementation. Kessler lists a range of potential problems associated with the establishment of performance criteria, the assessment of whether those criteria have been met, and the linkage between assessment and pay award (Kessler and Purcell, 1992; Kessler, 1994, pp. 484–90; see also Meyer, 1987; Marsden and Richardson, 1994).

Consider the establishment of performance criteria. First, quantifiable criteria are difficult to set where there is no tangible end product and where a range of stakeholders may have different views about which criteria are appropriate (as in the public sector services, for example). Similarly it is difficult to identify valid performance criteria where the work is highly speculative and uncertain in terms of outputs (e.g., R & D) or, on the other hand, where it provides little scope for on-going variation and performance improvement (e.g., routine clerical work). Kessler (1994, p. 485) notes that in the latter circumstances, the criteria selected are often behavioural traits (introducing the problem of subjectivity in assessment) rather than objectives or tasks. Second, focusing on individual performance goals may run counter to attempts at developing teamwork; but setting group goals raises the problem of the free-loader. Third, if employees focus on those aspects of the job where performance is measured, other aspects may be neglected, as well as the exercise of initiative and flexibility being inhibited.

Turning to performance assessment. Kessler suggests it is prey to the twin vices of subjectivity and inconsistency. First, given rates of change, performance criteria, particularly those related to tasks and targets may be undermined and require revision. Judgement has to be exercised about whether, and how, objectives should be revised. Second, not only is the appraisal process itself inherently subjective, but subjectivity and inconsistency can be compounded in situations where appraisal is used for different ends (e.g., management development, pay awards and promotion). Third, the social and political realities of organisations often make it easier for a manager not to rank subordinates harshly – or on the other hand to rank the inadequate highly (to remove them via promotion) and the competent as below average (in order to prevent promotion out of the department). Further, if subordinates are ranked on a normal distribution, those found 'satisfactory' may be demoralised, if they considered their performance was above average or even outstanding. Finally, appraisal, if taken seriously, is very time consuming and many managers are reluctant to devote the required time to it – particularly if this activity is not prioritised in their own appraisals (see Chapter 7).

Kessler (1994, pp. 488–90) further points out that the link between performance and pay may become distorted. First, the nature of the link may be unclear to recipients. Second, due to financial constraints, the amount of the performance-related pay, particularly if underpinned by a cost of living increase, may be small. If so, not only may it have little incentive effect, but may actually demotivate, if significantly out of line with raised expectations. Further, the potential demotivat-ing effect may be exacerbated if the limited money available inhibits managers in differentiating sharply in pay terms between average and outstanding performers.

In the light of all these difficulties it is highly questionable whether, in accountancy terms, performance-related pay contributes much to financial flexibility. As discussed in Chapter 4, it is ironic, given senior management's present apparent enthusiasm for PRP, that their own recent massive pay rises appear only weakly, if at all, associated with company performance and that declining corporate performance is very rarely associated with pay cuts for directors – an acid test for true financial flexibility! Nevertheless, the symbolic value of PRP as part of a cultural change programme, signalling a move away from bureaucratic to market oriented values, cannot be discounted (see Chapter 6 and 7).

Conclusions: the ideological agenda of flexibility and HRM

Several broad conclusions emerge from the preceding analysis of the themes and empirical evidence for the 'flexible specialisation' and the 'flexible firm' models.

1. The concept of flexibility is poorly specified and conflates very different changes in work organisation, such as multiskilling, job enlargement, cost controls and labour intensification (Pollert, 1991, p. 3). Poor conceptual specification muddies the waters of rigorous empirical testing.
2. Even in the light of 1, empirical evidence in support of flexible specialisation, in particular, and post-Fordism, in general, is inconsistent and fragmentary.
3. With the arguable exception of the public service sector, there is little evidence to support the strategic use of core–periphery strategies by employers in the UK, if a rationalistic view of strategy is adopted. Such increases in numerical flexibility that have occurred over the last decade and a half (mainly in the increase of part-time working and sub-contracting) appear to have been pragmatic and opportunistic following traditional labour segmentation practices. Even Atkinson, father of the flexible firm model, admitted that 'although the observed changes were widespread, they did not cut very deeply in most firms, and the outcome was more likely to be marginal, *ad hoc* and tentative rather than a purposeful and strategic thrust to achieve flexibility' (Atkinson and Meager, 1986, p. 29).
4. While there is evidence that employers, particularly in manufacturing, are seeking enhanced flexibility from their employees, this appears to be at the margins of craft skills rather than true multiskilling and to have involved job enlargement for semi-skilled employees rather than upskilling. There is evidence that the objective is increased management control over the deployment of labour and consequent labour intensification, with QWL outcomes secondary if not incidental.

That said, there has been a recent attempt to rescue the model of the flexible firm. Procter *et al.* (1994) argue that the research evidence that consistently points to employers' ventures into manpower flexibility as *ad hoc* and opportunistic, is derived from designs, or interpreted in a way that assumes strategy formation to be 'explicit', developed consciously and purposefully and made in advance of specific decisions to which it applies (Mintzberg, 1978, p. 935). In other words, strategy is conforming to the 'classical' model discussed in Chapter 4. Yet, as already seen, it is debatable whether this model *does* represent managerial behaviour in an uncertain and politicised environment. If, instead, strategy is seen from the perspective of the processual model, as a 'pattern in a stream of decisions' (Mintzberg, 1978, p. 935) is it possible to identify implicit manpower strategies adopted by employers, whether or not they conform with the flexible firm model? One problem with this approach, of course, as the rationalists might argue, is that any sets of decisions taken over a period of time can be regarded as reflecting strategy, but one has to wait (possibly for years) before one can say anything about its nature. Further, a strategy that is implicit and visible only after the event would be unlikely to systematically guide employer behaviour in the short term (Hunter *et al.*, 1993, p. 400).

If one views strategy as emergent and reflects on employer behaviour over the last fifteen years, two trends may be detected. First, in almost every sector of industry, in the context of recession, tough competitive conditions and government attempts to cut back public spending, not to mention the official watchdogs' controls on privatised industries, the strategy seems to be to downsize in the interests of cost control and financial viability. In conditions of recovery and growth employers' decision-making over types of contract appears more influenced by clear and stereotyped models of the behavioural characteristics of each type of worker, rather than detailed cost comparisons (Hunter *et al.*, 1993, p. 394). Thus

> Employers saw full-time permanent direct employees as easiest to manage, the most flexible to deploy across different tasks within the establishment, the most committed and the most likely to stay with the organisation. They became experienced and more effective workers and proved more rewarding to train where employers had bundles of tasks that could be made into a full-time permanent job. Temporary employees were seen as less committed and reliable than permanents, with commitment varying directly with the length of the contract. Agency temps were seen as the most problematic, invaluable in plugging emergency gaps but unlikely to have the loyalty to the firm or experience of its operation to become a more central part of its regular workforce. Part-time permanents were seen as more committed but offering less continuity across the working day or week, more difficult to manage, and less suitable for promotion or for use in positions of authority ... Employers thought that most men preferred full-time permanent work and were more likely to leave other jobs if such work became available. Conversely, they expected more women to be looking for part-time or temporary work because of domestic commitments and sometimes took this into account in the design of working hours (especially part-time temporary workers on twilight shifts). (Hunter *et al.*, 1993, p. 394)

Decisions about manpower contracts and usage then appear to rest on a weighing of the costs and benefits associated with each of these stereotypes in the light of immediate organisational requirements.

Nevertheless, a further question remains. If flexibility appears to be a generic label for very different practices, and these largely to reflect change at the margin rather than any radical restructuring of work, how do we account for the popularity of these debates among academics and, more importantly, why has 'flexibility' become such a fashionable buzz word for managers and embodied in HRM models?

As far as academics go it is easy to be cynical. The flexible specialisation debate provided a new focus for issues about industrial structure and work organisation at a time when the labour process debates stimulated by Braverman's (1974) *Labor and Monopoly Capital* were beginning to flag. It breathed new life into a dying corpse. Furthermore, for academics of a more managerialist position, the flexible firm model and its testing offered a research focus that looked practical, relevant, consistent with government economic policy and hence likely to attract funding. The very conceptual sloppiness of the concept allowed plenty of room for manoeuvre, to subsume under a flexibility banner whatever issues seemed to generate the most interest and potential pay-off. In an enterprise culture who can blame impecunious academics for flexing their own entrepreneurial muscles by starting up their own small businesses? This issue in relation to academics' hyping of HRM generally is considered further in Chapter 9.

Nevertheless I would concur with the critiques developed by Pollert (1991) and Hyman (1991) that the academic popularity of these debates stemmed from their empathy with the times. Pollert (1991) argues that the concept of flexibility resonates with the neo-classical revival and its assertion of the need to overturn rigidities that undermine the 'natural' workings of free markets. Furthermore she suggests that the flexibility debate can be located within the conservative tradition of industrial society theory, rejecting a conception of capitalism as a system of conflicting class relations and interests, emphasising instead a model of social integration and equilibrium. In other words:

> the concept has become the latest tool for a 'radical' break theory, in the tradition of previous post-industrial theories. The implication of a radical break from the past, in the preoccupation with newness and change and the absence of a [sic] historical perspective on the significance of work flexibility and labour market flexibility in previous periods, has consolidated a nostalgic picture of past stability and functional harmony, compared to present flux and uncertainty. At the same time, flexibility as a panacea of restructuring promises a new period of equilibrium and growth; the flexibility debate thus provides a discourse on a further stage of functional adjustment leading out of crisis. (Pollert, 1991, p. xx)

Hyman (1991), on a rather different tack, also presents a case for the functionality of the flexibility debates. Recalling Marx's characterisation of capitalist dynamism ('All that is solid melts into air') and the present context in national and international political and economic relations of a 'sustained phase of disturbance and disruption', he argues that flexibalisation derives its appeal not simply as a one-off process of removing entrenched rigidities, but 'as a means of adapting institutions and expectations to the certainty of uncertainty; of reforming Marx's original vision of capitalist dynamism' (Hyman, 1991, p. 282). To this effect he cites Streeck's (1987, p. 290) judgement:

> the particular experience of the 1980s seem to have given rise to a widely shared expectation that strong turbulences and uncertainties will become a permanent feature of economic life for the foreseeable future. This alone can explain why for many employers flexibility has turned from a capacity to master a limited set of concrete adjustment

problems into a value itself – a permanent property of economic organisations that is sought almost for its own sake in a situation in which adaptation seems to consist above all in increasing the general capacity to adapt.

The question remains, as Hyman points out, as to whose priorities will triumph in identifying and dismantling existing rigidities and in choosing to implant new sources of stability.

It is with this question in mind that we can look again at the relationship between the realities and rhetoric of flexibility and those embodied in the 'hard' and 'soft' models of HRM.

The rigidities that the 'hard' model of HRM addresses are those signified by standard forms of employment and traditional demarcations that inhibit the employer achieving the optimum utilisation of labour in pursuit of strategic objectives. If the strategy involves asset management – this may point to a pragmatic exploitation of the possibilities offered by labour market segmentation to achieve enhanced financial flexibility. If the strategy calls for a 'value added' approach – coopting core employees into practices of modified functional flexibility may be a preferred strategy. Either way, cost control to secure competitive advantage is likely to involve some measure of labour intensification. 'Porosity' in employment can be tackled either by numerical flexibility (e.g., only employ staff for the hours or service required, via part-time, seasonal or subcontracted work) or by functional flexibility (e.g., by horizontal job enlargement or vertical job enrichment).

The rigidities that the 'soft' model addresses are those implicit in the lack of commitment stemming from over-fragmented jobs, where 'ownership' is of little meaning. A functional flexibility that promises enhanced job satisfaction and QWL for core employees may appear the answer here. And there is some evidence that the removal of 'frustrating' demarcation lines and even modest forms of job enlargement, combined with enhanced training opportunities, are real sources of satisfaction on the shop floor (Elger, 1991, p. 56; Newell, 1991).

The rhetoric of 'flexibility' also serves practical managerial functions. As Hakim (1990, p. 180) points out, the language of the flexible firm model provides managers with a verbal and visual picture that gives access to 'the inner logic of existing labour market strategies ... [that] disclose[s] the implicit structure of segmented labour markets ... so that underlying issues and processes can be opened up to debate'. In contrast the language may also mask behaviour. Not only can negative 'uncertainties' be translated into positive 'flexibilities', as Hyman suggests, but the potential labour intensification implicit in both numerical and functional flexibility can be masked by positive language associated with the latter: 'core' personnel, 'multiskilling', 'teamworking', 'responsiveness' and so on. Backgrounded are some of the negatives overtones of flexibility (uncertainty): loss of specialist skills, loss of quality, lack of 'ownership' and so forth.

If HRM, in either its 'hard' or 'soft' guise, involves the reassertion of managerial prerogative over the labour process, the strategies of flexibility reflect and constitute a path to this. Furthermore, the multi-faceted nature of the debate and languages of flexibility encompass employees as both resourceful humans (flexible specialisation, functional flexibility) and human resources (numerical and financial flexibility). The language too serves to integrate HRM concerns with labour *and* product markets. Flexibility, in the one, permits responsiveness to the sovereign customer in the other.

It is to this interface between organisations' markets – reflected in issues of JIT and TQM – that we turn in Chapter 7, in analysing the strategies and rhetoric of quality and customer sovereignty.

Notes

1. *Scale* economies exist when the costs of providing a common product decrease with the volume of output; *scope* economies if the cost of providing two distinct goods or services from the same firm is less than the cost of providing both separately. Scale economies are often seen as a result of reducing transaction costs through *vertical* integration and scope economies through *horizontal* integration.

2. In contrast Proctor *et al.* (1994) take an opposite view and argue that the forms of flexibility identified in the flexible firm operate on a different level from flexible specialisation and other forms of 'post-industrialism' and that to consider them together confuses rather than illuminates the flexible firm debate.

3. Hakim (1990) suggests that this argument 'confuses fact and value and engages in wishful thinking'. She cites Beechey and Perkin's (1987) evidence – admittedly for the period 1979–81 when ideas about employees as a key resource at the cutting edge of quality were less in vogue – that part-time workers are regarded as marginal by employers and many trade unionists, whether their work is central or marginal to particular product processes.

4. As Casey (1991, pp. 193–4) points out selectivity biases are evident in the surveys by the LRD, ACAS, ELUS and NEDO, and hence their findings have to be treated with caution. The WIRS 1, 2 and 3 surveys and the Warwick Company Level surveys may be treated with more confidence. For a discussion of the strengths and weaknesses of major survey studies conducted in the early to mid-1980s see also Legge (1988, pp. 32–5) and Hunter *et al.* (1993). Casey also warns against the use in all the surveys of the retrospective assessments of respondents when reporting changes in the use of various types of employment contract, citing the discrepancies between reported figures and actual data, upwards or downwards of as much as 20 per cent in a CBI study. He adds – rightly, I think – 'When a "fashionable" issue such as flexibility becomes the object of enquiry, it is not unlikely that respondents will stress change, regardless of whether they view this change as positive, as management respondents might, or negative, as union respondents might'.

5. 'Grimco' in fact comprised a new plant, with a greenfield site philosophy, located on an existing physically 'brownfield' site.

6

HRM: from compliance to commitment?[1]

A central plank of Guest's (1987) normative model of HRM is the development of employee commitment to the organisation. 'The rationale behind this can be found in the assumption that committed employees will be more satisfied, more productive and more adaptable' (Guest, 1987, p. 513). Explicitly, commitment is contrasted favourably with the 'resigned behavioural compliance', seen as characteristic of employment relationships under conventional personnel management (Ogbonna and Wilkinson, 1988, 1990). Commitment is portrayed as internalised belief, as generating constructive proactivity, of 'going one step further' on the part of employees. Compliance, in contrast, is seen as maintained by externally imposed bureaucratic control systems, as generating reactive rather than proactive behaviours, of working to contract, of even 'working to rule'.

The *development of commitment* has been seen as intimately connected to that other major concern of HRM, the *management of cultural change*. This is for two reasons. First, commitment is self-evidently intertwined with organisational culture from the moment we ask the question 'commitment to what?'. And, if it is *organisational* commitment that we are talking about (as opposed to commitment to family, profession or trade union) it must mean to either the structures, policies or shared values that comprise the organisation. While shared values or taken-for-granted assumptions may be considered as the organisation's culture, its structure and policies (whether HRM or strategic) may be seen as expressive of organisational culture. Either way, as Sathe (1983, p. 6) puts it

> People feel a sense of commitment to an organisation's objectives when they identify with those objectives and experience some emotional attachment to them. The shared beliefs and values that compose culture help generate such identification and attachment.

Second, commitment is often associated with those 'soft' HRM policies of participation, team working and briefing, multiskilling, developmentally oriented appraisal, reward and training policies thought to be generative as well as expressive of an individualistic 'high trust' organisational culture, as opposed to the collectivist 'low trust' cultures of stereotyped 'contracts manager' personnel management (Fox, 1974; Tyson and Fell, 1986; Guest, 1987). Or, to put it more critically, 'high trust' commitment policies 'by enabling employees to derive a sense of meaning and purpose from using their discretion to put corporate values into practice ... [enable] non-rational aspects of organisation [to be] colonized by management' (Willmott, 1993).

This chapter, therefore, will focus on questions of how organisational commitment might be developed and whether replacing compliance with commitment will improve organisational performance. What HR policies appear to be conducive to 'organisational commitment'? Can individuals be induced to be committed to a 'new' organisational culture? Can 'cultures' be changed? Does individual commitment to a new culture supportive of strategic objectives necessarily deliver to the 'bottom line'? To answer these questions, the problematic nature of the key concepts involved – organisational culture, commitment and performance – will be considered, and the difficulties in establishing their interrelationship. Then the correlates between organisational commitment and certain types of HRM policies will be examined, followed by the arguments for and against the feasibility of cultural management, in the light of recent UK case study evidence. The chapter will conclude by asking – even if it is feasible – whether the development of a 'strong' organisational culture and employees highly committed to it is necessarily a good thing for either senior management or their employees. But, before considering these questions, the scene will be set by a brief outline of the historical antecedents to an interest in employee commitment and cultural management, and why it has emerged as such a strong theme of HRM.

The human side of enterprise

Well before the publication of McGregor's (1960) book, organisation theory was concerned with the tensions between the instrumental rationality of bureaucratic systems and the affective needs of complex (wo)man (Schein, 1980). Or, to put it somewhat differently, the tensions inherent in a major contradiction in capitalist systems: the need to achieve both control *and* consent of employees, in order to secure not just the extraction, but the realisation of their surplus value. The influence of Taylor's (1911) scientific management and the subsequent development of Fordism in the 1920s (see Rose, 1975), based on notions of rational–economic man and formal organisation, had been counterbalanced by that of the Hawthorne studies in the 1930s (Mayo, 1933; Roethlisberger and Dickson, 1939) and the Ohio/Michigan studies of the 1940s and 1950s (Katz and Kahn, 1966; Stogdill, 1974) which revealed the importance of employees' social affective needs and of informal organisation – relationships and values within small unofficial work groups. Hitherto unquestioned assumptions about the rightness of rational management embedded in hierarchy were challenged by research that pointed to the effectiveness of open participative leadership (Likert, 1961, 1967; McGregor, 1960) and the dysfunctional side effects of Fordist work system design and bureaucracy generally (see, for example, Blauner, 1964; Selznick, 1949; Merton, 1957; Gouldner, 1954). This later research – both that of the neo-Human Relations writers (McGregor, Likert, Argyris and motivation theorists such as Maslow, Herzberg, Vroom, Porter and Lawler) and the structural–functionalist sociologists (Selznick, Merton and Gouldner) anticipated present interest in organisational commitment and culture in two ways. The neo-Human Relations school expanded the early concern with groups into a broader, organisation-wide perspective, focusing on how organisations might be developed to achieve a high trust climate in which employees would see commitment to organisational goal achievement as the route to achieving their own aspirations. From this grew the work of the organisational development consultants, in the 1960s and 1970s, which will be discussed below. The structural–functionalist sociologists – particularly Gouldner (1954) in his study of a gypsum mine – identified the existence and process of emergence of sub-cultures within an organisation, which could oppose and subvert the instrumental rationality of the formal organisation.

Organisational development

Organisational development (OD), in vogue in the 1960s and 1970s in the UK and US, had much in common with present day strategies of generating commitment via cultural management – but some significant differences as well. Like present day HRM strategies it was largely a response to the problem of organisational adaptation to rapid rates of change, both in technologies and social values in the 'swinging sixties' (Beer, 1972; Toffler, 1970). The rhetoric, though, as befitted the era of 'flower power', was more in terms of self-development and the challenge of innovation than of achieving competitive advantage. Furthermore many managers (and some academics!) found it difficult to pin down precisely what OD involved in comparison to normal operational activities conducted through normal bureaucratic channels. In theory, OD referred to systems of three interrelated elements: humanistic values, change processes (i.e., data gathering, organisational diagnosis and action interventions, such as sensitivity training or team building or work system redesign) and technology (i.e., techniques and methods emerging primarily from the behavioural sciences) (French and Bell, 1973). The processes and technology aimed to implant humanistic values throughout the organisation which, by placing organisational relationships on a new basis of openness, trust and collaboration, would (in theory) create a climate conductive to commitment and to a positive approach to the challenge of change. Hence, in the main, the emphasis was on human process issues – teambuilding, communications, interpersonal relationships – rather than on task-centred initiatives or specific work goals. To obtain a feel for the idealistic, not to say naive (and unconsciously sexist!) intentions of OD practitioners, it is worth quoting from supporters of that time.

Thus Tannenbaum and Davies (1969) suggested that OD values involved a movement (I quote):

- Away from a view of man as essentially bad, toward a view of him as essentially good.
- Away from avoidance or negative evaluation of individuals towards confirming them as human beings.
- Away from a view of individuals as fixed towards seeing them as being in process.
- Away from resisting and fearing individual differences toward accepting and utilizing them.
- Away from maskmanship and game-playing toward authentic behaviour.
- Away from the use of status for maintaining power and personal prestige towards use of status for organisationally relevant purposes.
- Away from distrusting people towards trusting them.
- Away from avoiding facing others with relevant data toward making appropriate confrontation.
- Away from avoidance of risk-taking towards willingness to risk.
- Away from a view of process work as being unproductive effort toward seeing it as essential to effective task achievement.
- Away from a primary emphasis on competition toward a much greater emphasis on collaboration.

Even in its heyday much scepticism was expressed by both managers and academics about the feasibility of implanting such 'sweetness and light' values into hard-nosed organisations that operated both as bureaucracies and political jungles. This scepticism was reinforced by encounters with managers who had experienced the unstructured T-groups as a supposed path to greater self-awareness and openness. They tended to fall into two categories: those who rejected the experience and dismissed it as a pseudo-psychoanalysis totally inappropriate to organisational realities and those who 'saw the light' and exuded an air of religious conversion. As a result, as mentioned in Chapter 1, OD was seen, on the one hand, as a form of devious manipulation, and on the other as 'wishy-washy' and ineffectual (see Blackler and Brown, 1980; Pettigrew, 1985).

Furthermore, major OD initiatives in British companies such as Shell, Pilkington and ICI were far from being unqualified successes, as evinced by some of the titles of books and chapters reporting their evaluation (Klein, 1976; Blackler and Brown, 1980; Warmington et al., 1977; Pettigrew, 1985). Hence of Shell, Blackler and Brown (1980) were constrained to ask 'Whatever happened to Shell's New Philosophy of Management?', while Pettigrew's account of OD in ICI's (then) Plastics Division is entitled 'The change strategy without political support'. Even of the relative success story of value change in ICI's (then) Mond division, Pettigrew (1985, p. 375) queries

> One also wonders whether the halting, meandering, some might say inefficient process of connecting developmental thinking and resources to issues of structure, systems, culture and management processes in Mond, needed to be as meandering as it surely was?

Furthermore – and perhaps this should stand as a warning to the present generation of 'transformational leaders' – he quotes Harvey-Jones' (initiator of OD in ICI's (then) Petrochemicals division and subsequently Chairman of ICI) wry comments about its demise in that division:

> I think PCD organisation is a sad case, because I really believed that I had started an irreversible force. I knew there would be attempts to halt it, but I really believed it wouldn't be easy to halt it. I was dead wrong – well 80% ... (Pettigrew, 1985, p. 257)

The relative lack of success of OD initiatives in effecting major and lasting cultural change, with the aim of generating commitment to new values, in the relatively small number of UK organisations in which it was tried, may be put down to several factors. First, the employee relations climate in the 1960s and 1970s was one of strong union power, backed up by (generally) tight labour markets. The OD philosophy of trust and collaboration, in spite of urging the need for openness and confrontation, essentially assumed an ultimate identification of organisation members' interests. This implicitly unitarist position flew in the face of the rampant pluralism of industrial relations in the 1960s and 1970s. Secondly, in spite of much talk of OD signalling the 'death of bureaucracy' (Bennis, 1966) in order to cope with an increasingly complex and changing environment, many of the initiatives were, in retrospect, surprisingly inward looking, involving schemes of management development, work system design, attempts at participation, almost as a good in their own right, without close attention as to how they were to deliver against market-driven organisational success criteria. The long-term nature of OD activities, combined with difficulties in clearly establishing to sceptics their contribution to organisational success criteria (and within a UK culture of financial short-termism) (Sisson, 1990, p. 8) rendered the initiatives at best marginal to mainstream personnel management activities, to be regarded as 'deviant' innovation (Legge, 1978), and at worst to be treated with a cynical contempt. Pettigrew (1985, p. 255), for example, in discussing the 'ambivalence and rejection' the OD unit encountered in the (then) Petrochemicals division of ICI, cites an OD practitioner's observation that captures well this marginality:

> I asked the managers what they thought the OD unit does? It wasn't a question of them saying, 'Oh my God. They're way out.' Wasn't that at all. Either they didn't know, or somebody had done a study on transport drivers for them, or somebody had sat in, as a process resource. Or nothing had happened, and they didn't have the faintest idea or interest in the OD unit.

Against this background of only very limited success of OD initiatives in the 1970s, how do we account for the resurgence of interest in cultural management to generate a climate of commitment in the 1980s and 1990s?

Basically the answer lies in those changes that stimulated the emergence of HRM in the 1980s. As discussed in Chapter 3, these changes in both product and labour markets, mediated by technological development and a swing to right-wing political ideologies, are signified by several buzz words: intensification of international competition, the Japanese Janus (threat/icon), culture of excellence, information technology, knowledge working, high value added, the enterprise culture. What unites these concepts is the notion that flexible, highly skilled individuals *committed* to organisational values consistent with strategic objectives, will deliver competitive advantage. The first step then is the consideration of what are appropriate organisational values and how transformational 'leadership' can transmit this vision in a manner that leads (if necessary) to mass conversion and commitment? In other words, can, and if so how do, senior managers manage culture to generate commitment in order to secure high performance? To explore these questions it is first necessary to consider further the concepts involved.

The problematic concepts: culture and commitment

What is commitment?

In much writing about cultural management and HRM (see, for example, Peters and Waterman, 1982; Tichy, 1983) it is assumed that the intention is to develop a strong, unitary, corporate culture, whereby organisational members share a commitment to values, beliefs, taken-for-granted assumptions that direct or reinforce behaviours considered conducive to organisational success. But as Coopey and Hartley (1991) have recently pointed out (echoing an earlier analysis by Salancik, 1977) 'commitment' in organisational behaviour has been conceptualised in two distinct ways.

The orthodox approach is to see commitment as referring to an individual's psychological bond to an organisation, as 'affective attachment and identification' (Coopey and Hartley, 1991, p. 19). The Porter *et al.* (1974) definition is frequently employed (see also Mowday *et al.*, 1982). They define commitment as the relative strength of the individual's involvement with, and in, a particular organisation. This is operationalised in terms of three factors: a strong desire to remain a member of the organisation; a strong belief in, and acceptance of, the values and goals of the organisation; and a readiness to exert considerable effort on behalf of the organisation. As Guest (1992a, p. 115) points out, such a definition is unhelpful in establishing the outcomes of affective commitment as it conflates process and outcome: 'It is difficult to relate variation in levels of commitment, defined and measured in this way, to dependent variables such as effort, performance and labour turnover, since these are contained in the definition.' Further, in spite of its orthodoxy, the 'effective identification' conceptualisation, as Salancik (1977, p. 3) points out, can only be used *after the event* to classify persons (via the Organisational Commitment questionnaire (OCQ)) as committed or not committed.

In contrast, other commentators, notably Becker (1960), Kiesler (1971) and Salancik (1977, 1982) see commitment as 'the binding of the individual to behavioral acts' (Kiesler and Sakumura, 1966). This approach, which has its roots in theories of cognitive dissonance and consonance (Festinger, 1957), and in the notion that individuals become committed as a result of 'side bets' (pension schemes, status, organisation-specific training) in the organisation which would be lost, at a cost to the individual, if he or she were to leave (Becker, 1960), argues that the degree of commitment a person develops derives from the extent to which behaviours are experienced as binding. Individuals are more likely to be bound to their acts when the latter are highly visible, when their outcomes are irrevocable and when the individuals perceive their acts as voluntary (Salancik, 1982).

Various refinements to attitudinal and behavioural commitment theories have been proposed. Mowday *et al.* (1982) have argued that a reciprocal relationship may exist between attitudinal and behavioural commitment whereby attitudes influence behaviour and vice versa. Allen and Meyer (1990) suggest that there are three components of attitudinal commitment: affective commitment which involves the idea of wanting to remain in the organisation having experienced membership positively; continuance commitment, involving needing to remain in the organisation because of accumulated 'side bets' and lack of alternative employment opportunities; and normative commitment, the feeling that one ought to remain with the organisation because of personal norms and values. To date their results suggest that whilst affective and continuance commitment may be distinguished empirically, there is no conclusive evidence of a normative commitment distinct from affective commitment. McGee and Ford (1987), building on this work, suggest that continuance commitment comprises two separate components, one concerned with sunk costs and the other with a lack of attractive alternatives. While a positive correlation has been found between sunk costs and affective commitment, a negative one emerges between lack of alternatives and affective commitment.

From the point of view of managing corporate cultures and developing personnel policies to generate commitment in the hope of achieving desired behavioural outcomes – low labour turnover and high job performance – these contrasting forms of commitment may have very different implications. Guest (1992a, p. 116) argues that McGee and Ford's (1987) findings point to affective commitment being linked to effort and continuance commitment to low labour turnover. Further, attitudinal commitment suggests the continuance of organisational membership – a precondition to developing any strong organisational culture – follows from a positive decision, resulting from organisational identification. Behavioural commitment suggests it is a passive result of prior decisions and actions which constrain the individual to stay. While both forms of commitment assume instrumental or calculative motivations, attitudinal commitment suggests that commitment is exchanged for valued organisational rewards, in contrast to behavioural commitment which involves a calculation of the costs of leaving rather than the rewards for staying with the organisation. The implicit emphasis of attitudinal commitment, though, that attitudes are prior to and influence behaviour, would suggest that managers interested in changing or reinforcing a culture should opt for re-educative (development and training, persuasive communications, role-modelling, counselling) or replacement strategies (recruitment, selection, intensive socialisation) designed to change beliefs (or recruit compatible beliefs) in the assumption that appropriate behaviour will follow. In contrast, if the 'behavioural acts and consistencies' (Coopey and Hartley, 1991, p. 19) conceptualisation is adopted, the preferred strategy might be to induce behavioural change, but through minimal use of material rewards (to inhibit behavioural compliance rationalised through instrumentality), and rely on the individuals involved to develop attitudes consistent with, and hence reinforcing, their new desired behaviours. For example, if the organisation wishes its employees to internalise the value of quality, a strategy might be to abolish the role of specialist on-line quality inspector and redesign jobs so that each operator is held responsible for monitoring and achieving a work standard 'right-first-time'. Based on theories of cognitive consistency, the argument would go that, assuming the operator had some choice in adopting the new role, and assuming that new behaviour was not elicited through promise of great rewards or threat of sanctions, the very enactment of the new behaviour would result in attitudes consistent with it and, hence, reinforcing of it (see Salancik, 1977, pp. 21–7 for a more detailed discussion).

But this is to consider only half of the generally linked concepts of 'organisational' 'commitment'. Assuming commitment is secured, what is the employee committed to? We will return to this issue at the end of the chapter. Suffice to say here that if we assume a pluralistic model of organisation, following Coopey and Hartley (1991), multiple and potentially competing 'organisational' foci of commitment might be identified: job, profession, department, union, quite apart from that monolithic abstraction 'the organisation' (this issue will be considered further in Chapter 8). Normative HRM models, in their preference for unitaristic rather than pluralistic frameworks, overcome this difficulty by backgrounding enacted sub-cultures in favour of managed corporate cultures. Further, a focus on commitment assumes that, fostered by consistent and reinforcing HRM policies, it *does* result in desired behaviours, which in turn enhance organisational performance. What evidence is there to support this potentially fragile chain of relationships?

It should be said at the outset that virtually all the research conducted on organisational commitment, *per se* has used the attitudinal conceptualisation and measure offered by Mowday *et al.* (1982). Further, as most of the studies are correlational and cross-sectional it is often impossible to establish whether the commitment identified (or lack of it) is a cause or effect. For example, does a job that meets expectations *cause* higher commitment or does high commitment to the organisation *encourage* an individual to 'see the job through the organisation's eyes' and to define it as meeting expectations?

Within these constraints, what has been established as giving rise to organisational commitment on the part of employees and what are the consequences of such commitment? Guest (1992a) provides an excellent review of much of the recent research evidence and I will briefly summarise his findings. First, it has been suggested that the causes of commitment fall into four categories: personal/individual characteristics, role-related experiences, work experiences and structural factors (Mowday *et al.*, 1979). To this may be added HRM policies. The evidence concerning personal characteristics hardly accords with the rhetoric and cultural values of the 'soft' HRM model, for commitment correlates positively with (older) age and lower education! Apart from this the strongest correlates are confirmed job expectations, work involvement, and a job design that provides scope for responsibility and for self-expression. In the case of confirmed job expectations and work involvement, unless the studies provide longitudinal analysis, it is open to interpret the results as effects just as much as causes of commitment. Nevertheless the 'soft' HRM model of true functional flexibility and multiskilling and of employee involvement policies does seem a way forward to generating commitment – in theory.

The consequences of commitment that have most extensively been researched are its impact on labour turnover, absenteeism and job performance (the latter usually assessed by the potentially suspect measure of supervisory ratings). From a 'soft' HRM model perspective low labour turnover is clearly a precondition to other policy initiatives. It is impossible to build a strong corporate culture without stability of membership and high turnover (or, perhaps more accurately, low labour stability) undermines the motivation to invest in training and multiskilling. Generally speaking, the longitudinal research studies show that the link between commitment and labour turnover is indirect. In other words, commitment is an important predictor of intention to quit, which is invariably the best predictor of actual labour turnover. Commitment provides, at best, no more than a small additional independent explanation of labour turnover. And, while studies show a strong relationship between satisfaction and commitment, the causality is not clearly from satisfaction to commitment (Guest, 1992a, p. 121). Turning to absence, Steers and Rhodes (1978) (cited in Guest, 1992a) have suggested that attendance is a function of motivation to attend and ability to attend. While organisational commitment may affect motivation, it will have little effect on ability. Indeed, competing commitments, for example, to family, may negatively affect ability to attend. Hence, it is not surprising that the research evidence suggests that the link between organisational commitment and absence is weak (see Guest, 1992a, p. 122).

Regarding job performance, the available evidence shows only a small significant positive correlation with commitment. Again satisfaction shows a stronger correlation with performance, but again the direction of causality is not always clear. As Guest (1992a, p. 123) points out, it may not be sensible, in any case, to expect a strong link between commitment and performance. While commitment may result in greater effort, according to expectancy theory, the link between effort and performance is mediated by a range of intervening and potentially disruptive variables.

This said, what research evidence is there that 'soft' HRM 'employee involvement' policies can generate commitment, even allowing for the difficulties in assessing the consequences of that commitment? Guest (1992a, pp. 127–8) distinguishes five main forms of involvement: improving provision of information to employees, for example, through briefing groups and company employee reports; improving the provision of information from employees, for example, through suggestion schemes and quality circles; changing the work systems and organisation, through the development of semi-autonomous work groups; changing incentives, for example, through employee share-ownership schemes and performance-related pay; and finally, changing employee relationships, through more participative leadership and greater informality. As Guest suggests, not all these approaches might be expected to improve organisational commitment for, if they improve the industrial relations climate, they may equally encourage a dual commitment – to the trade union (for a detailed discussion of this issue see Chapter 8).

As it is, presently there has still been relatively little research on the link between a cluster of employee involvement (EI) – or 'soft' HRM – policies and organisational commitment so conclusions must be tentative (Guest, 1992a, p. 127). There is evidence that employees generally welcome such initiatives, but there is no consistent evidence of their impact on motivation, performance or industrial relations outcomes (Kelly and Kelly, 1991). Further, with a few 'special case' exceptions, no relationship has been found between use of employee involvement initiatives and company and plant performance – possibly due to the number of potentially intervening variables (Edwards, 1987; Marginson et al., 1988 cited in Guest, 1992a).

Various arguments have been suggested for these (managerially speaking) disappointing results. Guest (1992a, pp. 127–8) argues that if commitment is being used as the intervening variable between employee involvement policies and expected improvements in performance, this may be on assumptions about the link between commitment and performance that have yet to be convincingly demonstrated. Further, there are issues of inadequate introduction and implementation. Kelly and Kelly (1991) point to four reasons for the limited success of such involvement initiatives to achieve employee attitude change: employees lack of choice about participating in such initiatives; their lack of trust of employers' motivations and ability (see in particular with reference to quality circles and performance-related pay) (Hill, 1991b; Kessler and Purcell, 1992); unequal status and outcomes; and lack of institutional supports (again with particular reference to quality circles and employee consultation). Marchington *et al.* (1994), on the basis of their research into employee involvement, found that employee attitudes to such initiatives are dependent, *inter alia*, upon the prior experiences they have of EI and work in general, management's approaches to employee relations and the recent and projected corporate performance of the organisation. They sensibly conclude that employee involvement initiatives are as much affected by the prevailing organisational culture and environment as they are sources of cultural change. (See also Marchington *et al.*, 1992, for a broader discussion of employee involvement in the UK.) As Guest (1992a, p. 128) put it

> Often techniques are introduced in a piecemeal way, more as the 'flavour of the month' than as part of a coherent strategy. One consequence of this is that they are not sufficiently embedded into company systems and quickly fall into disuse, especially in those contexts where line managers are less than enthusiastic about some of the initiatives.

Guest's comments virtually echo the explanations as to why the earlier OD experiments failed (see earlier in this chapter). But a practising manager (or better still, transformational leader) might discount these 'mere academic' objections, the product of positivistic, 'nit-picking' research. Even if commitment shows only a weak link to narrowly specified desired behaviours, surely commitment to a strong and appropriate organisational culture will act as motivator and guide to exemplary general work behaviour, and at the very least serve to integrate the organisation? Before considering initiatives and evidence on this score, some further academic 'nit-pickings' on the relationship between culture, commitment and performance must be considered.

What is organisational culture?

If senior managers seek to manage 'organisational culture,' what exactly is it that they are seeking to manage? Up to this point organisational culture has been defined in the most minimal way as a 'set of shared meanings, or taken-for-granted assumptions'. Such a simple definition cloaks a wide ranging debate about the problems in arriving at an adequate conceptualisation of organisational culture (see, for example, Pettigrew, 1979; Deal and Kennedy, 1982; Pondy *et al.*, 1983; Gregory, 1983; Smircich, 1983; Frost *et al.*, 1983; Meyerson and Martin, 1987; Meek, 1988; Whipp *et al.*, 1989; Turner, 1990). For example, is 'corporate' culture the same as 'organisational' culture? Is organisational 'climate' (often talked about in the 1970s by OD practitioners) and organisational 'culture' one and the same? How inclusive a concept is it – for example, what is *not* organisational culture?

For the purposes of this discussion two issues appear central: the epistemological position taken with regard to the concept, and its inclusivity. The position adopted with regard to epistemology determines whether one considers that culture can be 'managed' at all, or whether managers are merely deluding themselves. The issue of inclusivity determines what aspects of the organisation managers might seek to manipulate when they attempt to change or reinforce its culture, assuming they have already satisfied themselves on the prior epistemological question.

Organisational culture as variable or 'root metaphor'?

In a seminal early paper Smircich (1983) made the valuable distinction that, depending on whether we lean towards a positivistic, structural–functional or a phenomenological world view, we can either conceptualise organisational culture as a variable, something an organisation 'has', or as a process of enactment, a 'root metaphor', something an organisation 'is'. Studies of culture in comparative management, and of corporate culture, treat it as something an organisation 'has': either as an independent variable, as when a national culture is imported into an organisation via its membership, or as something produced by the organisation – its values, language and rituals – as a by-product to the production of goods and services. As Meek (1988) points out, this conceptualisation of culture derives squarely from the anthropological tradition of structural–functionalism which rests on a biological metaphor. This heritage gives rise to a particular focus: culture is seen as somehow unitary and the collective consensus of the organisation. The organic analogy also suggests that culture is defined functionally, as an instrument serving human biological and psychological needs (e.g., gives employees a sense of identity and direction), and as an adaptive-regulating mechanism that effects system stability (through facilitating integration). Furthermore, the organic functionalist perspective encourages the view that the 'head' of the organism (its senior management) has a directive role in developing the collective consciousness, and that 'healthy' ('strong') cultures are both reflective and facilitative of organisational adaption and growth ('success'). Given this epistemological perspective it is not surprising that Schein (1985a, 1985b, cited in Meek, 1988, pp. 196, 198) can state both that

> 'strong cultures' are somehow more likely to be associated with effectiveness than are 'weak' cultures, and that strong cultures can be deliberately created
> [and]
> organisational cultures are created by leaders, and one of the most decisive functions of leadership may well be the creation, the management, and – if and when that may become necessary – the destruction of culture.

In the use of the term 'corporate' culture many writers seem to be imputing a culture created by senior management for the lower orders to swallow (see, e.g., Schein, 1985b; Martin, 1985; Lorsch, 1985; Gordon, 1985). This approach to conceptualising organisational culture *as* corporate culture has been termed the 'integration' paradigm by Meyerson and Martin (1987), where the emphasis is on that which is shared, consistency across cultural manifestations, consensus among cultural members, a denial of ambiguity and a focus on leaders as culture creators.

In contrast, culture may be conceptualised as something emerging from social interaction – something an organisation 'is' (Smircich, 1983; Gregory, 1983). According to Smircich (1983) it may be regarded as a system of shared cognitions, of knowledge and beliefs, or as a system of shared symbols and meanings, or even as a projection of the mind's universal unconscious infrastructure. It is both produced and reproduced through the negotiating and sharing of symbols and meanings – it is both the shaper of human action and the outcome of a process of social creation and reproduction (Meek, 1988; Whipp *et al.*, 1989). If culture is seen in these terms, it is questionable to what extent – or even *whether* – senior management can successfully manipulate or unilaterally change it. As Meek (1988, p. 293) puts it

> If culture is regarded as embedded in social interaction, that is as something that is socially produced and reproduced over time, influencing people's behaviour in relation to the use of language, technology, rules and law, and knowledge and ideas (including ideas about legitimate authority and leadership) then it cannot be discovered or mechanically manipulated; it can only be described and interpreted. The researcher adopting the social emergent view of culture cannot suggest how it can be created or destroyed, the researcher can only attempt to record and examine how culture may be altered in the process of social reproduction. People do not just passively absorb meanings and symbols; they produce and reproduce culture and in the process of reproducing it, they may transform it. The social emergent approach to culture also moves the researcher away from the political and ideological interests of management, towards those of the organisational community as a whole.

To adopt this position is not to imply that senior managements can have no influence at all on their organisation's culture. Indeed, given shared understandings in industrial organisations about the meaning of hierarchy, it is likely that their voices will be more audible and influential than those of subordinate employees. But it does imply that theirs will not be the only voice, nor *necessarily* listened to and internalised. As there are likely to be competing voices, the process of social production and reproduction may spawn a variety of cultures, given people's different experience of reality. Corporate culture – that shared by senior management and presented as the 'official' culture of the organisation – may be only one of several sub-cultures within any organisation, and may be actively resisted by groups who do not share or empathise with its values. If the corporate culture makes no sense of the organisational realities experienced by the employees other than senior management, it will not become internalised outside that small sub-group.

But the distinction between culture as variable or root metaphor still leaves unanswered how it is to be demarcated from other social aspects of organisation. What is, and is not, organisational culture?

Inclusivity

Substantive definitions of culture range from the all-inclusive to those that exclude all but taken-for-granted assumptions. Thus, on the one hand we have Deal and Kennedy's (1982) 'it's the way we do things around here' and, on the other, Gregory's (1983) 'a system of meanings'. Deal and Kennedy's definition would view organisational culture as meshed into organisational structure, while Gregory's would see organisational culture as distinct from structure. Such a distinction is of more than academic interest. If management is to manage culture it needs to know what aspects of organisational life cause, comprise or are manifestations of organisational culture.

First, following Meek (1988), I would argue that it is important to remember that both 'culture' and 'structure' are abstractions of regularities from observations of actual behaviour, not tangible entities. Hence, we can define either abstraction as we find appropriate to our purpose. Geertz's (1973) distinction (cited by Meek, 1988, p. 204) seems helpful – that culture may be viewed as an ordered system of meanings and of symbols, in terms of which social interaction takes place, and to see structure as the pattern of social interaction.

Such a distinction is not inconsistent with Schein's (1984) well known conceptualisation of organisational culture. Schein defines it as

> the pattern of basic assumptions that a given group has invented, discovered or developed in learning to cope with its problems of external adaption and internal integration, and that have worked well enough to be considered valid, and therefore, to be taught to new members as the correct way to perceive, think and feel in relation to these problems.

Schein goes on to distinguish three levels of culture and their interaction (see Figure 6.1). Visible artifacts – the organisation's architecture, technology, office layout, dress codes, visible or audible behaviour patterns and public documents – are the surface level of culture, easy to identify but difficult to interpret without an understanding of the underlying logic. The 'why' of how a group behaves is explained by identifying the values that govern behaviour, the second level of culture. Yet such values, being identified through interviewing key members of the organisation and content analysing artifacts such as documents, are likely to represent accurately only the manifest and espoused values of the organisational culture. To understand a culture, Schein argues, it is necessary to penetrate the third level, the underlying taken-for-granted assumptions that determine how group

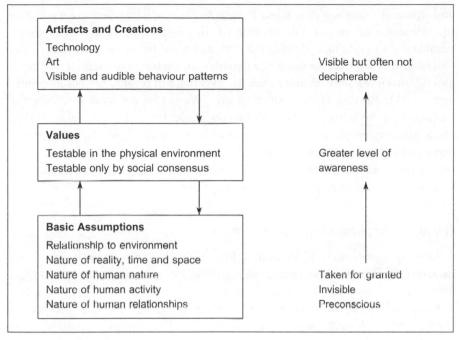

Artifacts and Creations
Technology
Art
Visible and audible behaviour patterns

Visible but often not
decipherable

Values
Testable in the physical environment
Testable only by social consensus

Greater level of
awareness

Basic Assumptions
Relationship to environment
Nature of reality, time and space
Nature of human nature
Nature of human activity
Nature of human relationships

Taken for granted
Invisible
Preconscious

Source: Schein (1985b).

Figure 6.1   Schein's model of levels of culture and their interaction

members perceive, think and feel. These assumptions are learned responses that
originate in espoused values and have resulted in successful adaptive behaviour,
such that the original values become so habitually validated that they drop from
conscious recognition. The basic assumptions which refer to the organisation's
relationship to its environment, the nature of truth and reality, the nature of human
nature, activity and relationships are, in Schein's view, the essence of organisational
culture; the artifacts and values being just manifestations of that culture.

Schein goes on to make the point that a culture only exists in the context of there
being a group to 'own' it, defined as a set of people who have been together long
enough to have shared significant problems, to have had the opportunity to solve
those problems and observe the consequences, and who have taken in and socialised
new members. The latter point is an important test of whether a given solution is
shared and perceived as valid, i.e., that a culture has developed.

Implications of definitional issues for cultural management

If organisational culture is seen as a variable rather than as a 'root metaphor', clearly
there is far more room for senior management to consciously mould it. If
organisational culture is seen as an inclusive catch-all concept, including artifacts

and espoused values as well as taken-for-granted assumptions, there are more levers for management to manipulate than if the former are considered merely manifestations of culture. If culture is seen as embedded in sets of people with a shared history and relative success in coping with problems of external adaptation and internal integration, then it argues the likelihood of organisational sub-cultures and points to the time factor in enacting any culture. Hence it is not surprising that the management initiatives that will be considered later have invariably, if often implicitly, conceptualised culture as a variable and focused on changing artifacts and espoused values. When evaluating the success of such initiatives, it is necessary to consider potential resistance from competing sub-cultures and to be aware of the resources invested in socialisation, including time.

Culture, commitment and performance

As already stated, there is an assumption in much of the popular 'excellence' literature (Peters and Waterman, 1982; Peters, 1987; Waterman, 1987; Morgan, 1988; Kanter, 1989) that 'strong' cultures, possessing particular values, contribute to exceptional levels of organisational performance. Let us leave aside for the moment the host of problematic issues embodied in such an assumption: the questionable equation of performance with dubious selected financial measures (Guest, 1992b); the worry that 'strength' is a dimension antithetical to the nature of culture as an interpretational phenomenon (Van Maanen and Barley, 1984), or that the trait-strength approach suffers from over-reliance on modal cultural profiles, ignoring the complex interaction of multiple sub-cultures to influence outcomes (Saffold, 1988). Let us assume that employees share a commitment to a range of values espoused by senior management, and that we can treat this as synonymous with a 'strong' culture. In attempting to demonstrate a linkage between strong cultures and organisational performance several issues have to be considered that are frequently neglected in much of the extant research (Saffold, 1988).

First, as Saffold (1988, pp. 549–50) points out, the relationship between culture and performance is not necessarily monotonic. Citing total institutions (Goffman, 1969) as a case in point, he argues that

> as cultural values are more fully elaborated, a greater range of organizational behaviour is brought under control. Initially this may enhance performance by ensuring that organizational priorities are uniformly established. But, if cultural controls multiply too greatly, resistance is likely to develop, causing performance to decrease.

Secondly, it is possible that a particular cultural value many not affect all performance-related organisational processes in the same direction. Sharing meanings may have a positive integrative effect, but at the same time inhibit an organisation's ability to learn and adapt (cf. Janis, 1972; Shrivastava, 1985; Coopey and Hartley, 1991) (I will return to this point later).

Third, even if we assume a monotonic, uni-directional effect of certain shared values on performance, attention (often lacking) must be paid to validation measures. Contrasting comparison groups, for example, are necessary to show that a cultural profile generally characteristic of high performing organisations (however defined) is not equally evident in average or low performing ones (Saffold, 1988; Guest, 1992b).

These problems stand even before we consider the immense difficulties of isolating the effects of any corporate culture from those of simultaneously interacting intervening variables on performance. Needless to say, if culture is treated as an all inclusive variable (and hence a meaningless one) much of this latter problem is circumvented, but to little analytical point.

Can culture be managed to generate commitment?

The case for the protagonists

If commitment is about 'binding individuals to behavioural acts', at least it can be said for managerial protagonists of cultural change that they are committed: they have put their money where their mouth is. Consider, for example, the cost of Austin Rover's 'Working with Pride' quality circle programme (Storey, 1987, 1992b) or Jaguar's initiatives to produce a 'cult of quality' (Whipp et al., 1989; Pettigrew and Whipp, 1991) or British Airways 'Putting the Customer First' and 'Putting People First' programmes. What do such programmes aim for?, how do they seek to achieve cultural change (or reinforcement); on what assumptions are their strategies based?

In considering such questions, we are dependent on published case accounts. The companies and industries that have attracted researchers over the last decade reflect very much the concerns of the enterprise culture. Thus there exist numerous accounts of cultural change in newly privatised industries, such as BT and British Airways (e.g., Clark et al., 1988; Young, 1989; Höpfl et al., 1992; Höpfl, 1993); in those public services, notably the NHS, newly subject to quasi-markets and managerialism (e.g., Coombs and Green, 1989; Kelly, 1991; Strong and Robinson, 1990; Pollitt, 1990, 1993); in engineering and in car manufacturing, whether on greenfield (e.g., Wickens, 1987; Newell, 1991) or brownfield sites (e.g., Hendry and Pettigrew, 1987; Pettigrew and Whipp, 1991); in banking and financial services (e.g., Hendry and Pettigrew, 1987; Pettigrew and Whipp, 1991; Knights and Willmott, 1987) and in retailing (Ogbonna and Wilkinson, 1988, 1990; Marchington and Harrison, 1991; Marchington, 1993).

The aim of cultural change programmes

I have referred to the aim of cultural change programmes throughout this chapter: to achieve employee commitment to those values senior management considers are facilitative to improved organisational performance. Following Ray (1986), cultural change strategies may be seen as an addition to other forms of control which organisations have tried to implement. Whereas bureaucratic control focuses on the social and organisational structure of the firm (e.g., structures of the internal labour market, appraisal and reward) (Edwards, 1979) and humanistic control on matching employee needs to 'satisfying task or work group life' (Mayo, 1933, 1945), both strategies aimed at increasing worker loyalty and ultimately productivity, cultural control

> implies that the top management team aims to have individuals possess direct ties to the values and goals of the dominant élites in order to activate the emotion and sentiment which might lead to devotion, loyalty and commitment to the company. (Ray, 1986, p. 294)

First, cultural control can supplement the other two forms. This is often done implicitly in broad brush HRM initiatives where performance-related pay may go hand-in-hand with enhanced communication and participation, along with training (e.g., in quality circles aimed at the internalisation and implementation of espoused values – as at BT). But, secondly, 'more than other forms of control ... corporate culture elicits sentiment and emotion, and contains possibilities to ensnare workers in a hegemonic system' through treating the organisation, à la Durkheim, as an appropriate site for an integrative moral order (Ray, 1986, p. 287).

What values do they seek to promote?

Pre-eminently *cultural* change programmes over the last decade have promoted the values of quality (of product or service) and the pre-eminence of the market place, sanitised into 'customer awareness/customer care' (see also Chapter 7). The other major values of cost effectiveness and flexibility (read labour intensification?) are promoted largely through systems of *bureaucratic* control, although the rhetoric of quality may enter such change programmes (see Chapter 5).

It is instructive to compare the statements of espoused values emanating from the range of organisations identified above and note their similarity. Privatised British Gas (in a patriotic red and blue booklet *Banishing Gripes*, sent free of charge to all customers) asserts 'British Gas is totally committed to giving you the best possible service' and specifies its standards, as does British Rail in its Passenger's Charter (also in patriotic blue and red): 'The Passenger's charter is a statement of our commitment to provide a high quality service for our passengers.' (One can only assume that BR dropped the recently acquired designation 'customer' in response to passengers' irritation at being so labelled, with the implications of consumer choice!)

An early advertising slogan of BT 'We answer to you' also asserts the primacy of the customer. Indeed, the whole concept of the Citizen's Charter is indicative of the Government's desire to bring concepts from the marketplace (i.e., the sovereignty of the customer) into the erstwhile non-market public sector.

However, private companies have echoed the same message, if with the competing one of cost-control. In the cases Pettigrew and Whipp (1991) explore, in the automobile, merchant banking, book publishing and life assurance industries, the pervading themes are a search for quality that will satisfy more discriminating customers (e.g., Jaguar) or the provision of the diversified range of services required by clients (e.g., Hill Samuel, Prudential). In retailing, too, 'customer care' combined with the provision of an up-market range of high value added products (e.g., Marks & Spencer, Sainsbury and Tesco) is the espoused value, although with the persistence of recession and recognition of market segmentation, some firms (e.g., Kwiksave) have interpreted 'customer responsiveness' as involving a reconsideration of the philosophy 'Pile 'em high, sell 'em cheap'. Marchington (1993), in his research on the retailing sector, cites one company's message, pinned up on the employee notice board: 'Customer Care is the Number One skill all employees must have. Our future success will depend on how well you apply this skill'.

Nevertheless the emphasis on quality has gone hand-in-hand with the espoused value of cost control as, in an environment of high interest rates and slowing of customer demand, it is perceived that even customers demanding quality are not price insensitive. The message of cost control may be conveyed symbolically (e.g., Castleman, Chief Executive of Hill Samuel, questioning division heads in 'public' regarding their cost projections and overruns, making the bank dining room self-service, cutting the number of company chauffeurs), but the real thrust generally lies in the messages conveyed by bureaucratic controls (e.g., appraisal systems, promotion policies, performance-related pay, the use of numerical flexibility).

Strategies to achieve culture change

In talking of cultural change, given the epistemological and inclusivity assumptions made earlier, I am assuming that senior managers attempt to change two *manifestations* of organisational culture: artifacts, including overt behaviour and espoused values. At best they seek to bind individuals to behavioural acts that are coherent with (newly) espoused values. This inevitably, then, involves the use of bureaucratic controls (e.g., structuring of the internal labour market, appraisal and promotion systems, training and payment systems) *as well as* managing meaning through rituals, symbols and so forth.

Hence the techniques used are those common to any strategy aimed at changing behaviour but with particular emphasis on their symbolic content. In most cultural change strategies one can recognise an implicit adherence to Lewin's (1951) change model and Chin and Benne's (1976) change strategies. In other words, the social system is viewed as a force field of driving and restraining forces in equilibrium; change is effected through a process of 'unfreezing' this system (by showing inadequacies of current beliefs) introducing change (via empirical–rational, normative re-educative and power–coercive strategies) and re-freezing it in its changed state (by developing reinforcing structures and control systems).

'Unfreezing' may occur through skilfully managed organisational trauma. In 1980 Michael Edwardes, the (then) BL chief executive, announced that Jaguar would close within a year, unless the unit broke even. In the same year, a new managing director and chairman, John Egan, was appointed. One of his early acts was the creation of a 'Black-Museum' displayed at plant level, of the worst product defects of the 1979–80 period and the inviting of US dealers to the tracks to put the case directly of the quality problem with the Series III model. (In this Egan was assisted by the rising levels of unemployment in the early 1980s.)

Introducing change may take place through empiricist–rational strategies (assumption: that individuals are rational and will follow rational self-interest given 'correct' information); normative re-educative strategies (assumption: that people's rationality and behaviour is influenced by social and sub-group norms, and that therefore re-education should not only provide 'correct information' about the 'facts' of the situation, but address socially supported beliefs and norms, working through groups rather than individuals); and power–coercive strategies (assumption: use of power to enforce behavioural change by exercise or threat of sanctions). Translated into management practice this generally results in three strategies, often simultaneously applied, but to different groups of people, at different levels in the hierarchy and at different stages in the change process. These are: re-education (including participative communication such as briefing groups, role modelling, quality circles, training and management development generally); replacement (e.g., selection, promotion and redundancy); and re-organisation (e.g., new structures, appraisal and reward systems).

Many companies have attempted to promote the values of quality and customer service through re-educative methods. Notable are British Airways' 'Putting People First' programme (Young, 1989; Höpfl et al., 1992; Höpfl, 1993); ICL's major management education programme in the early 1980s (Sparrow and Pettigrew, 1988a, 1988b; Sparrow, 1991); the 'new tech' training at GKN (Hendry and Pettigrew, 1988; Hendry, 1991); BR's 'Customer-Care' and TQM programmes (Storey, 1992b; Guest et al., 1993) and Lucas' TQM and JIT initiatives (Storey, 1992b); team building at Grampian Health Authority (Fullerton and Price, 1991). Role-modelling examples abound: not only the now legendary story of Colin Marshall, at British Airways, assisting at the check-in on the first day of the Super Shuttle service (Young, 1989), but of Turnbull, Chief Executive at Peugeot–Talbot, receiving customer complaint calls personally in 1990–1 (Pettigrew and Whipp, 1991). Role-modelling too plays a part in training initiatives, as in the use of senior managers, known for their participative style, taking question and answer sessions in Royal Bank of Scotland training courses – or even the use by Sainsbury of group role-play exercises, with check-out staff role-playing the customer. Briefing groups and quality circles, it is claimed, have been used effectively in car assembly particularly, and in engineering generally (e.g., Hardy Spicer, Jaguar, Nissan, Austin Rover) (Hendry and Pettigrew, 1988; Wickens, 1987; Pettigrew and Whipp, 1991). In summary, recent research by Storey (1992a, 1992b) based on a sample of fifteen household name organisations (e.g., Austin Rover, British Rail, ICI, NHS, Plessey, Whitbread) found that most were engaged in intensive and direct communications with employees as part of 'wide ranging cultural, structural and personnel strategies', aimed at 'conflict reduction through culture change'.

Replacement strategies are also in evidence. Well known are the selection policies of major engineering companies (e.g., Austin Rover, Nissan, Toshiba, Pirelli) (Willman and Winch, 1985; Wickens, 1987; Yeandle and Clark, 1989) that select not only for staff potential but for appropriate attitudes and values i.e., those supportive of flexibility and teamworking. The TSB and Abbey National have steadily increased the number of graduate trainees recruited in an effort to become more commercially oriented (see, e.g., Hendry and Pettigrew, 1987). Selective early retirement of senior or middle managers, perceived as averse to new, more commercially oriented values, has been used in many organisations e.g., at TSB., Shell, Smith and Nephew (see, e.g., Hendry and Pettigrew, 1987; Storey, 1992b).

Finally, major structural changes have been used to align organisations closely with the market place. In general terms this has involved decentralisation and increased operational autonomy for identified separate business units, and their change from cost to profit centres. In erstwhile public sector industries (e.g., British Gas, BT) this has often resulted in a (relatively late by industrial standards) move from functional organisation to business/market centred structures. (The same is true for the surviving public sector British Rail (see Guest et al., 1993).) The post-Griffiths reforms of the NHS and opting-out/grant maintained status for schools involve structural change similarly aimed at increased market responsiveness (see, e.g., Reed and Anthony, 1993a, 1993b; Fullerton and Price, 1991).

Such initiatives are often reinforced by the implantation of the new 'espoused values' into appraisal systems, backed up by the introduction of various forms of performance-related pay (see, for example, the 'new contracts' at BT and in the polytechnics/higher education section, also the use of performance-related pay on the shop floor at Black and Decker and Birds Eye Walls) (Kinnie and Lowe, 1990; Cannell and Wood, 1992; Kessler and Purcell, 1992; Kessler, 1994). Further details of the combinations of re-educative, replacement and re-organisation strategies may be found (notably in Pettigrew and Whipp, 1991; Storey, 1992b and Gowler et al., 1993).

Most of these strategies have received symbolic as well as instrumental expression. Identification with the organisation and its values is expressed by the vast expansion of company specific work wear, particularly in areas where there is direct contact with the customer (e.g., banks and building societies). Commercial orientation has resulted in changes in physical artifacts as evidenced by the redesign of banks and building societies from images that convey safeguarding money (metal grilles, high counters, mahogany and real marble) to selling money (carpets, glass screening, personal banking open plan area). Language has changed in the same direction too: British Rail passengers are now (ugh!) 'customers', as shall shortly be the students in institutions of higher education. Check-out personnel at supermarkets and fast food outlets are now encouraged to smile at customers and wish them a 'nice-day' (Ogbonna and Wilkinson, 1988, 1990). Above all, the transformational leaders have learnt the value of symbolic acts – as referred to earlier in this chapter and exemplified in the writings of that erstwhile supporter of OD, John Harvey-Jones (1988).

What is achieved?

I find it difficult to answer this question for, although we have accounts of such 'cultural change' initiatives involving 'high commitment' management practices, there are few, if any, systematic evaluations of the same. Has the reviving engineering culture of Jaguar, for example, survived take-over by Ford? Has the diversified, cost-conscious ethos that Castleman tried to develop in Hill Samuel survived his departure and its acquisition by TSB? We have no systematic evaluations that can answer this question. Further, the effects of any emergent enhancement of organisational performance in the private sector has been masked by those of the deep recession of the early 1990s.

What we can say on the evidence that we have is that the internalisation of any value demands its testing and reinforcement by relatively stable groups of employees over time, and their socialisation of newcomers into these values. The amount of delayering and redundancy in British industry since the late 1980s raises doubt as to whether these conditions have prevailed. Further, the assertion of the values of quality and customer care were very much part of the rejuvenation of manufacturing, the High Street boom, and the privatisation of public sector industries and services in the mid-1980s. While marketplace competition in manufacturing probably maintains support for the latter in manufacturing (note the number of household name manufacturing companies – Shell, Ford, ICI, Rover, etc. – heavily involved in TQM and the securing of BS 5750 – 'Quality Assurance') (see Chapter 7) there is the issue of the extent to which such values may be undermined by the competing ones of cost control, with the late 1980s and early 1990s recession, and the intervention of regulatory bodies (Ofgas, Oftel) affecting profitability. What of situations, as in the oil and chemical companies, where appraisal systems assert the primacy of cost control, while senior management rhetoric espouses quality and customer service? (The same might be said with equal force for companies as diverse as British Rail, the retail banks and the Big Five food supermarkets.)

What could be argued, if we take the 'behavioural consistencies' view of commitment, is that the *bureaucratic* controls (restructuring, redesign of working practices and control systems) that have induced new behaviour patterns *may* result in the eventual internalisation of the values embedded in the new structures and resultant behaviours. However, as argued earlier, in theory this internalisation is only likely to occur if the individuals involved feel they have some choice and discretion over their new behaviours and that the consequences of engaging in them are positive (see Chapter 7 for a discussion of the experience of JIT and TQM in manufacturing workplaces). If the individual has no choice (other than redundancy), or is heavily 'bribed' to participate, the required behaviour may result, but even espoused values of all but senior management remain unchanged. As for the taken-for-granted assumptions, it is debatable whether many of the work groups involved in cultural change programmes have had sufficient time to test and be reinforced in the new espoused values for these to be absorbed into unconscious assumptions. For example, to what extent did British Airways' 'Putting People First' espoused values stand the test of the redundancy programme and the Gap Closure and Sprint cost cutting exercises, in the light of revenue loss consequence on recession and the Gulf War?

On this very issue, Höpfl *et al.* (1992, p. 29) make some interesting observations. They consider that the redundancy exercise was not seen as a betrayal of the 'caring' values BA promoted during the 1980s. Three explanations are offered for this reaction. First, they suggest the culture change programmes of the 1980s ('Putting the Customer First . . .', 'Putting People First . . .', 'Customer First' teams, 'Managing People First', 'A Day in the Life', 'To be the Best') may not have been successful, that they 'engaged the mind but left hearts untouched'. Alternatively the redundancy exercise could be seen as expressive of and reinforcing espoused values rather than undermining them. Thus, because consistent with their 'customer service' principles, BA transformed their recruitment centre into an 'Advice and Support' Centre, offering a comprehensive and extended out-placement service, supported by very generous severance terms. Höpfl *et al.* (1992, p. 29) observe 'The Advice and Support Centre signalled the extent of BA's concern for its people in tough times', in a context where the external pressures driving the cut-backs – Gulf War and recession – were generally recognised and accepted as beyond the company's control. A third – and Höpfl *et al.* suggest the most likely explanation – has to do with the way in which the cultural change programmes were positioned.

> It was never the intention nor objective of the change process during the 1980s to encourage people to place company loyalty above commitment to family and friendships; it was in no sense a 'spiritual brainwashing' but rather an attempt to show people what BA believed in and enable individuals to make a conscious choice to opt in and feel good about their contributions [p. 29] . . . Culture was presented as a variable to be manipulated to improve performance. The workforce itself was not seen as a variable to be

manipulated. At root culture change programmes dealt with issues of survival ... Concern for the individual was set within this context of making sense of behaviour and experience in such a way as to serve the interests of the survival of the organisation. (p. 34)

The detractors' case

Several commentators (e.g., Anthony, 1990, 1994; Ogbonna and Wilkinson, 1990; Smith and Peterson, 1988) have expressed considerable scepticism as to whether organisational culture can be successfully managed in the way proponents of 'cultural change' strategies imply. As Smith and Peterson (1988, p. 121) warn 'cases do exist of organizations within which major changes in culture have been successfully accomplished ... and shown to persist ..., but they are rare'. Their reservations centre on three issues: epistemological and conceptual problems; paradoxes associated with 'cultural management'; empirical evidence.

Epistemological and conceptual problems

These arguments have largely been rehearsed. If we see culture as a 'root metaphor', as embedded in social interaction, and socially produced and reproduced over time, then it cannot be mechanically manipulated (Smircich, 1983; Meek, 1988). While there may be attempts by senior management to reshape the *manifestations* of culture (Schein, 1984, 1985a, 1985b), it is doubtful whether this will change organisational members' basic assumptions. This is for two reasons.

First, following Schein (and, as already argued), basic assumptions are learned responses that have originated in espoused values and, having resulted in successful adaptive behaviour, have become so habitually validated that they have dropped from conscious recognition. But this implies that groups have the opportunity to test espoused values over time. In turn, this suggests a certain stability of membership and of the surroundings in which the values are to be tested. Without these preconditions the 'sedimentation' of espoused values into basic assumptions is unlikely to occur. But how does this square with the 'cultural management' notion that cultures should be changed to match the organisation's current goals and circumstances? This introduces the first paradox, identified by Anthony (1994) that 'while interest in cultural change is explained by growing turbulence in markets and technology which is said to make it necessary, these may be the circumstances which make cultural change most difficult to achieve'. Furthermore, what are the implications of the flexible firm model and delayering for the prospects of achieving sedimentation?

Second, by definition, basic assumptions encapsulate moral values which are criteria of worth (see Figure 6.1, p. 188). The values that 'cultural management' seeks to change are largely instrumental ones in that, although containing a potentially moral dimension (e.g., 'quality', 'care') they are concerned with a means to an end (i.e., the 'bottom line'). If the integrative function of any culture rests largely on the spontaneous reciprocities, engendered by the shared moral meanings, that it conveys, it becomes problematic if the very instrumentality of the new 'espoused' values acts to negate their potentially moral dimensions. This is particularly likely if values that accord most readily with basic assumptions (e.g., 'care', 'autonomy') are juxtaposed with those that are more unequivocally instrumental (e.g., 'cost control'). In such circumstances it is questionable whether the instrumental espoused values will sit easily with basic moral assumptions.

Paradoxes of cultural management

It may be argued that the paradoxes embedded in the intentions and implementation of cultural management render it self-defeating (Anthony, 1990, 1994). As Anthony (1994) points out, if cultural control ('hegemonic' in Ray's terms) is regarded as a more effective substitute for rational bureaucratic control, it is interesting that the mechanisms by which messages of initiative, autonomy, innovation, risk taking and personal responsibility are conveyed – organisation-wide cascaded briefings, training days, appraisal systems – are themselves highly bureaucratic. Might not this, in itself, negate the messages that are being preached? And what of the infrastructures set up to monitor the success of 'high commitment' practices of teambuilding, multiskilling and so forth?

Second, the development of a new 'strong' culture is often seen as the task of the new leader (e.g., King and Marshall at BA, Egan at Jaguar, Castleman at Hill Samuel, Turnbull at Peugeot, Birch at Abbey National), as part of a strategy for revitalising the organisation. Such leaders, at least in the first instance, are often regarded as organisational deviants, representing a small sub-culture in battle with the strong (but perceived ineffective) dominant culture (e.g., Harvey-Jones at ICI, see Pettigrew, 1985). A classic example is the battle presently raging between post-Griffith's style NHS managers, representing the espoused management values of the primacy of the efficient allocation of resources to where they are judged to be best deployed and the professional clinician arguing the primacy of the delivery of best patient care as defined by clinicians. This raises the dilemma, which is the legitimate strong culture?

To quote Anthony (1990, p. 6) at some length

> there is no doubt that the allegiance of the [professionals] to a common culture is reinforced by a tradition of moral concern. In the National Health Service and the universities the internal values of health or education are shared by the inhabitants who influence the culture of their organisations because they regard its institutions as instrumental to their practices and to their concern with internal values. In these instances, culture is based upon identifiable values widely shared; they are not imposed by the institution although they may be reinforced by it. *Historically, the institution is secondary to the practice. In managed organisations the opposite is true: the institution comes*

first in time and any culture that follows is likely to have been imposed, often coercively, by a leader or founder, who may have charismatic qualities attributed to him or her. And the values and the culture are, of course, likely to be changed or obliterated with a change in the leadership; in the professions, culture is more likely to abide (added emphasis).

So here we have the paradox that a small sub-group (senior managers) are being called upon to create a 'strong' sub-culture to confront and overwhelm an existing, more widely shared strong culture, that is rooted in moral rather than instrumental values. Questions must inevitably be raised about the ethics of such initiatives, if only in the interests of democracy. And, in this context, Anthony (1995) reminds us of Jackall's (1988, pp. 195, 133) words: 'the fundamental requirements of managerial work clash with the normal ethics governing interpersonal behaviour ... [and] ... The logical result of alertness to expediency is the elimination of any ethical lines at all.' Perhaps we should consider these words as a prophetic warning of the role of a charismatic leader bent on the creation of his own 'strong' organisational culture in opposition to that of a strong occupational community. Consider, for example, Robert Maxwell, the *Daily Mirror* and its pension fund.

Third, Anthony (1990) argues that when a small senior management group attempts to superimpose a new set of espoused values upon subordinates that are discordant with the latter's sense of reality, the result may be that they act out the surface signals of the 'new culture' but cynically and without internalisation. Existing bureaucratic structures (hierarchy, appraisal, promotion ladders) ensure that negative, critical, even whistle-blowing feedback is unlikely to occur. On the contrary, the skilled performance enacted by employees may confirm senior management in its view that the new culture has taken, when all that is on show is a 'resigned behavioural compliance' (Ogbonna and Wilkinson, 1990, p. 14) supported by bureaucratic controls. Without negative feedback senior management is reinforced in the delivery of a message that may become increasingly at odds with employees' perceptions of organisational reality, and engender an increasing cynicism. In such circumstances the paradox will exist that as senior management become increasingly convinced that cultural change has taken place, other organisational members may become increasingly cynical and resistant to such influence attempts (cf. Harvey-Jones' rueful retrospective reflections on the failure of OD in ICI's Petrochemicals division, cited earlier).

Empirical evidence

Apart from that cited by Smith and Peterson (1988) in support of their contention of the rarity of cultural change, there are the methodological question marks over classic 'changing corporate culture' studies, cited earlier. The answer, one way or the other, awaits detailed longitudinal cases studies *and* follow up studies a decade later. Even then, for reasons already outlined, it is probable that researchers will find it easier to identify long-term changes in the manifestations of culture than in basic assumptions.

Recent case study evidence appears to suggest that cultural change initiatives appear more successful among their initiators – senior management – and their immediate collaborators – surviving middle managers – than further down the hierarchy. On the basis of his fifteen core cases, Storey (1992b, p. 215), for example, concludes that while there was

> very considerable evidence of transformation with line managers as the objects of change; there was much less evidence that this had as yet been carried through into similar behavioural and attitudinal changes at shopfloor level.

In a passage that echoes Salancik's (1977) comments about conditions facilitative or inhibiting in the achievement of commitment as 'behavioral acts and consistencies', Storey (1992b, p. 241) goes on to comment, with reference to supervisory reaction to the newly designated 'first line manager' role at Whitbread, that

> In consciously seeking to manage a change of culture, senior managers had manipulated some symbols to signify a new order, but these were insufficient to counterbalance the range of signs which persuaded the sceptical that things were pretty much the same. Hence the name change to 'first line manager' was not accorded very much significance by those who could glimpse little realistic future as a 'manager'. Without that glimpse even training courses on 'leadership' could make little impression. Those FLM's who had 'caught the management bug' had been receptive to the new set of symbols because they relished the planning and data-handling aspects of the role and they could envisage a future in a management career. It was those who had gone to the trouble of taking the old 'shift supervisor' name plates off their office doors. For the rest, the companies' paradigmatic shift (in Birds Eye, Whitbread and Eaton) had been too ambivalent to persuade most supervisors that they personally should buy into a new mode of operating. There were, on balance, simply too many contra-symbols (including middle and senior managers' general demeanour towards them) to overcome the power of inertia.

In the retailing sector, too, we have some evidence (admittedly of a less longitudinal nature than would be methodologically desirable) that points in the same direction. Ogbonna and Wilkinson (1990) point to the likelihood of 'resigned behavioural compliance' rather than changes in espoused values – let alone basic assumptions – among check-out staff when the managerial rhetoric of the 'customer is king', 'quality and service' is at odds with their experience of work as involving rude customers, monotony, and intense pressure for speed. While employees take pride in their ability to act out the espoused values of 'service with a smile' ('We are told to smile all the time ... sometimes it's very hard ... I succeed because I try to put up an act ... my mother thinks I'm very good at it and that I should have been an actress') Ogbonna and Wilkinson (1990, p. 13) claim that rarely do such values appear internalised

Rather, the motives behind the behaviour patterns displayed on the shopfloor were almost invariably either instrumental ('this disarms the customer') or under threat of sanction ('I smile because I'm told to'; 'you have to be very careful and polite because they can report you to the manager'). The check-out operator's job is, of course, highly visible and not smiling or even 'putting on a false smile' can result in being 'called into a room for a chat' with the supervisor. Random visits by bogus shoppers and head office managements reinforce the threat of sanctions for undesirable behaviour or expressing one's true feelings to difficult customers.

While the connection between bureaucracy and acting has been well made before (MacIntyre, 1981), following Salancik, these accounts raise two questions. Does continuous acting finally internalise the values being enacted? Possibly 'yes' where, as in the case of Whitbreads 'caught by the management bug' supervisors, behaviour was voluntary. Or, as one BA manager (cited in Höpfl *et al.*, 1992, p. 26) put it, 'I think there are different stages. One is that you start to spout a message, secondly that everybody starts to spout the message, and thirdly, you start to actually believe it, ... I think we are approaching the "believe it" stage'. Or, does the process of acting out a part at odds with perceptions of reality, merely enhance cynicism and, paradoxically, a deeper rejection of the newly proselytised values? This may well be true for Ogbonna and Wilkinson's check-out operators. Either way, it might be argued that the manipulation of values and symbolism to facilitate the extraction and realisation of surplus value raises issues about the mobilisation of bias and false consciousness as well as more general ethical issues (see Anthony, 1994).

Are strong cultures desirable?

Clearly a case may be made for the desirability of developing a strong organisational culture to which employees are committed – although the benefits may vary over time and between different groups of stakeholders. In a word, the attributed benefits are enhanced integration and, in some circumstances, adaptability. Strong culture can act as a 'moral glue' binding together a (possibly) differentiated organisation. This is particularly relevant when a penchant for tight–loose structures dissolves bureaucratic centralising controls other than the financial. Also, widely shared basic assumptions and espoused values can act as guidelines to facilitate, not just coordinated, but rapid decision-making. Strong commitment to shared values is particularly important when the relationship between an individual's actions and outcomes are uncertain or the instrumental pay offs are likely to be low. Furthermore by coopting an individual's commitment to espoused values and courses of action, and inducing a sense of personal responsibility for them, senior management inhibits that individual's ability to find fault with the same (Salancik, 1977, p. 445). However, the downside of a strong organisational culture is an inward looking, conformist, complacent organisation, sunk into a morass of group-think, rigid, rather than flexible in its outlook. Brunsson's (1982), Weick's (1969, 1987), Miller's (1993) and Coopey and Hartley's (1991) arguments are relevant here.

Following Brunsson's (1982) arguments, 'objective' ideologies (defined as ideas shared by all organisational members), when 'conclusive' (that is, clear, narrow and consistent) in one sense – speed of response – can promote adaptability. This is because decisions can be made quickly as the conclusive ideology – read 'strong culture' – acts as an effective filter on the acceptability of an action, eliminating lengthy discussion while generating commitment to implementing it. This is similar to Miller's (1993) argument that successful organisations over time, through positive reinforcement, become more focused or 'simple', in developing a homogeneous and mutually reinforcing set of world views, goals, structures, processes and culture that enhance success assuming their continued appropriateness to the environment. Weick (1987, p. 125) points out the advantages, in high-risk systems, such as air traffic control and nuclear power stations, of a rich culture of horror stories, aphorisms and histories, that 'register, summarise, and allow reconstruction of scenarios that are too complex for logical linear summaries to preserve'. This assumes though that either the stories 'hold the potential to enhance requisite variety among human actors' or, failing that, that the action required involves no radical departures from tenets of the strong culture, as conclusive ideologies rule out changes that challenge their assumptions.

Weick (1969, 1987), Coopey and Hartley (1991) and Miller (1993) point out the dangers of 'strong culture' in developing rigid and conformist thinking among its members. If environmental conditions change, the 'architecture of simplicity' that once enhanced success can trigger failure due to lack of mechanisms to sense the need for change and inappropriate responsiveness. While 'strong cultures' imply a convergence of goals and values, adaptability to rapidly changing conditions relies on people having different perceptions of environmental data (Weick, 1969). Coopey and Hartley argue for the advantage of multiple commitments within organisations – to job, career, profession, department and trade union. They suggest that competing ideologies 'stimulate individuals to think meaningfully about themselves and the world around them' (1991, p. 26), that creative tensions between heterogeneous viewpoints are ultimately more facilitative of flexibility and innovation than the complacency engendered by a shared, unchallenged view of reality. It might be said however that cultural – any change – programmes may initiate a re-examination of work roles and issues of personal identity, that challenge the erstwhile 'taken-for-granted' worlds of work and personal life (Höpfl et al., 1992, pp. 35–6).

The danger of complacency may be illustrated by the much quoted example of IBM in the early 1980s. IBM's narrow ideology of 'IBM is service' contained particular assumptions about the nature of product and service (mainframe, customised systems, salesmen as management consultants to customer-as-end-user, seeking quality of product and service) which were inappropriate when strategy dictated an entry into the personal computers market (standardised product, cost competition, dealer as customer) (Mercer, 1987). The very success of the IBM service ethic in its traditional markets inhibited an adaptive response from employees to new market opportunities and, in the early 1990s, led to unprecedented financial losses.

Yet conclusive ideologies, reflecting strong cultures, Brunsson argues, may in the long term be more amenable to radical shifts than the broad, ambiguous ideologies, often taken as symptomatic of a 'weak' culture. Superficially, while the latter might appear to allow more flexible responses on the part of the employee, their very vagueness fails to generate the necessary commitment for effective action. Nevertheless, such ideologies tend to survive as they are difficult to disconfirm, being apparently applicable to a wide range of situations. In contrast, the very precision of conclusive ideologies allows their disconfirmation as individuals' own experience of changed circumstances cannot be reconciled with their unequivocal prescriptions and justifications. Thus, in the early 1980s, many employees of BA could recognise the inappropriateness of their bureaucratic, technically oriented, almost militaristic culture in a world of high competition and threatened deregulation. The jokes that BA stood for 'British Ashtrays', 'Bloody Awful' and 'Bags Anywhere' originated with employees as much as with disgruntled passengers. In these circumstances, the ideology (culture) is likely to be questioned and replaced. Until a new ideology is in place, Brunsson suggests, it will be impossible for the organisation to take effective action as the period of transition will be marked by conflicts and uncertainties that will inhibit individuals' willingness to make a commitment to any one course of action and hinder coordination.

Hence, it could be said that the relationship between 'strong' cultures, employee commitment, and adaptability contains a series of paradoxes. Strong cultures allow for a rapid response to familiar conditions, but inhibit immediate flexibility in response to the unfamiliar, because of the commitment generated to a (now) inappropriate ideology. 'Weak' cultures, in contrast, when equated with ambiguous ideologies, allow flexibility in response to the unfamiliar, but cannot generate commitment to action. Yet strong cultures, through disconfirmation and eventual ideological shift may prove ultimately more adaptive to change, assuming the emergence of a new, strong yet appropriate culture. This may be at the cost of a transitional period when ability to generate commitment to any course of action – new or old – is minimal.

Given the different levels of culture that need to be penetrated if genuine cultural change is to be effected, it is tempting to ask whether it is worth it. Certainly, once values are internalised, organisational members have the desired controls 'built in' and self-maintaining. But, as evidenced by the case studies cited, this is both expensive and not always successful. There is a case to be made that where boundaries are to be specified to a relationship, behavioural compliance achieved through instrumentalities and external pressure (i.e., behavioural commitment) may be more cost effective than attitudinal commitment. Developing a 'strong culture' for peripheral employees may be an ineffective use of resources.

Conclusion

Having considered the problematic and multifaceted nature of employee commitment and cultural management, it is tempting to ask why managers should bother with either. Various explanations present themselves, depending on whether one takes an optimistic or rather more cynical view of the world.

First, commitment (in the sense of attitudinal commitment), in a democratic society, is a much more acceptable notion than resigned behavioural compliance (which effectively is the same as some forms of behavioural/continuance commitment). Most people prefer others to agree rather than disagree with them and senior management, I guess, is no exception, particularly when wedded to unitaristic beliefs of the organisation as a 'team' pulling together, 'a tight ship is a happy ship' – even a 'family' (note: with its patronising imagery of senior management as parents and employees as children – at worst rebellious adolescents). Certainly, memories of the adversarial nature of employee relations in the 1970s, of the perceived stubborn intransigence of an 'irrational' workforce resistant to change, of poor economic performance, quite reasonably stimulated the idea that there must be a 'better way'. Attitudinal commitment, with employees internalising managerial values seemed that way – whether expressed through the OD initiatives of the 1970s or the present programmes of cultural management. And, to some extent, senior management can interpret the changed behaviours in the 1980s in the light of developing attitudinal commitment. Hence 'empowering' 'core' workers via the creation of semi-autonomous work groups and observing rising levels of productivity in manufacturing plants adopting flexible working may be attributed to changes in workers' attitudes towards management and the organisation. A cynic though might suggest that employees are keeping their heads down in periods of recession and high unemployment and that flexible working results in the labour intensification that delivers enhanced productivity. Further, that low levels of labour turnover and absenteeism and lack of industrial action reflect fear of job loss and plant closure, rather than commitment to managerial values. In other words, the changes observed are examples of behavioural commitment (? compliance) rather than attitudinal commitment.

At the end of the day, such research evidence as we have suggests only a weak link between attitudinal commitment, labour turnover and job performance. Managers and academics alike might argue that such results are inconclusive, stemming as they do from artificial, positivistic, narrow research designs that fail to capture the rich and complex texture of organisational reality. Yet if we reject these findings we revert to assertions of belief and hope, often based on 'special case' anecdote. In the light of substantial evidence of increasing productivity, certainly in manufacturing industry, over the 1980s and before 1990s recession bit and of survey data of enhanced labour intensification (see, for example, Legge, 1988, Chapter 5; Layard and Nickell, 1988; Metcalf, 1988, 1989; Nolan, 1989; Nolan and Marginson, 1990; Guest, 1990; Edwards and Whitston, 1991) it might be suggested that management *has* achieved greater *behavioural* commitment to desired work practices. However, given many individuals' penchant for psychological reductionism in the interpretation of successful outcomes (see attribution theory), it is often natural to gloss behavioural commitment with the language of attitudinal commitment. This resonates too with the individualistic values of the enterprise culture. And what of cultural change – the vogue of the 1980s and still fashionable in the 1990s? Much of the rhetoric asserts positive messages about their organisations that senior managers hope financial markets will find persuasive. Many, no doubt, too find the image of a 'transformational leader' more appealing than that of the 'transactional manager'. Certainly activities associated with transactional management (e.g., cost cutting programmes) may be easier to swallow if coated in the rhetoric of transformational leadership.

Can organisational cultures be managed? Senior managers, by their position in the organisation, have a voice that will be heard if not necessarily listened to. Their best strategy is probably to build on existing deeply held beliefs, in such a way that the new message (e.g., 'customer service') resonates with an old belief (e.g., 'how I like to be treated as a customer') and the connections and positive consequences are spelt out. But to try to establish values that appear discordant with reality, as perceived by those on the receiving end, is probably a fruitless task. Calculative involvement might be a more cost effective aspiration. Again strategies to achieve behavioural commitment may bear more fruit than those aimed at securing attitudinal commitment.

Managing culture has sometimes been likened to 'riding a wave' (Morgan, 1988). The best the surf-rider can do is to understand the pattern of currents and winds that shape and direct the waves. She may then use them to stay afloat and steer in the desired path. But this is not the same as changing the basic rhythms of the ocean.

Note

1. Much of this chapter is based on an earlier publication, 'Managing culture: fact or fiction?' (see Legge, 1994).

7

HRM and quality: customer sovereignty in the enterprise culture?

The fourth element of Guest's HRM model is quality. Guest (1987, p. 515) sees quality as involving three dimensions: quality of staff, quality of performance, and a public image that the organisation has a reputation for high quality in its human resource management policies. The latter comprises high standards in recruitment, selection, training, appraisal and goal-setting, and in designing 'high quality challenging jobs for high calibre staff' (p. 515). Not only are these aspects of quality seen to be mutually reinforcing (for example, a good public image assists in the recruitment of high quality staff, high quality staff are likely to generate and achieve high performance standards, high performance standards may foster a good public image, thereby completing the virtuous circle) but they resonate with the other dimensions of Guest's model. The assumption of a high quality, well trained workforce underlies notions of flexible specialisation and functional flexibility; commitment and high quality performance may be mutually reinforcing; a business strategy of producing high value added goods and services would argue the appropriateness of HRM policies aimed at producing high quality employees who, in turn, would constitute 'the difference that made the difference'. Further, Guest's reference to 'public image' introduces the idea of consumption and the marketplace and, hence, indirectly, that of the customer.

That 'quality' was the buzz word of the 1980s and survives as a taken-for-granted assumption in the 1990s (albeit somewhat buffeted by the rigours of the recent recession, as consumers become more price sensitive), there is no doubt. Whether expressed in the up-marketing strategies of the major food retailers, such as Tesco, Sainsbury and Marks & Spencer, or in the enhanced quality consciousness of car and electronic goods manufacturers (see, for example, Jaguar's 'Pursuit of Perfection' and Austin Rover's 'Working with Pride' programmes of quality improvement); in the customer charters of the newly privatised industries (such as Southern Electric's 'Our commitment to customer care' or NW Water's 'Putting the customer first') as discussed in Chapter 6, quality of product or service appears to be the cultural value espoused by 'hard' and 'soft' models of HRM alike (if with differing enacted degrees of commitment).

The pursuit of this holy grail may be seen as a direct response to the Japanese icon, discussed in Chapter 3. For Japan's economic success was widely identified as resulting from the ability of its motor and consumer electronics manufacturers to produce goods that, in the late 1970s and early 1980s, outstripped the UK and US indigenous equivalents in terms of quality, reliability and value. Oliver and Wilkinson (1992, pp. 7–8) cite figures, drawn from the International Motor Vehicle Programme (IMVP) World Assembly Plant Survey, that highlight such Japanese superiority. Comparing the hours of actual working effort taken to assemble a car of equivalent specifications in terms of size, options and content, in the mid-1980s, on average Japanese car plants in Japan took 16.8 hours to assemble such a vehicle, European-owned plants in Europe took more than double this, at 35.5 hours. The best plant in Japan took 13.2 hours; the worst European plant 55.7 hours. That such superiority in productivity was not at the expense of quality was revealed by comparable figures for defects at assembly stage. The Japanese-owned plants in Japan averaged 51.1 assembly defects per 100 vehicles, compared to 76.4 in Europe. Further, from a consumer's point of view, Oliver and Wilkinson (1992, p. 9) point to the findings of a 1989 *Which?* survey. Of the top ten most reliable cars in the one–two year old age bracket, four were Japanese; in the three–five year old age bracket six were Japanese.

Recognition of such Japanese superiority and its stimulus to change, was made explicit, for example, at Ford Europe, when its President, after a trip to Japan in the late 1970s, allegedly returned 'in a state of shock' (Starkey and McKinlay, 1989) and instituted an 'After Japan' package of change initiatives involving quality circles and direct communication with employees. Ford's reaction introduces three aspects of the Japanese 'shock'. First, a recognition of the alarmist message about the extent of the productivity and quality gap; second, an interest in Japanese manufacturing methods and in the American 'quality' gurus (Deming, Juran) known to have assisted Japanese manufacturing industry after World War II; third, a belief that such manufacturing methods, stemming initially from American gurus, were transportable to Europe and the US. The latter 'message of hope' was reinforced in the mid- to late 1980s by evidence, from the survey cited above, that Japanese transplants in the US come close to equalling the productivity and quality levels of Japanese plants in Japan (Oliver and Wilkinson, 1992, p. 9). In the UK this message was reinforced by the performance of Japanese-owned assembly plants on greenfield sites, such as Nissan at Sunderland (Jones, 1990). Ford's subsequent US inspired programme of Employee Involvement and a change package entitled 'Mission Values and Guiding Principles' is redolent of both aspirations to higher quality and increased market share, along with a recognition of the need for different working practices. The 'Guiding Principles' assert that

- Quality comes first
- Customers are the focus of everything we do
- Continuous improvement is essential to our success
- Employee involvement is our way of life
- Dealers and suppliers are our partners
- Integrity is never compromised. (Storey, 1992b, p. 57)

The Guiding Principles highlight another stimulus for quality. As will be discussed below, a standard 'technical' definition of 'quality' is 'fitness for use' or 'conformance to the requirements of the customer' (Juran, 1988; Hill, 1991a, p. 400). As discussed in Chapter 3, the emergence of an enterprise culture in the 1980s promoted the values of free market discipline and customer sovereignty in private and public sectors alike. The leaflet that accompanied a recent electricity bill is heavy with the rhetoric of 'customer care'. Entitled *Norweb: Guaranteed Standards of Customer Service*, it contains a 'Message from the Chairman' (no doubt signalling a commitment to high quality service from the very top of the organisation).

The message reads

> From April 1st 1993, an improved appointments service is now available to all our customers. This re-affirms our commitment to provide guaranteed high standards of service to our customers and excellent value for money. If you want a visit from us or we want to visit you, we will offer at least a morning appointment (up to 1pm) or an afternoon appointment (after 12 noon). If you prefer a more exact time, we will offer a visit within a 2 hour band ...
>
> In addition Norweb is ahead of its targets on all its Overall Standards of Performance for the twelve month period ending 31st March 1993. We are confident that the performance on the Overall Standards for the year commencing 1st April 1993 will exceed our revised targets and further improve the level of service to our customers.

The leaflet goes on to list the standards of service, including the compensatory payments that will be made if they are not met. Further, the message is personalised by a picture of a smiling chairman (identified as Ken Harvey), along with the names of Customer Service Managers, and various heart-warming pictures of good-looking young mothers and children welcoming a beaming middle aged Norweb maintenance man (*sic*) in clean company workwear, shirt and tie, with an immaculate new white van, looking for all the world like our stereotype of an old-style village policemen. The leaflet shouts reassurance.

However, a close look at the claims made in this leaflet reveals themes that have been discussed in earlier chapters. Not only is there the language of quality ('high standards of service, excellent value for money') but of 'commitment' to customer service. The offer of an improved appointments system suggests recognition of the need for enhanced organisational responsiveness to the customer, not to mention the increase in flexibility that is required. As far as quality goes themes are touched on that will be considered throughout this chapter: that poor quality of goods or services has financial costs; that commitment to quality involves a commitment to continuous improvement and ever higher standards; that the organisation should be proactive rather than reactive *vis à vis* customers .

In considering the relationship between quality and HRM, this chapter will focus on the relationships between quality, business strategy and flexibility, and in particular on the Japanese manufacturing techniques of TQM and JIT and on so-called 'customer-driven' changes in the public sector services. To what extent are the espoused policies implemented and what are the outcomes to their various stakeholders? In what ways do they illustrate the interdependency of the integration, flexibility, commitment and quality dimensions of Guest's (1987) model? What is the relationship between 'quality' and the 'hard' HRM model? Does the pursuit of 'quality' (apparently so desirable) contain tensions, contradictions and dysfunctions? To explore these issues, it is first necessary to consider how 'quality' has been conceptualised in relation to products/services and work processes.

The nature of 'quality'

What do we mean by 'quality'? The *Oxford Paperback Dictionary* (1979, p. 659) suggests three meanings: a degree or level of excellence ('goods of high quality'); general excellence ('it has quality'); a characteristic, something that is special in a person, or thing ('she has the quality of inspiring confidence'). These very general definitions have been echoed by Juran *et al.* (1962, p. 1.2) ('a vague expression of general excellence, but without being specific enough to be classified'; 'distinguishing feature of a grade or product, e.g., appearance, performance, reliability'), but most of the 'quality' 'gurus' (i.e., those interested in the 'hard'/production management perspective on quality) give more precise definitions. Juran *et al.* (1962, p. 1.2), for example, list the following:

- Degree to which a specific product satisfies the wants of a specific customer ('market-place quality');
- Degree to which a class of product possesses potential satisfactions for people generally ('quality of design');
- Degree to which a specific product conforms to a design or specification ('quality of conformance');
- Degree to which a specific product is preferred over competing products of equivalent grade, based on comparative tests by consumers ('consumer preference');

subsequently arriving at the catch-all, 'fitness for use' (Juran, 1988). Crosby (1979) defines quality as 'conformance to requirements' or 'zero-defects', 'right first time'. Deming (1982) defines quality in terms of quality of design, quality of conformance and quality of the sales and service functions. Still other gurus, for example, Feigenbaum (1983) emphasises quality less as an outcome and more as a way of managing an organisation. His 'total quality system' emphasises that management must commit themselves to strengthening the quality improvement process itself; making sure that quality improvement becomes a habit; and managing quality and cost as complementary objectives (Dale et al., 1990, p. 9).

Although there is much overlap in these definitions, with a general emphasis on quality of design and quality of conformance, commentators divide on two issues. First, there is a distinction between those such as Crosby (and Deming) who believe that higher quality always reduces costs and raises profits (hence the title of Crosby's book, *Quality is Free*) and those, such as Juran, who believe that an optimum balance must be struck between the cost of quality and the value of quality for each quality characteristic of the product or services. In other words, while increased conformance to specification reduces losses due to defects and customer dissatisfaction, the cost of the controls needed for zero defects may be greater than the potential maximum value of the product/service in the marketplace. Second, commentators differ on the roles assigned to senior, middle management, workforce and quality professionals in contributing to quality improvements. For example, Juran places stress on the lead role played by quality professionals and middle management, with the role of the workforce being minimal; Deming and Feigenbaum, in contrast, emphasise the need to involve all the organisation's employees; Crosby emphasises the role of top management, supported by quality professionals, with the workforce merely reporting problems to them (Dale et al., 1990).

What is clear about these definitions that emphasise excellence, conformance to specification and, to a lesser extent, value for money, is that they derive from and are orientated towards manufacturing industries (not surprisingly, given their roots in America and their rediscovery in the wake of Japanese manufacturing successes). As such, though, it is debatable how relevant they are to the expanding service sector. Services differ from products in several significant ways. They are primarily intangible, making it impossible to stock services the same way as one might stock goods, and their attributes are difficult to demonstrate. Services are simultaneously produced and consumed; consequently firms cannot use inventories to manage fluctuations in demand. Customers are involved in the production of many services – whether personal, leisure or medical services – which creates additional quality control problems for managers, summed up in the classic medical joke that 'the operation was successful, but the patient died'. Further, services are generally extremely perishable and are better viewed as a process rather than an outcome like a product (for a detailed discussion see Bowen and Schneider, 1988; Reeves and

Bednar, 1994). Given both this recognised difference between products and services and the fact that, in advanced Western economies, it is the service sector that is expanding at the expense of manufacturing, an increasingly popular definition of quality (very much implied in some of the quotations in the Introduction to this chapter) is 'meeting and/or exceeding customers' expectations'. Although, on the surface, this definition has the advantage of being all-encompassing, responsive to market changes and so forth, it is highly problematic. Different customers may place different weights on the various attributes of a product or services; they may not know what their expectations are – or may have 'unrealistic expectations' (particularly in relation to state provided services, such as the NHS). Pre-purchase experience/attitudes are a factor too, along with differences in short- and long-term evaluation (see Reeves and Bednar, 1994).

Clearly, all these definitions have their strengths and weaknesses and different implications for managerial action. Reeves and Bednar (1994) suggest that in each organisation quality should be defined with reference to the nature of its output, in terms of its tangibility and extent of customisation. So, for example, quality can be defined as conformance to specification for output that is tangible and standardised. For output that is intangible and customised, quality can be defined as the extent to which output meets and/or exceeds customer expectations.

Finally, Wilkinson *et al.* (1992, pp. 2–3) identify three approaches to reviewing 'quality'. The first focuses on the 'soft' qualitative characteristics of the 'excellence' literature: customer responsiveness, competitive edge secured by employee participation and empowerment via teamwork. The second focuses on the 'hard' production aspects of quality design and conformance to specification, using statistical procedures to assess quality, set and control standards of performance. The third approach comprises a mixture of 'hard' and 'soft' approaches emphasising excellence and competitive advantage, the need for a scientific, 'ops. management' approach, but emphasising the importance of participation, empowerment and teamwork. It is the latter, involving management commitment, 'statistical process control' and 'teamworking' that forms the basis of the prime change initiative to secure quality: Total Quality Management (Oakland, 1989).

Total Quality Management

Quality Circles – or, how one swallow does not make a summer

Total Quality Management (TQM) should not be confused with its somewhat fragile precursor, Quality Circles (QC).

In the late 1970s and early 1980s, mainly but not exclusively in manufacturing industry, quality circles were the 'flavour of the month'. Quality circles, generally speaking, consist of a voluntary group of between six to eight people from the same department, who meet together for an hour every week, usually but not always led by their supervisor, in order to solve work-related problems that they directly and mutually experience. In theory, members of the circle, operating on an egalitarian basis, select the problems they wish to solve; collect necessary data; apply systematic, usually statistical, problem-solving techniques such as Pareto analysis, 'fishbone' diagrams, histograms, scatter diagrams to the problem in hand; present their findings and proposed solutions to management for approval; implement their solutions where feasible and monitor the outcomes. In setting up QCs a steering committee comprising representatives of a range of functions (personnel, training, production, finance), key senior line managers and staff specialists, and circle members, is likely to come into being to guide, publicise and monitor circle activities and progress. A facilitator, usually a junior or middle manager, is generally made responsible for the QCs' routine administration, development and progress, while training in participative as well as statistical techniques is likely to be offered to circle members (see Collard and Dale, 1989, for further details).

The popularity of QCs in the 1970s and early 1980s is attested by their rapid take-up. According to Collard and Dale (1989, p. 357) the first major example at Rolls Royce, Derby was reported in 1978. By 1981 Lorenz suggested that almost a hundred organisations were involved, while in 1985 Income Data Services put the number at 400. In 1982, the National Society of Quality Circles (NSQC) was formed, whose aim is 'to encourage the healthy development of quality circles in the UK by combining the experience and energy of people from its member organisations'. In 1988 the NSQC claimed 120 organisations as members and their newsletter circulated to 240 work locations (Collard and Dale, 1989, p. 357).

However, as with many 'flavours of the month', by the late 1980s their attractions were beginning to pale. Although Dale and various collaborators, between 1984 and 1986, on the basis of UK survey evidence (leaving aside the minority of organisations that abolished their QC programmes entirely), found that most had a high survival rate with only 20 per cent of circles failing, the other commentators were less sanguine. In the US, Ambler and Overholt (1982) found that 50 per cent of circles failed in the early 1980s, while Lawler and Mohrman (1985) 'simply dismissed circles in the USA as a fad which would pass away because they were unworkable' (Hill, 1991b, p. 542) In 1987 Bradley and Hill contacted eleven companies in the South East and Midlands of the UK, 'which had been among the British pioneers in the early 1980s', with mature programmes of more than four years' duration, with the aim of undertaking an in-depth evaluation study (Bradley and Hill, 1987; Hill, 1991b, p. 544). Only five of the firms still had QCs. Of these remaining five, one reported that its programme was on the verge of collapse and two others that they were dissatisfied with circles. Of the six that no longer had circles, four had not attempted new initiatives. Three of the companies overall, however, were in the early stages of implementing TQM. Further, as Marchington (1992) has pointed out, in his review of the evidence for employee involvement in

QCs, only a small proportion of the workforce of an organisation which boasts QCs actually takes part.

While not denying the successes of QCs – on the basis of survey evidence Dale and his collaborators report members' increased job satisfaction and involvement, better teamwork within the department, some improvements in quality and productivity – many of the benefits claimed were 'intangible' (Collard and Dale, 1989, pp. 364–6). Further, Bradley and Hill (1987) failed to find, even among participants, many positive changes in attitudes. Hill's (1991b) 1988 survey of a sample of members and non-members (n:146) in two establishments of an office automation company, a 'leading light of the British QC movement' (p. 547) found that while members were attached to and valued their circles, 'they still showed no greater job satisfaction, no more involvement in the company, and no more positive feelings towards management than their colleagues outside' (p. 548). Additionally, while some measurable cost savings were reported by management, the level of measurable return was seen as disappointing and declining over time.

> Those companies that kept them going chose to do so for 'social' rather than 'economic' reasons, believing that they were good for their members and the overall climate of human relations even if they no longer delivered significant financial or technical improvements.
> (Hill, 1991b, p. 548)

Various explanations have been offered for the relative lack of success of the QC movement. First, there was some ambiguity about the overt and covert objectives sought. Were QCs, via greater involvement, aimed at greater job satisfaction and better working relationships, with improved performance as a hoped-for spin-off? Or were they chiefly about eliciting behaviour conducive to better quality and productivity, irrespective of any attitudinal change? (Collard and Dale, 1989, p. 356). Or were they examples of pseudo-participation, a management ploy 'to bypass trade unions and create an individualistic relationship with employees, in order to increase the legitimacy of management in employees' eyes'? (Hill, 1991b, p. 543 citing Batstone and Gourlay, 1986, pp. 117–29). This ambiguity reflected the twin, but differing, motivations attributed to the introduction of QCs. In the late 1970s, they were seen on one hand, as a way of improving highly adversarial employee relations, via direct communication aimed at increasing employee involvement. Ramsay (1977, 1985, cited in Hill, 1991b, p. 543) argues that such participation represents a cyclical strategy on the part of employers. That is, senior management respond to perceived crises in employee relations by offering greater employee participation, only to reassert management prerogative when the crisis is over. Hence, by the middle of the 1980s when high unemployment and restrictive trade union and labour legislation had rendered employee relations less problematic, interest in QCs, as a vehicle for ameliorating problematic shop-floor relations, lost much of its point. On the other hand, QCs were seen in the late 1970s as a strategy for improving manufacturing quality, with realisation of the productivity/quality gap with Japan. By the end of the 1980s more encompassing strategies, such as TQM (see below) were sought to accommodate a broader conception of competitive advantage.

If failure lay partly in confusion and changing relevance of objectives, these in turn were reflected in the commitment (or lack of it) of the various stakeholders. Collard and Dale (1989, p. 369) list a range of technical and attitudinal reasons attributed to circle failure, including (in descending order of frequency) redundancies and/or restructuring caused by the economic situation; labour turnover; lack of cooperation from middle management, circle leaders' lack of time to organise meetings; circles ran out of projects to tackle; lack of cooperation from first-line supervisors; delay in responding to circle recommendations; circle members disillusioned with quality circle philosophy; circle members lacked time to carry out activities; over-ambitious projects tackled; lack of recognition; groups spread over too wide a work area; leader not following through initial training; failure to get solution implemented; inadequate training; lack of cooperation from functional specialists.

While recognising overlapping categories in this list, certain themes stand out. Although trade unions, such as the TGWU, have expressed opposition on the grounds that QCs may serve to undermine the authority of shop stewards and union organisation (Wintour, 1987), the evidence points overwhelmingly to a lack of junior and middle management support as a major reason for the relative failure of QCs on the ground. Bradley and Hill (1987, pp. 74–5) found that while senior management supported QCs, middle and junior management felt that participation was unnecessary if they were doing their jobs properly and, by implicitly criticising management performance, QCs undermined managerial prerogative. First-line supervision was concerned that QCs, if they fulfilled their aspirations for shop-floor democracy and critiqued established working methods, might result in calling into question the need for supervisors at all.

If managerial prerogative and job protection were covert agendas in this managerial foot-dragging, technical reasons for less than full participation could be used to cover these tracks.

The burdens involved in operationalizing participative management are usually ignored by its advocates. The middle managers, however, complained that these were unwelcome additional burdens in jobs that were already taxing. They asserted that quality circles dealt with minor problems, most of which managers had already recognized but had been prevented from solving for reasons of cost expediency; that rank-and-file employees were not competent to help on the important problems because of their limited formal education and job knowledge that was based on a narrow range of tasks; that regular circle meetings jeopardized departmental production targets; that managers had to give up time to deal with quality circle business which would have been better spent on more pressing issues. Quality circles were therefore seen to add to managerial workloads for comparatively small return. (Bradley and Hill, p. 75)

These, often genuine concerns, go a long way to explain other factors that contribute to circle failure; the facilitator being too junior and lacking authority to sanction expenditure at implementation stage; lack of facilitator support; lack of time for circle activities; running out of projects; a general lack of perceived rewards and, with it, a failure of motivation.

Hill (1991b, pp. 548–51) concludes that the fragility of QCs is less a question of management and employee attitudes and culture, than one of organisational design. 'In essence, circles disrupted managers' lives for small returns and created an organisational complexity that confused existing structures, and middle management had no reason to make them work.'

The small returns refer to the disruptive effects outlined above. The organisational complexity results from a failure to integrate QCs into the existing organisational hierarchy. Instead, a paralleled or dualistic structure is created that confuses normal lines of command and allocates responsibility to managers for overseeing circles without corresponding authority; separates the identification and solving of problems from the implementation of solutions, and fails to integrate managers' circle activity into the organisation's existing appraisal and reward system. This lack of integration into the mainstream of management, the absence of rewards and sanctions for quality of participation in QCs, the questionable calibre and/or very junior status of facilitators, by the late 1980s, called into question senior management's real, as opposed to espoused, commitment to QCs. As Hill (1991b, pp. 550–1) puts it, the message increasingly came over 'that the people at the top regarded quality improvement as an optional extra that was voluntary, divorced from normal managerial duties and with no penalties for those who choose to opt out'. At best, QCs might be seen as a transitional mechanism, sensitising organisations to issues of quality improvement and of extending the jobs of the shop floor (Lawler and Mohrman, 1985).

Enter TQM

As discussed in Chapter 4, increasingly the strategists' message is that corporate success is not measured in terms of organisational size, market share and profitability alone, but by an organisation's ability to add value to its inputs. This is achieved, so the argument goes, through developing distinctive capabilities, such as reputation or innovation, often derived from the unique character of the organisation's relationships with its suppliers, customers or employees, precisely identified and aimed at relevant markets. Hence the success in the 1980s of firm as diverse as Glaxo (innovation of the anti-ulcerant Zantac), Marks & Spencer ('architecture' of supplier and employee relations, reputation) and Reuters (reputation, incumbency positioning) (Kay, 1993). Without repeating arguments developed in Chapter 4, the important point for this discussion is that an increasing number of organisations have identified a reputation for quality as a route to the often greater profit margins of mid- or up-market positions (i.e., premium payment for *excellence*). Even where the market niche is acknowledged as distinctly down-market (The *Sun*, Casio watches, McDonald's hamburgers) quality is not irrelevant. Where profit margins are low, profitability depends on volume combined with cost minimisation. This, in turn, depends on the ability to maintain detailed control of product/service specification, such that quality will be maintained at a level preferred by consumers against competing products/services at a similar price (i.e., that it represents *value* for money). Consequently *both* strategies imply that achieving 'quality', at the standard aimed for, has implications for how the value chain and thus the organisation is to be managed. In Oliver and Wilkinson's (1992, p. 22) words, such aims 'imply a tightly integrated organisation, efficient in its use of resources so that it is price competitive, but simultaneously flexible enough to respond to customer requirements'. This points to Just-in-Time (JIT) systems as logically, not to say inextricably, linked to TQM.

This perspective on quality underlies the emergence of TQM. As pointed out by Dale *et al.* (1990, Figure 1.1), over the last thirty years, quality systems have evolved through four, increasingly proactive stages. Traditionally quality has been inspected after the event, when the complete product or brought-in components are screened for defects/conformity to specification. In this system there is no attempt at prevention other than identification of inadequate suppliers, operations or workers producing non-conforming products. The system is in-house and does not involve suppliers or customers directly. The outcomes are salvage, sorting and grading, identifying sources of non-conformance and taking corrective actions. A more sophisticated approach is quality control where various process control methods are instituted, such as a quality manual and process performance data, along with some intermediate stage product testing, some self-inspection by operators, and feedback of process information to operatives, setters and supervisors. A further stage is quality assurance, where a comprehensive system of planned actions such as statistical process control, use of quality costs data, systems audit and third party approvals are systematically used to prevent rather than just detect non-conformance. Finally, we reach the fourth stage, TQM.

So how does Total Quality Management (TQM) differ? In essence rather than remaining a more or less separate or imperfectly integrated control system, it is the *generation of structures and a culture of quality to pervade all aspects of the organisation*. This means that in theory quality management principles become the taken-for-granted assumptions that govern working relationships – vertically and horizontally – within the organisation, *and* with suppliers and customers. Various commentators have written in detail about TQM in theory and in practice (see Oakland, 1989; Dale and Plunkett, 1990; Hill, 1991a, 1991b; Oliver and Wilkinson, 1992; Sewell and Wilkinson, 1992; Garrahan and Stewart, 1992). With some minor variations in emphasis between commentators, TQM in *theory* would appear to emphasise the following:

1. Quality is defined as conformance to the requirements of the customer. As discussed earlier this involves effectiveness (i.e., 'fitness for use' – the product/service must meet the customer's needs) as well as efficiency (i.e., 'conformance to specification' – the product must do what it is designed to do).

2. The concept of customer is defined broadly; there are internal as well as external customers. The internal customers are those employees responsible for the next process, who have the 'right' to demand that inputs received conform to the agreed specifications, while they as 'suppliers' to the next process have the obligation similarly to meet the specifications of those responsible for that process.

3. Appropriate quantitative performance measures are used routinely to assess the quality of design and conformance and to initiate corrective action as soon as performance begins to deviate from specification. While market research and competitive bench marking of products and processes against other firms' performance is central to the former, statistical process control[1] is central to the latter.

4. TQM requires the involvement of all. This includes the continuous support of senior management to drive a culture of quality; their delegation of major responsibilities to interdepartmental and cross-functional middle management project teams; the enlisting of the commitment of 'empowered' workers, organised into teams and participating in decision-making, to take responsibility as 'suppliers' of zero-defect goods to internal customers. It also involves developing high trust relationships with external suppliers, based on long-term commitment, cooperation and mutual obligation (i.e., 'relational' as opposed to 'spot' contracting). But while the commitment and involvement of all in such a culture conducive to quality is essential, managers have the major responsibility for quality improvement and it is managerially designed control systems that are a major source of quality failure. Hence, as Oliver and Wilkinson (1992, p. 21) point out, TQM contains a source of potential tension – between local responsibility and centralised direction. This will be explored below.

5. The philosophy that underpins the above is a belief in '*kaizen*' or continuous improvement for the common good of internal and external customers alike. At one level this refers to the struggle to achieve 'zero-defects' but more broadly it encompasses the objectives of eliminating waste – waste of time/manpower, energy, materials and capital. TQM and JIT go hand in hand, as will now be discussed.

Just-in-time production

Enter just-in-time (JIT)

JIT production gained popularity throughout the 1980s but, unlike QCs, it is a fashion that has gained a widening rather than diminishing popularity. This may be because some proponents argue that many JIT techniques, albeit the 'Japanese' packaging, are not themselves new, but recognised attempts at overcoming some of the inefficiencies of Taylorist manufacturing systems (Graham, 1988). As it is, JIT is increasingly associated with 'best practice' in manufacturing systems. In *Management Today*'s regular reviews of 'Britain's Best Factories', by the beginning of the 1990s, of the sixteen companies identified as 'Britain's Best', ten operated a JIT system and all sixteen had some form of TQM in operation (Delbridge and Turnbull, 1992, p. 58).

> For many firms the question appears no longer to be whether to introduce JIT, but *how*. The adopting of these systems is seen as an imperative to survival. (Delbridge and Turnbull, 1992, p. 58, citing Womack *et al.*, 1990)

JIT production recalls the debate on flexible specialisation outlined in Chapter 5. First, it speaks of market specialisation as the sought-for reduction in machine set-up times (see below) permits a reduction in batch sizes, a major determinant of lead time and, hence, can allow greater customer responsiveness. Second, it raises questions about flexibility. Turnbull (1988a, p. 7) suggests a contradiction here. On the one hand, JIT has been seen both as a qualitatively different system of production – the 'lean' system of flexible specialisation (Womack *et al.*, 1990) – *and* as a method of eliminating the major problems of Fordist systems, by combining product diversity with mass production efficiencies, without any costly reskilling, but gaining access to the 'gold-in-the-heads' of workers and placing that knowledge in the service of rationalisation (Turnbull, 1988a, pp. 14–15). Which view one takes depends on the interpretation of the espoused theory and rhetoric in the light of the empirical evidence. Before considering such evidence, what it the theory of JIT and how does it relate to TQM?

The theory of JIT

Following Turnbull (1988a, p. 8) JIT production is aimed at 'securing time economies in the circuit of capital and new ways of extracting productivity improvements from the labour force'. This is done by increasing the rate of throughput through the organisation, thereby increasing the turnover ratio of capital (i.e., total sales divided by total assets) and total productivity. Thus the exact quantity of defect-free goods are produced just-in-time for sale in the market; sub-assemblies are produced just-in-time for final assembly; and brought components and materials arrive from supplier just-in-time to be made into sub-assemblies. Hence production is *pulled* through the plant in accordance with the configuration of final market demand rather than *pushed* by pre-determined fixed production schedules.[2]

The underlying philosophy of JIT is the elimination of waste – hence the designation of a 'lean' production system. This involves removing any non-value adding operation from the process. According to Oliver and Wilkinson (1992, p. 26) at Toyota there is a distinction between three types of waste: *muda, mura* and *muri*. *Muda* refers to seven types of waste; rework or repairs; overproduction (causing stock accumulations); inventory (excess stock); unnecessary motions by workers or machines; too much quality (overspecification); idle time; and double handling in the conveyance of materials. *Mura* refers to unevenness resulting from irregular schedules and volumes. This will inevitably result in *muda*, because for part of the day workers and machines will be operating below capacity. *Muri* refers to overburdening or the pushing of machines and/or workers beyond their tolerances with the result of incurring one of several of the types of *muda*.

As Oliver and Wilkinson (1992, pp. 29–31) point out, JIT is an extremely fragile system of production, vulnerable to the quality of components, the accuracy of scheduling, the efficiency and reliability of equipment, and the efficiency, flexibility and commitment of employees. As such it requires certain pre-conditions of production management and employee relations systems if it is to work in practice as in theory.

First, if goods are to be produced 'just-in-time' in fluctuating market conditions, then the system requires the ability to produce in relatively small batches, if so demanded. While small batches may be expensive in terms of set-up times, large batches incur the cost of tying up large amounts of capital in inventory. Hence in deciding what is the smallest, economically viable, batch size, set-up times are crucial and pressure is to reduce them as far as possible. This may be done by investing in multi-purpose machinery and tooling with quick change dies, pre-kitting, calibrated machine tools, automatic stop devices and so on. Apart from such 'technical' solutions, reducing set-up times calls for changes in the social systems as setting-up is included in the job description of direct production workers with the elimination of a separate (craft) grade of tool setters (i.e., a degree of functional flexibility is required). All this has implications for operator training. Oliver and Wilkinson quote Toyota's achievement in cutting the changeover of dies in its stamping shops from as much as ten hours to 165 seconds.

Second, JIT systems require a relatively simple, unidirectional workflow achieved by line layouts or group technology and the product form of organisation.[3] Without this there arise three different causes of stock accumulation: complexity, inflexibility and uncertainty. Complexity of workflow is likely to give rise to bottlenecks and to an inevitable stock accumulation as materials that are stationary as work-in-progress or buffer stocks tie up capital while gaining no added value. Inflexibility, that assumes set-up times as given and derives economical batch sizes from this, ties up stock in long runs. Uncertainty encourages stock accumulation via buffer stocks, unless quality assured supplies can be guaranteed along the complete value chain. This argues for a high trust collaborative relationship with suppliers, TQM throughout the organisation and standardisation of work tasks to allow for the required degree of synchronisation.

Third, in this context, it is easy to see the importance of TQM and its symbiotic relationship with JIT. Any cessation of supply halts the system and produces *muda*. Faulty raw materials, components or sub-assemblies have just this effect, as the absence of stocks brings the system to a halt. But importantly the relationship is a two-way one. The very fragility of the JIT system is an aid to achieving continuous improvement as any malfunction of equipment, materials or workers, in the absence of inventory, is instantly highlighted by bringing the system to a stop. This necessitates that the problem is examined and rectified rather than allowed to fester, protected by inventory. Further, given that the definition of quality used here implies 'quality at the right price', the elimination of waste, integral to JIT, is another aspect of achieving quality. Conversely, achieving 'zero defects', itself implies the elimination of waste, for example, the time and costs associated with reworking parts, rescheduling production and dealing with customer complaints and warranty claims. In addition, quality reduces costs by eliminating indirect grades of quality inspectors and increasing throughput. It allows production processes to be simplified because defective parts no longer need to be re-routed round rectification loops, while less waste assists in the elimination of buffer stocks to guard against quality problems (Turnbull, 1988a, pp. 8–9).

These production requirements of JIT have their corollary in the employee relations systems they assume. The drive to eliminate waste and seek continuous improvement relies heavily on employee input, whether achieved through employee involvement and empowerment or labour intensification. As already said, reducing set-up times requires operators to acquire new skills as their job descriptions expand. Group technology is often considered to achieve maximum effectiveness with teamworking and intra-team flexibility. TQM similarly argues that 'empowered' employees, within facilitating management control systems, should take responsibility for quality. The fragility of the system argues for employees' numerical and temporal flexibility, as allowable short-term buffers in response to larger than anticipated fluctuations in demand than can be coped with by the *kanban* system (Monden, 1983) (see also n. 2).

In summary, a number of beneficial outcomes theoretically derive from JIT, in harness with TQM; more efficient use of working capital, reduction in lead times and hence potentially greater customer responsiveness, improvements in quality and reductions in waste. Thus far the theory. But are these values achieved in practice and what, if any, is the potential downside?

TQM and JIT in action

Even this brief summary of the theory of TQM and JIT reveals incipient contradictions and tensions. First, both seem to argue for delegation and centralisation simultaneously. On the one hand, it suggested that employees are empowered in order to take responsibility at operational level for quality and continuity of production. This is symbolised by delegating to shopfloor operatives the authority to stop the line if they detect a problem that is impairing production (*jidoka*). On the other, it suggested that management have a pre-eminent role in the devising of systematic standardised systems for achieving quality that limit spontaneous initiative on the shopfloor. JIT's intolerance of uncertainty and complexity, as well as TQM's stress on 'conformance to specification' argues for a standardisation of tasks that further inhibits employee autonomy. Following the arguments developed in Chapter 6, developing a 'culture of quality', or any strong culture, equally points to standardisation of employees via highly selective recruitment practices and intensive socialisation in the preferred values. JIT, stressing the elimination of waste, could be argued to necessarily involve labour intensification, further reducing workers' autonomy. In what sense does teamworking both demand and inhibit flexibility? To what extent does a quality requirement argue for specialisation rather than upskilling functional flexibility? Does elimination of waste also refer to 'excessive' training costs? Is teamworking a vehicle for multiskilling and a focus for enhanced commitment and motivation or is it an instrument of cooptation, peer surveillance and management-by-stress (Parker and Slaughter, 1988)? Let us look at the evidence.

The case studies and surveys of JIT and TQM range from managerially written success stories, most famously, Wickens' and Jones' messianic accounts of Nissan (Wickens, 1987; Jones, 1990), through the balanced 'let us assess the pros and cons' accounts of academics within a pluralist tradition (e.g., Hill, 1991a, 1991b; Wilkinson *et al.*, 1992; Oliver and Wilkinson, 1992; Storey, 1992b) to the hostile critiques of labour process theorists (e.g., Turnbull, 1988a; Delbridge and Turnbull, 1992; and notably, Garrahan and Stewart, 1992). As the 'success' stories largely repeat the theory of TQM and JIT and claim that the organisation in question (Nissan, Lucas, Rank Xerox – see Wickens, 1987; White and Wyatt, 1990; Mercer and Judkins, 1990) has achieved or is well on the way to achieving many of their claimed benefits, I will say no more about them other than that it must be borne in mind that these accounts, though undeniably sincere, are written by those who have a vested interest in TQM's and JIT's success. What of the 'pluralist' and 'critical' accounts?

TQM and JIT – travelling hopefully but yet to reach the promised land?

Empirical studies in a pluralist tradition (e.g., Hill, 1991a, 1991b; Wilkinson *et al.*, 1992, 1993; Oliver and Wilkinson, 1992) point to widespread company experimentation with TQM and JIT, but with mixed outcomes. Hill's studies of TQM in four companies, in the office automation, automotive and precision engineering components industries, paints the most optimistic picture – perhaps by the way of contrast with his findings on the lack of success of QCs. He found far greater middle management involvement in TQM than with QCs, with TQM seen as more focused, coherent, relevant, less time consuming and delivering quicker and more substantial benefits. There was evidence of the growth of improvement teams, mainly among middle and junior managers of similar status on projects that ran horizontally across the organisation. There was some evidence of the delegation of TQM activities to the office and shopfloor and, in one case, the introduction of autonomous teamworking in a new automated assembly facility, in another the delegation of a relocation exercise involving design of the new layout, the move and installation of equipment to first-line supervisors and operatives. Further, every company considered that significant quality improvements had been achieved, whether measured in terms of reduction in the level of defects, reduced costs or increased customer satisfaction. Attitude surveys in at least one company indicated that two-thirds of employees reported a high level of personal commitment to improving quality, although, at the same time, all the organisations reported a lack of involvement on the part of some employees at all levels.

Such relatively positive results Hill (1991b) attributes to three factors. First, at least in initial stages, senior managers invested much time and personal commitment to TQM (although as the programmes developed they tended to maintain more of an oversight role than active involvement). Second, TQM (unlike stand-alone QCs) united routine management and managing innovation in one set of organisational arrangements and practices. Third, reflecting the first two factors, middle and junior managers could see that TQM directly affected their own interests: it helped them to manage more effectively, increased their own involvement and decision-making and, by performance in TQM activities being incorporated in appraisal systems, visible success was rewarded in career terms. Nevertheless, Hill (1991b, p. 564) reports evidence of some backsliding and lack of full commitment among certain middle and senior managers, and a fairly general failure to pursue the formal techniques of TQM amongst all levels of management.

Wilkinson et al. (1992, p. 14), in an examination of three companies in marketing communications, machine tools and retail finance sectors, paint a less optimistic picture. Summarising their results, they conclude:

Thus there is a pattern of adoption of TQM with consultants and expensive packages, an educational programme communicating missions and values, the establishment of quality teams and often a review committee (comprising senior management). The second phase is one of hope, with employees enthused by the ideas and their opportunity to influence their job and environment. However, the third phase can be described as one of disappointment and disillusion – some quantifiable financial returns, some evidence of commercialization, but not the gains expected by managers nor the influence employees hoped for. There are exceptions to this standard picture within our sample, but the fourth phase can be described even for the more successful TQM companies as a 'what now' phase. Continuous improvement, of course, is the TQM goal, but the evidence we have is that companies find it hard to sustain the momentum of the initiatives.

Such criticisms echo Hill's earlier comments about the fate of QCs, and the reasons for this lack of sustainability appear similar. Wilkinson *et al.* (1992, pp. 14–18) suggest four. First, that the TQM approach adopted by their case study companies, contrary to the philosophy, appeared narrowly conceived and bolted on to rather than integrated with key management policies, looking for immediate gains and hence adopting a 'quick-fix' approach, rather than seeking long-term cultural change. Second, TQM rather than uniting managers, may become an area for conflict between competing interest groups. In particular, production managers may see it as a vehicle for increasing their centrality to the organisation (see Chapter 9). Further, staff initiatives may be constrained by a highly centralised framework, even if the rhetoric speaks of decentralisation. In their financial services organisation, for example, 'TQM degenerated into staff papering over cracks which appear(ed) at the customer interface although they originate(d) in other parts of the organisation – such as administration centres' (Wilkinson *et al.*, 1992, p. 15). Third, being driven by senior management, in its early stages, TQM tends to be seen as part of management policy and outside the trade union sphere of influence. As a result, industrial relations issues, such as job control, working practices and pay, which may be important for its implementation at shop-floor level tend to be neglected in concentration on managerially-directed motivational and training initiatives. Finally, Wilkinson *et al.* (1992, p. 18) point to the tensions between the increased employee involvement prescribed by TQM (via educative programmes such as 'customer awareness'; work restructuring, such as teamworking, workers taking responsibility for quality control; committees, QCs, etc.) and a strong emphasis on reinforcing management control. 'In the sense that quality methods of working emphasise monitoring and control (with the differences that workers do it themselves), TQM ideas can also be used to reinforce a management style rooted in Taylorism.'

The cautionary note sounded by Wilkinson *et al.* (1992) is echoed by the findings of Oliver and Wilkinson's (1992) 1987 and 1991 surveys, each based on the responses of 66 manufacturing companies, drawn from the 1987 *Times* 1,000 index and the Microstat Extel respectively (i.e., response rates of 18 and 14 per cent respectively). Three findings stand out. First, the data demonstrate 'a clear *wish*' to adopt TQM and JIT manufacturing methods (with associated teamworking, SPC, QCs, etc.) and a very substantial use of the methods. However, the 1991 survey suggested that adoption of TQM and JIT had not been as fast as anticipated in 1987, and that there had been a decline in the usage of SPC and TQM, although a large rise in JIT. Further, the implementation dates reported in the second survey were more recent than in the first, 'suggesting that companies are either redefining what Japanese methods really are, or revising their perceptions of when they "really" started their programme of change, or most probably a combination of both' (p. 317). The implication is 'a gap between rhetoric and reality' (p. 317) which should be borne in mind when assessing the claimed spread of TQM and JIT.

Second, Oliver and Wilkinson cast some doubt on the claims of success for these methods. Not only are the success rates reported in 1991 lower than those reported in 1987, but such a finding, they considered, is consistent with anecdotal case study evidence. Tellingly they cite the different perceptions of John Parnaby, Lucas' Manufacturing Director, from the messianic vision of JIT in 1987:

> It is not the latest gimmick, it is fundamental and when completed there can be no other improvement since it completely tailors a manufacturing strategy to the needs of a market and produces mixed products in exactly the order required.

to the more down-to-earth view, that, implementing JIT

> is a balls-aching job. It cannot be anything other than that. You just have to grind your way through it. (Oliver and Wilkinson, 1992, pp. 317–18)

Third, Oliver and Wilkinson (1992, pp. 318–22) citing work by Williams *et al.* (1989) and Delbridge and Oliver (1991) suggest that the aggregate data on stock levels at sector level, show little evidence of a significant decline in stockholding, despite the claims by UK manufacturing companies to be implementing JIT. Of particular interest is Delbridge and Oliver's longitudinal study of stock turnover in the Japanese and Western car industries as it is in this sector of industry that TQM, in manufacturing, and JIT are claimed to be most widely and intensively developed. In a nutshell they found that stock turnover ratio figures (i.e., ratio of the value of total stocks to annual sales) showed little evidence that JIT and TQM were as yet making much impact on the stock turns of Western manufacturers. In spite of some improvement, the gap between Western and Japanese manufacturers (especially Toyota) showed little sign of narrowing and may even be widening. (Nor is there any evidence that the Japanese vehicle assemblers' performance is achieved at the cost of increased stockholding on the part of their suppliers. Indeed Japanese component suppliers' stock turn performance was improving faster than UK suppliers in the late 1980s in spite of the latters' claimed enthusiastic adoption of TQM and JIT at this time.) Further, while European assemblers showed lower stock turns than US manufacturers, within Europe, the UK volume producers showed some of the lowest stock turns. All this throws cold water on claims about the tangible outcomes of TQM and JIT in that sector of manufacturing industry where its adoption is widely reckoned to have been enthusiastic and advanced.

Taking these neutral studies together, from a managerial viewpoint, the verdict points to much enthusiasm, variable success in implementation and, as with most change initiatives in UK industry, the suspicion that in all but the exemplar companies, the underlying philosophies of TQM and JIT are compromised by economic exigencies and an endemic short-termism (Sisson, 1989, 1990) that both seeks a 'quick-fix' and lacks the stamina for the long haul of cultural change. Indeed, some commentators would argue that even in the exemplar companies, such as Nissan at Sunderland, the 'virtuous tripod' of quality, flexibility and teamwork is not what it seems. Commentators from a Marxist, labour process oriented perspective take a very different view of TQM and JIT.

TQM and JIT – control, exploitation and surveillance

Nissan at Sunderland, a vehicle manufacturer on a greenfield site in an area of decaying heavy industry and high unemployment is often referred to as an exemplar case study of the implementation of TQM and JIT and, indeed, of HRM generally. This, in no small measure, is due to the messianic account of the 'Nissan Way' penned by the plant's prominent Personnel Director, Peter Wickens. In *The Road to Nissan* he refers repeatedly to the 'tripod' of Nissan's success, namely flexibility, quality and teamwork (Wickens, 1987). These are spoken of in glowing terms, laced with words such as consensus, commitment and trust. However, critical theorists take a very different view – and of other vehicle assemblers and electronic plants where TQM and JIT techniques are most prevalent (Garrahan and Stewart, 1992; Turnbull, 1988a). They would suggest that flexibility equates with labour intensification and management-by-stress; quality with control and management-through-blame; teamworking with peer surveillance and management-through-compliance. Rather than flexibility, quality and teamwork representing a 'tripod of success', the critical theorists would argue that it represents a 'tripod of subjugation'. Their arguments are as follows.

The pursuit of quality, particularly in the context of waste-eliminating JIT, inevitably leads to the standardisation of the work process in order to achieve both conformance to specification and the elimination of uncertainty. At Nissan this is laid down as the 'Standard Operation', as is the supervisor's responsibility to ensure compliance with the standard operation, inculcation of subordinates in the rationale of *why* it must be complied with and the rooting out of 'abnormalities' (Nissan, 1987). The freedom of operators to innovate, even with the intention of improving quality or the production process, is highly circumscribed. At Nissan new methods can only be implemented after sanctioning at a *kaizen* meeting; similarly the Mazda training manual states

> For all work we perform in the workshop a work procedure sheet has been provided ... If the operator changes the work procedure at his discretion, he may put the process before and after that process in jeopardy, or increase the cost ... Therefore *the operator should always observe the specified work procedure faithfully*. If you have any doubts, you may propose a change to the team leader and *should never change the work procedure at your discretion*. (TGWU, 1989, original emphasis, cited in Delbridge and Turnbull, 1992, p. 62)

In other words, collective autonomy is limited to task design as opposed to task execution (Klein, 1991), and the implementation of suggestions is at management's discretion. As such, Garrahan and Stewart (1992, p. 10) liken *kaizen* meetings at Nissan to the 'games' identified by Burawoy (1979), in that they involve individuals, under the guise of participation and democracy, 'learning to participate in the agreement of preordained decisions'.

The worker's ability to buy 'parcels of time' through working up the line is similarly frowned on as this builds up the buffers that JIT is designed to eliminate. Effectively workers' rest time, achieved in this manner, is defined as waste to be eliminated. Such elimination contributes inevitably to labour intensification. The emphasis on standard procedures and the elimination of 'working up the line', in spite of the rhetoric of empowerment associated with workers taking responsibility for quality and participating in decision-making via *kaizen* meetings, in practice constrains their job discretion.

Further, the stress on quality standards and the elimination of waste has given rise to sophisticated visual and electronic systems of error detection that can trace faults back to the 'guilty' workgroup or even individual responsible. Sewell and Wilkinson (1992) describe a 'traffic-light' system in a Japanese-owned electronics factory, that shows a red card if an individual has made five or more mis-insertions on the previous shift, amber if between one and four, and green if no mis-insertions. By this method not only is an individual's absolute level of performance clearly signalled, but that performance in comparison with the rest of the workgroup. If an individual 'outperforms', his or her activities can be examined to see if a process innovation (although proscribed) has occurred that might be usefully adopted by all. If someone is consistently underperforming, the reason can be sought, even if it involves questions about the individual's private life. If all cards are on red or green management can deduce that the line is too fast or too slow for everyone and can adjust the speed to optimise on the elimination of waste, whether work in progress or defects. Amber cards signal a condonable level of error, but create a climate where workers feel pressured to make improvements – an approach that has been labelled as 'management-by-stress' (Slaughter, 1987). Significantly, Sewell and Wilkinson (1992, p. 110) quote one employee under this system as saying: 'OK, so no one likes to have a red card hanging over their head but it's when you see other people with red cards when yours is green that it really gets to you.' They conclude that 'the solitary confinement of Taylorism has been superceded by the electronic tagging of the Information Panopticon' (p. 109). Further control is exercised by appeals to the sovereignty of the customer and the satisfaction of his or her wants – or in Nissan's case to strive 'for a level of quality which matches *or exceeds* that expected by the customer' (Nissan, 1987, p. 2, added emphasis), the customer thereby being attributed with a surveillance role.

If TQM and JIT, in practice, may be seen as resulting in high levels of management control[4] and increased constraints on worker discretion, this goes hand in hand, so the critical theorists claim, with labour intensification and exploitation. JIT systems are notorious for the pace of work expected. Delbridge and Turnbull (1992, p. 67) cite a worker at Lucas Electrical, a UK automotive components manufacturer, as saying 'the rhythm of work is so constant. We now work flat out all the time, rather than when we want to'. Garrahan and Stewart (1992) suggest that the relatively high levels of labour turnover at Nissan, in spite of the area's high levels of unemployment, reflect the pace of work. This stems from the very logic of TQM and JIT. The idea of continuous improvement or *kaizen*, fundamental to TQM, dismantles the notion of fixed standard times, as the aim is to make the work process ever more efficient, that employees work towards ever lower time sequences for tasks. Labour and time are two resources that must not be wasted but utilised as fully as possible to add value to the product. Further, the fragility of JIT production processes necessitates that workers can cover for each other to the extent of being able to perform the range of standardised tasks that fall within their team's remit. However, although this flexibility is often presented as involving multiskilling and job enrichment, the critical theorists are quick to point out that in reality operators experience job enlargement and task accretion through the acquisition of a limited number of cognate tasks that result in a work pattern characterised by 'routine variety' (Garrahan and Stewart, 1992, pp. 60–1; Delbridge and Turnbull, 1992, p. 67). The nature of the job enlargement – taking on responsibility for some setting-up of machinery, inspection and cleaning – combined with required flexibility, effectively eliminate down-time or porosity in the working day and contribute to labour intensification. Further, such 'skills' as are acquired, being plant-specific, do little to enhance the worker's value in the general labour market but rather serve to develop his or her dependency on this 'exploitative' employer.

However, through Marxist eyes, labour intensification is not the only form of exploitation in TQM and JIT systems. The operation of *kaizen* committees, in which workers are expected to contribute their knowledge to improve the product and production process acts to appropriate that knowledge in the interests of capital without direct return to the worker. In 'mining the gold in the worker's head', *kaizen* is 'not an alternative to Taylorism but rather a solution to its classic problem of the resistance of workers to placing their knowledge of production in the service of rationalization' (Dohse *et al.*, 1985, p. 128). Furthermore it has been suggested that *kaizen* meetings, by *expecting* rather than encouraging workers to come up with ideas for improvements, are in themselves a source of stress through widening workers' responsibilities. The same might be said about the delegation of responsibility for quality at the point of production combined with the highly visible signalling of individual operator error.

Turning to teamworking, Parker and Slaughter (1988) have suggested that teams as constituted under TQM and JIT systems are a far cry from the semi-autonomous work groups of the 1960s and 1970s, designed to enhance worker control and job satisfaction. Rather teamworking is part of the overall management package which they term 'management-by-stress'. As such it includes the following elements:

1. A rewritten contract announcing that a new relationship exists between the company and its workforce.
2. Interchangeability, meaning the workers are required or induced (through pay-for-knowledge) to be capable of doing several jobs.
3. Drastic reduction of classifications, giving management increased control to assign workers as it sees fit.
4. Less meaning for seniority. In most cases seniority is explicitly undermined or modified. For example, if classifications are eliminated, opportunities to transfer to different classifications by seniority are also eliminated.
5. Detailed definition of every job step increasing management control over the way jobs are done.
6. Workers' participation in increasing their own workload.
7. More worker responsibility, without more authority, for jobs previously performed by supervisors.
8. A management attempt to make workers aware of the interrelatedness of the plant's departments and the place of the individual in the whole; an attempt by union and management to get away from the 'I just come to work, do my job and mind my own business' outlook.
9. An ideological atmosphere that stresses competition between plants and workers' responsibility for winning work away from other plants.
10. A shift towards enterprise unionism, where the union sees itself as a partner of management. (Parker and Slaughter, 1988, p. 5, cited in Garrahan and Stewart, 1992, p. 88)

Parker and Slaughter additionally make the point that the positive connotations attached to our everyday conception of teams, such as sport or surgical teams, rest on the assumption of the cooperation of *specialists*, rather than *interchangeable* members, towards a common goal. They add, tellingly

> In fact, the main place in our language where 'team' implies interchangeable members is where it refers to a team of horses – beasts of burden of equal capabilities yoked together to pull for a common end (determined by the person holding the whip). (Parker and Slaughter, 1988, p 4, cited in Garrahan and Stewart, 1992, p. 89)

Such conceptions may be compared with that of Nissan's Peter Wickens (1993, p. 86).

> A team begins with a group of individuals whose individual contributions are recognised and valued and who are motivated to work in the same direction to achieve clear, understood and stretching goals for which they are accountable. The best team results come with positive leadership and tough goals.

The critical theorists would suggest that, apart from facilitating labour intensification, teamworking acts as a self-policing device through peer surveillance and control while, at the same time, through providing a focus for collective solidaristic sentiment, 'manufactures consent' (Burawoy, 1979). At Nissan, peer surveillance takes the form of the 'Neighbour check' system of quality control. In other words, workers in their roles as 'customers' of the previous production process, and within work teams, are encouraged to identify defects caused by other workers and to allocate responsibility for such errors. The objective is to bring peer pressure within the team not to 'let down' a fellow team member. In practice workers feel they have to pick up each other's faults as the same thing will happen to them. Similarly it encourages competition between teams. 'Faults' are also exposed in *kaizen* meetings where, as one worker put it

> If you'd done anything wrong you got put in the middle and shouted at – 'You've done this wrong.' There are lads of 35 years old who would be shouted at by lads who are team leaders of 22 years old.

The 'Help Lamp' (or *jidoka*) at Nissan not only assists peer surveillance but self-regulation too. Theoretically workers have the power to stop the line to deal with process problems or product defects, before faulty work reaches another team ('customer') downstream. According to Garrahan and Stewart (1992, p. 105) this generates its own stress as operators feel that if they regularly stop the line they will be identified as incompetent. As a result they will rectify minor faults created by others upstream because, if the line is stopped for a minor defect, the resultant check of all the work might also reveal defects of their own making.[5]

Finally peer surveillance operates to control absenteeism. Under a JIT system there is no cover for absentees other than those team members present, hence there is a moral pressure not to 'let down' workmates. This is reinforced in some companies by prominently displaying a list of absentees, and their reasons for absence, along with messages of how fellow team members are 'hurt by absenteeism' (Parker and Slaughter, 1988, p. 106).

In the light of these criticisms of the nature of work under JIT and TQM why is there not more overt opposition on the part of workers who, from a Marxist perspective, are colluding in their own subjugation? Various explanations have been offered (see Delbridge and Turnbull, 1992; Sewell and Wilkinson, 1992; Garrahan and Stewart, 1992). First, the standardisation that applies to work processes also applies in the moulding of 'docile bodies' (Sewell and Wilkinson, 1992, p. 110). It has been widely recorded that at greenfield site operations, in particular, recruitment and selection is highly selective, with an emphasis on behavioural traits rather than relevant skills, and on the 'right attitude' to teamworking and flexibility (Townley, 1989, pp. 95–6; White and Trevor, 1983, pp. 103, 124; Delbridge and Turnbull, 1992, p. 61). Peter Wickens' (1987, pp. 175–8) discussion of the intensity of selection methods at Nissan is revealing – long questionnaires, 'enough to put off many of the less committed', intensive review of the same by supervisors and managers, skill modules and aptitude tests, with the aim that attention to quality, pride in the job and spirit of teamwork and cooperation within Nissan will be second to none. For those with the right attitude and motivation it will be a satisfying and rewarding environment. We look for and expect individual contribution to continually improve the company and its productivity and quality. (Recruitment material, cited in Wickens, 1987, pp. 175–6)

The result has been recruitment of a young 'green' labour force, without years of acculturalisation in traditional manufacturing methods in heavily unionised plants. Not inconsistently Garrahan and Stewart report of Nissan that dissent is met with a reaction of 'put up or shut up', a powerful inducement to passivity in an area of high unemployment. Further, selection policies are reinforced by intensive induction programmes spelling out the 'company way' (see, e.g., Alston, 1986).

Second, the development of the team leader role, responsible for production targets and the social organisation of the group, has been identified as a strategy for marginalising the role of the shop-steward on the shop floor. This is because the team leader becomes the 'ears and eyes' of management on the shop floor and the principal communicator between management and the workforce (see Delbridge and Turnbull, 1992, p. 63; Pollert, 1993). And, as is often quoted, 'He who communicates is King' (Wickens, 1987). In other words, the team and the team leader, rather than the union and the shop-steward (always assuming that plant *is* unionised) become the focus for any residual collective sentiment. Where the unions have been emasculated by a 'sweetheart' single-union deal and the introduction of 'company councils' with prior negotiating rights, as at Nissan, their marginalisation can become a *fait accompli*. Garrahan and Stewart (1992) take a bleak view of the fate of the AEU as a focus for a competing ideology at Nissan:

> There is no group with the cohesion of Nissan which is capable of providing a powerful counter view of the world. (p. 119)

> there is no social space for counter-ideologies of a collectivist and solidaristic kind. (p. 116)

(The issue of HRM and 'new realism' in industrial relations will be dealt with in detail in Chapter 8.)

Finally, given such selection policies, the attempted marginalisation of trade unions and the development of teamworking – all within the context of high residual unemployment – it is not surprising that many workers accept the JIT and TQM work systems for the benefits on offer. The acceptable face of teamworking – mutual support, participation, collective endeavour – is overtly attractive. Parker and Slaughter (1988, p. 4) admit that teamworking can genuinely appeal to workers because

> Through teamwork – everyone pulling together – we can increase productivity, improve quality, enhance job satisfaction and save jobs. Even allowing for some hype it seems too good not to try.

Garrahan and Stewart (1992, p. 116), harsh critics that they are, admit that many workers at Nissan approve of the company's stress on generating consensus and a 'family thing'. As they state 'a strong paternalistic management structure indulges those who are prepared to take sustenance from it'. This is particularly so when the stresses of the JIT and TQM working practices are seen, at the very least, as natural to a modern plant on a greenfield site, a symbol of managerial competence and the guarantor of job survival.

The rhetoric of quality in the service sector

In Chapter 6 mention was made of attempts at developing 'cultures of quality' in the retail supermarket chains, banks and building societies and in the newly privatised utilities and transport services. In all these sectors 'customer care' has been the watchword of the late 1980s and the 1990s summarised in widely recognised advertising slogans ('The Listening Bank' [Midland], 'The Friendly Bank' [Yorkshire], 'The Bank that Likes to Say Yes' [TSB], 'We Answer to You' [BT], 'Quality, Value, Service' [M&S], the 'Putting People First' (of the Citizen's Charters of the privatised utilities, public sector services and British Rail) and in programmes of cultural change and staff development (notably BA's 'Putting People First' programme and its 'Customer First' teams) (Young, 1989; Bruce, 1987). As reference has been made to these in Chapter 6, I will not dwell on them, except to raise two points.

First, given the marketplace ethos of the enterprise culture, the emphasis on quality of service, at least as a rhetoric, is hardly surprising because such industries are in direct, often face-to-face contact, with the immediate users of their services. The image of the organisation is conveyed very directly at the customer interface, in a situation where the latter often, but not invariably (cf. electricity, water and, at the time of writing, 1994, gas) has the option to go elsewhere. Reputation, a major source of competitive advantage, is all.

Second, there is mixed evidence as to whether quality is perceived by customers to have improved. A 1993 government inspired survey, monitoring the success of the Citizen's Charter initiative (see *Independent on Sunday*, 22 August 1993, 'Consumer poll cheers ministers'), reported high levels of satisfaction with the services of the Post Office, British Gas and British Telecom (91 and 89 per cent respectively reporting that these services had either improved or not deteriorated in the last year). The NHS scored 67 per cent, but the score went up to 88 per cent when family doctors were included in the category. By way of comparison supermarkets were included in the survey, and came out on top with a 91 per cent approval rating. However, 37 per cent saw the NHS and 26 per cent saw British Rail as in need of improvement. The problem with this survey and the subsequent annual review in 1994 (see *Independent on Sunday*, 20 March 1994) though is the suspicion of political bias in the wording of the survey questions ('improved or *not deteriorated*' inevitably will elicit more favourable responses than 'improved' alone) and in the mode of analysis (e.g., the inclusion of GPs in NHS ratings might be seen as allowing ministers to argue that this is a vindication of fund-holding reforms). Further, a series of boxes listing preferred methods of improving the quality of public services contained not only relatively neutral items (regular independent inspection, finding out what people want, giving people information about services) but those with overt ideological colouring (private sector competition, performance-related pay, performance 'league' tables). Private sector comparison (of supermarkets) enables ministers to point to the utility of market forces and competition. In contrast to these survey results are the reports of various consumer watchdogs such as the Transport Users' Consultative Committee, Oftel, Ofgas, often reporting a rise in complaints about the quality particularly of transport services and of consumer unfriendly practices by the organisations concerned. This is not exclusively dissatisfaction with the services of monopolies, such as investment-starved British Rail – if anything the major high street banks have come in for more criticism, with the suspicion that, in spite of the 'customer care' rhetoric, private customers are being made to pay for the banks' losses in overseas investments and property speculation in the 1980s. Further, a recent report from the National Consumer Council (*Paying the Price*, September 1993), on the basis of a MORI poll of nearly 2,000 consumers, found that the privatisation of water, telecommunications, electricity and gas industries, had benefited shareholders far more than domestic consumers (see *Independent*, 13 September 1993, 'Looking after the consumer', p. 18; 'State sell-offs "leave consumers worse off"', p. 24). In essence, domestic consumers, it argued, had borne more than their fair share of the costs of new capital investment; that many poor households continued to experience real hardship and that regulations needed to be made tighter not looser. BT, for example ('We answer to you') had competed for business markets by cross-subsiding at the expense of domestic users. In spite of these criticisms, it could be argued that such reports not only give undue prominence to the voice of 'professional' complainers and 'hard luck' cases, but merely reflect rising consumer expectations, themselves an expression of the internalisation of a 'quality' culture. (What cannot be denied, though, is the widespread anger at the size of salary increases that have been awarded to the Chairmen (*sic*) of the privatised industries at a time when their employees are subject to pay restraints (see, for example, reports in the *Independent, Guardian* and *Daily Telegraph* 4 January 1995–7 January 1995).)

In this section I wish to consider the issue of quality in two major public sector services, the NHS and education. As discussed in Chapter 5, the public sector services in the last fifteen years, being directly answerable to the government as paymaster, have become the test-bed for its experimentation with free market principles. This has resulted in four major thrusts. First, the introduction of quasi-markets for those parts of the public sector that could not be transferred directly into private ownership (e.g., schools and institutions of higher education would compete for students and be financed largely according to their relative success or failure in doing this; NHS would be divided into 'purchasers' – DHAs, fund-holding general practices – and 'providers' – hospitals, clinics, community units – 'purchasers' buying the services needed for their patients, using formal contracts to ensure that they obtained the best 'value for money' from among competing providers). Second, in theory, the decentralisation of the management and production of services, with control via bureaucratic hierarchy being (to some extent) exchanged for control via cultural management, targets and contracts (e.g., schools 'opting-out' of local authority control). Third, there has been much rhetorical emphasis on the need to improve service quality. Fourth, it has been emphasised that quality is inextricably linked with responsiveness to the individual service user/consumer (Pollitt, 1993, Chapter 7).

That the rhetoric of quality in response to the *individual* consumer has become the watchword of government spokespersons can be in no doubt. As I was preparing material for this chapter the Secretary of State for Health, Virginia Bottomley, announced that the private and voluntary sectors, which have (I quote) 'a magnificent tradition of providing high quality care', can bid to run the new secure units for disruptive children, the watchwords of this initiative being 'Care, quality, control and efficiency' (*Today* programme, 16 August 1993; *Guardian*, 16 August 1993). Successive education ministers through the 1980s have spoken of the importance of 'improving standards' in schools (via formal assessment of teacher performance, the national curriculum and testing) and of parental choice (to send their children to the 'best' schools, i.e., those in a locality which come higher up the league tables of testing scores, GCSE and 'A' level results and so forth) (Education Act 1980; *Teaching Quality*, Cmnd 8836, 1983; *Better Schools*, Cmnd 9469, 1985; Education Reform Act 1988). The assumption here is that the marketplace is somehow the arbiter of quality (allied with value); that schools can improve their 'quality' by opting-out of local authority control; that parental choice will result in support for the schools of 'good-reputation' and diminishing rolls for those perceived as inferior; and that in the NHS self-governing status for hospitals, the separating of the 'purchasing' and 'providing' roles of health authorities, fund-holding status for general practices, and the general introduction of managerialist as opposed to 'consensus management' organising principles will deliver higher levels of patient responsiveness (e.g., reduced waiting lists) and more effective use of resources (Griffiths, 1983; *Working for Patients*, CMM 555, 1989). But if a rhetoric of 'quality' has been employed, what does 'quality' mean in education and the NHS, and what evidence is there that 'quality' has improved?

Earlier in this chapter one definition of quality was 'conformance to the *requirements* of the customer', which involved 'effectiveness' (service must meet the customer's needs) and 'efficiency' (service must do what it is designed to do). This is, of course, rather different from 'meeting a customer's or consumer's *expectations*', as it implies that *management* defines what is required, if in consultation with the consumer, rather than the consumer being truly in the driving seat.[6] However, even this somewhat restricted definition becomes problematic in relation to public services as the customer has different characteristics and is in a different situation than a customer for private sector goods and services (Pollitt, 1990). First, the concept of 'customer' is individualistic; but the consumer of public sector services is also (nearly always) a citizen, which has collectivist connotations. For a customer the *caveat emptor* ('buyer beware') rule usually applies; a citizen has rights that speak less of efficiency and effectiveness and more of justice, representation and equal treatment. The entrepreneurialist notion of risk taking and making 'profits through exploiting the ignorance of other traders' (Parsons, 1988, p. 36) sits uneasily with a public service ethic. Second, while some public services are compulsory but not necessarily wanted by the consumer (primary and secondary school education, prisons), others may be wanted but unable to afford every potential consumer his or her desired access (hospital treatment, council housing). In most of the private sector more demand equates with greater income (if not profits); in the public sector services traditionally more demand increases costs without corresponding growth in income and, hence, a pressure on public sector management to limit demand and ration what they can provide rather than stimulating the public demand for their products (Pollitt, 1990, p. 124). Unlike many private sector products and services, public services often involve intensive, complex and long term interaction between the provider of the service and the consumer (education being a case in point). Finally, given that public sector services are in a political arena, with multiple and conflicting priorities held by different stakeholders, there is pressure on politicians to shy away from clearly defined objectives for these services. Vagueness and ambiguity allow the building and maintaining of coalitions of support, are less likely to give hostages to fortune and allow a basically unchanged policy to be presented as something new when public opinion demands change (Pollitt, 1990, pp. 121–2).

In the light of all this it is inherently difficult to define and deliver what meets customers' needs, let alone to provide services that do what they are designed to do. Hence in the political context of the enterprise culture surrogates of quality have been adopted (test scores, GCSE results, length of time on hospital waiting lists, number of screening tests performed by GPs) that, in a similar manner to JIT, *appear designed to eliminate waste*.

Following Pollitt's (1990) arguments, both the education and health services in the 1980s and 1990s have been subjected to the imposition of neo-Taylorist policies if latterly, with the introduction of Citizen's Charters, with a more 'caring' image. The central thrust of these policies, endlessly reiterated in official documents, is to set clear targets, to develop performance indicators to measure the achievement of these targets and to focus, by means of appraisal, merit awards and even performance-related pay on those who get 'results'. The strengthening, incentivising and enhancing the accountability of line management is a dominant theme (Pollitt, 1990, p. 56). These policies are designed to deliver in terms of quasi-TQM and JIT objectives. In other words 'results' have been defined less in terms of the 'effectiveness' of the service (which might involve such issues as the distinctiveness of their ethical base, their possible redistributive goals, tracking those in need who may not be receiving adequate treatment, questioning whether it is appropriate to pursue a big 'want' inefficiently rather than a lesser one efficiently) and more in terms of the efficiency of delivering conformance to narrowly defined surrogates for quality. These surrogates invariably equate quality with delivery, i.e., the achievement of quantitative targets that focus on economy and efficiency, or the elimination of waste, to use JIT terms. Thus 'results' for the general manager of a hospital often boils down to getting more patients through fewer beds at lower unit costs or, in universities, to process higher numbers of students at lower unit cost (Harrison *et al.*, 1989; Jarratt, 1985). The Citizen's Charter for schools (*The Parent's Charter*) and hospitals (*The Patient's Charter)* (note in both cases the individualistic use of the singular form) clearly reflects this. In the *Patient's Charter*, for example, quality as effectiveness is expressed in general 'motherhood' statements

> creating a better health service ... means a service that always puts the patient first, providing services that meet clearly defined national and local standards in ways responsive to people's views and needs ... offers, respect for privacy, dignity and religious and cultural beliefs.

The real emphasis, reflected in the objective of being 'highly efficient, representing really good value for money' is on quantitatively expressed standards of delivery, for example

> To be guaranteed admission for treatment by a specific date no later than two years from the day when your consultant places you on a waiting list ...
> When you call an emergency ambulance it should arrive within 14 minutes if you live in an urban area, or 19 minutes if you live in a rural area...
> In outpatients clinics you will be given a specific appointment time and be seen within 30 minutes of that time.

Or from the *Parent's Charter*

> From Summer 1992 all parents will receive a written report on their child's progress at least once a year.
> (Note, incidentally, the assumption of two-parent families).

Whether quality as conformance to specification delivers quality as 'fitness for use' is debatable. In the context of 'value for money' (e.g., cutting staff levels and funding) the administrative burden of testing and report writing cuts into teaching time. Clearing waiting lists has raised the issue of whether quick one-off operations, such as varicose veins, are drawing resources away from life-threatening conditions. Furthermore, the 'standards of delivery' themselves are not unambiguous. You may wait no longer than two years after your consultant places you on a waiting list, but how long might you have to wait before seeing a consultant?

As with TQM and JIT in manufacturing, the rhetoric in relation to public services has been one of decentralisation, customer responsiveness and the empowerment of line managers and customers alike (see, for example, the rhetoric in the 1979 *Patients First* document, or in the notion of fund-holding GPs or, in education, talk about giving parents choice and control, or about promoting education's responsiveness to the needs of industry). Also like TQM and JIT, a critical analysis would suggest that the customer responsiveness, empowerment and decentralisation that has occurred (e.g., retraining of NHS receptionists, extended visiting hours, personalised nursing, financial delegation to schools and for individual institutions to opt out of LEA control) is more than counterbalanced by the centralisation inherent in delivering conformance to specification and the elimination of waste.[7] In education, the imposition of a national curriculum and testing in schools, the requirement on universities to implement the managerialist and cost cutting reforms ('value for money and accountability') of the Jarratt report, the introduction of formal staff appraisal in both schools and universities, the imposition of research selectivity and teaching audit exercises in universities, the creation of the UFC (Universities' Funding Council) and now HEFCE (Higher Education Funding Council of England) to replace the UGC (Universities' Grants Commission), point to massive central control. In the NHS centralisation is evident in the battles over competitive tendering (between the (then) DHSS and those District Health Authorities determined to retain their own in-house ancillary services) and in the selection of general managers (DHSS intervening to improve chances of non-NHS candidates) and reflected in central initiatives (e.g., in 1986 to reduce waiting lists, various new review procedures) (Pollitt, 1990, p. 68). In the 1989 decentralisation of *Working for Patients*, centre–periphery tensions are apparent, in that of the new apparently decentralising structures (e.g., self-governing status for hospitals) the White Paper states that 'the overall effect of these changes will be to introduce for the first time a clear and effective chain of management command running from Districts, through Regions to the Chief Executive and from there to the Secretary of State' (CMM 555, 1989, para 2–6, cited in Pollitt, 1990, p. 68). Some decentralisation to line management has been matched by a centralisation of control over professional groups, aimed at inhibiting their potentially wayward autonomy. The upshot is that, in the context of producing 'value for money' services (eliminating 'waste'/cutting back on unit funding), professionals have experienced labour intensification comparable to that of the shopfloor workers in TQM- and JIT-driven manufacturing, resulting in 'widespread demoralisation ... and a deep resentment and suspicion of the way they are being treated' (Pollitt, 1990, p. 178).

The 'quality' employee

The rhetoric of high value added or zero-defect products and of 'customer care' at the organisation–market interface, generally includes a mantra about the importance of well-trained, skilled and committed employees. This is almost tautological. *Not* to advocate the importance of training and skills development would be tantamount to proclaiming that employees were of little value and not worth investing in. Demands for employees' commitment to the organisation and responsiveness to the external customer logically demand a reciprocal commitment to the employee and responsiveness to her demands as internal customer. If quality of product or service ultimately depends on the quality of the employee, we have to look to its underpinnings – that is society's and organisations' commitment to developing skills appropriate to a national economic policy and organisational corporate objectives.

And here we have the same lack of coherence and fragmentation that marks so many so-called HRM initiatives. It is well recognised that the UK compared to its major competitors, traditionally, at national level, has a poor record in providing vocational education, post-secondary and university training to its citizens (see Storey and Sisson, 1993, Table 2.3). Nor, traditionally, has this been compensated for by increased in-company training (see Storey and Sisson, 1993, Table 2.4). The background to failures in the UK educational and national vocational training systems have been variously attributed to the class system, traditionally protected markets, the union-dominated time-served craft apprenticeship system and the 'voluntarist' bias towards training provision in this country (Keep, 1989). This was not assisted by the typically low levels of education of British management (Handy, 1987; Mangham and Silver, 1986; Storey *et al.*, 1991).

But, undeniably, in the latter half of the 1980s and in the 1990s initiatives are being undertaken that place training issues, at national level at least, somewhat higher on the agenda. First, quite apart from the rhetoric about 'quality' and standards in our schools, participation rates in post-16 year old education have risen steadily. This may be due, of course, to higher levels of unemployment for young people and the withdrawal of benefit entitlement for 16–18 year olds. Numbers in higher education – particularly among mature students – have increased enormously. Secondly, there have been a whole tranche of government inspired initiatives, such as the setting up of the National Council for Vocational Qualifications (NCVQs) and Training and Enterprise Councils (TECs) to develop competence-based training provision and certification, not to mention the much decried Youth Training Schemes (YTS) (for details and critique, see Keep, 1994). In companies product-market competition and new production methods have inevitably called into question the adequacy of traditional training provisions and Rainbird (1994) cites examples of continuous in-company training aimed at flexible working (but see Chapter 5), organisational development, customer care and so forth. Storey and Sisson (1993, Chapter 7) cite well known examples of adult 'open' learning (such as Ford's Employee Development and Assistance Programme) and point to investment in management development via management competencies programmes, target-setting, company-sponsored MBAs and even self-development. So does this mean that the rhetoric of quality is being underwritten by a revolutionised investment in training and education for employees?

While not wishing to decry the efforts that are being made it has to be pointed out that they are building on a very low base, that the case study accounts we have tend to be from exemplar companies (i.e., they are representative of the 40 per cent of employers who were found to have a training budget in the *Training in Britain* survey (IDS, 1990) rather than the *60 per cent* that did not) (Rainbird, 1994, p. 360), and that the direct resources devoted to training, while not so obviously out of line with international competitors as once thought (Holden and Livian, 1992) are still 'very modest' (Sisson and Storey, 1993, p. 169; Hyman, 1992). It might be argued, of course, that direct training expenditure is not always a good indicator of training activity. The Japanese often record low levels of direct expenditure precisely because their intensive and well-planned training is fully integrated into everyday work practices (Sisson and Storey, 1994, p. 170).

The real problem, Sisson and Storey (1993, pp. 170–4) assert, on the basis of their comparative study between quality-loving Japanese and UK companies (Storey *et al.*, 1991), is that, unlike in Japan, it is rarely the case that a critical measure in managers' appraisal is how well they are developing their subordinates. Rather, they suggest, managers are evaluated on how well they are seen to 'shoulder responsibility' and to meet financial and production targets. And, as we saw in Chapter 4, in many cases such targets will reflect the short-termism endemic in UK financial institutions. The picture Sisson and Storey (1993, pp. 171–2) paint of the training 'strategy' that results again betrays a fragmented *ad hocery*.

> From time to time a new training initiative may be launched and staff development becomes a relatively high profile activity. But, given the next downturn in the business cycle the traditional priorities reassert themselves and training once again becomes a mere nice-to-have but 'cannot be afforded, luxury'.[8] Supervisors and staff themselves rarely act as a constituency to complain about this. On the contrary, they are far more likely to be complicit in the process. Reading the signs about 'what counts' ordinary members of staff routinely declare themselves 'too busy' to be trained. Their supervisors and departmental line managers resist attempts to take any of their staff from normal duties ...
>
> Ironically, when begrudgingly, training does take place, because it has been pared and timed to cause minimal disruption the resulting experience is often unsatisfactory. Trainees at first line management level, for example, will rightly observe that the training has come too late, or that it is insufficiently targeted at their specific needs. *These problems are not purely technical failings of the kind the prescriptive texts warn about. On the contrary, they are logical outcomes of the endemic training problems in Britain of the kind outlined in this section* (added emphasis).

I have quoted this extract from Storey and Sisson at length because it exactly sums up my own experience of training in relation to a TQM initiative in a large chemical company and the training initiatives of a public sector organisation that is a past master in delivering the rhetoric of quality.

Yet here we are confronted with an irony, not to say contradiction. Earlier I talked of 'society's and organisations' commitment to developing skills appropriate to a national economic policy and organisational objectives'. It could be argued that this is *precisely* what is happening. In other words, a few exemplar companies such as British Airways, British Telecom, British Rail, BP, ICI, National Westminster Bank, Philips Electronics and Shell, committed to various TQM or 'customer care' programmes have invested in training schemes that at the very least have heightened employee awareness of quality issues or changed the presentation of the services on offer. Undoubtedly too where firms have seen competitive advantage to lie in BS5750 certification investment in the training requirements for accreditation has occurred, even in recession (Green and Felstead, 1994). But such initiatives are the exception to the general rule of low, fragmented and spasmodic training investment coupled with a preference for poaching skills as and when needed. But this befits a government economic strategy that demands cut-backs in government spending and preaches the virtues of low labour costs and abolishes wages councils, which enforced minimum rates of pay for around 2.5 million workers (see Chapter 8), while in the same breath advocating 'quality'. It is consistent too with the strategy of organisations that compete on cost and are constrained by short-term financial targets. In such organisations, as we have seen in relation to the public sector, cost cutting actions and a rhetoric of 'quality' are reconciled by defining quality as 'value for money'.

Conclusions

Much of the writing on quality in relation to HRM – for example that of Guest (1987) which introduced this chapter – tends to adopt what Wilkinson *et al.* (1992) termed the 'soft' qualitative approach of the 'excellence' literature. From this standpoint quality is invariably considered from a consumer's viewpoint as 'fitness for use' or quality of design, with a backgrounding of the producer's hard waste-reducing aspects of conformance to specification in the theoretically quality-enhancing environment of JIT (or the 'value for money' environment of public expenditure reductions). From the 'soft' perspective on quality it is easy to see a correlation between high quality products and services and the developmental, mutuality models of 'soft' HRM. However, as discussed in this chapter, conformance to specification in the context of waste elimination points more directly to the 'hard' HRM model of employee relations policies being used to drive business/government strategy, if at the costs of reduced autonomy and labour intensification for direct workers, be they car assembly operatives, teachers or doctors.

The tensions between different aspects of quality and the 'hard' and 'soft' models of HRM can be seen clearly in the reaction of public sector professionals to the managerialist neo-Taylorist initiatives of the past decade and a half. Traditionally the conditions of employment enjoyed by professionals in the public sector education and health services contained many aspects of a stereotypical 'Japanese' 'soft' HRM employment policy and culture – lifetime employment, promotion on the basis of seniority laced with merit, notions of community and collegiality that enabled high levels of personal empowerment and autonomy, allied with consensus management and peer review. Many would say that this resulted in task/client centred cultures of excellence. The government initiatives have effectively moved employment policies towards a much 'harder', more contractually oriented stance. In higher education, for example, tenure has been weakened and performance-related pay introduced, in the context of the monitoring devices of research selectivity exercises and the teaching quality audit, both of which serve to inhibit autonomy, standardise output, and intensify work. In the NHS it is proposed to give every consultant a more detailed, locally negotiated job description and to modify their distinction awards so that 'consultants must demonstrate not only their clinical skills but also a commitment to the management and development of the service' (*Working for Patients*, CMM 555, 1989, p. 44). Every GP now has specified the minimum number of hours she or he must devote to the surgery (*Patient's Charter*, 1991).

As a consequence professionals, generally speaking, have been resistant to many of the supposedly customer oriented (read, cost control) reforms in the public sector, and have fought rearguard actions whenever possible. For example, university academics having conceded appraisal, negotiated that it should be used at least formally as an instrument of staff development, rather than being officially part of the promotion system (Townley, 1990/1). Similarly 'doctors have repeatedly frustrated the government's hopes that some form of management or clinical budgeting could be introduced to most health authorities' (Pollitt *et al.*, 1988) although Pollitt (1990, p. 70) queries how successfully resistance can be maintained after the implementation of the provisions of the 1989 White Paper, with its major increase in management authority and redefinition of clinical autonomy.

Movement towards a 'harder' face of HRM in pursuit of quality as conformity to waste-eliminating specification has been assisted by the rhetoric of the enterprise culture and the market place (du Gay and Salaman, 1992). The customer, who is sovereign, is associated with positive empowering images of choice and satisfaction.

Customers are constituted as autonomous, self-regulating and self-actualizing individual actors, seeking to maximize the worth of their existence to themselves through personalized acts of choice in a world of goods and services (du Gay and Salaman, 1992, p. 623).

This positive image of the customer operates at two levels. The 'customer' in a JIT system is every worker accepting raw material, components or sub-assemblies from a subcontractor or another team, with the right (obligation) to reject the same if they are not satisfactory. Hence an image of empowerment may be used to mask an experience of reduced autonomy and labour intensification. Further, as arbiters of quality, 'customers are made to function in the role of management ... as customer satisfaction is now defined as critical to success' (du Gay and Salaman, 1992, p. 621). Thus the increase of administrative controls from the centre can now be re-represented as management through customer responsiveness. As the worker is also a customer, Taylorist controls can be presented, by sleight-of-hand, as the encouragement of self-control and even (as is appropriate in a customer) of 'ownership' (Wickens, 1993, pp. 87–8). Further, 'waste' is a product that a consumer, by definition, has rejected, or does not want and, therefore, logically and necessarily has to be eliminated.

The prevalence of the language of the customer and of enterprise serves to coopt organisational stakeholders who have a vested interest in the changes that are encompassed by the quality umbrella. In manufacturing, TQM and JIT have been a bandwagon by which line management can assert its centrality and authority. In the public sector services, the following have all gained from the new managerialism/customer responsiveness direction of public services: management consultants; cleaning, laundry, catering, refuse collection and leisure firms who have gained contacts for hitherto 'in-house' public-service work; accountancy firms developing auditing of public services: and above all public servants and private sector managers who have assumed many of the new senior public service management positions created during the various restructurings. And, as Pollitt (1990, p. 137) tellingly observes

> New institutions and practices themselves help to remould old interests and stimulate the construction of new ones ... Head teachers, senior social workers, nursing officers, police chief inspectors/captains and many others have been taught to think of this dimension. Even more significant have been the effects on 'consumers'. Once council tenants buy the freeholds of their houses their status, obligations and reference groups all change ... Some, at least, of the architects of public service managerialism realised this very well. Far from being a purely technical exercise, *the articulation of what I have termed neo-Taylorism was in part an attempt at shaping a new set of organisational and political constituencies* (added emphasis).

The same might be said of the managers in charge of TQM and JIT, of the team leader, and of the marginalised trade unions in plants such as Nissan. Not for nothing does Reed (1995) refer to TQM as an 'intellectual or governmental technology', one geared 'to realising a "paradigm shift" in social values and managerial forms such that the principles and practices of bureaucratic rationality were to be replaced by those constitutive of market rationality'.

To such 'political' issues we now turn in Chapter 8.

Notes

1. Following Oliver and Wilkinson's (1992, pp. 24–5) excellent summary, statistical process control rests on the principle that products display two sorts of variations: that which is inherent in the process and which ought not to create any product out of tolerance (i.e., it is random) and that which is due to a specific cause, and which will create faulty products.

   SPC then involves first working out the extent of a process's random variation and then regularly sampling the process's output, using the samples to chart the behaviour of the production process, in order to detect trends that indicate that the process is producing variation that is not random, even if such output might still be within tolerance. Information is used to initiate corrective action before faulty output is produced. Minimising variation in components not only reduces scrap and reworking cost, but can significantly improve performance of the assembled product as all the parts 'match' more exactly.

2. In the early days of debate about the 'Japanisation' of British Industry (see, for example White and Trevor, 1983) JIT systems of production were sometimes considered to be synonymous with Toyota's *kanban* systems of production. In fact this represents just one aspect of JIT, aimed at handling small variations (up to 10 per cent) in demand. Under the *kanban* system, materials in special containers are tagged by two production cards (the *kanban*) which initiate production and accompany the materials through the factory. If market demand dips, *kanbans* cease to be issued and containers carrying no *kanban* are ignored. Conversely an upturn in demand from the market triggers the issuing of 'extra' *kanban* tickets from the final assembly stage that 'pull' the necessary sub-assemblies and components through the factory to meet final demand.

3. Group technology is where families of machines, dedicated to the production of specific and usually similar products are 'grouped' together, as operations are organised on a product rather than a functional basis. Functional organisation in production management terms, is where, in contrast, equipment is laid out according to what function it serves (e.g., all lathes together, all milling machines together) irrespective of the product worked on.

4. Note Wickens' (1993, p. 86), Personnel Director of Nissan, admission that 'If we are to achieve long-term high quality, we need to combine two elements – commitment of the workforce and *control of the process*' (added emphasis).

5. A further reason for reluctance to stop the line is its potential to result in unwanted overtime in order to achieve targets. Overtime is the allowable buffer for any unanticipated disruption in the fragile JIT/TQM system (Turnbull, 1988a, p. 15). As even Wickens (1993, p. 80) admits 'lean production shifts the buffer from being stock in production to the workers' personal time'. Note also, a trade unionist's comment 'Our willingness to make up after hours the production lost during the shift ... makes us the buffers ... It is not that Japanese production methods have done away with unnecessary buffers; it has simply shifted the cost of these' (Robertson, 1992).

6. It should be noted that in spite of the rhetoric, the Conservative government's Citizen's Charters did not usually extend citizen's legal rights, although they did spell out existing rights and, beyond the law, what the citizen has a right to expect – that is, the *government's* view of citizens' expectations. And, while many public sector services have

extended complaints systems, open to *individual* users, there has been little or no enhancement of systems of users' *collective* representation (Pollitt, 1993, p. 185).

7. Pollitt (1993, pp. 181–2) notes the paradox that while the Conservative governments' rhetoric is focused on the benefits of *free* markets, the quasi-markets in the public sector are highly managed, being artificial constructions running to the rules, definitions and formulae invented by government and Whitehall. For example, it was government which insisted that the numbers of patients waiting for operations for more than two years was a key target for reduction, even if that led to increases in average waiting times for those elsewhere on the lists and the rumour that less urgent operations are now being done before more urgent ones. ('Citizens Charter: some progress ... could try harder', *Independent on Sunday*, 20 March 1994).

8. While this assertion is supported by evidence of cutbacks in the number of apprentices and other trainees in manufacturing industry during the recession of the early 1980s, recent research by Green and Felstead (1994) suggests that only a small reduction in training has occurred during the recession of the early 1990s. This they attribute to the many regulations (e.g., Health and Safety Act, Financial Services Act) that provide a floor for training provision and the fact that recession-intensified competition has meant that firms have 'increasingly to fly the flag of quality in order to retain or expand market share'. Hence the training requirements of the BS5750 were widely cited in their research. Nevertheless, Green and Felstead (1994, p. 216) also add that

> Even in our sample, which in its construction was biased towards users of WRFC (Work Related Further Education) courses, we found a large minority of firms which had no training plan, or which reduced their training primarily as a cost-cutting strategy to outlast the recession.

8

HRM and 'new realism' in industrial relations?[1]

The 'soft' normative model of HRM is depicted as individualistic, with committed employees working flexibly and 'beyond contract' in pursuit of competitive advantage. The 'hard' model implies that employees are a resource to be used like any other, at management's discretion, in whatever way best achieves strategic objectives. Both models appear at odds with depictions of the 'traditional' British industrial relations system as wedded to voluntaristic collective bargaining, joint regulation and established procedures for the protection of workers' hard won rights. Can an employee be committed to both organisation and trade union simultaneously, particularly if workplace employee relations are adversarial rather than collaborative? How does functional flexibility square with multi-unionism and associated demarcation lines between jobs and with union territoriality? Can numerical flexibility ever be compatible with union positions on job security? And how does the unitaristic stance of HRM sit with the pluralism of 'traditional' industrial relations? Can HRM and 'traditional' British industrial relations cohabit?

Even to pose such a question assumes that something called 'traditional' industrial relations still exists in the UK, in spite of a decade and a half of the enterprise culture, with the associated restrictive trade union legislation and major economic recessions. What is 'traditional' industrial relations, and does it still exist? What changes have occurred, why, and can they be reversed with a change of government? If the industrial relations system now exhibits a 'new realism', is this compatible with HRM? To these interrelated questions we now turn.

Models of 'traditional' industrial relations

Strictly speaking when I talk of 'traditional' industrial relations I am referring to the dominant pre-1979 *models* for analysing the 'institutions of job regulation'

(Flanders, 1965) just as much as to the institutions themselves. For the purposes of this chapter, following Gospel and Palmer (1993, p. 3), industrial relations may be defined as 'processes of control over the employment relationship, the organisation of work, and relations between employers and employees'. 'Traditional' industrial relations may be seen in terms of how those institutions associated with the employment relationship and the processes of job regulation (e.g., employers' associations, management, trade unions, collective bargaining, industrial action) are perceived according to conventional pre-1979 assumptions about their 'proper' enactment. Again following Gospel and Palmer (1993, Chapter 2) the conventional perspectives on industrial relations prior to 1979 (i.e., those shared by the Labour party, centre parties and the centre and left-wing of the Conservative party) were those of liberal collectivism and corporatism.[2] If we take their respective positions on conflict and cooperation, management's, trade unions' and government roles, liberal collectivism and corporatism share much common ground. Both perspectives view group conflicts on economic interests as inevitable and potentially beneficial, both see the management role as a coordinator of interest groups and both identify a constructive role for trade unions. The emphasis however differs. The liberal collectivist view sees group conflict as potentially beneficial if institutionalised through *collective bargaining*. Corporatists see it as beneficial if institutionalised by *incorporating* the different interests into *decision-making bodies*. The liberal collectivists see management's coordinative role as representing the employers' interests and institutionalising conflict through collective bargaining, the trade unions doing likewise for workers' interests. Corporatists emphasise management's role as representing owner interests and helping to build corporate arrangements, trade unions helping to incorporate workers onto governing bodies. Where the two conventional perspectives differ is in the role assigned to the state. Whereas liberal collectivists recognise the role of the state as the 'first among equals' but consider that its role in the economy should be *minimised*, corporatists emphasise its role as an active *interventionist* in the national interest (see Gospel and Palmer, 1993, Table 2.1, and Chapter 2 for a further discussion of these distinctions). The Donovan Commission of the late 1960s, advocating the need for procedural reforms and restructuring of collective bargaining, but without changes in labour law that might undermine the voluntaristic bases of British industrial relations, represents 'traditional' industrial relations in its liberal collectivist style. The labour relations policies of the 1974–9 Labour government, promoting pro-union and employee protection legislation, industrial democracy and the 'Social Contract' incomes policy – not to mention 'beer and sandwiches at No. 10' for trade union leaders – represents 'traditional' corporatist industrial relations.

Post-1979, with the election of a radical reforming Conservative administration, such views of what constituted 'industrial relations' came under ideological attack. I have already discussed the nature of the enterprise culture in Chapter 3, with its stress on individualism, *laissez faire* and the free market. Suffice to say at this point that the Conservative governments throughout the 1980s and early 1990s have vociferously advocated and tenaciously implemented a 'liberal individualist' policy towards industrial relations. In comparison to liberal collectivism and corporatism, liberal individualism views *individual* conflicts on the economic terms of employment as inevitable, but considers that this can be resolved through well designed *individual* contracts of employment. Management's role is one of leadership, enhancing general interests through economic development. Group conflict is seen to result from the harmful actions of trade unions manipulating, with solidaristic rhetoric, a 'conscript' army of reluctant members. The trade unions' role, as an institutional impediment in the operation of free markets (not to mention that of disguising from workers their own best interests) is harmful. At best unions are unnecessary. The state's role, *in theory*, is first among equals, and its role in the economy should be minimised. (We shall consider later whether the Conservative government's role *in practice* has been non-interventionary) (see Gospel and Palmer, 1993, Table 2.1 and Chapter 2, for more details).)

The collision of these different ideologies and the resultant legislative and economic programmes of the Conservative governments in the 1980s and early 1990s, have inevitably led to changes in the institutions and processes associated with the employment relationship and job regulation over this period. In what ways have they changed, and to what extent? And, importantly, can all the changes observed be attributed to the industrial relations policies of the Conservative government or are there other factors at work irrespective of government policy? This question needs to be addressed, if the assumption is made that a change of government could automatically allow a reversion to the industrial relations scenarios of pre-1979. First, though, what change has taken place?

Post-1979 changes in industrial relations institutions

Six major and interrelated changes have occurred since 1979. These are:

1. A decline in trade union membership and density.
2. A decline in, and ultimate abolition of, the closed shop.
3. A decline in trade union recognition.
4. A decline in the coverage and scope of collective bargaining, particularly in the private sector.
5. A shift from multi-employer to single-employer bargaining; a shift from multi-establishment to single-establishment bargaining.
6. A decline in the number of strikes, in the number of workers involved in strike action, and in the number of working days lost.

The statistics paint a clear picture of trade union membership and density decline (see Tables 8.1 and 8.2). In 1979 trade union membership stood at a peak of 13,289 million, by 1992 it had fallen to 9 million (*Employment Gazette*, June 1994). By Autumn 1992, according to the Labour Force Survey, it had fallen still further to 7,540 million.[3] Similarly, in the WIRS survey samples of 1980, 1984 and 1990, establishments with union members fell from 73 per cent in both 1980 and 1984 to 64 per cent in 1990, all of this decline being in the private sector (Millward *et al.*, 1992, pp. 58–60). In 1979 trade union density (i.e., union membership as a percentage of the employed workforce) stood at 55.8 per cent; by 1987 it had fallen to 46.3 per cent (Waddington, 1992; *Employment Gazette*, June 1991).[4] The figures from WIRS surveys tell the same story. In their samples union density fell from 58 per cent in 1984 to 48 per cent in 1990, representing a rather larger fall for manual (66 per cent to 53 per cent) than non-manual workers (51 per cent to 43 per cent) (Millward *et al.*, 1992, pp. 60–7). Recent Labour Force Survey figures suggest the downward trend continues: in Autumn 1992 trade union density for all employees had declined from 39 per cent in Spring 1989 to 35 per cent in Autumn 1992 (for all employment, from 34 per cent in Spring 1992 to 32 per cent in Autumn 1992) (IRS Employment Trends, June 1993). By 1994 only 31 per cent of employed workers belonged to a union (*Employment Gazette*, June, 1994).

One reaction to falling union membership and its implications for declining union power has been a wave of recent and defensive union mergers, somewhat

Table 8.1 Trade union membership in the UK, 1979–92

Year	Number of unions at end of year	Total membership at end of year (thousand)	Percentage change in membership since previous year	Cumulative fall in membership since 1979 (thousand)
1979	453	13,289	+1.3	
1980	438	12,947	−2.6	342
1981	414	12,106	−6.5	1,183
1982	408	11,593	−4.2	1,696
1983	394	11,236	−3.1	2,053
1984	375	10,994	−3.2	2,295
1985	370	10,821	−1.6	2,468
1986	335	10,539	−2.6	2,750
1987	330	10,475	−0.6	2,814
1988	315	10,376	−0.9	2,913
1989	309	10,158	−2.1	3,131
1990	287	9,947	−2.1	3,342
1991	275	9,585	−3.6	3,704
1992	268	9,048	−5.6	4,241

Source: Employment Gazette (June 1994).

Table 8.2 Trade union density, 1970–87

Year	Male	Female	Total
1970	59.0	31.2	48.5
1972	59.6	31.1	48.8
1973	60.4	32.4	49.6
1974	60.0	32.9	49.4
1974	61.2	34.1	50.4
1975	62.7	36.4	52.0
1976	64.7	38.3	54.0
1977	66.2	39.4	55.3
1978	68.0	39.1	56.1
1979	66.9	40.4	55.8
1980	65.0	39.9	54.5
1981	64.6	40.6	54.4
1982	63.3	39.9	53.3
1983	62.3	39.3	52.3
1984	59.1	38.0	49.8
1985	58.3	37.3	49.0
1986	56.5	36.2	47.4
1987	55.2	35.7	46.3

Source: Waddington (1992); *Department of Employment Gazette* (June 1991).
Note: The denominator for calculating density excludes the self-employed, members of the armed forces and the registered unemployed.

different from the expansionary and rationalising activities of the Transport and General Workers Union (TGWU), the General Municipal and Boiler Makers Union (GMB) and the Manufacturing Science and Finance Union (MSF) in earlier years. Notable are the mergers of the print unions, NGA and SOGAT in 1990 to form the Graphical Paper and Media Union (GPMU); of the engineers and electricians, AEU and EETPU, to form the Amalgamated Engineering and Electricians Union (AEEU) in 1992; the seamens' and rail unions (NUS and NUR) to form the National Union of Rail, Maritime and Transport Workers (RMT) in 1990 and, above all, in July 1993, of the three public service unions (COHSE, NALGO and NUPE) to form the largest union in the UK – UNISON.

It should be noted that trade union membership (of unions affiliated to the TUC) is now largely a public sector phenomenon with nearly three out of every four members hailing from the public sector.

Decline in, and ultimate abolition of, the closed shop

As will be discussed below, compulsory trade union membership, the closed shop, has been one of the chief foci for legislative attack since 1979, culminating in its abolition in 1990, consistent with the EU Social Chapter provision, which emphasises the right to join or not to join a trade union. Even before its abolition, the closed shop was in steep decline. Thus the results of the successive WIRS surveys indicate that whereas some form of closed shop covered 5 million employees in 1980, the equivalent figure for 1990 was 0.5 million (Millward *et al.*, 1992, p. 102). In the case of manual workers, 20 per cent of establishments had a closed shop arrangement in 1984, compared with only 4 per cent in 1990. For non-manual workers the respective figures were 9 per cent and 1 per cent. Evidence also suggests that the decline was steepest in the public sector, in particular, in the nationalised industries. Over 80 per cent of nationalised industry workplaces had manual closed shops in 1984, in 1990, less than 1 per cent (Millward *et al.*, 1992, p. 98).

Nevertheless, there has been higher stability in employer-endorsed unionism (management strongly recommends that all or some workers are members of unions). According to the WIRS surveys, in 1984 employer-endorsed unionism existed in just over 15 per cent of establishments and in 1990 this was the same for manual workers, but somewhat less for non-manual workers. The highest incidence of such encouragement was in the nationalised industries and, to a lesser extent, in the public services sector where it related to both manual and non-manual employees. However, the extent of such encouragement was very much lower in 1990 than in 1984, especially in central government (Millward *et al.*, 1992, p. 99).

Decline in trade union recognition

The WIRS survey data point to a substantial decline in recognition from 1984. The figure for all workplaces and all employees fell from 66 per cent in 1984 to 53 per cent in 1990. Thus, by 1990, only just over half the workplaces in the survey were ones in which the employer recognised one or more unions for collective bargaining over basic pay for some of the employees present. This contrasts strongly with the WIRS figures from the 1980–4 period, when there was stability in the overall figures. However, the decline was very much concentrated in particular sectors – engineering and vehicle industries, printing and publishing – with little change in other sectors. Further, the decline was notable also in smaller establishments, with fewer than 200 employees, and establishments independent of any larger organisation. In the larger establishments there was 'hardly any change' (Millward *et al.*, 1992, p. 72).

Derecognition, generally speaking, has been limited. As Gall and McKay (1994) conclude, 'there is no stampede'. Overall only 3 per cent of all workplaces which had no recognised unions in 1990 had previously recognised unions at some stage since 1984. These amounted to just over 1 per cent of all workplaces in 1990. In the public sector, nearly all the cases were in the education sector, reflecting the government's abolition of the teachers' negotiating machinery in 1987 (Millward *et al.*, 1992, p. 74). However, two caveats must be recognised. The data on the timing of derecognition, with a substantial concentration in 1989, suggests that it may be a 'growing phenomenon' (Millward *et al.*, 1992, p. 74; Gregg and Yates, 1991, pp. 364–5; see also Gall and McKay, 1994). Second, when the WIRS 'panel' of trading sector workplaces, which were surveyed in both 1984 and 1990 are examined, nearly a fifth of those which recognised unions in 1984 no longer did so in 1990.

Data from the second Warwick Company Level 1992 survey is consistent with that of WIRS 3. Almost one in five of the companies surveyed reported that recognition for negotiating purposes had been partially or wholly withdrawn on existing sites, that is, those which they had continued to operate over the previous five years. In three-quarters of the cases this was at some sites, but in one-quarter it was at most or all sites. Such changes were more likely to have occurred among UK domestics, rather than among UK or foreign-owned multinational companies. Some 80 per cent of companies reported taking over one or more operating sites as going concerns in the past five years. Of these companies over 90 per cent had maintained the *status quo*, 63 per cent maintaining union recognition and 28 per cent maintaining non-recognition. The remainder were split 3:2 between those withdrawing recognition and those granting fresh recognition. 80 per cent of companies reported opening at least one new site over the previous five years. Amongst these companies, just over 40 per cent had granted union recognition at all or some sites opened, but in almost 60 per cent of cases no union recognition had been granted to the largest group within the workforce. Of those companies already recognising unions, just under 40 per cent had granted recognition at all new sites opened, but over one-third had not recognised unions at any new site opened. Recognition at new sites was more common amongst UK- than overseas-owned companies and in manufacturing and other production sectors than in the services sector. It was strongly associated with bargaining arrangements covering all establishments in a company, whereas recognition at some or no sites was strongly associated with site-level bargaining. In a similar manner the withdrawal of recognition at existing sites was strongly associated with establishment-level bargaining and the factors cited most as bringing about derecognition were diminishing union membership and privatisation (Marginson *et al.*, 1993, pp. 55–7). The authors of the survey conclude

> Overall, the balance of these findings points towards a diminution of recognition for negotiating purposes, least marked amongst companies' existing sites and those that they take over, but most noticeable amongst new sites opened. Comprehensive recognition of unions across all sites within a company now only occurs in a minority of large companies. (p. 57)

Decline in the coverage and scope of collective bargaining

The fall in the proportion of the total workforce covered by collective agreements in the 1980s was substantial, according to WIRS survey data. The aggregate proportion of employees covered by collective bargaining fell from 71 per cent to 54 per cent between 1984 and 1990. In private sector manufacturing there was a fall from 64 per cent to 51 per cent and from 41 per cent to 33 per cent in the service sector. As Millward et al. (1992, pp. 93–4) noted this means that in the private sector as a whole, coverage declined from a majority of employees (52 per cent) to a minority (41 per cent). In the words of the WIRS research team, this represents 'one of the most dramatic changes in the character of British industrial relations that our survey series has measured' (Millward et al., 1992, p. 93). Further, the WIRS surveys reveal that the scope of bargaining has contracted within the unionised sector. Fewer issues were subject to joint regulation in 1990 than in 1980, although much of this contraction occurred in the earlier part of the decade. In particular, employment levels and closely related issues were ones that management most commonly succeeded in removing from the bargaining agenda.

A further indication of the weakening of trade unions in collective bargaining is indicated by the fall in the proportion of workplaces with recognised unions that had a representative on site, from 82 per cent in 1984 to 71 per cent in 1990. Moreover, representatives were less likely to be appointed by competitive elections and more likely to emerge as the only person willing to take on the role (Millward et al., 1992, pp. 111, 137, 352).

However, while the scope and coverage of collective bargaining has declined overall, an important caveat should be noted. In workplaces where trade union representation and collective bargaining persisted, 'surprisingly little altered'. To quote the WIRS researchers

> Change occurred more because the proportion of workplaces operating the British 'system' of industrial relations declined so markedly, rather than because there was a uniform decline in trade union representation and collective bargaining across all sectors and types of workplaces. (Millward et al., 1992, p. 350)

A shift in bargaining levels

The shift from multi-employer to single-employer bargaining, although encouraged by the Conservative governments, has been long running (see *IRRR*, 1989a, 1989b). It reflects a view on the part of employers that multi-employer bargaining has the potential to be both inflationary and inflexible. The argument for its decline is that (a) pay and conditions should be related to company profitability and local labour market conditions, (b) changes in payment systems and working practices are slow to come about as the industry tends to move at the pace of the slowest, (c) it is an abdication to an external body of control of pay and conditions of a company's 'most important asset', (d) it gives trade unions too much power as they can bring to bear their limited resources on to one set of negotiations (Storey and Sisson, 1993, pp. 209–10).

The shift from multi-establishment to single-establishment bargaining has also been marked in the 1980s. This has been especially true for large enterprises with dispersed plants operating in different labour markets. However, where the range of production is diverse and the processes of production are highly interdependent then centralised bargaining still tends to be favoured (Storey and Sisson, 1993, p. 211). Centralised bargaining also persists in the unionised sector (Millward et al., 1992, p. 355). Nevertheless, any decentralisation of decision-making in bargaining matters is largely illusory. Most key bargaining issues have to be agreed within parameters set by head office and any potential deviations cleared with head office (Kinnie, 1985a, 1985b; Marginson et al., 1988; Millward et al., 1992, pp. 209, 355–6; Marginson et al., 1993, pp. 58–61).

At the same time, where collective bargaining has survived, there have been moves to widen the bargaining units at any given level. On greenfield sites this has been expressed in employers' preference for single-union agreements (see below). On established, multi-union sites, where historically there may have been a number of separate bargaining units (e.g., for craftsmen, process and clerical workers) there have been moves in some companies towards 'single-table' bargaining, that is, one joint negotiating body and one set of negotiations covering manual and non-manual workers, with an integrated pay structure (Kessler and Bayliss, 1992, p. 181).

Decline in strike action

Whether measured in terms of number of strikes, number of workers involved in strike action or in number of working days lost, strike action has steadily declined since the 1979 'Winter of Discontent' with two exceptions: the Miners' strike in 1984 and the 'Summer of Discontent' in 1989 (see Table 8.3). The annual average number of disputes in the 1970s was 2,631 compared to 1,129 in the 1980s; the annual average number of working days lost in the 1970s was 12.9 million compared to 7.2 million in the 1980s (the latter figure reflecting the very lengthy miners' strike) (Employment Gazette, cited in Gospel and Palmer, 1993, p. 226). The contrast between the 1979 'Winter of Discontent' and 1989 'Summer of Discontent' is striking. In the former there were 2,126 stoppages and 29,474 working days lost in strikes; in the latter, 701 stoppages and 4,128 working days lost. With the onset of recession in the early 1990s strike action fell even further. In 1993 the provisional figures were a mere 211 stoppages and 649 days lost (all figures for working days lost expressed in thousands) (Employment Gazette, August 1994).

It should be noted that reductions in strike incidence between the 1970s and 1980s occurred in all OECD counties, as did a lower incidence of strike activity in the second than in the first half of the decade. Further, reductions in the UK's incidence were not larger than those of its main competitors (see Kessler and Bayliss, 1992, Table 11.5). This is important if seeking to attribute the causes of such a reduction solely to post-1979 Conservative government policy (see below).

Table 8.3 UK strike statistics, 1974–93

Year	Working days lost (000)	Working days lost per 1,000 employees[a]	Workers involved (000)	Stoppages
1974	14,750	647	1,626	2,946
1975	6,012	265	809	2,332
1976	3,284	146	668	2,034
1977	10,142	448	1,166	2,737
1978	9,405	413	1,041	2,498
1979	29,474	1,273	4,608	2,125
1980	11,964	521	834	1,348
1981	4,266	195	1,513	1,344
1982	5,313	248	2,103	1,538
1983	3,754	178	574	1,364
1984	27,135	1,278	1,464	1,221
1985	6,402	299	791	903
1986	1,920	90	720	1,074
1987	3,546	164	887	1,016
1988	3,702	166	790	781
1989	4,128	182	727	701
1990	1,903	83	298	630
1991	761	34	176	369
1992	528	24	148	253
1993	649	30	385	211

[a] Based on the latest available mid-year (June) estimates of employees in employment.
Source: *Employment Gazette* (June 1994).

Summary

So, what does this series of interrelated statistics amount to? In a nutshell, fall in union membership and density, assisted in part by the decline in the closed shop, both reflect and stimulate a decline in trade union recognition. Lack of recognition inevitably diminishes the coverage of collective bargaining, and low density encourages employers to restrict its scope. Lack of union recognition, combined with decreased membership and density, inevitably inhibits union organisation and financial strength (Willman, 1990; Kessler and Bayliss, 1992, pp. 146–9) and undermines both the willingness and the ability to undertake strike action. As perceived effectiveness is reckoned to be the most powerful inducement on an employee's decision to join a union, and as successful strikes are the most visible evidence of that effectiveness (Kelly, 1990, p. 59) lack of successful strike action, combined with some very notable union defeats, in turn inhibits union recruitment. It might also be argued that shifts in bargaining level have a similar effect as they undermine broader solidarities and encourage workers to focus on the fate and well-being of their own company/plant irrespective of the interests of fellow workers/unionists. In other words, the changes in 'traditional' industrial relations from a liberal collectivist perspective centre around the undermining of voluntaristic collective bargaining. And what of the survival of that other form of 'traditional' British industrial relations: 'corporatism'? Before considering the impact of such changes on the employment relationship, and the death of corporatism, how and why did the changes already identified occur?

The employment context post-1979: recession and the enterprise culture

In summarising the institutional changes in 'traditional' liberal collectivist industrial relations institutions, in the 1980s and early 1990s, it is clear that the decline in trade union membership and density both reflects and stimulates the other changes identified. So, a first question is to establish the reasons for this decline.

Reasons for the decline in trade union membership and density

Three main explanations have been offered: secular changes in the composition of the workforce; changes in the incentives and opportunities for workers to organise and for employers to resist unionisation; inadequate organising efforts on the part of the unions (Kelly, 1990, p. 33). The first two explanations focus on the demand for, and the third on the supply of, union services. So what is the nature of these explanations and evidence for their support?

The changing composition of the workforce?

Summarising Kelly (1990), it is often claimed that changes in the composition of the workforce largely account for the decline in union membership. In other words, shifts in employment from private sector manufacturing and public sector industries to private sector services (and with overall stagnation in public sector services), and the rise in overseas-owned workplaces have resulted in a decline in traditionally well organised groups: male, full-time, relatively well paid manual workers in large plants, and a rise in groups with traditionally lower union density: women, part-time, white collar and the low paid in smaller workplaces. While this explanation is highly relevant to industrial unions in high density, declining industries which are unable to expand into other job territories (e.g., mining, steel, railways), it is by no means a complete explanation for the massive falls in union memberships in the 1980s.

First, the compositional trends supposedly inimical to trade union membership pre-date membership decline. For example, while manufacturing employment in Britain began to decline absolutely from 1966, losing 1 million jobs by 1979, union membership in manufacturing rose by 1 million in that period. In the decade of union growth, 1968–79, 61 per cent of the extra 3 million members were white collar and 52 per cent were women. Second, similar compositional trends in advanced capitalist societies in the western world correlate not only with very different outcomes but very different trends in union densities. For example, with similar sectoral composition, in 1989 the US had union density of 25 per cent compared to Sweden's 89 per cent; with similar workforce composition, and union densities each of around 29 per cent, that of the US has fallen to below 20 per cent while Canada's has risen to 40 per cent (Kelly, 1990, p. 35). Third, the standard explanations as to why compositional changes should result in lower union membership – that women, white collar and part-time workers have different priorities and interests compared with male, manual, full-time workers, and that unions fail to address these, while sectoral shifts in capitalist societies have led to a decline in collectivist attitudes – are not fully supported by survey evidence. Kelly (1990, pp. 36–8) argues that the evidence suggests that the interests of women trade unionists are not especially homogeneous by virtue of gender, but rather reflect such factors as labour market location, type of labour process and union socialisation. Similarly 'white collar' and 'part-time' workers are heterogeneous categories containing groups with very different propensities to organise (cf. teachers and retail workers). Further, as far as ideological shifts go, British trade union popularity among the general public tends to be *inversely* related to union growth and major reviews of attitudinal and opinion data in the 1980s, in spite of governmental trumpeting of the values of individualism and enterprise, show strong support for the principle of trade unionism among the general population and employees (Curtice, 1987; Gallie, 1988; Rentoul, 1989 cited in Kelly, 1990, p. 38). The reasons most frequently cited by non-trade unionists for not being in a union are that they are in a job where there is no union available or where membership is not required, or if there is a union available they have not been able to join (Gallie, 1988, 1989; Payne, 1989; Stevens *et al.*, 1989, cited in Kelly, 1990, p. 38). This suggests that changes in the structure of employment towards smaller workplaces and *management* attitudes towards collectivism, supported by restrictive legislation (see below) underlies non-joining. So what other factors account for membership decline?

Recession and unemployment?

Generally speaking, inflation and low or falling unemployment correlate with trade union growth while low inflation and high or rising unemployment correlate with membership stagnation or decline (Bain and Price, 1983). The first scenario, overall, matches the 1970s, the second (with the exception of the years 1988–90) matches the 1980s and 1990s. Unemployment rose from 1.3 million in 1979, to a peak of 3.3 million in 1986, dropping to 1.6 million in 1990, following the inflationary boom of the late 1980s, only to rise to over 3 million by January 1993. Arguably the whole country has experienced the meaning of unemployment. The recession of 1979–81 decimated the heartlands of UK manufacturing industries in the Midlands and North, resulting in a fall in manufacturing employment of approaching 25 per cent between 1979–85 (Hawkins, 1987, p. 54) and hitting male full-time manual workers particularly hard. Throughout the period the mining industry has been massively run down, prior to privatisation, accelerated by the effects of the 1984–5 strike and the implications of privatisation of electricity generation. The recession of the early 1990s impacted on the private service sector in the South that had grown substantially in the boom years of the late 1980s, squeezing the jobs, not only of part-time women workers but of full-time male professionals in the financial services industries. Throughout the period, but accelerating with the competitive climate of the early 1990s, many middle managers experienced previously unimagined unemployment, through massive delayering, as organisations sought to reduce overheads and equated 'leanness' with 'fitness'. With the exception of the late 1980s, when the relaxation of monetarism and expansionary, election oriented budgets produced an inflation rate of over 10 per cent by 1990, inflation has fallen from a peak of 18 per cent in 1980 to a low of around just over 2 per cent in 1994. Further, earnings across the whole economy, but especially in manufacturing and private service sectors, have increased in real terms throughout the 1980s, if with some slowdown in the recession of the early 1990s.

The argument that decline in trade union membership is related to unemployment, low inflation and rise in real earnings is three-fold. First, the unemployed lack both the incentive and cash to maintain union membership. Secondly, for those in employment there has been less incentive to unionise, as employers have been prepared to concede real wage increases. Thirdly – an argument favoured by Kelly (1990, pp. 39–40), a declared Marxist – rising unemployment coupled with anti-union legislation, in particular that undermining and eventually banning the closed shop (see below), allows employers to inhibit union membership, either by raising its costs (through non-recognition, victimisation) and/or by raising the benefits of non-membership through a series of 'soft' HRM policies, substituting for recognition and collective bargaining. This latter argument will be considered in more detail below. Suffice to say here, in support of Kelly, that the WIRS 3 survey, conducted in 1990, did find a relationship between management attitudes unfavourable towards trade unions (more likely to be found in larger, manufacturing establishments) and union failures to recruit new members (Millward et al., 1992, p. 68). Further as already shown, while derecognition has been limited, it appears to be a rising trend.

The supply of union services?

A further argument Kelly (1990, pp. 40–1) presents to account for declining union membership is unions' inadequate efforts at recruitment. He cites several studies in support of this. Kelly and Heery (1989) found that recruitment, on average, was ranked as only the sixth most time consuming activity of full-time union officers, a finding supported by a more comprehensive TUC study (TUC, 1989a). The 1984 WIRS 2 survey found that 85 per cent of establishments without recognised unions for manual workers, and 90 per cent of establishments without recognised unions for non-manual workers had not been visited by a union official within the past five years (Millward and Stevens, 1986). Not much had changed by 1990. Only 12 per cent of establishments had been subjected to (unsuccessful) recruitment efforts in private sector non-union workplaces in the six years prior to the 1990 survey (Millward et al., 1992, p. 68). TUC surveys of two local labour markets found that most non-union establishments had no record of any approach by a union organiser (TUC, 1989b) and McLoughlin and Gourlay (1989) found that 84 per cent of non-union electronics plants in their survey reported that there had been no recruitment attempts in the 1980s.

Further evidence of the inadequacy of union recruitment attempts through most of the 1980s has been the TUC's initiative, in 1987, to set up a Special Review Body to examine membership and recruitment into the 1990s, along with its encouragement of unions to offer a wider range of financial, legal and other services to workers in order to attract and retain them in membership.

Reasons for the growth of non-recognition and decline in the closed shop, in coverage and scope of collective bargaining and in strike action

As already suggested, there is a clear connection between decline in trade union membership and density, in the decline of the closed shop and in the decline of collective bargaining and strike action and the growth of non-recognition. Insofar as the latter are seen to be indirectly caused by membership decline, the causes of such decline in part account for these related trends. However, other factors appear equally important, in particular the post-1979 Conservative government's support of a liberal individualist approach to industrial relations, that has strengthened the employers' hand in their relationship with both trade unions and employees.

Changes in collective and individual legislation

As briefly touched upon in Chapter 3, the Conservative governments of the 1980s and early 1990s advocate the virtues of free markets (and hence of deregulation and privatisation) and the evils of those institutions seen to inhibit their operation. Trade unions, throughout this period have been defined as such and hence seen as not worthy of incorporation but as the 'enemy within', a power to be constrained if not broken. Military analogies abound: not only the 'enemy within', but 'entrenched' (attitudes), 'militant' (union leaders, shop stewards), 'conscripted' (trade union membership) and notably, 'The mining dispute cannot be settled. It can only be *won*' (cf. Dunn, 1990).

Throughout the 1980s and 1990s employment legislation has been enacted to undermine the props to collective bargaining and trade union recognition while at the same time to introduce new flexiblities in managing individual employees. (Excellent summaries are provided in Kessler and Bayliss, 1992, Chapter 5; Gospel and Palmer, 1993, pp. 254–60; in Lewis, 1991 and in Blyton and Turnbull 1994; Chapter 6.) An important feature of the legislative changes has been the consistency and relentlessness of their step-by-step eating away at union and some individual employment protection rights, while strengthening individual members' rights against trade unions..

The major initiatives have been as follows. The *Employment Act 1980* repealed procedures for aiding trade union recognition and extending collective agreements. It gave employers legal remedies against secondary picketing, and made it more difficult to introduce and maintain the closed shop. Public funds were made available to encourage unions to hold postal ballots for the election of officers and for important policy decisions. The *Employment Act 1982* tightened the law on closed shops by requiring reviews in secret ballots and by outlawing union-labour-only contracts. Trade unions were made liable for asset sequestration if they instigated industrial action that was not protected by the statutory immunity applying to acts done in contemplation or furtherance of a trade dispute. Selective dismissal of strikers was now legal and 'political' strikes outlawed. The *Trade Union Act 1984* placed constraints on how unions conducted their internal affairs, with the intention of 'democratising' unions and undermining the position of 'entrenched' interests, militants and so forth. Union executives had to submit themselves for election by secret ballot every five years and unions had to hold a secret ballot every ten years if they wished to retain a political fund. Pre-strike ballots were required before calling an official strike, if unions were to retain immunity from civil action for damages. The *Employment Act 1988* continued the attack on unions, by strengthening the rights of individual employees *vis à vis* union actions. Workers were allowed to apply for court orders instructing unions to repudiate industrial action organised without a secret ballot. Unions were banned from disciplining members for refusing to support industrial action. Post-entry closed shop was declared unenforceable. All senior officials had to be elected by secret ballot. A new Commissioner for Rights of Trade Union Members was created with the duty to support and fund union members' court action against their unions. The *Employment Act 1989* amended the statutory provisions on time off work for trade union duties, principally by restricting the range of issues for which paid time off can be claimed. Finally, the *Employment Act 1990* removed all legal protection from the closed shop by making refusal of employment on grounds relating to union membership illegal. It made nearly all forms of secondary action illegal, by removing immunity for organising industrial action if that action was not in contemplation or furtherance of a trade dispute or if the action was in support of an employee dismissed while taking any unofficial industrial action. Employers were given greater freedom to dismiss any employee taking unofficial industrial action and made unlawful industrial action to secure the reinstatement of selectively dismissed strikers. Unions were made responsible at law if any official (including shop stewards) called for industrial action. The law on balloting was further tightened.

After the 1992 election victory the Conservative government introduced a further tranche of labour legislation, in the *Trade Union Reform and Employment Rights Act 1993*, that arguably struck even harder at the principles of collectivism. Individuals were given the right to join any union of their choice, thus undermining the TUC's Bridlington agreements concerning poaching and union territorial rights. Members were also required to give periodic written consent for the deduction of union dues directly from their pay packets by employers (the 'check-off') thus potentially undermining both membership numbers and union finances.[5] ACAS' requirement to encourage collective bargaining was removed. Requirements about postal balloting before any strike action were further tightened and unions were required to provide employers with at least seven days' notice of official industrial action. Individuals were to be allowed to seek an injunction against a union or individual promoting unlawful industrial action resulting in public service disruptions. New controls on union elections were introduced.

Turning to individual employment law the government's stated aim has been to reduce what it sees as rigidities in the labour market, and to introduce new flexibilities in support of the employer. The upshot of the changes (enacted through the *Employment Act 1980, Wages Act 1986, Employment Act 1989* and the *Trade Union Reform and Employment Rights Act 1993*) has been to limit employees' unfair dismissal and maternity rights; to first reduce the functions of wage councils in fixing minimum enforceable wage rates in industries where collective bargaining is weak, by restricting them to fixing a single rate of pay and removing young workers from their coverage (1986) before, in 1993, abolishing 26 wage councils altogether;[6] to repeal laws regulating young people's hours of work; to exempt small firms from the requirement to provide written statements of disciplinary procedures and, again, increasing the qualifying period for bringing complaints of unfair dismissal. Against this, after reducing maternity leave rights and rights to reinstatement in 1980, they were restored and extended under pressure from EU directives in 1993.

Such changes have been compounded by the government's opposition to the EU Social Charter, safeguarding the rights of part-time workers, maternity leave and placing restrictions on overtime working. This culminated in its negotiation, at the Maastricht summit in 1991, of 'opt-out' rights in relation to the Social Chapter of the treaty, which committed all other EU counties to an extension of social legislation. British workers are now some of the least protected in the EU (see Chapter 10).

In summary, in spite of the *laissez faire* traditions of liberal individualism, the successive Conservative administrations have *intervened*, ostensibly to *deregulate* the labour market by dismantling the props to union membership, collective bargaining and industrial action. Paradoxically, in Gospel and Palmer's (1993, p. 257) words 'it has sought to *regulate* collective relations at work and to introduce the threat of common law interventions into industrial relations'. Such state intervention, though, is a denial of corporatism. The institutions of collectivism are not seen as representing workers' interests and hence have no place on national decision-making bodies. Hence the very clear governmental marginalisation of union leaders and the TUC throughout this period. In the area of individual and protective labour law, true to its principles, the government, with a few EU driven exceptions, has deregulated industrial relations.

Nevertheless, one should be wary of overestimating the effect of such legislative changes on industrial action and on the conduct of industrial relations generally. However, the legislation created a hostile and inhibitive climate that may have influenced union officials' and memberships' attitudes and behaviours. Certainly, Freeman and Pelletier (1990) estimated that changes in UK labour laws had reduced union density by 1–1.7 percentage points per year from 1980 to 1986, which cumulatively amounted to 9.4 percentage points – effectively the entire decline in UK density in that period. But, as Blyton and Turnbull (1994, p. 109) query, 'is legislation the *cause* of union decline and membership losses the *effect*, or the other way round?'. After all the government adopted a step-by-step approach to legislative reform and the decline in union density slowed after 1983 when one would have expected, according to Freeman and Pelletier's argument, that it would have accelerated (Waddington, 1992, pp. 310–11; see also Disney, 1990). Further, the effect of narrowing unions' legal immunity in calling strike action is difficult to assess because, particularly in the second half of the 1980s and in the early 1990s, industrial action has been running at such a low level that there has been insufficient occasions on which the law might have been tested for its practical significance to have emerged. And, as mentioned earlier, the incidence of strikes has been falling in all other OECD countries over the decade, although some were untouched by 'Conservative' legislation. Also, as far as the UK goes, although secondary action and picketing were curtailed in the 1980 Act, it was not until the 1984 Act on balloting that the main inhibitive legal provisions were in force and, hence, only in the second half of the decade that they could exercise an influence (Kessler and Bayliss, 1992, pp. 232, 217).

Privatisation and the creation of quasi-markets

Again this has been referred to briefly in Chapters 3, 5 and 7.

Since 1979 Conservative governments have pursued, and continue to pursue, a consistent policy of deregulating erstwhile regulated markets (e.g., telecommunications, finance) and privatising commercial monopolies. Where complete privatisation is politically unacceptable ('The Health Service is safe in our hands') other tactics have been employed to imitate the discipline of the market. Thus we have seen the introduction of cash limits as a control on overhead and pay levels; compulsory competitive tendering, leading to the contracting out of services (often to non-unionised companies), 'trust' status for hospitals, 'fund-holding' general practices, and contractor–provider relationships in the NHS; the 'opting-out' of schools and pressure to attract business sponsorship; imposition of priority financial targets coupled with the spread of accounting criteria and commercialisation; appointment of businessmen to managerial posts; attempts to decentralise national pay bargaining; introduction of performance-related pay in local authorities (as well as in the privatised monopolies) and so on (Kelly, 1990, pp. 51–3; Parsons, 1988). Above all, as employer or holder of the purse strings, throughout this period the successive governments have been prepared to withstand major strikes in nationalised industries and public sector services as in steel, coal, railways, civil service, education, health and local government. Symbolic of the government's stance was the withdrawal of trade union recognition and the banning of individual trade union membership among staff at GCHQ (1984), which precipitated widespread industrial action in the Civil Service, and the withdrawal of teachers' negotiating rights in 1987.

The effects of privatisation have been to release employers from a statutory obligation to recognise trade unions and consult employees through various mechanisms. (However, WIRS 3 found little evidence that trade union negotiating rights had, in practice, been extensively withdrawn, Millward et al., 1992, p. 359). However, 'market disciplines' have led to widespread job loss in both privatised industries (e.g., BT and British Gas) and in public sector services such as the NHS. 'Contracting out' has not only led to job loss in the public sector services but to a substitution of full-time jobs in a unionised sector for often part-time jobs in non-unionised companies, now undertaking ancillary services, and hence reduction in pay levels (Kelly, 1990, p. 56). Taken together job loss through cutting overhead and 'contracting out' has reduced trade union membership, while 'contracting out' has diminished the coverage and scope of collective bargaining.

The marginalisation and loss of power of trade unions

To what extent do the changes in 'traditional' industrial relations institutions, given their generative context, add up to a loss of trade union power? If this has occurred, to what extent is there a 'new realism', a recognition on the part of trade unions that their relations with employers must be on a new, collaborative footing?

A loss of power?

In spite of the changes identified, up to the 1990s recession, it was *just* about possible on the part of the optimistic to query the extent to which unions had lost the power they enjoyed in the 1970s. With the exception of the depths of the 1979–81 recession, real earnings had risen throughout the 1980s. Further, with the fall of unemployment in the late 1980s and with increasing recognition of an endemic skills shortage and a demographic downturn in the labour supply just around the corner (see Atkinson, 1989), days lost through strike action once again started to rise in the 'Summer of Discontent' (1989), with some notable successes (e.g., at BT, ICI and at Ford) (see Kelly, 1990, p. 45). Furthermore up to the mid-1980s the pattern of union recognition remained remarkably stable (Millward and Stevens, 1986; Edwards and Marginson, 1988). In spite of the overall decline in union membership some unions, in the 1980s, in entertainment/media, post/telecommunications, banking and in the public sector had seen small rises in membership (Kelly, 1990, p. 32).[7] Further, as already reported, even as late as 1990, the WIRS 3 survey found that in workplaces where trade union representation and collective bargaining persisted, 'surprisingly little altered' (Millward *et al.*, 1992, p. 350).[8]

Furthermore, some plausible arguments could be offered in support of a continuation of union power in spite of recession. First, the underlying assumptions that unemployment produces a reserve army of labour and, second, that recession strengthens employers' ability to resist strike action appeared questionable to the pluralistically oriented academics of the early to mid-1980s (see Batstone, 1984; Batstone and Gourlay, 1986; Martin, 1987).

The arguments go as follows. Companies do not conform to a price auction model of labour recruitment in their primary labour markets because of the large transaction costs (e.g., of recruitment, selection, training, administration of differential wages, union opposition) involved. In particular, as the costs of training increase and the significance of job-related experience – including 'tacit skills' (Manwaring and Wood, 1985) – grows, the costs of substituting recruits from the unemployed for the presently employed increase. Further, the unemployed are not directly substitutable for the employed; not only do they tend to be either younger or older, but they tend also to have lower levels of education, are less likely to be skilled and to be concentrated in particular labour markets (Martin, 1987, pp. 223, 232). It is then in employers' interests to isolate the workplace from the wider labour market and to promote retention and cooperation of employees through the development of the internal labour market, via 'soft' HRM policies.

In practice, if substitution of the unemployed for the employed occurs, it is more likely to do so in the secondary labour market, where required skill levels are often lower, job insecurity higher, and union coverage and effectiveness lower. In the mid-1980s evidence was debatable whether employers in the primary labour market were engaging in widespread subcontracting of peripheral activities, or in the use of non-core labour *in recession*. If flexibility was their aim, and demand was low, employers were more likely to shift work away from the secondary, back into the primary labour market (MacInnes, 1987b, p. 121). Use of secondary labour, the evidence then suggested, was more likely to be associated with *rising demand and recovery*.

The second argument questions whether employers are better able to resist threats of strike action in periods of recession, as work stoppages are less costly in conditions of falling demand. Batstone and Gourlay (1986, pp. 4–6) pointed to the limitations of this assumption. First, even in a recession there will be some companies experiencing buoyant demand when work stoppages would be costly, assuming they wish to maximise profitability or market share. Secondly, slack demand may place a company in a very competitive situation, as far as retaining or extending market share is concerned. For such employers, a stoppage could be costly as potential customers might switch to alternative suppliers. Thirdly, if employers anticipate recovery, they may wish to build up stocks to meet the upturn. Fourthly, if both the employer and unions recognise the weakness of the employer's competitiveness position, both may cooperate in an attempt to regain profitability or market share and to secure jobs. The situation in which an employer may refuse to concede to strike action is where acceding to demands would prevent even a long-run return to profitability, and where surplus capacity and multiplant structure allows threats of individual plant closure to be made and one plant played off against another. In such a situation, too, an employer may decide to close production altogether in the UK and source from overseas. Except for the final strategy, most of these threats depend for their effectiveness on weak union organisation and coordination between the different plants.

Hence, so the argument goes, when companies face market problems, it is rational for them to seek union and employee cooperation, particularly given the philosophy underlying the development of internal labour markets, rather than risk the potential costs of confrontation. Hence, the reduction in work stoppages and days lost need not *necessarily* be interpreted as reflecting a loss of union power.

One is tempted to suggest that such interpretations, persuasive as they might have seemed at the time, emerged mainly because the traditionally pluralist/collectivist industrial relations academics, familiar with the growth of unionism in the 1970s, could not quite believe in the audaciousness and radicalism of the Conservative government's industrial relations policy (nor in the return of successive Conservative governments!). In fairness to these interpretations, they took place at a time when the economy was reviving, before much of the Conservative industrial relations legislation had been enacted, and before WIRS 3 detected the changing patterns of trade union recognition and decrease in the coverage and scope of collective bargaining that had not been apparent from WIRS 2 (1984) survey data. Nevertheless, with the prolonged nature of the recession of the early 1990s and the slowness of recovery and with hindsight over the 1980s and early 1990s, few would even attempt to make such a case today, for the following reasons.

Enter a 'new realism' and 'new industrial relations'?

As noted by Kelly (1990, p. 42), following Lukes (1974), employer/union power is manifested in three ways: who wins industrial actions; who succeeds in controlling the agenda of industrial relations (e.g., scope of collective bargaining); who succeeds in moulding employees' definition of their interests and ideological stance. On all three counts, since the end of the 1970s, unions have lost ground.

First, their ability to mobilise employees for strike action has declined sharply, whether measured in terms of numbers of stoppages, days lost and workers involved (see Table 8.3, p. 256). In recession, employees have not been prepared to embark on strikes which they felt could not be won and might only accelerate plant closure. Such perceptions have been reinforced by spectacular defeats of erstwhile strong unions: railways (1982), mining (1985), printing (1986), TV-AM (1987), teachers (1987), P&O Ferries (1989). In particular, the defeat of the National Union of Mineworkers in 1985, previously regarded as unbeatable since its strike victory and its role in the fall of the Conservative government in 1974, gave rise to a widespread public opinion that if the miners could be defeated, anyone could be. As John Monks, General Secretary of the TUC, put it, retrospectively, in 1991

> After all, the miners had been the one group that the Conservative Government had feared and had avoided fighting earlier in the decade; so when the miners were defeated there was an important sense of an era of traditional trade union activity coming to an end and a realization that if the Government could take on the miners they could take on anyone else. (Monks et al., 1991/2, p. 75)

Hence unions have been unable to mobilise effective resistance to plant closure and redundancies, and have often been forced to watch employees opt for voluntary redundancy packages, in the belief that this will give them first opportunity to secure the remaining jobs in the local labour market, prior to a flood of competitors following an anticipated wave of future compulsory redundancies and possible plant closure.

Further, there is much evidence that throughout the 1980s, partly through strategies of functional and numerical flexibility and of JIT, (see Chapters 5 and 7) that work intensification has occurred, particularly in manufacturing (see Layard and Nickell, 1988; Legge, 1988; Metcalf, 1988, 1989; Nickell et al., 1989; Nolan and Marginson, 1990; Guest, 1990; Edwards and Whitston, 1991). Unions have been unable to resist the changes in working practices that have resulted in such intensification.

Turning to the control of the industrial relations agenda, again, in the 1980s, the unions appear to have lost out at both a macro and micro level. Not only did the successive Conservative governments refuse to engage in any form of dialogue with union leaders, but at plant level, as already discussed, the scope and coverage of collective bargaining diminished. In particular, while New Technology Agreements, negotiated between employers and unions were emerging in the 1970s, the introduction of new technology in the 1980s was marked by an absence of negotiation and relatively little consultation (Daniel, 1987; Edwards, 1987; Legge, 1989b). Managers kept the implementation of technical change and investment issues generally out of the bargaining arena (Marginson et al., 1988). Unions generally welcomed rather than resisted technical change and investment as a guarantor against plant closure (Daniel, 1987). Throughout the 1980s there has been a significant increase in management initiatives to increase direct employee involvement, and survey evidence would suggest that in plants experiencing serious economic problems and with traditionally above average levels of union organisation, this has involved attempts to by-pass the unions (Millward and Stevens, 1986; Millward et al., 1992; Batstone, 1984; Batstone and Gourlay, 1986; Legge, 1988, pp. 45–9). While the WIRS 3 survey of 1990 found that consultation continued to be more common in workplaces where trade unions were recognised than where they were not, union representatives were consulted less often and being given less information (Millward et al., 1992, pp. 170–1, 354).

Storey's (1992b) case study evidence also points to unions' diminished influence over the industrial relations agenda. Most of the companies he researched did not engage in a frontal assault on the unions, nor did they have a policy to displace them. Rather their stance was generally firmer, even more aggressive and, in relation to new initiatives, seemed to marginalise the unions. Storey (1992b, pp. 250–1) quotes significant comments from both a senior personnel manager and a shop steward, at Rover, about the 'Working with Pride' Programme:

> The unions were invited to the party but they didn't seem to want to come. So, the party went ahead without them.

> Yes, I've heard about the invitation to a 'party'. The trouble is it had already started and in any case it was not the kind of party which we wanted to go to. 'Working with Pride' is a nice fancy label but the reality is not so very different to what they have tried to serve up to us before. Basically, they want more work out of fewer men.

Finally, Kelly (1990, p. 42) has argued that, from a Marxist point of view, the spread of 'new realism' among trade union members and leadership and the willingness to accept legislative controls on union activities 'could signify a more profound, ideological weakening of union power'.

Although the TUC initially led campaigns and demonstrations in opposition to the Conservative government's first programmes of labour legislation, the massive election defeat of the Labour party in 1983, followed by the miners' defeat in 1985, resulted in a sea-change of opinion on the part of the TUC and the more 'moderate' union leaders (notably of the engineers, electricians and the GMB). In 1984 the TUC launched the TUC Strategy Document, advocating the need for collaboration with government and employers and the need to promote a more positive, more 'modern', less adversarial image if unions were to win new members among the expanding sectors of the economy where union membership and density were traditionally low. The 'new industrial relations' (NIR) backgrounds much collectivist ideology, with its acceptance of single-union deals (anti-solidaristic), 'no-strike' clauses, the breaking down of traditional demarcation lines and the acceptance of flexible working, its support for direct employee involvement, staff status and employee development (often involving such 'individualistic' policies as appraisal and performance-related pay) and, above all, of cooperation rather than confrontation between trade unions and employers (Bassett, 1986; Beaumont, 1990, 1992; Lucio and Weston, 1992). While it is arguable how widely accepted the 'new industrial relations' is throughout the union movement – and, in particular, in the public sector – leaders of major general and craft unions, such as John Edmonds (GMB), Bill Jordan (AEU) and Alan Tuffin (UCW), along with John Monks, the General Secretary of the TUC, now routinely speak its language. For example:

John Edmonds
Traditional collective bargaining will not deliver better training, better promotion opportunities, fully-fledged equal rights, or a forum for quality issues and improvements in products and services. Hence, we were led on to consider changing the structures for consultation with employers ... The British system is too conflict based to allow sensible handling of the wider agenda at the moment. Issues such as training ought not to be conflict issues. It is difficult to see how they can be tackled within the present IR framework. The present institutions actually *create* conflict – almost out of anything. The British industrial relations system is lousy, its awful. It doesn't work. (Storey *et al.*, 1993, pp. 67, 69)

Two significant documents, the joint GMB/UCW (1990) paper entitled *A New Agenda: Bargaining for Prosperity in the 1990s* and the consultative document of the Involvement and Participation Association (1992) entitled *Towards Industrial Partnership* epitomise the values of 'new industrial relations'. The first advocates a 'new agenda' of employment issues arguing for less emphasis on collective bargaining over pay, and more attention to the 'rights of individuals', such as training rights, equal opportunity rights, having a worthwhile satisfying job through work restructuring, and job security (Storey *et al.*, 1993, pp. 66–8). The second is a joint declaration between leading industrialists (for example, David Sainsbury, Denis Cassidy and Sir Brian Nicholson) and union leaders (such as Bill Jordan, Leif Mills, Alan Tuffin and John Edmonds) committing the signatories to certain principles. The declaration states that managers should declare job security as a key corporate objective, agree to 'gainsharing' the results of success, and recognise the legitimacy of the employee's right to be informed, consulted and represented. It is proposed that trade unions in return renounce rigid job demarcations and commit themselves to flexible working; give sympathetic consideration to the continental model of representation of the whole workforce by means of the election of representatives to new works councils; and recognise and then copromote employee involvement methods (Storey *et al.*, 1993, p. 63).

Summary

From the evidence presented it would appear that the combined effects of compositional changes in the workforce, Conservative governments' policies of monetarism and market deregulation (which directly or indirectly have promoted recession and unemployment, restrictive collective and deregulatory individual labour legislation, privatisation and quasi-markets), employers' attitudes and behaviours and even the stance taken by the union's themselves have resulted in the erosion of 'traditional' British industrial relations, whether of the liberal collectivist or corporatist traditions (Metcalf, 1991). Unions have not only lost power, but, as a result, significant representatives of its leadership are questioning the continued relevance of traditional priorities and institutions, given the changing structure of British industry and an increasingly competitive global economy. Even if 'little has altered' *institutionally* where trade union representation and collective bargaining persists (Millward *et al.*, 1992, p. 350), the fact that this state of affairs represents increasingly diminishing sectors of an economy in which there is a general recognition of declining union power has meant that the institutions are shadows of their former selves and increasingly marginalised (Storey, 1992b, Chapter 9).

Given that structural changes and adverse cyclical factors in the economy are as responsible for the decline in 'traditional' liberal collectivist industrial relations as Conservative governments' policy, it is unlikely that a change of government could restore this form of pre-1979 *status quo*. Since the 1987 election defeat the Labour party has come to appreciate that too close an identity with the unions is harmful to its election prospects – just as unions are recognising that a considerable proportion of their membership – and potential membership – do not vote Labour. The erstwhile symbiotic relationship between party and unions of the 1970s has become more distanced both constitutionally and by mutual consent, and both party and unions accept that many of the legislative changes introduced under Conservative governments are here to stay. Thus any future Labour government would not go back to the pre-1979 legal situation, partly for electoral reasons and partly because of EU requirements. It is likely it would keep much of the present law on the closed shop and balloting, although some of the law on immunities, secondary action and total sequestration would be amended. A Labour government is presently committed to introducing law on minimum wage protection, training rights, equal opportunities and on many of the measures found in the European Social Charter and Chapter (Gospel and Palmer, 1993, pp. 258–9). However, a future Labour government (or Labour/Liberal Democrat coalition) may be more tempted to restore 'a macro corporatism under the new banner of Social Partnership' (Gospel and Palmer, 1993, p. 274), rather than seek to prop up a liberal collectivism whose relevance is increasingly being questioned by 'moderate' union leadership. Some commentators question whether even corporatism is on the cards (Kessler and Bayliss, 1992, p. 242).

So, the issue that now needs to be addressed is the extent to which HRM is compatible with the *eroded* 'traditional' industrial relations system that now exists, and with the 'new realism' and 'new industrial relations' exhibited by some large unions.

HRM and 'new realism' in industrial relations

HRM: a threat to unions?

As Guest (1989b) points out, if HRM rests on individualistic and unitaristic assumptions, there is a *prima facie* case that, in theory at least, it must be incompatible with the collectivist and pluralistic assumptions of traditional British industrial relations. Indeed, in the very attempts – at least of the 'soft' mutuality model of HRM – to develop a collaborative and constructive organisational climate, HRM poses a threat to unions in four ways. First 'soft' model HRM policies, through their emphasis on establishing commitment on the part of the individual employee, tend to by-pass the collective modes of representation and negotiation of unions, via attitudinally oriented selection and socialisation procedures, individualised forms of appraisal and reward, direct employee communication and so forth. Secondly, if, as in 'soft' model HRM, employees *are* treated as the organisation's most valuable assets, the need for a union as a protection against arbitrary and exploitative management action is reduced and the role of existing unions is thereby diminished and unions marginalised. Thirdly, HRM policies may obviate the need for a union at existing non-union plants and on greenfield sites. Fourthly, if HRM policies do generate high levels of organisational commitment on the part of employees, is it feasible for them to maintain commitment to a potentially competing focus of loyalty – that of the union?

Evidence from Storey's (1992b) case studies would support the view that, in unionised establishments (with some notable exceptions such as the 'jointist', 'bargaining for change' approach adopted at Ford) unions *are* being by-passed in the development of HRM initiatives. As Storey points out this is in a context of downplaying traditional industrial relations, if without any well-worked out agenda to displace them. Unions appear marginalised for two reasons. On the one hand employers are taking a generally 'tougher', 'standing no nonsense' approach to unions, although rarely engaging in a frontal assault. This does not encourage a joint development of HRM initiatives. Secondly, because personnel departments are rarely the main drivers of HRM-type change programmes and are often on the sidelines themselves, given that they are cast in the role of chief mediators with the unions, their own lack of involvement (and sometimes hostility to HRM) does not facilitate a more proactive role on the part of the unions. The upshot, in Storey's view, is that typically in his case study companies, traditional personnel departments and unions, in a symbiotic relationship, maintain a shell of traditional industrial relations practices 'in ticking over mode', while greater efforts and enthusiasm, on the part of line managers, are devoted to HRM-type new initiatives (see Storey, 1992b, especially Chapter 9). However, whether in practice it is the *HRM* initiatives that marginalise the unions, rather than managements' 'studied neglect' (Storey, 1992b, p. 260) consequent on a general recognition of unions' loss of power is debatable, given, as Guest (1989b, p. 55) suggests, that 'initiatives which appear impressive when described in the company head office become heavily diluted in practice ... [so that] HRM issues are rarely pursued to the point where the industrial relations system is seriously challenged'.

Evidence that 'good' management, represented by 'soft' model HRM practices, reduces employees' need for union recognition, rests on two sources: much cited exceptional cases, such as Marks & Spencer, and WIRS and Warwick Company Level survey data (Marginson *et al.*, 1988; Millward *et al.*, 1992; Marginson *et al.*, 1993). The latter, however, sends mixed messages. To some extent foreign-owned workplaces seem to fit this pattern, possessing a greater specialist personnel management presence, high non-union employee representation, higher disclosure of information to their employees, a lower incidence of lower paid employees and a more pronounced decline in union recognition than in comparable indigenous companies (Millward *et al.*, 1992). Against this, taking non-unionised industrial and commercial workplaces generally, WIRS 3 found no evidence for the emergence of alternative models of employee representation, but higher labour turnover, a more common incidence of low paid employees, wider differentials between the highest and lowest earners, workforce reductions more likely to be achieved by compulsory redundancy than by less painful methods, dismissals more frequent, and a lack of dissemination of information to employees than in comparable unionised companies (Millward *et al.*, 1992, pp. 363–5). While good management might reduce the role of the union, the lack of a union presence, in spite of managements' claims of good or very good employee relations in the non-union sector, appears associated with at best a more informal and at worst a more arbitrary management style (Millward *et al.*, 1992, p. 363).

Similarly, the second Warwick Company Level 1992 survey found that, in general, non-union companies were no more likely than companies recognising unions at all or some sites to use a range of methods to communicate with employees, to communicate information about business performance to employees, to have profit-sharing and/or employee share ownership schemes or to use (other) forms of performance-related pay. Indeed, companies recognising unions were significantly more likely to use a greater range of methods of employee communication, to provide information about investment plans to employees and to utilise forms of task participation. Where companies had derecognised unions at existing or acquired sites, striking differences in practice were evident between the four-fifths of companies where derecognition was confined to some sites, and the one-fifth where it extended across most or all sites. The use of forms of employee communication, involvement and participation amongst the first group was, if anything, less widespread than amongst companies recognising unions. In the second group (the 'soft' HRM group?), however, intensive use of forms of employee communication and greater use of forms of financial participation were evident, but not of forms of task participation (Marginson *et al.*, 1993, pp. 61–6).

Considering, specifically, greenfield sites, Guest (1989b, p. 48) suggests that employers have four main options in terms of union recognition:

1. Adopt a unitarist individualistic HRM policy and have no union and no collective arrangements.
2. Adopt a unitarist perspective with no independent trade union, but provide a collective voice through some form of company consultative council.
3. Accept a pluralist perspective, but plan it carefully, seeking a single-union agreement, signed on the company's terms and possibly containing pendulum arbitration.
4. Accept the traditional pluralist perspective in the UK and recognise unions who can demonstrate significant membership.

As Guest points out, which option is adopted by employers will be influenced by many factors such as the policy of the country of ownership, 'any established policy in existing plants in the UK, local traditions and union strength, government grants and policies, the advice of professional consultants and the profile of the company and the attendant publicity that this implies' (Guest, 1989b, p. 48). Generally speaking the evidence suggests that unions have found it hard to gain recognition on greenfield sites and in new companies. Kessler and Bayliss (1992, p. 98) from their interviews with senior personnel managers and union leaders, suggest that employers often hold different attitudes to unions in existing plants, from that held towards union recognition in a new or unorganised plant:

> If they can avoid recognition they will, and if they cannot they often have a strong preference for a single union ... They may have a good working relationship with unions where unions are recognised, but nevertheless keep them out or only admit the one they select on greenfield sites. *They want whatever arrangement gives them the greater freedom to take successful initiatives* (added emphasis).

Typically on greenfield sites recognition has been resisted. Where it has occurred – often on Japanese-owned sites such as Nissan at Sunderland or Toyota at Derby, where their high public profile dictated some sort of union presence – it has been on management terms: a single-union agreement, the union being chosen by management; management largely determining procedural arrangements (e.g., non-strike agreement, binding conventional or pendulum arbitration), absence of traditional 'status quo' clauses and agreement on management's freedom in operational matters, including the flexible use of labour (Kessler and Bayliss, 1992, p. 153). Country of origin of plant ownership may influence whether recognition, even on this basis, is granted or not. Traditionally US companies, with a culture of anti-unionism and individualism, pursue a non-union path. Japanese companies, according to one of Kessler and Bayliss's (1992, p. 180) union interviewees, tend to follow whatever is the local attitude – thus they follow US companies in Scotland and are anti-union, but in the North-East and in South Wales they recognise unions because other employers do so. Such unions, however, are generally seen by both management and employees as having a marginal role, on the one hand lacking independence and the 'teeth' to resist management proposals and thus, on the other, seeking to maintain some presence by actively supporting managements' HRM style policies. Not surprisingly, in such plants union density figures are low – the AEU figures at Nissan in Sunderland being variously estimated at around 15 per cent in its initial years (Garrahan and Stewart, 1992, p. 68) and 25 per cent (Guest, 1989b, p. 48) (see also Chapter 10, n. 4).

It is debatable the extent to which non-unionised greenfield sites or new companies pursue 'soft' HRM style policies as a general rule. The WIRS 3 evidence cited earlier would suggest it may be the exception rather than the rule. The second Warwick Company Level 1992 survey found that there were clear differences on new sites between companies which displayed a consistent approach, recognising unions at all or no sites, and those companies which varied in their approach. Only the first group of companies were more likely to use a greater range of means of communication with employees, to utilise forms of financial participation and to use performance-related pay as compared with the general picture amongst unionised companies (Marginson et al., 1993, pp. 65–6). The evidence Guest (1989b, pp. 48–51) cites is fragmentary and, on his own admission, needs treating with caution. Non-unionism does not automatically equate with 'soft' HRM – indeed it can go hand-in-hand with an opportunistic and authoritarian manage-ment style. The case study evidence we have is biased towards the well known but exceptional Japanese-owned plants where there is evidence of HRM policies and practices – and equally, at best, of only a very marginalised role for unions. (For a general discussion of industrial relations in greenfield sites, see Guest and Rosenthal, 1993.)

Finally, turning to the issue of 'dual commitment'. Can employees socialised to give commitment to the organisation also give it to a competing source of loyalty – the union? Guest (1992a, p. 124) argues that, logically, if commitment to company and to trade union are caused by different extremes of the same variables, then dual commitment is not possible. However, if they are caused by the same dimension of particular variables (e.g., high potential for work involvement, older rather than younger workers), then dual commitment *is* possible, as it is if they are caused by different variables. The body of research that Guest summarises appears to conclude that dual commitment is possible, where the industrial relations climate is cooperative and non-adversarial but, nevertheless, the levels of commitment shown to either company *or* union are generally low. Hence the paradox. If the pursuit of HRM polices leads to a cooperative industrial relations climate, dual commitment is feasible but relatively meaningless if such policies marginalise or coopt the trade unions involved. On the other hand, if HRM policies (or the lack of HRM policies) fail to generate employee commitment to the organisation and, hence, provide opportunities for unions to present themselves as an alternative focus for commitment, the evidence suggests in practice this does not occur.

HRM: the union response

Throughout this chapter, the emphasis has been on the implications for unions not only of compositional, sectoral, legislative and economic developments in the 1980s and early 1990s, but of 'soft' model HRM policies. Little attention has been paid to the reactions of unions to 'hard' model HRM although, arguably, such policies have been most prevalent in the public sector where trade unionism has its largest presence. And, indeed, very different union responses may be identified depending on whether the union in question perceives employers' developing 'soft' or 'hard' HRM policies. In the former case some unions, notably craft unions such as the former AEU and EETPU, have collaborated with management particularly on greenfield sites to such an extent that their 'new industrial relations' posture virtually equates with, and is compatible with, 'soft' HRM. On the other hand, public sector unions have shown outright opposition to the 'hard' HRM policies arising from compulsory competitive tendering, various forms of 'opting-out', market testing and so forth.

Lucio and Weston (1992) suggest that TUC policy documents reflect three different union responses to HRM initiatives, that in turn correspond to three different interest groups among their affiliate membership. The first, which reflects the craft-based engineering (AEU) and electricians' (EETPU) unions (now merged to form the AEEU), argues the need for a 'realistic' approach to relations with employers that reflects a 'progressive social partnership'. This 'market unionism' position accepts that traditional adversarial industrial relations has contributed to the failure of the British economy, and that workers' involvement with management in seeking the most efficient forms of production is the way forward, combined with attracting inward investment on greenfield sites. Hence the AEU and EETPU have been to the forefront in striking single-union deals on greenfield sites. Their strategy has been to approach managements rather than employees to gain a presence within new plants. 'Single-union' representation has been agreed with management on the understanding that the union's presence 'would be complementary not contradictory to the development of the new practices' (Lucio and Weston, 1992, p. 80). Second, conflict was to be avoided via no-strike agreements and binding arbitration. Third, unions would support new forms of worker involvement at company level (e.g., advisory and company councils) and in the workplace (e.g., teamworking and quality circles), 'even though this meant that the union would no longer be considered the single channel of workers' interests' (Lucio and Weston, 1992, pp. 80–1). In return unions were to be given commitments *vis à vis* training facilities to be offered to employees and their own greater involvement in management decision-making in such areas as job evaluation and work study. A flavour of the collaborative stance of the AEU and EETPU can be gauged by the following quotation from the General Secretary of the EETPU, Eric Hammond.

> I have no hesitation in advising trade unionists to explore with their management and with their fellow workers how forming such [quality] circles can bring benefit to them as individuals as well as to their organisation. Such involvement would improve personal satisfaction and pride in the job as well as boosting our national performance at the level where a real remedy to our problems lies – in the plant and in the company. (cited in Beaumont, 1992, p. 121)

This trade union stance appears miles away from traditional liberal collectivism and the partnership role envisaged with management is perfectly compatible with 'soft' HRM policies such as those developed on foreign-owned greenfield sites. Indeed, it is the workers organised by the engineers and electricians that arguably have the most to gain from HRM, constituting the 'core' skilled workers of a manual labour force, and the likely beneficiaries of any programmes of genuine multiskilling.

The second response, which Lucio and Weston (1991, p. 81) echoing Beardwell (1991/2, p. 1), term 'making Donovan work' has been identified in the policy pronouncements of the GMB (General Municipal and Boilermakers' Union) and of its General Secretary, John Edmonds. Basically this involves embracing the 'soft' HRM policies that propose the development of individual workers as an organisation's most important asset, but, in contrast to the 'market unionism' of the AEU and EETPU, it attempts to mould such initiatives through collective bargaining and to assert the union's role in policing management practices and dealing with employee grievances, if implementation falls short of rhetoric. At its core is the intention to extend collective bargaining into areas that affect its more broadly-based and diversified membership, namely those of individual rights and benefits such as training, career development and promotion, skill enhancement and so on. In other words the GMB's position, outlined in *New Agenda* (1992) and *Towards Industrial Partnership* (1992) is similar to the Harvard school's 'mutuality', neo-pluralist approach to 'transforming' American industrial relations (Kochan *et* al., 1986). As Lucio and Weston (1992, p. 82) put it, although superficially similar to the AEU and EETPU's form of 'market unionism' in its willingness to seek cooperation rather than confrontation with employers, this stance is pragmatic rather than idealistic, conditional rather than wholehearted. With it goes a recognition that the present institutions of collective bargaining may be inadequate to deal with the wider agenda of 'individualistic' issues and that a 'German' model with statutory rights for individuals and their representation may be the way forward.

A flavour of this approach is caught in some recent statements of John Edmonds, in discussion with John Storey and Nicholas Bacon (Storey et al., 1993, pp. 65–9).

John Edmonds
HRM promises new relationships. It is intended to give people an opportunity, an employer can't just say, 'sorry the market has changed'. Isn't HRM meant to be about *adjusting* to markets? You can't cop out on this. If people mean what they say, then let them deliver on employment security ... If you value people you don't sack them. If you want them to contribute their initiative you don't give them negative vibes that they are disposable. HRM exponents can't have it both ways. Either they mean it all or they don't. If they don't mean it then let them shut up, if they do mean it then they should follow it through.

I'm just talking the language and logic of human resource management and playing it back. It requires a different attitude to management. The good thing about human resource management from our point of view is that it give us a handful of high cards to play. We can say, 'OK, we recall the HR Director's last speech, and we intend to play it back to you with a commentary. That bit means job security, that bit means training'... *Let us use some of the attractive ideas of HRM. But let us also run them fully through and expose any inconsistencies between the underlying principles and actual practice* ... If appraisal is intended to identify problems for the individual and create further opportunities for the individual to develop, for example by designing an individual training plan or an individual career path plan, then that is smashing. In other words, our stance on appraisal is governed by the intent behind it. If, on the other hand, it is intended to be oppressive, or linked to salary in a subjective way without transparent and accepted rules, then it is wrong and we will oppose it. The first set of uses we see as consonant with human resource management. But arbitrariness will destroy a team fast. *Again, for us it's a matter of playing back the fundamental principles* (added emphasis).

Furthermore Edmonds recognises the need for broader institutions of representation and reform of existing collective bargaining institutions.

I don't subscribe to the view that trade unions should be the sole conduit for information to the workforce. I simply don't agree with that. It does not do the steward any good anyway because it can separate the stewards from the members – for example when having to deliver a redundancy message ... In any case a manager would be stupid to rely on the union to transmit his or her messages. But the communications shouldn't operate in such a way that the stewards do not know what's going on. The stewards can also play a constructive role in giving critical feedback. You cannot get proper feedback unless there is a representative structure.

... In workplaces without recognition the collective bargaining package does not get us very far. Hence, in small workplaces without recognition we need alternative services ...

... Traditional collective bargaining will not deliver better training, better promotion opportunities, fully fledged equal rights, or a forum for quality issues and improvements in product and services. Hence we are led on to consider changing the structures for consultation with employers. Either we need to move into the European mainstream or devise something new and better ourselves.

It would appear from these lengthy extracts that the GMB would collaborate with management in developing 'soft' HRM policies, but would keep a wary eye out for 'soft' HRM rhetoric masking 'hard' HRM or opportunistic employee relations management. The problem with this position lies in its ambiguity. Is the GMB's policing and monitoring role compatible with securing management's consent to enlarging the agenda of collective bargaining? Are the roles of collaborator and resistance fighter mutually compatible? How long will genuine cooperation last, if potential confrontation waits in the wings?

The third position Lucio and Weston (1992, pp. 84–6) identify is 'holding on to independence', and is very much associated with the TGWU (Transport and General Workers' Union). Facing massive membership decline and turnover[9] the TGWU's early response was one of outright opposition to HRM associated practices such as quality circles, teamworking, and direct employee involvement. In 1989 the then General Secretary stated that

> a new era of crafty Rambo managers has come into existence which seek to ignore or deliberately disrupt union organisation and collective bargaining procedures, by bringing in their schemes based on fake committees and centred on the individual worker, not the organised worker, with the aim of undermining established working practices and bargaining methods. (TGWU, 1989 cited in Lucio and Weston, 1992, p. 85)

That the TGWU was in the vanguard of opposition to HRM is not surprising, given that its membership of unskilled and semi-skilled workers are more likely to be in the periphery rather than the core of any organisation's internal labour market. The TGWU membership are precisely those employees that are more likely to experience the 'hard' model HRM practices, whether or not dressed up in 'soft' HRM model forms and rhetoric. However, as Lucio and Weston point out, this unequivocal opposition has been undermined by the very vulnerability of the union to recession and sectoral changes. As a result the union has seen 'hard' HRM style changes in working practices being forced through by managements, with or without agreement. Furthermore decentralisation of industrial relations both at bargaining and production levels, combined with the TGWU's traditionally highly decentralised structure, has made it difficult to maintain a coordinated response. Not all local-level TGWU representatives have challenged the introduction of HRM practices; many have pragmatically accepted their introduction as a condition of plant survival. Hence the union's position has changed from outright opposition to 'regulating' best practice and accommodating HRM development on a local *ad hoc* basis, on the understanding that the 'independence' and traditions of the union at the workplace will be respected (TGWU Biannual Conference, 1991). This shifting stance reflects a lack of union power rather than any diminution of ideological opposition to HRM.

Finally, there is the case of the public sector unions. As discussed earlier in this chapter, and in Chapter 7, the public sector and, particularly, public sector services have borne the brunt of ideologically-driven government initiatives, based on the philosophy of the free market: decentralisation, opting-out of schools and hospitals, stringent financial controls, compulsory competitive tendering, marketing testing and a 'private' sector managerial culture of cost effectiveness (in government rhetoric 'value for money'). The associated HRM initiatives from numerical flexibility to performance-related pay have a distinctly 'hard' faced HRM appearance, but, as discussed in Chapter 7, are masked by the 'soft' HRM rhetoric of commitment and responsiveness to consumers of high quality services. And here is the rub. Public sector unionism has fought hard to stave off the massive structural changes consequent on an adherence to 'marketplace' disciplines. Of the thirteen strikes of over half a million working days lost in the 1980s, eleven were in the public sector – local government, civil service, the NHS, railways, education, the Post Office, steel and coal mining[10] (Kessler and Bayliss, 1992, p. 211). As a result 'initially HRM and the new management practices were largely on the fringe of debates' (Lucio and Weston, 1992, p. 86).

However, this changed when unions perceived that the major structural changes were being underpinned by HRM style changes in working practices (flexible working, performance-related pay) combined with challenges to their traditionally centralised collective bargaining, consequent on decentralisation and quasi- (or full) privatisation. Again, the initial stance was opposition, but the unions' hands have been tied on two scores. As indicated in Chapter 7, the strategies of 'hard' HRM have been masked by a rhetoric of the 'soft' HRM values of quality and commitment – for example, flexible working practices have been systematically tied to quality of service debates and the quality of individual performance. This makes it difficult for the public sector unions to challenge 'hard' HRM initiatives without appearing to jeopardise quality of service to the consumer (Lucio and Weston, 1992, p. 86). Second, partly given the influx of private sector personnel into the higher grades of the public sector, opposition to such initiatives as performance-related pay have not been uniform. Hence, according to Lucio and Weston (1992, p. 87) the public sector unions, like the TGWU, have now been forced to abandon headlong opposition to HRM practices in favour of monitoring developments and regulating best practice. Nevertheless, again, an ideological opposition persists on the part of public sector unions, even if with a recognition that many HRM practices have to be accommodated rather than resisted.

Summary

From this analysis it would appear that the greater the extent to which unions adhere to a liberal collectivist view of employee relations the more likely it is that in theory they will regard HRM as a threat undermining the institutions of collective bargaining. If 'soft' HRM undermines via cooptation and marginalisation, 'hard' HRM undermines via marginalisation, non-recognition and, in extreme cases, derecognition. But, even in the cases of those unions (e.g., TGWU, UNISON) which do not embrace the ideology of 'new industrial relations' there perforce has been some reluctant accommodation to HRM practices. As Beaumont (1992, pp. 123–4) suggests the essence of such unions' approach to HRM is 'decentralised policy with national union guidelines'. This rests on the following assumptions:

1. British unions are concerned about HRM developments as potentially undermining union organisation and collective bargaining arrangements;
2. product and labour market circumstances will inevitably lead some employers to favour such initiatives;
3. the case for membership involvement (or not) must be made at the individual organisational level on a situation-by-situation basis;
4. hopefully local-level negotiators will be wary about such involvement through the inclusion of appropriate safeguards and obtaining of certain quid pro quos.

If this is the reactive, foot-dragging accommodation of traditional British industrial relations (and arguably, in particular, of those unions confronting 'hard' model HRM initiatives) that of the unions associated with 'new industrial relations' (AEU and EETPU, now AEEU) appears far more proactive and ready to support managerially – or jointly – sponsored 'soft' HRM practices. In spite of the GMB's commitment to bringing developmental individualistically oriented HRM initiatives within the scope of collective bargaining, its very recognition of the inadequacy of the traditional confrontational structures of collective bargaining for this task, suggests that its stance is not incompatible with 'soft' HRM. Whereas traditional British industrial relations and 'hard' HRM appear ideologically incompatible, with any 'practical' accommodation based on the exercise of managerial prerogative over weakened unions, both ideologically and practically, 'new industrial relations' and 'soft' model HRM appear compatible, even if the weaker partner runs the risk of being absorbed up by the more dominant one, or of a breakdown occurring through disappointed expectations.

Conclusions

Perhaps in deference to postmodernist approaches to organisational analysis, it is fashionable to characterise both traditional industrial relations and human resource management in terms of metaphors.

Thus, traditional industrial relations has been likened to 'trench warfare' (Dunn, 1990) and potentially to a cut-off 'lagoon' (Beardwell, 1991/2). HRM, in contrast, has been variously described as a 'journey' (Dunn, 1990), an expression of the 'American Dream' (Guest, 1990b), and potentially as a 'wolf in sheep's clothing' (Keenoy, 1990a). According to Dunn, the imagery of trench warfare paints a depressing picture of traditional industrial relations – of a static war of attrition, characterised by a *modus vivendi* of 'live and let live', interspersed by frontal assaults that generally inflicted great losses on both sides in return for very little gain, resulting in disillusionment on the part of most participants. Beardwell's image of a 'lagoon' is more ambiguous – although possibly a haven of tranquillity, it also conjures ideas of stagnation, of cut-off irrelevancy and shallowness. On the whole, as Dunn points out, the images of HRM – of a 'journey' and the 'American Dream' convey far more positive messages – of movement, progression, hope of goal achievement, of a common goal, of adventure. Keenoy's image of a 'wolf in sheep's clothing', however, sounds a note of caution – of HRM deliberately cultivating an innocuous image the better to achieve its ruthless intentions.

In many ways, these images reflect the themes of this chapter. Traditional industrial relations, as Keenoy (1991) suggests, rests on the assumption of differential interests between employer and employee, of an endemic socio-economic conflict. This is at odds with 'soft' HRM's assumption of mutuality, of the reciprocal interests of employer and employee, in their survival against the competition. Hence the incompatibility between traditional industrial relations and HRM. In contrast 'new industrial relations' accepts many of the messages embodied in the HRM imagery of the 'journey' and the 'American Dream': of management and employees travelling together to a better world of greater mutual prosperity. Those unions developing a 'new industrial relations' might well join Beardwell in seeing the traditionalists as being 'cut-off' from the 'new realities' of conducting industrial relations in the Darwinian environment of the 1980s and 1990s. Such traditionalists, however, often experiencing the 'harder' face of HRM – as in the public sector services, or among vulnerable, peripheral employees in the private sector – might more readily identify HRM as a 'wolf in sheep's clothing'.

If traditional industrial relations and HRM are incompatible, and if 'new industrial relations' and HRM can live happily together, Dunn's and Beardwell's metaphors point to a third scenario: coexistence. Trench warfare allowed two hostile forces, for much of the time, to live and let live – the trenches ran parallel and the inhabitants often did not meet directly. So, as Storey's (1992b) research work suggests, HRM initiatives often run side by side with conventional industrial relations systems each supported and serviced by different management groups. And, in his imagery of the ecology of the estuary, Beardwell (1991/2, p. 6) makes a similar point:

At times of strong flood the estuary is filled with a tidal stream that reaches both far upstream and high along the restraining banks. Occasionally, the tide breaches these constraints. On the ebb, the flow runs back and leaves whole areas of flats, saltings and marshes. At each point of the tide, while there is a predominant flow, there remain many micro environments which flourish in a habitat which either adapts to or is untouched by the main currents. In this way the non-union firm could flourish at the height of strong unionisation in the 1970s, and the unionised firm continues to be an observable fact in the 1990s.

Beardwell's conclusion can also serve as that to this chapter

The point at issue for traditional industrial relations is whether there has been a major shift in the ecological balance of the estuary, so that, instead of being subjected to tidal flows, it has become cut-off – a lagoon. In these circumstances, over time, wholly different flora and fauna may emerge.

This is the issue considered in Chapter 10.

Notes

1. I am very grateful for the valuable comments of David Guest, Birkbeck College, London and of Alan Whitaker, Behaviour in Organisations, Lancaster University, on a earlier draft of this chapter.
2. Clearly both unitarist and radical perspectives may be viewed as 'traditional' in that both have long histories – as does the liberal individualism of post-1979 Conservative governments. However, in the debate about 'new industrial relations' and 'new realism' the tendency is to treat as 'traditional' industrial relations the institutions associated with voluntaristic collective bargaining (liberal collectivism) in dialogue with basically collaborative and supportive state intervention.
3. Figures for union membership and density tend to be lower if one uses sample survey methods (e.g., WIRS, Labour Force Survey) rather than actual recorded figures, such as appear in the *Employment Gazette*. The problem with the latter is the time lag, of over a year, in their appearance. For a full discussion of the discrepancies between LFS, WIRS and Department of Employment figures, and why they occur, see Kessler and Bayliss, 1992, pp. 137–9.
4. It should be noted that density figures are somewhat lower if density is calculated in terms of working population, *including* the unemployed, rather than in terms of those in employment. Hence the comparable figures for the working population would be 53.4 per cent in 1979 and 41 per cent in 1987.
5. Loss of 'check-off' arrangements is potentially a crippling blow to union membership and finances, given membership lapses when the check-off stops, unless the individual member contacts the union or vice versa. It is argued that due to inertia and the present climate the former is unlikely while, given unions' long dependence on the check-off, any alternative becomes more and more difficult and expensive to organise – a real vicious circle. According to Kessler and Bayliss (1992, p. 258) one of their respondents reckoned that without the check-off the TUC's union membership would be halved. For

an interesting discussion of the role of the 'check-off' in employee relations and union organisation see Kessler and Bayliss (1992, pp. 258–60).

6. Since the abolition of wages councils a survey by the Low Pay Network in 1994 found that one-third of the jobs formerly covered by wages councils were paying less than the rate the councils would have set. Yet, contrary to the Conservative government's rationale in abolition, there is little evidence that this has made employers more willing to recruit. Employment in hotels and catering – a key former wages council sector – has fallen by 27,000 since abolition. The survey concludes that the fall in pay rates may be pushing more people into means-tested social security benefit and increasing the amounts to which those already entitled are reliant. It estimates that a quarter of Family Credit recipients could be former wages council workers. The report concludes:

> This dependence on means-tested benefits is not only unhelpful to families (who can face a marginal tax rate of 97 per cent and thus find it difficult to work their way out of poverty), it also increases the fiscal problems associated with rising benefit requirements and lower yield from employment. (Reported in 'Low-paid worse off after end of council protection', *Independent*, 30 August 1994)

(See also Dickens *et al.*, 1993).

7. After 1986, with falling unemployment more unions went back into (temporary) growth than in the years 1980–6. Nevertheless, although this trend was in the predicted direction, it was insufficient to arrest overall membership decline (Kelly, 1990, p. 39).

8. And, interestingly, some of the labour legislation intended to allow the 'silent majority' of union members to disavow militancy, political affiliation and coercion by an 'out-of-touch' 'militant' leadership, has backfired on its initiators. Thus pre-strike ballots (most of which have gone in favour of the unions) have strengthened negotiators' hands. Balloting for union officers has tended to confirm incumbents in their posts and increased their legitimacy. Ballots on political funds have all gone in favour of unions with such funds and may even have encouraged some unions to institute such funds for the first time (Undy and Martin, 1984; Fosh and Heery, 1990; Gospel and Palmer, 1993, p. 259).

9. According to TUC statistics, the TGWU has experienced one of the largest percentage and absolute reductions in membership of affiliated unions in the 1979–89 period (see Kessler and Bayliss, 1992, Table 8.2).

10. As I wrote the first draft of this chapter (5 November 1993) the civil service was engaged in a one-day protest strike against market testing. As I revise this chapter in August 1994, we are in the grip of the RMT signallers' strike.

9

HRM: modernist project or postmodern discourse?

In concluding this critical analysis of human resource management, it seems appropriate to locate it in a much broader socio–cultural context than that considered in Chapter 3. As a socio–cultural artifact itself, what does HRM reflect or represent? Undeniably, HRM, as represented in the body of literature analysed here, is a product of the 1980s and early 1990s. There are no problems with its periodisation. But how do we typify that period? As one of mature capitalism or 'radical modernity' (Giddens, 1990), or of 'disorganised capitalism' (Offe, 1985; Lash and Urry, 1987) or of that equally fashionable movement of the 1980s, 'postmodernism'? And what are the epistemological implications of the typifications we choose? How will they affect what we judge to be the 'reality' and significance of HRM? Before we can begin to consider such questions we need to gain some understanding of the concepts involved. What do we mean by 'modernity' or 'modernism'[1] and by that trendy buzz word of the chattering classes: 'postmodernism'? Because postmodernism is so frequently defined in opposition to it, let us start by considering what is meant by modernism.

The modernist project

Modernism (and, similarly, postmodernism) refers to both a period of time and an epistemological position, that has generated certain modes of social organisation and cultural expression. We can place it in time as emerging from the 17th century onwards and, arguably, dominating the world until the present day, spawning the institutions of industrialism, capitalism, the nation state and surveillance. As a theory of knowledge, or epistemology, modernism is identified with a positivistic technocratic knowledge base that facilitated the emergence of such institutions. Modernism has been identified with rationality, optimism, authoritarianism and élitism. It has been identified with rationality because it rests on a rationalistic, positivistic, technocratic knowledge base that seeks efficiency through standardisation, order and control. It is often seen as optimistic because this knowledge base has generated a belief in linear progress, in the possibility and desirability of change 'for the better', in the emancipation of humanity from poverty, ignorance and prejudice. Optimism and authoritarianism go hand-in-hand with modernism's propensity for grand 'totalising' meta-narratives or large-scale theoretical interpretations of purportedly universal truth and application. Rationalism, optimism and authoritarianism are expressed in modernism's belief in the rational planning of ideal social orders. Finally, élitism as well as the other values, is reflected in the rational, bureaucratic, hierarchical systems that modernism has identified as instruments and guarantors of order, control and efficiency. And, all four values are recognisable themes in the 'auratic' (Benjamin, 1969) art forms associated with modernist artists, architects and musicians, whose work, developed to unfold an autonomous inner logic of academic aesthetics – 'art for art's sake', and truth to the possibilities of the (aesthetic) materials – is far divorced from popular culture and understanding, reserved for the appreciation of an élite artistic establishment.

To clarify these bald statements, it is helpful to explore in more detail three aspects of modernism: its knowledge base, its reconceptualisation of time and space and its institutions. To illustrate how these aspects of modernism are reflected in an organisational context, that great archetype of modernism – Fordism – will also be considered.

The knowledge base of modernism

The roots of modernism lie in the epistemology of the Enlightenment, that constituted a fundamental break with traditional foundations of knowledge and associated social institutions. In traditional, pre-modern societies, knowledge arose from and was validated by the repeated experience of generations and dogma derived from divine law. Knowledge was characterised by unquestioning belief and re-enactment. In contrast, modern societies are characterised by a critical questioning, derived from the rationalism of the Enlightenment. The philosophers of the 17th century Enlightenment proposed that valid knowledge rested on deductive reasoning or positivism. Knowledge, they argued, can only be derived from constructing general laws or theories which express relationships between directly observable phenomena. Observation and experimentation will then show whether or not the phenomena fit the theory. But the truth of a proposition, strictly speaking is not made more probable by the accumulation of confirming evidence. Rather, scientific advance results from the testing and falsifying of propositions, which are then replaced by new, theory-derived hypotheses, which themselves are subject to test and falsification.

This critical reasoning has given rise to a dynamic tension in modernism. On the one hand, deductive reasoning is seen as the vehicle for accumulating ever greater knowledge of and control over the material world and, through resultant increases in efficiency, achieving continuous material progress. This is 'instrumental rationality', that in a world of uncertainty, constraints and opportunities, facilitates the choice of actions that will yield preferred outcomes, given competing alternatives. The preferred outcome is usually that of 'performativity' or the optimisation of input/output relationships. This aspect of critical reasoning is expressed in the prevailing institutions of modernism, industrialism and capitalism and lies at the heart of what has been termed 'systemic modernism' (Cooper and Burrell, 1988, pp. 95–7).

On the other hand, there is the critical, emancipating aspect of rationality because no knowledge can rest on an unquestioned foundation, even the most well-established theory can only be regarded as valid 'in principle'. Otherwise it would relapse into dogma and become separated from the very sphere of reason which determines what validity is in the first place. Hence, 'all science rests upon shifting sand' (Popper, 1962) or, as Marx put it, 'all that is solid melts into air'. Furthermore, a belief in progress has contributed to this instability, as reflexivity does not stop at the testing of theoretical propositions. Rather social practices and institutions are constantly examined and 'improved' in the light of incoming information about them, thereby constitutively altering their character. Hence not only is there no stable social world to know, but that knowledge of that world contributes to its unstable character (Giddens, 1990). The view of reason and rationality that takes nothing on trust (including the fruits of 'systemic modernism') has been termed 'critical modernism' (Cooper and Burrell, 1988, p. 97). It finds reflection in meta-narratives as varied as Marxism and the Bauhaus movement in design and architecture.

This distinction between 'systemic' and 'critical' modernism is crucial when we come to consider the characteristics of postmodernism. For naive commentators, in identifying the reflexivity of postmodernism, tend to see this as a negation of modernism, full stop, as they equate modernism solely with its systemic and not its critical reflexive form. I will consider later the epistemological differences between 'critical modernism' and postmodernism.

The knowledge base of modernism is reflected in three characteristics that distinguish modern from traditional societies: the rapidity of change; the scope or globalisation of change and the intrinsic nature of modern social institutions, such as the nation state, the dependence of production on inanimate power sources, the commodification of products and wage labour (Giddens, 1990).

The reconceptualisation of time and space

The dynamism of modernity, therefore, partly derives from the reflexivity inherent in its rational knowledge base. But rationality also stimulates changes by its reordering of time, space and their interrelationships (Giddens, 1990; Harvey, 1989).

In traditional societies time was associated with very localised space. 'When' and 'where' were closely connected because it was impossible to tell the time of day or year without reference to other socio–spatial markers e.g., the position of the sun. Given its spatial embedding, time was often perceived as cyclical rather than linear. With the invention and diffusion of the mechanical clock (itself a product of rationality) it was possible to express a uniform dimension of 'empty' time, quantified in such a way as to permit the precise designation of 'zones' of the day (e.g., the 'eight hour day', the 'lunch hour', 'overtime'). Time was still connected with space until the uniformity of time measurement was matched by uniformity in the social organisation of time (e.g., the standardisation of calendars and time zones). These processes brought into being a uniform and linear time across space, facilitating the development of notions of continuity and a sense of future oriented potentiality, rather than cyclicality and regression. The conception of time as homogeneous and universal underpinned the engines of capitalist decision-making – rate of return on capital over time, interest rates, hourly wage etc.

Just as the mechanical clock and calendars allowed for and represented the creation of a uniform and linear conception of time, so maps, based on the principles of perspectivism (which emerged in the mid-15th century), allowed for and represented space as something 'usable, malleable and capable of domination through human action' (Harvey, 1989, p. 254).

In traditional societies space and place (physical settings of social activity as situated geographically) coincided. In relatively isolated 'known' worlds, spatial organisation reflected confused, overlapping patterns of religious, political and legal obligations and rights contained within roughly drawn territorial boundaries. Continuous world-wide space with fixed spatial coordinates was unknown – space outside parochial worlds was conceptualised as a mysterious cosmology, whether populated by heavenly hosts or 'sinister figures of myth and imagination' (Harvey, 1989, p. 241). The 16th century voyages of discovery were a major factor in changing this conception, producing as they did information of a globe that was finite and potentially knowable. Geographical knowledge became a valuable commodity as increasingly money-driven and profit-conscious societies sought to achieve political and economic control over far distant 'new' lands. The development of perspectivism which conceives of the world from the standpoint of the 'seeing eye' of the individual assisted these developments. Perspectivism emphasises the science of optics and the ability of the individual to represent what she or he sees as 'objective' and 'truthful'. In modern societies, at least up to the 20th century, this 'objectivity' and 'truthfulness' became valued as the cornerstone to achieving accurate navigation, determining property rights in land and political boundaries, securing rights of passage and transportation – all of which have economic as well as political importance. 'Scientific' mapping allows space to be represented as stable and uniform. This is a necessary precondition to its representation as amenable to rational ordering. Rational ordering is fundamentally an expression of modernistic control.

Although by their homogenisation, time and space have been separated, principles of rationality and control have provided the bases for their recombination. The development of technologies that replace animate with inanimate power (wind, water, coal/steam-mechanical; oil, electricity/electro–mechanical; oil, electricity, chemical, nuclear/electronic, avionics) and the science of materials have allowed the conquest of time over space. Four examples may illustrate this.

First, technology, the product of the critical reasoning referred to above, through speeding up systems of communication (transport, telecommunications) sometimes appears to have shrunk the world to a 'global village'. Not only can we talk to the other side of the world as though in the same room but, within the constraints of time zones, we can observe its inhabitants 'live'. We consume on a daily basis not only information but consumer durables and non-durables from all over the world, transcending our 'local' seasonality. Time annihilates space.

Secondly, time and movement tend to dominate our thinking about the uses of space. Space has become less a medium for living, than for moving through – as evidenced by such mundane symbols of modernism as the car and street names and house numbers (Lash, 1990).

Thirdly, in industrialised capitalist societies (see below) time also dictates an individual's location in space – as evidenced by conceptions of 'clocking in', the 'working day and week', 'lunch hour', 'free time', 'overtime' and so on. For many commuters this dictation of time over space is represented by the railway timetable, which signals the requirement of being on a specified platform, at a specified time, if one wishes to avoid the risk of missing a train and being 'late' for work.

Finally, time dominates space in the rationalistic Fordist work organisation that is characteristic of industrial capitalism. In developing the assembly line, with fragmented tasks, mechanical handling, uniformity and standardisation of product and process, Ford aimed to maximise efficiency by minimising time-related inputs to the product. 'In effect he used a certain form of spatial organisation to accelerate the turnover time of capital in production. Time could then be accelerated (speed up) by virtue of the control established through organising and fragmenting the spatial order of production' (Harvey, 1989, p. 266). Considerations about time and velocity therefore dictated the rational ordering of space (and people) in his factories.

Reconceptualising time and space, expressed through instruments of rationality (mechanical clocks, 'modern' calendars and maps) stimulates change through providing an environment that is conceptualised as amenable to control and for human 'benefit'. Homogeneous time, allied with technology, allows the conquest and rational ordering of space rendered equally homogeneous by technology. The pace and scope of change, characteristic of modernism, rests on this reconceptualisation. It also lies at the heart of the development of the characteristic institutions of modernity: industrialism, capitalism, the nation state, and systems of surveillance (Giddens, 1990).

The institutions of modernity

Industrialism refers to the application of inanimate sources of power and associated machinery to production. It involves a regularised social organisation of production (resting on the concepts of homogenised time and space referred to above) in order to coordinate human activity, machines and inputs and outputs of raw materials and goods and services (Giddens, 1990, p. 56). This social organisation of production is characterised by a division of labour, within a factory system, urbanisation and the geographical concentration of industry and population and changes in occupational structure. Although industrialism now transcends any single economic system, it emerged within and is particularly associated with capitalism. As an expression of modernism it is imbued with the spirit of scientific rationalism and is the engine of material progress via the technical and social innovation associated with economic growth.

Capitalism is characterised in its 'pure' form by private ownership and control of the means of production, i.e., capital; directing economic activity to making profits; a market framework that regulates this activity; the appropriation of profits by the owners of capital (subject to state taxation); the provision of labour by workers who are free agents (Abercrombie *et al*, 1984, p. 30). While capitalism has assumed various forms in different countries and over time, partly as a result of state intervention and partly due to increasing economic concentration ('monopoly' capitalism) and the rise of institutional ownership ('finance' capitalism), the forms it takes reflect the contradictions inherent in its basic features and attempted modes of resolution.

Contradiction is a Marxist notion, and the following analysis is essentially Marxist (one of the grand 'meta-narratives'). Capitalism, it is argued, has three basic features (see Harvey, 1989, p. 180). First it rests on the assumption of the desirability, not to say inevitability, of growth for its survival as an economic system. This, because growth, in the short term, is the guarantor of profitability and the accumulation of capital, whatever other social, political and ecological consequences are implied in the long term.

Second, growth is achieved by the extraction of the surplus value of labour in production and its realisation in the marketplace; surplus value being that remaining when the worker's costs of subsistence have been extracted from the value of what she or he produces. This does not necessarily mean that the workers inevitably get just the bare minimum for physical survival – for, as discussed in Chapter 1, the worker must also support capital in the realisation of value as purchaser and consumer of its products. This means that capitalism seeks to control both the labour process (that is, the social organisation of production) in the workplace and patterns of consumption and exchange in the market place. Such control is attempted in two ways. On the one hand, there is capital's economic domination in the workplace and labour market. This is not adequate in itself, as it is likely to result in worker resistance and damaging class struggle over labour control and market wages. Hence, on the other, there is attempted ideological domination, whereby through the institutions of civil society (family, schools, churches, the media) the consent of the dominated classes is sought (Gramsci, 1971). Today this is seen most clearly through the use of advertising to promote and direct forms of consumer demand and even personal identity (the prosperous householder consuming all manner of consumer durables and non-durables) that are supportive of economic growth and hence of private industry and commerce. (This was referred to in Chapter 1, in the discussion about 'hegemonic' control and 'manufacturing consent' (Burawoy, 1979, 1985).)

Third, capitalism implies continuous technological and organisational change as 'the coercive laws of competition push individual capitalists into leap-frogging innovations in search of profit' (Harvey, 1989, p. 180). Because the ability to achieve this dynamic would be severely impeded by worker resistance and/or their inability to consume, modes of incorporation and representation become increasingly crucial to the perpetuation of capitalism. This both enables and necessitates that it is presented as being the socio–economic system that represents 'progress'. Again, this is part of the process, referred to in Chapter 1, as 'obscuring the commodity status of labour' (Burawoy, 1979).

Marx argued that these three characteristics of capitalism were inconsistent and contradictory, and would lead to periodic crises of overaccumulation. Over-accumulation, defined as a condition in which idle capital and labour supply could exist without coming together to generate wealth, is indicated when spare productive capacity, excess of inventories, surplus money capital and high unemployment coexist. The recessions of the 1970s and early 1980s, following the oil shocks, would be typical expressions of overaccumulation, likewise the recessions of the early 1990s, following the overheating of world economies in the late 1980s. From a Marxist perspective, overaccumulation represents the seeds of the decay and overthrow of capitalism. From capitalism's point of view, overaccumulation may be contained and managed in ways that maintain a capitalist social order. Capitalism's meta-narrative, in contrast to Marxist predictions, proposes three ameliorative strategies (Harvey, 1989, pp. 181–4).

First, the quickest-acting (but potentially most dangerous to that very social order capitalists seek to preserve) is to manage the supply side of the economy via devaluation. Capital (by inflationary erosion of money, defaults on loans, 'writing off' capital equipment), commodities (by 'sales', built-in obsolescence, EU food mountains) and labour (by labour intensification, lower health and safety standards, unemployment) may all be devalued. Marxists would argue that the most severe form of depreciation (but potentially dysfunctional through disrupting social order) is war between protagonists of competing capitalist systems (e.g., World War I). However, as we have seen in the UK between the late 1970s and early

1990s, controlled devaluation through managed deflationary policies is an important option in managing overaccumulation.

Second, as was seen in the long, steady period of growth, post-World War II, in Western capitalist economies, overaccumulation was contained by a form of macroeconomic control that, in itself, epitomised some of the underlying values of modernism. States committed to a utilitarian conception of progress ('the greatest happiness to the greatest number') adopted Keynesian programmes of demand management to enable a sharing of the benefits while minimising dysfunctional side effects of capitalism's unrestrained pursuit of rationality in Fordist (see below) production systems. Hence Keynesian demand management was instituted to control the pace of technological and organisational change (mainly through corporate monopoly power) to keep class conflict within bounds (collective bargaining and state intervention) and to balance mass production and consumption.

Such macroeconomic control was (and is) supported by a third strategy: the absorption of overaccumulation through what has been termed 'temporal' and 'spatial displacement' (Harvey, 1989, pp. 182–4).

'Temporal displacement' refers to switching resources from present to future use (e.g., long-term public and private investment in physical and social infrastructure) or an acceleration in turnover time (speed with which investment returns profit) so that speed-up this year absorbs excess capacity from last year. Switching resources from present to future use, it is argued, depends on the availability of credit and 'fictitious capital formation' (that is, capital that has a nominal money value on paper, but which at a given moment in time is not backed by any 'real' collateral). But this fictitious capital is converted into real capital if and when its investments provide useful assets or commodities.

Hence this palliative tends to be short-term unless there is continuous displacement via continuously accelerating rates of fictitious capital formation and ever-increasing amounts of long-term investment. Keynesian policies after World War II had this effect by increasing state sponsored indebtedness. Speed-ups too tend to have only short-term effects unless turnover time is continuously accelerated, implying massive write offs of past assets due to necessary investment in newer 'faster' technologies.

Spatial displacement involves the absorption of excess capital and labour through geographical expansion (e.g., overseas investment in 'underdeveloped' countries). This too rests on fictitious capital formation and a credit system backed up by state fiscal, monetary and sometimes, military power (e.g., Hong Kong, South Korea). Again this is a short-term solution, partly because the world is finite, but also because the progressive expansion of capitalism throughout the world increases the area within which the overaccumulation problem may arise. Combining time–space displacements though provides longer-term, more effective respite (note, for example, the enhanced role of credit in capitalist societies, even the re-scheduling of

Third World debts until the 21st century, and international collusion with the US budgetary deficit). However, when and if this fails for the reasons already given, massive devaluation through de-industrialisation is likely to emerge as the residual alternative.

It is out of these crises of capitalism and the strategies of temporal and spatial displacement to absorb overaccumulation that 'radical modernity' or the post-modern period of 'disorganised capitalism' is said to have merged (see below).

The nation state and surveillance. Modernity's reconceptualisation of space and of the nature of authority (from divine to secular), and the rise of industrialism, enabled the development of the nation state. The nation state may be characterised as a secular rational–legal authority holding monopoly (and, hence, centralised) control over the means of violence within specified territorial boundaries (Giddens, 1990, p. 58). The reconceptualisation of space allowed 'frontiers' to be replaced by 'borders' and nation states' mutual recognition of each other's borders sanctions the autonomy claimed by each state to exercise ultimate authority within its own borders. Such authority, expressed in a far more effective concentration of administrative power than in pre-modern communities, is intimately connected with the more intensive surveillance of subject populations by the control of information and social supervision (Foucault, 1977). Such surveillance is an instrument of one of the nation state's central aims: to produce a common culture in which local differences have been homogenised and 'deviance' controlled (Bauman, 1990), or the 'bio-mass' managed in the state's interests (Foucault, 1980).

Together, the institutions of industrialism, capitalism, the nation state and surveillance, in interaction, provide the dynamism of modernity. The interests of the nation state and capitalism often converge. Thus, the nation state, in alliance with capitalism, has assisted in the latter's commodification and cooptation of labour. As the state monopolised the control of the means of violence (whether nuclear bombs or police-controlled water-cannon and tear gas) violence, technically, was moved from the labour contract and, in place of the servitude of the 'whole person' as in pre-modern feudal systems, nominally free 'abstract' labour could be hired as a commodity (expressed in 'hours', 'hands' or 'skills') in the marketplace. State schools (children in neat lines, differentiated by exam performance, responding to bells), the legislative framework, including social welfare provision, Keynesian intervention, assisted in its cooptation. This regulation, as well as the cooptation of labour, was achieved by systems of surveillance (note the myriad uses in the UK of individuals' National Insurance numbers) that until the post-modern period, rested on the concentration of administrative power within national boundaries. This power was both reflected in and supported by the raising of tax revenues that are reliant on the generation of wealth by the capitalistic, industrialised economy. The nation state has further sought to maintain internal integration and maintain territorial boundaries through warfare that itself has become industrialised (note, for example, the relationships between government and defence contractors, the organisation of the Alamo project, NASA, etc.). War between nation states in the 19th and 20th centuries often reflected imperialist ambitions consistent with and supportive of the globalising tendencies of capitalism. Clearly capitalism and industrialism are mutually reinforcing.

Fordism. Fordism illustrates well many of the characteristics of modernism discussed above.

'Fordism', came into being in America in Henry Ford's car assembly plant at Dearborn, Michigan. Commodified, 'abstract' labour, expressed in 'empty' time (the 'eight hour' day) was purchased by that symbol of modernity, money ('five dollar' day). Labour was purchased to perform tasks redolent of an instrumental rationality and the logic of performativity. Tasks were specialised and fragmented and the input of valuable time was optimised, in relation to output, via organisation based on work study and mechanisation. Work in progress, via automation, came to the stationary worker to add value, rather than the worker losing time by seeking out the work. Time organised space. The Tayloristic separation between management, conception, control and execution not only expressed an instrumental rationality but a hierarchical ordering of social relations in the labour process, consistent with élitism and authoritarianism. The mechanisation involved was itself an expression of industrialism as much as the division of labour, factory system and geographical urbanised concentration of car production.

But these aspects of Ford's organisational and technological innovations were already part of well established trends. What distinguishes Fordism from earlier forms of industrialism is the explicit recognition that mass production depends on the mass consumption of standardised products. This is because such production is dependent on heavy investment in fixed capital which requires stable demand conditions to be profitable. This ties in Fordism with the major institutions and underlying themes of modernism.

First, although not confined to capitalist economies (Lenin being a well known advocate of Taylorist and Fordist principles) Fordism provided, for over fifty years, an engine for *growth* in capitalist systems.

Second, the recognition of the requirement for mass consumption went hand-in-hand with an optimistic belief in a 'better' form of industrial society. The five dollar, eight hour day was not only designed to secure labour compliance to new levels of work discipline required by the assembly line, but to provide income and leisure to enable the mass consumption of mass produced goods. This required *surveillance* to ensure that workers knew how to spend their money 'properly'. Hence Ford's early experiment of sending 'social workers' into the homes of his workers 'to ensure that the "new man" of mass production had the right kind of moral probity, family life, and capacity for prudent (i.e., non-alcoholic) and "rational" consumption to live up to corporate needs and expectations' (Harvey, 1989, p. 126).

Fourth, the very symbol of early mass consumption of a standardised product – the Model-T Ford car – was one instrument of modernity's *time-space compression*.

Fifth, the need to maintain mass consumption, in the context of capitalism's recurring problem of overaccumulation and the consequent threat of devaluation, stimulated *nation states* to develop forms of economic intervention (Keynesianism, national socialism) directed at demand management. Keynesianism through *temporal displacement* (public investment of 'fictitious' capital on physical and social infrastructure) was vital to the growth of both mass production and mass consumption, through the guarantee of relatively full employment. Full employment, combined with nation states' provision of a social wage through tax expenditures on social security, health care, education and housing was expressive of a commitment to a planned progressive 'better' society, even if the latter enhanced the scope of *surveillance*.

Sixth, resistance to Fordist production systems in Europe in the inter-war years was largely overcome by the perceived need for a thoroughgoing rationalisation of work processes to improve efficiency in a total war effort. In other words, the *industrialisation of warfare* and diffusion of Fordism went hand-in-hand – even if this form of mass consumption of standardised goods was essentially a form of devaluation.

The postmodernist discourse[2]

Is modernism dead?

Several commentators exhibit a healthy scepticism suggesting that a core value of modernism – bureaucratic rationality with its attendant principles of hierarchy and performativity – are alive and well in our globalised, so-called 'post-modern' world (see, for example, Thompson, 1993). Nevertheless a critique of classical modernism has surfaced concerning its practical consequences and its continued theoretical relevance.

The 'practical consequences' critique is that while acknowledging the positive side of modernism, whether we look to emancipation or instrumental rationality, we should be aware of its negative consequences. The Holocaust can be seen as just as much an expression of modernism as rising material living standards in the First World (Bauman, 1991).[3] The contradictions of capitalism (not to mention the collapse of that other great meta-narrative, Communism) raises doubts about the continuity of economic growth, not to mention the political instabilities of the world divided into the rich 'haves' (First World) and poor 'have nots' (Third World). Even if growth is sustained there is the danger that its pursuit will lead to ecological disasters (Perrow, 1984). Technocratic rationality and the industrialisation of warfare carries at best the threat of large-scale destruction and, at worst, nuclear conflict triggering ecological disasters. Increasing surveillance can facilitate the sectional control of political power and the rise of totalitarianism (Giddens, 1990, pp. 171–3).

Such negative consequences appear inherent in modernism's commitment to an instrumental rationality that backgrounds alternative value-laden criteria for action. 'Irrational' ethical concerns sit uneasily with the promotion of the instrumental rationality that energises growth, scientific advance and so on. The optimistic modernist retort would be that the application of scientific progress combined with a search for some agreement as to substantive rationality (what ends should be sought) on a global basis, can provide a means of avoiding the negative consequences of modernism. Indeed, the very reflexivity of modernism, in its critical emancipatory mode, it is argued, is capable of generating alternative utopian models of a 'radical modernity' that suggest the possibility of a new world order comprising a post-scarcity economic system, demilitarisation, multilayered democratic participation and humanisation of technology (see Giddens, 1990, pp. 163–73).

The continued theoretical relevance of modernism has been called into question by commentators who identify the erosion of the institutions of modernism and a questioning of its rationalistic base. Some commentators would argue that we now live in a period of time in which changes in social institutions signal an epoch after and an abandonment of modernism (Lash and Urry, 1987). For example, it has been argued that the First World is moving into a post-industrial society (Bell, 1974), in which capitalism is increasingly 'disorganised' (Offe, 1985) and the nation state is 'too small for the big problems of life, and too big for the small problems of life' (Bell, 1987). Further, underlying this, is a questioning of the epistemology of modernism – of deductive reasoning, of the existence of transcendal truths and of the validity of meta-narratives – such that a rupture with and negation of modernism has occurred (Hassard, 1993). The rise of relativism, it is argued, is expressed in a move from meta-theory, narrative and depth, to language games, image and surface, away from production, originality and authority towards reproduction, pastiche and eclecticism, away from purpose and design, toward play and chance (Harvey, 1989, pp. 340–1). Indeed one commentator has likened postmodernism to 'the twilight of the real' (Wakefield, 1990).

Hence, as already suggested, postmodernism, like modernism, refers to both a period of time and an epistemological position. Differentiating between the two, Parker (1992) refers to the former as post-(hyphen) modernism and to the latter as postmodernism (one word). Post-modernism suggests that we are living in a period that follows on from and is different to that of the modern world of organised capitalism, industrialism and the dominance of nation states and their systems of surveillance. Confusingly, depending on the degree of discontinuity identified in the emergence of new or evolving social institutions, the 'post-modern' period has also been labelled as one of late or 'radical' modernity (Giddens, 1990; Callinicos, 1989). For proponents of modernism assert not only the continuities of institutions (e.g., of time–space compression, new forms of capitalism reflected in globalisation) but argue that such changes that are occurring are a product of the very reflexivity that is a hallmark of the critical reasoning that is the knowledge base of modernism. Either way, what are the characteristics of this 'post-modern' ('radical modernity') world and of post-modern institutions?

Postmodernism, on the other hand, asks how can we use a postmodern epistemology or theory of knowledge to analyse organisations and management – including HRM – in a different way (Parker, 1992, p. 2). To use Cooper and Burrell's (1988, p. 106) much cited phrase, this might involve a focus on the 'production of organisation, rather than the organisation of production'.

Let us look in a bit more detail at these two different perspectives on post-modernism/postmodernism.

The post-modern period and organisation

The reconceptualisation of time and space and, in particular, the conquest of space by time, reflects and enables a major characteristic of post-modernism/'radical modernity': the globalisation of its institutions.

Globalisation has been defined as 'the intensification of world wide social relations which link distant localities in such a way that local happenings are shaped by events occurring many miles away and vice versa' (Giddens, 1990, p. 64). Thus a local labour market in the north-east of England (Sunderland) can be affected by decisions made in Tokyo by Nissan; villages in the Third World may be affected by changes in world money and commodity markets; a localised happening, for example, the death of a tycoon or the actions of a trader in the money markets, may trigger company collapses throughout the world (Robert Maxwell, Nick Leeson).

Globalisation of the institutions of modernism rests on the annihilation of space by time. All globalisation depends on rapid and simultaneous access to pooled information on the part of individuals spatially widely separated from one another (Giddens, 1990, p. 78). This is seen clearly in the ways in which capitalism seeks to reconcile the imperative of growth with its consequence of potential over-accumulation. As already discussed, time and space displacement are a major mechanism and central to capitalism's globalisation. The resultant transnational corporations that span the world and have budgets bigger than all but the largest nation states are fuelled by pooled information systems. Indeed a modern definition of organisation is 'an information processing system' (Galbraith, 1973).

Industrialism's globalisation can be seen in the expansion of the global division of labour, not at the organisational level of job tasks, but in regional specialisations in terms of industry, skills and production of raw materials (Giddens, 1990, p. 76). The extraction and realisation of surplus value by globalised capitalism stimulates the development of a world economic order, countries specialising as providers of cheap labour and commodities (Third World) or skills that enable the production of high value added goods (First World). Sophisticated differentiation occurs within these broad categories: note the alarm in erstwhile First World countries at the rise of a super-league of industrial powers (e.g., Germany and Japan) and their relegation to the ranks of a 'screwdriver' economy. Shifting interactive patterns of industrialisation and de-industrialisation can now only be understood within the framework of a global economy. Not surprising then is the declining use and impact of Keynesian economic policies at the level of the national economy.

The dominant culture of systemic modernism has been a materialistic utilitarianism. Hence economic prosperity has been at the forefront of the political agendas of the most powerful nation states in modern times. So, partly in response to the globalisation of the economic order, nation states have joined in compensatory global/supra-nation alliances (OECD, EU) to increase their influence collectively over the world economic order and, by politico–military alliances (UN, NATO), over the world state system. The treaty concerning monetary union and social legislation between the twelve nation states of the European Union, signed at Maastricht in December 1991 is a case of the former, as is the proposed expansion of EU membership to erstwhile Eastern European states. The UN sanctioned economic and military action in the Gulf in 1990–1 is an example of the latter. Problems of ecology (Chernobyl, destruction of the rain forests), scarcity of resources (oil) and the securing of global political stability, in order that economic and social 'progress' may not be jeopardised, all encourage concerted action, on a global basis, between nation states.

The perceived need for such action is reinforced by the industrialisation and globalisation of warfare. As the conflicts of the 20th century have shown, local conflicts have escalated into global wars. In the present day, the need for containment of local disputes (e.g., in Bosnia) is made ever more pressing by all countries' access (including the economically backward) to technologically advanced weaponry and by the threat of nuclear proliferation (particularly with the collapse of the Soviet Union).

The potential of enhanced surveillance in a 'global village' should be recognised. It is not only the nation state that now exercises such powers, but globalised political and economic institutions seek them to manage global problems (e.g., population movement, by immigration/refugees, from economically backward to advanced parts of the world; drug trafficking).

It is against this background of globalisation and deregulation, at the level of the nation state, that the emergence of 'disorganised capitalism' may be seen (Offe, 1985; Lash and Urry, 1987). Lash and Urry consider that the changes outlined above have resulted in various socio–politico–cultural effects. In the First World, with the shift away from labour intensive manufacturing to the service sector, there has been a decline in the traditional working class of male manufacturing workers and in traditional class consciousness and loyalties, a decline in the nation state and the 'death' of inner cities. Compensationally, there has been the rise of a distinctive service class of knowledge workers in media-based industries and the growth of smaller plants, a more flexible labour process, increased feminisation of the workforce, and the requirement for a more 'mentally' skilled workforce. All such developments are seen as underpinned by increasingly sophisticated information technologies that have accelerated the modernist trend of time–space compression. The result has been, in the First World, of increased differentiation in consumption patterns along with an increased de-differentiation in production. It is against this representation of a post-modern world that regulationist and flexible specialisation theorists (e.g., Aglietta, Kern and Schumann, Piore and Sabel) argue the case for the emergence of new regimes of production and accumulation (see Chapter 5).

Clegg (1990, p. 181) succinctly summarises what, in organisational terms, such post-modern regimes might look like, in comparison with their modern predecessors:

> Where the modernist organization was rigid, postmodern organization is flexible. Where modernist consumption was premised on mass forms postmodernist consumption is premised on niches. Where modernist organization was premised on technological determinism, postmodernist organization is premised on technological choices made possible through 'de-dedicated' micro-electronic equipment. Where modernist organization and jobs were highly differentiated, demarcated and de-skilled, postmodernist organization and jobs are highly de-differentiated, de-demarcated and multiskilled. Employment relations as a fundamental relation of organization upon which has been constructed a whole discourse of the determinism of size as a contingency variable increasingly give way to more complex and fragmentary relational forms, such as subcontracting and networking.

Clegg further suggests, on the basis of empirical analysis, that these post-modern organisational characteristics have emerged (to meet seven organisational imperatives)[4] in Japan, South Asia, Sweden and Italy. In particular, he considers Japanese organisation, the icon of 'soft' model HRM theorists, to epitomise this model of post-modern organisation. It should be noted though that from a *postmodern* standpoint, this *post-modern* perspective still sees the world in terms of a modernist, realist and positivistic epistemology. In other words, the post-modern world is seen as the most recent development of the inherent logic of modernist socio–economic arrangements, not as an alternative to it.

Postmodernism and organisation

Postmodernism as a theoretical perspective rejects both the modernist realist ontology and positivistic epistemology. In other words it rejects modernism's belief in the existence of fundamental truths, in the power of reason and observation, in meta-narratives about progress and universal design and its absorption in the machine metaphor (Gergen, 1992, p. 211). It rejects a 'distal' way of thinking that privileges results and outcomes, the bounded 'finished' and 'ready-made', in favour of a 'proximal' mode that deals in the continuous unbounded and 'unfinished' processes that emphasise the partiality and precariousness of action (Cooper and Law, 1995).

To explore what this means, we need to step aside for a moment from the gurus of excellence that up to now have informed HRM and look briefly at the work of four French philosophers and the implications of their ideas for the way we look at the world generally and organisations in particular. The philosophers are Derrida, Baudrillard, Lyotard and Foucault.

According to postmodernist philosophers, modernism's belief in fundamental truths 'out there' that may be discovered by deductive reasoning and experimentation and then presented in a language subservient to this reality ('logocentrism') is fundamentally flawed due to the 'undecidability' or uncontrollability of meaning (see Derrida, 1973, 1976, 1978, 1981, 1982 and Cooper's, 1989, analysis of his ideas). 'Logocentrism' pivots social action upon the idea of an original 'logos' or prefixed metaphysical structure (e.g., an internal reasoning agent with mind, soul, reason) which validates and gives meaning to social action. But, given its fixed point of origin, logocentrism 'censors the self-errant tendencies of the text' (Cooper, 1989, p. 482) privileging unity and identity over separation and difference. In contrast, for Derrida, language and text are not so much a means of communicating pre-existing 'facts' or thoughts, but a set of sounds and marks upon which meaning is imposed. That meaning is ultimately 'undecidable', is because not only are texts structured around binary oppositions ('good'/'bad', 'formal'/'informal') in which one term dominates the other ('male'/'female') but the relationship between opposing terms is one of mutual definition ('black'/'white'). To use Cooper's (1989, p. 483) expression, they 'inhabit' each other. Hence individual terms 'give way to a process where opposites merge in a constant undecidable exchange of attributes' (Norris, 1987, p. 35, cited in Cooper, 1989, p. 483). Derrida shows, for example, how the ancient Greek term *pharmakon* is intrinsically undecidable since it could mean both remedy and poison and good and bad simultaneously (Cooper, 1989, p. 486).

Meaning is made further undecidable by the deconstructive reading of the text. Modernism would assert just one reading of a text – that intended by the author, the subject of the writing. In contrast a Derridean position would 'de-centre' the subject and assert the primacy of the reader(s). What each reader understands the text to be is equally valid. Further, in reading a text, a reader might choose to deconstruct or overturn the hierarchies within it ('her'/'his'). But the reflexive logic of deconstruction does not allow this reversal to result in a new and permanent, if opposite, hierarchy. This would be merely another instance of prioritising structure over process, in which opposing terms are kept separate and discrete rather than inhabiting each other. The process of deconstruction must be continuous – a process Derrida terms 'metaphorisation'. As Hassard (1993, p. 11) puts it 'the superordinate term [is] defined only in contrast to the subordinate term, which itself serves to threaten constantly the former's hegemony ... seemingly unique terms submit to a process which sees them combine in a continual exchange of "undecidable" characteristics'.

Derrida's (1973) concept of *differance* gives further insight into the idea of a text's 'undecidability'. Derrida proposes that the meaning of any word or phrase is derived from a process of *deferral* to other words or phrases that *differ* from itself (i.e., *differance* embodies the idea to *defer* or postpone, in time, and to *differ* in space). Hence *differance* should be understood as a continuous absence of a deferred meaning as well as the difference of opposed meanings. Cooper (1989, p. 489) illustrates this, taking again Derrida's example of the *pharmakon*:

> In terms of difference, the *pharmakon* does not simply include the two opposing meanings of 'poison' and 'remedy'; these are not just structurally different *from* each other, instead they actively *defer* each other, the deferred term being postponed for the present, waiting for an opportunity to flow back to the medium from which it was severed.

The nature of *differance* as undecidable movement which cannot be pinned down, is well caught by Gergen's (1992, p. 219) analysis of the words 'let's be logical about this; the bottom line would be the closing of the Portsmouth division'. He shows that the meaning of such words is not transparent, but rests on the meanings we attribute to words like 'logical', 'bottom line' and so forth. But this in turn requires that we *defer* to other words. To answer what 'logical' means, for example, we have to consider other terms like 'rational', 'systematic', 'coherent'. But we could have chosen other terms and, even for the terms we have chosen, there are multiple meanings, bearing the 'trace' (to use Derrida's term) of many other words and contexts, ' in an ever-expanding network of significations'. 'What seemed on the surface to be a simple straightforward piece of wise advise, on closer inspection can mean virtually anything' (Gergen, 1992, p. 219). Hence the essence of undecidability is the existence of contradictory, if postponed, or marginalised meanings within a single term, meanings that can be surfaced and prioritised at the reader's volition.[5]

Derrida's ideas then call attention to both instabilities in our understanding of the world but also the possibility of reading it in any way we like. These themes resonate with the ideas of three other postmodernist French philosophers: Baudrillard, Lyotard and Foucault.

Baudrillard (1981, 1983) argued that Marx's analysis of capitalism as concerned with commodity production is outdated, as capitalism is now concerned predominantly with the production of signs, images and symbols rather than the commodities themselves. In post-modern societies 'simulcra' – or replications so perfect that it becomes virtually impossible to recognise the difference between the original and a copy – have encouraged the confusion between representations and the 'real'. Indeed, given modern media-based techniques, representations may appear more real, or 'hyper-real', compared to the 'real thing'. In this post-modern world, according to Baudrillard, our shifting identities are defined by our patterns of consumption, rather than by our roles as producers, but it is images that we primarily consume rather than purely the use value of goods and services. While modern society was characterised by an explosion in forms of social differentiation, Baudrillard argues that post-modern society experiences implosion, or de-differentiation (Kellner, 1988). Hence, our tastes, erasing distinctions between high and popular culture (e.g., Pavarotti mingling opera with the football of the World Cup) are eclectic, playful and transient, focusing on style, rather than substance and immediate gratification rather than long-term aspiration. Time–space compression disrupts any sense of linear continuity or spatial boundaries (e.g., use of video, global village – itself a Derridean contradiction!). Hence history becomes a repository of images to be mined by politicians, the leisure industry and advertisers, which are more readily consumed when presented through shock tactics, such as pastiche or collage forms, or as a spectacle (e.g., Spielberg films, Disneyland). Truth and fiction, fact and artifact are confounded, as the 'real' world looks a pale copy of a media created 'hyper-real' world (e.g., UK royal family as soap stars, virtual reality). Not surprisingly, then, Harvey (1989, p. 291) can write of Baudrillard's vision of a 'hypereal' world, that

> This, of course, is the kind of environment in which deconstructionism can flourish. If it is impossible to say anything of solidity and permanence in the midst of this ephemeral and fragmented world, then why not join in the [language] game?

The relativism of this perspective also emerges in the writings of Lyotard (1984). Lyotard too conjures with ideas about indeterminacy and language games. Lyotard argues that modernity is primarily a form of knowledge rather than, as in Baudrillard's view, a condition of society. Modernist knowledge, as already discussed, used deductive reasoning to establish truths on which could be built grand totalising narratives, whether in the spirit of systemic modernism (wealth creation, performativity) or of critical modernism (Habermas's view of the emancipation of the subject and the 'language of the community') (Habermas, 1972, 1974; Burrell, 1994). Lyotard argues that, in contrast, postmodern knowledge is based on indeterminacy, as quantum theory and microphysics 'reveal the world as a network of self-referential structures ... far from uncertainty decreasing with more precise knowledge ... the reverse is the case: uncertainty increases with precision' (Cooper and Burrell, 1988, p. 98). Hence postmodern discourse is the 'search for instabilities' (Lyotard, 1984, p. 53), and involves the rejection of grand totalising narratives.

From this position, Lyotard argues that knowledge is based on nothing more than a number of distinct discourses each with its own rules and structures, and defined by its own particular knowledge criteria. No one discourse is privileged. Rather, in a postmodern society, actors struggle with an infinite number of language games within a society characterised by diversity and conflict. It is the contest between competing discourses that gives vitality to social life, 'through maintaining a state of continuous difference and provocation' (Cooper and Burrell, 1988, p. 99). It is on these ideas that Lyotard builds a paradigm for the practice of theory. In 'doing science' he argues, we only enter a number of language games with our colleagues, in which, in a form of 'serious play', we seek to advance our own position and block – or seek alliances with – other players. In this representation of 'science in action', Lyotard's work is complementary with that of actor network theorists (such as Callon, 1986; Latour, 1987) who both embrace Derridean 'undecidability' and *differance* in their adherence to relativism and contradiction[6] and a prioritising of the proximal over the distal in their discourse on organisation (see Cooper and Law, 1995).

Finally, there is the contribution of Foucault (1972, 1973, 1977, 1980, 1981, 1985 and 1986) (see also Dreyfus and Rabinow, 1982; Burrell, 1988; Eribon, 1992; Townley, 1993, 1994). While recognising that the shifts in his work between his archaeological and genealogical periods may themselves be analysed in terms of Derridean *differance* and contradiction (Burrell, 1988), Foucault's central concern is to make strange or problematic the familiar, refusing to begin his analyses with supposedly self-evident concepts, such as 'individual' or 'organisation'. A proper understanding of a solution can only be achieved by seeing how language, expressive of power/knowledge, structured a problem in the first place. As with Derrida, then, language is not a means of communicating pre-existing facts but a vehicle for construction and deconstruction, of making the familiar extraordinary. In problematising the familiar, Foucault engages with three concepts, in particular: power, knowledge and subjectivity (Townley, 1993, 1994).

For Foucault power does not reside in persons or institutions, provoking such questions as 'who has power?' or 'where, or in what, does power reside?' Rather it may be identified in a network of relationships that are systematically interconnected. Power, then, is relational and becomes apparent when exercised through the practices, techniques and procedures that give it effect. Hence, the question Foucault asks is 'how is the power exercised and identified?' This view of power underlies his conceptualisation of the power/knowledge relationship, which in turn owes much to his notion of 'governmentality'. 'Governmentality' is a neologism derived from a combination of government and rationality. It rests on the ideas that, first, government refers not just to institutions but the activity aimed at shaping or influencing the conduct of people and, second, that something must be known before it can be governed. As Townley (1993, p. 520) puts it:

> Programs of government, for example, require vocabularies, ways of representing that which is to be governed, ways of ordering population (i.e., mechanisms for the supervision and administration of individuals and groups). Rationality is dependent upon specific knowledges and techniques of rendering something knowable and, as a result, governable. Governmentality, therefore, is a reference to those processes through which objects are rendered amenable to intervention and regulation by being formulated in a particular conceptual way.

Knowledge and power, then, to use Cooper's expression 'inhabit' each other:

> The exercise of power itself creates and causes to emerge new objects of knowledge and accumulates new bodies of information ... the exercise of power perpetually creates knowledge and, conversely, knowledge constantly induces effects of power ... It is not possible for power to be exercised without knowledge, it is impossible for knowledge not to engender power. (Foucault, 1980, p. 52)

This 'inhabiting' is revealed most clearly in Foucault's double-faceted use of the word 'discipline' – as both a body of knowledge and as a system of control and correction. The 'inhabiting' or intertwining of knowledge-power again asserts the postmodern position that procedures for the formation and accumulation of knowledge are not neutral instruments for the presentation of the 'real', but creators of a reality. Hence, power-knowledge is not negative, but creative: 'in fact, power produces; it produces reality, it produces domains of objects and rituals of truth' (Foucault, 1977, p. 194). The relational nature of power means too that it should not be seen just as creating and disciplining oganisational subordinates – superordinates are as much disciplined and created as their subordinates in that everyone is enmeshed in many disciplinary practices.[7] As Burrell (1988, pp. 232–3) puts it, 'as individuals, we are incarcerated within an organisational world [and] the reality of organisations is that they reflect and reproduce a disciplinary society'.

Finally, there is Foucault's use of the concept of subjectivity, of the individual. Foucault regarded the human subject not as 'given', but as a product of power/ knowledge disciplinary practices. (For example, once the human body was conceptualised as a machine in the 18th century, it became a target for manipulation and training (Burrell, 1988).) When human beings lose their privileged epistemological position, become 'decentred', 'no longer self-directing but ... instead a convenient location for the throughput of discourses' (Hassard, 1993, p. 15), the focus of analysis becomes the 'knowability' of the individual, the process by which the individual is constructed or produced (Townley, 1993, p. 522). How the individual becomes known or named is through the processes involved in the construction of knowledge – processes of classification, codification, categorisation, precise measurement and so forth. The individual becomes an object of knowledge, a product of discourse (see Foucault's discussions on the criminal, madman, sexual identity) (Townley, 1993, pp. 522–3).

To summarise this, postmodernism, as a theory of knowledge, in its simplest terms, boils down to the following. The 'real' is not 'out there' to be discovered, but is created through discourses emergent from power/ knowledge relations, 'collectively sustained and continually renegotiated in the process of making sense' (Parker, 1992, p. 3). Language is not a neutral vehicle for communicating independent 'facts', but itself constitutes or produces the 'real'. The real is not absolute and singular but relative and multiple. Symbol and image, representations can be 'hypereal' or more 'real' than so called 'reality'. In looking at the world we must be reflexive – continually critical of our own assumptions, to the extent of endlessly deconstructing the structures we have created, but in the belief that anything goes rather than that, through a critical reflexivity, we may find an ultimate truth (the position of critical modernity).[8] This relativistic – some would say, ultimately, solipsistic world view – is not to everyone's taste, and the criticisms centre on its neglect of the objective, materialistic basis of 'real' power relations in society and of the role of social institutions in patterning behaviour and privileging some discourses above others. For unrepentant modernists the 'anything goes' position of the fully fledged postmodernist is not only factually wrong but an abrogation of responsibility (Callinicos, 1989; Thompson, 1993; Tsoukas, 1992). Postmodernism then embraces contradiction and paradox and approaches enquiry in the spirit of ironic self-reflection or 'playful seriousness'. As Gergen (1992, p. 216) has it, this offers a new role to organisation theorists:

> Rather than founders of the 'last word' (where in the beginning was the word of God), we should perhaps view ourselves as balloon craftsmen – setting aloft vehicles for public amusement.

It is in this spirit, as a tentative postmodernist, that I now come to the point of this chapter: is HRM a modernist project or postmodernist discourse?

Deconstructing HRM?

The question mark signifies a problem with this proposal. As several writers before me have suggested, given that academic writing and, indeed, universities are conventionally rationalistic endeavours, based on a positivistic epistemology, the danger is ever present that the writer inadvertently finds herself discussing postmodern ideas using the structure and language of modernism (Burrell, 1993; Parker, 1992). Sentences are logically constructed, a 'rational' argument (note that word!) is presented, chapters follow in coherent order. As Burrell points out, when academics write books they are often not entirely indifferent to questions of performativity and hierarchy: 'let's hope this book sells well and is well reviewed, in order that I might ascend the rungs of academic hierarchy and bask in the bottom-line of enhanced peer-group prestige'. And, as Foucault suggests, the disciplinary practices in which we are enmeshed in our organisational world offer little prospect of escape: publishers, rhetoric apart, want standardised (but entertaining), newly packaged, blockbusters that sell well. Perhaps their realisation of the importance of packaging, however, betrays sympathy with Baudrillard's position!

This raises a serious problem with this book, however. Isn't the development of a rational argument, as has been undertaken in preceding chapters, a negation of postmodern epistemology? Even if I knew how to develop a discourse consistent with postmodern epistemology (and, Derrida, notably, has tried to do so) would this not be pointless, given the traditional argument against relativistic scepticism: how can a discussion negating the concept of truth itself be true? (Gergen, 1992, p. 215). Note, in my very citation of sources I yet again reproduce the practices of positivism and further undermine my position as a potential postmodernist commentator. But enough of this navel-gazing. I shall follow Gergen's advice about engaging in serious play and enjoy the contradictions in which I have entangled myself, hoping to provide some public entertainment (after all, analytical insight is a bit of a modernist notion!).

HRM as a modernist project

HRM and positivism

Certainly, with a few exceptions (Keenoy, Anthony), most commentators on HRM have researched and written on it from the unquestionably modernist perspective of positivism. Positivism, with its realist ontology, seeks to explain and predict what happens in the social world by searching for regularities and causal relationships between its constituent elements. As discussed earlier in the chapter, its epistemology is hypothetico–deductive. To a greater or lesser extent this is the logic that reigns in much of the research on HRM, even when it is case study-based and fails to adhere to the strict canon of positivism, methodologically speaking (see, for example, Storey, 1992b; Pettigrew and Whipp, 1991). The research aims at discovering what is really going on 'out there': is HRM as a strategic and coherent model being implemented? what is the popularity and prevalence of different HRM practices? what 'factors' can account for the outcomes observed?

Three examples of positivism in action are the well known models of Beer *et al.* (1985), Devanna, Fombrun and Tichy (1984) and Guest (1987). The Beer *et al.* (1985, p. 16) model is described by the authors as a 'broad causal mapping of the determinants and consequences of HRM policies' (see Figure 9.1). Devanna *et al.* (1984) suggest four 'generic functions' of HRM, selection, appraisal, reward and development that act as independent variables, in a cycle of human resource interventions on the dependent variable of performance (see Figure 9.2). Guest (1987), in discussing the development of his own model makes quite explicit its underlying positivistic assumptions. He speaks in terms of theory development (mainly motivation theories) from which can be derived the 'main dimensions' of HRM, which in turn can provide 'the basis for formulating measurable criteria against which to assess whether or not an organisation is practising human resource management' (p. 598). His 'policy framework' identifies HRM policies, HRM outcomes and organisational outcomes, with an implicit assumption of a potential causal relationship. The modernist enlightenment spirit of research and factual knowledge being the instrument to achieve progress is evident in Guest's (1987,

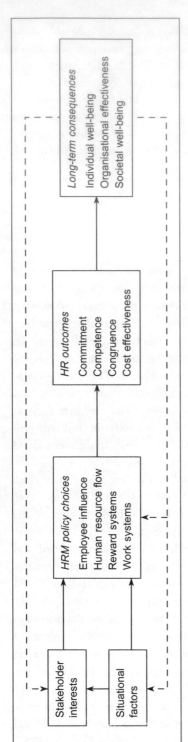

Source: Beer *et al.* (1985).

Figure 9.1 Beer *et al.*'s model of determinants and consequences of HRM policies

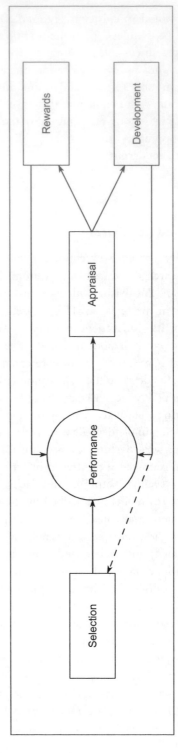

Source: Devanna *et al.* (1984).

Figure 9.2 Devanna *et al.*'s model of the four generic functions of HRM and their causal interactions

p. 510) aim 'to develop a set of testable propositions and finally to arrive at a set of prescriptive policies'. This he achieves in subsequent work in which four models of the causes of effective human resource management, labelled organisational integration, policy integration, functional integration and process integration 'were operationalised and tested in a regression analysis against a range of qualitative and quantitative measures of HRM effectiveness ... the theoretical and policy implications of these results are discussed' (Guest and Peccei, 1994, p. 219).

HRM: Unity, rationality and performativity

The content of HRM normative models similarly expresses the epistemology of modernism reflecting the themes of unity, rationality and performativity. The unitaristic values of HRM, discussed in Chapters 3 and 8, suggest the existence or desirability of a systemic coherence in organisations that either occurs naturally or can be manufactured through cultural management – a highly modernistic and optimistic way of viewing the world. Further, as discussed in Chapter 4, the notion of external integration between business strategy and HRM, rests squarely on rationalistic models of business strategy formation. Similarly, the idea of internal integration – that HRM policies should be mutually consistent and supportive of business strategy – asserts values of coherence and logical ordering, the cornerstones of rationality. HRM's engagement with the concept of flexibility (see Chapter 5) betrays a commitment to the modernist principle of design for betterment and to contingency principles (match organisation structure to environmental contingencies) that are both positivistic and rationalistic. Performativity pervades the positivistic models of HRM – whether in their rationale (to achieve competitive advantage in increasingly uncertain, competitive and global markets) or in their evaluation (contribution to effectiveness, translated into measures of 'bottom line' performance) (see, for example, the 'excellence' writers as well as the 'bottom line' assumptions embodied in contingency theories). As discussed in Chapter 7 'soft' *and* 'hard' models of HRM's prioritisation of quality can be seen in terms of performativity. In the 'soft' model, increasing value added is a strategy to achieve competitive advantage and long-term 'bottom line' success. In the 'hard' model, quality equates with 'value for money' and cost effectiveness – measures that scream of performativity.

What, though, of the argument of the excellence school of writers (Peters and Waterman, Kanter, etc.) that HRM should reclaim the soft 's' and focus on the informal aspects of organising – values, management through people, transmitting a vision and so on? Indeed some commentators (Peters and Waterman, 1982) have suggested that concentrating on the informal 'softer' side of organising equates with managing the ambiguous, amorphous – even the irrational and, in particular, the irrationality of cultures. Are we seeing a hint of the postmodern here? Yes and no.

I would suggest that, while the generation of employee commitment can be analysed from a postmodern standpoint, in Foucauldian terms (see below), in the hands of the prescriptive writers on cultural management, it remains firmly within a modernist frame. As will be clear from Chapter 6, the 'soft' HRM model's concern with developing employee commitment and a reinforcing 'strong' organisational culture is squarely aimed at performativity – delivering 'bottom line' results which, in a competitive world, demand that the employee 'goes the extra mile'. Further, the role of the transformational leader is often presented as centred in changing compliance to commitment. The transformational leader (invariably a man) is the hero of the hour, fending off Japanese attack, and rallying the troops to achieve success against the odds (read Jaguar, BA, etc.). *He* may be presented almost as an icon of critical modernity, as questioning the old order of inefficient non-participative bureaucracies, dinosaurs of state industries, distinctly non-dancing giants, to use Kanter's phrase (e.g., Richard Branson, Bill Gates). If so, from a postmodern Baudrillardian standpoint the hypereal radical image masks the unglamorous conventional reality. Such 'critical' anti-heroes in fact have more in common with 19th century entrepreneurs and are fully in tune (not to say, 'turned on') by the meta-narrative of capitalism and all that that entails in terms of performativity. Furthermore, some commentators would consider that the 'maleness' of transformational leadership inherently predisposes it in favour of the masculine logic embedded in notions of objectivity and reason (Calás and Smircich, 1992, p. 241). A postmodernist would point to the logocentrism implicit in transformational leadership (language being used to transmit a real sense of mission) and its assertion of a conventional hierarchy of binary opposites (leader/led, male leader/female employees) that cry out for Derridean deconstruction (leader as servant? 'soft' HRM values as 'feminine'?) (see below).

From an epistemological perspective then, the argument that HRM – at least in terms of its normative model – is essentially modernist, rests on its adherence to a positivistic epistemology and to the values of rationality and performativity. If HRM is about designing organisation structures and personnel policies to achieve competitive advantage in a world of increasingly competitive and uncertain global markets, it is difficult to see how it can be anything other than, epistemologically speaking, a modernist project in a world of late modernity. No matter that Clegg (1990) identifies many HRM-associated organisational initiatives as characteristic of post-modern organisation. As discussed earlier, such an identification is at the level of *periodisation* not of epistemology and whether such a period is referred to as one of late or radical modernity or of post-(hyphen) modernity, the mode of analysis is positivistic and realist. Nevertheless, the optimistic tone of 'soft' model HRM, about the developmental potential and value of employees exudes modernist notions of progress and improvement, while the 'hard' model's insistence on the primacy of the 'bottom line' asserts the performativity dear to systemic modernism. So, post-modern (late modern) in period and modernist in epistemology? But is this the whole story of HRM?

HRM may be seen as a postmodernist discourse in three senses. First, we can apply Derridean ideas about the undecidability or uncontrollability of meaning to HRM as a form of representation and we can attempt to deconstruct the hierarchies in the normative texts. Second, we can use Foucauldian ideas about power/knowledge and subjectivity to rethink HRM 'as a discourse and set of practices that attempt to reduce indeterminacy involved in the employment contract' (Townley, 1993, p. 518). Third, using ideas from actor network theory we can analyse how HRM might be seen as a discourse created to support the interests of a loose network of stakeholders.

HRM as discourse

Throughout this discussion of HRM it is evident how frequently commentators have recourse to colourful and memorable imagery and metaphor. Armstrong (1987), for example, invited us to consider whether HRM was a case of the 'emperor's new clothes' or of 'old [personnel] wine in new [HRM] bottles'. Keenoy (1990a) questioned whether HRM was a case of 'the wolf in sheep's clothing'. Guest (1990b) analysed HRM in terms of the 'American Dream'. Keenoy and Anthony (1992, p. 239) likened human resource managers to 'shamans [i.e., priests] [who] cannot be expected to do the chores'. In considering this imagery one is struck by two aspects. First, is the extent to which it is Biblically derived or has religious overtones[9] and, secondly, the recurring theme that HRM presents itself in a deceptive but 'new' packaging. Putting these two ideas together and applying Derrida's ideas about the 'trace' of many other terms ('networks of signification' according to Gergen) the reader can interpret this imagery as implying that HRM involves supernatural/magical/divine intervention, packaged in a consumer-friendly, but glitzy form. Keenoy and Anthony (1992, pp. 238–9) come close to Baudrillard's ideas about the ready consumption of the hypereal [HRM] in preference to the more mundane real [Personnel Management] when they write

> There should be little wonder ... that there are parts of the organisation that personnel management cannot reach, because its engagement in practical control makes it impossible to avoid the contradictions between apparent and espoused values that aspirations to cultural change reveal. HRM is not so disadvantaged. It is concerned with the management of beliefs, with the manufacture of acquiescence in corporate values, with the production of images ... If this is the case, if the symbolic rather than the social construction of 'reality' *is* the central concern of strategic HRM, then the separation of powers between personnel and human resource management is necessary: shamans cannot be expected to do the chores. Consequently, it is no good carping about the differences between image and reality if it is the business of HRM to shift perceptions of reality ...

It is interesting to note that in this quotation Keenoy and Anthony themselves revert to the representational world of the media – in this case advertising – in their adaptation of the famous beer commercial, 'that it refreshes the parts other beers cannot reach'. Hence the text can be read as asserting the values of consumption over those of production – itself a postmodern theme.

In looking at the language used to represent HRM one is struck by the degree (as in much rhetoric) to which binary oppositions are employed. In the examples cited above, we have 'old' and 'new', 'wolf' and 'sheep', 'wine' (a liquid to be contained) and 'bottle' (a structure of containment). In an extract quoted at length in Chapter 3, HRM was identified with the use of 'tough love'. We also have the oppositions contained in the 'brilliant ambiguity' (Keenoy) of the very phrase 'human resource management' (see also Chapter 3). Above all we have the oft-cited opposition between the 'hard' and 'soft' models of HRM.

This latter example is particularly interesting as it has structured much of the debate about HRM in the UK. In a sense, a process of 'metaphorisation', to use Derrida's term, has been on-going in reversing the hierarchy contained in this discourse. A starting point is that in a patriarchy 'hard' (a masculine characteristic), is likely to take precedence over 'soft' (a feminine characteristic) certainly in the external world of work. And this was how it started – with 'standard modern' styles of employee relations in the majority of UK companies (see Chapter 2), backgrounding the softer 'sophisticated paternalism', associated with industries where female staff or knowledge workers were prevalent (Marks & Spencer, IBM). Partly inspired by the Japanese icon, itself something of a culture shock, the 'soft' model of HRM was then talked up, backgrounding the 'hard' model that

Rhetoric	Reality
Customer first	Market forces supreme
Total quality management	Doing more with less
Lean production	Mean production
Flexibility	Management 'can do' what it wants
Core and periphery	Reducing the organisation's commitments
Devolution/delayering	Reducing the number of middle managers
Downsizing/right-sizing	Redundancy
New working patterns	Part-time instead of full-time jobs
Empowerment	Making someone else take the risk and responsibility
Training and development	Manipulation
Employability	No employment security
Recognising contribution of the individual	Undermining the trade union and collective bargaining
Teamworking	Reducing the individual's discretion

Source: Sisson (1994b, p. 15).

Figure 9.3   Sisson's model of rhetoric and reality in HRM

superficially resembled discredited 'standard modern' practices. Now, in the light of empirical work and critique of the 'soft' model, and in the context of recession, the 'hard' model of HRM is receiving more attention (see Guest, 1995).

Perhaps it is going too far to see conscious and continued efforts on the part of commentators to reverse or overturn the hierarchies implicit in the binary opposition of 'hard'/'soft'. However, many commentators, not just Keenoy and Anthony, cited earlier, have seen the contradictions embedded in HRM discourses and practices. In a relatively early paper, Legge (1989) spoke of the language of the 'soft' model of HRM being used to mask the contradictions of capitalism implicit in the 'hard' model. More recently, Sisson (1994b) shows how the rhetoric of the 'HRM organisation' may be used to mask the reality of the harsh face of managerial prerogative in the service of capitalism (see Figure 9.3).

HRM: the exercise of power/knowledge

This brings us to Foucault's ideas about power/knowledge and how they might be used to make strange the 'normal' activities of personnel/HRM. In an interesting analysis, Townley (1993, 1994) uses a Foucauldian approach to explore how the indeterminacy in the employment contract and in the employee herself are rendered known and governable. HRM, she suggests may be seen as the construction and production of knowledge, a discipline or discourse which

> serves to render organizations and their participants calculable arenas, offering, through a variety of technologies, the means by which activities and individuals become knowable and governable. HRM disciplines the interior of the organization, organizing time, space and movement within it. (Townley, 1993, p. 526)

The management of work and employees requires the coordination of large numbers of people and the ability to differentiate between them. Townley uses Foucault's ideas on disciplinary practices or techniques to manage people en masse to re-examine processes of selection, appraisal, work design, job evaluation and surveillance. In the following discussion, I will summarise her analysis.

Management's first task is to locate individuals conceptually in time and space. Foucault identified three ways in which this could be done: by enclosure (the creation of space closed in on itself e.g., the boundary between employment and non-employment), by partitioning (each individual has his or her own place and each place an individual, e.g., core/periphery, manual/non-manual) and ranking (the hierarchical ordering of individuals e.g. appraisal, promotion). To compare individuals or jobs a common denominator must be established. The basis for comparison may be either through developing a taxonomy (taxinomia) (Chapter 2 in this book is replete with them) or establishing an order through measurement (mathesis). For example, a job evaluation system ensures the ordering of a population: 'through the reduction of activities to a taxonomy of job factors, and their subsequent translation into numerical representation or mathesis, the population of jobs becomes ordered to be filled by suitable personnel' (Townley, 1993, p. 528).

Townley points out that other familiar tools of HRM – skills inventories, performance appraisal systems, attitude measurements, personality tests – are all arrangements for ranking, which facilitates the serial ordering of individuals. Such classification techniques serve to locate individuals in relation to the whole and in doing so operates to reduce individuality. Judging individuals according to comparative scalar models not only acts as a disciplinary process but as a normalising one. Ranking organises individuals round two poles – the positive and the negative (note, again, the appearance of a binary opposition). Hence, 'the distribution according to ranks or grades has a double role: it marks the gaps, hierarchises qualities, skills and aptitudes but it also punishes and rewards' (Foucault, 1977, p. 181, cited in Townley, 1993, p. 530).

Townley (1993, pp. 530–3) goes on to show how disciplines attempt to codify and enumerate time, space and movement in the labour process via the use of timetables, job analyses and descriptions, task and skill specifications, appraisal systems using behavioural observation scales and attitudinal measurement. To ensure that both time and activity are rendered productive, there is the organisation of activity into a series or temporal sequence, with each stage successfully graded from the others and leading to a seemingly logical progression (e.g., as in MBO or Human Asset Accounting). This process Foucault refers to as the capitalisation of time – the process of relating time and activity to cost.

Finally, the individual at work must be made visible, not only indirectly, through making the labour process known, but also directly. This is achieved through what Foucault terms the examination, which constitutes the individual as an object of knowledge through scientific study and the confession, which produces information that become part of the individual's self-understanding.

Foucault's most famous example of the examination derives from Jeremy Bentham's plan for the Panopticon penitentiary in the late 18th century. Essentially, it was for a building on a semicircular pattern with an inspection lodge at the centre and cells around the perimeter. Prisoners, in individual cells (note 'enclosure' and 'partitioning') were open to the surveillance of guards but, by a carefully contrived system of lighting and wooden blinds, the guards would be invisible to the inmates. Control was to be maintained by the constant sense that prisoners were watched by unseen eyes and, hence, that their only rational option was continuous obedience in the 'all-seeing place'. As Foucault (1977, p. 201) himself put it, the Panopticon acted

to induce in the inmate a state of conscious and permanent visibility that assures the automatic functioning of power. So to arrange things that the surveillance is permanent in its effects, even if it is discontinuous in its action; that the perfection of power should tend to render its actual exercise unnecessary; that this architectural apparatus should be a machine for creating and sustaining a power relation independent of the person who exercises it; in short, that the inmate should be caught up in a power situation of which they themselves are the bearers.

Panoptic forms of examination, acting simultaneously to individualise and standardise, are very evident in the operation of HRM. In Chapter 6, the role of selection, training and appraisal techniques in achieving a workforce attitudinally compatible with and willing to maintain the desired corporate cultures was discussed. Strong company cultures in themselves are part of the examination process, as they both facilitate the identification of deviants and prescribe the behaviours necessary for success. The forms of electronic, peer group and even customer surveillance associated with JIT and TQM, that were discussed in Chapter 7, also form part of the examination process. But because of the all-pervasive nature of power/knowledge relations and everybody's involvement in their reproduction, the examination process serves to monitor the surveyors just as much as those surveyed. A subordinate's poor performance raises questions about the competence of her manager; poor sets of financial figures can mean that heads will roll in the boardroom. I am reminded of a quotation cited in Purcell (1989, p. 85):

> We asked Malcolm Bates of GEC how many years a manager would fail to meet his budget before expecting to lose his job. His response was telling and only partly tongue in cheek: 'How many years? You mean how many months. He might last for six months or he might not.'

If the examination allows the inspector 'to measure in quantitative terms and to hierarchise in terms of values the abilities, level and the nature of individuals' (Townley, 1993, pp. 533–4), the confession – the individual's acknowledgement of his or her actions or thoughts – yields further knowledge to assist in the process of governance (e.g., via open ended questions at selection or appraisal interviews). Further, the introspection involved in the confession can be harnessed by management to develop self-monitoring subjects, prepared to present an appropriate identity. In Chapter 7 we saw how electronic and peer surveillance encouraged introspection and self-monitoring on the part of those subjected to it. Examination and confession together can give rise to the individual consciously acting out a socially constructed performance. While conscious that it is an act, Ogbonna's check-out operators would be an example of this, as well as Hochschild's (1983) emotional labourers – flight attendants.

Thus, HRM is amenable to analysis from a postmodern Foucauldian perspective. This perspective highlights how HRM acts to impose order on the inherently undecidable – the employment contract. Paradoxically such an analysis reveals HRM to be an expression of modernism, its discourse being permeated by concepts of rationality, ordering, measurement and grading. That such a postmodern analysis of HRM only serves to highlight its modernism is characteristic of postmodernism's penchant for reversals and contradictions.

The hyping of HRM?

In *Science in Action* (1987) Bruno Latour contrasts the study of scientific outcomes or 'ready-made' science with that of the process of 'doing science', or science-in-the-making. Those studying 'ready-made' science or 'black-boxed' scientific outcomes, would hold as self-evident that science and rationality go hand-in-hand; that a distinction can be drawn between human actors in the scientific community and the technology and other material artifacts necessarily involved; that science is a progressive force 'for good'; and that science is about the representation of reality. Ready-made science would hold as self-evident such positivistic statements as 'once the machine works people will be convinced' and 'when things are true they hold'. In other words, science, *par excellence*, is an expression of modernism. Those studying science-in-the-making, however, take an opposite view. From a postmodern perspective, Latour argues that the process of scientific discovery resembles 'organised persuasion', persuasion that utilises 'literary inscriptions' and is engaged in by actors who build 'networks of association' that tie in other actors. Latour shows, for example, in the case of Louis Pasteur, how actors as different as bacilli, farmers, the French government and Pasteur himself became tied into a network of association that was increasingly difficult to resist or challenge. Scientific fact-making, although often represented in terms of the lone scientific genius or hero is, on the contrary, a collective business in which resistances must be overcome and allies recruited by 'translation' of interests or borrowing the forces of another. To do this humans translate and enrol others and are aided in this by their ability to label, codify and simplify. Thus paper work 'inscriptions' are the key, because together with devices and compliant people they allow 'action at a distance' and increase the power of the centre over the periphery. A key objective in this action is to make one's work indispensable for others, an 'obligatory point of passage'. Hence Latour suggests that the earlier quoted positivistic statements should be reversed: 'the machine will work when all relevant people are convinced' and 'when things hold they start becoming true'.

Now is not the time to go further into actor network theory (for an excellent short account see Law, 1992; see also Cooper and Law, 1995). Suffice to say, though, that its deconstruction of conventional accounts of scientific work may be applied loosely to the making-of-HRM as a discourse and practice.

Who are the actors in attempts to create a 'black-box' status for HRM? How do they attempt to make familiarity – at least with its rhetoric – an obligatory point of passage for 'progressive' management, consultants and so on? More loosely, why do behaviours that either resemble the old normative models of personnel management (i.e., 'soft' model HRM) or, in practice, come close to the opportunistic 'standard modern' practice of personnel management (i.e., 'hard' model HRM) require a new representation, involving actors as diverse as operational management techniques (JIT, TQM), government (privatisation, legislative change), academics (the new 'HRM' professors and journals), IT, senior management and the unemployed? To answer this, in an age of consumer sovereignty, we need to ask who are the 'buyers' and 'sellers' of HRM, and what is the project? How, in this marketplace, are potential buyers and seller brought together into a mutually advantageous relationship (or in Latour's terms 'enrolled' in a network of strong association)?

Apart from consultants and Conservative governments, I would identify three major groups, or human actors, that have a vested interest in hyping HRM: academics, line managers and, more ambiguously, personnel managers themselves. All three can act variously as 'buyers' or 'sellers' (as will be discussed below). What is being bought is higher education and research funding, work intensification, competitive survival and managerial legitimacy. In such transactions the rhetoric – or language games – of HRM is the reality of the commerce.

To take *academics* first. It has already been pointed out in Chapter 3 that HRM has become big business in institutions of higher education, spawning new chairs, new journals and new degree courses, not to mention a burgeoning number of HRM texts, collections of critical papers and so forth. Perhaps most indicative is the trend for erstwhile lecturers in Industrial Relations, on achieving promotion, to change their title to one that incorporates HRM. (I won't mention names to spare the guilty!) Indeed, even where there has been no title change (e.g., Keith Sisson, Professor of Industrial Relations and Director of the IRRU, University of Warwick) there has nevertheless been a recognition that HRM cannot be ignored (Professor Sisson, for example, was the founding editor of the new *Human Resource Management Journal*). Why has this occurred?

If we take Latour's injunction that 'the machine will work when all relevant people are convinced', it was clear in the early 1980s that the academic machine of industrial relations – and indeed industrial relations in the country as a whole – had a severe credibility problem, following the 'Winter of Discontent' and a Conservative election victory. The rhetoric employed in the 1991 Green Paper on Proposals for the Further Reform of Industrial Relations and Trade Union Law captures the climate that the government both drew on and fostered at that time:

> It was a widely held view in the 1960s and 1970s that the severity and damaging consequences of Britain's industrial relations problems were exceeded only by their intractability ... in many cases union leaders were seen to be both irresponsible and undemocratic in exercising their industrial power. (Department of Employment, 1991, p. 1)

Such a climate inevitably had implications for research funding. I well remember in the early 1980s, a leading industrial relations research unit, Warwick's IRRU, being placed under government investigation as being 'unfairly biased in favour of the unions' (Rothschild, 1982, p. 87, see sections 9–16, 11–10; see also Hyman, 1989).

Strong hints were made that unless the research became more 'managerially oriented', long term (then) SSRC funding would be under threat. Undeniably too, interest in and support for old-style institutional industrial relations studies has been dealt a blow by successive Conservative governments' programmes of restrictive legislation throughout the 1980s designed to 'curb the unions' and the fall in union membership and militancy occasioned by sectoral changes, combined with two major recessions and high residual unemployment. The 'new realism' of industrial relations, it might be said, is matched by a new realism among academic staff.

The beauty of the 'machine' of HRM is that it allows discipline-based research in organisational behaviour and industrial relations to enrol allies, that is achieve research funding for projects, which, while conceptually interesting from their disciplinary point of view, can be given the commercial gloss of relevance demanded by most funding bodies. Hence, for example, the titles of three projects, which I have recently refereed, that successfully achieved funding from the Leverhulme Trust: 'HRM in a Professional Partnership Firm'; 'HRM and JIT in Japanese Manufacturing Plants'; 'When Greenfield Sites Turn Brown: The Evolution of HRM'.

Further, most funding bodies these days require evidence that the researcher has some promise of access. How much easier to gain access to look at an interesting organisational experiment (JIT? TQM? Teambuilding? – all non-human actors in the HRM network) in a greenfield site owned by an exemplar organisation than to seek access to research an industrial relations' 'problem' in a brownfield, unionised manufacturing organisation engaged in exercises of plant closure and downsizing? An added bonus for the hard pressed academic (and who in the last fifteen years has had a good word to say for this beleaguered group?) is that, as far as teaching goes, discipline-based teaching material can be repackaged into a form more in tune with the interests and relevancy requirements of other potential allies, that is the increasing numbers of self-funded business studies undergraduates and MBA students. Indeed, the academic's own marketability in consultancy arenas can be further enhanced by extending organisational behaviour interests into areas of business strategy via the wonderfully inclusive umbrella of researching organisational change – and we all know that *strategic* integration is integral to HRM. Indeed the utility of HRM to academics, struggling to meet the various demands of government-inspired research selectivity exercises, student-led funding and the teaching quality audits (not to mention the miserly pay awards that might propel some towards consultancy activities), is such that if it did not exist, we would have had to invent it. Certainly, in our roles as writers and consultants, I sometimes think we have! 'When things hold they start becoming true', as Latour stated.

But what of the product or 'machine' that the academics have sold? To the funding councils and MBA students the relationship between HRM and competitive advantage, wrapped up in the paper of quality and the string of flexibility, has been the product on offer. But that is not all. Nostalgia for our discipline origins, not to mention the labour process heyday of the later 1970s and early 1980s, made some academics more prone to seeing HRM as one more variant on personnel management's old function as a mediator of the contradictions of capitalism rather than as the key to competitive advantage. Additionally, academic careers can be forwarded by a critical dissection (or I should say 'deconstruction?') of new orthodoxies. Hence, as shown throughout this text, a large critical literature has emerged that has focused on deconstructing the contradictions and rhetoric of HRM (see, for example, Legge, 1989a; Keenoy, 1990a, 1990b; Guest, 1990b; Delbridge and Turnbull, 1992; Sewell and Wilkinson, 1992; Keenoy and Anthony, 1992). Nor should it be assumed that academics adopting a critical stance represent a different group from those successful with the research funding bodies. Quite the contrary. If 'the machine will work when all relevant people are convinced' then successful academics have to develop an entrepreneur's sensitivity to consumer taste and market niches and an awareness that research proposals will be reviewed by academics of a radical as well as managerialist predisposition who need to be enrolled to strengthen the network of association. Hence they know well that the secret of obtaining research funding (apart, of course, from proposing a methodologically sound study) is to construct a proposal that will enrol the very different potential actors in their support. Academics, in developing and marketing the product of HRM, have had to be as customer oriented in their product development and marketing as any other competitor in the enterprise culture.

Turning to *line managers*, in Chapter 3 I referred to Fowler's (1987) comment that HRM represented the discovery – or enrolment in Latour's terms – of personnel management by chief executives. Storey's (1992b) case study research in his large 'mainstream' UK organisations to some extent bears this out (see especially, Chapter 7). As already discussed in Chapter 4, in Smith and Nephew, Ford, Bradford Council and Peugeot, senior management were increasingly giving 'HRM issues' a high profile in their general deliberations on business strategy, while, at the same time, maintaining that personnel policy itself had been taken over by the executive (Storey, 1992b, pp. 171, 204). For example,

> Every month the Executive Committee of Ford of Europe (i.e., the vice president's board of directors) moves, in the afternoon, from the board room to a more relaxed atmosphere to discuss the 'people' issues of involvement, appraisal, employee relations, etc.. In total it adds up to a very considerable proportion of the board's time. (Director of Manufacturing, Ford of Europe) (Storey, 1992b, p. 203)

Further, the achievement of competitive advantage (the 'truth' or 'bottom line' in business networks) has been seen to involve non-human actors, that is operational management techniques, such as JIT, TQM, MRP and CAM and organisational design initiatives (not just the development of new team-based work systems, consequent on the operations management changes, but strategic initiatives as such as decentralisation to single business units and the 'delayering' of swathes of middle management 'support' staff, redefined as 'overhead'). The enlistment of these non-human actors is designed to serve as we have seen potentially incompatible ends: cost cutting, quality enhancement and increased flexibility and customer awareness both inside and outside increasingly permeable organisational boundaries. Such changes, where undertaken strategically rather than pragmatically, are consistent with the 'hard' model of HRM. And, according to Storey, line managers are not only central actors in enrolling such non-human actors, but may use them to both protect and enhance their roles and career prospects. The creation of a new network to establish a new credible engine to achieve competitive advantage is particularly desirable in a context of massive managerial job loss through delayering and downsizing.

Storey's argument accounting for line managers' involvement in HRM initiatives has already been summarised in Chapter 4. The upshot of all this is that line management has a vested interest in enrolling the rhetoric of HRM and its associated techniques. If the line manager is to demonstrate that she has graduated from being an old-style reactive 'mere' production manager (ripe for delayering), to a new proactive manufacturing (or better still 'business') manager, she must demonstrate that she is responsible for coordinating and directing *all* resources – or actors – in the business unit, including people, in pursuit of 'bottom line' results. The language of HRM is a most appropriate vehicle to demonstrate optimum resource utilisation in pursuit of the bottom line – yet with an acceptable face. Again, to quote one of Storey's (1992b, p. 201) departmental managers, in a process company, in response to a question on changes in his role:

> Oh [it has changed] quite significantly. The old progress chasing game has gone, I am much clearer about what my contribution is. I look outwards to the customer but I also get involved with the motivation of teams. In a sense what is new is that employee relations now have to be seen to make sense in a market context.

In these few lines the rhetoric of commitment, customer care (quality?) and strategic integration trip neatly off the tongue and is enrolled in the action of role and career enhancement.

Munro's (1994) in-depth case study research on rhetorics employed by middle-ranking line managers is consistent with this view. Embedded in a broader, sophisticated argument about governmentality effects and surveillance, he argues that middle managers are enrolling 'quality', that cornerstone of the 'soft' HRM model, as an expertise and rhetoric to protect themselves and their status as their traditional position is eroded via delayering, outsourcing and so on. Munro argues that professionalising over quality enables managers to represent themselves as the 'voice of the customer' and hence as representing the 'real' bottom line interests of the company in a competitive environment. Further, surveillance paths can be constructed around concepts of quality rather than standard costs and if control over the lines of surveillance is likely to remain in the hands of middle managers, as the holders of the expertise of quality, then the result is likely to create a new province ruled by middle managers and radiate a governmentality effect over employees, through talk of 'empowerment' and the like ... re-representing the customer affirms the governing rights of middle managers. (Munro, 1994, p. 146)

Finally, to turn to *personnel managers* themselves. Traditionally, personnel managers have suffered from problems of achieving credibility, recognition and status in the eyes of other management groups and employees (see Chapter 1). This has resulted in a willingness to adopt different roles and rhetorics to suit the contingencies of the times and to exploit possible bases of power (see Chapters 2 and 3). As already discussed in Chapter 1, the post-war consensus on full employment, combined with an upsurge in union membership and militancy, and the development of supportive employment law in the 1970s, gave rise to a valuable but ambiguous source of legitimacy for personnel managers, as mediators, not to say shock absorbers of trade union pressure, and policemen of line managers' propensity to *ad hoc* decision-making that, in the multisite organisations, might upset the apple cart. As we have seen this role has been variously referred to as the 'contracts manager' (Tyson and Fell, 1986), the 'consensus negotiator' (Torrington, 1989) and, more recently, 'the regulator' (Storey, 1992b). That this was an ambiguous source of legitimacy stemmed from two interrelated factors. First, such personnel managers were perceived as having a symbiotic relationship with the unions, the 'enemy within', and as such were not truly part of the management team (Batstone, 1980). Second, they were regarding as performing a gatekeeping function, a barrier between trade unions and access to strategic management considerations – with the result that such personnel specialists themselves became segmented into an isolated department and excluded from strategic management decisions (Marginson *et al.*, 1988).

However, as should be clear from the whole tenor of this text, 'managing the unions' as a source of even an ambiguous legitimacy has become increasingly vulnerable following two major recessions, persistently high levels of residual unemployment, falling union membership and restrictive labour legislation. By the late 1980s the most perspicacious personnel managers realised that need for a new rhetoric to assert credibility and enrol potential supporters, and one that would perform the dual, if paradoxical, function of highlighting a new specialist contribution, while simultaneously locating themselves unequivocally within the management team. At first glance HRM hardly fits the bill – after all a key emphasis is the vesting of people management in line management of 'having to "give HRM away"' in order to maintain a presence' (Storey, 1992b, p. 186). But skilful interweaving of the rhetorics of the 'hard' and 'soft' models maintains the paradox. While the 'hard' model uses the rhetoric of strategic integration, 'the subsumption of personnel under the prevailing (usually management accounting) business logics of the senior team', the latter 'emphasises the unique qualities of the human resource and thus seeks to unlock its potential through the use of an altogether distinctive set of techniques' (Storey, 1992b, p. 169). HRM, in other words, has the potential for personnel managers to have their cake and eat it. The subtle shifts of emphasis in backgrounding or highlighting the 'team member' or 'distinctive contribution' aspects of HRM are conveyed in two attributions of personnel directors' special qualities (made by line colleagues) cited in Storey (1992b, pp. 182–3):

> DT [the personnel and corporate affairs director] is very much a team-player. As for a 'distinctive personnel contribution', as you put it, I don't know. In fact, I'm not really sure what these personnel people actually do. But if we didn't have [DT] we would certainly miss him, well I would ... We've got a very good manpower planning system in place now, we used to have chronic overmanning – that's now a thing of the past. We have cut the number of locations by half and that was achieved without a single dispute; our people are now fully flexible.

> Chris has brought a breath of fresh air to the board. Our 'analysis' of people-management issues in the past was clouded by our obsession with relative remuneration packages and the like. We now have a much wider vista; talk of retention, development and career planning has become more meaningful and more serious. Oddly our people-management polices now seem to make far more business sense. The board feels more in control of the massive culture change which we are undoubtedly undergoing.

Shifts of emphasis there may be but integration with business strategy is a common theme in both discourses – the 'truth' that allies will validate.

Storey (1992b), with reference to his sample of 'mainstream' UK organisations, is the first to admit that a fully fledged adoption of HRM rhetoric and values was evident in only two of his fifteen core cases (although more widespread in his panel firms). Support for this finding is echoed in WIRS 3, where Millward *et al.* (1992, p. 29) found that fewer than 1 per cent of their workplace respondents said they were called 'human resource' managers, and in the Second Warwick Company Level survey, where only 9 per cent of correspondents had 'human resource' in their titles as compared to 63 per cent who had 'personnel' in their title (Marginson *et al.*, 1993, Table 4.1). Further, a continuing commitment to the 'regulator' role was evident among a hard core that could dismiss HRM initiatives as a passing fad.[10] As Storey (1992b, p. 187) points out this might be accounted for by the nature of the organisations involved: large, unionised and proceduralised. Nevertheless, even in this context, the writing is on the wall. Storey suggested that at least half the personnel managers and directors had aspirations to move towards the HRM changemaker role.

Conclusion

From a managerialist view, HRM is a phenomenon of late modernity – or the post-(hyphen) modern age – both in terms of its periodisation and its realist, positivistic epistemology. Nevertheless, from a critical perspective, it can be deconstructed from a postmodernist standpoint engaging in notions of social construction, actor network theory, the hypereal and language games.

If we look to the future, from a modernist perspective, is HRM likely to deliver to the 'bottom line' in such a way that it becomes 'taken-for-granted' in British industry? What is its future – and that of employee relations in general – likely to be in the next decade in the UK? This will be considered in the final short 'Epilogue' conclusion.

From a postmodern perspective, we have focused on HRM as a rhetoric or discourse that has been 'hyped' as something new and consistent with the demands of the enterprise culture, to serve the interests of three groups seeking legitimacy in a hostile climate. It has been in their interests to 'talk-up' HRM as a coherent new strategy that paves the way to achieving competitive advantage. The 'brilliant ambiguity' (Keenoy, 1990b) of the language of HRM has facilitated their endeavours.

But, herein lies a danger. Without doubt the language of HRM – and its close cousin, the language of excellence – is that of managerial triumphalism. Managers create missions for their organisations, they change their cultures, they act as transformational leaders that gain the commitment of employees to the values of quality, service, customer sovereignty, that is translated into 'bottom line success'. In the interests of achieving these values, employees must take responsibility, become 'empowered' – as also are the supreme arbiters, the customers. So, what do we have? The rhetoric, if not the practice, asserts that we are *all* managers: the employee becomes 'responsibly autonomous' to manage the operational variances in JIT and TQM systems; in service sector industries 'customers are made to function in the role of management' (du Gay and Salaman, 1992, p. 621); even in higher educational institutions there is much talk of student-managed learning. Now at one level we might recognise this as a rhetoric masking the intensification and commodification of labour (Keenoy and Anthony, 1992), but at another level it raises the question of, who are the 'real' managers?

Paradoxically then a rhetoric adopted to enhance managerial legitimacy might prove to be the thin edge of the wedge for at least some of its advocates.

So, what is the future for HRM?

Notes

1. In some writing it may appear that 'modernism' and 'modernity' are used interchangeably (and, similarly, 'postmodernism' and 'postmodernity'). However, for the purist, *modernisation* refers to the economic, social and technological innovations associated with the rise of capitalism; *modernity*, to the cultural experience of modern social life and the institutional forms through which it is articulated and communicated (Reed, 1992, p. 290) and *modernism*, to the answering wave of experimental movements

in the arts and cultural forms linked to capitalist metropolitan centres (Hebdige, 1989, p. 49). Frequently, though, and especially in the case of *modernism* and *postmodernism* the terms are used to embrace an amalgam of period, institutional forms and all related forms of socio–cultural–aesthetic expression. It is in this sense that, in this chapter, I use modernism and postmodernism as all-embracing, generic terms.

2. 'Discourse' refers to the way in which things are discussed and the argumentation and rhetoric used to support what is said. It also refers to 'reading between the lines' – what remains unspoken or taken-for-granted, such as assumptions or evasions. Crucially, discourse analysis deals with issues of representation. That is, it starts with the premise that words do not merely reflect what is being talked about, but they actually construct and even constitute what is being talked about. Feminist writers, for example, show how the structure of language literally constructs a 'man-made' patriarchal world (Spender, 1980).

3. This is well caught in a quotation from Feingold (cited in Bauman, 1991, p. 8):

> [Auschwitz] was also a mundane extension of the modern factory system. Rather than producing goods, the raw material was human beings and the end product was death, so many units per day marked carefully on the manager's production charts. The chimneys, the very symbol of the modern factory system, poured forth acrid smoke produced by burning human flesh. The brilliantly organised railroad grid of modern Europe carried a new kind of raw material to the factories. It did so in the same manner as with other cargo. In the gas chambers the victim inhaled noxious gas generated by prussic acid pellets, which were produced by the advanced chemical industry of Germany. Engineers designed the crematoria; managers designed the system of bureaucracy that worked with a zest and efficiency more backward nations would envy. Even the overall plan itself was a reflection of the modern scientific spirit gone awry. What we witnessed was nothing less than a massive scheme of social engineering ...

4. These organisational imperatives are:
   1. Articulating mission goals, strategies and main functions.
   2. Arranging functional alignments.
   3. Identifying mechanisms of coordination and control.
   4. Constituting accountability and role relationships.
   5. Institutionalising planning and communication.
   6. Relating rewards and performance.
   7. Achieving effective leadership. (Blunt, 1989, cited in Clegg, 1990, p. 184)

5. Gergen (1992, pp. 210–20) captures well the 'undecidability' of meaning, in deconstructing his Portsmouth example. He writes
   To affirm something is to set in motion a chain of signification that simultaneously confirms its negation. (In simplest terms, for example, the exhortation 'Let's be logical about this ...' is to make reference to the possibility of irrationality, which possibility is affirmed by the nature of the exhortation itself ... which is not logically grounded.)

6. Paradox and contradictions are very evident in Latour's (1987, pp. 258–9) statement of the 'Methods' and 'Principles' of 'Science in Action'. For example, in 'Rules of Method':

Rule 3: Since the settlement of a controversy is the *cause* of Nature's representation, not its consequence, we can never use this consequence, nature, to explain how and why a controversy has been settled.

In 'Principles'

First principle: the fate of facts and machines is in later users' hands; their qualities are thus a consequence, not a cause, of a collective action.

7. Look at the UK Royal Family, for example!
8. The distinction between the reflexivity of critical modernity and that of postmodernism is paralleled by their different perspectives on alienation and identity. From a critical modernist perspective alienation is considered within the meta-narrative of Marxism, and presupposes a coherent rather than a fragmented sense of self from which to be alienated. This contrasts with the fragmented sense of self of postmodernism that denies alienation, as no 'true' or fixed sense of self exists. Harvey (1989, pp. 54–5) draws out this distinction well in terms of critical modernism/postmodernism theories:

It is only in terms of such a centred sense of personal identity that individuals can pursue projects over time, or think cogently about the production of a future significantly better than time present and time past. Modernism was very much about the pursuit of better futures, even if perpetual frustration of that aim was conducive to paranoia. But postmodernism typically strips away that possibility by concentrating upon the schizophrenic circumstances induced by fragmentation and all those instabilities (including those of language) that prevent us even picturing coherently, let alone devising strategies to produce, some radically different future.

9. It is interesting that the *Oxford Paperback Dictionary* defines 'shaman' as '(in primitive religion) a person regarded as having direct access to, and influence in, the spiritual world which enables him to *guide souls, cure illnesses, etc.*' (added emphasis).

This sounds remarkably like a transformational leader striving for company turnaround!

10. But, note, 'industrial relations' is not a popular job title – only 1 per cent of respondents in both the WIRS 3 and Second Warwick Company Level survey claimed it in their job titles (Millward *et al.*, 1992, p. 29; Marginson *et al.*, 1993, Table 4.1).

10

Epilogue: the future of HRM?

In the 1980s, in the academic analysis of survey and case study data on employee relations, there was much preoccupation with questions of change and continuity (for a summary, see Legge, 1988). While case study data, particularly of greenfield sites or newly privatised industries, sparkled with evidence of new HRM initiatives, survey data – until WIRS 3 and the second Warwick Company Level survey at least – stubbornly showed a marked continuity in terms of the maintenance of traditional structures of employee relations. By the end of the decade a synthesising orthodoxy had emerged, that while the *form* of employee relations had broadly survived in the majority of workplaces, the *content* had changed (Blyton and Turnbull, 1994).

Spiral time?

In discussing such debates, Blyton and Turnbull (1994, pp. 9–12) made some insightful observations with which I concur. All periods, they argue, are characterised by change *and* continuity. Change is likely, by its nature, to receive more attention, as being newsworthy, relevant and so on (Dastmalchian *et al.*, 1991, p. 11). It is also likely to be more apparent if a relatively short time scale and a linear view of time is adopted. From this perspective, the fifteen years of Conservative government appear marked by massive changes from and discontinuities with the employee relations scene of the 1960s and 1970s. However, a longer time scale and cyclical view of time might well have identified continuity with employee relations in the 1930s. Hence perspectives resting on a linear or cyclical view of time both have their limitations. The former suffers from a naivety that overemphasises the uniqueness of the present and the latter from a cynicism that is sceptical of any real underlying change – a *'plus ça change, plus c'est la même chose'* position. Blyton and Turnbull (1994) consider that a more constructive approach may be found by

356

adopting Filipcova and Filipec's (1986) and Burrell's (1992) idea of 'spiral time'. From this perspective, time incorporates elements of both the linear and cyclical; movement along the spiral involves progression, continuity and reversal, 'the short term [can represent] a single twist of a longer term spiral' (Blyton and Turnbull, 1994, p. 12). From this perspective, surveying employee relations over the last decade and a half they conclude

> Nothing changes yet everything is different: as we twist around the spiral of capitalist economic development we experience progression and return, never a return to exactly the same point but always to a place that is familiar. (Blyton and Turnbull, 1994, p. 298)

Quite so. I would argue here that an underlying continuity is the function itself of personnel management – whether dressed in 'hard' or 'soft' model HRM clothes – to mediate the contradictions of capitalism, to realise the surplus value through obscuring the commodity status of labour (see Chapter 1). A further continuity appears to be the close resemblance, in practice if not in theory, of 'hard' HRM and the opportunistic, pragmatic 'standard modern' employee relations style (see Chapter 2). A progression might be the attempts to achieve both control and consent (themselves underlying continuities) through the implementation of 'soft' model HRM. A reversal or return might be identified in the WIRS 3 findings about employee relations practices in non-unionised firms,[1] which appear depressingly reminiscent of the 'traditional' industrial relations style which unreformed pluralists were accustomed to regard as something of yesteryear (see Chapters 2 and 8).

So, perhaps, to ask 'what is the future of HRM?' is to pose the wrong question. As Eliot reminds us, in the The Four Quartets:

> Time present and time past
> Are both perhaps present in time future,
> And time future contained in time past.

Nevertheless, a few concluding observations may be offered.

Bleak house and hard times

Although there is plenty of case study evidence and, latterly from WIRS 3, survey evidence, for a considerable adoption of practices associated with HRM in UK organisations, there are question marks as to whether this adoption has much depth. From the analysis in Chapters 4–8 it would appear that the most thoroughgoing adoption of approximately 'soft' model HRM appears in relatively few – latest estimates suggest no more than 70–80 (IRRR, 1991) – largely foreign-owned, greenfield sites and in a small number of brownfield sites, mainly in car and electronic assembly, that are in a direct fight for survival with Japanese competition (Sisson, 1994b, p. 42), and in chemical plants (Wilkinson et al., 1993). As for the adoption of 'hard' model HRM, the public sector services are prominent. However, even with this generalisation, two caveats must be entered. First, where the 'soft' model apparently has been introduced, to what extent does that form (e.g., 'empowered' TQM oriented 'teams') and rhetoric (e.g., 'customer care') mask 'hard' practice (e.g., labour intensification, cost minimisation, coercive surveillance)? Further, under the pressure of recession and need for tight cost controls, to what extent do the exemplar greenfield sites turn brown (Nissan's lay-offs, Pirelli's 'capping' of skill module acquisition)? Secondly, bearing in mind the analysis presented in Chapter 4, how many of these initiatives can truly be called *strategic* – the *sine qua non* of the normative models of HRM? Possibly, in some of the most heralded greenfield sites and, at least initially, in the public sector (see Chapters 5 and 7), but in the majority of cases where HRM initiatives appear, there is far more of a 'suck it and see' approach that resembles the familiar gibes about the 'flavour of the month' that greeted the OD experiments in the 1960s and 1970s. The evidence we have of the implementation of practices associated with HRM, in the vast majority of cases, at best resembles a 'thinking pragmatism' rather than any well thought out, coherent and strategic plan (Legge, 1995). In which case, given that strategic integration and coherence in both 'hard' and 'soft' HRM models is *the* defining characteristic of 'true' HRM, can one say, in any real sense, that HRM has been implemented, except in a tiny minority of exemplar cases?

Then there is the paradox noted by Sisson (1993, 1994b) and Guest (1995) and in Chapter 8. In theory, with its emphasis on individualism, HRM is an alternative approach to and, indeed, incompatible with, traditional collectivist industrial relations. Hence it might be expected that survey evidence would reveal a greater prevalence of HRM-associated practices in non-union as opposed to unionised organisations. Indeed this is what Storey (1992b, p. 44) predicted at the outset of his empirical research on the adoption of HRM by 'mainstream' UK organisations. In fact, on the basis of WIRS 3 findings (Millward *et al.*, 1994, pp. 363–5), the *exact opposite seems to be the case*. HRM initiatives were more frequently associated with unionised workplaces. In contrast, in non-unionised workplaces (as compared to unionised) there were fewer procedures and fewer health and safety representatives, fewer channels of information and consultation, less information from management and fewer personnel specialists. Although respondents were more likely to describe workplace climate as 'good' or 'very good' than in unionised organisations, there were more compulsory redundancies, more dismissals, higher labour turnover, higher accident rates, more low pay and a greater dispersion of pay. Claims to industrial tribunals for unfair dismissal and other alleged mistreatment were no less common than in union workplaces. Pay also appears to be both more often performance-related and market-determined, with greater use of freelance and temporary contracts. Marginson *et al.* (1993) similarly found no support for a non-union HRM strategy. For example, non-union firms were no more likely to pursue employee involvement – indeed unionised companies were significantly more likely to use a greater range of methods of employee communication, to provide information about investment plans to employees and to utilise forms of task participation. The only possible exceptions were the very small number of cases on greenfield sites where there had been a centrally agreed strategy to derecognise all unions and where some thought had been given to the strategic choice of what might be put in their place.

For those who consider the salvation of UK industry to lie in its universal and thoroughgoing adoption of 'soft' model HRM, this is bad news. The picture WIRS 3 paints is not even, strictly speaking, one of 'hard' HRM, which would imply a considered strategy and coherence. Rather it smacks of a pragmatic viewing of labour as a variable cost, at least in recession. Leading commentators, such as Sisson (1993) and Guest (1995) take an equally gloomy view, the former referring to such organisations as 'Bleak House' and the latter as the 'Black Hole: no HRM and no industrial relations'. In such a context it is interesting that the Citizens' Advice Bureaux (1993) have recently reported a large increase in complaints about unfair dismissals and that, in a recent opinion poll survey (cited in Blyton and Turnbull, 1994, p. 305) almost half the respondents said that they would leave the country if they could, and less than one in ten could identify anything about their country of which they were proud. So much for the managerial triumphalism of the gurus of the enterprise culture.

What is really disturbing, though, is that the 'Bleak House' scenario may become more rather than less prevalent. The arguments for and against this prediction are as follows:

First, as discussed in Chapter 8, not only is there a fall-off in union recognition, but a rise in derecognition. This is borne out in both WIRS 3 and in the second Warwick Company Level 1992 survey (Millward et al., 1992, Marginson et al., 1993). Second, the evidence suggests that this is an upward trend. Disney et al. (1993), in their analysis of the WIRS surveys, have shown that the pattern of recognition at new plants has changed. They argue that the industrial relations climate at the time of start-up is a crucial factor and that it was different in the 1980s compared with the 1970s. As a result it was 28 per cent less likely, other things being equal, that a union would be recognised at a new establishment set up in the 1980s compared with one set up in the 1970s. More specifically, WIRS 3 shows that in 1990 only 24 per cent of establishments less than ten years old recognised a union. This compares with 45 per cent of establishments less than ten years old in 1980. If we look only at establishments employing more than fifty people and where, traditionally, the probability of a union presence is greater, the percentage recognising a union in the 1980s was 41 per cent (Guest and Hoque, 1993). Marginson et al. (1993) reveal a similar pattern in the second Warwick Company Level 1992 survey. Of the 140 companies in their sample, 59 per cent that had opened a new site did not recognise a union at the site, including 38 per cent of otherwise unionised companies.

In other words, the dominant pattern in new establishments is not to recognise a union. In which case, if the 'Bleak House' employee relations scenario is associated with non-unionised workplaces, its prevalence, other things being equal, is likely to spread.

Secondly, 'soft' model HRM is essentially aimed at developing a highly skilled, highly committed, functionally flexible workforce that is highly productive in producing high value added goods and services. As has been reiterated throughout this text, but particularly in Chapter 4, the political, financial and educational institutions of the UK interact in a vicious circle to produce an economy based on low investment, low cost, low skill, low technology, low value added goods and services – but relatively high unit labour costs (Nolan, 1989; Brown and Walsh, 1991). Both Sisson (1994b) and Blyton and Turnbull (1994) are eloquent on this score. As Sisson argues (1994b, pp. 21–2), we have a set of financial institutions – investment trusts and pension funds, threat of take-over in the form of large conglomerates anxious to maintain the price/earnings ratio of their shares – that has put considerable pressure on companies to maintain dividends and deliver short-term financial results, at the expense of any investment strategy – whether in people or in technology – that smacks of the long term and the uncertain. This has been exacerbated by the adoption of organisation structures which have reinforced short-term thinking – that is a multidivisional pattern which, coupled with a tradition of corporate head offices emphasising control rather than development, has reinforced an emphasis on 'number-driven' rather than 'issue-driven' planning (McKinsey and Co., NEDO, 1988) (see also Chapter 4). The general lack of long-term thinking and investment leads inevitably to labour being regarded as a variable cost to be minimised.

Nor is this bleak picture completely alleviated by the evidence we have of inward investment into the UK (for an interesting discussion, see Marginson, 1994). *Not all the news is bad – far from it.* Inward investment, particularly into areas of high unemployment resulting from the collapse of extractive and heavy manufacturing industry, has involved welcome job creation. Further, *it cannot be emphasised too strongly* that case study evidence and evidence from WIRS 2 and 3 and the first and second Warwick Company Level surveys suggest that overseas-owned multi-nationals are associated with a stronger specialist personnel management presence, with better pay and conditions and with the advanced manufacturing techniques, which are often associated with innovatory labour practices, than many UK-owned companies (note some of the exemplar greenfield site cases such as Nissan of Sunderland). However, as we have already seen in relation to that case, there may be another side of the story – the exploitative face of multinational activity, based on enhanced bargaining power deriving from an ability to 'divide and rule'. Thus Marginson (1994, p. 66) points to multinationals' ability to switch – or credibly threaten to switch – production from one location to another; dual sourcing of products and services from locations in different countries, enabling multinationals to minimise disruption caused by local industrial disputes; the remoteness of corporate decision-makers from trade union negotiators, left to deal with local managers negotiating to a centrally determined mandate; the scale of financial resources behind multinationals and the lack of financial transparency in decisions of the future of local operations. Confronting such power are workforces and trade unions whose differences of interest and difficulties in developing effective organisational and communication links across national borders impedes the development of common policy and a united front. Further, the ability of multinationals to pursue enlightened employee relations policies in their own plants often goes hand-in-hand with driving such hard bargains with sub-contractors that the latter may be pushed into treating labour as a variable cost. 'Soft' HRM policies on the part of large multinational plants may be predicated on 'bleak house' policies on the part of their hard-pushed suppliers (Blyton and Turnbull, 1994, p. 229; see also, Mitter, 1985.).

More worryingly, though, in the long term, is the evidence that the attractiveness of the UK for inward investment, in terms of labour supply, rests on the availability, within the EU market, of a relatively cheap, unprotected, semi-skilled workforce (Marginson, 1994, pp. 73–7). The activities multinationals are choosing to locate in the UK tend to be relatively low skilled assembly and sub-assembly operations involving routinised and standardised production methods (Young and Hamill, 1988; Auerbach, 1989; Nolan, 1989). The decision of Ford to scale down its R & D activity in the UK, transferring a large part of it to Germany, is indicative (*Financial Times*, 1992). The UK is not only a low direct (*but not unit*) labour cost country, when compared with other industrialised Western economies (Brown and Walsh, 1991), but emerges substantially lower, in comparison to most other EU countries, when the indirect costs of statutory social welfare, training and holidays are taken into account. Relatedly, companies based in the UK are subject to few statutory constraints on how they manage their workforces, and employees enjoy fewer substantive rights regarding pay, benefits and working time as compared with other advanced economies within the EU. Not only does it appear that employers across Europe indicate that they perceive the UK as having the weakest employment protection legislation within the Union (Commission of the European Communities, 1993) but the UK Conservative government's opting-out of the Social Chapter in the Maastricht Treaty in 1991 was based on the assumption that absence of such statutory constraints combined with low social costs gives the UK a comparative advantage in the eyes of multinational investors.

That the present Conservative government considers low labour costs (rather than high value added) and the potential for the unfettered exercise of managerial prerogative to be the 'jewels in the crown' of the UK economy, is yet another example of its endemic short-termism. As Blyton and Turnbull (1994, pp. 305–6) rightly point out

The main shortcoming of the state's labour market strategy over the past 15 years is not that it is leading to Britain becoming 'the Taiwan of Europe' as some observers have suggested, but rather that it would be impossible to maintain even that position in the face of the strong cost-based competition from Taiwan itself. There is no long-term security in a competitive strategy based on low-investment, low-cost, low-skill, low-technology, low-value added products. There will invariably be countries that can manufacture and export mass-produced, low technology goods to the market cheaper than Britain. It is alarming that the structure of the British economy now resembles that of a semi-peripheral country, specialising in sectors that are not research intensive.[2]

Further, such a strategy gives rise to some unfortunate vicious circles in UK-owned industries (Blyton and Turnbull, 1994, pp. 300–1). Low pay does not encourage employee commitment as, not unnaturally, employees are likely to look elsewhere for better pay. This, in turn, does not encourage management to invest in training, preferring to poach specialist skills as and when needed (Henley and Tsakalotos, 1992), further reducing industry's commitment to training and, hence, ability to create the skill base required for a high value added economy. This further exacerbates the vicious circle. 'Many British companies are encouraged to produce relatively low quality goods and services because low paid consumers cannot afford better' (Sisson, 1994b, pp. 41–2). This is hardly a fertile institutional and cultural soil in which 'soft' HRM might thrive, but exactly appropriate to the burgeoning of 'bleak houses' and 'black holes'.

New messiahs or false prophets?

The conventional wisdom to guard against such a scenario becoming even more of a reality than it presently is, is to express hope in a revitalised trade union movement, in the safeguards provided by EU membership and in a change of government. On all three counts optimism has to be guarded.

In Chapter 8, the decline of trade unionism was recognised. If one is an optimist, one might identify some grounds for its recovery. First, unions are now more popular than they have been for years (Waddington, 1992). However, this in itself reflects their marginalisation as part of the reason for their enhanced popularity may be their lower profile, linked to a sharp reduction in strike activity, and in the fact that it is no longer possible to use them as a scapegoat for the industrial and employment problems of the UK. Secondly, it could be argued that if the 'black hole' employee relations scenario becomes increasingly prevalent, along with a retreat from the welfare state, conditions are recreated that gave rise to the trade union movement in the first place – a real reversal in the spiral of time. The need is to attract new members, while retaining current members, to persuade managers at new establishments that they should recognise a trade union, and to convince managers at existing plants that they wish to retain trade unions and continue to recognise them (Guest, 1995).

Guest (1995) suggests three strategies of revitalisation. The first, aimed at existing members, is the 'Quality of Working Life' strategy, set within the agenda of the European Social Chapter. This would rest on assumptions of pluralism and of the value of partnership, on the promotion of issues such as health and safety, skill formation, job design and working hours with the idea of securing mutual benefits for employee and the organisation, assuming an economic strategy of high skills, high commitment and high value added. Good in principle, if unions can persuade employers that such a programme is not one-sidedly in favour employees' interests, but is of mutual benefit. Unions' use of the rhetoric of quality might be important here.

The second strategy is that of the 'Friendly Society', for unions to emphasise their role in providing financial, legal and possibly social support to individual members. This might be aimed at new members, in the light of the trend among employers – particularly in non-unionised 'black hole' companies – to offer short-term contracts with limited or non-existent social and welfare benefits. The difficulty with this approach is the chicken and egg problem: that it will require financing, which only increased membership can provide, but with that membership being sought among employees who are least able to cope with higher union dues.

The third strategy is the *proactive* support of 'soft' HRM as a route to a highly committed and flexible workforce, that might have pay-offs, in terms of job security and employability via training, to the employee and high productivity, via commitment and flexibility, to the company. Unions, Guest (1995) argues, might find a new 'compelling' ideology in the notion of 'community' and 'corporate citizenship', or 'co-determination and co-ownership'. They might strongly advocate and monitor the implementation of soft 'HRM'. As discussed in Chapter 8, some unions, notably the GMB, have already taken tentative steps along a path of proactive support for HRM, 'appropriating management's own model', as Guest puts it. While this looks feasible in workplaces already unionised – particularly those already experimenting with HRM practices – it is difficult to see how it might be effected in non-union settings that apparently show no interest in 'soft' HRM, or if interested, are so committed to a philosophy of individualism as to exclude any possibility of a union presence.

The inclination or ability of the union movement to wholeheartedly embrace such strategies is questionable. Blyton and Turnbull (1994, pp. 302–4) provide a very persuasive analysis of some of the problems involved. They argue that while unions generally recognise many of the challenges they face and the need for new strategic thinking (Terry, 1991), they encounter a 'Catch 22' situation when it comes to implementing such initiatives as Guest outlines. Unions need to recruit more members, but the very dwindling membership base, a product of sectoral change and economic recession, reduces the income that is required to mount effective recruitment campaigns. Further, the biggest potential for membership growth lies in those private sector service industries which traditionally are difficult to organise and have lacked union organisation and, partly in consequence, suffer from low pay. Yet low pay does not encourage the payment of unions' subscriptions, particularly if it is unclear to potential members what unions, with their diminished power, can achieve for them in return (Willman, 1989).[3] Additionally, the provision to reform 'check-off' arrangements in the Trade Union Reform and Employment Rights Act 1993 is likely to lead to a further fall in union membership and funds.

If funds are in short supply, it is imperative that they are used to most effect (i.e., to increase the membership base and thereby initiate a virtuous circle of revenue generation, which may finance recruitment drives, generating further revenue and so on). However, as Blyton and Turnbull point out, unions' policy has often suffered from a short-termism and lack of coherency and coordination akin to managements'. In other words, rather than coordinated recruitment initiatives to organise new members in expanding sectors of the economy, the unions have adopted a 'market share' approach, focused on competing for members in relatively well organised sectors, via single-union 'sweetheart' deals, or redistributing existing memberships via mergers and amalgamations. The former strategy seems particularly ill-advised. Not only does it advertise to the public a lack of unity and common front in the union movement as a whole (underlined by the weaknessess of the TUC as a confederating body) but if the conditions attaching to the 'sweetheart' deals are perceived by the workforce as severely compromising the union's independence, recruitment is likely to be low.[4]

Finally, there is the prospect of a changed employee relations climate deriving from EU membership and a possible change of UK government. Admittedly, prior to the Maastricht Treaty of 1992, the track record of the EU in the area of employment had been somewhat modest. Although the European Court of Justice had made some significant judgements in areas of health and safety and equity issues, progress in other areas (e.g., employee participation in decision-making) had been slow. This had been attributed to employer opposition (voiced through employers' associations and major transnational corporations), the watering-down of Directives and failure of member states to comply with EU regulations and the lack of Europe-wide concerted pressure from the unions, divided as they are by different structures, ideologies and levels of organisation. Particularly in recession, national bodies, whether states themselves, employers' organisations or unions have tended to put first perceived national above pan-European interests (Blyton and Turnbull, 1994, p. 308).

However, the Maastricht Treaty may prove something of a watershed, particularly when the advanced European economies emerge from recession. The Social Charter, adopted by all member states, except in the UK, in 1989, and the accompanying Action programme, sought protection, in such areas as equity issues, health and safety, worker information, consultation and participation rights. The principles of the Social Charter were subsequently endorsed in a separate Protocol on social policy (the 'Social Chapter') included as an annex to the Maastricht Treaty on political union. As we know the UK refused to endorse the Social Charter and 'opted-out' of the Social Chapter. However, this 'opt-out', in the long term, may be less significant than, first, the extension of qualified majority voting to cover working conditions, worker information and consultation rights, gender equality and assistance for the unemployed as well as health and safety issues and, secondly, the recognition that the UK's 'opt-out' decision precludes it from impeding the development, in the other eleven states, of those social and employment policy issues that are decided by majority voting. Before Maastricht, such issues required unanimous agreement among member states and, in practice, proposals were often blocked by individual states (particularly the UK). Now there is an increased likelihood that, however vaguely drafted in order to be applicable under different systems of national legislation and practice, draft Directives, currently held up in the European council, will now reach EU statute books. Although lacking the force and immediacy of a Regulation[5] the Directive to establish European Works Councils has particular symbolic importance, endorsing the legitimacy of collective representation at a time when, in the UK, government has sought to undermine it and promote individualism (Blyton and Turnbull, 1994, pp. 307–15; Ramsay, 1991, Addison and Siebert, 1992). Nevertheless, the potential significance of the Social Chapter should perhaps not be overestimated as the protocol includes a significant contingency clause: any potential Europe-wide social measures are subject to 'the need to maintain the competitiveness of the Community economy'. Current increasing concern over this competitiveness 'may result in the scaling down – or even the implicit abandonment – of the Commission's social policy agenda' (Hall, 1994, pp. 301, 307).

Although the UK has 'opted-out' of the Social Chapter, Blyton and Turnbull suggest that it is debatable whether the UK can stand aside indefinitely and still remain a member state. A future Labour government is committed to embracing the Social Chapter. Irrespective of this, however, is the effect of the creation of a single European market. It is likely that large UK transnational companies operating in Europe will wish to introduce into the UK employee relations systems compatible with those being introduced by agreement in Europe. This is particularly likely in companies which operate with a single management structure within Europe and a divisional structure organised internationally, along product lines, rather than by local national subsidiaries, and where growth has occurred via the development of greenfield sites rather than by acquisition or merger (Marginson, 1992). The perceived need in Europe-wide corporations to develop employee commitment to intra-firm 'customers' may encourage the development of Europe-wide communication channels – unless the corporation is more wedded to a 'divide and rule' approach. Although there seems little likelihood of the development of cross-national collective bargaining within Europe, both because of the 'divide and rule' inclinations of multinationals, differing bargaining structures and latent nationalism of managements, employees and unions alike, there are indications of a greater degree of inter-union contact and information exchange within Europe (Blyton and Turnbull, 1994, pp. 312–14). Blyton and Turnbull (1994, pp. 314–15) further suggest that Europe is important in demonstrating that economic success, based on a philosophy of secure employment, high skill and high value added, is not only compatible with collectivism and social protection, but that these factors might actually unpin such a strategy and underwrite its success.

Conclusion

As argued in Chapter 3, HRM in the UK, as both a rhetoric and a series of initiatives, is very much a product of the 'enterprise culture'. In the late 1980s, before descent into recession, it appeared part of the 'feel good' scenario that embraced rampant consumerism and the so-called 'Thatcher economic miracle'. In the cold light of the 1990s, HRM and the enterprise culture both appear tarnished – not least in the eyes of those managers simultaneously suffering the twin shocks of the 1990s, negative equity in property combining with the job insecurity consequent on delayering and downsizing. 'Soft' model HRM appears a shallow rooted plant, save in the most exceptionally fertile soil. While there is some evidence from WIRS 3 and the second Warwick Company Level survey that the presence of specialist personnel managers is associated with policies and practices often associated with 'soft' model HRM and that the extent to which these are endorsed at board level is strongly influenced by the presence of a personnel director on the main board, the link between such practices and performance outcomes is more difficult to establish (Guest and Hoque, 1994a). Further, Guest and Peccei (1994), in their NHS study, found a lack of evidence of any relationship between the existence of a professional specialist personnel department and perceived personnel effectiveness. Indeed, in a somewhat contrary analysis of WIRS 3 data, Fernie et al. (1994) even argue that the practices generally associated with 'soft' HRM and 'new industrial relations', generally speaking, do not contribute to a better employee relations climate than that found in traditional workplaces.[6] In the light of the preceding analysis the depressing thing is that these equivocal findings are not a complete surprise. 'Hard' HRM, in many cases, appears to have supplanted 'soft' HRM, but like any weed, is not noted for its planned and systematic planting – rather it grows wild when and where conditions suit. The enterprise culture, too, although debatably responsible for some increases in efficiency in the much diminished UK manufacturing base (Legge, 1988),[7] appears unable to ameliorate high endemic levels of unemployment and to be associated with a retreat from the welfare state and a growing number of organisations descending into a 'black hole' of employee relations practice reminiscent of yesteryear. The union response, generally speaking, has been ineffectual in halting, let alone reversing, trends inimical to employees' well-being.

The present Conservative government's opt-out of the Social Chapter, to quote Sisson (1994b, p. 42) is not only consistent with, but positively encourages 'a vicious circle of low pay, low skill and low productivity'. While the rhetoric of the present Labour opposition is encouragingly pro-European and in support of 'community' values and of a high skill, high value added economy that can fund social spending – rhetoric is cheap. Yet to appear are detailed policy commitments and implementation strategies that spell out how such aspirations are to be achieved in the context of a tax-shy electorate and a fundamentally weak economy. Further, at the 1994 TUC conference, the Labour party's distancing from the trade unions (reflected in a refusal to endorse the RMT signallers' strike and some equivocation on minimum wage commitments) combined with a further swing to the Right, with the election of Tony Blair as leader, raises questions about what policies it will *wish* to deliver, if elected.

Against this background, the widespread implementation of the 'soft' normative model of HRM appears as a mirage, retreating into a receding horizon.

Notes

1. Although WIRS 3 talks of the 'smaller size of the typical non-union workplace' (Millward *et al.,* 1992, p. 363) the figures have yet to be broken down by size for a detailed analysis of the difference in industrial relations practices between large and small institutions. But, as Sisson (1993, p. 207) points out, it would take a very substantial polarisation around a relatively small number of large establishments to explain away the overall differences between the union and non-union sectors. In any case, it would mean that there was even less evidence of good practice in small and medium firms in the non-union sector.

2. It is interesting, in this context, that with the exception of chemicals and pharmaceuticals, *British*-based multinationals are engaged in sectors characterised by relatively low technology and low skill: food, drink, tobacco, paper and textiles in manufacturing, and in hotels, leisure and finance in services. Such sectors are not research intensive (Stopford and Turner, 1985; Sisson *et al.,* 1992).

3. There is evidence of a decline in the union mark-up throughout the 1980s and that where single table bargaining has been established, any positive impact of trade unions on wage levels has been eliminated (Metcalf, 1993).

4. Union (AEU) membership at Nissan in Sunderland, for example, has never exceeded 50 per cent of the workforce and is reported by Garrahan and Stewart (1992, p. 128) to have grown from less than one in five to only around 30 per cent, 'even with management encouragement'.

5. Whilst a Regulation has immediate binding power across the EU, Directives require each member state to pass legislation to implement the proposals. Further, this opens up the possibility for some dilution of the proposals if members seek to legislate only to cover minimum compliance with the Directive (Ramsay, 1991, p. 557).

6. This deliberately provocative study should, perhaps, be taken with a pinch of salt. Not only do the researchers conveniently background the statistic that over 90 per cent of the sample thought management–employee relations were good, but they underplay the

problem that besets many correlational studies – the unequivocal attribution of the direction of causality. Furthermore, even they have to admit a strong positive relationship between two-way, interactive employee involvement – a defining feature of 'soft' HRM models – and a good employee relations climate.

7. EC data suggests that Britain's relative position in terms of both labour costs and productivity within the EC has remained unchanged over the period 1981–91 (Commission of European Communities, 1993).

Bibliography

Abbegglen, J.C. and Stalk, G. (1985) *Kaisha: The Japanese Corporation*, New York: Basic Books.

Abercrombie, N., Hill, S. and Turner, B.S. (1984) *The Penguin Dictionary of Sociology*, Harmondsworth: Penguin.

Abernathy, W., Clark, K.B. and Kantrow, A.M. (1981) 'The new industrial competition', *Harvard Business Review*, 59(5): 69–77.

Abrahamson, E. (1996) 'Management fashion', *Academy of Management Review*, 21(1): 254–85.

ACAS (1988) *Labour Flexibility in Britain: The 1987 ACAS Survey*, Occasional Paper, 41, London: ACAS.

Ackers, P. and Payne, J. (1998) 'British trade unions and social partnership: rhetoric, reality and strategy', *International Journal of Human Resource Management*, 9(3): 529–49.

Ackroyd, S. and Proctor, S. (1998) 'British manufacturing organization and workplace relations: some attributes of the new flexible firm', *British Journal of Industrial Relations*, 36(2): 163–83.

Addison, J.T. and Siebert, W.S. (1992) 'The Social Charter: whatever next?', *British Journal of Industrial Relations*, 30(4): 495–513.

Aglietta, M. (1979) *A Theory of Capitalist Regulation*, London: New Left Books

Aglietta, M. (1984) 'Long term trends in the American economy and possible future', in L. Lindberg, A. Lejins and K. Engberg (eds), *American Futures, Conference Paper 4*, Stockholm: The Swedish Institute of International Affairs: 17–29.

Ahlstrand, B. and Purcell, J. (1988) 'Employee relations strategy in the multi-divisional company', *Personnel Review*, 17(3): 3–11.

Alchian, A.A. and Demsetz, H. (1972) 'Production, information costs and economic organization', *American Economic Review*, 62(11): 777–95.

Allen, K. (1991) 'Personnel management on the line: how middle managers view the function', *Personnel Management*, 23(6): 40–3.

Allen, N.J. and Meyer, J.P. (1990) 'The measurement and antecedents of affective, continuance and normative commitment to the organization', *Journal of Occupational Psychology*, 63(1): 1–18.

Alston, J.P. (1986) *The American Samurai: Blending American and Japanese Management Practices*, New York: de Gruyter.

Alvesson, M. (1993) 'Organizations as rhetoric: knowledge-intensive firms and the struggle with ambiguity', *Journal of Management Studies*, 30(6): 997–1015.

Alvesson, M. (1995) *Management of Knowledge-intensive Companies*, Berlin/New York: de Gruyter.

Ambler, A. and Overholt, M. (1982) 'Are quality circles right for your company?', *Personnel Journal*, 61: 829–31.

Amin, A. (1991) 'Flexible specialization and small firms in Italy: myths and realities', in A. Pollert, (ed.), *Farewell to Flexibility?*, Oxford: Blackwell: 119–37.

Ansoff, H. (1965) *Corporate Strategy*, Harmondsworth: Penguin.

Anthony, P. D. (1990) 'The paradox of the management of culture or "he who leads is lost"', *Personnel Review*, 19(4): 3–8.

Anthony, P. D. (1994) *Managing Culture*, Milton Keynes: Open University Press.

Anthony, P. D. (1995) 'Talking culture'. Unpublished working paper.

Argyris, C. and Schön, D. (1978) *Organizational Learning*, Reading, Mass.: Addison-Wesley.

Armstrong, M. (1987) 'Human resource management: a case of the emperor's new clothes?', *Personnel Management*, 19(8): 30–5.

Armstrong, P. (1989) 'Limits and possibilities for HRM in an age of management accountancy', in J. Storey (ed.), *New Perspectives on Human Resource Management*, London: Routledge: 154–66.

Arthur, J. B. (1992) 'The link between business strategy and industrial relations systems in American steel minimills', *Industrial and Labor Relations Review*, 45(3): 488–506.

Arthur, J. B. (1994) 'Effects of human resource systems on manufacturing performance and turnover', *Academy of Management Journal*, 37(3): 670–87.

Arthur, M. (1994) 'Rover managers learn to take a back seat', *Personnel Management*, 26(1): 58–63.

Atkinson, J. (1984) 'Manpower strategies for flexible organisations', *Personnel Management*, 16(8): 28–31.

Atkinson, J. (1989) 'Four stages of adjustment to the demographic downturn', *Personnel Management*, 21(8): 20–4.

Atkinson, J. and Meager, N. (1986) *New Forms of Work Organisation*, IMS Report, 121, Brighton: Institute of Manpower Studies.

Auerbach P. (1989) 'Multinationals and the British economy', in F. Green (ed.), *The Restructuring of the British Economy*, London: Harvester.

Bacon, N. and Blyton, P. (2000) 'High road and low road teamworking: perceptions of management rationales and organizational and human resource outcomes', *Human Relations*, 53(11): 1425–58.

Bain, G. S. and Price, R. (1983) 'Union growth: dimensions, determinants and destiny', in G. S. Bain (ed.), *Industrial Relations in Britain*, Oxford: Blackwell, 3–33.

Baird, L. and Meshoulam, I. (1988) 'Managing the two fits of strategic human resource management', *Academy of Management Review*, 13(1): 116–28.

Baldamus, W. W. (1961) *Efficiency and Effort*, London: Tavistock.

Balkin, D. B. and Gomez-Mejia, L. R. (1987) 'The relationship between organizational strategy, pay strategy and compensation effectiveness', *Working paper*, University of Colorado at Boulder.

Bamber, G. J. and Lansbury, R. D. (eds) (1993) *International and Comparative Industrial Relations: A Study of Market Economies*, London and New York: Routledge.

Barham, K., Fraser, J. and Heath, L. (1988) *Management for the Future*, Berkhamsted and London: Ashridge Management College and FME.

Barker, J. R. (1993) 'Tightening the iron cage: concertive control in self-managed teams', *Administrative Science Quarterly*, 38(3): 408–37.

Barney, J. (1991) 'Firm resources and sustained competitive advantage', *Journal of Management*, 17(1): 99–120.

Baron, J. and Krebs, D. (1999) 'Consistent human resource practices', *California Management Review*, 41(3): 29–53.

Barrett, M. (1980) *Women's Oppression Today*, London: Verso.

Bartlett, C. A. and Yoshihara, H. (1988) 'New challenges for Japanese multinationals: is organization adaptation their Achilles heel?', *Human Resource Management*, 27(1): 19–43.

Bassett, P. (1986) *Strike Free. New Industrial Relations in Britain*, London: Macmillan.

Batstone, E. (1980) 'What have personnel managers done for industrial relations?', *Personnel Management*, 12(6): 36–9.

Batstone, E. (1984) *Working Order*, Oxford: Blackwell.

Batstone, E., Ferner, A. and Terry, M. (1984) *Consent and Efficiency*, Oxford: Blackwell.

Batstone, E. and Gourley, S. (with H. Levie and R. Moore) (1986) *Unions, Unemployment and Innovation*, Oxford: Blackwell.

Batt, R. (2000) 'Strategic segmentation in front line services: matching customers, employees and human resource systems', *International Journal of Human Resource Management*, 11(3): 540–61.

Batt, R. (2002) 'Managing customer services: human resource practices, quit rates, and sales growth', *Academy of Management Journal*, 45(3): 587–97.

Baudrillard, J. (1981) *For a Critique of the Political Economy of the Sign*, St Louis, Mass.: Telas.

Baudrillard, J. (1983) *Simulations*, New York: Semiotext (e).

Bauman, Z. (1990) 'Modernity and ambivalence', *Theory, Culture and Society*, 7: 2–3.

Bauman, Z. (1991) *Modernity and the Holocaust*, Oxford: Polity (first published 1989).

Bean, R. (1994) *Comparative Industrial Relations: An Introduction to Cross-National Perspectives*, London and New York: Routledge.

Beardwell, I. (1991/2) 'The "new industrial relations"?: a review of the debate', *Human Resource Management Journal*, 2(2): 1–7.

Beaumont, P. B. (1990) *Change in Industrial Relations*, London: Routledge.

Beaumont, P. B. (1992) 'Annual review article 1991', *British Journal of Industrial Relations*, 30(1): 107–25.

Beaumont, P. B. (1993) *Human Resource Management, Key Concepts and Skills*, London: Sage.

Becker, B. E. and Gerhart, B. (1996) 'The impact of human resource management on organizational performance: progress and practice', *Academy of Management Journal*, 39(4): 779–801.

Becker, B. E. and Huselid, M. A. (1998) 'High performance work systems and firm performance: a synthesis of research and managerial implications', in G. R. Ferris (ed.), *Research in Personnel and Human Resource Management*, Vol. 16, Greenwich, Conn.: JAI Press, 53–101.

Becker, B. E., Huselid, M. A., Pickus, P. S. and Spratt, M. F. (1997) 'HR as a source of shareholder value: research and recommendations', *Human Resource Management*, 36(1): 39–47.

Becker, H. S. (1960) 'Notes on the concept of commitment', *American Journal of Sociology*, 66: 289–96.

Beechey, V. and Perkins, T. (1987) *A Matter of Hours: Women, Part-time Work and the Labour Market*, Cambridge: Polity.

Beer, M. and Spector, B. (1985) 'Corporate wide transformations in human resource management', in R. E. Walton and P. R. Lawrence (eds), *Human Resource Management, Trends and Challenge*, Boston: Harvard Business School Press, 219–53.

Beer, M., Spector, B., Lawrence, P., Quinn Mills, D. and Walton, R. (1985) *Human Resource Management: A General Manager's Perspective*, Glencoe, Ill.: Free Press.

Beer, S. (1972) *Brain of the Firm: The Managerial Cybernetics of Organization*, London: Allen Lane.

Bell, D. (1974) *The Coming of Post-Industrial Society*, Harmondsworth: Penguin.

Bell, D. (1987) 'The world and the United States in 2013', *Daedalus*, 116.

Benjamin, W. (1969) *Illuminations*, New York: Schocken.

Bennett, A. and Smith-Gavine (1988a) 'The percentage utilization of labour index (PUL)', in D. Bosworth (ed.), *Working Below Capacity*, London: Macmillan.

Bennett, A. and Smith-Gavine (1988b) 'Index of percentage utilization of labour', *Bulletin to Co-operating Firms* 53 (March).

Bennis, W. G. (1966) *Changing Organizations*, New York: McGraw-Hill.

Best, S. and Kellner, D. (1991) *Postmodern Theory: Critical Interrogations*, London: Macmillan.

Better Schools, Cmnd 9469 (1985) London: HMSO.

Birley, S. and Westhead, P. (1990) 'Growth and performance contrasts between "types" of small firms', *Strategic Management Journal*, 11(7): 535–57.

Blackler, F. H. M. (1995) 'Knowledge, knowledge work and organizations: an overview and interpretation', *Organization Studies*, 16(6): 1021–46.

Blackler, F. H. M. and Brown, C. A. (1980) *Whatever Happened to Shell's New Philosophy of Management?: Lessons for the 1980s from a Major Socio-Technical Intervention of the 1960s*, Farnborough: Saxon House.

Blauner, R. (1964) *Alienation and Freedom*, Chicago: University of Chicago Press.

Block, F. (1985) 'Economy and nostalgia', *Dissent*, (Fall), 498–500.

Blunt, P. (1989) 'Strategies for human resource development in the Third World', opening address to the *International Human Resource Development Conference*, University of Manchester, 25–28 June.

Blyton, P. and Turnbull, P. (eds) (1992) *Reassessing Human Resource Management*, London: Sage.

Blyton, P. and Turnbull, P. (1994) *The Dynamics of Employee Relations*, London: Macmillan.

Boselie, P., Paauwe, J. and Jansen, P. (2001) 'Human resource management and performance: lessons from the Netherlands', *International Journal of Human Resource Management*, 12(7): 1107–25.

Boselie, P., Paauwe, J. and Richardson, R. (2003) 'Human resource management, institutionalization and organizational performance: a comparison of hospitals, hotels and local government', *International Journal of Human Resource Management*, 14(8): 1407–29.

Bowen, D. E. and Schneider, B. (1988) 'Services marketing and management: implications for organizational behaviour', *Research in Organizational Behavior*, 10: 43–80.

Boxall, P. F. (1992) 'Strategic human resource management: beginnings of a new theoretical sophistication?', *Human Resource Management Journal*, 2(3): 60–79.

Boxall, P. (1996) 'The strategic HRM debate and the resource-based view of the firm', *Human Resource Management Journal*, 6(3): 59–75.

Boxall, P. and Purcell, J. (2003) *Strategy and Human Resource Management*, Basingstoke: Palgrave – now Palgrave Macmillan.

Boyacigiller, N. and Adler, N. (1991) 'The parochial dinosaur: organization science in a global context', *Academy of Management Review*, 16(2): 262–90.

Bracker, J. (1980) 'The historical development of the strategic management concept', *Academy of Management Review*, 5(2): 219–24.

Bradley, K. and Hill, S. (1987) 'Quality circles and management interests', *Industrial Relations*, 26(1): 68–82.

Braverman, H. (1974) *Labor and Monopoly Capital*, New York: Monthly Review Press.

Brewster, C. (1995) 'HRM: The European dimension', in J. Storey (ed.), *Human Resource Management: A Critical Text*, London: Routledge, 309–31.

Brewster, C. and Burnois, F. (1991) 'Human resource management: a European perspective', *Personnel Review*, 20(6), 4–13.

Brewster, C. and Hegewisch, A. (eds) (1994) *Policy and Practice in European Human Resource Management*, London: Routledge.

Brewster, C. and Larsen, H.H. (1999) *Human Resource Management in Northern Europe*, Basingstoke: Macmillan – now Palgrave Macmillan.

Brewster, C. and Tyson, S. (eds) (1991) *International Comparisons in Human Resource Management*, London: Pitman.

Brewster, C., Gill, C. and Richbell, S. (1983) 'Industrial relations policy: a framework for analysis', in K. Thurley and S. Wood (eds), *Industrial Relations and Management Strategy*, Cambridge: Cambridge University Press, 67–72.

Brewster, C., Mayrhofer, W. and Morley, M. (2000) *New Challenges for European Human Resource Management*, Basingstoke: Macmillan – now Palgrave Macmillan.

Brown, B. and Perry, S. (1994) 'Removing the financial performance halo from *Fortune*'s "Most Admired Companies"', *Academy of Management Journal*, 37(5): 1347–59.

Brown, J. and Duguid, P. (1991) 'Organizational learning and communities of practice: toward a unified view of working, learning and innovation', *Organization Science*, 2(1): 40–57.

Brown, W. and Walsh, J. (1991) 'Pay determination in Britain in the 1980s: the anatomy of decentralization', *Oxford Review of Economic Policy*, 7(1): 44–59.

Brown, W., Deakin, S., Nash, D. and Oxenbridge, S. (2000) 'The employment contract: from collective procedures to individual rights', *British Journal of Industrial Relations*, 38(4): 611–29.

Bruce, M. (1987) 'Managing people first – bringing the service concept into British Airways', *Industrial and Commercial Training* (March/April): 21–6.

Brunsson, N. (1982) 'The irrationality of action and action rationality: decisions, ideologies and organizational actions', *Journal of Management Studies*, 19(1): 29–44.

Buller, P. F. (1988) 'Successful partnerships: HR and strategic planning in eight top firms', *Organizational Dynamics* (Fall): 17–43.

Buller, P. F. and Napier, N. K. (1993) 'Strategy and human resource management integration in fast growth versus other mid-sized firms', *British Journal of Management*, 4(2): 77–90.

Burawoy, M. (1979) *Manufacturing Consent*, Chicago: University of Chicago Press.

Burawoy, M. (1985) *The Politics of Production*, London: Verso.

Burrell, G. (1988) 'Modernism, post-modernism and organizational analysis 2: the contribution of Michel Foucault', *Organizational Studies*, 9(2): 221–35.

Burrell, G. (1992) 'Back to the future: time and organization', in M. Reed and M. Hughes (eds), *Rethinking Organization*, London: Sage, 165–83.

Burrell, G. (1993) 'Eco and the Bunneymen', in J. Hassard and M. Parker (eds), *Postmodernism and Organizations*, London: Sage, 71–82.

Burrell, G. (1994) 'Modernism, postmodernism and organizational analysis 4: the contribution of Jürgen Habermas', *Organizational Studies*, 15(1): 1–19.

Burrell. G. (1997) *Pandemonium – Towards a Retro Organization Theory*, London: Sage.

Burrell, G. and Morgan, G. (1979) *Sociological Paradigms and Organizational Analysis*, London: Heinemann.

Butler, J. E. (1988) 'Human resource management as a driving force in business strategy', *Journal of General Management*, 13(3): 316–38.

Cadbury, E. (1912) *Experiments in Industrial Organization*, London: Longman.

Calás, M. B. and Smircich, L. (1992) 'Re-writing gender into organizational theorizing: directions from feminist perspectives', in M. Reed and M. Hughes (eds), *Rethinking Organization, New Directions in Organization Theory and Analysis*, London: Sage, 227–53.

Callinicos, A. (1989) *Against Postmodernism*, Cambridge and Oxford: Polity and Blackwell.

Callon, M. (1986) 'The sociology of an actor network', in M. Callon, J. Law and A. Rip (eds), *Mapping the Dynamics of Science and Technology*, London: Macmillan.

Cannell, M. and Long, P. (1991) 'What's changed about incentive pay?', *Personnel Management*, 23(10): 58–63.

Cannell, M. and Wood, S. (1992) *Incentive Pay*, London: IPM.

Capelli, P. (1985) 'Competitive pressures and labour relations in the airline industry', *Industrial Relations*, 22(3): 316–38.

Capelli, P. and McKersie, R. B. (1987) 'Management strategy and the redesign of work rules', *Journal of Management Studies*, 24(5): 441–62.

Casey, B. (1991) 'Survey evidence on trends in "non-standard" employment', in A. Pollert (ed.), *Farewell to Flexibility?*, Oxford: Blackwell: 179–99.

Casey, B., Lakey, J., Cooper, H. and Elliot, J. (1991) 'Payment systems: a look at current practice', *Employment Gazette* (August): 53–8.

Castells, M. (1996) *The Rise of the Networked Society: The Information Age, Vol. 1*, Oxford: Blackwell.

Chakravarthy, B. S. (1984) 'Strategic self-renewal: a planning framework for today', *Academy of Management Review*, 9(3): 536–47.

Chandler, A. D. (1962) *Strategy and Structure: Chapters in the History of the American Industrial Enterprise*, Cambridge, Mass.: MIT Press.

Chandler, A. D. (1977) *The Visible Hand: The Managerial Revolution in American Business*, Cambridge, Mass.: Harvard University Press.

Charlwood, A. (2004) 'The new generation of trade union leaders and prospects for union revitalization', *British Journal of Industrial Relations*, 42(2): 379–97.

Child, J. (1985) 'Managerial strategies, new technology and the labour process', in D. Knights *et al.*, (eds), *Job Redesign, Critical Perspectives on the Labour Process*, Aldershot: Gower: 107–41.

Child, J., Loveridge, R., Harvey, J. and Spencer, A. (1984) 'Microelectronics and the quality of employment in services', in P. Marstrand (ed.), *New Technology and the Future of Work*, London: Frances Pinter: 163–90.

Chin, R. and Benne, K. D. (1976) 'General strategies for effecting changes in human systems', in K. D. Benne, W. G. Bennis, R. Chin and K. E. Corey (eds), *The Planning of Change*, New York: Holt, Rinehart & Winston.

Christianson, R. (1986) 'Human resources in the emerging growth environment', *Human Resource Planning*, 9(4): 161–5.

Citizens' Advice Bureaux (1993) *Job Insecurity*, London: Social Policy Section, Citizens', Advice Bureaux.

Clark, J. (1993) 'Full flexibility and self-supervision in an automated factory', in J. Clark (ed.), *Human Resource Management and Technical Change*, London: Sage, 116–36.

Clark, J., McLoughlin, I., Rose, H. and King, R. (1988) *The Process of Technological Change*, Cambridge: Cambridge University Press.

Clark, R. (1979) *The Japanese Company*, New Haven, Conn: Yale University Press.

Clark, T. and Fincham, R. (eds) (2002) *Management Consulting*, Oxford: Blackwell.

Clegg, S. (1990) *Modern Organizations: Organization Studies in the Postmodern World*, London: Sage.

Clegg, S. and Dunkerley, D. (1980) *Organization, Class and Control*, London: Routledge & Kegan Paul.

Cockburn, C. (1985) *Machinery of Dominance: Women, Men and Technical Know-How*, London: Pluto.

Cohen, R. and Kennedy, P. (2000) *Global Sociology*, Basingstoke: Macmillan – now Palgrave Macmillan.

Cohen, Y. and Pfeffer, J. (1986) 'Organizational hiring standards', *Administrative Science Quarterly*, 31(1): 1–24.

Collard, R. and Dale, B. (1989) 'Quality circles', in K. Sisson (ed.) *Personnel Management in Britain*, Oxford: Blackwell, 356–77.

Collinson, D. L. (1987) 'Who controls selection?', *Personnel Management*, 19(5): 32 5.

Collinson, D. L. (1988) *Barriers to Fair Selection: A Multi-Sector Study of Recruitment Practices*, Equal Opportunities Commission Research Series, London: HMSO.

Collinson, D. L. (1991) '"Poachers turned gamekeepers": are personnel managers one of the barriers to equal opportunities?', *Human Resource Management Journal*, 1(3): 58–76.

Collis, D. J. and Montgomery, C. A. (1995) 'Competing on resources: strategy for the 1990s', *Harvard Business Review*, 73(4): July/August, 118–28.

Colvin, G. (1992) 'How to pay the CEO right', *Fortune* (6 April): 28–36.

Commission of the European Communities (1993) *Employment in Europe: 1993*, Luxembourg: Office for Official Publications of the European Communities.

Constable, J. and McCormick, R. (1987) *The Making of British Managers*, London: British Institute of Management.

Coombs, R. and Green, G. (1989) 'Work organization and product change in the service sector: the case of the UK health service', in S. Wood (ed.) *The Transformation of Work?*, London: Unwin Hyman.

Coombs, R. and Jones, B. (1988) 'Alternative successors to Fordism', Paper presented at the conference on *Society, Information and Space*, Swiss Federal Institute of Technology, Zurich (21–22 January), Manchester and Bath: UMIST and Bath University, mimeo.

Cooper, R. (1989) 'Modernism, postmodernism and organizational analysis 3: The contribution of Jacques Derrida', *Organizational Studies*, 10(4): 479–502.

Cooper, R. and Burrell, G. (1988) 'Modernism, postmodernism and organizational analysis: an introduction', *Organization Studies*, 9(1): 91–112.

Coopey, J. and Hartley, J. (1991) 'Reconsidering the case for organizational commitment', *Human Resource Management Journal*, 1(3): 18–32.

Cooper, R. and Law, J. (1995) 'Organization: distal and proximal views', in S. Bacharach (ed.), *Research in the Sociology of Organizations*, Greenwich, Conn.: JAI Press.

Coutts, K. and Godley, W. (1989) 'The British economy under Mrs Thatcher', *Political Quarterly*, 60(2): 137–51.

Crosby, P. B. (1979) *Quality is Free*, New York: McGraw-Hill.

Cross, M. (1988) 'Changes in working practices in UK manufacturing 1981–88', *Industrial Relations Review and Report*, 415 (May) 2–10.

Crouch, C. (2001) 'A Third Way in industrial relations?', in S. White (ed.), *New Labour: The Progressive Future?* Basingstoke: Palgrave.

Crouch, C., Finegold, D. and Sako, M. (1999) *Are Skills the Answer? The Political Economy of Skill Creation in Advanced Industrial Societies*, Oxford: Oxford University Press.

Crystal, G. S. (1991) *In Search of Excess: The Overcompensation of American Executives*, New York: W. W. Norton.

Cully, M., Woodland, S., O'Reilly, A. and Dix, G. (1999) *Britain at Work*, London: Routledge.

Cuming, M. W. (1975) *The Theory and Practice of Personnel Management* (3rd edn), London: Heinemann.

Curtice, J. (1987) 'Interim report: party politics', in R. Jowell *et al*, (eds), *British Social Attitudes: the 1987 Report*, Aldershot: Gower/SCPR.

Cyert, R. M. and March, J. G. (1963) *A Behavioral Theory of the Firm*, Englewood Cliffs, N.J.: Prentice Hall.

Daft, R. L. and Weick, K. E. (1984) 'Toward a model of organizations as interpretation systems', *Academy of Management Review*, 9(2): 284–95.

Dale, B. G. and Plunkett, J. J. (eds) (1990) *Managing Quality*, London: Philip Allan.

Dale, B. G., Lascelles, D. M. and Plunkett, J. J. (1990) 'The process of total quality management', in B. G. Dale and J. J. Plunkett (eds), *Managing Quality*, London: Philip Allan, 3–18.

Daniel, W. W. (1987) *Workplace Industrial Relations and Technical Change*, London: Frances Pinter.

Dasey, R. (1981) 'Women in computing', *Women and Training News*, 3 (Summer).

Dastmalchian, A., Blyton, P. and Adamson, R. (1991) *The Climate of Workplace Relations*, London: Routledge.

Deal, T. E. and Kennedy, A. (1982) *Corporate Cultures*, Reading, Mass.: Addison-Wesley.

Delaney, J. T. and Huselid, M. A. (1996) 'The impact of human resource management practices on perceptions of organizational performance', *Academy of Management Journal*, 39(4): 241–6.

Delbridge, R. (2003) 'Workers under lean manufacturing', in D. Holman, T. D. Wall, C. W. Clegg, P. Sparrow and A. Howard (eds), *The New Workplace: People, Technology and Organisation*, Chichester: Wiley, pp. 19–36

Delbridge, R. and Oliver, N. (1991) 'Narrowing the gap?, Stock turns in the Japanese and western car industries', *International Journal of Production Research*, 29(10): 2083–95.

Delbridge, R. and Turnbull, P. (1992) 'Human resource maximization: the management of labour under just-in-time manufacturing systems', in P. Blyton and P. Turnbull (eds), *Reassessing Human Resource Management*, London: Sage, 56–73.

Delery, J. (1998) 'Issues of fit in strategic human resource management: implications for research', *Human Resource Management Review*, 8(3): 289–309.

Delery, J. and Doty, D. (1996) 'Modes of theorizing in strategic human resource management: tests of universalistic, contingency, and configurational performance predictions', *Academy of Management Journal*, 39(4): 802–35.

Deming, W. E. (1982) *Quality, Productivity and Competitive Position*, Cambridge, Mass.: MIT Press.

Department of Education and Science (1983) *Training Quality*, Cmnd 8836, London: HMSO.

Department of Employment (1991) *Industrial Relations in the 1990s – Proposals for Further Reform of Industrial Relations and Trade Union Law*, Cm. 1602, London: HMSO.

Department of Health (1989) *Working for Patients*, Cmm 555, London: HMSO.

Department of Health and Social Security (1979) *Patients First: A Consultative Paper on the Structure and Management of the National Health Service in England and Wales*, London: HMSO.

Derrida, J. (1973) *Speech and Phenomena*, Evanston, Ill.: North-Western University Press.

Derrida, J. (1976) *Of Grammatology*, Baltimore, Md: Johns Hopkins University Press.

Derrida, J. (1978) *Writing and Difference*, London: Routledge & Kegan Paul.

Derrida, J. (1981) *Positions*, Chicago: University of Chicago Press.

Derrida, J. (1982) *Margins of Philosophy*, Brighton: Harvester.

Devanna, M. A., Fombrun, C. J. and Tichy, N. M. (1984) 'A framework for strategic human resource management', in C. J. Fombrun et al,, *Strategic Human Resource Management*, New York: Wiley.

DfEE (2000) *Opportunity for All: Skills for the New Economy*, London: DfEE.

Dickens, R., Gregg, P., Machin, S., Manning, A. and Wadsworth, J. (1993) 'Wage councils: was there a case for abolition?', *British Journal of Industrial Relations*, 31(4): 515–29.

DiMaggio, P. and Powell, W. (1983) 'The iron cage revisited: institutional isomorphism and collective rationality in organizational fields', *American Sociological Review*, 48(2): 147–60.

DiMaggio, P. and Powell, W. (eds) (1991) *The New Institutionalism in Organizational Analysis*, Chicago: University of Chicago Press.

Disney, R. (1990) 'Explanations of the decline in trade union density: an appraisal', *British Journal of Industrial Relations*, 28(2): 165–78.

Disney, R., Gosling, A. and Machin, S. (1993) 'What has happened to trade union recognition in Britain?', LSE, CEP *Discussion Paper*, 130, London.

Doeringer, P. B. and Piore, M. J. (1971) *Internal Labor Markets and Manpower Analysis*, Lexington, Mass.: Heath.

Dohse, K., Jurgens, U. and Malsch, T. (1985) 'From "Fordism", to "Toyotism"?, The social organization of the labour process in the Japanese automobile industry', *Politics and Society*, 14(2): 115–46.

Donaldson, T. and Preston, L. E. (1995) 'The stakeholder theory of the corporation: concepts, evidence and implications', *Academy of Management Review*, 20(1): 65–91.

Dreyfus, H. L. and Rabinow, P. (1982) *Michel Foucault: Beyond Structuralism and Hermeneutics*, Brighton: Harvester.

Drucker, P. (1961) *The Practice of Management*, London: Mercury Books (first published 1954).

Drucker, P. (1988) 'The coming of the new organization', *Harvard Business Review*, 66(1): 45–53.

Drucker, P. (1989) *The New Realities*, London: Heinemann.

DTI (1998) *Fairness at Work*, London: DTI.

du Gay, P. (1996) *Consumption and Identity at Work*, London: Sage.

du Gay, P. and Salaman, G. (1992) 'The cult(ure) of the customer', *Journal of Management Studies*, 29(5): 615–33.

Dunlop, J. and Weil, D. (1996) 'Diffusion and performance of modular production in the US apparel industry', *Industrial Relations*, 35(4): 334–55.

Dunn, S. (1990) 'Root metaphor in the old and new industrial relations', *British Journal of Industrial Relations*, 28(1): 1–31.

DuPuy, F. (1999) *The Customer's Victory*, Basingstoke: Macmillan – now Palgrave Macmillan.

Dyer, L. and Shafer, R. (1999) 'Creating organizational agility: implications for human resource management', in P. Wright, L. Dyer, J. Boudreau and G. Milkovich (eds), *Research in Personnel and Human Resource Management (Supplement 4: Strategic Human Resources Management in the Twenty-First Century)*, Stamford, Conn. and London: JAI Press.

Easterby-Smith, M. (1990) 'Creating a learning organization', *Personnel Review*, 19(5): 24–8.

Easterby-Smith, M. and Lyles, M. (eds) (2003) *Blackwell Handbook of Organizational Learning and Knowledge Management*, Oxford: Blackwell.

Easterby-Smith, M., Burgoyne, J. and Araujo, L. (eds) (1999) *Organizational Learning and the Learning Organization: Developments in Theory and Practice*, London: Sage.

Edelman, L. F., Bresnen, M., Newell, S., Scarbrough, H. and Swan, J. (2004) 'The benefits and pitfalls of social capital: Empirical evidence from two organizations in the United Kingdom', *British Journal of Management*, 15, S59–S69.

Edwards, P. K. (1987) *Managing the Factory*, Oxford: Blackwell.

Edwards, P. K. and Marginson, P. (1988) 'Trade unions, pay bargaining and industrial action', in P. Marginson, P. K. Edwards, R. Martin, J. Purcell and K. Sisson, *Beyond the Workplace: Managing Industrial Relations in the Multi-Establishment Enterprise*, Oxford: Blackwell.

Edwards, P. K. and Whitston, C. (1991) 'Workers are working harder': effort and shopfloor relations in the 1980s', *British Journal of Industrial Relations*, 29(4): 593–601.

Edwards, P. K. and Wright, M. (2001) 'High involvement work systems and performance outcomes: the strength of variable, contingent and context-bound relationships', *International Journal of Human Resource Management*, 12(4): 568–85.

Edwards, R. (1979) *Contested Terrain. The Transformation of the Workplace in the Twentieth Century*, London: Heinemann.

Elger, T. (1991) 'Task flexibility and intensification of labour in UK manufacturing in the 1980s', in A. Pollert (ed.), *Farewell to Flexibility?*, Oxford: Blackwell, 46–66.

Eribon, D. (1992) *Michel Foucault*, London: Faber & Faber.

Evans, S., Ewing, K. and Nolan, P. (1992) 'Industrial relations and the British economy in the 1990s: Mrs Thatcher's legacy', *Journal of Management Studies*, 29(5): 571–89.

Fairclough, N. (1991) 'What might we mean by "enterprise discourse"?', in R. Keat and N. Abercrombie (eds), *Enterprise Culture*, London: Routledge, 38–57.

Farnham, D. (1990) *Personnel in Context* (3rd edn), London: IPM.

Fayol, H. (1949) *General and Industrial Management*, London: Pitman (first published in 1916).

Feigenbaum, A. V. (1983) *Total Quality Control*, New York: McGraw-Hill.

Felstead, A. (1991) 'Franchising: a testimony to the "enterprise economy" and economic restructuring in the 1980s?', in A. Pollert (ed.), *Farewell to Flexibility?*, Oxford: Blackwell, 215–38.

Ferner, A. and Hyman R. (eds) (1992) *Industrial Relations in the New Europe*, Oxford: Blackwell.

Fernie, S., Metcalf, D. and Woodland, S. (1994) 'Does HRM boost employee-management relations?', *Working Paper*, 548, Centre for Economic Performance and Industrial Relations Department, London School of Economics.

Festinger, L. (1957) *A Theory of Cognitive Dissonance*, Stanford, Ca.: Stanford University Press.

Filipcova, B. and Filipec, J. (1986) 'Society and concepts of time', *International Social Science Journal*, 107: 19–32.

Financial Times (1992) 'Developing cars across borders', (27 February).

Finegold, D. and Soskice, D. (1988) 'The failure of training in Britain: analysis and prescription', *Oxford Review of Economic Policy*, 4(3): 21–53.

Fineman, S. (ed.) (1993) *Emotion in Organizations*, London: Sage.

Fineman, S. and Sturdy, A. (2001) ' "Struggles" for the control of affect resistance as politics *and* emotion', in A. Sturdy, I. Grugulis and H. Willmott (eds), *Customer Service*, Basingstoke: Macmillan – now Palgrave Macmillan: 135–56.

Fitzgerald, L., Johnston, R., Brignall, S., Silvestro, R. and Voss, C. (1991) *Performance Measurement in Service Businesses*, London: Chartered Institute of Management Accounting.

Flanders, A. (1965) *Industrial Relations: What's Wrong with the System?*, London: Faber.

Flood, P. C., Turner, T., Ramamoorthy, N. and Pearson, J. (2001) 'Causes and consequences of psychological contracts among knowledge workers in the high technology and financial services industries', *International Journal of Human Resource Management*, 12(7): 1152–65.

Fombrun, C., Tichy, N. M. and Devanna, M. A. (eds) (1984) *Strategic Human Resource Management*, New York: Wiley.

Fosh, P. and Heery, E. (1990) *Trade Unions and their Members*, London: Macmillan.

Foucault, M. (1972) *The Archaeology of Knowledge*, London: Routledge.

Foucault, M. (1973) *The Birth of the Clinic*, London: Tavistock.

Foucault, M. (1977) *Discipline and Punish*, London: Allen Lane.

Foucault, M. (1980) *Power/Knowledge*, Brighton: Harvester.

Foucault, M. (1981) *The History of Sexuality, 1: The Will to Knowledge*, Harmondsworth: Penguin.

Foucault, M. (1985) *The History of Sexuality, 2: The Use of Pleasure*, New York: Pantheon.

Foucault, M. (1985) *The History of Sexuality, 3: The Care of the Self*, New York: Pantheon.

Foulkes, F. K. (1975) 'The expanding role of the personnel function', *Harvard Business Review*, 53(2): 71–84.

Foulkes, F. K. (1986) (ed.) *Strategic Human Resource Management, A Guide for Effective Practice*, Englewood Cliffs, N.J.: Prentice Hall.

Foulkes, F. K. and Morgan, H. M. (1977) 'Organizing and staffing the personnel function', *Harvard Business Review*, 55(3): 142–54.

Fowler, A. (1987) 'When chief executives discover HRM', *Personnel Management*, 19(1): 3.

Fox, A. (1966) *Industrial Sociology and Industrial Relations*, Research Paper 3, Royal Commission on Trade Unions and Employers' Associations, London: HMSO.

Fox, A. (1974) *Beyond Contract: Work, Power and Trust Relations*, London: Faber & Faber.

Fox, S. (1990) 'Strategic HRM: postmodern conditioning for the corporate culture', *Management Education and Development*, 21(3): 191–206.

Fox, S. and McLeay, S. (1992) 'An approach to researching managerial labour markets: HRM, corporate strategy and financial performance in UK manufacturing', *International Journal of Human Resource Management*, 3(3): 523–54.

Freeman, R. and Pelletier, J. (1990) 'The impact of industrial relations legislation on British union density', *British Journal of Industrial Relations*, 28(2): 141–64.

French, W. L. and Bell, C. H. (1973) *Organization Development*, Englewood Cliffs, N.J.: Prentice-Hall.

Friedman, A. L. (1977) *Industry and Labour*, London: Macmillan.

Friedman, A. L. (1984) 'Management strategies, market conditions and the labour process', in F. H. Stephen (ed.), *Firms, Organization and Labour*, London: Macmillan, 176–200.

Friedman, M. (1970) 'The social responsibility of business is to increase profit', *New York Times Magazine*, 13 September.

Frost, P. J., Moore, L. F., Louis, M. R., Lundberg, C. C. and Martin, J. (eds) (1983) *Organizational Culture*, Beverly Hills: Sage.

Fullerton, H. and Price, C. (1991) 'Cultural change in the NHS', *Personnel Management*, 23(3): 50–3.

Galbraith, J. R. (1973) *Designing Complex Organizations*, Reading, Mass.: Addison-Wesley.

Gall, G. and McKay, S. (1994) 'Trade union derecognition in Britain, 1988–1994', *British Journal of Industrial Relations*, 32(3): 433–48.

Gallie, D. (1988) 'Employment, unemployment and social stratification', in D. Gallie (ed.), *Employment in Britain*, Oxford: Blackwell.

Gallie, D. (1989) 'Trade union allegiance and decline in British urban labour markets', ESRC/ SCEL *Working Paper* 9, London.

Gardner, T. M., Wright, P. M. and Gerhart, B. (1999) 'The HR-firm performance relationship: can it be in the mind of the beholder?' Working Paper, Center for Advanced Human Resources Studies, Cornell University, Ithaca, NY.

Garrahan, P. and Stewart, P. (1992) *The Nissan Enigma: Flexibility at Work in a Local Economy*, London: Mansell.

Geary, J. (1992) 'Employment flexibility and human resource management', *Work, Employment and Society*, 6(2): 251–70.

Geertz, C. (1973) *The Interpretation of Culture*, London: Hutchinson.

Gennard, J. and Kelly, J. (1994) 'Human resource management: The views of personnel directors', *Human Resource Management Journal*, 5(1): 15–32.

Gergen, K. J. (1992) 'Organization theory in the postmodern era', in M. Reed and M. Hughes (eds), *Rethinking Organization*, London: Sage, 207–26.

Gerhart, B., Wright, P. M., McMahan, G. C. and Snell, S. A. (2000) 'Measurement error in research on human resources and firm performance: how much error is there and how does it influence effect size estimates?', *Personnel Psychology*, 53(4): 803–34.

Gibbons, M., Limoges, C., Nowotny, H., Schwartzman, S., Scott, P. and Trow, M. (1994) *The New Production of Knowledge: The Dynamics of Science and Research in Contemporary Societies*, London: Sage.

Giddens, A. (1990) *The Consequences of Modernity*, Cambridge and Oxford: Polity and Blackwell.

Giddens, A. (1998) *The Third Way*, Cambridge: Polity.

Giddens, A. (2000a) *Runaway World: How Globalization is Reshaping our Lives*, London: Routledge.

Giddens, A. (2000b) *The Third Way and Its Critics*, Cambridge: Polity.

Gittleman, M., Horrigan, M. and Joyce, M. (1998) ' "Flexible" workplace practices: evidence from a nationally representative survey', *Industrial and Labor Relations Review*, 52(1): 99–115.

Glover, I. A. and Kelly, M. P. (1987) *Engineers in Britain: A Sociological Study of the Engineering Dimension*, London: Allen & Unwin.

Glueck, W. F. (1974) *Personnel, A Diagnostic Approach*, Dallas, Texas: Business Publications.

Godet, M. (1987) 'Ten unfashionable and controversial findings on Japan', *Futures* (August) 371 84.

Goffman, E. (1969) 'The characteristics of total institutions', in A. Etzioni (ed.), *A Sociological Reader on Complex Organizations*, New York: Holt, Rinehart & Winston.

Golden, B. R. (1992) 'The past is the past – or is it? The use of retrospective accounts as indicators of past strategy', *Academy of Management Journal*, 35(4): 848–60.

Golden, K. A. and Ramanujam, V. (1985) 'Between a dream and a nightmare: on the integration of the human resource management and strategic planning processes', *Human Resource Management*, 24(4): 429–52.

Golzen, G. (1988) 'How "company culture" can block innovation', *Financial Times* (24 January).

Goodman, J., Armstrong, E., Davis, J. and Wagner, A. (1977) *Rule Making and Industrial Peace*, London: Croom Helm.

Goold, M. and Campbell, A. (1987) *Strategies and Styles*, Oxford: Blackwell.

Gordon, G. G. (1985) 'The relationship of corporate culture to industry sector and corporate performance', in R. H. Kilmann, M. J. Saxton and R. Serpa, *Gaining Control of the Corporate Culture*, San Francisco: Jossey Bass.

Gospel, H. F. and Palmer, G. (1993) *British Industrial Relations* (2nd edn), London: Routledge.

Gospel, H. F. and Wood, S. (2003) (eds) *Representing Workers: Trade Union Recognition and Membership in Britain*, London: Routledge.

Gouldner, A. W. (1954) *Wildcat Strike*, New York: Antioch Press.

Gowler, D., Legge, K. and Clegg, C. (1993) (eds), *Case Studies in Organizational Behaviour and Human Resource Management*, London: Paul Chapman.

Graham, I. (1988) 'Japanization as mythology', *Industrial Relations Journal*, 19(1): 69–75.

Gramsci, A. (1971) *Selections from Prison Notebooks*, London: New Left Books.

Granovetter, M. S. (1973) 'The strength of weak ties', *American Journal of Sociology*, 78, 1360–80.

Granovetter, M. S. (1985) 'Economic action and social structures: the problem of embeddedness', *American Journal of Sociology*, 91(3): 481–510.

Green, F. and Felstead, A. (1994) 'Training during recession', *Work, Employment and Society*, 8(2): 199–219.

Greenwood, R. and Hinings, C. R. (1996) 'Understanding radical organizational change: bringing together the old and the new institutionalism', *Academy of Management Review*, 21(4): 1022–55.

Gregg, P. and Yates, A. (1991) 'Changes in wage-setting arrangements and trade union presence in the 1980s', *British Journal of Industrial Relations*, 29(3): 361–76.

Gregg, P., Machin, S. and Symanski, S. (1993) 'The disappearing relationship between directors' pay and corporate performance', *British Journal of Industrial Relations*, 31(1): 1–9.

Gregory, K. (1983) 'Native view paradigms: multiple cultures and culture conflicts in organizations', *Administrative Science Quarterly*, 28(3): 359–76.

Grey, C. (2003) 'The real world of Enron's auditors', *Organization*, 10(3): 572–6.

Grey, C. and Mitev, N. (1995) 'Re-engineering organizations: a critical appraisal', *Personnel Review*, 24(1): 6–18.

Grint, K. (1994) 'Reengineering history: social resonances and business process reengineering', *Organization*, 1(1): 179–201.

Grint, K. and Willcocks, L. (1995) 'Business process re-engineering in theory and practice: business paradise regained?', *New Technology, Work and Employment*, 19(2): 99–109.

Grugulis, I., Vincent, S. and Hebson, G. (2003) 'The rise of the "network organisation" and the decline of discretion', *Human Resource Management Journal*, 13(2): 45–59.

Guardian (2004) 'Inside the grim world of the gangmasters', 27 March.

Guest, D. E. (1987) 'Human resource management and industrial relations', *Journal of Management Studies*, 24(5): 503–21.

Guest, D. E. (1989a) 'Personnel and HRM: can you tell the difference?', *Personnel Management*, 21(1): 48–51.

Guest, D. E. (1989b) 'Human resource management: its implications for industrial relations and trade unions', in J. Storey (ed.), *New Perspectives on Human Resource Management*, London: Routledge, 41–55.

Guest, D. E. (1990a) 'Have British workers been working harder in Thatcher's Britain?, A re-consideration of the concept of effort', *British Journal of Industrial Relations*, 28(3): 293–312.

Guest, D. E. (1990b) 'Human resource management and the American dream', *Journal of Management Studies*, 27(4): 378–97.

Guest, D. E. (1991) 'Personnel management: the end of orthodoxy?', *British Journal of Industrial Relations*, 29(2): 149–76.

Guest, D. E. (1992a) 'Employee commitment and control', in J. F. Hartley and G. M. Stephenson (eds), *Employment Relations*, Oxford: Blackwell, 111–35.

Guest, D. E. (1992b) 'Right enough to be dangerously wrong: an analysis of the *In Search of Excellence* phenomenon', in G. Salaman *et al*, (eds), *Human Resource Strategies*, London and Milton Keynes: Sage/Open University Press, 5–19.

Guest, D. E. (1995) 'Human resource management, trade unions and industrial relations', in J. Storey (ed.), *Human Resource Management: A Critical Text*, London: Routledge, 110–41.

Guest, D. E. (1997) 'Human resource management and performance: a review and research agenda', *International Journal of Human Resource Management*, 8(3): 263–76.

Guest, D.E. (1998) 'Is the psychological contract worth taking seriously?', *Journal of Organizational Behavior*, 19, S1, 649–664.

Guest, D.E. (1999) 'Human resource management – the workers' verdict', *Human Resource Management Journal*, 9(3): 5–25.

Guest, D.E. (2001a) 'Industrial relations and human resource management', in Storey, J. (ed.), *Human Resource Management, A Critical Text (Second edition)*, London: Thomson Learning, 96–113.

Guest, D.E. (2001b) 'Human resource management: when research confronts theory', *International Journal of Human Resource Management*, 12(7): 1092–1106.

Guest, D.E. and Conway, N. (1997) *Employee Motivation and the Psychological Contract*, London: CIPD.

Guest, D.E. and Conway, N. (1998) *Fairness at Work and the Psychological Contract*, London: CIPD.

Guest, D.E. and Conway, N. (2000) *The Psychological Contract and the Public Sector*, London: CIPD.

Guest, D.E. and Conway, N. (2001) *Organisational Change and the Psychological Contract*, London: CIPD.

Guest, D.E. and Conway, N. (2004) 'Exploring the paradox of unionised worker dissatisfaction', *Industrial Relations Journal*, 35(2), 102–21.

Guest, D.E. and Hoque, K. (1993) 'Are greenfield sites better at human resource management?', LSE, CEP *Discussion Paper*, 435, London.

Guest, D.E. and Hoque, K. (1994a) 'Yes, personnel does make a difference', *Personnel Management*, 26(11): 40–4.

Guest, D.E. and Hoque, K. (1994b) 'The good, the bad and the ugly: employment relations in non-union workplaces', *Human Resource Management Journal*, 5(1): 1–14.

Guest, D.E. and Peccei, R. (1994) 'The nature and causes of effective human resource management', *British Journal of Industrial Relations*, 32(2): 219–42.

Guest, D.E. and Peccei, R. (1998) *The Partnership Company*, London: IPA.

Guest, D.E. and Peccei, R. (2001) 'Partnership at work: mutuality and the balance of advantage', *British Journal of Industrial Relations*, 39(2): 207–36.

Guest, D.E. and Rosenthal, P. (1993) 'Industrial relations in greenfield sites', in D. Metcalf and S. Milner (eds), *New Perspectives on Industrial Disputes*, London: Routledge.

Guest, D.E., Mackenzie Davey, K. and Patch, A. (2000) 'The employment relationship, the psychological contract and knowledge management: securing employees' trust and contribution', *Proceedings of the Knowledge Management Concepts and Controversies Conference*, University of Warwick, 9th–10th February.

Guest, D.E., Michie, J., Conway, N. and Sheehan, M. (2003) 'Human resource management and corporate performance in the UK', *British Journal of Industrial Relations*, 41(2): 291–314.

Guest, D.E., Peccei, R. and Fulcher, A. (1993) 'Culture change and quality improvement in British Rail', in D. Gowler, K. Legge and C. Clegg (eds), *Case Studies in Organizational Behaviour and Human Resource Management*, London: Paul Chapman, 126–33.

Gunz, H. and Whitley, R. (1985) 'Managerial cultures and industrial strategies in British firms', *Organization Studies*, 6(3): 247–73.

Habermas, J. (1972) *Knowledge and Human Interests*, London: Heinemann.

Habermas, J. (1974) *Theory and Practice*, London: Heinemann.

Hakim, C. (1988) 'Self-employed in Britain: a review of recent trends and current issues', *Work, Employment and Society*, 2(4): 421–50.

Hakim, C. (1990) 'Core and periphery in employers' workforce strategies: evidence from the 1987 ELUS survey', *Work, Employment and Society*, 4(2): 157–88.

Hall, M. (1994) 'Industrial relations and the social dimension of European integration: Before and after Maastricht', in R. Hyman and A. Ferner (eds), *New Frontiers in European Industrial Relations*, Oxford: Blackwell, 281–311.

Hall, P. and Soskice, D. (eds) (2001) *Varieties of Capitalism: The Institutional Foundations of Comparative Advantage*, Oxford: Oxford University Press.

Hamel, G. and Prahalad, C. (1994) *Competing for the Future*, Boston, Mass: Harvard Business School Press.

Handy, C. B. (1984) *The Future of Work*, Oxford: Blackwell.

Handy, C. (1987) *The Making of Managers*, London: MSC/NEDO/BIM.

Hannan, M. T. and Freeman, J. (1988) *Organizational Ecology*, Cambridge, Mass.: Harvard University Press.

Hanson, M. T., Nohria, N. and Tierney, T. (1999) 'What's your strategy for managing knowledge?', *Harvard Business Review*, 77(2): March–April, 106–16.

Harrison, S., Hunter, D. J., Marnoch, G. and Pollitt, C. (1989) *The Impact of General Management in the National Health Service*, Milton Keynes: Open University/Nuffield Institute for Health Service Studies.

Harvey, D. (1989) *The Condition of Postmodernity*, Oxford: Blackwell.

Harvey-Jones, J. (1988) *Making it Happen: Reflections on Leadership*, London: Collins.

Hassard, J. (1993) 'Postmodernism and organizational analysis: an overview', in J. Hassard and M. Parker (eds), *Postmodernism and Organizations*, London: Sage, 1–23.

Hatch, J. and Clinton, A. (2000) 'Job growth in the 1990s: a retrospect', *Monthly Labor Review*, December, 3–18.

Hawkins, K. (1987) *Unemployment* (3rd edn), Harmondworth: Penguin.

Hay, C. and Watson, M. (1998) 'The discourse of globalization and the logic of no alternative: rendering the contingent necessary in the downsizing of New Labour's aspirations for government', Paper presented at the Annual Conference of the Political Studies Association, University of Keele.

Hebdige, D. (1989) 'After the masses', *Marxism Today* (January): 48–53.

Heery, E., Kelly, J. E. and Waddington, J. (2003) 'Union revitalisation in Britain', *European Journal in Industrial Relations*, 9(1): 79–97.

Held, D., McGraw, A., Goldblatt, D. and Perraton, J. (1999) *Global Transformations*, Cambridge: Polity.

Hendry, C. (1991) 'Manufacturing change at Belma Joints', in K. Legge, C. Clegg and N. Kemp (eds), *Case Studies in Information Technology, People and Organizations*, Manchester and Oxford: NCC/Blackwell, 35–47.

Hendry, C. (1993) 'Personnel leadership in technical and human resource change', in J. Clark (ed.), *Human Resource Management and Technical Change*, London: Sage, 78–100.

Hendry, C. and Pettigrew, A. (1986) 'The practice of strategic human resource management', *Personnel Review*, 15(5): 3–8.

Hendry, C. and Pettigrew, A. (1987) 'Banking on HRM to respond to change', *Personnel Management*, 19(11), 29–32.

Hendry, C. and Pettigrew, A. (1988) 'Multi-skilling in the round', *Personnel Management*, 20(4): 36–43.

Hendry, C. and Pettigrew, A. (1990) 'Human resource management: an agenda for the 1990s', *International Journal of Human Resource Management*, 1(1): 17–44.

Hendry, C. and Pettigrew, A. (1992) 'Patterns of strategic change in the development of human resource management', *British Journal of Management*, 3(3): 137–56.

Hendry, C., Jones, A., Arthur, M. and Pettigrew, A. (1991) *Human Resource Development in Small to Medium Sized Enterprises*, Sheffield: Department of Employment.

Hendry, C., Pettigrew, A. and Sparrow, P. (1988) 'Changing patterns of human resource management', *Personnel Management*, 20(11), 37–41.

Hendry, J. (1990) 'The problem with Porter's generic strategies', *European Management Journal*, 8(4): 443–50.

Henley, A. and Tsakalotos, E. (1992) 'Corporatism and the European labour market after 1992', *British Journal of Industrial Relations*, 30(4): 567–86.

Henwood, D. (1996) 'Work and its future', *Left Business Observer*, 72 (Internet edn).

Herman, S. M. (1968) *The People Specialists*, New York: Knopf.

Herzberg, F. (1966) *Work and the Nature of Man*, Cleveland: World Publishing.

Heskett, J., Sasser, E. and Schlesinger, L. (1997) *The Service Profit Chain*, New York: Free Press.

Hickson, D. J., Butler, R. J., Cray, D., Mallory, G. R. and Wilson, D. C. (1986) *Top Decisions: Strategic Decision-Making in Organizations*, Oxford: Blackwell; San Francisco: Jossey-Bass.

Hill, C. W. L. and Hoskisson, R. E. (1987) 'Strategy and structure in the multiproduct firm', *Academy of Management Review*, 12(2): 331–41.

Hill, P. (1971) *Towards a New Philosophy of Management*, Epping: Gower Press.

Hill, S. (1991a) 'How do you manage a flexible firm: the total quality model', *Work, Employment and Society*, 5(3): 397–415.

Hill, S. (1991b) 'Why quality circles failed but total quality management might succeed', *British Journal of Industrial Relations*, 29(4): 541–68.

Hirst, P. and Thompson, G. (1999) *Globalization in Question* (2nd edn), Cambridge: Polity.

Hirst, P. and Zeitlin, J. (1991) 'Flexible specialization versus post-Fordism: theory, evidence and policy implications', *Economy and Society*, 20(1): 1–55.

Hochschild, A. R. (1983) *The Managed Heart: Commercialization of Human Feeling*, Berkeley: University of California Press.

Hodson, R. (2001) *Dignity at Work*, Cambridge: Cambrige University Press.

Hofstede, G. (1980) *Culture's Consequences: International Differences in Work Related Values*, Beverly Hills: Sage.

Holden, L. and Livian, Y. (1992) 'Does strategic training policy exist? Some evidence from ten European countires', *Personnel Review*, 21(1): 12–23.

Holloway, J. (1987) 'The red rose of Nissan', *Capital and Class*, 32: 142–64.

Holman, D. (2003) 'Call centres', in D. Holman, T. D. Wall, C. W. Clegg, P. Sparrow and A. Howard (eds), *The New Workplace, A Guide to the Human Impact of Modern Working Practices*, Chichester: Wiley, 115–35.

Hope Hailey, V. (2001) 'Breaking the mould? Innovation as a strategy for corporate renewal', *International Journal of Human Resource Management*, 12(7): 1126–40.

Höpfl, H. J. (1993) 'Culture and commitment: British Airways', in D. Gowler, K. Legge and C. Clegg (eds), *Case Studies in Organizational Behaviour and Human Resource Management*, London: Paul Chapman, 117–25.

Höpfl, H. J., Smith, S. and Spencer, S. (1992) 'Values and valuations: corporate culture and job cuts', *Personnel Review*, 21(1): 24–38.

Hosmer, L. T. (1995) 'Trust: the connecting link between organizational theory and philosophical ethics', *Academy of Management Review*, 20(2): 379–403.

House of Lords (1985) *Report from the Select Committee on Overseas Trade*, London: HMSO.

Howell, C. (2004) 'Is there a Third Way for industrial relations?', *British Journal of Industrial Relations*, 42(1): 1–22.

Hudson, R. (1989) *Wrecking a Region: State Policies, Party Politics and Regional Change in the North East of England*, London: Psion.

Hunt, J. W. and Lees, S. (1987) 'Hidden extras: how people get overlooked in takeovers', *Personnel Management*, 19(7): 24–8.

Hunter, L. and MacInnes, J. (1992) 'Employers and labour flexibility: the evidence from the case studies', *Employment Gazette* (June): 307–15.

Hunter, L., McGregor, A., MacInnes, J. and Sproull, A. (1993) 'The "flexible firm": strategy and segmentation', *British Journal of Industrial Relations*, 31(3): 383–407.

Huselid, M. A. (1995) 'The impact of human resource management practices on turnover, productivity, and corporate financial performance', *Academy of Management Journal*, 38(3): 635–72.

Husted, K. and Michailova, S. (2002) 'Diagnosing and fighting knowledge-sharing hostility', *Organizational Dynamics*, 31(1): 60–73.

Hutton, W. (1995) *The State We're In*, London: Jonathan Cape.

Hyman, J. (1992) *Training at Work*, London: Routledge.

Hyman, R. (1987) 'Strategy or structure?, Capital, labour and control', *Work, Employment and Society*, 1(1): 25–55.

Hyman, R. (1989) 'Why industrial relations?', in R. Hyman, *The Political Economy of Industrial Relations. Theory and Practice in a Cold Climate*, London: Macmillan, 3–19.

Hyman, R. (1991) 'Plus ça change?, The theory of production and the production of theory', in A. Pollert (ed.), *Farewell to Flexibility?*, Oxford: Blackwell, 259–83.

Hyman, R. and Ferner, A. (eds) (1994) *New Frontiers in European Industrial Relations*, Oxford: Blackwell.

Ichniowski, C., Shaw, K. and Prennushi, G. (1997) 'The effects of human resource management practices on productivity: a study of steel finishing lines', *American Economic Review*, 87, 291–334.

Industrial Relations Review and Report (IRRR) (1989a) 'Developments in multi-employer bargaining: I', Report 440 (May): 6–11.

IRRR (1989b) 'Decentralized bargaining in practice: I', Report 454 (December).

IRRR (1992) 'Single union deals in perspective', Report 523 (November): 6–15.

Institute of Personnel Management (1963) 'Statement on personnel management and personnel policies', *Personnel Management* (March).

Jackall, R. (1988) *Moral Mazes: The World of Corporate Manager*, New York: Oxford University Press.

Jackson, S. E., Schuler, R. S. and Rivero, J. C. (1989) 'Organizational characteristics as predictors of personnel practice', *Personnel Psychology*, 42(4): 727–86.

Jahoda, M. (1972) *Marienthal. The Sociography of an Unemployed Community*, London: Tavistock (first publ. Leipzig, 1933).

Janis, I. (1972) *Victims of Groupthink*, Boston: Houghton Mifflin.

Jaques, E. (1964) *The Time-Span Handbook*, London: Heinemann.

Jaques, E. (1990) 'In praise of hierarchy', *Harvard Business Review*, 68(1): 127–33.

Jarratt Report (1985) Committee of Vice-Chancellors and Principals of the Universities of the UK, Steering Committee for Efficiency Studies in Universities, *Report*, London: CVCP.

Jenkins, C. (1973) 'Is personnel still under powered?', *Personnel Management*, 5(6): 34–5.

Jenkins, R. (1986) *Racism and Recruitment*, Cambridge: Cambridge University Press.

Johnson, S. (1991) 'The small firm and the UK labour market in the 1980s', in A. Pollert (ed.), *Farewell to Flexibility?*, Oxford: Blackwell, 239–55.

Jones, A. K. V. (1990) 'Quality management the Nissan way', in B. G. Dale and J. J. Plunkett (eds), *Managing Quality*, London: Philip Allan, 44–51.

Jones, B. (1988) 'Work and flexible automation in Britain: a review of developments and possibilities', *Work, Employment and Society*, 2(4): 451–86.

Jones, B. (1989) 'Flexible automation and factory politics: Britain in contemporary perspective', in P. Hirst and J. Zeitlin (eds), *Reversing Industrial Decline*, Leamington Spa: The Berg Press, 95–121.

Jones, B. and Rose, M. (1986) 'Re-dividing labour: factory politics and work re-organization in the current industrial transition', in K. Purcell, S. Wood, A. Waton and S. Allen, (eds), *The Changing Experience of Employment: Restructuring and Recession*, London: Macmillan, 33–57.

Jucius, M. J. (1975) *Personnel Management* (8th edn) Homewood, Ill.: Irwin.

Juran, J. M. (1988) *Juran on Planning for Quality*, New York: Free Press.

Juran, J. M., Seder, L. A. and Gryna, F. M. Jr. (eds) (1962) *Quality Control Handbook* (2nd edn), New York: McGraw-Hill.

Kakabadse, A. and Tyson, S. (eds) (1993) *Cases in European Human Resource Management*, London: Routledge.

Kamoche, K. and Mueller, F. (1998) 'Human resource management and the appropriation-learning perspective', *Human Relations*, 51(8): 1033–60.

Kanter, R. M. (1984) *The Change Masters: Corporate Entrepreneurs at Work*, London: Allen & Unwin.

Kanter, R. M. (1989) *When Giants Learn to Dance*, New York: Simon & Schuster.

Kanter, R. M., Stein, B. A. and Todd, J. D. (1992) *The Challenge of Organizational Change*, New York: Free Press.

Kaplan, R. and Norton, D. (1996) *The Balanced Scorecard: Translating Strategy into Action*, Boston, Mass: Harvard Business School Press.

Kaplan, R. and Norton, D. (2001) *The Strategy Focused Organization*, Boston, Mass: Harvard Business School Press.

Katz, D. and Khan, R. L. (1966) *The Social Psychology of Organizations*, New York: Wiley.

Kay, J. (1993) *Foundations of Corporate Success. How Business Strategies Add Value*, Oxford: Oxford University Press.

Keat, R. (1991) 'Introduction: starship Britain or universal enterprise?', in R. Keat and N. Abercrombie (eds), *Enterprise Culture*, London: Routledge, 1–17.

Keat, R. and Abercrombie, N. (eds) (1991) *Enterprise Culture*, London: Routledge.

Keenoy, T. (1990a) 'HRM: a case of the wolf in sheep's clothing', *Personnel Review*, 19(2): 3–9.

Keenoy, T. (1990b) 'HRM: rhetoric, reality and contradiction', *International Journal of Human Resource Management*, 1(3): 363–84.

Keenoy, T. (1991) 'The roots of metaphor in the old and new industrial relations', *British Journal of Industrial Relations*, 29(2): 313–28.

Keenoy, T. (1999) 'HRM as a hologram', *Journal of Management Studies*, 36(1): 1–23.

Keenoy, T. and Anthony, P. (1992) 'HRM: metaphor, meaning and morality', in P. Blyton and P. Turnbull (eds), *Reassessing Human Resource Management*, London: Sage, 233–55.

Keep, E. (1989) 'A training scandal?', in K. Sisson (ed.), *Personnel Management in Britain*, Oxford: Blackwell, 177–202.

Keep, E. (1994) 'Vocational education and training for the young', in K. Sisson (ed.), *Personnel Management* (2nd edn), Oxford: Blackwell, 299–333.

Keep, E. and Rainbird, H. (2000) 'Towards the learning organization?', in S. Bach and K. Sisson (eds), *Personnel Management* (3rd edn), Oxford: Blackwell, 173–94.

Kellner, D. (1988) *Jean Baudrillard: From Marxism to Postmodernism and Beyond*, Cambridge: Polity.

Kelly, A. (1991) 'The enterprise culture and the welfare state: restructuring the management of the health and personal social services', in R. Burrow (ed.), *Deciphering the Enterprise Culture*, London: Routledge.

Kelly, J. E. (1999) 'Social partnership in Britain: good for profits, bad for jobs and unions', *Communist Review*, 30, 3–10.

Kelly, J. E. (1990) 'British trade unionism 1979–89: change, continuity and contradictions', *Work, Employment and Society*, 4 (Special Issue): 29–65.

Kelly, J. E. and Heery, E. (1989) 'Full-time officers and trade union recruitment', *British Journal of Industrial Relations*, 27(2): 196–213.

Kelly, J. E. and Kelly, C. (1991) 'Them and us: social psychology and the "new industrial relations"', *British Journal of Industrial Relations*, 29(1): 25–48.

Kelly, J. E. and Willman, P. (2004) (eds) *Union Organization and Activity*, London: Routledge.

Kern, H. and Schumann, M. (1984) *Das Ende der Arbeitsteilung?*, Munich: Beck.

Kern, H. and Schumann, M. (1987) 'Limits of the division of labour: new production and employment concepts in West German industry', *Economic and Industrial Democracy*, 8: 151–70.

Kerr, J. L. (1982) 'Assigning managers on the basis of the life cycle', *Journal of Business Strategy*, 2(4): 58–65.

Kerr, J. L. (1985) 'Diversification strategies and managerial rewards: an empirical study', *Academy of Management Journal*, 28(1): 155–79.

Kerr, J. L. and Slocum, J. W. (1987) 'Managing corporate culture through reward systems', *Academy of Management Executive*, 1(12): 155–79.

Kessler, I. (1990) 'Flexibility and comparability in pay determination for professional civil servants', *Industrial Relations Journal*, 21(3): 194–208.

Kessler, I. (1994) 'Performance pay', in K. Sisson (ed.), *Personnel Management* (2nd edn), Oxford: Blackwell, 465–94.

Kessler, I. and Purcell, J. (1992) 'Performance related pay – objectives and application', *Human Resource Management Journal*, 2(3): 34–59.

Kessler, S. and Bayliss, F. (1992) *Contemporary Industrial Relations*, London: Macmillan.

Kieser, A. (1997) 'Rhetoric and myth in management fashion', *Organization*, 4(1): 49–74.

Kiesler, C. A. (1971) *The Psychology of Commitment: Experiments Linking Behavior to Belief*, New York: Academic Press.

Kiesler, C. A. and Sakumura, J. (1966) 'A test of a model for commitment '. *Journal of Personality and Social Psychology*, 3: 349–53.

Kinnie, N. (1985a) 'Local managers' control over industrial relations: myth and reality', *Personnel Review*, 14(2): 2–10.

Kinnie, N. (1985b) 'Changing management strategies in industrial relations', *Industrial Relations Journal*, 16(4): 17–24.

Kinnie, N. and Lowe, D. (1990) 'Performance related pay on the shopfloor', *Personnel Management*, 22(11), 45–9.

Kinnie, N., Purcell, J. and Hutchinson, S. (2000a) 'Managing the employment relationship in call centres', in K. Purcell (ed.), *Changing Boundaries in Employment*, Bristol: Bristol Academic Press, 163–94.

Kinnie, N., Purcell, J. and Hutchinson, S. (2000b) ' "Fun and surveillance": the paradox of high commitment management in call centres', *International Journal of Human Resource Management*, 11(5): 967–85.

Kirkbride, P. S. (ed.) (1994) *Human Resource Management in Europe*, London: Routledge.

Klein, J. A. (1991) 'A re-examination of autonomy in the light of new manufacturing practices', *Human Relations*, 44(1): 21–38.

Klein, L. (1976) *A Social Scientist in Industry*, Epping: Gower Press.

Klein, N. (2000) *No Logo*, London: Flamingo.

Knights, D. and McCabe, D. (2000) 'Bewitched, bothered and bewildered: the meaning and experience of teamworking for employees in an automobile company', *Human Relations*, 53(11): 1481–517.

Knights, D. and Morgan, G. (1990) 'The concept of strategy in sociology: a note of dissent', *Sociology*, 24(3): 275–43.

Knights, D. and Willmott, H. (1987) 'Organizational culture as management strategy: a critique and illustration from the financial services industry', *International Studies of Management and Organization*, 17(3): 40–63.

Kochan, T. and Barocci, T. (1985) *Human Resource Management and Industrial Relations: Text, Reading and Cases*, Boston: Little, Brown.

Kochan, T. and Dyer, L. (1992) 'Managing transformational change: the role of human resource professionals', paper for the Conference of the International Industrial Relations Association, Sydney.

Kochan, T. and Dyer, L. (1995) 'HRM: An American view', in J. Storey (ed.), *Human Resource Management: A Critical Text*, London: Routledge, 332–51.

Kochan, T., Katz, H. C. and McKersie, R. B. (1986) *The Transformation of American Industrial Relations*, New York: Basic Books.

Kochan, T., McKersie, R. B. and Capelli, P. (1984) 'Strategic choice and industrial relations theory', *Industrial Relations*, 23(1): 16–39.

Korczynski, M. (2002) *Human Resource Management in the Service Sector*, Basingstoke: Palgrave – now Palgrave Macmillan.

Kuhn, R. L. (1982) *Mid-sized Firms Success Strategies and Methodology*, New York: Praeger.

Labour Market Trends (2000) June, London: ONS.

Labour Market Trends (2004) London: ONS.

Labour Research Department (LRD) (1986) 'Flexibility', *Bargaining Report*, 56 (November) 5–12.

Lane, C. (1990) 'Vocational training and new production concepts in Germany: some lessons for Britain', *Industrial Relations Journal*, 21(4): 247–59.

Lash, S. (1990) *Sociology of Postmodernism*, London: Routledge.

Lash, S. and Urry, J. (1987) *The End of Organized Capitalism*, Cambridge and Oxford: Polity and Blackwell.

Lashley, C. (1997) *Empowering Service Excellence*, London: Cassell.

Latour, B. (1987) *Science in Action*, Milton Keynes: Open University Press.

Lave, J. and Wenger, E. (1991) *Situated Learning: Legitimate Peripheral Participation*, Cambridge: Cambridge University Press.

Law, J. (1992) 'Notes on the theory of the actor-network-ordering, strategy, and heterogeneity', *Systems Practice*, 5(4): 379–93.

Lawler, E. and Mohrman, S. (1985) 'Quality circles after the fad', *Harvard Business Review*, 63(1): 64–71.

Lawrence, P. R. and Lorsch, J. W. (1967) *Organization and Environment*, Boston: Graduate School of Business Administration, Harvard University.

Layard, R. and Nickell, S. (1988) 'The Thatcher miracle?', LSE, Centre for Labour Economics, Discussion Paper 343, London: LSE.

Legge, K. (1978) *Power, Innovation and Problem-Solving in Personnel Management*, London: McGraw-Hill.

Legge, K. (1986) 'Women in personnel management: uphill climb or downhill slide?', in A. Spencer and D. Podmore (eds), *In a Man's World*, London: Tavistock.

Legge, K. (1988) *Personnel Management in Recession and Recovery: A Comparative Analysis of What the Surveys Say, Personnel Review*, 17(2) (monograph issue).

Legge, K. (1989a) 'Human resource management – a critical analysis', in J. Storey (ed.), *New Perspectives on Human Resource Management*, London: Routledge, 19–40.

Legge, K. (1989b) *Information Technology: Personnel Management's Lost Opportunity?, Personnel Review*, 18(5) (monograph issue).

Legge, K. (1993) 'The role of personnel specialists: centrality or marginalization', in J. Clark (ed.), *Human Resource Management and Technical Change*, London: Sage, 20–42.

Legge, K. (1994) 'Managing culture: fact or fiction?', in K. Sisson (ed.), *Personnel Management* (2nd edn), Oxford: Blackwell, 397–433.

Legge, K. (1995) 'Rhetoric, reality and hidden agendas', in J. Storey (ed.), *Human Resource Management: A Critical Text*, London: Routledge, 33–59.

Legge, K. (1998) 'Is HRM ethical? Can HRM be ethical?', in M. Parker (ed.), *Ethics and Organizations*, London: Sage, 150–72.

Legge, K. (2000a) 'The ethical context of HRM: the ethical organisation in the boundaryless world', in D. Winstanley and J. Woodall (eds), *Ethical Issues in Contemporary Human Resource Management*, Basingstoke: Macmillan, 23–40.

Legge, K. (2000b) 'Personnel management in the lean organization', in S. Bach and K. Sisson (eds), *Personnel Management (Third Edition)*, Oxford: Blackwell, 43–69.

Legge, K. (2001) 'Silver bullet or spent round? Assessing the meaning of the "high commitment management"/performance relationship', in J. Storey (ed.), *Human Resource Management, A Critical Text (Second edition)*, London: Thomson Learning, 21–36.

Legge, K. (2002a) 'The making of an icon: the deconstruction and construction of September 11th', Paper presented at the 18th EGOS Colloquium, Barcelona, July.

Legge, K. (2002b) 'On knowledge, business consultants and the selling of total quality management', in T. Clark and R. Fincham, R. (eds), *Critical Consulting*, Oxford: Blackwell, 74–90.

Legge, K. (forthcoming 2005) 'Ethics at work', in M. Korczynski, R. Hodson and P. Edwards (eds), *Social Theory at Work*, Oxford: Oxford University Press.

Legge, K., Clegg, C. and Kemp, N. (eds) (1991) *Case Studies in Information Technology, People and Organizations*, Manchester/Oxford: NCC/Blackwell.

Leidner, R. (1993) *Fast Food, Fast Talk*, Berkeley, Calif.: University of California Press.

Lengnick-Hall, C. A. and Lengnick-Hall, M. L. (1988) 'Strategic human resources management: a review of the literature and a proposed typology', *Academy of Management Review*, 13(3): 454–70.

Leonard, D. (1998) *Wellsprings of Knowledge: Building and Sustaining Competitive Advantage*, Boston, Mass: Harvard Business School Press.

Lewin, K. (1951) *Field Theory in Social Science*, New York: Harper.

Lewis, R. (1991) 'Reforming industrial relations: law, politics and power', *Oxford Review of Economic Policy*, 7(1): 60–75.

Likert, R. (1961) *New Patterns of Management*, New York: McGraw-Hill.

Likert, R. (1967) *The Human Organization*, New York: McGraw-Hill.

Lindblom, C. E. (1959) 'The science of muddling through', *Public Administration Review*, 19: 79–88.

Linn, P. (1987) 'Gender stereotypes, technical stereotypes', in M. McNeil (ed.), *Gender and Expertise*, London: Free Association Books, 127–51.

Lipman-Blumen, J. (1984) *Gender, Roles and Power*, Englewood Cliffs, N.J.: Prentice-Hall.

Long, P. (1984) *The Personnel Specialists: A Comparative Study of Male and Female Careers*, London: IPM.

Long, P. (1986) *Performance Appraisal Revisited*, London: IPM.

Lorange, P. and Murphy, D. (1984) 'Bring human resources into strategic planning: systems design considerations', in C. Fombrun, N. Tichy and M. Devanna (eds), *Strategic Human Resource Management*, New York: Wiley, 275–96.

Lorsch, J. W. (1985) 'Strategic myopia: culture as an invisible barrier to change', in R. H. Kilmann, M. J. Saxton and R. Serpa, (eds), *Gaining Control of the Corporate Culture*, San Francisco: Jossey Bass.

Lovas, B. and Ghoshal, S. (2000) 'Strategy as guided evolution', *Strategic Management Journal*, 21(9): 875–96.

Lowendahl, B. (1997) *Strategic Management of Professional Service Firms*, Copenhagen: Copenhagen Business School Press.

Lukes, S. (1974) *Power – A Radical View*, London: Macmillan.

Lupton, T. (1964) *Industrial Behaviour and Personnel Management*, London: IPM.

Lyon, D. (1994) *The Electronic Eye*, Cambridge and Oxford: Polity.

Lyotard, J.-F. (1984) *The Postmodern Condition: A Report on Knowledge*, Manchester: Manchester University Press.

MacDuffie, J. P. (1995) 'Human resource bundles and manufacturing performance: organizational logic and flexible production systems in the world auto industry', *Industrial and Labor Relations Review*, 48(2): 197–221.

MacInnes, J. (1987a) 'Why nothing much has changed: recession, economic restructuring and industrial relations since 1979', *Employee Relations*, 9(1): 3–9.

MacInnes, J. (1987b) *Thatcherism at Work*, Milton Keynes: Open University Press.

MacIntyre, A. (1981) *After Virtue: A Study of Moral Theory*, London: Duckworth.

Mackay, L. (1986) 'The macho manager: it's no myth', *Personnel Management*, 18(1): 25–7.

Mackay, L. (1987) 'Personnel: changes disguising decline?', *Personnel Review*, 16(5): 3–11.

McCabe, D. L. and Dutton, J. E. (1993) 'Making sense of the environment: the role of perceived effectiveness', *Human Relations*, 46: 623–43.

McGee, G. W. and Ford, R. C. (1987) 'Two (or more?) dimensions of organizational commitment: re-examination of the affective and continuance commitment scales', *Journal of Applied Psychology*, 72: 638–41.

McGregor, A. and Sproull, A. (1992) 'Employers and the flexible workforce', *Employment Gazette*, 100, 225–34.

McGregor, D. (1960) *The Human Side of Enterprise*, New York: McGraw-Hill.

McKinsey and Co./NEDO (1988) *Performance and Competitive Success: Strengthening Competitiveness in UK Electronics*, London: McKinsey/NEDO.

McLoughlin, I. and Gourlay, S. (1989) 'Innovation and change in Roseland: a survey of high tech establishments', *Occasional Paper*, Kingston Business School (October).

McWilliams, A. and Smart, D. (1995) 'The resource-based view of the firm: does it go far enough in shedding the assumptions of the S-C-P paradigm?',*Journal of Management Inquiry*, 4(4): 309–16.

Machin, S. (2000) 'Union decline in Britain', *British Journal of Industrial Relations*, 38(4): 631–45.

Maister, D. (1994) *Managing the Professional Service Firm*, New York: Free Press.

Mangham, I. and Silver, M. S. (1986) *Management Training: Context and Practice*, London: ESRC.

Mangum, G. L. and Mangum, S. L. (1986) 'Temporary work: the flipside of job security', *International Journal of Manpower*, 7(1): 12–20.

Manning, K. (1983) 'The rise and fall of personnel', *Management Today* (March): 74–7.

Manwaring, T. and Wood, S. (1985) 'The ghost in the labour process', in D. Knights *et al.*, (eds), *Job Redesign, Critical Perspectives on the Labour Process*, Aldershot: Gower, 171–96.

Marchington, M. (1985) 'The macho-myth...', Letters, *Personnel Management*, 17(6): 61.

Marchington, M. (1992) *Managing the Team: A Guide to Successful Employee Involvement*, Oxford: Blackwell.

Marchington, M. (1993) 'Close to the customer: employee relations in food retailing', in D. Gowler, K. Legge and C. Clegg (eds), *Case Studies in Organizational Behaviour and Human Resource Management*, London: Paul Chapman, 134–43.

Marchington, M. (2001) 'Employee involvement at work', in J. Storey (ed.), *Human Resource Management, A Critical Text* (2nd edn), London: Thomson Learning, 232–52.

Marchington, M. and Grugulis, I. (2000) '"Best practice" HRM: perfect opportunity or dangerous illusion?', *International Journal of Human Resource Management*, 11(6): 1104–24.

Marchington, M. and Harrison, E. (1991) 'Customers, competitors and choice: employee relations in food retailing', *Industrial Relations Journal*, 22(4): 286–99.

Marchington, M. and Loveridge, R. (1983) 'Management decision-making and shop-floor participation', in K. Thurley and S. Wood (eds), *Industrial Relations and Management Strategy*, Cambridge: Cambridge University Press, 73–82.

Marchington, M. and Parker, P. (1990) *Changing Patterns of Employee Relations*, Brighton: Harvester Wheatsheaf.

Marchington, M., Goodman, J., Wilkinson, A. and Ackers, P. (1992) *New Developments in Employee Involvement*, Employment Department, *Research Series*, 2, London: HMSO.

Marchington, M., Wilkinson, A., Ackers, P. and Goodman, J. (1994) 'Understanding the meaning of participation: views from the workplace', *Human Relations*, 47(8): 867–94.

Marginson, P. (1991) 'Change and continuity in the employment structure of large companies', in A. Pollert (ed.), *Farewell to Flexibility?*, Oxford: Blackwell, 32–66.

Marginson, P. (1992) 'European integration and transnational management-union relations in the enterprise', *British Journal of Industrial Relations*, 30(4): 529–45.

Marginson, P. (1994) 'Multinational Britain: employment and work in an internationalized economy', *Human Resource Management Journal*, 4(4): 63–80.

Marginson, P., Armstrong, P., Edwards, P. and Purcell, J. with Hubbard, N. (1993) 'The control of industrial relations in large companies: an initial analysis of the second company level industrial relations survey', *Warwick Papers in Industrial Relations*, 45, IRRU, School of Industrial and Business Studies, University of Warwick (December).

Marginson, P., Edwards, P.K., Martin, R., Purcell, J. and Sisson, K. (1988) *Beyond the Workplace: Managing Industrial Relations in Multi-Plant Enterprises*, Oxford: Blackwell.

Marquardt, M. and Reynolds, A. (1994) *The Global Learning Organization*, Burr Ridge, Ill.: Irwin.

Marris, R. (1964) *The Economic Theory of Managerial Capitalism*, London: Macmillan.

Marsden, D. and Richardson, R. (1994) 'Performing for pay? The effect of "merit pay", on motivation in a public service', *British Journal of Industrial Relations*, 32(2): 243–61.

Marsden, D., Morris, T., Willman, P. and Wood, S. (1985) *The Car Industry: Labour Relations and Industrial Adjustment*, London: Tavistock.

Martin, H. J. (1985) 'Managing specialized corporate cultures', in R. H. Kilmann, M. J. Saxton and R. Serpa (eds), *Gaining Control of the Corporate Culture*, San Francisco: Jossey Bass.

Martin, R. (1987) 'The effect of unemployment upon the employed: a new realism in industrial relations?', in S. Fineman (ed.), *Unemployment, Personal and Social Consequences*, London: Tavistock, 219–34.

Martinez Lucio, M. and Weston, S. (1992) 'Human resource management and trade union responses: bringing the politics of the workplace back into the debate', in P. Blyton and P. Turnbull (eds), *Reassessing Human Resource Management*, London: Sage, 215–32.

Martinez Lucio, M. and Stuart, M. (2004) 'Swimming against the tide: social partnership, mutual gains and the revival of "tired" HRM', *International Journal of Human Resource Management*, 15(2): 410–24.

Maslow, A. H. (1943) 'A theory of human motivation', *Psychological Review*, 50, 370–96.

Mayo, E. (1933) *The Human Problems of an Industrial Civilisation*, New York: Macmillan

Mayo, E. (1945) *The Social Problems of an Industrial Civilization*, Cambridge, Mass.: Harvard University Press.

Meegan, R. (1988) 'A crisis of mass production?', in J. Allen and D. Massey (eds), *The Economy in Question*, London: Sage.

Meek, V. L. (1988) 'Organizational culture: origins and weaknesses', *Organizational Studies*, 9(4): 453–73.

Megginson, L. C. (1972) *Personnel – A Behavioral Approach to Administration* (revised edn) Homewood, Ill.: Irwin.

Melian-Gonzalez, S. and Verano-Tacorante, D. (2004) 'A new approach to the best practices debate: are best practices applied to all employees in the same way?', *International Journal of Human Resource Management*, 15(1): 56–75.

Mercer, D. (1987) *IBM: How the World's Most Successful Company is Managed*, Homewood, Ill.: Irwin.

Mercer, D. S. and Judkins, P. E. (1990) 'Rank Xerox: a total quality process', in B. G. Dale and J. J. Plunkett (eds), *Managing Quality*, London: Philip Allan, 297–306.

Merton, R. K. (1957) *Social Theory and Social Structure* (revised edn) Glencoe, Ill.: Free Press.

Metcalf, D. (1988) 'Trade Unions and economic performance: the British evidence', LSE Centre for Labour Economics, *Discussion Paper*, 320, London: LSE.

Metcalf, D. (1989) 'Water notes dry up: the impact of Donovan reform proposals and Thatcherism at work on labour productivity in British manufacturing industry', *British Journal of Industrial Relations*, 27(1): 1–31.

Metcalf, D. (1991) 'British unions: dissolution or resurgence?', *Oxford Review of Economic Policy*, 7(1): 18–32.

Metcalf, D. (1993) 'Industrial relations and economic performance', *British Journal of Industrial Relations*, 31(2): 255–83.

Meyer, H. (1987) 'How can we implement a pay for performance policy successfully?', in D. Balkin and L. Gomez-Mejia (eds), *New Perspectives on Compensation*, Englewood Cliffs, N.J.: Prentice-Hall.

Meyerson, D. and Martin, J. (1987) 'Cultural change: an integration of three different views', *Journal of Management Studies*, 24(6): 623–47.

Miles, R. E. and Snow, C. C. (1978) *Organizational Strategy, Structure and Process*, New York: McGraw-Hill.

Miles, R. E. and Snow, C. C. (1984) 'Designing strategic human resources systems', *Organizational Dynamics* (Summer): 36–52.

Miller, D. (1990) *The Icarus Paradox*, New York: HarperCollins.

Miller, D. (1993) 'The architecture of simplicity', *Academy of Management Review*, 18(1): 116–38.

Miller, P. (1987) 'Strategic industrial relations and human resource management – distinction, definition and recognition.', *Journal of Management Studies*, 24(4): 347–61.

Miller, P. (1991) 'Strategic human resource management: an assessment of progress', *Human Resource Management Journal*, 1(4): 23–39.

Miller, P. and Norburn, D. (1981) 'Strategy and executive reward: the mismatch in the strategic process', *Journal of General Management*, 6(4): 17–27.

Miller, S. (1993) 'The nature of strategic management', in R. Harrison (ed.), *Human Resource Management, Issues and Strategies*, Wokingham: Addison-Wesley, 3–33.

Mills, D. Q. (1985) 'Planning with people in mind', *Harvard Business Review*, 63(4): 97–105.

Mills, P. (1986) *Managing Service Industries*, Cambridge, Mass: Ballinger.

Millward, N., Bryson, A. and Forth, J. (2000) *All Change at Work?* London: Routledge.

Millward, N. and Stevens, M. (1986) *British Workplace Industrial Relations – 1980–1984* The DE/ESRC/PSI/ACAS Survey; London: Gower.

Millward, N., Stevens, M., Smart, D. and Hawes, W. R. (1992) *Workplace Industrial Relations in Transition* The ED/ESRC/PSI/ACAS Surveys, Aldershot: Dartmouth.

Mintzberg, H. (1978) 'Patterns in strategy formation', *Management Science*, 24(9): 934–48.

Mintzberg, H. (1987) 'Crafting strategy', *Harvard Business Review*, 65(4): 65–75.

Mintzberg, H. and Walters, J. A. (1985) 'Of strategies, deliberate and emergent', *Strategic Management Journal*(6): 257–72.

Mitter, S. (1985) 'Industrial restructuring and manufacturing homework: immigrant women in the UK clothing industry', *Capital and Class*, 27.

Monden, Y. (1983) *Toyota Production System*, Atlanta, Ga.: Industrial Engineering and Management Press.

Monks, J., Gilbert, R. and Beardwell, I. (1991/2) 'Is there a "new industrial relations"?', *Human Resource Management Journal*, 2(2): 74–82.

Moore, W. (1969) 'Climbers, riders, treaders', in B. Rosen, H. Crockett and C. Nunn (eds), *Achievement in American Society*, Cambridge, Mass.: Schenkmann Publishing.

Morgan, G. (1986) *Images of Organization*, London: Sage.

Morgan, G. (1988) *Riding the Waves of Change: Developing Managerial Competencies for a Turbulent World*, London: Sage.

Morgan, G. (2001) 'Transnational communities and business systems', *Global Networks*, 1(2): 113–30.

Morris, J. and Burgoyne, J. G. (1973) *Developing Resourceful Managers*, London: Institute of Personnel Management.

Morris, T. and Wood, S. (1991) 'Testing the survey method: continuity and change in British industrial relations', *Work, Employment and Society*, 5(2): 259–82.

Moult, G. (1990) 'Under new management: the practice of management in a world without certainties', *Management Education and Development*, 21(3): 171–82.

Mowday, R. T., Porter, L. W. and Steers, R. M. (1982) *Employee–Organization Linkages: The Psychology of Commitment, Absenteeism and Turnover*, New York: Academic Press.

Mowday, R. T., Steers, R. M. and Porter, L. W. (1979) 'The measurement of organizational commitment', *Journal of Vocational Behavior*, 14, 224–47.

Mroczkowski, T. and Hanaoka, M. (1989) 'Continuity and change in Japanese management', *California Management Review* (Winter): 39–53.

Mumford, E. and Hendricks, R. (1996) 'Business process re-engineering RIP', *People Management*, 3(9): 22–9.

Munro, R. (1994) 'Governing the new province of quality', in A. Wilkinson and H. Willmott (eds), *Making Quality Critical*, London: Routledge, 127–55.

Murray, R. (1989) 'Fordism and post-Fordism and "Benetton Britain"', in S. Hall and M. Jacques (eds), *New Times*, London: Lawrence & Wishart.

Nahapiet, J. and Ghoshal, S. (1998) 'Social capital, intellectual capital and organizational advantage', *Academy of Management Review*, 23(2): 242–66.

National Research Council (1991) *Pay for Performance*, Washington: National Academic Press.

NEDO (1986) *Changing Working Patterns: How Companies Achieve Flexibility to Meet New Needs*, London: NEDO.

Newell, H. J. (1991) *Field of Dreams: Evidence of 'New' Employee Relations in Greenfield Sites*, D.Phil. Dissertation, University of Oxford.

Newell, S., Robertson, M., Scarbrough, H. and Swan, J. (2002) *Managing Knowledge Work*, Basingstoke: Palgrave – now Palgrave Macmillan.

NHS Management Enquiry (1983) *The Griffiths Report*, London: DHSS/HMSO.

Nickell, S., Wadhwani, S. and Wall, M. (1989) *Union and Productivity Growth in Britain 1974–86: Evidence from UK Company Accounts Data*, London: LSE. Centre for Labour Economics, *Discussion Paper*, 353.

Niland, J. R., Lansbury, R. D. and Verevis, C. (eds) (1994) *The Future of Industrial Relations: Global Change and Challenges*, Thousand Oaks, London and New Delhi: Sage.

Nissan (1987) *Workshop Management.*

Niven, M. M. (1967) *Personnel Management 1913–1963*, London: IPM.

Nkomo, S. M. (1984) 'Prescription vs practice: the state of human resource planning in large U.S. organizations.', paper presented at the Southern Management Association meeting (14–17 November) New Orleans.

Nolan, P. (1989) 'Walk on water? Performance and industrial relations under Thatcher', *Industrial Relations Journal*, 20(2): 81–92.

Nolan, P. and Marginson, P. (1990) 'Skating on thin ice?, David Metcalf on trade unions and productivity', *British Journal of Industrial Relations*, 18(2): 225–47.

Nolan, P. and O'Donnell, K. (1991) 'Restructuring and the politics of renewal: the limits of flexible specialization', in A. Pollert (ed.), *Farewell to Flexibility*, Oxford: Blackwell, 158–75.

Nonaka, I. and Takeuchi, H. (1995) *The Knowledge Creating Company: How Japanese Companies Create the Dynamics of Innovation*, Oxford: Oxford University Press.

Noon, M. (1992) 'HRM: a map, model or theory?', in P. Blyton and P. Turnbull (eds), *Reassessing Human Resource Management*, London: Sage, 16–32.

Norris, C. (1982) *Deconstruction,Theory and Practice*, London: Methuen.

Norris, C. (1987) *Derrida*, London: Fontana.

Oakland, J. (1989) *Total Quality Management*, Oxford: Butterworth–Heinemann.

Offe, C. (1985) *Disorganized Capitalism*, Cambridge and Oxford: Polity and Blackwell.

Ogbonna, E. and Wilkinson, B. (1988) 'Corporate strategy and corporate culture: the management of change in the UK supermarket industry', *Personnel Review*, 17(6): 10–14.

Ogbonna, E. and Wilkinson, B. (1990) 'Corporate strategy and corporate culture: the view from the checkout', *Personnel Review*, 19(4): 9–15.

Ohmae, K. (1989) 'Managing in a borderless world', *Harvard Business Review*, 67(3): 52–61.

Okubayashi, K. (1986) 'Recent problems of Japanese personnel management', *Labour and Society*, 11(1).

Oliver, C. (1997) 'Sustainable competitive advantage: combining institutional and resource-based views', *Strategic Management Journal*, 18(9): 697–713.

Oliver, N. and Wilkinson, B. (1992) *The Japanization of British Industry, New Developments in the 1990s* (2nd edn), Oxford: Blackwell.

Oram, M. and Wellins, R. (1995) *Re-engineering's Missing Ingredient: The Human Factor*, London: IPD.

Osterman, P. (1994) 'How common is workplace transformation and who adopts it?', *Industrial and Labor Relations Review*, 47(2): 173–88.

Ouchi, W. (1981) *Theory Z*, Reading, Mass.: Addison-Wesley.

Paauwe, J. (1996) 'Key issues in strategic HRM: lessons from the Netherlands', *Human Resource Management Journal*, 6(3): 76–93.

Paauwe, J. (2004) *HRM and Performance*, Oxford: Oxford University Press.

Paauwe, J. and Boselie, P. (2003) 'Challenging "strategic HRM" and the relevance of the institutional setting', *Human Resource Management Journal*, 13(3): 56–70.

Paauwe, J. and Richardson, R. (2001) 'Editorial introduction: human resource management and performance: confronting theory and reality', *International Journal of Human Resource Management*, 12(7): 1085–91.

Parker, M. (1992) 'Post-modern organizations or postmodern organization theory?', *Organization Studies*, 13(1): 1–17.

Parker, M. (ed.) (1998) *Ethics and Organizations*. London: Sage.

Parker, M. and Slaughter, J. (1988) *Choosing Sides: Unions and the Team Concept*, Boston: Labour Notes.

Parsons, S. (1988) 'Economic principles in the public and private sectors', *Policy and Politics*, 16(1): 29–39.

Patterson, M., West, M., Lawthom, R. and Nickell, S. (1997) 'Impact of people management practices on business performance', *Issues in People Management No. 22*, London: IPD.

Payne, J. (1989) 'Trade union membership and activism among young people in Britain', *British Journal of Industrial Relations*, 27(1): 111–32.

Perrow, C. (1984) *Normal Accidents, Living with High Risk Technologies*, New York: Basic Books.

Petch, S. (1990) 'Performance related pay-problems for the trade unions', paper given to TUC Seminar on PRP (21 January).

Peters, T. J. (1987) *Thriving on Chaos*, New York: Harper & Row.

Peters, T. J. (1992) *Liberation Management*, New York: Macmillan.

Peters, T. J. and Waterman, R. H. Jr. (1982) *In Search of Excellence, Lessons from America's Best Run Companies*, New York: Harper and Row.

Pettigrew, A. M. (1973) *The Politics of Organisational Decision Making*, London: Tavistock.

Pettigrew, A. M. (1979) 'On studying organizational cultures', *Administration Science Quarterly*, 24(4): 570–81.

Pettigrew, A. M. (1985) *Awakening Giant*, Oxford: Blackwell.

Pettigrew, A., Sparrow, P. and Hendry, C. (1988) 'The forces that trigger training', *Personnel Management*, 20(12): 28–32.

Pettigrew, A. and Whipp, R. (1991) *Managing Change for Competitive Success*, Oxford: Blackwell.

Pfeffer, J. (1994) *Competitive Advantage Through People*, Boston, Mass: Harvard Business School Press.

Pigors, P. and Myers, C. A. (1969) *Personnel Administration* (6th edn), New York: McGraw-Hill.

Pil, F. K. and MacDuffie, J. P. (1996) 'The adoption of high involvement work practices', *Industrial Relations*, 35(3): 423–55.

Piore, M. and Sabel, C. (1984) *The Second Industrial Divide*, New York: Basic Books.

Polanyi, M. (1966) *The Tacit Dimension*, New York: Doubleday.

Pollert, A. (1987) 'The "flexible firm": a model in search of reality (or a policy in search of a practice)?', *Warwick Papers in Industrial Relations*, 19, IRRU, School of Industrial and Business Studies, University of Warwick.

Pollert, A. (1988a) 'The "flexible firm": fixation or fact?', *Work, Employment and Society*, 2(3): 281–316.

Pollert, A. (1988b) 'Dismantling flexibility', *Capital and Class*, 34 (Spring): 42–75.

Pollert, A. (ed.) (1991) *Farewell to Flexibility?*, Oxford: Blackwell.

Pollert, A. (1993) 'HRM, team working and industrial relations: management panaceas and shopfloor realities at Choco-Co', paper presented at the 11th EGOS Colloquium, Paris (June).

Pollitt, C. (1990) *Managerialism in the Public Services*, Oxford: Blackwell.

Pollitt, C. (1993) *Managerialism in the Public Services* (2nd edn), Oxford: Blackwell.

Pollitt, C., Harrison, S., Hunter, D., and Marnoch, G. (1988) 'The reluctant managers: clinicians and budgets in the NHS', *Financial Accountability and Management*, 4(3): 213–33.

Pondy, L., Frost, P.J., Morgan, G. and Dandridge, T. (1983) *Organizational Symbolism*, Greenwich, Conn.: JAI.

Poole, M. (1973) 'A back seat for personnel', *Personnel Management*, 5(5): 38–41.

Popper, K. (1962) *Conjectures and Refutations*, London: Routledge & Kegan Paul.

Porter, L., Steers, R., Mowday, R. and Boulian, P. (1974) 'Organizational commitment, job satisfaction and turnover among psychiatric technicians', *Journal of Applied Psychology*, 59: 603–9.

Porter, M. E. (1980) *Competitive Strategies: Technologies for Analyzing Industries and Firms*, New York: Free Press.

Porter, M. E. (1985) *Competitive Advantage: Creating and Sustaining Superior Performance*, New York: Free Press.

Porter, M. E. (1987) 'From competitive advantage to corporate strategy', *Harvard Business Review*, 65(3), 43–59.

Porter, M. E. and Miller, V. E. (1985) 'How information gives you competitive advantage', *Harvard Business Review*, 63(4): 149–60.

Power, M. (1997) *The Audit Society: Rituals of Verification*, Oxford: Oxford University Press.

Preece, D. (1993) 'Human resource specialists and technical change at greenfield sites', in J. Clark (ed.), *Human Resource Management and Technical Change*, London: Sage, 101–15.

Priem, R. and Butler, J. (2001) 'Is the resource-based "view" a useful perspective for strategic management research?', *Academy of Management Review*, 26(1): 22–40.

Proctor, S. J., McArdle, L., Rowlinson, M., Forrester, P. and Hassard, J. (1993) 'Performance related pay in operation: a case study from the electronics industry', *Human Resource Management Journal*, 3(4): 60–74.

Proctor, S. J., Rowlinson, M., McArdle, L., Hassard, J. and Forrester, P. (1994) 'Flexibility, politics and strategy: in defence of the model of the flexible firm', *Work, Employment and Society*, 8(2): 221–42.

Purcell, J. (1981) *Good Industrial Relations: Theory and Practice*, London: Macmillan.

Purcell, J. (1982) 'Macho managers and the new industrial relations', *Employee Relations*, 4(1): 3–5.

Purcell, J. (1987) 'Mapping management style in employee relations', *Journal of Management Studies*, 24(5): 533–48.

Purcell, J. (1989) 'The impact of corporate strategy on human resource management', in J. Storey (ed.), *New Perspectives on Human Resource Management*, London: Routledge, 67–91.

Purcell, J. (1994) 'Personnel earns a place on the board', *Personnel Management*, 26(2): 26–9.

Purcell, J. (1995) 'Corporate strategy and human resource management', in J. Storey (ed.), *Human Resource Management: A Critical Text*, London: Routledge, 63–86.

Purcell, J. (1997) 'Pulling up the drawbridge: high commitment management and the exclusive corporation', Paper presented to the Cornell Conference, 'Research and Theory in Strategic HRM: An Agenda for the 21st Century', October.

Purcell, J. (1999) 'Best practice and best fit: chimera or cul-de-sac?', *Human Resource Management Journal*, 9(3): 26–41.

Purcell, J. and Ahlstrand, B. (1994) *Human Resource Management in the Multi-Divisional Company*, Aldershot: Dartmouth.

Purcell, J. and Gray, A. (1986) 'Corporate personnel departments and the management of industrial relations: two case studies in ambiguity', *Journal of Management Studies*, 23(2): 205–223.

Purcell, J. and Sisson, K. (1983) 'Strategies and practice in the management of industrial relations', in G. S. Bain (ed.), *Industrial Relations in Britain*, Oxford: Blackwell, 95–120.

Rainbird, H. (1991) 'The self-employed: small entrepreneurs or disguised wage labourers?', in A. Pollert (ed.), *Farewell to Flexibility?*, Oxford: Blackwell, 200–14.

Rainbird, H. (1994) 'Continuing training', in K. Sisson (ed.), *Personnel Management* (2nd edn), Oxford: Blackwell, 334–64.

Ramsay, H. (1977) 'Cycles of control', *Sociology*, 11(3): 481–506.

Ramsay, H. (1985) 'What is participation for? A critical evaluation of "labour process" analyses of job reform', in D. Knights, H. Willmott and D. Collinson (eds), *Job Redesign*, Aldershot: Gower, 52–80.

Ramsay, H. (1991) 'The community, the multinational, its workers and their charter: a modern tale of industrial democracy?', *Work, Employment and Society*, 5(4): 541–66.

Ramsey, H., Scholaris, D. and Harley, B. (2000) 'Employees in high-performance work systems: testing inside the black box', *British Journal of Industrial Relations*, 38(4): 501–31.

Ray, C. A. (1986) 'Corporate culture: the last frontier of control?', *Journal of Management Studies*, 23(3): 287–97.

Reed, M. I. (1992) *The Sociology of Organizations*, Brighton: Harvester Wheatsheaf.

Reed, M.I. (1995) 'Managing quality and organizational politics: TQM as governmental technology', in I. Kirkpatrick and M. Martinez Lucio (eds), *The Politics of Quality: Management of Change in the UK Public Sector*, London: Routledge.

Reed, M.I. and Anthony, P. D. (1993a) 'Southglam: managing organizational change in a district health authority', in D. Gowler, C. Clegg and K. Legge (eds), *Case Studies in Organizational Behaviour and Human Resource Management*, London: Paul Chapman, 177–89.

Reed, M.I. and Anthony, P. D. (1993b) 'Between an ideological rock and an organizational hard place', in T. Clarke and C. Pitelis (eds), *The Political Economy of Privatisation*, London: Routledge.

Reed, M. I. (1996) 'Expert power and control in late modernity: an empirical review and theoretical synthesis', *Organization Studies*, 17(4): 573–97.

Reeves, C. A. and Bednar, D. A. (1994) 'Defining quality: alternatives and implications.', *Academy of Management Review*, 19(3): 419–45.

Reich. R. B. (1991) *The Work of Nations*, New York: Knopf.

Rentoul, J. (1989) *Me and Mine: The Triumph of the New Individualism?*, London: Unwin Hyman.

Ritzer, G. and Trice, H. M. (1969) *An Occupation in Conflict*, Ithaca, N.Y.: Cornell University Press.

Robertson, D. (1992) 'New management techniques – the development of a trade union counter strategy', TIE/Vauxhall Shop Stewards' Committee Conference (30 January–2 February).

Roethlisberger, F. J. and Dickson, W. J. (1939) *Management and the Worker*, Cambridge, Mass.: Harvard University Press.

Rogaly, J. (1977) *Grunwick*, Harmondsworth: Penguin.

Rogers, E. W. and Wright, P. M. (1998) 'Measuring organizational performance in strategic human resource management: problems, prospects, and performance information markets', *Human Resource Management Review*, 8: 311–31.

Rose, M. (1975) *Industrial Behaviour: Theoretical Development Since Taylor*, Harmondsworth: Allen Lane.

Rothschild, Lord N. (1982) *An Enquiry into the Social Science Research Council*, Cmnd 8554, London: HMSO.

Rowland, K. and Summers, S. (1981) 'Human resource planning: a second look', *Personnel Administration* (December): 73–80.

Rubery, J., Tarling, R. and Wilkinson, F. (1987) 'Flexibility, marketing and the organization of production.', *Labour and Society*, 12(1): 131–51.

Rugman, A. (2000) *The End of Globalization*, London: Random House.

Rustin, D. (1989) 'The politics of post-Fordism or the trouble with new times', *New Left Review*, 54–77.

Sabel, C. (1982) *Work and Politics*, Cambridge: Cambridge University Press.

Sabel, C. (1989) 'The reemergence of regional economics, in P. Hirst and J. Zeitlin (eds), *Revising Industrial Decline?* Leamington Spa: The Berg Press, 17–70.

Saffold, G. S. (1988) 'Culture traits, strength and organizational performance: moving beyond "strong" culture', *Academy of Management Review*, 13(4): 546–58.

Salaman, G. (2001) 'A response to Snell: the learning organization: fact or fiction?', *Human Relations*, 54(3): 343–59.

Salancik, G. R. (1977) 'Commitment and control of organizational behavior and beliefs', in B. M. Staw and G. R. Salancik (eds), *New Directions in Organizational Behavior*, Chicago: St Clair Press.

Salancik, G. R. (1982) 'Commitment is too easy!', in M. L. Tushman and W. L. Moore (eds), *Readings in the Management of Innovation*, London: Pitman.

Salvati, M. (1989) 'A long cycle in industrial relations', *Labour*, 3(1): 42–72.

Sanz-Valle, R., Sabater-Sanchez, R. and Aragon-Sanchez, A. (1999) 'Human resource management and business strategy links: an empirical study', *International Journal of Human Resource Management*, 10(4): 655–71.

Sathe, V. (1983) 'Implications of corporate culture: a manager's guide to action', *Organizational Dynamics* (Autumn).

Schein, E. H. (1980) *Organizational Psychology*, Englewood Cliffs, N.J.: Prentice-Hall.

Schein, E. H. (1984) 'Coming to a new awareness of organizational culture', *Sloan Management Review* (Winter): 3–16.

Schein, E. H. (1985a) 'How culture forms, develops and changes', in R. H. Kilmann, M. J. Saxton and R. Serpa (eds), *Gaining Control of the Corporate Culture*, San Francisco: Jossey Bass.

Schein, E. H. (1985b) *Organizational Culture and Leadership*, San Francisco: Jossey Bass.

Schneider, B., Bowen, D. and Davis, E. (1993) 'The service organization: human resources management is critical', *Organizational Dynamics*, 21(4): 39–52,

Scholte, J. A. (2000) *Globalization: A Critical Introduction*, Basingstoke: Macmillan – now Palgrave Macmillan.

Schuler, R. S. and Jackson, S. E. (1987) 'Linking competitive strategies with human resource management practices', *Academy of Management Executives*, 1(3): 209–13.

Scott, M. C. (2001) *The Professional Service Firm*, Chichester: Wiley.

Scullion, H. (1995) 'International HRM', in J. Storey (ed.), *Human Resource Management: A Critical Text*, London: Routledge, 352–82.

Selznick, P. (1949) *T.V.A. and the Grass Roots*, Berkeley, Ca.: University of California Press.

Senge, P. (1990) *The Fifth Discipline*, New York: Random House.

Sennett, R. (1998) *The Corrosion of Character*, New York: Norton.

Sewell, G. (1998) 'The discipline of teams: the control of team-based industrial work through electronic and peer surveillance', *Administrative Science Quarterly*, 43(2): 397–428.

Sewell, G. and Wilkinson, B. (1992) 'Empowerment or emasculation? Shopfloor surveillance in a total quality organization', in P. Blyton and P. Turnbull (eds), *Reassessing Human Resource Management*, London: Sage, 97–115.

Shrivastava, P. (1985) 'Integrating strategy formulation with organizational culture', *Journal of Business Strategy*, 5: 103–11.

Shrivastava, P. (1986) 'Is strategic management ideological?', *Journal of Management*, 12(3): 363–77.

Sisson, K. (ed.) (1989) *Personnel Management in Britain* (1st edn), Oxford: Blackwell.

Sisson, K. (1990) 'Introducing the Human Resource Management Journal', *Human Resource Management Journal*, 1(1) (Autumn): 1–11.

Sisson, K. (1993) 'In search of HRM?', *British Journal of Industrial Relations*, 31(2): 201–10.

Sisson, K. (ed.) (1994a) *Personnel Management* (2nd edn), Oxford: Blackwell.

Sisson, K. (1994b) 'Personnel management: paradigms, practice and prospects', in K. Sisson (ed.) *Personnel Management* (2nd edn), Oxford: Blackwell, 3–50.

Sisson, K. and Scullion, H. (1985) 'Putting the corporate personnel department in its place', *Personnel Management*, 17(12): 36–9.

Sisson, K. and Storey, J. (1993) *Managing Human Resources and Industrial Relations*, Milton Keynes: Open University Press.

Sisson, K., Waddington, J. and Whitson, C. (1992) 'The structure of capital in the European Community: the size of companies and the implications for industrial relations', *Warwick Papers in Industrial Relations*, 38, IRRU, School of Industrial and Business Studies, University of Warwick.

Slaughter, J. (1987) 'The team concept in the US auto industry: implications for unions', *Labour Notes*,

Smircich, L. (1983) 'Concepts of culture and organizational analysis', *Administrative Science Quarterly*, 28(3): 339–58.

Smith, C. (1989) 'Flexible specialization, automation and mass production', *Work, Employment and Society*, 3(2): 203–20.

Smith, D. (1988) 'The Japanese example in south-west Birmingham', *Industrial Relations Journal*, 19(1): 41–50.

Smith, P. and Morton, G. (2001) 'New Labour's reform of Britain's Employment Law: the devil is not only in the details but in the policy too', *British Journal of Industrial Relations*, 39(1): 119–38.

Smith, P. and Peterson, M. (1988) *Leadership, Organizations and Culture*, London: Sage.

Smith, R. (1982) 'Women and occupational élites: the case of newspaper journalism in England', in C. F. Epstein and R. L. Coser (eds), *Access to Power: Cross-National Studies of Women and Elites*, London: Allen & Unwin, 237–48.

Smith-Cook, D. and Ferris, G. R. (1986) 'Strategic human resource management and firm effectiveness in industries experiencing decline', *Human Resource Management*, 25, (3): 441–58.

Sparrow, P. R. (1991) 'Developing a human resource management strategy: International Computers Ltd.', in K. Legge, C. Clegg and N. Kemp (eds), *Case Studies in Information Technology, People and Organisations*, Oxford and Manchester: NCC/Blackwell.

Sparrow, P. R. (2004) *Globalising HRM*, London: Routledge.

Sparrow, P. R. and Hiltrop, J. (1994) *European Human Resource Management in Transition*, London: Prentice-Hall.

Sparrow, P. R. and Pettigrew, A. (1988a) 'Strategic human resource management in the computer supplier industry', *Journal of Occupational Psychology*, 61(1): 25–42.

Sparrow, P. R. and Pettigrew, A. (1988b) 'Contrasting HRM responses in the changing world of computing', *Personnel Management*, 20(2): 40–5.

Sparrow, P. R. and Pettigrew, A. (1988c) 'How Halfords puts its HRM into top gear', *Personnel Management*, 20(6): 30–4.

Special Issue (1993) 'Knowledge Workers and Contemporary Organizations', *Journal of Management Studies*, 30(6): November (Guest editors: Frank Blackler, Michael Reed and Alan Whitaker).

Special Issue (1995) 'The Manager and Morality', *Organization*, 2(2): May.

Special Issue (1998) 'Trust in Organizations', *Academy of Management Review*, 23(3).

Special Issue (1999) 'Human and Inhuman Resource Management: Saving the Subject of HRM', *Organization*, 6(2): May (Guest editors: Maddy Jansens and Chris Steyaert).

Special Issue (2000a) 'Practice-based Theorizing on Learning and Knowing in Organizations', *Organization*, 7(2): May (Guest editor: Silvia Gherardi).

Special Issue (2000b) 'Analyses of Britain's 1998 Workplace Employee Relations Survey', *British Journal of Industrial Relations*, 38(4): December (Guest editors: Paul Marginson and Stephen Wood).

Special Issue (2001) 'Knowledge Management: Concepts and Controversies', *Journal of Management Studies*, 38(7): November (Guest editors: Jacky Swan and Harry Scarbrough).

Special Issue (2003a) 'Trust and HRM in the New Millennium', *International Journal of Human Resource Management*, 14(1): February (Guest Editors Rachid Zeffane and Julia Connell).

Special Issue (2003b), 'Ethics, Politics and Organizing', *Organization*, 10(2): May (Guest editor: Martin Parker).

Special Issue (2003c) 'Knowledge and Professional Organizations', *Organization Studies*, 24(6): July (Guest editors: Bob Hinings and Huseyin Leblebici).

Special Issue (2004a) 'Knowledge Construction and Creation in Organizations', *British Journal of Management*, 15: May (Guest editors: Haridimous Tsoukas and Nikos Mylonopoulos).

Special Issue (2004b) 'Human Resource Management in China Revisited', *International Journal of Human Resource Management*, 15(4) & (5): June and August (Guest editor: Malcolm Warner).

Spender, D. (1980) *Man Made Language*, London: Routledge.

Stacey, R. D. (1993) *Strategic Management and Organizational Dynamics*, London: Pitman.

Stacey, R. D., Griffen, D. and Shaw, P. (2000) *Complexity and Management*, London: Routledge.

Starbuck, W. (1992) 'Learning by knowledge-intensive firms', *Journal of Management Studies*, 29(6): 713–40.

Starkey, K. and McKinlay, A. (1989) 'Beyond Fordism? Strategic choice and labour relations in Ford UK', *Industrial Relations Journal*, 20(2): 93–100.

Steedman, H. and Wagner, K. (1987) 'A second look at productivity, machinery and skills in Britain and Germany', *National Institute of Economic Review* (November).

Steers, R. M. and Rhodes, S. R. (1978) 'Major influences on employee attendance: a process model', *Journal of Applied Psychology*, 63: 391–407.

Stevens, M., Millward, N. and Smart, D. (1989) 'Trade union membership and the closed shop in 1989', *Department of Employment Gazette*, 11: 615–23.

Stogdill, R. M. (1974) *Handbook of Leadership*, New York: Free Press.

Stoney, C. and Winstanley, D. (2001) 'Stakeholding: confusion or utopia? Mapping the conceptual terrain', *Journal of Management Studies*, 38(5): 603–26.

Stopford, J. and Turner, L. (1985) *Britain and the Multinationals*, Chichester: Wiley.

Storey, J. (1987) 'Developments in the management of human resources: an interim report', *Warwick Papers in Industrial Relations*, 17, IRRU, School of Industrial and Business Studies, University of Warwick (November).

Storey, J. (ed.) (1989) *New Perspectives in Human Resource Management*, London: Routledge.

Storey, J. (1992a) 'HRM in action: the truth is out at last', *Personnel Management*, 24(4): 28–31.

Storey, J. (1992b) *Developments in the Management of Human Resources*, Oxford: Blackwell.

Storey, J. and Bacon, N. (1993) 'Individualism and collectivism: into the 1990s', *International Journal of Human Resource Management*, 4(3): 665–84.

Storey, J. and Sisson, K. (1993) *Managing Human Resources and Industrial Relations*, Milton Keynes: Open University Press.

Storey, J. and Bacon, N. with J. Edmonds and P. Wyatt (1993) 'The "new agenda", and human resource management: a roundtable discussion with John Edmonds', *Human Resource Management Journal*, 4(1): 63–70.

Storey, J., Okazaki-Ward, L., Edwards, P. K., Gow, I. and Sisson, K. (1991) 'Management careers and management development: a comparative analysis of Britain and Japan', *Human Resource Management Journal*, 1(3): 33–57.

Streeck, W. (1985) 'Industrial relations and industrial change in the motor industry: an international view', Public lecture, Industrial Relations Research Unit, University of Warwick.

Streeck, W. (1987) 'The uncertainties of management in the management of uncertainty', *Work, Employment and Society*, 1(3): 281–308.

Streeck, W. (1997) ' German capitalism: does it exist? Can it survive?', in C. Crouch and W. Streeck (eds), *Political Economy of Modern Capitalism*, London: Sage, 33–54.

Strong, P. and Robinson, J. (1990) *The NHS: Under New Management*, Milton Keynes: Open University Press.

Swart, J. and Kinnie, N. (2003) 'Sharing knowledge in knowledge-intensive firms', *Human Resource Management Journal*, 13(2): 60–75.

Tannenbaum, R. and Davis, S. M. (1969) 'Values, man and organization', *Industrial Management Review*, 10(2): 67–86.

Taylor, F. W. (1911) *Principles of Scientific Management*, New York: Harper.

Taylor, P. and Bain, P. (1999) 'An assembly line in the head: the call centre labour process', *Industrial Relations Journal*, 30(2): 101–17.

Terry, M. (1989) 'Recontextualizing shopfloor industrial relations: some case study evidence', in S. Tailby and C. Whitson (eds), *Manufacturing Change*, Oxford: Blackwell.

Terry, M. (1991) 'Annual review article 1990', *British Journal of Industrial Relations*, 29(1): 97–112.

TGWU (1989) 'Lessons from Langley for Ford: co-ordinators, group leaders and teamworking', Report prepared by Mike Gosling for the TGWU 1/1107, Dagenham Branch (June).

Thomason, G. F. (1975) *A Textbook of Personnel Management*, London: IPM.

Thomason, G. F. (1984) *A Textbook of Industrial Relations Management*, London: IPM.

Thompson, M. (1992) *Pay for Performance in the Employer Experience*, Sussex: Institute for Manpower Studies.

Thompson, P. and McHugh, D. (1990) *Work Organizations*, London: Macmillan (3rd edition, 2002).

Thompson, P. (1993) 'Postmodernism: fatal distraction', in J. Hassard and M. Parker (eds), *Postmodernism and Organization*, London: Sage, 183–203.

Thompson, P., Warhurst, C. and Callaghan, G. (2001) 'Ignorant theory and knowledgeable workers: interrogating the connections between knowledge, skills and services', *Journal of Management Studies*, 38(7): 923–42.

Thurley, K. (1981) 'Personnel management in the U.K.: a case for urgent treatment', *Personnel Management*, 13(8): 24–9.

Thurley, K. and Wood, S. (eds) (1983) *Industrial Relations and Management Strategy*, Cambridge: Cambridge University Press.

Tichy, N. (1983) *Managing Strategic Change*, New York: Wiley.

Tichy, N., Fombrun, C. and Devanna, M. A. (1982) 'Strategic human resource management', *Sloan Management Review*, 23(2) (Winter): 47–61.

Toffler, A. (1970) *Future Shock*, London: Bodley Head.

Torrington, D. (1989) 'Human resource management and the personnel function', in J. Storey (ed.) *New Perspectives on Human Resource Management*, London: Routledge, 56–66.

Torrington, D. (1994) *International Human Resource Management*, London: Prentice-Hall.

Torrington, D. and Hall, L. (1987) *Personnel Management, A New Approach*, London: Prentice-Hall.

Townley, B. (1989) 'Selection and appraisal: reconstituting 'social relations'?, in J. Storey (ed.), *New Perspectives on Human Resource Management*, London: Routledge, 92–108.

Townley, B. (1990/1) 'The politics of appraisal: lessons of the introduction of appraisal into UK universities', *Human Resource Management Journal*, 1(2): 27–44.

Townley, B. (1993) 'Foucault, power/knowledge, and its relevance for human resource management', *Academy of Management Review*, 18(3): 518–45.

Townley, B. (1994) *Reframing Human Resource Management. Power, Ethics and the Subject at Work*, London: Sage.

Tsoukas, H. (1992) 'Postmodernism, reflexive rationalism and organization studies: a reply to Martin Parker', *Organization Studies*, 13(4): 643–9.

TUC (1989a) *TUC Survey of Union Officers 1989*, London: TUC.

TUC (1989b) *Organizing for the 1990s*, London: TUC.

TUC (1999) *Partners for Progress: New Unionism in the Workplace*, London: TUC.

Turnbull, P. (1988a) 'The limits to Japanization – just-in-time, labour relations and the UK automotive industry', *New Technology, Work and Employment*, 3(1): 7–20.

Turnbull, P. (1988b) 'Leaner and possibly fitter: the management of redundancy in Britain', *Industrial Relations Journal*, 19(3): 201–13.

Turner, B. A. (ed.) (1990) *Organizational Symbolism*, Berlin and New York: de Gruyter.

Tyson, S. (1985) 'Is this the very model of a modern personnel manager?', *Personnel Management*, 17(5): 22–5.

Tyson, S. (1987) 'The management of the personnel function', *Journal of Management Studies*, 24(5): 523–32.

Tyson, S. and Fell, A. (1986) *Evaluating the Personnel Function*, London: Hutchinson.

Undy, R. (1999) 'New Labour's "industrial relations settlement": the Third Way?', *British Journal of Industrial Relations*, 37(2): 315–36.

Undy, R. and Martin, R. (1984) *Ballots and Trade Union Democracy*, Oxford: Blackwell.

Upton, R. (1987) 'The bottom line: Bejam's ingredients for success', *Personnel Management*, 19(3): 26–9.

Van Maanen, J. (1991) 'The smile factory: work at Disneyland', in P. Frost, L. Moore, M. Louis, C. Lundberg and J. Martin (eds), *Reframing Organizational Culture*, Newbury Park, Calif.: Sage.

Van Maanen, J. and Barley, S. (1984) 'Occupational communities: culture and control in organizations', in B. M. Staw and L. L. Cummings (eds), *Research in Organizational Behavior*, Greenwich, Conn.: JAI Press.

Waddington, J. (1992) 'Trade union membership in Britain 1980–87: unemployment and restructuring', *British Journal of Industrial Relations*, 30(2): 287–324.

Waddington, J. (2003) 'Heightening tensions in relations between trade unions and the Labour Government in 2002', *British Journal of Industrial Relations*, 41(2): 335–58.

Wakefield, N. (1990) *Postmodernism: The Twilight of the Real*, London: Pluto.

Walby, S. (1986) *Patriarchy at Work*, Oxford: Polity.

Walby, S. (1990) *Theorizing Patriarchy*, Oxford: Blackwell.

Walsh, T. (1991) '"Flexible" employment in the retail and hotel trades', in A. Pollert (ed.), *Farewell to Flexibility ?*, Oxford: Blackwell, 104–15.

Walton, R. E. (1985) 'Toward a strategy of eliciting employee commitment based on policies of mutuality', in R. E. Walton and P. R. Lawrence (eds), *Human Resource Management, Trends and Challenges*, Boston: Harvard Business School Press, 35–65.

Walton, R. E. and Lawrence, P. R. (eds) (1985) *Human Resource Management, Trends and Challenges*, Boston: Harvard Business School Press.

Walton, R. E. and McKersie, R. B. (1965) *A Behavioral Theory of Labor Negotiation*, New York: McGraw-Hill.

Warmington, A., Lupton, T. and Gorfin, C. (1977) *Organizational Behaviour and Performance*, London: Macmillan.

Waterman, R. H. Jr. (1987) *The Renewal Factor: Building and Maintaining Your Company's Competitive Edge*, London: Bantam.

Watson, T. J. (1977) *The Personnel Managers: A Study in the Sociology of Work and Industry*, London: Routledge & Kegan Paul.

Watson, T. J. (1983) 'Towards a general theory of personnel and industrial relations management', *Occasional Paper Series*, (2), Trent Business School, Nottingham.

Watson, T. J. (1986) *Management, Organization and Employment Strategy. New Directions in Theory and Practice*, London: Routledge & Kegan Paul.

Watson, T. J. (2004) 'HRM and critical social science analysis', *Journal of Mangement Studies*, 41(3): 447–67.

Wedderburn, K. W. (1986) *The Worker and the Law* (3rd edn), Harmondsworth: Penguin.

Weick, K. (1969) *The Social Psychology of Organizing*, Reading, Mass.: Addison Wesley.

Weick, K. (1987) 'Organizational culture as a source of high reliability', *California Management Review*, 29(2): 112–27.

Weick, K. (1995) *Sensemaking in Organizations*, Thousand Oaks, Calif.: Sage.

Weick, K. and Westley, F. (1996) 'Organizational learning: affirming an oxymoron', in S. R. Clegg, C. Hardy and W. R. Nord (eds), *Handbook of Organization Studies*, London: Sage, 440–58.

Wensley, R. (1982) 'PIMS and BCG: new horizons or a false dawn?', *Strategic Management Journal*, 3(2): 147–58.

Wernerfelt, B. (1984) 'A resource-based view of the firm', *Strategic Management Journal*, 5(2): 171–80.

Werther, W. (1985) 'Job 1 at Ford: employee co-operation', *Employee Relations*, 7(2): 10–16.

Westergaard, J. and Resler, H. (1975) *Class in a Capitalist Society: A Study of Contemporary Britain*, London: Heinemann.

Whipp, R. (1992) 'Human resource management, competition and strategy: some productive tensions', in P. Blyton and P. Turnbull (eds), *Reassessing Human Resource Management*, London: Sage, 33–55.

Whipp, R., Rosenfeld, R. and Pettigrew, A. (1989) 'Culture and competitiveness: evidence from two mature UK industries', *Journal of Management Studies*, 26(6): 561–85.

White, I. and Wyatt, M. (1990) 'A case study of Lucas Industries' approach to supplier integration', in B. G. Dale and J. J. Plunkett (eds), *Managing Quality*, London: Philip Allan, 270–80.

White, M. and Trevor, M. (1983) *Under Japanese Management*, London: Heinemann.

Whitley, R. (1992) *Business Systems in East Asia: Firms, Markets and Societies*, London: Sage.

Whitley, R. (1999) *Divergent Capitalisms: The Social Structuring and Change of Business Systems*, Oxford: Oxford University Press.

Whittaker, D. H. (1990) 'The end of Japanese-style employment?', *Work, Employment and Society*, 4(3): 321–47.

Whittington, R. (1989) *Corporate Strategies in Recession and Recovery: Social Structures and Strategic Choice*, London: Unwin Hyman.

Whittington, R. (1991) 'The fragmentation of industrial R and D', in A. Pollert (ed.), *Farewell to Flexibility?*, Oxford: Blackwell, 84–103.

Whittington, R. (1993) *What is Strategy and Does it Matter?*, London: Routledge.

Wickens, P. D. (1987) *The Road to Nissan*, London: Macmillan.

Wickens, P. D. (1993) 'Lean production and beyond: the system, its critics and the future', *Human Resource Management Journal*, 3(4): 75–90.

Wildavsky, A. (1975) *Budgeting, A Comparative Theory of the Budgeting Process*, Boston: Little, Brown.

Wilkinson, A. and Marchington, M. (1994) 'TQM: Instant pudding for the personnel function?', *Human Resource Management Journal*, 5(2): 33–49.

Wilkinson, A., Marchington, M., Goodman, J. and Ackers, P. (1993) 'Refashioning industrial relations: The experience of a chemical company in the 1980s', *Personnel Review*, 22(2): 22–38.

Wilkinson, A., Marchington, M., Goodman, J. and Ackers, P. (1992) 'Total quality management and employee involvement', *Human Resource Management Journal*, 2(4): 1–20.

Wilkinson, B. (1983) *The Shopfloor Politics of New Technology*, London: Heinemann.

Williams, K., Cutler, T., Williams, J. and Haslam, C. (1987) 'The end of mass production?', *Economy and Society*, 16(3): 405–39.

Williams, K., Williams, J. and Haslam, C. (1989) 'Why take the stocks out?, Britain vs Japan', *International Journal of Operations and Production Management*, 9(8): 91–105.

Williamson, O. E. (1975) *Markets and Hierarchies: Analysis and Antitrust Implications*, New York: Free Press.

Williamson, O. E. (1985) *The Economic Institutions of Capitalism*, New York: Free Press.

Willman, P. (1989) 'The logic of "market share", trade unionism: is membership decline inevitable?', *Industrial Relations Journal*, 20(4): 260–70.

Willman, P. (1990) 'The financial status and performance of British trade unions 1950–88', *British Journal of Industrial Relations*, 28(3): 313–27.

Willman, P. and Winch, G. (1985) *Innovation and Management Control, Labour Relations at BL Cars*, Cambridge: Cambridge University Press.

Willmott, H. (1993) '"Strength is ignorance; slavery is freedom": managing culture in modern organizations', *Journal of Management Studies*, 30(4): 515–52.

Willmott, H. (1994) 'Business process re-engineering and human resource management', *Personnel Review*, 23(3): 34–46.

Winkler, J. (1974) 'The ghost at the bargaining table: directors and industrial relations', *British Journal of Industrial Relations*, 12(2): 191–212.

Winstanley, D. and Woodall, J. (eds) (2000) *Ethical Issues in Contemporary Human Resource Management*, Basingstoke: Macmillan – now Palgrave Macmillan.

Wintour, P. (1987) 'Japanese quality control idea a threat to unions?, *Guardian* (10 January).

Womack, J. P., Jones, D. T. and Roos, D. (1990) *The Machine that Changed the World: The Triumph of Lean Production*, New York: Rawson, Macmillan.

Wong, D. (1993) 'The permanent search for temporary staff', in D. Gowler, K. Legge and C. Clegg (eds), *Case Studies in Organizational Behaviour and Human Resource Management*, London: Paul Chapman: 75–81.

Wood, S. and Kelly, J. (1982) 'Taylorism, responsible autonomy and management strategy', in S. Wood (ed.), *The Degradation of Work?*, London: Hutchinson, 74–89.

Wood, S. J. (1989a) 'New wave management?', *Work, Employment and Society*, 3(3): 379–402.

Wood, S. (ed.) (1989b) *The Transformation of Work? Skill Flexibility and the Labour Process*, London: Unwin.

Woodall, J. and Winstanley, D. (2001) 'The place of ethics in HRM', in J. Storey (ed.), *Human Resource Management, A Critical Text (Second edition)*, London: Thomson Learning, 37–56.

Working for Patients, Cmm 555 (1989) London: HMSO.

Wright, P. and Gardner, T. M. (2003) 'Theoretical and empirical challenges in studying the HR practice-firm performance relationship', in D. Holman, T. D. Wall, C. W. Clegg,

P. Sparrow and A. Howard (eds), *The New Workplace: People, Technology and Organisation*, Chichester: Wiley, 311–28.

Wright, P. M. and Snell, S. A. (1998) 'Towards a unifying framework for exploring fit and flexibility in strategic human resource management', *Academy of Management Review*, 23(4): 756–72.

Wright, P. M., Dunford, B. B. and Snell, S. A. (2001a) 'Human resources and the resource based view of the firm', *Journal of Management*, 27(6): 701–21.

Wright, P. M., Gardner, T. M., Moynihan, L. M., Park, H. J., Gerhart, B. and Delery, J. E. (2001b) 'Measurment error in research on human resources and firm performance: additional data and suggestions for future research', *Personnel Psychology*, 54(4): 875–901.

Wright, P. M., McMahan, G. C. and McWilliams, A. (1994) 'Human resources and sustained competitive advantage: a resource-based perspective', *International Journal of Human Resource Management*, 5(2): 301–26.

Yeandle, D. and Clark, J. (1989) 'A personnel strategy for an automated plant', *Personnel Management*, 21(6): 51–5.

Youndt, M., Snell, S. A., Dean, J. and Lepak, D. (1996) 'Human resource management, manufacturing strategy, and firm performance', *Academy of Management Journal*, 39(4): 836–66.

Young, D. (1989) 'British Airways: putting the customer first', Ashridge Strategic Management Centre (July).

Young, S. N. H. and Hamill, J. (1988) *Foreign Multinationals and the British Economy*, London: Croom Helm.

Zeithaml, V. and Bitner, M. (1996) *Service Marketing*, New York: McGraw-Hill.

Zemke, R. and Schaaf, D. (1989) *The Service Edge: 101 Companies that Profit from Customer Care*, New York: NAL Books.

Author index

Subject index

business strategy   xvi, 3, 6, 14, 25, 93–6,
    104, 105, 133–68, 170–4
  and business life cycles   140–3, 151–2,
    153
  definitions of   133–4
  and HRM fit   3, 14, 23, 24, 25, 28,
    140–67
  and management styles   141–51;
    analyser   146–7, 148, 150; cost
    leadership   19; cost reduction   23,
    33, 141, 144–5, 152; defender   141,
    146–7, 148, 150; financial
    control   148–9, 150, 171; high value
    added   19; innovation   141, 144–5,
    152; prospector   141, 148, 146–7,
    148, 150; quality enhancement   141,
    144–5, 152; strategic control   148–9,
    150; strategic planning   148–9,
    150
  and models of: classical   71, 135, 139,
    140, 151, 165, 170–1, 174, 195, 204;
    evolutionary   136, 138, 140, 171;
    processual   71, 136–7, 139, 140,
    151, 171, 204; systemic   138–40, 151,
    171, 172–3
  national business systems   2, 6, 22, 34
  and pragmatism   150
  and 'short-termism'   6, 22, 31, 34, 40,
    171–3, 213, 259, 273, 360, 361

Cadbury, Edward   52, 61
Cadbury Schweppes   77, 149
call centres   2, 7, 9, 11, 13, 34, 39
capital
  circuit of   56, 57–8, 59
  mobility   6
  social   14, 19
capitalism   2, 15, 33, 38, 39, 64, 74, 123,
    316, 320, 321–4, 325, 326, 340
  contradictions of   xv, 56–60, 69, 70, 80,
    108, 210, 321–2, 343, 349, 357
  and over accumulation   322–3
  devaluation   322
  displacement   323–4, 326
  disorganised   1, 139, 181, 316, 324, 327,
    329
  see also globalisation, industrialism,
    labour intensification, nation state,
    surplus value and surveillance
car industry   see motor manufacturing

chaebol   6
chaos theory   7
China   1, 5, 41
Citizen's Charters   227, 266, 269, 270, 275,
    277–8
Civil Service   99, 120
closed shop   see legislation and trade
    unions
Coca-Cola   37
collective bargaining   6, 14, 16, 41, 75, 77,
    280, 281, 294, 297, 299, 301, 308–10,
    312, 323
  coverage   281, 285–6, 288, 292–6, 298
  levels   285, 286–7, 288
  scope   281, 285–6, 288, 292–6
  single employer 281, 286, 367
  single table   287
collectivism   xvi, 14, 15, 16–17, 18, 59, 74,
    75–6, 77, 78, 79–80, 81–4, 89, 111,
    166–7, 209–10, 265, 277–8, 290, 295,
    358, 365
  see also trade unions
commitment   xv, xvi–xvii, 19, 31, 32, 34,
    39, 59, 76, 77, 96, 103, 104, 105, 106,
    108, 110, 116, 125, 130, 164, 165–6,
    209–10, 214–19, 224–40, 279, 339–40,
    350
  affective   214–15, 239–40
  antecedents of   217
  behavioural   215–16, 239–40
  continuance   215
  dual   165–6, 218
  outcomes   215, 218–19
  and performance   19, 225
communications   8, 17, 76, 77, 78, 103,
    106, 114, 154, 216, 226, 227, 228–9,
    265, 304–5, 306
  see also involvement
competitive advantage   1, 3, 7–8, 14, 19, 20,
    22, 23, 24, 34, 41, 96, 98, 104, 105, 109,
    115, 116, 122, 126, 161–2, 214, 246,
    274, 339, 340, 350, 353
complexity theory   7
compliance   see behavioural compliance
compulsory competitive tendering 196,
    201
Confederation of British Industry
    (CBI)   208
Confederation of Health Service Employees
    (COHSE)   283

economy, UK
  of scale 179, 208
  of scope 179–80, 208
  see also Conservative government,
    enterprise culture and
    'short-termism'
Edmonds, John 301, 309–10
Edwardes, M. 228
education see training
education sector 266–71, 275, 296, 311
efficiency 4, 52–3, 54, 55, 56
Electrical, Electronic, Telecommunication
    and Plumbing Union (EETPU) 198,
    283, 307–8, 309, 312
  see also AEEU
electronics industry 92, 172, 193, 242, 261
Emilia Romagna 181, 189
emotional labour see labour
employability 176, 363
employee behaviour 29, 30
  'black box' 4, 29, 30, 32, 33
employee commitment see commitment
employee involvement see involvement
employee participation see participation
employee relations see human resource
    management, industrial relations,
    personnel management and trade
    unions
employee relations strategy 8, 34, 71,
    152–60
  see also business strategy
employee relations style xvi, 70–100,
    110–11, 113, 123
  definitions of 71–2
  models of: adversarial 75;
    cooperative 78; constitutionalist 74,
    77, 78, 79, 88, 92; consultative 74,
    76–7, 78, 79, 80, 88, 92, 93, 97, 99;
    development/resource 19, 23, 79,
    88; hybrid 17; individual
    rights 15–16; investment
    orientation 80, 84, 88, 95, 99, 111;
    labour control/commodity 79–80,
    88, 95–6; 'macho' 51, 73, 74, 99,
    127; opportunism/pragmatism xiv,
    xv, 72, 78, 85, 93, 94, 96, 98, 148,
    154, 171–3, 190; partnership
    orientation 15–18 34, 80, 84, 88;
    pluralist 16, 17, 18, 21, 73–4, 75,
    123, 213, 216, 297; radical 47, 73–4,

75, 77, 314; share ownership 17;
  socio-economic
    management 15–16; sophisticated
    modern 74, 76; sophisticated
    paternalist/human relations 74,
    75–6, 77, 78, 79, 81, 88, 92, 97, 111,
    123, 342; stakeholding 15–18, 33;
    standard modern 72, 74, 78, 79,
    173, 342, 347, 357; unitarist 16, 17,
    21, 46, 47, 73–83, 75, 76, 77, 78, 111,
    117, 127, 213, 239, 314
  and organisation wide 89–92:
    organisational context 92–6;
    ownership 92, 96–8
  typologies of 73–89
  see also human resource management and
    personnel management
employee satisfaction 12, 19, 32
Employers' Labour Use Strategies survey
    (ELUS) 190, 191–2, 194, 196, 208
employment 4–7, 9, 10, 42
  core 8, 88, 107, 126, 182, 189–90, 195,
    202, 239
  female 15, 117, 191, 205, 289–90, 342–3
  homeworkers 192
  male 191, 205
  non-standard 8, 37, 191–7, 201–2
  part-time 132, 191–2, 194–5, 204, 205
  periphery 8, 36, 88, 107, 126, 182, 183,
    189–90, 195, 202, 239
  policy 23, 24
  relations reform 2, 15
  self-employed 191, 194–5
  temporary 191, 192–3, 194–5, 196,
    205
  see also flexibility and unemployment
Employment Act (1980) 120, 293, 294
Employment Act (1982) 120, 293
Employment Act (1988) 293
Employment Act (1989) 293, 294
Employment Act (1990) 293
Employment Relations Act (1999) 17
empowerment 34, 129, 239, 246, 252, 255,
    261, 271, 275, 351, 353, 358
engineering industry 79, 93, 172, 198, 225,
    228, 229, 284
Enron 33
enterprise culture see culture
equal opportunities 54, 64, 91
equal pay 64

Labour government (1997–) 2, 16, 17, 18
see also New Labour
Labour government, party (pre-1995) 51, 53, 280, 302, 365, 367
'Old Labour' 15, 16
Labour Force Survey (LFS) 190, 191, 282, 314
Labour Research Department (LRD) survey 190, 194, 197, 208
leadership 73, 125, 159, 214, 220, 234, 240, 263, 281
participative 211, 218
transactional 118
transformational 7, 118, 125, 213, 219, 240, 340, 353, 355
learning organisation see organisation structure
Leeson, Nick 328
legislation xvii, 16, 41, 51, 54–5, 61–2, 64, 120–1, 248, 279, 291, 293–5, 302–3, 351
ballots 293, 294, 302, 315
closed shop 291, 293, 302
picketing, secondary 16, 294, 302
political funds 293, 315
recognition 293
trade union immunities 293, 302
Lever Brothers 52
Leverhulme Trust 348
Lex 149
Lincoln Electric 141
Lockheed 125
Lucas Industries 228, 256, 259, 262

Maastricht Treaty 1992 361, 364–5
see also Europe
management
authority 73
by blame 260
by stress 256, 260, 261, 271
development see training
legitimacy 139, 353
line xvi, 47–8, 49–50, 54, 63, 65, 66 8, 85–6, 109, 113, 167–70, 193, 235, 249–50, 257, 258, 271, 273, 274, 304, 350–1
see also control, employee relations style, first line managers and personnel management

Managerial, Scientific and Finance Union (MSF) 283
manufacturing
employment 2, 192–7, 204
industries 7, 11, 14–15, 25, 116, 117, 132, 172, 186–7, 240, 245, 258–9, 286, 289, 291, 299
markets 56, 57, 92–3, 93–6, 117, 119–20, 122, 128, 187, 297–8
financial 22, 171, 187
labour 6, 19, 23, 35–6, 77, 78, 117, 182, 183, 226
product 78, 93–6, 99, 117, 183
stock 6
market economies
coordinated (CMEs) 6, 18, 31, 41
liberal (LMEs) 6, 18, 22, 31, 41
Marks & Spencer 3, 22, 48, 76, 84, 90, 97, 161, 227, 241, 250, 266, 304, 342
Marshall, Sir Colin 139, 228, 233
Marxism 22, 39, 56, 57–8, 61, 206–7, 259–60, 262, 264, 291, 300, 318, 321–3, 355
Maxwell, Robert 234, 328
McDonaldization 2, 38–9
McDonald's 40, 42, 123, 251
mergers 22, 155–6
metaphors 74, 123, 129, 313–14, 341–3
see also symbolism
Mickey Mouse 37
Midland Bank 266
modernism 3, 35, 316–26, 355
critical 317–18, 333
critique of 326–8
institutions of 321–6
knowledge base 317–18
and meta-narratives 34–7, 317, 318, 321, 326, 327, 330–1, 333, 340
and performativity 3, 318, 325, 336, 339, 340
pre-modern 3
systemic 318, 329
and time–space compression 5, 318–20, 323–4, 326
modernity 316
late 316, 327–8, 340
radical 324, 327–8, 340
motor manufacturing 9, 80, 198, 225, 228, 241–2, 259–60, 284
multinationals see organisation structure

multiskilling   *see* skill
mutuality   xvi, 103, 105, 106, 110, 129, 132, 160, 173

nation state   6, 37, 324–5, 326, 327, 329
National Association of Local Government Officers (NALGO)   283
National Consumer Council   267
National Council for Vocational Qualifications (NCVQ)   272
National Graphical Association (NGA)   283
National Health Service (NHS)   120, 176, 225, 229, 233, 246, 266–8, 271, 275, 296, 311, 366
National Minimum Wage   16, 294
National Union of Mineworkers (NUM)   74, 121
National Union of Public Employees (NUPE)   283
   see also UNISON
National Union of Railwaymen (NUR)   283
National Union of Seamen (NUS)   283
National Westminster Bank   176, 274
NATO   329
negotiation   *see* collective bargaining
Netherlands   40
New Labour   2, 4, 15, 16, 17
   partnership   15–18
   social democracy   15
   stakeholder society   15–18, 33, 39
'new realism'   *see* trade unions
new technology   *see* information technology
Next   3
NGOs   4
Nicholson, Brian   301–2
Nike   37
Nissan   77, 200, 229, 229, 243, 256, 259, 260–6, 276, 277, 277, 305–6, 328, 358, 360, 367
No Logo   37–9
Norsk Data   166–7

OECD   287, 295, 329
Ofgas   230, 267
Oftel   230, 267
oil shocks   55, 115, 138, 322

organisation structure   8, 222, 227
   centralised   271
   critical function   89–90
   decentralised   159, 168, 176, 268, 271
   diversified   72, 89–92, 98, 159, 161–2, 172
   institutional isomorphism   8, 24, 41
   'lean'   8, 9, 22, 33
   learning   10, 12, 18–23, 40
   multidivisional   89–90, 135, 172, 173, 360
   multinationals   6, 34, 187, 188, 328–30, 361, 365, 367
   multiplant   72, 78, 80, 86, 89–90, 159
   postmodern   330–1
organisational
   change   9, 36, 40, 86, 157, 159, 168, 202, 227–30, 236–9; *see also* culture
   competencies/knowledge   8, 19, 20, 22, 24, 33, 40
   competitiveness   24
   design   xvii, 1, 4–7, 7–9, 33, 34, 54, 168, 175–7, 250, 349, 358; *see also* flexibility *and* organisation structure
   development   54, 110, 114, 124, 211–14, 219, 234–5, 240
   learning   10, 13, 19–23, 54, 157, 165
   outcomes: balanced scorecard   32, 40
   ownership   39, 92, 97–8, 160, 285, 304, 305, 360–1
   performance   24, 25–34, 153, 174, 218, 224, 225, 230; *see also* competitive advantage
   size   152, 153
   strategies   6, 8, 24, 31
   structures   6

Panopticon   261, 344–5
Parnaby, J.   259
partnership   15–18
Partnership Fund   17
part-time workers   *see* employment
Pasteur, Louis   346
participation   76–7, 103, 209, 226, 246, 248, 249, 252
patriarchy   55, 60–4, 69, 342, 354
Pavarroti, Luciano   333
pay   19, 26, 32, 46, 103, 164, 165, 286
   low   99, 304, 315, 348, 358

National Minimum wage 16
performance-related 26, 99, 159, 201–3,
    218, 219, 226, 227, 229, 267, 269–70,
    296, 305, 306, 311, 358–9
  see also reward
Pepsi 37
performance
  outcomes 4
personnel management xiv, xv–xvi, 23,
    43–69, 109–14, 126
  ambiguities xv, 44, 52, 60, 63, 64–9
  and conformist innovation 55
  contradictions xv, 43, 52
  corporate 90–2, 97, 156–7, 159
  credibility 40, 44, 51–2, 60, 64, 69, 168,
      351
  definition of 3, 43, 51–2
  and deviant innovation 54, 110, 213:
      firefighting 49, 67–8, 69, 87, 159;
      success criteria 65, 67
  directors 91–2, 97, 159–60, 366
  expertise 65–6, 67
  history of 52–5
  and HRM 2, 3
  models of: critical–evaluative xv, 44, 47;
      descriptive–behavioural xv, 3, 44,
      47–50, 51, 122;
      descriptive–functional xv, 44,
      45–7, 84
  policy espoused 71–2, 85, 98, 154–5,
      253; 'in use' 71–2, 154–5
  roles 52–5; acolyte of benevolence 52,
      55, 59; architect 55, 84–6, 87, 88,
      91; advisor 87; changemaker 88,
      92, 352; clerk of works 55, 67,
      84–6, 87, 88, 59 155; consensus
      negotiator 53, 55, 60, 63, 66, 351;
      contracts manager 55, 66, 84–6, 87,
      88, 351; gatekeeper 66;
      handmaiden 87, 88, 89, 155;
      humane bureaucrat 52, 55, 69;
      legal wrangler 54, 55, 59, 63, 64;
      manpower analyst 55, 59, 63;
      mediator 59–60, 64, 349, 351, 357;
      organisational diagnostician 86;
      regulator 88, 351, 352; social
      reformer 52, 59; social worker 62
  scapegoating of 65, 66, 67
  specialists 44, 46, 47–50, 51–2, 54, 55,
      59–60, 61, 63, 64, 65, 66, 67, 68–9,

      84–6, 97, 101, 155–6, 168–9, 173–4,
      304, 350–2, 358, 366
  status of 49–50, 62, 64, 86
  stereotypes of 47–8, 49–50, 68–9
  vicious circles of 67–8
Peugeot-Talbot 169, 198, 228, 349
Philips Electronics 274
Pilkington 54, 116, 212
Pirelli 199, 229, 358
Plessey 149, 198, 229
P&O Ferries 299
population ecology 136
positivism xvii, xviii, 3, 26, 31, 69, 220,
    316–17, 337–9, 340
post-industrial society 34, 177, 181, 208,
    327
postmodernism xvii, xviii, 37, 123
  as epistemology 3, 330–6
  and HRM 3, 341–53
  as periodisation xvii, 181, 328, 330,
      340
  time–space compression 330, 333
  see also deconstruction, discourse *and*
      rhetoric
Post Office 266, 311
private service sector 14–15, 17, 22, 117,
    132, 179, 245, 289, 291
privatisation 3, 37, 99, 120, 205, 225, 226,
    230, 242, 267, 286, 291, 295–6
production *vs* consumption 37–9
professional groups 233–4, 245, 271, 275
profit sharing 26, 29, 77
promotion 63, 64, 76
Prudential 227
'psychological contract' 4, 32
public sector 9–10, 12, 14, 15, 16, 17, 57,
    97, 99, 119–20, 190, 192, 196, 197, 201,
    202, 204, 227, 229, 266–71, 274, 275,
    276, 283, 284, 284, 295–6, 311

Quakerism 52, 61–2, 97
quality xv, xvi, xvii, 32, 104, 107–8, 113,
    116, 117, 130, 207, 208, 226–7, 230,
    232, 241–78, 348, 350
  circles 31, 76, 125, 218, 219, 226, 228,
      246–50, 256–8, 258, 308, 310
  definitions of 244–6
  employee 272–4
  of life 36, 37–9
  in service sector 266–71

statistical process control 246, 251, 258–9, 277, 328
   see also Total Quality Management
strategic business units (SBUs) 169
strategy *see* business strategy
STC 149
strikes 53, 58, 65, 120–1, 281, 287–8, 295, 296, 297, 298, 299, 311, 330
   miners' 74, 99, 287, 293, 299, 311
   see also industrial conflict, 'Summer of Discontent' *and* 'Winter of Discontent'
subcontracting 8, 189–90, 192, 193–4, 196–7, 201, 204
   see also employment *and* flexibility
'Summer of Discontent' 287, 297
supervision *see* first line managers
suppliers 8, 36, 250, 251, 252, 253, 255, 361
   insourcing 8, 36
   outsourcing 8, 23, 34, 36, 37
surveillance 9, 35, 263–4, 324–5, 326, 327, 344–5, 350, 358
   peer 31, 36, 256, 260, 263–4
   see also Panopticon
symbolism 34, 37, 221, 222, 229–30, 235, 236, 335
   brands 37–9
   see also metaphors

Taiwan 115, 362
Tarmac 149
Taylorism 23, 25, 53, 57, 81, 96, 171, 179, 180, 186, 188, 210, 253, 258, 260, 262, 269, 275, 276, 325
teachers 99, 189, 268, 276, 284, 290, 296, 299
teams 73, 358
   leaders 35–6, 265, 276
   working 8, 11, 19, 31, 32, 35–6, 84, 166–7, 168, 197, 200, 203, 207, 209, 211–12, 228, 246, 248, 252, 255, 256, 259, 262–3, 265, 308, 310, 349
Tesco 3, 227, 241
Texas Instruments 148
Thatcherism 16, 51, 119, 366
Theory Y 124
Theory Z 118
Tie Rack 187
T-Groups 212
'Third Way' 2, 14–18

Third World 7
time
   linear 318–19
   span of discretion 176
   spiral 356–7
   time–space compression 320, 323–4, 326, 328, 333
Todd, Ron 117
Toshiba 229
Total Quality Management (TQM) xvii, 8, 31, 116, 168–9, 206, 228, 231, 244, 246–7, 250–2, 255–63, 270, 271, 274, 276, 277, 345, 346–7, 348, 349, 353, 358
   definition of 251–2
   in practice 256–66
   in theory 250–2
   see also just-in-time
Toyota 254, 259, 277, 306
'tough love' 127–8, 163
Trade Union Act (1984) 120–1, 293, 295
Trade Union Reform and Employment Rights Act (1993) 121, 294, 364
trade unions xvii, 14–15, 18, 31, 41, 50, 53, 65, 66, 75, 76, 77, 93, 95, 120–1, 280
   check-off 294, 314, 364
   closed shop 281, 283–4, 288, 292–6
   decline 288, 289
   density 281, 282–3, 288, 289–92, 295, 306, 314
   derecognition 80, 284, 305, 359
   enterprise unionism 263
   finances 288, 294, 314, 364
   marginalisation 265, 276, 296–9, 300, 302, 303, 306
   market unionism 307, 308
   membership 16, 281, 288, 289–92, 295, 296, 314, 351
   modernisation 16
   and multinationals 360–1
   and 'new realism' xvii, 296, 303–11
   and no strike agreements 301
   and partnership 15–18
   and pendulum arbitration 305
   and personnel management 351
   and pluralism 16, 279
   power 3, 286, 288, 296–300, 302
   public sector 16, 311
   recognition 14, 15, 75, 78, 80, 97, 281, 284–5, 288, 291, 292–6, 297, 298, 304, 304–5, 359–60, 362